T0274867

Angels Against the Sun

Praise for

Angels Against the Sun

"General Douglas MacArthur, driven from the Philippines at the start of World War II, famously vowed to return—and James M. Fenelon has captured that epic slugfest in magnificent detail. In his extraordinary new book *Angels Against the Sun*, Fenelon drops readers into the heart of the fight in a story filled with banzai charges, jungle warfare, and the block-by-block battle to retake Manila, the former Pearl of the Orient. His laser focus on the story of the 11th Airborne Division illuminates the commanders and the grunts who battled not only a fanatical enemy but also the sweltering tropical landscape, insects, and disease. *Angels Against the Sun* is both a testament to the fortitude of these daring soldiers as well as a helluva great read."

> —**James M. Scott,** Pulitzer Prize finalist and author of *Black Snow* and *Rampage*

"This fast-paced narrative effectively blends the real-world paratrooper perspective of the author with a valuable assortment of historical records, resulting in a gripping tale that sheds light on an outfit whose deeds have too often been neglected."

> —**Jared Frederick,** co-author of *Fierce Valor: The True Story of Ronald Speirs and His Band of Brothers*

"A riveting, superb account of extraordinarily courageous American airborne troops in some of the toughest fighting of the Pacific War."

> —**Alex Kershaw,** author of *Against All Odds* and *The Longest Winter*

"A fierce must-read for any history buff! The 11th Airborne Division are the forgotten paratroopers of WWII. While other parachute units fought in Europe as welcoming liberators, James Fenelon describes how the 11th Airborne slugged it out against a fanatical enemy in the Philippine jungles. This book is for any WWII enthusiast who wants to discover the little known history of those who wore jump wings and glider badges in the Pacific."

> —**Andrew Biggio,** bestselling author *of The Rifle*

ANGELS AGAINST THE SUN

A WWII Saga of Grunts, Grit, and Brotherhood

JAMES M. FENELON

REGNERY
HISTORY

Regnery History books may be purchased in bulk at special discounts for sales promotion, corporate gifts, fund-raising, or educational purposes. Special editions can also be created to specifications. For details, contact the Special Sales Department, Regnery History, 307 West 36th Street, 11th Floor, New York, NY 10018 or info@skyhorsepublishing.com.

Regnery History™ is an imprint of Skyhorse Publishing, Inc.®, a Delaware corporation.

Hardcover ISBN: 978-1-68451-200-3
First paperback ISBN: 978-1-68451-507-3
eBook ISBN: 978-1-68451-206-5

Library of Congress Cataloging-in-Publication Data is available on file.

Visit our website at www.regneryhistory.com.
Please follow our publisher Tony Lyons on Instagram @tonylyonsisuncertain.

10 9 8 7 6 5 4 3 2 1

Cover design by John Caruso
Cover photo by Brian Monnone

Printed in the United States of America

To the lost

Fiery the Angels rose, and as they rose deep thunder roll'd around their shores, indignant, burning …

—William Blake, "America: A Prophecy"

11th AIRBORNE DIVISION
May 1944 Organization

8,530 troops

MANEUVER UNITS

511th Parachute Infantry Regiment	187th Glider Infantry Regiment	188th Glider Infantry Regiment
1,931 troops	1,651 troops	1,651 troops
1st Battalion A, B, C Cos.	**1st Battalion** A, B, C Cos.	**1st Battalion** A, B, C Cos.
2nd Battalion D, E, F Cos.	**2nd Battalion** E, F, G Cos.	**2nd Battalion** E, F, G Cos.
3rd Battalion G, H, I Cos.		

FIRE SUPPORT UNITS

Division Artillery	457th Parachute Field Artillery BN	674th Glider Field Artillery Battalion	675th Glider Field Artillery Battalion
111 troops	464 troops	386 troops	386 troops
4X 75mm Howizters	20X 75mm Howizters	12X 75mm Howizters	12X 75mm Howizters

COMBAT SUPPORT UNITS

127th Airborne Engineer Battalion	152nd Anti-Air/Anti-Tank Battalion	221th Medical Company	511th Signal Company
418 troops	510 troops	208 troops	129 troops

SUSTAINMENT UNITS

408th Quatermaster Company	711th Ordnance Company	Division Headquarters	Division Headquarters Company
87 troops	74 troops	115 troops	77 troops
MP Platoon 37 troops	**Recon Company (later a platoon)** 106 troops	**Parachute Maintenance Company** 131 troops	**Division Band** 58 troops

11th AIRBORNE'S MANEUVER UNITS
Organization

511th Parachute Infantry Regiment

1,931 paratroopers
- 1 HQ & HQ company (186 men)
- 1 service company (155 men)
  - 3 infantry battalions

530 soldiers per battalion
- 1 HQ company (149 men)
  - 3 rifle companies

127 soldiers per company
- 1 HQ company (16 men)
  - 3 rifle platoons

37 soldiers per rifle platoon
- 1 HQ section (7 men)
- 1 60mm mortar squad (6 men)
  - 2 rifle squads

12 soldiers per squad
- 1 squad leader
- 1 assistant squad leader
- 7 riflemen
- machinegun team (3 men)

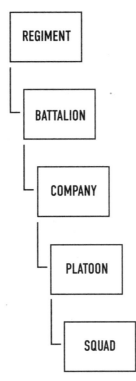

REGIMENT

BATTALION

COMPANY

PLATOON

SQUAD

187th & 188th Glider Infantry Regiments

1,651 glider-troopers (each)
- 1 HQ & HQ company (291 men)
- 1 service company (82 men)
  - 2 infantry battalions

639 soldiers per battalion
- 1 HQ company (174 men)
  - 3 rifle companies

155 soldiers per company
- 1 HQ company (28 men)
- 1 weapons platoon (33 men)
  - 2 rifle platoons

47 soldiers per rifle platoon
- 1 HQ section (11 men)
  - 3 rifle squads

12 soldiers per squad
- 1 squad leader
- 1 assistant squad leader
- 7 riflemen
- machinegun team (3 men)

Contents

May You Beat Your Dog Tags Home

On a gray morning in May of 1944, the equally gray SS *Sea Pike* slipped her moorings in San Francisco Bay. The lumbering liberty ship glided past Alcatraz Island, then picked up steam as she passed under the Golden Gate Bridge. Soldiers crowded the decks, craning for a view of the waking city. They were sailing across the Pacific, away from their homes and their families, to islands most of them had never heard of, much less ever wanted to visit. They were destined to wage war across inhospitable terrain, where they'd battle rain, heat, mud, disease, insects, leeches, rats—the very jungle itself—and, of course, the Imperial Japanese Army.

The United States fielded twenty-seven divisions in the Pacific: six from the Marine Corps and twenty-one from the Army. This book is about one of them: the Army's 11th Airborne Division—nicknamed the Angels. It is an account of the troopers' daily lives: the follies of youth, the oddities of Army life, the consequences of both inspiring and poor leadership, as well as the tribulations of jungle warfare and the desperation to survive amid the clatter of machineguns and the crump of hand grenades.

The 11th Airborne Division's campaigns were spearheaded by squads and platoons engaging the enemy at extremely close ranges. This book chronicles those brutal slugging matches between small units fighting in terrain that often reduced the efficacy of modern weapons. Neither side gave quarter in what was close to a war of annihilation, and I made no effort to shelter readers from the resulting ferocity. If we want to understand what is asked of men and women serving in uniform, we ought to feel strongly about knowing what they endure. Time and distance provide a comfortable gap from which passing judgement is easy, as is underestimating the stresses of no sleep, little food, a relentless enemy, and an overwhelming desire to make it home. I invite readers to immerse themselves in the complicated nuances of the Pacific War from the perspectives and experiences of the American infantrymen whose boots were calf-deep in the mud. Theirs was a journey of discovery, privation, terror, hate, and ultimately, heartbreaking transformation.

This is a work of nonfiction. Anything between quotation marks, as well as all *italicized* thoughts, come from a letter, diary, memoir, interview, or other historical document. Period and veteran accounts use the language of the day, and I have not edited them for content. Extensive information on sources can be found in the endnotes.

Some notes about conventions: this book uses the twenty-four-hour military clock to avoid confusion between morning and afternoon. For instance, 11:00 a.m. is 11:00; 11:00 p.m. is 23:00. When referring to the US Army Air Forces (which changed its name from the US Army Air Corps in mid-1941), I use the shorter, modern term "Air Force" instead of the period-correct plural Air Forces.

As I put the final touches on this manuscript, the US Army announced the reformation of the 11th Airborne Division. They'll serve as arctic warfare specialists in climates and conditions far removed from the tropical crucible where the division's history was forged. I know they'll accomplish their mission with the same dash and dedication as did their World War II forebearers.

James M. Fenelon
Texas, 2022

Prologue

Leyte Island, Philippines.
10:00, Monday morning, November 27, 1944

The single-file column of American paratroopers trudged down a narrow jungle trail thick with ankle-deep mud. The vegetation gleamed green under an incessant drizzle that had turned the track into a quagmire and made every step a chore. Hunched against the weight of their packs, they were a staggered line of olive-clad sameness, their helmets and equipment making one man indistinguishable from the next.

It was their first patrol into enemy territory, and they were on edge. Each man eyed the dense vegetation on both sides of the trail; it was a mottled emerald wall, uncomfortably close—almost claustrophobically so—and ideal concealment for an ambush.

Every sound or movement drew their attention. The mystique of their adversaries' jungle fighting prowess was built on years of battlefield success and effective propaganda. The Japanese—the fabled supermen of Asia who survived for days on a ball of rice, carried

samurai swords, and were merciless in victory—were infamous for
their cunning use of camouflage and surprise attacks. It was easy to
imagine them lurking in the shadows, like jaguars waiting to pounce.

Private Norman Honie, a twenty-year-old Hopi Indian from
Arizona, led the column downhill toward a small clearing on the edge
of a river. Before stepping out from the undergrowth, he took a knee
and slowly raised his rifle. After years of training for and anticipating
this very moment, there they were: two Japanese soldiers crouching
just a few dozen feet away on the riverbank, washing their clothes.

Honie's squad leader, Sergeant Mike Olivetti, signaled to the men
behind him: enemy sighted. He then hunched his way back down the
line to Lieutenant James E. Wylie, reporting the pair of Japanese up
front.

"Kill the sons of bitches and move the column forward," said the
lieutenant without hesitation. Behind them was Charlie Company's
full complement of more than a hundred and thirty men, and he
wanted to keep them moving. But when the column halted, the men
plunked down like a row of dominos. Burdened with full packs, rifles,
mortars, machineguns, and as much ammunition as possible, any
pause was an opportunity to get off their feet.

Olivetti nodded and reversed his route.

A minute later, the *Pop! Pop!* of two shots ring out. They were
followed almost immediately by an unexpected barrage of rifle fire.

What's happening? Is it an ambush? Wylie and the men up the
trail had no idea. Honie, clutching a bleeding wound, stumbled past.
He didn't stop to answer questions; he kept moving down the line of
wide-eyed troopers, in search of a medic.

Wylie yelled his men into action. The next squad dropped their
packs, grabbed a few extra bandoleers of ammunition, and charged
into the clearing. There, they found men sheltering behind stumps
and fallen trees. Olivetti lay in a heap, dead.

Sergeant Colbert Renfroe threw himself to the ground and squeezed off a few shots at the far bank. He couldn't see the enemy, but the incoming fire snapped in from that direction. He knew the Japanese used smokeless powder in their ammunition, and the lack of muzzle flashes made them almost invisible in the thick undergrowth.

All around Renfroe, men were getting hit. Lieutenant Wylie was the next to die.

Troopers started leapfrogging back toward the trail but were cut down by bursts of machinegun fire. Renfroe glanced at several of his comrades hesitating on the high ground, but when he looked back again, they were gone. With the Japanese advancing on both flanks, the main column had withdrawn farther up the hill. Seizing the opportunity, Japanese troops occupied the hill and set up a second machinegun to block the isolated troopers' escape route. The American company was now split in two.

With Wylie lying dead a few feet away, Platoon Sergeant Elton Henry took charge of the unfolding disaster. He rallied the remaining men into a circular perimeter to defend the small clearing.

They held off the attackers but were soon running out of ammunition. With most of his men wounded or killed, and no sign of reinforcements, Henry's choices were simple: stay put and die, or risk a bullet in the back while escaping the growing enemy encirclement. He chose to run.

The closest cover was across the river where the heavily overgrown bank provided better concealment. Following Henry's order, Renfroe, who'd been hit twice in the legs and once in the back, splashed across the stream. Halfway across, he took shelter on a small spit of dirt to help his friend, Bob Godwin. Godwin had been shot in the head, and Renfroe tried in vain to stem the bleeding. The two men had enlisted together back home in Georgia; Godwin's death was a personal tragedy, but there was no time to mourn. Renfroe slid back

xxii **ANGELS AGAINST THE SUN**

into the water, joining several other troopers wading their way to the far bank. The first of their group scrambled up onto a rock and was shot in the chest. As the dead man pitched back into the water, the troopers abandoned that route and threw themselves downstream.

Riding the current, Private Newton Terry's conscience gnawed at him. In the melee, he had abandoned a badly wounded comrade, Francis Perez. Perez, not wanting to be taken alive, had begged to be shot, but Terry couldn't do it. Horror stories of Japanese atrocities flashed through his mind—there was no telling what would happen to the helpless Perez. It was too much for Terry to stomach, and as the rest of his battered platoon slipped away downstream, he waded back against the current to find his friend. It was the last anyone ever saw of him or Perez.

MEANWHILE, BACK ON THE HILL, the rest of Charlie Company had dropped their packs at the sound of gunfire. Unsure of what was happening at the front of the column, they moved forward. Private George Floersch's squad started toward the clearing—just as the shout of "Grenade!" sent everyone diving for cover.

The blast occurred simultaneously with the warning. A trooper staggered back up the trail screaming, his face and torso a bloody mess of shrapnel and gravel.

Floersch glimpsed movement to his left. He snapped his rifle up and squeezed the trigger.

"I got one, Dutch, I got one!" he yelled to Herman 'Dutch' Wagner. Floersch's adrenaline surged, and he later recalled feeling "giddy with excitement."

Japanese troops were flanking them. The squad tried to reach their buddies in the clearing, but enemy movement on their left brought them to a halt.

"There were so many Japs that I couldn't shoot fast enough," recalled Floersch. "I couldn't even take aim. I just pointed and pulled the trigger."

From over the rise, Floersch saw a rifle muzzle tracking him. He leveled his own rifle and fired. His target's helmet flew off as the man's face exploded.

The squad then engaged another group of Japanese bounding forward along the river's edge. A trooper next to Floersch darted down the slope to get a better vantage point, then fell under a hail of rifle fire.

Floersch reloaded and kept shooting.

PFC Samuel 'Sammy' Dragoo wanted to help the wounded trooper who was laying out in the open. He yelled for Floersch to go with him.

There's no way I'm going out there with the Japs crawling around all over, Floersch thought.

"For Christ's sake!" screamed Dragoo, sprinting forward alone.

He made it five steps before a bullet cut him down.

With the enemy swarming up the hill, Floersch retreated to avoid being surrounded. He paused at a wounded Japanese soldier that he'd shot a few minutes earlier.

"I promptly put my rifle to his side and fired five times. I don't know why," he later admitted. "One shot at muzzle range would have been enough. ... Maybe I was angry for our wounded and killed, or maybe I enjoyed killing—I felt very powerful with that M1 rifle."

Captain Thomas 'Big Tom' Mesereau, Charlie Company's towering six-foot-four commander, hunkered down near Floersch to ascertain the situation. Seeing Dragoo writhing in pain and enemy movement on both flanks, it didn't look good.

Mesereau sent Floersch back to find the regimental commander, Colonel Orin 'Hard Rock' Haguen, and give him an update.

"Tell Tom we're withdrawing," said Haugen after hearing Floersch's report. They needed to pull back, regroup, and figure out what was happening.

Heading back down the trail, Floersch ran past curious troopers who could hear the shooting but were oblivious to what was happening.

They asked, "What's going on down there? Is anyone shot?" Floersch kept moving.

Returning to the fray, he passed the body of Private Delmar Stam, a buddy who'd purchased a pearl-handled revolver back in the States. "He said he was going to kill a lot of Japs with it," remembered Floersch. "It was still in his holster."

Floersch gave Mesereau the message to withdraw. The captain nodded, responding, "Cover me and bring my rifle while I get Dragoo."

Fire power! thought Floersch *Fire power!* as he squeezed off shots in rapid succession. *Keep their heads down!*

Mesereau slithered out to the wounded man, rolled him onto his own back, and crawled back with him. Medics rushed forward to relieve the captain and aid Dragoo.

Floersch trailed the group as they withdrew, leaving the isolated platoon behind. About seventy-five yards into the jungle, Floersch and Private Daniel D. Hart were told to stay put and wait for any survivors to join them.

Seconds later, the pair heard shooting erupt up ahead. Down the trail, Floersch saw troops working their way toward them. The rain and dense undergrowth made it hard to identify who they were. But flashes of tan uniforms made it clear.

"Hart," whispered Floersch, "let's go, it's Japs!"

Floersch fired a few rounds to discourage pursuit, and the two of them ran up the hill as bullets sliced overhead. At the top, they found bodies and equipment strewn all over. A Japanese machinegunner had the hilltop covered, and bursts of fire chased the two troopers as they scurried across. Floersch made it. Hart did not.

With Charlie Company scattered into multiple groups, and their first combat action devolving into disaster, they'd been initiated into the savage realities of war in the Pacific: the jungle was unforgiving and the enemy unrelenting.

PART I

The Drums of War

Chapter 1

You're in the Army Now

201 Edward Street, Brisbane, Australia.
11:30, Thursday, May 11, 1944

The heels of Major General Joseph M. Swing's paratrooper boots clicked together as he snapped to attention and saluted the Supreme Commander of the Southwest Pacific Area, General Douglas MacArthur. MacArthur's spotless, almost austere office was dominated by a dark mahogany desk fronted by two plush leather chairs flanking a small side table and a standing chrome ash tray. On the wall behind MacArthur, as if looking over his shoulder, was a framed painting of George Washington.

MacArthur smiled and greeted Swing warmly. "Joe, I'm glad to see an old familiar face."

The two men were acquaintances but hadn't seen each other in years, and Swing appreciated the sincere welcome.

MacArthur had been in Brisbane since mid-1942 after being chased out of the Philippines by the Japanese. From this eighth-floor office, he was orchestrating his island-hopping campaign to push his adversaries back to Tokyo. Swing, the fifty-year-old commander of the 11th Airborne Division, had recently arrived with three of his staff officers to prepare for his unit's entrée into MacArthur's offensive.

After thirty minutes of explaining the strategic overview, MacArthur had one piece of advice for Swing: "Joe, we don't do it over here the way the Marines do it, or the way they do it over in Europe. We use a little military common sense on how we get our men killed. We don't do it by massive brute force. Anybody can fight that way."

Swing nodded. As an advocate of tactical finesse himself, he understood, but he also knew that the Japanese would get a vote.

WITH OVER THIRTY YEARS in uniform, Swing was well prepared to lead his men through the trials of combat. In a profession where force of character often outweighs intellect, he'd developed the tactical acumen and mental fortitude to navigate the inevitable friction of war. Swing's rigid posture carried his six-foot frame well, and he moved with a purposeful, long gait. His dark blue eyes and close-cropped white hair lent themselves to his practiced, stern demeanor.

"He personified a general officer," said Lieutenant William Weber, one of Swing's subordinates. "He was ruggedly handsome, tall, and well built."

He was also quiet, which added to his facade of command and kept others guessing. When he spoke, his orders were pointed and concise. He had little tolerance for verbosity and rarely conducted a meeting that lasted more than fifteen minutes.

"If he said, 'Frog,' something jumped," admitted one his officers. Of his intensity, another observed, "You could almost see flames shooting out his eyes."

Lieutenant Colonel Douglas Quandt described him as "impatient with mediocrity," with a temper to match, "though," he added, "its displays are of the flash-flood type: brief and devastating." But Quandt also noted that Swing could be "tactful and charming—no one more so—but when he considers the cost of being so excessive, he will not bother to display either trait."

Born in Jersey City, New Jersey, on February 28, 1894, Swing received his commission as an artillery officer in 1915 upon graduation from West Point. While he ranked in the top quarter of his class, his classmates—including Dwight D. Eisenhower—believed that if he had focused on his studies rather than on football, stunt riding, "rough-housing," and his infamous "mischief and practical jokes," he'd have been one of the top graduates. The focus and self-discipline would come soon enough.

Brigadier General Joseph M. Swing, pictured in late 1942

Swing's first assignment as a twenty-two-year-old junior officer was in General John 'Black Jack' Pershing's 1916 expedition into Mexico. There, he witnessed Pershing's propensity for decisive action and leading from the front—traits he and another young lieutenant named George Patton harnessed for their own leadership styles.

The search for Pancho Villa and his guerrilla band gave Swing the opportunity to observe many innovations, such as the use of rickety biplanes for reconnaissance, wireless telegraphs for communication, and movement of troops via trucks and armored cars. It was the beginning of a mechanized evolution, but with the often-temperamental technology came a series of logistical blunders that Swing logged as cautionary tales of poor planning.

In 1917, he served as a captain with the 1st Infantry Division in the slaughterhouse of the First World War. If his experiences in Mexico molded his leadership style and spawned an interest in modernization, it was the mire of the trenches that taught him static positions and senseless frontal assaults were no way to defeat an enemy.

Swing became the aide to the Army's Chief of Staff, General Payton C. March, in 1918. In June of that year, newly promoted to major, he married the general's daughter, Josephine.

Swing spent the next two decades steadily advancing through the ranks and playing polo, a sport for which he had a deep passion, and which was also a favorite of the Army's social elite. By the time America joined the war in 1941, Swing had earned the one star of a brigadier general and subsequently took command of the 82nd Infantry Division's horse-drawn artillery. Six months later, under the leadership of Major General Matthew B. Ridgway, the 82nd transitioned into the Army's first airborne division, specializing in dropping its infantrymen, howitzers, and supporting units into combat via parachutes and gliders. Inserting troops behind the enemy was a tremendous new capability—and Swing embraced it.

As the Army grew to meet the requirements of fighting wars in both Europe and Asia, Swing earned a second star on his collar. In February 1943, he was assigned to command and form his own airborne division.

SWING'S 11TH AIRBORNE DIVISION was built from the ground up at Camp Mackall, North Carolina. The first to arrive were the cadre: the officers and sergeants transferred from other units to provide the nucleus of expertise. Together they underwent an intensive program to prepare for their role in training the raw recruits who would arrive in a few weeks. The 11th was the first of the airborne divisions to be formed with recruits all training together as units. The initial thirteen weeks of basic training that turned civilians into soldiers were to be followed by an additional twelve weeks of unit training—where soldiers learned to fight as a team.

On Thursday, February 25, Swing's headquarters issued his first General Order: activating the division. It consisted of three core infantry regiments—one of paratroopers and two of glider troops —as well as supporting units of administrative personnel, quartermasters, signals, ordnance, medics, engineers, artillery, military police, anti-aircraft gunners, and even a band.

Once the full complement of troops arrived, Swing's manpower would be just over 8,300, giving him a unit roughly 60 percent the size of a standard infantry division. The reduced numbers reflected the Army's doctrine of using airborne units as shock troops to be dropped behind enemy lines in support of a ground campaign. Intended to link up quickly with friendly units and return to base to prepare for the next mission, they lacked the self-supporting logistics of regular divisions. But as Swing and his men would learn, the doctrine was based on theory, and once their boots hit the ground, the anvil of combat would dictate their reality.

RECRUITS ARRIVED BY THE TRAINLOAD at Hoffman, North Carolina, where they were met by the cadre and trucked ten minutes to camp. Their first day was filled with disappointing revelations.

These early arrivals filled the ranks of the glider units. Confusion was followed by shock: none of them had volunteered for airborne assignment, nor had most ever been in an aircraft, let alone flown in one without an engine.

Towed over the battlefield and released in an aircraft with no engines or parachutes?

They also found the camp's facilities to be less than satisfactory.

One of the recruits later recalled, "My first impression on seeing Camp Mackall was one of surprise, thinking that these tar-paper shacks must be the temporary buildings till the regular barracks were put up. It did not take long to find out otherwise. It was nice being able to see what was going on outside of the buildings without going to a window—just look through the cracks."

SIMULTANEOUSLY ARRIVING AT MACKALL were the division's parachute troops: the 511th Parachute Infantry Regiment, the 457th Parachute Field Artillery Battalion, and Charlie Company of the 127th Airborne Engineer Battalion. They'd filled their ranks in January before the 11th Airborne was formed and arrived as nearly complete units, though they needed more recruits to be at full strength.

These units were composed entirely of men who'd volunteered for parachute training. Some of them had joined the Army willingly while others were drafted, but all had raised their hands to serve with the Army's newest and most elite: the parachute troops.

Recruiting pamphlets described them as "ultramodern fighting men of Uncle Sam's modern Army" who "must be agile, athletic, actively aggressive." Interested recruits were advised that volunteers who passed selection would master all infantry weapons, handle explosives, learn how to ride motorcycles and drive trucks, and would operate tanks and even locomotives. Those needing extra encouragement were informed that, once through the rigorous training, they would receive an extra $50.00 a month as jump pay. Among the listed qualification requirements was the caveat, "Recent venereal disease disqualifies."

Motivations for volunteering fell into a few common categories. "I thought I would get to fight quicker," said eighteen-year-old Jerry Davis, "and you got $50 extra for jump training."

Another volunteer sought personal challenge, admitting, "I wanted to see if it was as tough as it was cracked up to be."

Richard Laws, a teenage bakery salesman from Detroit, Michigan, was still boiling after the attack on Pearl Harbor. He volunteered, "because I knew it would put me in contact with those Japs."

As an additional incentive, parachute troops wore a distinct uniform that rivaled the Marine Corps: they ditched the Army's unflattering "bus driver hat" in favor of jaunty garrison caps with a parachute insignia. They pinned silver jump wings on their chests and bloused their pants over the top of high-calved, brown leather jump boots—their most prized status symbol.

The largest of Swing's parachute units was the 2,000-man 511th Parachute Infantry Regiment, commanded by a dark-haired, thirty-six-year-old chain-smoking colonel named Orin D. Haugen. His pleasantly wide face and thin lips belied an inner fire that he fed with an insatiable competitive nature. He wanted to be the best, and he wanted his men right behind him.

He aspired to serve others from an early age and spent his freshman year seeking a future in ministry at St. Olaf, a Lutheran college in Minnesota. But the next year, he transferred to Cornell University before attending West Point.

By all reports, Haugen was a self-made man. Described by his own family as "not an exceptionally bright student," he buckled down at West Point to graduate with honors in his 1930 class. To overcome his lack of natural athleticism, he dedicated himself to rigorous exercise and lung-bursting cross-country runs. His West Point classmates respected Haugen's "bull-dog tenacity" but also noted that his "distaste for disciplinary measures" often put him at odds with the faculty. Haugen favored discipline that helped obtain goals over the nit-picky, pedantic rituals designed

Colonel Orin D. 'Hard Rock' Haugen

to reinforce an already-inherent power structure. He was interested in results, and the means—so long as they were legal and fair—were of less concern.

A year after graduation, Haugen wed Marion Sargent, a twenty-five-year-old avid equestrian. The two shared a love of riding, and Marion won shelves of trophies while Orin excelled at polo.

In 1940, after assignments in Texas and Hawaii, Haugen's restless spirit, which one of his peers likened to a sea-roaming Viking, led him to volunteer for the newly formed parachute troops. Promoted to captain, he commanded a company in the Army's first organized parachute battalion. Haugen found a home among the rough-and-tumble volunteers. His lead-by-example mentality helped grow their esprit-de-corps. When the Army expanded its doctrine of dropping a battalion of troops behind enemy lines to regiments, and then entire divisions, Haugen's career followed a similar upward trajectory. By late 1942, he was a lieutenant colonel assigned to command the 511th PIR forming at Camp Toccoa, Georgia.

Nestled at the southern end of the Blue Ridge Mountains, Toccoa was home to several parachute units in the process of filling their own ranks. Lieutenant Miles W. Gale, a twenty-seven-year-old jump school graduate from West Bend, Wisconsin, recalled driving through the main gate and up to the 511th area to report to Haugen as a member of his cadre. He found the barracks still under construction.

"Bulldozers and graders were chewing up the ground preparing for road paving. Concrete was being poured for slabs," he said.

Farther down the hill, the call-and-response cadence of exercise echoed as a group of paratroopers conducted their daily calisthenics. The camp was in the shadow of a 1,735-foot mountain named Currahee.

Gale reported to Haugen and received his first order: procure equipment for the regiment's boxing team. Haugen wanted to instill a fighting spirit with bi-weekly bouts.

The volunteers were a cultural mix, arriving from training centers and induction stations across the country. Private Mike Polidoro, from Boston, found the thick southern accents of Sergeants Byron New and Robert Durkin impossible to decipher.

"No excuse!" Sergeant New yelled in Polidoro's face; disobeying an order was punished with push-ups.

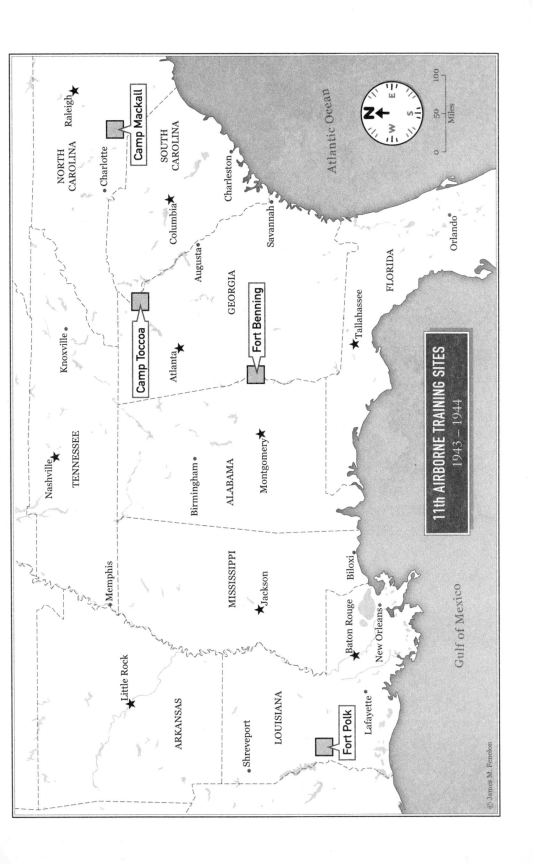

11th AIRBORNE TRAINING SITES
1943 – 1944

Atlantic Ocean

Gulf of Mexico

NORTH CAROLINA
Raleigh
Charlotte
Camp Mackall

SOUTH CAROLINA
Columbia
Charleston
Savannah

Knoxville
Camp Toccoa
Atlanta
Augusta
GEORGIA
Fort Benning
Tallahassee

FLORIDA
Orlando

TENNESSEE
Nashville

Birmingham
ALABAMA
Montgomery

Memphis
MISSISSIPPI
Jackson
Biloxi
Baton Rouge
New Orleans

Little Rock
ARKANSAS

Shreveport
LOUISIANA
Lafayette
Fort Polk

0   50   100
Miles

N

© James M. Fenelon

"I was constantly in mud up to my elbows," lamented Polidoro. "Hell, I wasn't disobeying, I just couldn't understand them."

The confusion cut both ways. During roll call, Private Bernard Majstrowicz had to answer to "Master Son-of-a-Bitch," because his first sergeant was unable, or unwilling, to pronounce his Eastern European name.

George Doherty thought his high school Junior ROTC experience would give him an edge over his fellow recruits. He'd already glimpsed life in the service while captaining the rifle team, as well as patrolling the streets of Riverside, California, to enforce black-out restrictions. Captivated by the movie *Parachute Battalion*, Doherty volunteered and was inducted in Los Angeles on February 23, 1943—three days after his eighteenth birthday.

But upon debarking from the train with other recruits, Doherty was swiftly put in his place by Sergeant Joe Chitwood, a swaggering paratrooper of the cadre who met them at the station. After a short welcome speech, Chitwood approached Doherty. "How about you soldier, are you a good man?"

Doherty replied in the affirmative. Chitwood nodded, "Okay, get down and give me twenty-five."

Doherty struggled after the first five push-ups, prompting Chitwood to grab him by the back of his belt and lift him up and down repeatedly to finish the remaining twenty. It was a lackluster start.

Haugen and the cadre initiated physical training immediately, followed by marching for hours in close order drill. Described as "demanding, extensive, and tough," the program put the recruits through their paces. Walking was forbidden; squads and platoons ran in formation from point A to B. The men were "hurting and hungry all the time."

Leroy D. Butler, who gave up his draft-deferred job as a signalman for Southern Pacific Railroad to enlist as a paratrooper, recalled his time at Toccoa, noting, "Everything was double time, double time, double time, push-ups, push-ups, push-ups."

Another trooper had similar recollections. "They made us run from one place to another—we weren't allowed to walk. We were always trying to avoid the mud." When recruits hesitated to get muddy, Sergeant Al Barreiro yelled, "Come on, come on, Jocko! Keep going, you guys. Better men than you are dying in mud like this."

The cadre hazed and pushed the volunteers to exhaustion; they could quit anytime for reassignment back to the regular infantry. It was a test of fortitude to determine who wanted to be there. The tradition had been established in 1941 that "the paratroops would be hard to get into and easy to get out of."

Soon after arriving, Charles Thollander wrote to his girlfriend, "I am lying on my bunk thoroughly disgusted with this camp and also exhausted after the two hardest days in my life. Not that we work all day—but every morning, in the cold, we have 30 or 40 minutes of calisthenics. They alone tire me more than the hardest day's work I ever did in my life. It's just like one of the fellows said this morning—compared to this, football practice is like playing marbles. Every man in this hut is an athlete, and they all agree on that . . . . But the boys take it in the right spirit, because we know that it is good for us and will make us tough."

Shared hardship and misery soon created bonds among those far from home and seeking friends. Peers dubbed each other with the honored tradition of nicknames: Red, Pinky, Blacky, Whitey, Hog Ears, Rocky, Tex, Old Woman, Honest Dan, Deacon, Burpie, Duck Butt, Heeb, Half Man, Cue Ball, and so on. Leroy Butler, at twenty-six-years-old, earned the predictable moniker 'Pops.'

As one trooper recalled, the names were often "crude, undignified, derogatory, and insulting." They were probing for weaknesses; if a man couldn't take a humorous verbal ribbing, how would he take the rigors of combat?

Haugen earned a semi-affectionate nickname as well: 'Hard Rock'—often shortened to simply 'Rock,' but none of his men called him either to his face. Nicknames were used among peers and maybe by the chain of command, but never by subordinates.

Many of the regiment's troopers were away from home for the first time and embraced the rough language of soldiering. Thollander again shared his observations in a letter home: "I never heard so much swearing in my life." Indeed, profanity became ubiquitous and provided a shorthand for referring to their new circumstances. "Shit on a shingle," or "SOS," was the ever-present chipped beef over toast they would eat for the duration of their service; "chickenshit" was shorthand for tedious or petty Army rules; "rat's ass" was a step of senselessness below that, even lower than a chicken's shit; "SNAFU" was one of many colorful acronyms to describe current events: Situation Normal, All Fucked Up.

Barracks life meant unavoidable friction and personality clashes. An exasperated Thollander tried to roll with it. "I have to laugh at some of these guys in here. Spoiled, conceited, and everything else. One guy is always asking stupid questions. So stupid that I want to slug him as soon as he opens his mouth." Another trooper admitted, "I can't say that we all got along like blood brothers, because it would not be true. There were people I didn't like, and I'm sure there were people who didn't care for me, but we worked hard together."

IT WASN'T LONG before Haugen led his troops in six-mile round trip runs to the summit of Mount Currahee. The gasping pace—up hill and down—averaged just over ten minutes a mile, and if a trooper fell behind or quit, he was sent packing.

"Ten pounds of red mud stuck to each boot double timing up and down that damned mountain," complained Corporal Louis Meeker. "[On one run] Floyd Zobel was to my left, and the guy in the middle began to stumble on the way back down. A slight rain made everything slick and red-mud gooey. Zobel grabbed the man's left arm, and I got his right, and we held him up. We finished the run like that, and we all made it."

One of Haugen's platoon leaders, Lieutenant Arthur Fenske, was an avid cross-country athlete and ran sections of the mountain backwards, both to impress his men as well as to keep an eye on them.

The exertions were grueling, but there was encouragement, too. "You are the best!" Haugen often shouted to his troopers as he ran beside them. He expected no more from his men than he did himself—give 100 percent and try to be better than the day before. The cadre made hand-painted signs and posted them throughout the training area. "Paratrooper's fancy boots GET THE GALS!" Another near the basketball court read, "AMERICAN PARATROOPERS HAVE THE BEST WEAPONS ON EARTH!" For further inspiration, they decorated the mess hall with photographs of paratroopers in action and draped brightly colored cargo chutes from the ceiling.

The troopers eyed the cadre's silver wings and jump boots with envy. They were the fraternity badges of winners. "Whatever it was that they were trying to project worked," remembered a trooper. "We all would have killed to remain in or be associated with this kind of outfit."

The longer the men endured the training, the more their leaders' quality became apparent. Haugen understood that now was the time for his officers to gain their men's respect. Once in combat, it would be too late. Hard, realistic training built both self-confidence in the men and trust in their leadership.

"We have swell officers, the best and toughest in the Army," opined Thollander. "When one of the officers noticed that I didn't have any gloves during our exercises, he gave me his and didn't wear any himself. It is so cold here that you freeze all over as soon as you step outside the door."

One of those officers enduring the winter conditions with his men was Major Edward 'Slugger' Lahti, commander of the 3rd Battalion. Lahti moved with the confidence of a bull elephant on the march. His gaze was dissecting, and his block of a head was defined by a rugged jawline with a dimpled chin, reminiscent of two knuckles of a large fist. He was as dedicated as Haugen to the pursuit of excellence, and he'd personally interviewed each volunteer before accepting him into his battalion. It was an intimidating conversation, with the recruit reporting to Lahti's selection panel, then stripping off his overcoat to stand at attention in just his boxershorts while answering questions. Lahti sought all-stars, and he was particularly interested in physically fit men who'd played team-based athletics.

Born in 1913 as the youngest of six children to Finish immigrants, Lahti was one of many Horatio Alger stories the Army could take credit for. He grew up in an impoverished home in rural Oregon, where the family subsisted largely on their father's fishing. Lahti joined the National Guard at fifteen, motivated by the pay and the opportunity to play on its softball team.

In 1931, seeking further opportunity, he enlisted in the regular Army. The next year, he took a series of competitive exams for West Point, which started him on the path to obtain one of the few coveted appointments granted to talented, hardworking enlisted men. He passed all the tests, but it wasn't until March 1934, after earning one of the Army's highest scores, that he entered the Academy. As a cadet, Lahti excelled on the parade ground and sports field alike. He ranked near the top of plebes in conduct and discipline and played on the soccer and baseball teams for three years, lettering in both each year. He cemented his 'Slugger' nickname when he hit a triple with bases loaded against Navy.

Commissioned as an infantry officer, Lahti volunteered for parachute duty in 1942, not long after his promotion to Major. Upon completing jump school, he reported to the 511th Parachute Infantry Regiment, where one of his junior officers described his bearing as "blunt and rough ... devoid of pretensions of any sort."

IN LATE FEBRUARY, the parachute units moved to Camp Mackall to receive their final allotment of recruits and join the rest of the 11th Airborne Division for basic training. Stories of their cocky attitude had preceded them, and Swing's reception was less than welcoming.

Egos and aggressive attitudes are a natural biproduct—if not the desired outcome—of rigorous training. Confronting an enemy in combat requires a healthy amount of self-assurance, but when combined with youthful exuberance and immaturity—and no immediate outlet—that self-confidence often manifested itself in rowdy drinking and fist fights. Lots of fist fights, particularly with non-paratroopers.

"People used to wonder why we were wilder than other soldiers, and I can tell you," wrote one paratrooper. "The thing that distinguished us most from other soldiers was our willingness to take chances and risks in a branch of the Army that provided a great, new, almost unexplored frontier. In other days, paratroopers would have been the type of men to sail with Columbus.... Each man had supreme faith in his ability to take care of himself, whatever the odds. For this reason, paratroopers were at times a quarrelsome lot, because they could never believe that anybody could beat the hell out of them."

James 'Bull' Hendry agreed. "Fights were a rather commonplace part of our lives. We had been instilled with a firm conviction that we could whip anyone or anything."

Officers and sergeants mostly ignored the fisticuffs and, in some cases, even encouraged them. "Occasionally, some disciplinary action was deemed necessary," admitted Hendry, "but it was rare."

Swing was no stranger to hellraising himself, however, and his views on discipline may have been motivated by his own past carousing.

One of his contemporaries later told a story of when the two of them were stationed in Hawaii together. "I was billeted temporarily in the BOQ [Bachelor Officer Quarters], a dreadful place with thin, tar-paper walls. Major Swing was also staying there for some reason. Saturday nights, he and this infantry officer buddy would get skunked. They'd start roughhousing. Well, I'm damned if Swing didn't literally throw this fellow right through the wall."

Swing took preemptive action to deflate the inflated pride of his new units, whom he allegedly referred to as "Goddamn rowdy paratroopers." He stripped the officers and cadre of their distinctive status symbol: their highly polished jump boots. They'd now wear lace-up canvas leggings and field shoes like the rest of the division—who enjoyed no unique uniforms or hazardous duty pay. The motivation for Swing's scheme, designed to remind the paratroopers they were no better than the division's glider troops, was multifold: improved morale, better discipline, and probably a desire for uniformity. As the hallmark of a traditional military mindset, uniformity was a hobgoblin to paratroopers who wanted to stand out. The stage was set for a tumultuous relationship.

Captain Henry 'Butch' Muller, one of Haugen's officers, recalled their reaction to Swing's uniform restriction: "We were in a state of shock." He described wearing the Army's traditional footwear as "dreadful."

"It made you feel limp and unimportant to have pants flapping loose," agreed a trooper. "There was more to the boots than the way they shined. It was the go-to-hell way they wrinkled around the ankles, and the high curve of the bulldog toes, and the aggressive squeak of them when you moved across a quiet room. They were symbols of the crap a man endured to become a jumper. Civilians seemed to get a kick out of them, too, asking a hundred questions about them. Fast women liked them under their beds, and more timid women liked to dance with them, and maternal women liked them under their dining room tables. The boots just naturally got around, and it was nice to be in them."

Depriving the troopers of their boots was the type of old school chickenshit many of the men wanted to escape by volunteering for parachute units. As trivial as it may have seemed to outsiders, Haugen's troopers endured exacting physical demands to earn their place in an elite regiment, and those hard-won boots played no small part in their rite of passage.

Swing's efforts to strike a balance between esprit-de-corps and respect for authority required a nuanced touch. The fifty-year-old general was in charge of more than eight thousand men whose average age was nineteen. In addition to their immaturity, few of them sought Army careers, making them unresponsive to promotion opportunities, and they were often unmoved by regulations that made little sense to their civilian logic. They were willing to engage the Germans or the Japanese, but their tolerance for engaging with Army nonsense ran thin. They wanted to end the war as soon as possible and get back to their lives.

If Swing's reception of the paratroopers was lukewarm, the feeling was mutual.

Swing had designed the division insignia worn on the left shoulder by all the troops under his command. The three-inch-tall patch, a shield of dark blue, contained a white numeral eleven within a centered red circle; a white border, held aloft by two oblique wings, outlined the circle. The shield was topped by an arced blue tab, with AIRBORNE stitched in white.

As striking as the design was, the paratroopers weren't impressed. The 101st Airborne Division had a screaming bald eagle on their patch; the 17th Airborne had a black and gold silhouette of an eagle's talon on theirs.

Regarding the red dot centered on their patch, the men of the 511th observed, "The 101st got the head, the 17th got the claws, and we got the asshole."

"It cannot be truthfully said that we field grade officers liked the general in those early days," said Major W. K. 'Ripcord' Walker, an officer in one of Swing's glider regiments. "We were awed by his presence, respected and admired him, but the liking came later."

"Anyway," he added, "it wasn't necessary that we like him."

WITH EVERYONE WEARING the same footwear, the division settled into the routine of basic training. The Army took nothing for granted. The curriculum started with the fundamentals of making a bed: forty-five-degree folded corners and tight enough to bounce a quarter. John Bandoni benefited from the instruction and was thrilled at having his own bed (he had slept on the couch in his family's living room since he was a kid). As many recruits now had more than one pair of shoes for the first time, there were routine reminders to rotate between pairs. The rudimentary lessons, which were reinforced during daily inspections, also covered the proper way to wear a uniform.

Private Joseph Russell Vannier, standing proudly in formation for his first battalion inspection, learned attention to detail was critical. One of his trouser legs dangled over his canvas legging, his tie was tucked into his shirt incorrectly, and it appeared he'd shined just one of his shoes. After being berated for his slovenly appearance, Vannier heard an officer whisper, "That's about the saddest sack of shit I ever witnessed."

Vannier wasn't alone in digesting the cruelties of Army life. Private Dick Ostrom was in his barracks when his twenty-one-year-old platoon sergeant, Buford Atkinson, known as Sergeant At, entered. "Has anybody here been to college?" the sergeant shouted. "If so, fall out in front of the barracks."

Ostrom and two others perked up and raised their hands.

"Can't you understand English?" bellowed Atkinson. "I didn't say raise your hands, I said fall out!"

The three men hustled outside.

They must be short of officers and they are going to pick us because of the year of college, thought Ostrom. *I've only been in the Army for a very few weeks and here I'm going to be an officer already. My parents will be so proud.*

Sergeant At continued his instructions to the rest of the platoon. "Fall out in front of the barracks opposite those three college boys."

With the two groups facing each other, Atkinson revealed, "These college boys are going to police [clean] up the area. I want the rest of you dumb bastards to watch and see if you can learn something."

Crawling under the barracks to pick up trash, Ostrom vowed to never again call attention to himself.

THE DAYS BLED TOGETHER as recruits started each morning at 05:45 (they were allowed an extra hour of sleep on Sundays), followed by cadre-led runs, calisthenics, and marching in formation before breakfast. They were taught the fundamentals of marksmanship, basic first aid, grenade throwing, and map reading. For every interesting block of instruction, there seemed to be ten more that were as dull as an elementary school graduation ceremony: barracks fire drills, personal hygiene, field sanitation, malaria control, and use of foot powder. Then there were the ridiculous air raid drills. Each unit had designated air raid wardens and assigned dispersion areas in the event of an enemy aircraft attack. In case the Axis managed to make its way to North Carolina undetected, the air raid warnings were coded "yellow" for practice and "blue" for actual.

Guard duty was an ever-present monotony that rotated through the ranks. Shifts started in the late afternoon and ran until dawn. Guards wore a pressed uniform, including a necktie, and carried a filled canteen, a flashlight, and a rifle. Until the recruit had completed his marksmanship course, his weapon remained empty. Guards walked their circuitous routes without variance, checking doors each time they passed to ensure they were locked. The men were advised to be "especially watchful for fires."

THEY COMPLETED BASIC TRAINING in late June, and as the heat and humidity soared, the next twelve weeks of building unit cohesion commenced. Tactical field exercises were conducted, first at platoon level, then growing in complexity to company and battalion size. The men ran through day and night infiltration courses and learned close quarters shooting and urban combat tactics. They practiced camouflage, scouting, and patrolling. They trained to provide covering fire while another squad or platoon advanced against the enemy. Instructors taught them about demolitions, calling for artillery fire, handling prisoners, and identifying aircraft as friend or foe.

Toward the end of basic training, the parachute units rotated through Fort Benning's jump school to get their personnel fully qualified. Not long after they returned, Swing relaxed his prohibition against jump boots. As later events would reveal, he might have been playing a card from up his sleeve.

The glider units, meanwhile, went to a nearby air base for training. They started with basic knot tying, then advanced to loading and lashing equipment into the CG-4A cargo gliders. Jeeps, howitzers, and trailers all had to be loaded to respect the glider's center of gravity, then secured to prevent shifting in flight—which would result in calamity for everyone onboard. The men also took their first ride in the lumbering, engineless aircraft. The flights did little to endear the "egg crates" to the troopers. As they were towed to release altitude, the racket of canvas slapping against the fuselage's metal skeleton frayed already-jittery nerves. A trooper describing his first glider ride said, "The Air Force had some formula involving wings, vacuum, and other factors to explain what holds those things up. Little did they know that I grabbed the bench seat on either side of me and held them up out of sheer terror."

Trooper Rod Serling showing off his well-earned wings and boots

IN LATE JULY, General Swing returned from a trip to North Africa, where he'd been temporarily attached to Allied Forces HQ in Algiers. He had been there to help his former West Point classmate, General Dwight Eisenhower, coordinate the airborne operation spearheading the invasion of Sicily. The July 10, 1943, night drop had been a near disaster. High winds and navigational errors scattered paratroopers all over the island, and gliders were released prematurely, forcing many to ditch in the ocean. But that paled in comparison to the tragedy that unfolded the next night: twenty-three C-47 cargo planes were shot down by friendly fire. On the heels of a German air raid, the armada had flown over US Navy ships whose uninformed gun crews unleashed their multi-barreled anti-aircraft guns. The lives of 157 paratroopers and aircrew were lost in the confused melee.

Swing arrived back at Camp Mackall determined to apply the lessons he'd learned. He extended the division's work week to forty-eight hours, with the additional time dedicated to night training. A typical exercise, designed to improve assembling in the dark after a night drop, had the men load into trucks and trailers to replicate a C-47 or glider load plan. The drivers bumped across the landing fields to deliver their cargo in the haphazard pattern of an actual airdrop. The men sprang from the trucks, first figuring out where they were, then joining the rest of their company at pre-designated rendezvous points before marching to an objective for a mock attack at dawn.

Swing was omnipresent. He visited units in the field and scoured their offices on base to ensure that officers and sergeants were out participating in training; they'd have to get their paperwork completed after hours. Given the division's reduced headcount, Swing wanted every man to be front-line ready, regardless of his job.

He pushed his officers hard. 'Ripcord' Walker described Swing's leadership style as "cruel to be kind." Swing embraced the adage that sweating during training meant less blood spilled in combat. As he put it, he wanted a lean division, whittled down "until only the steel and whalebone remain."

"From the first, he made it plain that letters of commendation and appreciation would be extremely rare around that shebang," Walker continued. "Superior work, he informed us, would be standard in his command."

While Swing ensured that his officers ran their men through night maneuvers at least twice a week, he also demanded the training be practical and focus on marches and field problems. Extraneous after-hours training in the classroom was to be avoided.

"I want your people free to be with their families when their day's work is done," Swing advised. "These few months are the last for many of them."

ON FRIDAY AFTERNOONS, Swing led all the officers on an hour-long, five-mile hike. Formally noted on the training schedule as "The General's Walk," it was known in the division as a "Swing Session." Swing's adjutant general trailed the parade of officers in a jeep, noting the names of anyone unable to keep up.

"If you fell out three times, you were bounced out of the division," said one of the officers.

At six feet tall, Swing's long strides set a quick pace that created a rubber-band effect for those at the back of the formation. Trotting was often required to avoid falling behind, and the "brisk exercise walk," as Swing described it, often ended with a run through the camp's obstacle course.

The battle of wills between Swing and his paratroopers continued. Captain Stephen 'Rusty' Cavanaugh, one of Haugen's company commanders, who kept his red hair in a tight buzz cut, recalled, "Our regiment was not beloved by many in the division staff. We were felt to be mavericks and troublemakers and prone to feel superior to the rest of the division—which, of course, we were." Cavanaugh claimed Swing "always put the 511th officers at the end, because that's the toughest place to run."

Haugen used the taunt as an opportunity to show off his unit's fitness. "When it was over," Cavanaugh continued, "and the rest of the officers were huffing and puffing, we'd take off and sprint back to our regimental area, Colonel Haugen leading the way."

Foot marches were common throughout the division and much dreaded by the men. At the end of basic training, all personnel had to complete an eighteen-mile march in full combat equipment within six hours. But that was just one trek among many; foot marches became so routine the men grumbled that despite all their elite training, they were all just "glorified infantrymen."

The emphasis on tactical marches reflected the limitations of aerial delivery. Swing's units would have scant motor transportation in the field, and though gliders could bring in jeeps, those were almost exclusively for use by medics or for towing artillery.

The distances of the marches varied. Some were as short as five miles or as long as twenty-five, with the brisk speed averaging four miles an hour. The time requirements forced a steady pace, which created an accordion effect as each man sped up or slowed down to keep up or maintain tactical distance to the man in front of him. Short sprints were often necessary, and carrying full packs and weapons created a constant level of discomfort. Steel helmets seemed to get heavier with each step, equipment straps bit into flesh, back muscles burned, and boots rubbed blisters. Some men carried belt-fed machineguns or mortars. There was no comfortable way to tote such beasts; they dug into shoulders no matter how well positioned. Water was rationed so the men wouldn't empty their canteens in the first few miles.

The foot marches were not just confined to Swing's infantry units, the traditional ground pounders. An aspiring paratrooper in the 457th Parachute Field Artillery Battalion recalled a twenty-mile march with their 75mm pack-howitzers. The cannoneers were racing the other gun crews and moving under the additional weight of their combat packs, radios, shovels, and weapons. "You haven't lived until you've tried to pull a fourteen-hundred-pound pack howitzer with wooden spoke, steel-rimmed wheels through deep sand," he wrote.

During another fast-paced march led by 'Slugger' Lahti, William MacKay, lugging a forty-four-pound 81mm mortar tube, was flagging. He shouted to his buddy Herbert Whitehead, "Hey, Whitehead, I'm going to unbutton my pants and let my dong hang out!"

"How come you're going to let your dong hang out, MacKay?" Whitehead yelled back.

"If I'm gonna work like a horse, I'm gonna look like a horse!"

Lahti, trying to conceal his laughter, got the point and slowed the pace.

Unsurprisingly, the marches leant themselves to Haugen's competitive nature. If he was going to have the best regiment in the division, one measure was having the fastest regiment in the division. He led the men on a blistering twenty-five-mile night march, completing the grueling marathon-length route in just six and a half hours. Moving that fast meant taking fewer breaks and trucking along at almost a jog. A trooper recalled it was so bad that "a couple of guys had blood coming through their boots."

Pride and determination got them to the finish. They were learning as much about themselves as about each other, and the completion of each march revealed who had the fortitude to be relied on.

In the middle of one march, Hugh Harrison relieved a fatigued buddy of a .50 caliber machinegun's sixty-pound receiver. Harrison wasn't a member of the machinegun section, but he hoisted the block of metal onto his shoulder anyway and leaned into the march. When troopers offered to spell him of it, he refused. At the finish, Harrison's shoulder was rubbed raw, staining his uniform with blood. A witness later reflected, "Men just outdid themselves that night and refused to quit."

They were starting to jell.

Haugen often balanced the training's intensity with well-earned rewards. After the long, record-setting march, the exhausted men collapsed into their barracks to find fifty-five-gallon drums filled with ice-cold beer.

Few things feel as good as completing a backbreaking march. Slipping off heavy equipment and releasing aching feet from the confines of warm combat boots are simple but undeniable pleasures. The event itself was misery, but being done with it and enjoying a cold beer with comrades made it worth every painful step.

"The men griped about the long marches," an officer admitted, "but on weekends they bragged about the toughness of the training, that they could march farther and faster than any other troops."

IF THE EXERTION AND EXHAUSTION didn't drive home what their new profession required, the accidental deaths did.

The first occurred in mid-August when a twin-engine C-47 cargo plane developed mechanical trouble, forcing Hard Rock's troops to jump as it descended. Eight of them made it out in time, but the last two men to exit were too low for their chutes to deploy.

Less than a month later, tragedy struck again when a CG-4A glider crashed during a demonstration for visiting dignitaries. The fatalities included the two pilots and four of Swing's artillerymen.

"Now the men are—in some units—beginning to refuse to fly," wrote Major Henry A. Burgess in a letter home. Burgess, a Harvard graduate who grew up on a ranch in Wyoming, understood his men's concerns. "You can't help but sympathize with them, but nevertheless they get court-martialed if they refuse to fly. Charges are drafted on the grounds that they refuse to obey the lawful command of a commissioned officer."

Ten more troopers died when their pilot aborted their night drop and attempted to land with an engine out. He overshot the runway, and in pulling up, clipped a pine tree, which spun the aircraft into the ground.

The death of nineteen-year-old Private Guilio F. 'Ju-Ju' DiPangrazio, on the night of November 19, 1943, hit the ranks of Hard Rock's men deeply. During their first tactical night jump as a unit, DiPangrazio's parachute failed to open.

"It was an awakening moment for all of us," said a trooper. "We were not invincible."

Equipment failures were rare but did occur, and Haugen ordered the men of DiPangrazio's company to make a second night jump before the implications sank in. There was nearly a second fatality as a result.

First Lieutenant Robert H. Kliewer, a twenty-six-year-old jump-master, was so focused on his men's welfare and checking their equipment that he forgot to check his own. Leading his men out of the aircraft, Kliewer realized almost too late that he failed to connect his chute's static line. Tumbling toward the ground, he violently snatched the handle of his reserve parachute. It was a rough landing, but he made it.

DiPangrazio's death was a tragedy, but it also galvanized a deeper ethos amongst the paratroopers. More than one of them came to a secret, maybe even unconscious, realization about their comrade's death: it fortified their culture of sacrifice and superiority. They were willing to risk their lives just to get into the battle. It was a spirit characterized in the morbid refrain of their favorite drinking song, "Gory, gory, what a helluva way to die!"

BUT NOT ALL OF SWING'S UNITS enjoyed that same esprit-de-corps, as many men resented their unilateral glider assignments. Additionally, the drudgery of basic training weighed down morale as men

Paratroopers exit a C-47 in flight during a training jump

realized the Army often appeared to cherish sweeping, mopping, digging, inspecting, scrubbing, polishing, marching, and exercising above all else. The camp's condition didn't help, either. The facilities were so primitive—the barracks had no indoor plumbing—and the heat was so oppressive, the men referred to it as "Guadalmackall," in reference to the horrors of the bitter fighting that had occurred on the island of Guadalcanal in 1942.

It was during this low period that Swing initiated a contest to christen the division with a nickname. As the submissions came in, it became apparent now wasn't the time. "Dehydrated," read one. "Rat Race Division," read another. The division historian decided the more profanely imaginative were unprintable, and the contest was soon dropped.

Swing's next attempt to raise morale was more successful, and units were soon fielding sports teams to compete in football, baseball, basketball, swimming, and boxing. The sports appealed to the young men's sense of fun competition and provided a welcome distraction from Army life.

As such, it wasn't until a Monday morning during the summer of 1943 that the division earned its nickname. Like most, it was born of circumstance rather than design. Before roll call, Lieutenant Colonel Douglas 'Tangle Foot' Quandt routinely asked his commanders, "Any of your angels in jail?"

It wasn't a rhetorical question.

As the troopers completed basic training, they were rewarded with weekend passes into town. With freedom to shrug off the shackles of authority, if even for a few hours, came the testing of boundaries. Fights and drunken behavior were the most common infractions. But some high-spirited troopers were more inventive, like the two stowaways who hopped on a passing freight train for a free ride back to camp. Perturbed when the train didn't slow down at their destination—and with bottles of alcohol in each hand preventing a jump—they uncoupled their carriage to make their escape.

There was also the story of an entire platoon who went on the war path in retaliation for a taxi driver robbing one of their drunk buddies. They swarmed into the cab company's parking lot and overturned all the taxis.

So Quandt never knew what to expect on a Monday morning.

"How many of your angels are in jail?" he would ask the next officer.

"None, sir, not this weekend," was the hoped-for response.

The sarcastic sobriquet soon caught on with the division staff, and even Swing occasionally referred to the troops as "My angels."

THE 11TH AIRBORNE'S initial training phase culminated in December 1943, with a multi-division-sized exercise to seize the Knollwood Army Auxiliary Airport near Pinehurst, North Carolina. Transports carrying paratroopers and others towing gliders lifted off at midnight from four airfields and navigated a complex, two-hundred-mile flight route. The goal: to drop the troops on multiple moon-bathed landing zones. Over the course of the next five days, Swing's men secured objectives, received resupplies by airdrop, and evacuated simulated casualties from the secured airport. With the entire division and nearly two thousand tons of supplies delivered by air, it was a resounding success.

Over a series of days starting on Sunday, January 2, 1944, rumors of heading into combat ran rampant amongst the troops when they were loaded onto twenty-two trains heading west, destination unspecified. Those speculations were dashed when their journey ended in Louisiana. At Camp Polk, they would face batteries of individual tests and unit exercises as one of the final milestones before combat deployment.

The men were impressed upon arrival. These were no cramped tar-paper shacks, but roomy buildings with indoor plumbing—both showers and latrines! No more braving the elements or urinating in a bottle in the middle of the night.

"We were housed in 'real' barracks, which were two-story," recalled Harold 'Hal' Jones. "For once, we were living high!"

The food was better, too, and there was more of it, and troops were delighted to find the post exchange well stocked with soft drinks and beer.

The paratroopers wasted no time introducing themselves to Camp Polk's other residents, the tankers of the Army's recently formed armored divisions. Tank units, with their origins rooted in the US Cavalry's rich history, considered themselves elite. Haugen's men, however, had a different pecking order in mind.

A squad of troopers purchased Armored Forces pillowcases at the post exchange. Emblazoned with a frilled border and embroidered tanks, the souvenir keepsakes were intended to be sent home to wives and sweethearts. The troopers stationed themselves outside the entrance and made a show of spit-shining their jump boots with the pillowcases. It was an invitation. And it was accepted.

Brawls between the two groups became a reoccurring problem for the base commander and local police. Troops from both units relished the "knuckle maneuvers."

John Curcio was a smaller paratrooper with a unique fighting style: he'd suffer a few punches to close the gap on his opponent, then, grabbing the man's groin, he'd give a violent twist to end the melee. "He lost very few fights," noted one of his buddies.

Tom Granillio, a hulk of a man who played tackle on the 511th's football team, cemented his legendary status at Camp Polk: after throwing an armored division military policeman (MP) over a jeep, it took six more MPs to subdue and arrest him. A few hours later, Granillio wrestled the barred window out of his cell and escaped from the stockade.

THE ARMY GROUND FORCE'S tests commenced with a week of individual assessments. Swing's men were run through graded lanes to ensure they had mastered disassembling and reassembling their weapons, throwing hand grenades, donning gasmasks, placing land-mines, administering first aid, and other basic skills.

In the first week of February, the troops marched out to the Calcasieu Bayou for unit-level testing. Observers graded them as they executed a series of squad, platoon, company, battalion, and regi-mental tactical exercises under simulated combat conditions. Noise and light discipline were enforced as the troops dug field positions, attacked, defended, and finally withdrew. There were tests for the artillery, engineer, and signal units as well, and each were put through their paces.

"The salient feature of the maneuvers was the rain," said one trooper. Edward A. Hammrich agreed, recalling, "We had everything as far as weather conditions: snow, sleet, rain, and hail. The mud was up to our—well, let's say it buried a jeep. Need I say more?" Between each three-day exercise, troopers had twenty-four hours to get some sleep, get warm, eat, and burn off any blood-sucking ticks with cigarettes.

Some of the "farm boys," according to Hammrich, used the time to hunt for wild pigs. Having blank ammunition, they had to impro-vise. Affixing their bayonets to their rifles, they threw them like javelins, which required closing in on the wounded animal and finishing it off with rifle butts or knives.

When one of his men suggested a "bayonet drill," Henry Burgess' troopers went after a farmer's hogs with their bayonets. Burgess turned a blind eye to the slaughter; almost thirty hogs were skewered and then eaten.

"We learned that our bayonets were rather stiff and could be broken unless you withdrew your bayonet quickly," said Burgess. They also learned that the government had to reimburse the farmer for lost income.

AFTER PASSING the readiness exercises, however, nothing happened. No deployment orders, no re-assignment, nothing. By March, it became clear the War Department would be keeping the Angels at Camp Polk longer than expected.

Swing took advantage of the extended stay to qualify more of his troops as parachutists. Having as many men trained in parachuting as possible would give him the flexibility he needed when combat conditions dictated how his division would be deployed.

Swing assigned 'Hard Rock' Haugen to set up the Angels' own jump school at a nearby air base. Haugen, the most senior parachute officer in the division, was the natural choice, but Swing should have predicted what happened next.

Haugen approached the assignment with his typical zeal, his four-week course of instruction mirroring the Army's parachute school at Fort Benning. With instructors from his own regiment, there was an extensive focus on physical conditioning as well as hazing. Haugen and his men were products of such rituals, and in their minds, those rituals worked. In addition to training men to jump out of planes, they viewed it as their responsibility to separate those who wanted to be there from the posers. Inducing stress through harassment and physical exertion wasn't personal, it was Haugen's best tool to forge the warriors he thought the division needed. Swing disagreed.

It was over dinner and drinks that the issue came to a head.

"Swing was in a hurry [to get more men qualified], as time was short before we were to go overseas," recalled Major Henry Burgess, who was present. "Swing thought Haugen had been spending too much time on physical conditioning, which was really unnecessary at that point, and too little on the jumping phase."

The two men argued their points, loudly and with passion: Swing as a division commander who wanted his orders carried out, and Haugen with the stubbornness of a Spartan mule. The other guests slipped from the room as the debate grew in intensity. Neither man backed down, and Haugen stormed out.

The next morning, there was more yelling in Swing's office. What exactly was said, only Swing and Haugen would ever fully know, but the debate ended with Haugen refusing to modify his curriculum and Swing relieving him of running the school. The course would now be run by the twenty-five-year-old Burgess, who, while a capable officer, had never jumped from a plane in flight himself.

Burgess got his orders: he'd have a maximum of two weeks per class, with ground training the first week and jump qualification the second.

Swing launched his own campaign to muster volunteers for the division-run school. He couldn't order men to attend; they had to volunteer.

"We're going to have our own jump school right here at Camp Polk!" bellowed Swing to a gathered group of quartermasters, MPs, medics, and signal troops. "You won't have to go to Benning and go through all of that rigamarole for weeks and weeks. You'll get those shiny jump boots and that extra fifty bucks a month."

Swing apparently understood the allure of those boots after all.

He completed his pitch with a strong call to action: "Now, how many of you fighting sons of bitches want to be paratroopers? Raise your hands!"

Several, including Richard L. Hoyt, a thirty-three-year-old signal officer, raised their hands. Hoyt's training was far less than two weeks, as he later recalled, "We had two days of orientation and then we went up and jumped."

THAT SWING VIEWED PARACHUTING into combat as nothing more than a unique commute—where gravity did most of the work—was likely a combination of personal experience and his traditional Army perspective. While he wore US Army paratrooper wings, he hadn't gone through parachute school to earn them, nor had he made the requisite five jumps.

At the outbreak of World War II, with the airborne concept in its infancy, jump-qualified senior officers were scarce. In mid-1942, as commander of the 82nd Airborne Division's artillery, Swing and his commander, General Matthew Ridgway, traveled to Fort Benning to earn their wings.

Their training was short and to the point. Under the tutelage of a parachute officer, the men were given "about a half hour of basic instruction and demonstration: a few minutes' work in a suspended parachute harness, a few jumps from a raised platform to simulate the shock of hitting the ground, a few practice exits from the door of the C-47, and a rudimentary briefing on how to maneuver the parachute with risers, collapse it on the ground, and shuck the harness."

An hour later, the group was aloft and made its jump. Ridgway had a jarring landing, but Swing landed just fine, quipping, "I'd rather fall off an airplane than a polo pony."

BURGESS MANAGED THE JUMP SCHOOL with instructors from Swing's other parachute units, the 457th Parachute Field Artillery Battalion and the 127th Airborne Engineer Battalion's Charlie Company. Hard Rock refused to let any of his men participate. Swing visited the site to inspect Burgess' program. The instructors had built mock aircraft fuselages and elevated platforms to rehearse aircraft procedures and practice landing falls. Swing was satisfied.

An officer in one of Burgess' first classes remembered the condensed schedule: "Monday, we jogged and tumbled off the mockup... Tuesday, we jogged and tumbled and hung in the harness... Wednesday was jump day and we entrucked at dawn for DeRidder Army Air Base.... We completed the required five jumps, including a night jump, during the rest of the week."

The extended stay at Camp Polk gave the men time to speculate on their future, especially where and when they'd be going to combat and who would or wouldn't survive. Two airborne divisions had already left for Europe, and a parachute regiment had been sent to fight in the Pacific. Some reasoned that thousands more troops would be needed to overcome Hitler's Atlantic Wall, others that the Pacific's island-hopping campaigns were ill-suited to parachute and glider operations. Many opined that Louisiana's swampy terrain and humidity were ideal for learning jungle warfare.

"We presumed that Polk was selected for the 11th, and then we were slated for the Pacific," said General Albert Pierson, Swing's assistant division commander. "But when we arrived at Polk, we found another division that was shipped later to Europe."

Rumors ceased in mid-April when Swing restricted everyone to camp. Instructions followed for commanders to prepare for movement and for the men to remove the division patch, along with all airborne insignia, from their uniforms. No parachute wings were to be worn. The paratroopers grumbled as they stuffed their jump boots into duffle bags and laced up canvas leggings over standard Army field shoes. Many assumed it was more of Swing's petty games, but in reality, the War Department wanted it kept secret that airborne troops were being deployed.

When they weren't loading cargo or packing equipment, the men attended censorship lectures. Posters were tacked up in the barracks to remind all, "Loose lips sink ships."

"We began to load up on a troop train heading north," said Private Leroy 'Pops' Butler, "still not knowing where we were going."

After a few hours, the train veered west. "We finally knew," he continued. "We were going to fight the Japs."

THERE WERE MIXED EMOTIONS about heading to the Pacific. Some of the men were excited; having enlisted in response to the attack on Pearl Harbor, they were eager to fight the Japanese. Paratrooper Jerry Davis, reading about the maelstrom of German artillery barrages in Europe, considered heading west a lucky draw. Most, however, were indifferent, as one trooper recalled, "Strangely, we did not discuss our destination too much. We had trained long and hard. We had believed we were going to Europe—but really, what's the difference? We had to fight till victory, so let's get started."

By April 28, 1944, Swing's eight thousand-odd troopers had debarked at Camp Stoneman, roughly thirty miles east of San Francisco. The men received tropical inoculations and instruction on life aboard a troop ship. They learned where the onboard life rafts were, how to lower them into the ocean, and how to use the survival kits found in each. They practiced climbing up and down rope nets and learned how to properly don a lifejacket and to jump from a sinking ship.

The camp served hearty food and attempted to keep the men occupied with plenty of movies, stage acts, and concerts. But after several days on a cramped train with periodic stops for calisthenics and little else to do but stare out the window, the men were restless. Above all, the looming realities of combat weighed on many.

With San Francisco so close, it seemed absurd to spend what might be their last nights in the States on a military post.

Several of Haugen's paratroopers jumped the fence, risking AWOLs for a last night on the town. They returned to camp with their hair dyed peroxide blonde, ears pierced, and one swashbuckler sporting a nose ring.

Harry Wagers, from Haugen's 3rd Battalion, blacked out in his bunk after he and a buddy drank too much beer. A punch in the face woke him up. He'd been so drunk that he had climbed down from his top rack and urinated on a sleeping corporal in the bunk below. The corporal's fist woke Wagers, sending him stumbling across the room.

"The division accumulated a record number of AW-104s [non-court-martial offenses] during that period, including one myself," admitted six-foot-three Lieutenant Leo Crawford, one of Hard Rock Haugen's platoon leaders.

Crawford and a fellow officer took offense when non-parachute officers walked into Camp Stoneman's officer club wearing jump boots. Insults were exchanged, a scrap ensued, and the next morning, after a reprimand by Haugen, Crawford had to go see Swing.

"I reported to General Swing bearing a black eye," said Crawford, "which I had tried ineffectually to conceal with borrowed sunglasses."

"Are you an officer?" asked Swing.

"Yes, sir," Crawford replied.

"You look like a damned hoodlum to me," Swing barked back.

Crawford was fined $125 and transferred to one of the glider infantry regiments. He was upset about leaving his men but relieved that he'd still be going to the Pacific with the division.

Crawford's brawl wasn't an isolated incident. A group of troopers happened upon some non-airborne men wearing jump boots, and to make matter worse, they were scuffed and dirty. As George Doherty remembered, "They were wearing 'our' jump boots, while we were wearing leggings—this was a NO! NO!"

The fracas ended when Haugen's troopers retreated victoriously with several of the culprits' jump boots as their prize.

When Haugen learned that a Marine unit had established a camp record by completing a twelve-mile march in under four hours, he decided to put his men's excess energy to use. He set a blazing pace—his regiment completed the trek under three hours, securing another bragging right for the regiment.

With their time at Stoneman complete, the 11th Airborne Division transitioned into becoming shipment #1855, another anonymous group of GIs leaving the States for an undisclosed island in the Pacific.

The troops of #1855 would depart on several ships sailing from San Francisco. The first would debark on May 5, 1944, with the rest staggered over the next several weeks.

Lines of troops snaked up the gangplanks. Each man had his name checked against the manifest. Straining under the weight of a rifle and two duffel bags, the men shifted uncomfortably and waited to board. Red Cross volunteers handed each a ditty bag containing a toothbrush, toothpaste, cigarettes, and gum.

Senior officers were assigned staterooms in the ship's fantail, but below deck, the conditions were spartan. The bunks were stacked five high with barely three feet between them. There were no mattresses, just stretched canvas roped into place on iron frames, and each man had a hook to hang his gear. With so many troopers shuffling aboard, maintaining order was a chore; the men were told to climb into their bunks and wait for additional instruction.

Many took their last glimpse of the States as they steamed past Alcatraz Island and under the Golden Gate Bridge. With their destination still unknown, almost all of them marked the occasion with a traditional coin toss into the ocean for good luck.

Of their departure, a trooper wrote to his parents, "Perhaps the most memorable part of our voyage was that first day off the coast of California as we headed toward the horizon.... Overhead, a flew blimps and planes seemingly escorting us out to sea. When they suddenly departed, I felt much like a baby bird just tossed from its nest!"

The 11th was sailing into a combat zone where the blood-stained tide was changing. After a series of stunning victories that had placed almost one-tenth of the globe under Emperor Hirohito's banner, the Japanese lines—stretching thousands of miles in any direction from Tokyo—were crumbling. The Allies were regaining territory on multiple fronts, overland from the east in Burma and on two parallel routes of advance through the Pacific: one led by Army General Douglas MacArthur, the other led by Navy Admiral Chester W. Nimitz. The two American warlords were launching mutually supporting operations to seize a series of islands, both to shorten their supply lines and secure land-based airfields from which they could continue their campaigns.

MacArthur's advance, in particular, was slicing through Japan's economic sea lanes and threatening to cut off access to vital resources. The Emperor's war machine required the rubber, oil, tin, and rice from his seized territories in the Dutch East Indies. Japanese military leaders understood the danger, and as the battles on Guadalcanal and New Guinea had shown, they would fight viciously to keep their supply routes open.

The Angels were heading into a fray unlike anything they could imagine, and left behind in the ship's wake were their youth and innocence—for those who came back would never be the same.

Chapter 2

Bugs, Breasts, and Beer!

Oro Bay, New Guinea.
Friday, May 26, 1944

Twenty-one days after departing San Francisco, the first ship dropped anchor off New Guinea's east coast. The rest of the division continued to sail in during the next three weeks.

It had been a long, uncomfortable voyage, and the men were ready to get back on land. Temperatures soared in the crowded cargo holds, and blackout conditions at night reduced ventilation, making it worse. The stifling heat, described as "unbearable," allowed fitful sleep at best, and many men slept on deck. On Lieutenant Miles Gale's ship, the SS *Sea Pike*, the sailors relished washing down the decks before sunrise.

"At 4:00 a.m., the decks were watered down with fire hoses and sleepers would wake up in the middle of a river. There was a lot of salty language directed at the hose crew who delighted in waking the deck sleepers."

The ghastly latrines stunk with a rank combination of sweat, cigarettes, and urine. Keeping clean was almost impossible. One of

Haugen's paratroopers recalled, "For washing and shaving, salt water only was available—it lathered not at all." Some of the men tried to launder their uniforms by throwing them overboard tied to a rope, a technique that was abandoned after the sea claimed their clothes.

Everyone agreed the food was atrocious, a rare example of consensus amongst troops who made a sport out of disagreement. They were fed two meals a day: a breakfast of overcooked, dehydrated potatoes with green powdered eggs, and hot dogs or Spam for dinner. Both were slopped into the men's mess kits after they waited in line for hours. On good days, they got an orange for lunch.

The monotonous daily routine at sea consisted of morning calisthenics, weapons cleaning, and four hours of repetitive instruction on anything from hygiene, malaria, first aid, aircraft recognition, treatment of POWs, military courtesy, and articles of war to map reading, gas mask drills, or a geographic orientation to the Pacific. The training day ended with a second session of calisthenics and dinner.

There was plenty of time for entertainment, though. The troopers organized skits, concerts, and boxing matches to help pass the time. Occasionally, the crew set up a movie projector on deck, and men watched from both sides of a stretched sheet, half enjoying the reversed film. Crossing the equator provided another distraction as the men graduated from pollywogs to shellbacks in the time-honored naval tradition. Officiated by a sailor dressed as King Neptune, the ceremony subjected selected officers and men to rituals of spankings, hot tar, and other embarrassments while troopers hooted and hollered in delight.

The Angels' destination was announced a few days after sailing from San Francisco. Many had hoped Australia would be their first port of call, and there was disappointment and confusion when the PA system broadcast that they were going to New Guinea. It was the same on every ship—most men had no clue where the island was located. Invariably, at least one joker assured his buddies it couldn't be that far from Old Guinea.

The ships anchored in Oro Bay, and the men clambered over the sides and down cargo nets to transports ready to bring them ashore. The sailors were relieved to be rid of the troopers. It had been a grudging relationship at best. The troopers booed loudly at the sailors' failed attempts to hit floating targets during gunnery practice, and they considered the captain's use of the loudspeakers to address his sailors as an unacceptable interruption. After each, "Now hear this, now hear this," the troopers yelled in unison, "48! 49! 50! Some shit!" The bizarre chant's origin seems to have been lost to history.

As the transport craft chugged toward shore, the troopers' initial impressions of the island were favorable. Paratrooper George Doherty later recalled, "We got our first glimpse of the tropics, lush jungle so green and thick it looked like a solid wall."

Edward 'Big Ed' Hogan concurred, adding, "The land rose rather steeply from the water's edge, sometimes at an angle of 45 degrees or higher, with the trees and dark green jungle growth everywhere. At various levels, there were small hutments, and in the evening, the lights from the hutments presented a tranquil sight. It was a far cry from the Detroit River back home."

Swing, having already arrived from his meeting with MacArthur, was waiting for them near the village of Dobodura. Their camp was in a broad jungle basin about fifteen miles inland from the bay, on the edge of a former US airfield.

Once ashore, Doherty's initial excitement "gave way to the oppressive heat and humidity.... Perspiration broke out and soaked us to the skin." As the troopers were driven down dusty roads to camp, they passed a ten-foot-tall hand-painted sign that read:

"DOBODURA-TOKYO ROAD 'There are many roads to Tokyo; we will neglect none of them.' Pres. Roosevelt."

The Angels were finally on the war path—or so they thought.

EACH UNIT FOUND piles of cots and heaps of twenty-by-twenty pyramidal tents waiting for assembly. While the Air Force had left the airfield and some dirt roads, it was up to the Angels to lay out and establish their camp.

A trooper, Corporal Cecil C. Robson, stands in front of a typical tent on New Guinea; note the wood frame for storing the men's mess kits

Swing's engineers developed a framing system for the tents that tightened their musty canvases and raised them off the ground. The design became a division standard, and each unit constructed their frames accordingly. Troopers armed with machetes waded through the sea of eight-foot kunai grass and into the nearby jungle to cut down bamboo and haul it back to camp. Their harvest was cut to length and used as framing. Once the tents were up, each lodged four soldiers with room for their cots, footlockers, and weapons.

"Even with the side rolled up to catch a nonexistent breeze," said Miles Gale, "those were very tight quarters."

Work parties cleared vegetation to create areas for company formations and calisthenics. Showers were rudimentary contraptions built from aircrafts' external fuel tanks. The tanks were hoisted up on poles with a hanging wire to open the valves that were fed chlorinated water pumped from a nearby creek. Bathing was scheduled by unit, with each having three days a week designated for their usage.

The demand was high, and the water precious, so a formal memo documented the shower procedure: "All bathers will wet up, turn water off, soap well, and shower off."

The latrines were even more basic: dug-in fifty-five-gallon oil drums with a seat cut out of scrap lumber. They were installed on the edge of camp, as far from the tents as reasonable.

"This setup didn't encourage you to 'sit and think,' and with the addition of the odor, it was not a pleasant place to visit," wrote one of Haugen's officers. Miles Gale shuddered at the thought of the stench for decades after the war. To manage sanitation and odor, daily work parties poured aviation fuel into the drums of excrement and set the mess alight.

"In five or ten minutes, the fire would burn out and odor around the latrine would be almost bearable," recalled Bill Porteous, who had the unpleasant chore of conducting the task.

Like the tents, the latrines needed to adhere to Swing's approved design and be uniformly aligned to his liking. This created a lot of frustration as digging the pits for the barrels was no small task. In Major Edward 'Slugger' Lahti's recollection, Swing "seemed to change his mind almost daily.... The many changes in the lineup of latrines required a great deal of unnecessary work. It was very discouraging for those in charge."

Swing wanted the camp as orderly as any base back in the States, and he invested in making it as comfortable as possible. He had the labor and a jungle full of materials at his disposal, and just as importantly, all the work kept the men busy and out of trouble.

The men constructed huts in the local style, and with the help of Papuan labor, they built thatched roof kitchens, mess facilities, chapels, day rooms, and even clubs. Haugen's men dubbed their sergeants' lounge Club 91 for the ninety-one non-commissioned officers in the regiment who had exclusive access. Some of the huts had corrugated tin sheets added to the sides, giving them the semblance of permanence. To reduce the mud, dirt roads were covered with sand by engineers hauling dump trucks up from the beach.

In addition to making the base resemble a State-side post, Swing ran it like one too, maintaining a forty-four-hour training week. Guard duty was conducted in the regulated manner, with armed troops pacing off their assigned route while wearing their tan service uniforms and shined boots or shoes. Buglers blared the daily calls, twice each, one facing east and another west, ensuring they were heard by all. Church worship services were conducted regularly and included special services, such as Rosh Hashanah, by denomination.

At the same time, Swing established another jump school to qualify more parachutists. Henry Burgess was again in charge and took the opportunity to earn his wings. With the number of required jumps reduced from five to three to minimize injuries, Swing was getting closer to his goal, with almost 75 percent of the enlisted men parachute-qualified. Enough had gone through the division's schools that Swing modified the designation of his glider infantry regiments to paraglider infantry regiments, in recognition of their dual airborne capability. Even though the Army did not officially recognize the new designation, it was a welcome boost in morale.

The Air Force also made twelve gliders available, and select groups of grumbling paratroopers became glider-qualified while acquiring some respect for the men who had to fly in the fragile aircraft. The school's drop zone was near Soputa Military Cemetery, where the rows of wooden crosses marking the graves of men killed during the battle for New Guinea served as a sober reminder of what lay ahead.

There were also opportunities to learn from those who had already been in the thick of fighting. A few members of the Angels' reconnaissance platoon were sent to the prestigious Alamo Scout School, while others attended the Australian-run jungle survival school. The Aussies had mastered the jungle at great cost. The Angels took their lessons to heart, including setting up a small sniper group armed with scoped bolt-action Australian Enfield rifles.

The Angels learned how the war in the Pacific was fought. The Australians' and veterans' anecdotes were consistent: a GI who failed to respect the "no quarter asked, none given" rules put himself and his buddies at risk. The Japanese had dictated the terms: the string of atrocities committed by Imperial troops were well publicized, starting with their decapitation and murdering of Chinese prisoners and civilians, up to the more recent revelations of brutalizing American and Philippine prisoners during the Bataan death march. But their ruthlessness was not just reserved for post-battle victory. The US Marines' experience on Guadalcanal in 1942 revealed the enemy's aversion to surrender, preferring instead to fight to the literal last man. Wounded Japanese were notorious for blowing themselves up to kill as many Allied soldiers as possible, and fake surrenders were a common deception. The trick of waving a white surrender flag, only to gun down those accepting the capitulation, occurred several times during the combat on New Guinea. The Angels were entering an "anything goes" campaign, and woe to the soldier who failed to steel his heart for it.

Training exercises emphasized patrolling and refined the Angels' tactics. The maneuvers took place in the Owen Stanley mountains, which 'Big Ed' Hogan described as "the ugliest mountains in the world. They were positively eerie. A good part of the time, the peaks were covered with fog or clouds."

Eerie they were, as thousands of Allied troops had died in them repelling the Japanese who had invaded in 1942. The bitter fighting, some of the most punishing of the entire war, pushed the Japanese back to the island's west coast, where the battle continued.

Abandoned equipment, crashed aircraft, unexploded booby traps, and human remains were common encounters. A trooper in Doherty's battalion recalled, "I remember that when we worked through exercises there, we commonly came across human skulls and bones." The men also learned to recognize the putrid smell of rotting flesh as they trudged past Japanese corpses.

The possibility of stumbling upon Japanese stragglers while battling centipedes, fire ants, mosquitos, leeches, and the stifling heat combined to make the training both realistic and wholly unpleasant.

George Doherty recalled that entering the shoulder-deep primordial swamps "was a very scary situation, because you could imagine stepping into a bottomless hole and being swallowed up by the brackish water, and even worse was our imaginations that were running wild about long slithering snakes or crocodiles that could tear you apart."

There were lots of rats, too. "I swear, as big as cats," recalled one trooper. "God almighty, they scared the living hell out of you. They were all over the place."

New Guinea introduced the Angels to the realities of jungle warfare, and they soon realized that the swamps of Louisiana had more in common with the plains of Kansas than the dense, unforgiving terrain of the Pacific Islands.

There were some humble reminders that common sense usually beat brute force. Leroy Butler recalled his patrol crossing a wide river that emptied into the ocean. "Being tough paratroopers," he wrote, "we held our equipment high over our heads and forded the river. On the opposite side, we sat down to rest and dry ourselves."

Feeling proud of their accomplishment, they watched as a five-foot-tall Papuan approached the river from the same direction they had just come from. "When he reached the river," continued Butler, "he turned and walked straight out into the ocean, turned and walked parallel to the shore, and turned back toward the beach, never getting into water deeper than his knees."

To rehearse bringing their full firepower to bear, combat teams—composed of an infantry battalion augmented with howitzers, engineers, heavy machineguns, and medics—conducted three-day live-fire exercises. Acting as a single unit, they completed a series of battlefield tasks: moving into and establishing a defensive perimeter, radioing for aerial resupply drops, and attacking a defended airfield with multiple assault parties.

The exercises proved invaluable. Mistakes were noted and lessons shared across the division to be learned and corrected. Failures were those of troops new to combat: individuals making too much noise during movement or bunching too closely together; commanders being unaware of where their subordinate units were or losing contact with adjacent units; lieutenants positioning flank security poorly and exposing their machineguns and artillery sites; patrol leaders getting lost; and officers sending verbose, unclear messages. It was better to hone these tactics in the relatively quiet jungles of New Guinea than in combat against an enemy who had been at war for over ten years.

Training with real ammunition formed the Angels into a cohesive fighting team, and they were as prepared for combat as any unit could be. But the realistic training came at a price. One of Haugen's men was killed by flying debris from an explosion during a field exercise. A demonstration of Japanese hand grenades killed a captain, and six others were severely wounded when a rifle grenade detonated prematurely. Two men were accidently shot and killed by their own squad during live fire exercises, and several others were wounded by mortar shrapnel.

Beyond those hazards, troopers thought the island itself was trying to kill them. Even with the swamps surrounding the camp drained, warding off insects and disease was a constant battle. The men slept under nets to defend against "bomber-size mosquitoes," and upon rising, they dusted their ankles and socks with insecticide powder. They continued the daily habit started during their Pacific voyage of taking Atabrine tablets to keep malaria at bay, with the noticeable side effect that it turned their skin and the whites of their eyes yellow. Everyone smelled like a pungent perfume of sweat and "bug oil," the Army-issued insect repellent.

Swing's strict policy was for the men in the field to wear their cotton field uniforms with their sleeves rolled down. The men complained about it, preferring to roll up their sleeves in the heat, but the practice was yet another preventative tactic against malaria, dengue fever, and scrub typhus. The threat was real, and despite their best efforts, several men died of scrub typhus after being bitten by mites while on jungle exercises.

Additionally, all the water was treated to prevent disease. In camp, chlorinated water was available in rubber lined lister bags, and in the field, disinfecting halazone tablets were dropped into canteens after filling them from streams. Chaplain Lee 'Chappie' Walker despised the taste. He likened it to "something like a liquefied rubber tire." He longed for the "unadulterated joy of a cool, clear, pure, unspoiled, pristine flavor of a simple glass of water!" It would be well over a year before Chappie got to enjoy that modest pleasure.

Some found the conditions and intensity of the training too much. One man in paratrooper Jerry Davis' unit committed suicide; another had a nervous breakdown, requiring evacuation.

COMBATING IDLE BOREDOM was almost a greater challenge than combating the elements. With evenings and weekends off, there was plenty of time for relaxation, but unlike their brethren in the European theater, men in the Pacific were stuck where they were. A rear-area base was still on an island in the middle of nowhere, barren of all youthful distractions. Here, there were no weekend passes to London or Paris, and no nearby villages with pubs, wine, or champagne. And women were as rare as a refreshing breeze.

Any romantic illusions the troopers might have had about landing in a tropical paradise populated by beautiful hula-dancers were dashed upon arrival. The aboriginal tribesmen, referred to by the Angels as "Fuzzie Wuzzies" due to their kinky, clay-coated hair, were, as one trooper unkindly noted, "just plain ugly." The men were initially captivated by the Papuans' dress, which for the women was little more than a skirt. With most of the troopers never having seen a naked breast, the bare-chested women were an instant curiosity. Troopers snapped photos by the dozens, but the women, surely sensing the adolescent chicanery, often fled from the camera. The initial interest faded, and there was little interaction with the local tribes, but GIs did barter with them, trading cigarettes, Hershey bars, or chewing gum for bananas or coconuts.

There was a small contingent of American women from the Women's Army Corps on the island. Their compound was well guarded, however, with some sources claiming no less than three rings of barbed wired fences. Those WACs interested in dating servicemen gravitated to officers, leaving the enlisted men to fashion far-fetched tales of conquest that included pole-vaulting, tunneling, and even clinging to the underside of supply trucks.

Gambling was a popular pastime. The cooks in Hard Rock's 3rd Battalion ran an after-hours casino in the mess tent, complete with music and craps tables, and it was a hopping spot on pay day. In addition to poker and dice, some games of chance took on a local flair. Doodlebug racing required participants bring their own insect, the bigger the better, as everyone agreed that size equated to speed. The beetles were placed in the center of a large circle drawn in the sand, and whoever athlete crossed the line first claimed their prize of beer or cigarettes.

Although the Army provided beer, the twelve-ounce, 3.2 percent alcohol beers available for purchase from the quartermaster were strictly rationed. Each man could buy up to twenty-four a month, but just three at a time within a three-day period. Keeping them cold was impossible.

Enterprising free-market capitalists stepped in to fill the void and satiate demand. Two men in Mile Gale's platoon, Claude 'Pappy' Ledford and his buddy, Doug Pierson, rummaged through damaged aircraft to salvage tubes and valves to build their still. Shrewdly, they hid it in the jungle behind the latrines, where the awful odors discouraged the curious. With some stolen fruit, they were in business. Ledford named their brew "Old Saddlebags," and after a few days, they had a canteen full of the white lightning. They shared it with their platoon. Each man took a sip, choked it down, and passed it on, eyes watering.

Moonshine production became a division-wide cottage industry, with bootleggers selling it in recycled beer bottles for up to $20.00 a "jug," almost $300 in today's dollars. Some commanders hunted down and destroyed the stills; others turned a blind eye in exchange for a discrete jug or two. The cat and mouse game became a sport unto itself, offering its own distraction from the island's boredom. One plucky trooper fermented a brew of canned cherries, pineapples, raisins, prunes, and coconut juice in a fifty-five-gallon drum buried under the support beam of his tent; the squad smirked each time an officer inspected their quarters.

Swing was sensitive to his men's plight, and his most ambitious effort to maintain their morale was also the Angels' biggest construction project: an open-air amphitheater with enough bench seating for the entire division. The combat engineers spearheaded the task, supervising work parties and installing a generator-powered PA system.

Upon completion, it sat twelve thousand spectators and was used for boxing matches, movies, concerts, and USO shows.

As 'Big Ed' Hogan recalled, "Movies were shown several nights a week.... The theatre was outdoors, and the only thing covered was the projector. It was always a good idea to bring your poncho in case of rain."

To improve the concerts' verve, Swing reorganized the division's two bands, combining the artillery's and Haugen's into a single ensemble. Conducted by Warrant Officer John Bergland, the ninety-member orchestra belted out popular tunes by Glenn Miller, Jimmy Dorsey, and other well-known big-bands. The band had a nice gig, but Swing insisted they be qualified for truck driving, radio communicating, and pushing out supplies for aerial delivery. In combat, there would be little need for music and plenty of need for extra hands.

Sports were a big morale booster. Just as in the States, units fielded both baseball and football teams, although the temperature was often so extreme that the football games were played with ten-minute quarters to avoid heat exhaustion. Haugen's football team led the division, thanks in no small part to his coach: six-foot-four 'Big Tom' Mesereau, the captain of Charlie Company. Mesereau had been playing football for at least nine of his twenty-three years. An All-State athlete from Englewood, New Jersey, he'd been recognized for his athletic accomplishments before entering West Point as a seventeen-year-old cadet in 1939. There, he ran track and lettered as a tackle three out of his four years on the football team. Haugen's roster also included a veteran kicker from Missouri University.

The biggest sporting draw, however, was the Friday night fights. One division document estimated that 80 percent of the men stepped into the boxing ring for a bout at one point or another. And if it was worth playing, in Hard Rock's opinion, it was worth winning.

It took just a few losses to the glider units for Haugen to start "raising hell" with the 511th's coach, Lieutenant Preston D. Carter. A former NCAA National Middleweight champion, Carter finally suggested Haugen find a more suitable coach, and he was replaced by another lieutenant, Foster D. Arnett.

Haugen didn't care what Arnett had to do, but he made it clear losing to the glider riders was unacceptable. Fighters were paired from across the division by weight class and a five-point scale from amateur to professional. The idea was to prevent mismatches and give the audience—and the gladiators—a fair fight. But competitive spirits ran high, and coaches often slipped a larger or more experienced fighter into a bout. The glider riders had more professionally ranked boxers than Hard Rock's team, which had two: Calvin 'The Fox' Lincoln and 'Irish Gene' Kirk. The Fox, a trim redhead, and the tattooed Kirk were both despised by the glider troops.

The Fox liked to keep his lightning-fast left hand lowered, inviting a right hook from his opponent, who never failed to take the bait—and always regretted it.

"[The Fox] would fight anyone, anytime, anywhere, and without regard to his opponents' size and record," said Arnett.

Arnett's most lethal fighter was Sergeant William Ransdell from Colorado. Ransdell was a reluctant boxer who preferred to stay out of the ring. But when he stepped in, he was a beast, infamous for his three single-punch knockouts.

Arnett, who was serving a stint at the division officers' mess hall after getting into a non-sanctioned fist fight with another officer, took advantage of his demotion to sneak his fighters in for steak after tournaments. That lasted until Swing found out about it and sent him packing back to the 511th. Haugen had to have been happy with Arnett's team as they took the division title, then went on to defeat all comers from the neighboring 33rd Infantry Division and win the New Guinea Championship.

● ◎ ●

Much to the aggravation of both the troopers and their commanding general, the division was required to provide a rotating shift of stevedores down at the harbor. The troopers, conscious of their elite status as combat troops, thought unloading supply ships was "humiliating." The dock work exacerbated a growing morale problem.

When the division landed on New Guinea, Swing promised they'd see action soon enough, telling his men to "think, eat, and dream of war." Months passed. All they'd done was sit through interminable lectures and conduct training exercises, and now they were hauling freight. Maintaining a sharp edge required the potential of training paying off, but with no imminent mission, a "deadly monotony" settled in. One of Haugen's officers described his men as "wild horses, over-trained and eager to get into the fight."

The restless troopers, already referring to themselves as "noncombatants," added "labor battalions" to their growing list of self-derogatory adjectives.

But youth can always find a way to salve the tedium of inaction.

"I ought to shoot that thing down," said a trooper, squinting over his rifle sights at a colony of large fruit bats silhouetted against the setting sun.

"You're a chicken if you don't!" came the immediate taunt.

The jibes grew louder, and finally, the man squeezed off a shot. The bullet grazed a bat, and the rest of the platoon snatched up their rifles and opened fire. The fusillade downed a couple more of the creatures and also brought down the wrath of several officers, who swarmed into the tents to apprehend the sharpshooters.

Haugen was incensed by his men's poor judgement. Opening fire in such a manner, and in an area still considered a combat zone, was reckless. He confiscated their ammunition and disciplined the entire 3rd Battalion for the misconduct. Group punishment or "collective motivation," intended to inspire peer pressure for future compliance, has always been a questionable leadership tactic. It is despised by the innocent and ignores the fact that troublemakers rarely consider the repercussions of their actions; it can also backfire with the group, closing ranks against authority.

The sentence was a Hard Rock specialty: a fast-paced march in full equipment. Sitting a few hundred miles below the equator, New Guinea is hot and humid, and as Mile Gale put it, they were all in a "constant state of sweat." The grueling march under the blazing sun was agonizing, and several men collapsed with heat exhaustion. Four of the cases were so serious they never returned to duty. The punishment reinforced Haugen's already polarizing reputation, and "ruthless martinet" was a description later leveled at him by a fellow officer.

DOWN AT THE HARBOR, the Angels took the liberty to compensate themselves for what they viewed as a lack of fair wages. They were paid to fight the enemy, not unload cargo. They rationalized that, as they were in the Army and were unloading Army supplies, taking some of those supplies wasn't stealing, it was merely reallocation. They reallocated by the ton.

"Personally," said First Lieutenant Randolph W. Kirkland, "I thought this thievery to be a just and righteous thing. The rear area scum certainly saw to it that none of the good things reached the combat troops."

Kirkland, a twenty-four-year-old intelligence officer from South Carolina, was a mechanical engineer by schooling. He'd waved his General Electric draft deferment and joined the parachute infantry. He was five-feet, ten-inches tall, trim, with green eyes and dark brown hair. He wore his cap at a jaunty angle that complemented his tight-lipped smirk of a smile. His sardonic knack for recognizing the absurdities of Army life, combined with his lack of pretense, gave him an easy empathy for the plights of enlisted men.

First Lieutenant Randolph W. Kirkland, Jr.

The thefts ranged from pilfering cans of Coca-Cola, coffee, and fruit to heists by the truckload. Serving as transport drivers, a few Angels made detours to camp with a goldmine of frozen Australian beef. By the time the loss was discovered by the harbor's quartermasters, all the evidence had been consumed.

Haugen, however, drew the line. Upon hearing of steak available in the officer's mess tent, he yelled, "I don't want you officers to eat any better than the enlisted men!" He didn't care about stealing from rear echelons, but if there wasn't enough for everyone, don't bother.

Swing largely turned a blind eye to the mischief. When Colonel Stanley Bachmani, the base commander, called to complain about troopers loafing on the job and stealing anything not nailed down, Swing took none of it.

"Stanley, you have over twenty-seven thousand base commandos down there, and I resent the hell out of your calling on me for support unloading ships," he said. "My men are angels compared to that outfit you have under your command." The reallocations continued unabated.

But tensions flared again after a group of Haugen's troopers stole a generator and lights to replace their kerosene lanterns in camp. The stunning set-up, described as "Times Square on New Year's Eve," drew too much attention, and it was soon moved to Swing's head-quarters. That lasted only a few nights before Bachmani reclaimed the generator. "Sparks flew, but no court martial charges," admitted one of the perpetrators.

Bachmani's quartermasters gave Swing his own nickname, 'Ali Baba,' short for Ali Baba Swing and his eight thousand thieves.

Swing's officers enjoyed playing the game as well. Major Henry Burgess, while visiting an Air Force base to coordinate aircraft for the division's jump school, spotted an unguarded refrigerator.

"I decided I wanted that refrigerator," said Burgess. It was quickly and quietly loaded into a jeep, covered with a tarp, then transferred back to camp. Burgess figured the best way to avoid the heat of having such a rare, luxurious item was to gift the icebox to Swing, who didn't ask where it came from.

Some of the stealing was to make up for shortages, or short-sightedness, in the division's authorized allocation of equipment. The division was meant to travel light, but some troopers thought the War Department made them too light.

Lieutenant William 'Buzz' Miley, one of Haugen's platoon leaders, and Norm Norton, Miley's platoon sergeant, organized a "moonlight requisition" to better arm their men. Pistols were in high demand, as only ten were authorized for the entire regiment. The stories of Japanese creeping into foxholes at night spooked everyone. A Colt .45 pistol at the ready was an ideal remedy. After Miley confirmed the location of several crates of pistols at Oro Bay, he launched his raid.

"After dark, we made two trips to the tents," Miley said. "On the first trip, we timed the walk-around guard, and one volunteer noted that the guard's carbine had no magazine inserted. We liberated three wooden cases the first time and four on the second and last trip." The .45 caliber automatic "foxhole comforters" were issued that night to a very grateful platoon.

There was at least one instance where sticky-fingered temptation overcame common-sense plausible deniability. One night in late October, Sergeant Charlie Ford was put on guard shift to watch over a tent containing a case of Schenley's Whisky. The stash was reserved for the officers, but Ford knew each bottle could fetch as much as fifty bucks on the black market. Before his shift ended, he lifted two bottles and buried them for later recovery.

As other guards rotated through their shifts, they each helped themselves to a bottle. In the morning, when the heist was discovered, the officers demanded an investigation.

Major Walter 'The Sheriff' Magadieu, Swing's provost marshal, hit a dead end questioning Ford, who claimed he was just an ignorant farm boy from Mississippi.

"I wasn't really sure what liquor was," shrugged Ford innocently.

"Son," said Magadieu, "I'm not really buying all of that horseshit, but that was one hell of a dumb thing putting enlisted men guarding the officer's booze."

All the culprits caught in Magadieu's net—Ford was not among them—were stripped of their rank, transferred to another unit, and punished with three months of confined labor. But their sentences were soon commuted by unfolding events.

ON MONDAY, OCTOBER 12, 1944, Swing received orders from MacArthur's HQ to ready the division for movement. MacArthur was preparing a massive operation to retake the Philippines, starting with Leyte, but to Swing's disappointment, there was no combat mission for the Angels. They would land a few weeks after the initial wave had secured the beach.

MacArthur's ground commander, Lieutenant General Walter Krueger, was hesitant to commit Swing's undersized division to the battle. With only seven infantry battalions—compared to nine in a regular division—and without tanks or heavy artillery, the Angels might have been more trouble than they were worth. If they failed to sustain their own campaign, they'd become a logistical burden.

Swing was frustrated with Krueger's unwillingness to shake his conventional mindset. As Swing later said, "It was very hard to get him to relax and realize there were other ways of doing things than bing, bing, bing, right down the line." Swing's men were getting restless. With the US invasions of Saipan, Guam, Peleliu, and Angaur, the war was moving closer to Japan without them. The division was as ready as any unit fielded by the Army, and Swing wanted a chance to prove it.

Eight days later, MacArthur launched Operation KING II against the Japanese-held island of Leyte. The landing fulfilled MacArthur's well-publicized promise made nearly two and a half years earlier: "I shall return."

And return he did, heralded with a four-hour naval gunfire barrage by one of the largest armadas ever assembled. Once secured, Leyte's central location would divide the Japanese forces in the Philippines and provide airfields from which land-based aircraft could support operations across the entire chain of islands. MacArthur viewed retaking the Philippines as a moral obligation after his defeat there in 1942, as well as a military necessity in his island-hopping campaign. Securing bases in the Philippines would allow the Allies to sever Japanese supply routes through the South China Sea and add another link in the vital logistics chain for the advance on Tokyo.

The Angels were told nothing, but with news of the invasion, excited rumors spread through camp that they were finally headed to combat. Only a small group of Swing's staff knew the truth.

In early November, the troopers collapsed their cots, struck, folded, and stacked their tents, and packed all their non-essential items into foot lockers. The engineers dismantled the showers and latrines; those would be packed for transport, too. No one knew where they were going, but seeing that the ships weren't combat loaded—priority items loaded last to be the first off—told them plenty: they'd be sitting this one out.

They loaded over seventeen hundred tons of supplies, including rations, tents, hammocks, shovels, and 274 cases of toilet paper. Five months after their arrival, the men took landing craft from Oro Bay out to their awaiting ships. Peeking at Navy manifests only revealed that the destination of their convoy was code-named "Accumulation." On Saturday, November 11, 1944, Task Unit 79.15.1 sailed at 08:00 in the morning. After two days at sea, their destination was announced over the loudspeakers: Leyte.

PART II

'Rat's Ass!'

Chapter 3

"We Can Still Win"

Leyte Gulf.
07:20, Saturday, November 18, 1944

The sun had been up for three hours when the rattle of anchor chains punctuated the end of the Angels' voyage. While escorting destroyers lingered offshore, the cargo ships slipped into their assigned anchorage points some 1,700 yards off Leyte's Bito Beach. Once moored, their formation placed them in a row perpendicular to the shoreline, with each ship assigned a section of the beach four football fields wide in which to conduct its unloading.

"Now hear this ... Man your debarking stations ... Man your debarking stations."

Below deck, the troops shouldered their gear and readied themselves for departure. On deck, the sailors went to work.

Each of the large attack transport ships carried its own fleet of eighteen or more landing craft, capable of ferrying men, jeeps, artillery, and other cargo to shore. Tannoy loudspeakers squawked commands as crews lowered the landing craft over the sides into the swells below. Once in the water, cockswains nestled their craft next to the ship like nursing whales, waiting for the troops to climb down. The priority was getting them ashore; their supplies would follow.

Just twenty minutes after dropping anchor, Leroy Butler watched his buddies disappear over the gunwale. Readying himself, he gripped the thick cargo net and glanced down, momentarily distracted by the distance to the landing craft below. He swung his leg over the side, as did the man next to him, and the pair started their descent. Butler moved quickly but carefully down the cargo net, mentally repeating, *Hands on vertical, feet on horizonal ... Hands on vertical, feet on horizonal*, lest his fingers fell victim to the next man's boots.

Everyone and everything were moving. The ship rolled in the swells, swinging the cargo nets back and forth against its steel sides. Below, the landing craft bobbed up and down as the cockswain struggled to keep it close to the ship. A steady dribble of soldiers crawled down the net as soon as there was space.

The men had to time their jump at the bottom of the net in consideration of their equipment's shifting weight and the unpredictable movement of both craft. But with the cascade of troopers, they had to move fast. Those already in the boat helped to steady the net for those that followed, and Butler made it down safely.

The cockswains waited for their landing craft to be crowded to capacity before gunning the engine and heading to the beach. The ride was bumpy but short. It was standing room only. To stay on their feet, the men near the gunwales held on to the sides, and those who couldn't held on to those who could.

As the landing craft nosed ashore, the front ramps dropped, and the troops splashed out. Even though the Angels landed on a secure beach, the armada's arrival drew attention, and over the course of several hours, multiple Japanese air raids swept into the bay.

Each sighting of enemy aircraft provoked an emergency broadcast to all ships: "Flash Red, Control Yellow; Flash Red, Control Yellow." The warning sent crews scrambling to general quarters.

Gunners on the USS *Thuban* hurled hundreds of 20mm and 40mm anti-aircraft rounds skyward, the double and quad barrels punching shells at the incoming bombers. Little black clouds of bursting flak chased the Japanese planes as sailors swiveled their guns to track the flight path.

"There was shooting all over the place," Private Deane Marks recalled, "with nothing getting hit." Marks, originally from St. Paul, Minnesota, was a machinegunner who appreciated the art of automatic weapons fire. He and the troopers watching the drama unfold cheered the arrival of several American P-38 twin-engine fighters roaring overhead to pounce on the raiders. The *rat-tat-tat* of machineguns echoed back to shore, and three of the enemy aircraft cartwheeled into the ocean disappearing in flaming splashes.

Those on the beach were spellbound, some by the extraordinary action, and others by the realization that, for the first time, they'd seen a human life taken in violence.

ONCE ASHORE, sergeants herded the troops together for rollcall, making sure no one was left onboard, then organized them into work details to unload the incoming cargo. Those not working mingled in groves of coconut trees to keep the beach clear. For soldiers used to the assured footing of solid ground, the exhibition of the US Navy conducting a full maritime debarkation was an impressive site.

Signal lamps winked out morse code from ship to ship while booms winched cargo nets filled with crates out of the holds and lowered them into the vessels moored alongside. The bay churned with craft chugging troops and supplies ashore or returning for their next complement. Colored flags, posted on the beach to help guide craft ashore, fluttered in the breeze.

Underlying the activity was a sense of urgency, the men spurred by the knowledge that the lumbering cargo ships were easy targets for prowling Japanese aircraft. Kamikaze attacks, unleashed for the first time a few weeks prior, put everyone on edge.

"The Navy made no bones about wishing to be rid of us," recalled a trooper, "and in a hurry."

The sooner the unloading was completed, the sooner the ships could depart for the safety of the open sea. Nonetheless, cockswains and work parties went about their duties with a professional calm that ensured the smooth, well-practiced transition of men and materiel from ship to shore.

The USS *Monrovia* emptied its holds of 1,244 troops—including General Swing—and all its cargo in just over four hours. It was a personal best for the ship's crew, who unloaded 130 tons an hour.

After the Navy got the cargo to the beach, it was the Army's responsibility to offload it. The 11th, in addition to a handful of jeeps and cargo trucks, had brought thirty days of rations, ammunition, fuel, medical supplies, and batteries.

Landing ships belly up to the beach on Leyte to disgorge their supplies by the ton

Furthermore, several massive Tank Landing Ships (known as LSTs for Landing Ship, Tank, or by their crews as Large, Slow Target) nuzzled through the surf to ground themselves on the beach. These flat-bottomed beasts, equipped with two massive clamshell doors in the bow, were longer than a football field and capable of transporting almost two thousand tons of cargo. It would take days to unload these monsters.

Work parties, stripped to the waist, waded into the surf, forming human chains that extended from each side of the wide-mouth cargo ships back to shore. Crates were passed down the line from man to man, hand to hand.

One observer described the scene as "turmoil," with the ships "expelling men and machines" at a fantastic rate, and "jeeps, trucks, and DUWKs [amphibious vehicles] running up and down the beach."

The urgency to empty the cargo holds, combined with rough seas and a steady drizzle of rain, contributed to the frenetic pace. The men, toiling to keep up, piled equipment and supplies right on the beach, rather than carry them up farther into the dunes.

That worked until the tide came in.

Troopers splashed out into the surging waves to retrieve boxed rations, barrels of fuel, and dozens of the division's precious parachutes packed in tin containers. At least those floated.

Swing's quartermaster troops ranged up and down the beach, trying in vain to regain control and get everything organized. Now the troopers joined the sailors in eyeing the sky warily for enemy aircraft. The shoreline had become a massive ammo dump, with crates of artillery and mortar shells strewn all over the place. A few well-placed bombs could ignite the whole mess.

THE ANGELS SPENT their first night on Leyte in makeshift bivouac sites dotted along the beach. Many sought shelter from the rain under the palm trees, but when the wind picked up, falling coconuts drove them elsewhere. Likewise, low ground, initially eyed for its protection from the wind, was surrendered to flooding.

There was nothing to do about it but to dig into their canvas backpacks, pull out their rubberized ponchos, and wrap up for a miserable night on the ground. The more determined scrounged cots

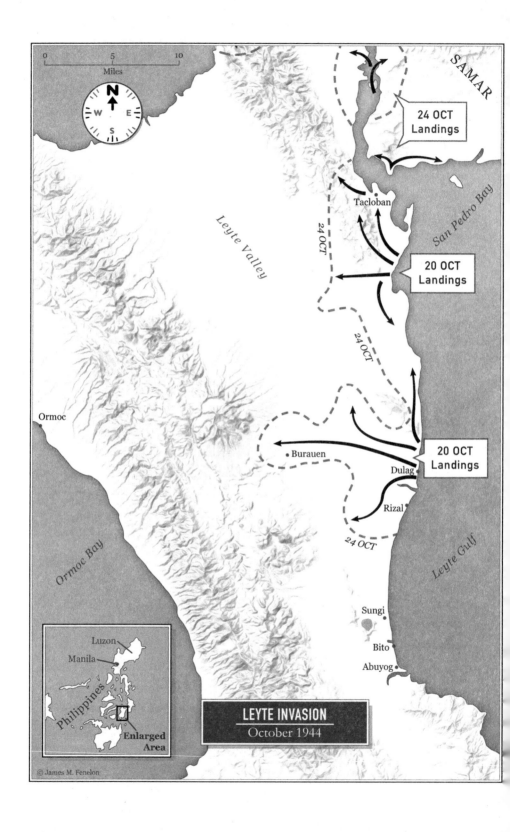

LEYTE INVASION
October 1944

from the piles of equipment littering the beach to spend the night in relative comfort.

Deane Marks, sitting in the dark under his poncho, was distracted from the drizzling rain by another Japanese air raid out in the bay.

"[They] were fun to watch because the searchlights would pick up the Nip bombers at around eight or nine thousand feet, and then the Army 'Ack Ack' would start shooting." Bright, laser-like tracers arced up, stabbing through the dark and seeking the enemy aircraft, but ultimately, Marks was unimpressed.

"Never saw them hit a thing," he commented wryly.

● ● ●

By the time the 11th Airborne landed, the battle for Leyte had been raging for thirty days. MacArthur's legions of four infantry divisions had landed on the east coast of the island, pushing the Japanese steadily inland. But despite initial success, the campaign's progress had slowed. The Japanese still held the west coast, which was only approachable from the north or south due to the rugged central mountain range splitting the island's 115-mile length. To a mechanized army, the thickly vegetated mountains' sharp, four-thousand-foot ridgelines and plunging ravines were a dividing barrier hindering a westward attack.

Reasons for the delays were numerous, beginning with the weather. MacArthur's staff dismissed engineering reports and underestimated the torrential showers that dumped thirty-five inches of rain in forty days. Leyte Valley, consisting mainly of rice paddies and swamps, became even more soupy from mountain streams overflowing, which flooded rivers and reduced roads to muddy quagmires. Most importantly, the three airstrips near the villages of Buri, Bayug, and San Pablo—collectively called the Burauen airstrips—became useless bogs. Getting land-based aircraft was critical for MacArthur's campaign, as the Navy's aircraft carriers would remain offshore for only so long. The original plan was to use the Burauen airstrips to support the Army on the ground, but without hardstands or steel matting, the 17,500-pound P-38 fighters sunk into the mire up to the top of their wheels. To ready the fields for heavier bombers would require an eight-inch base layer of sand and dredged coral topped by the steel matting. Rain, poor drainage, and the faulty assumption that the Japanese had improved the airstrips during their occupation all combined to delay their use. Further exasperating the efforts was a shortage of the labor crews that were desperately needed to maintain the island's deteriorating roads. In early November, construction efforts at the Burauen airstrips had been largely abandoned and shifted to an airfield farther north, where a token presence of land-based fighters and bombers juggled supporting ground operations and interdicting Japanese shipping. The lack of dedicated air support put a more onerous burden on the infantry to go toe-to-toe with the Japanese.

Compounding the campaign's delays were the growing number of American casualties and the lack of replacements. It was partly a self-induced problem, as MacArthur's staff was inexplicably using the wrong numbers to calculate losses. Instead of tracking a unit's effective strength—the number of troops actually fit for duty—they were using the *assigned* strength numbers and comparing that to how many men the unit *should* have had at full strength (a status rarely enjoyed by combat units). The week before the Angels arrived on Leyte, the staff's math determined MacArthur's forces were just 2,163 men shy of full strength. However, the effective strength numbers revealed they were short by roughly twelve thousand, nearly an entire division. Furthermore, at the campaign's current rate of attrition, thousands of more losses could be expected before securing the island.

But the arrival of fresh troops had been erratic, and when they did arrive, they did so in dribs and drabs. MacArthur's ground commander, Lieutenant General Walter Krueger, had requested 18,800 replacements, including over fourteen thousand infantrymen. During the campaign's entirety, however, he received just over five thousand. Having already committed his two reserve divisions, he needed every man who could pull a trigger.

With the manpower shortages becoming critical, the Angels' arrival couldn't have been timelier. Swing's division, initially placed in reserve for use on Luzon, would now be pressed into service.

Of course, the campaign's primary hinderance wasn't the weather, terrain, or math: it was the Japanese.

THREE HUNDRED MILES northeast of Leyte, on the island of Luzon, Tomoyuki Yamashita studied MacArthur's campaign progress. The fifty-nine-year-old general's office was at Manila's Fort McKinley, the former American base built in 1901 and occupied by the Japanese since January 1942. While Yamashita had been in Manila only a few weeks, he assessed the reports from Leyte with a practiced and professional eye. Having been commissioned after graduating in 1908 from the Japanese Army Academy in Tokyo—the nation's equivalent of West Point—he'd been a soldier for almost forty years. His current assignment to repel the Americans from the Philippines was just the latest in a long, accomplished career, but Yamashita harbored suspicions it would be his last.

At 220 pounds, Yamashita was a big man. "Built like a bear," said one biographer. He kept his head shaved, owning his baldness, which heightened his already oblong face. His wide-set eyes and pug nose

General Tomoyuki Yamashita on Luzon

inspired the Filipinos to call him "Old Potato Face." Others were even less kind, describing him as a "pig-faced man."

Despite his detractors' jabs, Yamashita had a serious and well-trained mind. The son of a doctor, he had graduated fifth in his class at the Academy and sixth out of fifty-six at the War College. He was a poet, writing under the pen name *Daisan*, or Giant Cedar. He had also traveled extensively, serving as a military attaché in Switzerland, where he took the opportunity to study World War I's European battlefields. He returned to Europe several times, including leading a military commission on a six-month inspection tour of Germany and Italy, just a few months after Japan joined the Axis pact in late 1941. While there, he met Hitler, who failed to impress. "He may be a great orator on a platform," said Yamashita, "with his gestures and flamboyant way of speaking, but standing behind his desk listening, he seems much more like a clerk."

Yamashita's glimpse of European industrialization and the morass of Germany's campaign in Russia was sobering. He advised the members of his delegation, "I must ask you not to express opinion in favor of expanding the alliance between Japan, Germany, and Italy."

"Never suggest in your report that Japan should declare war on Great Britain and the United States. We must not and cannot rely upon the power of other nations," he warned them. "We must have time to rebuild our defense system and adjust the whole Japanese war machine. I cannot repeat this to you often enough."

His advice was ignored. The Japanese plunged forward into their conquest of Asia, and once the die was cast, the dutiful Yamashita fell in line, directing his intellect and energy toward victory for the Emperor. In February 1942, he cemented his reputation as a skilled tactician by sacking British-held Singapore. The skillful campaign earned him the sobriquet "the Tiger of Malaya," a metaphor the poet loathed. "The tiger attacks its prey in stealth," he complained, "but I attack the enemy in fair play."

Attack he did, and perhaps in fair play, but certainly with a fury-prodded urgency. To speed his infantry across the Malay Peninsula and into the attack of Singapore, he equipped those without motorized transport with eighteen thousand bicycles. His force advanced some seven hundred miles in eight weeks, and after a brief siege, Yamashita handed the British one of their most humiliating defeats in history. Over eighty thousand Commonwealth troops were captured.

The victory, so close on the heels of the attack on Pearl Harbor and simultaneous conquests across the Pacific, boosted the notoriety of Japanese military dominance.

Yamashita's success generated talk of his appointment as war minister, which, in turn, spun the machinations of political intrigue. The prime minister, Hideki Tojo, viewed Yamashita as a rival for the Emperor's favor and had the Tiger of Malaya assigned to the backwater region of Manchuria. Yamashita accepted the side-lining appointment gracefully and set about preparing for an unlikely attack from Russia. The Russians had a treaty with Tokyo, and even if they wanted to break it, they were too busy defending themselves against Germany to do much else. Upon arrival at his new headquarters, Yamashita rotated his desk to face the Imperial Palace in Tokyo.

By the fall of 1944, however, with the Allies grinding across the Pacific, Tojo was ousted as prime minister. His successor dusted off Yamashita and ordered him, by way of Tokyo, to the Philippines to prepare for the looming battle there.

During briefings in Tokyo, Yamashita began to understand the enormity of the task ahead. When he asked how many islands were in the Philippines, he was astonished by the answer: "More than seven thousand."

It was impossible to defend against the innumerable possibilities that so many islands offered the enemy, but both Yamashita and General Yoshijiro Umezu, chief of the Imperial Army's general staff, agreed that the battle would be won or lost on the main island, Luzon.

"If you can crush the Americans on Luzon," Umezu said, "we can still win."

There were two tactical options to meet the Americans in battle. The first, "annihilation on the beachhead," meant attacking them as soon as they landed; the second, "resistance in depth," required falling back farther inland to more favorable, defensible terrain. There was spirited debate about which was better. Those who had seen the devastation of American naval guns felt it was useless to defend a beach against such firepower and advocated a battling withdrawal to lure the Americans inland to face the fortifications there. Others felt the Americans would be most vulnerable when trying to gain a defended shore. Imperial General Headquarters settled the arguments, mandating the Philippines be defended by resistance in depth.

From their perspective in Tokyo, the situation looked promising. There were almost 432,000 Japanese troops garrisoned in the Philippines, and Manila was a primary supply depot, not just for the Philippines, but also for Borneo and Singapore. It was well stocked with ammunition and food. But Yamashita's experience had taught him to balance others' optimism with his own skepticism. On the battlefield, troops and their supplies had to be moved at the correct moment to disrupt the enemy's plan. Making this happen on land was difficult enough, but orchestrating it across a chain of islands was another challenge entirely.

Yamashita's reservations were well founded. In early October, when he arrived in Manila, he found that he had inherited a mess. His predecessor, Lieutenant General Shigenori Kuroda, had been relieved of command based on accusations of operational delinquencies and spending his time playing golf and reveling with prostitutes rather than preparing for the inevitable return of the Americans. Kuroda's derelictions became apparent as Yamashita surveyed Manila's defenses, which lay virtually untouched since ousting the Americans in 1942. He also found discipline lacking within the ranks, and the severe treatment of the local population had fostered a widespread guerrilla movement—both of which would come back to haunt him.

Yamashita's bleak assessment was not shared by all, however. On October 20, 1944—eleven days after he arrived—the Americans landed on Leyte, and many of the Japanese officers had a prevailing sense of optimism, even hubris.

One commander exclaimed, "Good, they have picked the place where our finest troops are located."

"We were determined to take offensive after offensive and clean up American forces on Leyte Island," said Major General Yoshiharu Tomochika. "We seriously discussed demanding the surrender of the entire American Army after seizing General MacArthur."

But the realities were hard to ignore. Yamashita and his staff's unfamiliarity with their battlefield was made clear when, upon hearing of the American landings, Yamashita's chief of staff asked, "Where is Leyte?"

Yamashita issued the *Shō Ichi Go* plan—Victory Operation Number One—calling for cooperation between the Imperial Army, Air Force, and Navy to attack the American invaders. Three days later, however, much of the Japanese Navy was resting on the bottom of Leyte Gulf—sunk by the US Navy. In a decisive defeat, the fleet lost nine destroyers, six heavy cruisers, four light cruisers, four aircraft carriers, and three battleships. Tokyo-based propaganda downplayed the stinging rout, confusing matters for the defenders, who were falsely led to believe the Americans had lost several ships—including eleven aircraft carriers, enough to cripple their campaign. The Japanese fared little better in the air, losing over six hundred aircraft to American raids. With his air and naval support in tatters, Yamashita's forces would bear the brunt of the fighting on land alone.

That was fine with Lieutenant General Sosaku Suzuki, Yamashita's fifty-three-year-old ground commander on Leyte. Suzuki had discounted help from the Navy and Air Force from the beginning. A career Army officer since 1912, his mistrust of the sister service ran deep, and he planned accordingly. He also followed his own counsel, ignoring the Imperial General Headquarters' mandate for 'resistance in depth.' Instead, Suzuki opted for a hybrid defense. He told his officers, "The main battle is fought in numerous isolated areas of our choice, rather than on the coast under naval bombardment. Nevertheless, there is some effectiveness in resistance along the beaches and, therefore, part of the troops must suffer premature losses." His troops had spent the last seven months building three lines of successive defensive positions, starting on the east coast and moving inland, giving them positions to fall back on. Suzuki had supplies pre-positioned in the central mountains and had jungle trails improved to facilitate his troops' movement.

JAPANESE INTELLIGENCE INITIALLY SUGGESTED the Americans had landed two divisions on Leyte. In response, Suzuki ordered several infantry battalions to be shipped from surrounding islands to reinforce his troops already there. The convoys landing on the west coast at Ormoc Bay provided him more than five divisions on the island and confidence of victory.

But by early November, it had become clear that the intelligence was incorrect, and Suzuki's optimism misplaced. The Americans had landed four divisions in their first wave. Repelling them would require more men and materiel than expected.

Yamashita advocated to his superiors that Leyte be abandoned to focus on defending Luzon, a strategy he had favored since his arrival. The American landing on Leyte, he reasoned, was just a steppingstone for attacking the main island. By his logic, the loss of naval support exacerbated the already-challenging problems of reinforcing Leyte. The Americans' air power was wreaking havoc on the troop transports navigating between the islands, and the Navy lacked the ships to provide effective escort. Why continue to throw away troops and supplies that would be vital for the battle on Luzon?

He was overruled.

Field Marshal Count Hisaichi Terauchi, whose command encompassed the Philippines, Malaya, Burma, and French Indochina, ordered the reinforcement efforts to continue. Terauchi feared that if the Americans established airfields on Leyte, their air superiority would be complete, making it that much harder to defend Luzon. Leyte was where Terauchi wanted to destroy the Americans.

Yamashita balked at the order, but Terauchi told him it came directly from the Imperial Palace.

"If our Emperor has consented to this plan," Yamashita replied, "there is nothing else to do but proceed with it stubbornly."

The Emperor and the government leadership in Tokyo viewed Leyte as their opportunity for a great 'decisive battle' against the enemy. While the ultimate direction of the war was impossible to ignore, they believed a significant victory would crush the Americans' will to fight and provide a way to end the war on Japanese terms. This pending triumph was key to avoiding the humiliation of an unconditional surrender. But first, Yamashita had to get more troops to the island.

The Japanese convoys, hampered by American air raids, achieved limited success but managed to deliver another forty-five thousand men and several thousand tons of supplies to Ormoc Bay. Ten thousand of those troops arrived just a week prior to the Angels' landing, bringing the total number of Japanese reinforcements close to sixty thousand.

Suzuki planned to fight on his own terms, using Leyte's rugged central mountain range to his advantage. The terrain played to his forces' strengths while negating the Americans' advantages in artillery, mechanization, and air support. His camouflaged supply trails led deep into the jungle, and from ridge-top redoubts, his men could wage a grinding battle of attrition.

His soldiers knew what was expected of them. Imperial Army manuals on island defense stated the Emperor's expectations clearly: "All personnel must be able to fight continuously for days without sleep, rest, food or drink. . . . All difficulties must be overcome, and the spirit of the offensive remain unflagging to the bitter end." The manual equated defending each island to protecting the homeland, and its final point was unambiguous: "The Army operates on the principle of defense to the death when defending an island.

● ● ●

After their first night on the beach, Swing and his staff moved the division command post up the coast to a collection of huts labeled *Sungi* on the map. It was time for the 11th Airborne to get into the war, and it was here that Swing formalized his first field order. The mission appeared simple enough: replace another division already in defensive positions at the base of the mountains.

To cut off the Japanese landings at Ormoc Bay, General Krueger planned a five-division squeeze play: two divisions would push across the northern part of the island while the 7th Infantry Division would attack from the south. Swing's 11th, with another division on its right flank, would hold blocking positions along the central mountain range to prevent Suzuki's units from escaping the Americans' anvil.

For the 7th Infantry to get into position, the Angels needed to take over their current sector so they could cross over to the west coast and then advance north for their attack. The 7th held a front thirty-one miles wide with almost fourteen thousand men. Swing, with little more than half that manpower, had to figure out how to do the same.

Word of the Angels' first combat assignment disseminated rapidly through the ranks.

Buford Atkinson—Sergeant At—ordered his men to assemble on the beach for the announcement. He knew rumors had been circulating since they'd left New Guinea and that his men wanted real news.

He gave them time to settle in, then kept his update short and to the point: "Monday morning, we replace the 7th Infantry Division in combat."

What Sergeant At's briefing lacked in detail was made up for by gravitas.

The platoon was silent. There it was. They were going to war.

'Big Ed' Hogan later recalled, "It was a somber thought, for each of us knew that for some, death could be just over the horizon ... and it was."

Leroy 'Pops' Butler took the news from a practical perspective. "I had some feeling of trepidation, but not really fear, because this was what we had been training for so hard, for so long, and now I was about to do the job I was trained to do."

A trooper in the same company as Hogan and Butler recalled the necessary combination of confidence and denial that all combat soldiers must embrace: "No one thought they would be killed. Kill the other son of a bitch was the attitude that prevailed."

Swing had six days to get his units in position.

IT WAS A SLOW START. Forty-eight hours after landing, Swing could say his division was ashore, but that was about it. His first challenge was simply to get his men off the beach.

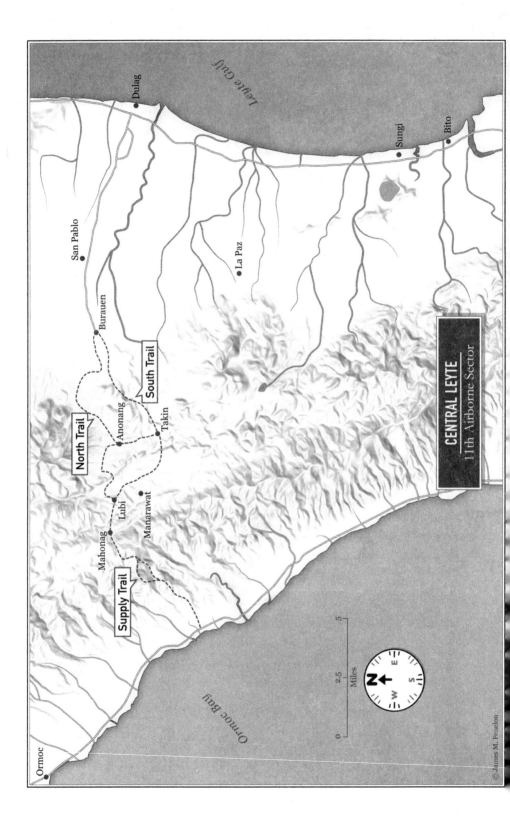

CENTRAL LEYTE
11th Airborne Sector

The 11th's landing site at Bito Beach, a long spit of sand about a hundred yards deep, had facilitated unloading cargo but was useful for little else. There was a reason it wasn't chosen for the initial landings: it was backed by a coconut grove that gave way to a densely vegetated swamp, and swollen rivers blocked exits to the north and south. The Angels and their stockpiles of supplies were boxed in.

To get his division on the move, Swing put his combat engineers to work. Their priority was to build a causeway across the swamp to get access to the one-lane, randomly paved coastal highway, and it had to be strong enough to support the weight of loaded cargo trucks. The engineers drove wooden pilings into the swamp, only to have dozens of them disappear into the muck. The running joke was that they would later emerge halfway around the world, maybe somewhere in Texas.

Simultaneously with the bridging efforts, work parties cleared nearly an acre of coconut grove for the division's maintenance area. Setting up water points, improving beach roads, establishing a sanitary dump, and installing generators and electrical systems all had to be completed for the 11th's rear-area base of operations.

They also carved out a temporary landing strip for the division's fleet of nine L-4 Piper Cubs and two L-5 Sentinels. Swing's artillery units used the small single engine aircraft circling above the battlefield for aerial observers to direct fire support. The planes were brought ashore in crates and assembled on the beach. At just twelve hundred pounds each, they would soon be worth their weight in gold.

ON MONDAY, the 20th of November, Hard Rock Haugen's paratroopers trickled into the 7th Infantry Division's line to take over their positions.

Since Haugen couldn't wait for the bridges to be completed, his troops were ferried one battalion at a time up the coast by landing craft and DUKWs, known as ducks to the troops. The open-topped, lightly armored amphibious transports carried up to twenty-four combat-equipped men. The DUKWs had a propeller and six wheels, allowing them to churn through water or across beaches and bogs.

The five-hundred-odd troops of Haugen's 1st Battalion climbed into the DUKWs for the fourteen-mile voyage up the coast. Their destination was the village of Dulag, the first link in the chain leading them into the mountains. From there, a combination of cargo trucks and combat boots would get them the ten miles inland to Burauen. They arrived just before sunset and went to work establishing the regimental command post from which Haugen would oversee the dispersion of his troops along the six-mile front.

As part of taking over the sector, Haugen dispatched several squads to guard bridges farther up the coast.

Private George Floersh and his squad arrived at their bridge to find it a rusting, iron antique. Its questionable integrity prompted the debate, *Why does this need guarding?*

On the side of the road was a faded canvas tarp, propped up by some metal ribbing from the back of a cargo truck; it would be their home for the next four days. Floersh's first combat assignment wasn't the glorious entrée into combat the parachute troops recruiting pamphlet had promised, but there were worse ways to start the war.

THE NEXT DAY, Haugen's two remaining battalions were delayed after torrential rains flooded or swept away pontoon bridges and turned roads to a thick muck. A two-mile section of the coastal highway became impassable, with trucks sinking into the mud and having to be winched out.

The effort to relieve the 7th Infantry became a start-and-stop affair with Swing's troops filtering into the line piecemeal, battalion by battalion, and in some cases, company by company.

Already accustomed to the Army's "hurry up and wait" routine, the men strung along the chain settled in for what seemed like just another SNAFU.

Dulag beach had been the landing site for two infantry divisions that had stormed ashore under fire in October. Since then, they had pushed well inland, clearing the area of Japanese, but there was plenty of evidence of the battle. Most of the palm trees were stripped of their vegetation by the offshore naval bombardment. Abandoned Japanese trenches, foxholes, and rifle pits, as well as machinegun and mortar positions, dotted the terrain.

Haugen's men stuck in Dulag occupied their time by exploring the area, gambling with the locals, or pilfering. Leroy Butler remembered, "Our entertainment consisted mostly of cockfights, which the natives had rigged for fleecing the unsuspecting GIs. The beat up, bedraggled looking bird would always win, while the suckers always bet on the sleek-looking rooster."

The rain didn't stop Haugen's 1st Battalion, already at Burauen, which had marched into the downpour at 07:00 under the command of Lieutenant Colonel Ernest 'Ernie' LaFlemme. Seven hours later, they were in their blocking positions. At the same time, and experiencing the same frustrating delays, battalions of Swing's paraglider infantry slogged into their positions. The hold-ups and hindrances annoyed everyone.

Swing wanted his division's transition into the line to go smoothly, and General Archibald Arnold, the 7th Infantry Division commander, wanted to be on the move for the big attack. He'd been able to commit just one of his three regiments to the west coast so far.

Swing's staff reminded Arnold that their troops' movements relied on the roads and available transportation. But the timetable wasn't Arnold's only irritation—Hard Rock, true to his nickname, was being hardheaded and refused to acknowledge Arnold's authority. Until the full relief had been completed, Arnold was still in command of the sector, but Haugen was running his own show. After complaints of the "misunderstanding" reached Swing, he visited Arnold to smooth over the situation.

That same day, news spread of the Angels' first fatality. He had died not at the hands of the enemy, but by drowning on a patrol trying to cross an overflowing river.

THE 23rd OF NOVEMBER—Thanksgiving—found Haugen's 3rd Battalion still back at Bito Beach. Joseph Vannier woke for breakfast at 04:00 in the pouring rain. They'd be boarding amtracks for Dulag that morning, and it was time to get moving. Thirty minutes later, with the sun's soft glow defining the ocean's horizon line, Vannier joined his squad for chow.

"[We] filed slowly along the mess lines, through mud jump boot deep, and with water dripping down steel helmets," Vannier later recalled. "Cooks ladled out slabs of cold boned turkey from open gallon cans into held-out mess kits."

The Army tried, but to Vannier, "the stringy slivers of buzzard-like meat, carefully packed in soupy gelatin and thoughtfully topped with a scoop of heated cranberries from the bogs of New England," was a far cry from a home-cooked meal with family and friends.

At the end of the line were large metal garbage cans full of coffee, already flavored with powdered milk and sugar. The rain diluted the concoction and cooled it, if it was ever warm in the first place. As the troopers filed by, the optimists dipped their metal canteen cups into the brown water. It was horrible. The taste reminded Vannier of a barracks song they used to sing at Camp Mackall:

The coffee that they serve you,
They say its mighty fine,
It's good for cuts and bruises,

It tastes like iodine …

Many of the men, their mess kits overflowing with rainwater, paused at the next station to dump the turkey, cranberries, and coffee into another waiting garbage can. It was hard to be thankful for cold, unappealing food in a downpour.

"Little did the men realize," Vannier said, "that in just a few days, they would gladly have traded their mother-in-law for some of that slop."

An hour later, while churning up the coast in the amtracks, they watched an American P-38 get the better of a Japanese Zero. With smoke trailing from the enemy aircraft, the men cheered.

"Our jubilation didn't last long," recalled Lieutenant Colonel Edward 'Slugger' Lahti, the 3rd Battalion commander. From the slow-moving amtrack, Lahti and his men watched as the wounded pilot pulled his aircraft around and headed straight for them.

"The pilot was determined to take someone with him," said Lahti. "At the last second, or so it seemed, he banked again and crashed into the side of a cargo ship, spewing flames all over the side of the deck."

The close call gave the men their first hint of the horrors to come. The war was getting closer.

WHEN MACHINEGUNNER DEANE MARKS ARRIVED at his foxhole, he studied the previous owner's handiwork with a critical eye. A foxhole was a personal space. Always a temporary home, but never reliably so, each occupant took a measured approach to his excavation. In the field, comfort was relative, and men spent a lot of time in their foxholes. It was where they'd sleep, eat, duck enemy fire, and, if the situation was dire enough, relieve themselves.

There were endless options for renovations. It could always be a little deeper or a little longer. Digging a grenade trap was a good idea, as was scratching a shelf into a wall. On Leyte, where the water level was often a few inches below the surface, foxholes all had one thing in common: they were wet and muddy. Drainage was a constant challenge; keeping feet dry was a near impossibility. Troopers often lined the bottom with branches and leaves in vain attempts to keep the mud at bay.

The same evening, while the Angels settled into the line and celebrated Thanksgiving, the Japanese launched a breakout attack on the west coast. However, for the next several days, there was little for the Angels to do.

"At this point, it was sort of a phony war," recalled Marks, awaiting some action. "We sort of sat around all day shooting the breeze, eating our C-rations, and improving our foxholes for better sleeping."

Although officers kept the men busy with local patrols, they found nothing. Swing's intelligence staff knew that elements of a Japanese division were still in the area, but no one knew exactly where. Locals reported a large concentration of Japanese troops several miles farther inland, but the staff thought those accounts were exaggerated.

The staff was wrong.

ON FRIDAY MORNING, Swing and the staff moved the division command post five miles inland to the San Pablo airstrip. MacArthur's engineers had previously abandoned the strip, one of the three near Burauen, as a lost cause. The airstrip's 4,920-foot runway was overgrown with weeds and slushed by poor drainage, but it was closer to the 11th's assigned sector, and Swing was happy to have it. The division's Piper Cubs were stationed a mile west at the Bayug airstrip, where the slightly higher elevation reduced flooding, allowing for the light-weight aircraft to take off and land.

Swing's signal company went to work setting up the division's message center, switchboard, and two radio nets. The crews hustled, wanting to get their communication equipment in place before the rain started again. Several radio sets had already been ruined by the torrential downpour, and they'd be hard to replace.

The first order of business remained the piles of supplies still littering Bito Beach. Quartermaster crews worked day and night to first move them inland, and then shelter them from the rain. Well away from the main supply dump, they dug trenches to store stocks of petrol and oil in case of a potential fire.

The parachute maintenance section learned an expensive lesson upon discovering that over fifteen hundred personnel parachutes and two thousand cargo chutes had been ruined. It was a costly mistake made through a combination of faulty packing and leaving them in the rain. Parachutes were unique to the division, and getting them replaced required imposing on a complicated supply chain that started back in the States.

In all, it took the work parties five days to clear the beach. It was toiling work and a constant battle to protect the stores from the high tide, rain, and sticky fingers.

Armed guards patrolled the makeshift depot against foxes in the henhouse as well as other units taking advantage of the chaos. Captain Thomas Jordan, a supply officer, stopped a group of GIs at gunpoint from driving off the beach with a truckload of the Angels' rations.

AFTER A WEEK on the island, on Saturday, November 25, Swing issued his second field order. While the two paraglider regiments held in place, Haugen's paratroopers were to push west across thirty miles of jungle to the west coast. The squeeze play—the double envelopment of Ormoc Bay—had started, and Hard Rock's troops were finally on the offensive. They would cut over the spine of the central mountains to secure trails the Japanese might use to attack east. In case his intent wasn't clear, Swing ended his instructions to Haugen with, "Destroy by offensive action all hostile forces encountered."

Their first objective was the village of Lubi, located approximately eight miles west of Burauen. There were two trails to get there, a northern and a southern route. Haugen sent companies down both. The one hundred and thirty men of Able Company had already departed the previous day via the north trail, while another company, with a Filipino guide, patrolled the southern route. Other companies would follow at intervals; however, due to the poor trail conditions and steep terrain, Haugen estimated a five-day trek to get to Lubi. But Able Company made better progress on the north trail than expected, stopping for the day after making six miles.

HAUGEN WAS ALREADY LEARNING the challenges of controlling his units' movement deeper into the island. The rain and steep terrain hampered radio communications, and a glance at the map made it clear they were headed into uncharted territory: vast blank swaths were labeled "Clouds" or "No Photographic Coverage." On most maps, the areas more than fifteen hundred yards inland from the coast were empty. Persistent fog and low clouds had foiled pre-invasion efforts to map the island's interior via photo reconnaissance. Missing from these blank sections of the map were vital terrain features to help orientate patrols.

A soldier unable to locate himself on the battlefield is operating blind. A map and compass are basic tools of the trade, with a map's terrain details providing essential cues to pinpoint a location. Without them, he cannot effectively communicate his position to others nor radio for artillery support, guide in reinforcements, or direct airstrikes. The danger of fratricide is high.

Army engineers issued "Leyte Specials"—rudimentary black and white maps with line drawings attempting to capture enough detail to be helpful. But they were basic, with a note at the bottom warning, "Scaled distances may be at variance with actual ground

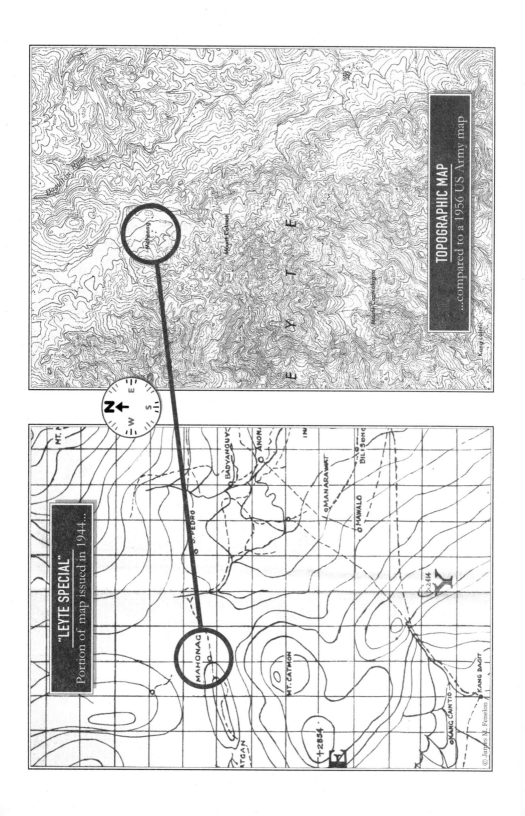

distances." The maps barely hinted at the severity of the topography Haugen's men were about to encounter. They soon discovered that entire ridge lines were missing, marked trails were wildly inaccurate, and some village locations were off by several thousand yards.

As the troopers headed west out of Burauen, they crossed farmers' fields of peanuts and yams. Behind them was the might of a modern arsenal: tanks, artillery, destroyers, and aircraft carriers; to their front loomed the jagged blue-green peaks of the central mountains disappearing into the low clouds, where almost all the advantages belonged to the Japanese.

To Haugen, the enemy situation was just as vague as his maps. The latest intelligence reports estimated that the Japanese held the Ormoc area with up to forty thousand troops. Additional reserves, estimated to be at least a division in size, were located somewhere to Haugen's front, and it was suspected they were moving east to capture the Burauen airstrips. If that prediction was true, the paratroopers would be the first to find out.

LESS THAN TWENTY-FOUR HOURS after getting his new mission, Haugen and his staff trailed behind the men of Charlie Company as they pushed west through the morning drizzle. They were following the same northern route to Lubi previously taken by two other companies. Neither of those patrols had seen any sign of the Japanese.

It was a tiresome slog. The trails, crisscrossed with tangled vines, were little more than muddy animal paths weaving between towering trees. Of the nearly impenetrable vegetation, Miles Gale, the twenty-seven-year-old lieutenant from Wisconsin, recalled, "The easiest way to travel through the jungle was to stick to the existing narrow trails made by animals and natives. Cutting new paths through the thick undergrowth with machetes was hot, arduous work. Chopping also disturbed many insects that could bite and sting."

The troopers had loaded themselves down like pack mules. The riflemen wore full cartridge belts with eighty rounds of .30-06 caliber ammunition, along with two bandoleers with another ninety-six rounds. Everyone had clipped a couple of hand grenades to their belts and carried two full canteens. Their small backpacks contained three days of rations and whatever else they could cram in there. Some men had even stuffed gum, cigarettes, and candy bars into their gas mask bag. Those that had it worst carried the thirty-one-pound belt-fed machineguns, or a 60mm mortar whose barrel, bipod, and baseplate were usually distributed amongst the squad to spare the bearer the full forty-five pounds. The men rotated the heaviest loads during their ten-minute rest breaks that took place once an hour.

The men realized, like a lot of green troops, that they had packed too much. The first thing to go were gas masks, pulled from their bags and discretely discarded into the underbrush. In the rain, their wool GI blankets had become waterlogged bricks, and so were ejected next. Books, shelter-halves, extra underwear, and socks were also ditched.

The value of an item was eyed afresh, its worth directly proportional to its weight.

"We threw the top part of our mess kits away," said a trooper. "We threw away our knife and fork; we just kept a spoon and the bottom part of the mess gear. If anything weighed too much, we eliminated it."

Some men left the mortar shells they were carrying alongside the trail, a decision they would later regret. Most had the foresight to keep their rubberized ponchos, which would prove invaluable as a sleeping bag, tent, ground cloth, improvised litter, or burial shroud.

The trail of discarded equipment reminded leads to better inspect their men before patrols to ensure they weren't carrying too much.

That afternoon, one of the division's Piper Cubs flew over and dropped a case of colored smoke grenades to the units on the trail. With the useless maps, a new tactic was implemented: each day at 10:00 and 16:00, a spotter would fly over Haugen's marching route and look for yellow smoke drifting up through the jungle canopy. The pilot marked the location on his map as closely as possible.

Just before the 16:00 overflight, small arms and mortar fire clattered through the jungle. The front of the column had bumped into a Japanese patrol. It was a hit-and-run engagement and was over quickly. It left everyone spooked, but no one was hurt.

They popped their yellow smoke grenade, reported in, and set up a perimeter for the night. At 07:30 the next morning, they were again moving toward Lubi. To avoid a potential ambush after yesterday's skirmish, their six-foot-four commander, Captain 'Big Tom' Mesereau, had them moving across some high ground to avoid the trail. Private George Floersch was up front, hacking a path through the thick vegetation with his machete; it was exhausting work, and after twenty minutes, Herman 'Dutch' Wagner replaced him. Deciding the creeping pace was too slow, the company moved back onto the trail, and Lieutenant James E. Wylie's platoon moved up to lead Charlie Company.

Private Norman Honie was on point as the column nosed downhill toward a small clearing. The twenty-year-old Hopi Indian from Arizona took a knee. He had seen movement.

There, just a few dozen feet in front of him, were two Japanese soldiers washing their clothes.

Honie slowly raised his rifle.

Chapter 4

The Mud Rats

Leyte Mountains.
16:20, Monday, November 27, 1944

Following a few hours behind Charlie Company was the 1st Battalion commander, Lieutenant Colonel Ernest 'Ernie' LaFlamme, and the hundred-and-fifty-odd men of his headquarters' company. They had stopped to set up a perimeter for the night when, shortly after 16:00, two survivors from Charlie Company blundered into their lines, setting off booby traps and breathlessly reporting the firefight two miles up the trail. LaFlamme was still trying to understand what had happened when, twenty minutes later, a group of thirty-nine troopers and two officers stumbled in. Another nine exhausted men, including Colbert Renfroe, found LeFlemme's perimeter after floating down river to flee the melee. The fact that only three still had their rifles indicated how frantic their escape had been.

LaFlamme wanted more details, but none of the survivors could locate the site of the battle on any of the maps, nor did they know what had happened to the troopers up front before they withdrew.

They thought the Japanese had wiped out the entire company, and wild rumors to that effect quickly spread. The actual number of casualties or who was on the run remained unclear. Hard Rock's whereabouts were also a mystery, and Captain 'Big Tom' Mesereau, along with most of the other men, remained unaccounted for.

LaFlamme radioed Swing's HQ with an update and requested medical supplies be brought up to aid the wounded, but with the sun setting, there was little else to do except hold tight until morning. Moving at night in these mountains guaranteed getting lost, walking into an ambush, or both.

Major 'Slugger' Lahti disagreed. He insisted LaFlamme dispatch troops immediately. LaFlamme balked, opting instead to wait for first light. It was an argument between battalion commanders—peers— and the mess was LaFlamme's. Lahti huffed away, ensuring his intelligence officer noted the conversation and LaFlamme's refusal to act.

Haugen, with Mesereau and thirty-odd men, had, in fact, withdrawn up a ridgeline about five hundred yards from the firefight. The group, with six wounded in tow, dug in under sporadic enemy rifle fire. They'd have to defend in place until help arrived.

Twenty-one-year-old Private E.V. Schoener—one of Hard Rock's bodyguards—later recalled, "Darkness was setting in, and the rain was constant as the able bodied were digging a protective perimeter of foxholes around the wounded.... Everybody was rain soaked, cold, shivering, and perplexed."

To a man, they'd been stunned. The battle had unfolded at a furious pace, and with action always besting inaction, the Japanese gave the paratroopers a humble lesson.

Lying in their shallow, muddy foxholes, the troopers reflected upon their baptism of fire. Some wondered why they'd lived while others hadn't. Several thanked God; a few cursed him. Some steeled themselves for the fight ahead; others questioned why they were there or wallowed in self-pity, pondering their chances of getting home alive.

Why am I here? Is this how it's going to end?

In their foxhole, Schoener and John West alternated two-hour vigils so the other could sleep.

"At about 02:00, I took my turn," remembered Schoener, "but began shivering uncontrollably.... I could not hold my rifle steady. I was in a state of hypothermia."

Darkness provided a respite from the day's sweltering temperatures and the soul-sucking 100 percent humidity, but the twenty-degree temperature drop brought a different discomfort. The change was enough to leave the exhausted, soaked-to-the-skin troopers—whose bodies had been drained of adrenaline from the day's ordeal—chilled to the bone.

West, seeing Schoener shivering, whispered, "Settle back, Scooter. I'll take it for a while longer."

Schoener settled back into their foxhole, wrapping himself up in his wet poncho. "My gratitude has never ceased over the years," he said.

One of the wounded died during the night while the other five remained in critical condition. The regimental surgeon, thirty-seven-year-old Major Wallace 'Doc' Chambers, did what he could but had little to work with. He laid his patients on top of ponchos to get them out of the muck and kept them as comfortable as possible by pairing the lightly wounded men with the more serious cases. Sharing a shallow foxhole, the pair's body heat staved off the night chill, and they could whisper back and forth, reminding the other he wasn't alone. In between rounds of triaging the wounded, 'Doc' Chambers would curl up in the mud for a nap.

DAYLIGHT FAILED TO YIELD any new information about the missing men. Just after sunrise, 'Ernie' LaFlamme dispatched a sixty-man rescue patrol up the trail, but five hours later, they returned with bad news.

They had run into the Japanese perimeter—manned by an estimated two hundred troops—and after a sharp firefight, they couldn't break through to where they suspected the remnants of Charlie Company were laid up. Lieutenant Merkel Varner had charged into the enemy lines but hadn't been seen since, and another trooper had been killed.

One of Swing's L-4 spotter aircraft was also up at dawn, flying low and scouring the jungle for survivors. The pilot, using his onboard hand-cranked radio, established contact with Haugen and Mesereau's group. Unfortunately, the thick jungle canopy prevented him from pinpointing their location. Confirmation of the men with Mesereau, plus the others who'd been accounted for, left some twenty troopers either dead or missing. The survivors were still surrounded, and their location had only been vaguely determined.

SIMULTANEOUSLY, SWING HAD OTHER PROBLEMS competing for his attention. The Angels had completed their relief of the 7th Infantry Division, and the pincer attack against Ormoc Bay was well underway. For his part, Swing needed to keep his units moving deeper into the mountains to cut off escape routes, and he elected not to inform his higher headquarters about the status of his lost men. As desperate as it might have been, the plight of Mesereau's group couldn't hold up the ongoing mission. This came at the same time as a stream of intelligence reports suggesting the Japanese might drop paratroopers somewhere near Swing's airstrips. Potentially corroborating this was an unconfirmed report from a civilian that ten Japanese had landed in his yard. Additionally, in a bizarre series of events, three enemy transport aircraft attempted to belly-land with well-armed raiding parties onboard. One crashed at Buri, killing all aboard, another crashed offshore farther north, and the third splashed down in the shallows off

Bito Beach with all but one of the Japanese escaping into the jungle. The Angels found several satchels of demolitions onboard and dispatched patrols to chase them down.

Unsure if these were isolated sabotage attempts or scouts of a larger operation, Swing ordered increased security at outposts, bridges, and supply depots. As an additional precaution, Swing's higher headquarters placed several Sherman tanks under his command. Swing split up the additional firepower and formed mobile defense forces to protect the airstrips.

Furthermore, a map found on a dead Japanese soldier added to the puzzle: lines drawn on the map converged at the San Pablo strip where Swing had his command post, while another arrow coming in from the southeast pointed at the neighboring Dulag strip. The arrows presumably indicated air routes to drop paratroops.

Swing opted to dismiss the intelligence, thinking an airdrop too fanciful. However, Major Henry 'Butch' Muller, the Angels' intelligence officer, believed a raid was imminent. Swing shrugged off the warning and focused on the task of pushing west to flush the Japanese out of the mountains and herd them toward the coast—where the converging American divisions would finish them off.

ON WEDNESDAY, November 29, approximately forty-eight hours after Charlie Company's firefight, Haugen's and Mesereau's group was still surrounded, but they had at last been located.

An observation aircraft circled under scattered clouds until the pilot spotted signal mirror flashes through a break in the trees.

Talking over the radio in the clear—without the benefit of code words—the pilot asked whoever was flashing the mirror to confirm their identity by answering, "Where did you train?"

"M...A...C...K...A...L...L," the mirror signaled in Morse code.

"That's when we went in and started dropping blood plasma and food," Swing recalled. "That was pretty nerve racking."

The pilot flew as low as possible to shove much-needed medical supplies out the window. Unable to pinpoint the location on the black and white maps, he was able to circle the spot on an aerial photograph. It was enough: comparing it with other known points, such as the Manarawat plateau southwest of Lubi, a compass azimuth and distance were plotted.

Manarawat plateau was occupied by a company of Haugen's paratroopers who had set up a perimeter at the summit. Covered in six-foot-tall kunai grass, it formed a narrow, two-hundred-yard-long mesa that rose approximately a hundred and fifty feet above the surrounding riverbed. It was defendable terrain, and with some work, would be a good place to air drop supplies to the 511th.

With Hard Rock isolated and two battalions of paratroopers changing course to converge on the plateau, Swing's priority was to re-establish the 511th's chain of command and keep them moving. Lieutenant Colonel Norman E. Tipton, Haugen's second-in-command, took charge of the regiment but needed to be closer to the front so he could better organize both the attack westward as well as a rescue mission. The thirty-five-year-old from South Carolina had spent three years in Panama before the war and knew that hiking through the jungle to Manarawat would take him at least two days, so he opted for faster means.

Tipton shrugged into a parachute and folded himself into the cramped backseat of a single-engine L-5 Sentinel. With his static line anchored inside the cabin—his feet dangling out the open doorframe— and the aerial photograph shoved into his cargo pocket, they bounced down the muddy airstrip for takeoff.

Tipton's pilot made one low pass over Manarawat for him to get a better feel for what he was about to do, and then circled up to one thousand feet. Tipton awkwardly edged off the backseat to tumble out of the aircraft. It was a much different experience than jumping from a roaring twin-engine C-47. The slower cruising speed of the L-5 required a higher drop altitude as absence of the forward throw from a more powerful aircraft meant the chute needed more time to open. Tipton notched the Angels' first descent into combat with a good landing.

Once on the ground, Tipton assigned Captain Patrick W. Wheeler's George Company to rescue Mesereau's beleaguered group. Wheeler and Mesereau had been classmates at West Point. The two officers were close, having played football together, and the day after their graduation, Mesereau had attended Wheeler's wedding. Wheeler was keen to find his friend, but it was getting dark, and they'd have to wait until morning.

Attempting to reach Mesereau's group from the opposite direction would be the job of the 511th's remaining battalion, the 2nd, commanded by Lieutenant Colonel Norman M. 'Shippo' Shipley. Shipley's men left their blocking positions at Burauen and moved down the north trail to join the rest of the regiment at Manarawat.

But in Mesereau's perimeter, Haugen had run out of patience. Earlier that morning, while rescue efforts were still being planned, he decided he'd been away from his regiment long enough and he, with a dozen men, slipped out.

'Scooter' Schoener accompanied the group. "We left our rations and most of our ammo with Captain Mesereau, who was left in command of the position." Schoener took point and led the group out. With steam rising from the wet jungle floor, they weaved through the thick vegetation, finding a trail fifty yards outside the perimeter. They followed it east, back toward Burauen.

"About mid-day, we heard Japanese soldiers chopping and jabbering," continued Schoener. "Since we were not about to engage the enemy, we kept on going until nightfall when we came upon a river flat.... Without digging in, we rested there until dawn."

AT 08:00 THE NEXT MORNING, Captain Wheeler's rescue patrol headed down the plateau. Wheeler planned to move up the north trail until they got to a spot where they would cut overland in search of Mesereau's ridge. One of Wheeler's troopers, Private Harry 'Bloody' Swan, recalled the trepidation of heading out "somewhat blind."

"We knew that we had to be very careful that we didn't get into a similar situation as Charlie Company," he said.

Each man had the same inner dialogue: *Are the Japanese using Charlie Company as bait? Are they waiting for us? They must know rescuers are on the way, right?*

Stan Young, a mortarman with Wheeler's patrol, was more focused on the present. "I had no idea where we were. We wound our way through jungle, uphill and down, through creeks and valleys."

The patrol labored for nine hours to traverse the six miles to Mesereau's perimeter. They arrived at the spit of high ground an hour before sunset, passing dozens of Japanese corpses on their way up the steep hill. The bodies lay in contorted positions; having been searched for documents, their shirts were ripped open and their pants pulled down. Bits of equipment and useless discoveries had been discarded, littering the macabre scene.

Mesereau was relieved to see his old classmate. After holding out for three days against multiple Japanese attacks, his men were low on water, ammunition, and grenades. 'Doc' Chambers had run out of sutures and was using thread from the men's field sewing kits to stitch wounds. Worse yet, most of the bottles of blood plasma that had been airdropped shattered on impact. Chambers strained what liquid was left through a mosquito net, filtering out the broken glass. With only three good bottles and just one adaptor tube, he rotated it amongst the patients for infusions. He also diluted the plasma with water to make what he had last longer. He figured, *They won't die from the glass, but they'll sure die if we don't get some fluids back in them.*

Off to the side was a rain-soaked pile of the dead, their paratrooper boots sticking out from under bloody ponchos.

As it was too late in the day to ready the wounded for travel before dark, Wheeler's company took over the perimeter, allowing the survivors to get what rest they could. The men on watch were told to be quiet and to stay in their foxholes.

"It pelted rain incessantly all night," recalled Stan Young. "None of us had [rain] jackets or shelter of any kind. I have been chilly before, but never wetter."

"It was a miserable night," agreed 'Bloody' Swan.

IN THE GRAYING DAWN of first light, Stan Young and several of the other troopers who had arrived with Wheeler paired up to transport the wounded. They slipped out of the perimeter and headed to Manarawat with armed escorts. The trek to the plateau was judged too ambitious for the group to make in one go, so their first destination would be Anonang, a village where they would rest for the night.

"The fellow we carried out had a back wound and was in a great deal of pain," said Young. "We had to be extremely careful that he did not hit the ground, a tree, or a rock," he said. "On several occasions while going up a hill, we became so exhausted we could no longer move. Our wounded patient, noticing our condition, bravely instructed us to set him down—which, on one occasion, we did, for perhaps three or four minutes. He just gritted his teeth and groaned."

Meanwhile, the rest of Wheeler's group, able to move faster, took a more direct route back to Manarawat. They were following a streambed when the distinct chatter of a Japanese Nambu machinegun sent troopers scrambling for cover. Sergeant Harry A. Cheney collapsed in the first hail of bullets.

A second dug-in Japanese machinegun opened fire, followed by several bolt-action rifles, elevating the cacophony. Cheney lay sprawled in the water, but the ferocious enemy salvo prevented anyone from getting to him.

PFC James M. Massey, Floyd Frantz, and Bob Perkins—together a .30-caliber belt-fed machinegun crew—tried to escape the fusillade by scrambling up the steep, muddy riverbank, but it was slippery work. Frantz had crawled to the top, and Massey was pushing Perkins up the bank. A bullet thudded into Perkins' hip, taking a chunk of Massey's hand with it. Massey gave Perkins a final shove and slid back down into the stream to snatch up his machinegun.

"With nowhere to go, I wrapped my folded poncho around the barrel jacket and started firing—first come, first served," he later wrote.

He fired in short bursts, walking the rounds into the two enemy machinegun positions, shredding the crews. The volume of Japanese fire dropped, but Massey kept shooting until he emptied the full ammo belt of 150 bullets.

He ditched the machinegun and switched to his carbine, squeezing the trigger as fast as he could.

"Hold on, Rebel. We're moving up," yelled Lieutenant William 'Buzz' Miley, while rallying his men for a counterattack.

"For the first time in the action," Massey confessed, "I had time to think and true fear took over. There seemed to be so many Japs in front of me that they almost replaced the tree line. Of course, there weren't, but at the time, I'd have sworn to it."

Behind him, the rest of the company had fallen back to better positions to recover from the pandemonium. As the Japanese swarmed forward, Miley and Massey took to their heels to join the main element.

Captain Wheeler directed the mortar crews to unlimber their 60mms at a fork in the stream. 'Bloody' Swan took a knee to provide covering fire while they assembled the three mortars. Wheeler knew they'd have to withdraw uphill to get out of the kill zone and wanted the enemy fire suppressed before his men started the exposed climb.

Sergeants got the crews organized, and soon high-explosive rounds were thumping out of all three tubes, the shells bursting on target. The Japanese screamed as the first volley's shrapnel sliced through their ranks.

During the melee, the Japanese guns' staccato bursts sent rounds zipping down the streambed and ricocheting off boulders. Captain Wheeler scooped up a bazooka and sprinted forward in a crouch until he could see the barricaded machinegun. He snapped the weapon to his shoulder and aimed. "All I could see was the gun and the black aperture between the covering logs and the lip of a hole," said the captain.

A quick squeeze of the trigger sent the rocket racing down range. The blast decimated the machinegun emplacement, and the incoming fire dropped enough for the troopers to get to safety.

The mortar crews, firing a shell every two seconds, exhausted their ammunition before throwing their forty-five-pound mortars over their shoulders to join the uphill dash.

While they suffered one man killed and four wounded, the company's swift response to the attack prevented more casualties and left behind an estimated sixty enemy dead. Sadly, Cheney's body was never recovered.

WHEELER'S MEN REORGANIZED and rendezvoused with Able Company, the two groups forming a joint perimeter for the night.

It had been a long, sobering trek for Able. They'd departed Manarawat two days prior and spent that time in single file, silently hiking up and down steep mountains. The four- or five-yard interval between each man discouraged conversation, and they kept their attention on the thick vegetation crowding the trails, which allowed for an easy enemy ambush.

One trooper recalled, "Even though others were there with you, it was lonely on that jungle combat trail." Visibility was limited, and the column of troops spread out. "It was often difficult to keep track of the others there with you," he continued. "Occasionally, you might see the man ahead glance back to make sure that the others were still there. Or maybe you would look about to make sure that you were not alone."

Another man remembered the smell of rotting vegetation and the slimy mud. "Footsteps of men who preceded us left four-inch-deep depressions filled with rainwater," he said. "Our footsteps squished out the water, making the trail muddier and sloppier than ever."

Going up sharp hills often required climbing on all fours, using rifle butts for leverage, or forming human chains to pass mortars and machineguns up to the next man. Traversing downhill meant digging heels into the muck or clinging to underbrush to avoid sliding. It was slow, demanding work, requiring hourly breaks. The rest halts also provided an opportunity to remove leeches, which were as ubiquitous as the mud.

"These tiny, black, thread-like blood suckers were thick on the bushes along the trail," commented a trooper. "You would not be aware you had picked one up until you felt or noticed a pendulous grape growing on your chest, arm, or leg." A lit cigarette held against the squishy parasite was the favored removal technique.

Steve M. 'Heggy' Hegedus remembered wading through a steep-sided river during the patrol. "You could see the sky only by looking straight up," he recalled.

The man in front turned to him with a single vertical finger held to pursed lips. *Be quiet.*

Hegedus turned to the trooper behind him, made the same gesture, and continued forward to find the source of heightened caution: a corpse.

A corporal from Charlie Company lay on his back, eyes open, seeing nothing. The grotesque sight of a man shot multiple times in the chest jarred the troopers. It was the first time many of them had seen a dead body—and the war suddenly became very real. Twenty feet farther on, slumped at the base of a fallen tree, was the body of a lieutenant, his gray face drained of life. The Japanese had searched both men and stripped them of their paratrooper boots.

While several troopers fanned out to set up a protective perimeter, Hegedus' sergeant drew a detailed map to help later recovery of the bodies. Hegedus and the rest of the squad hacked out a grave for the corporal. The riverbank's thick, fibrous tree roots made it arduous work.

"We tried like hell, but we barely got down a foot," lamented Hegedus.

They wrapped the corporal in a poncho and slid him into the shallow grave, only to find it was too short. They tried to bend his knees, but rigor mortis made that impossible. The squad stood in a circle, contemplating what to do next. One man advised the group, "Stand back."

He leapt up and landed on the corporal's chest, forcing the corpse into the hole. The squad solemnly shoveled mud over the body.

Next, they propped the lieutenant's poncho-wrapped body into a sitting position between the exposed, flared vertical roots of an immense tree.

"We covered him with enough mud until no part of the poncho was visible," said Hegedus. The group paused to say a prayer for the dead before resuming their trek.

WHILE CHARLIE COMPANY was being rescued, 'Hard Rock' Haugen's patrol made it out of the mountains. After spending the night at a Filipino guerrilla camp a few miles west of Burauen, Haugen reported to Swing at the San Pablo airstrip on Friday morning, December 1. While the content of their conversation remains unconfirmed, they surely discussed Charlie Company's battle, and it may be where an alternate narrative of what happened on the north trail originated.

Members of the lead platoon who had been in the brunt of the firefight believed they'd bumped into a large enemy unit that had reacted faster, carving the American force in two. But at some point, a story was circulated that Charlie Company—and Haugen's staff—had been led into an ambush by a traitorous Filipino guide whom Haugen later had executed. Another version of the story said someone else shot the guide when he approached the encircled troopers with Japanese surrender terms. However, none of the survivors mentioned a local guide, and they disagreed with the characterization of the battle as an ambush.

A lone trooper descends into the jungle drop zone at Manarawat after jumping from an L-bird

After the meeting, Haugen stuffed himself into the back of an L-5 for the flight to Manarawat and what would be his thirty-eighth parachute jump. Upon landing, he resumed command from Tipton and found the plateau bustling with activity.

Men slashed at the towering kunai grass with machetes while L-5s puttered overhead at a thousand feet, making dozens of sorties to drop twenty-one of Swing's combat engineers one at a time. They were followed by their equipment bundles of picks, shovels, axes, and explosives. Soon after they landed, explosions echoed through the surrounding valleys as the engineers blew up old stumps and demolished trees to expand the drop zone's footprint. With the entire regiment converging there to get resupplied, clearing the plateau would ease recovery of the airdropped cargo.

Stan Young and the litter party bearing Charlie Company's wounded made it to the base of the plateau after resting two nights at Anonang. Even with the respite, they were absolutely drained. They'd followed streams when possible to ease their journey, but carrying the full weight of a wounded man up and down the steep mountains was shattering work.

"The going was, as I said, very tiring," admitted Young, "but further, the sand from these streams was wreaking havoc with our boots. I had sand in my boots, and eventually the soles wore right through; next was the soles of my feet. The last half mile or so was utter agony."

Troopers bolted down from the plateau to relieve the group of the wounded. Young and the other litter bearers had to be carried up the hill as well. Eleven of them, having worn through their boots, were taken to the growing field hospital to receive care for their shredded feet.

WITH THEIR ARRIVAL AT MANARAWAT, Swing's paratroopers out-marched the range of their own 75mm artillery. They also had 155mm 'Long Tom' howitzers nestled back in Leyte Valley, but despite the howitzers' fourteen-mile range—the shell's velocity covered that distance in just over twenty-six seconds—they hadn't been much use. The poor maps and the sporadic, small-unit combat made the threat of fratricide too high. Swing, a career artilleryman, wanted his troops to profit from heavy firepower. Getting howitzers up the narrow jungle trails, however, would have been a time-consuming, back-breaking exercise, and the advance couldn't wait. The solution was a combination of initiative and the unique capabilities of his division.

Swing tapped Colonel Nicholas Stadtherr's 457th Parachute Field Artillery Battalion to prepare a battery of four 75mm howitzers for an airdrop. Swing figured they might have to abandon the howitzers in the jungle later, but in the meantime, they'd provide the firepower to keep his offensive moving.

Adopted by the Army in 1927, the M1A1 75mm, with a five-mile maximum range, drew sneers from conventional artillerymen, but airborne troops valued it for its simple operation and reliability. Referred to as a pack howitzer, it was designed to be dismantled into seven components for transportation by mules over rough terrain; its easy disassembly made it ideal for parachute delivery.

Nevertheless, air dropping the howitzers, even in pieces, required a stauncher transport than a single-engine observation aircraft. Specifically, the Angels needed a C-47—the Air Force's venerable variation of the twin-engine DC-3. To drop a full battery of howitzers and artillerymen simultaneously required twelve C-47s, but there were just six of them supporting the seven divisions on Leyte. With all the demands and required coordination between multiple units, Colonel Stadtherr would be lucky to get his hands on just one.

Stadtherr, from the backseat of an L-bird, had reconnoitered the plateau's six-hundred-foot-long drop zone and determined that if they dropped low enough, they'd hit it. To pull it off, the pilot would have to be spot-on: the flight path required following a crescent-shaped canyon, leveling out over the drop zone after navigating a blind curve, and then hurriedly pulling up to avoid a mountain.

In case of fortune favoring the bold, Stadtherr obtained permission to press an idle air-sea rescue C-47 into service. The pilot, despite never having flown an airdrop, readily agreed.

Each disassembled howitzer was packed into nine equipment bundles, six of which were strapped into special "pararacks" bolted to the C-47's underside. The six bundles would be salvoed simultaneously as the other three were pushed out the port-side cargo door when the aircraft passed over the drop zone. They were all daisy-chained together, linked by canvas straps, to ensure they didn't drift apart during descent.

The artillery crews and a skeleton HQ staff would jump with their carbines, three days of rations, and a few small tents to keep the artillery shells out of the rain. They would also bring canvas bags and tarps to protect their recovered parachutes. With so many chutes ruined during the beach landing, Swing had to carefully manage what he had left.

Stadtherr had a plane, but his attempts to get the artillery dropped met with weather delays and cancellations. Clouds were often too low over the airfield or obscured the plateau, restricting the pilot's ability to find the drop zone. Stadtherr radioed Swing's HQ to keep them apprised and share his annoyance: "Bastards would not let me take off this PM."

Finally, the weather cleared, and Stadtherr personally jump-mastered each pass, ensuring the equipment and troopers were rigged correctly and that the pilot flew low enough. Each sortie roared over Manarawat at six hundred feet, and as the bundles were ejected, five men leapt from the cargo door. The short drop zone prevented more men from exiting before the plane banked hard left and was back over the jungle. It took seven sorties over three days to drop the full complement of artillerymen, four howitzers, and 260 rounds of ammunition.

ON DECEMBER 4, in the middle of the artillery airdrops, Swing clarified Haugen's next objective: the 511th would move deeper into the mountains to seize the Mahonag Pass. Filipino guerrillas reported that two thousand Japanese were located somewhere near Mount Mahonag, where they also believed that Lieutenant General Sosaku Suzuki had hidden his troops' main supply base.

To get at them, Swing needed a reliable way to get food and ammunition in and the wounded out. On the same day that he ordered Haugen to attack Mahonag, he also dispatched his thirty-year-old operations officer, Lieutenant Colonel Douglas 'Tangle Foot' Quandt, to the plateau. Quandt would oversee the set-up of a forward command post and orchestrate the Angels' resupply.

Quandt squeezed into the back of an L-5 for the jump in, while later that afternoon, Swing's assistant division commander, General Albert 'Uncle Al' Pierson, landed in a Piper Cub. The combat engineers had completed the rough airstrip earlier that morning, and Pierson was their first customer. Swing still commanded the division from San Pablo, but his two staff officers at Manarawat would be his eyes on the ground to coordinate the main offensive as more units moved forward.

Quandt's first concern was establishing reliable communications. They needed a system more dependable than liaison pilots relaying messages to Haugen's advancing troopers. Initially, a seven-man team from the division's signal company attempted to run a wire network out to Haugen from Burauen. They'd departed along the southern trail, feeding out a communications wire from a backpack-mounted spool. But packing in the heavy commo wire to facilitate a telephone line to the front was impractical. The team overcame that issue by using bright orange signal panels to coordinate with pilots circling overhead to drop more wire. After toiling uphill and down for three days, they had used twenty miles of wire to cover just six miles of trail. With more men needed to guard such a long communication line against the Japanese, the effort to reach the plateau was abandoned.

Instead, an officer, two radio operators, and a code clerk parachuted into Manarawat with a portable field radio. The team quickly realized that although San Pablo was well within their radio's reach, the steep and always-wet terrain hampered transmissions. Swing ordered platoons from his 152nd Airborne Anti-Aircraft Battalion to leave their heavy guns behind and move inland. These men followed Hard Rock's troops along the north trail to form a series of communication relay stations. Codenamed 'Godfrey,' each station was numbered, beginning with Godfrey 1 at San Pablo. As one station was established, another platoon passed through to set up the next.

With Manarawat in the middle of enemy territory and Haugen's paratroopers poised to move, Swing needed trigger pullers to provide perimeter security for the medics, signal troops, and staff officers. The day after Quandt arrived, the sky over the plateau again buzzed with L-5s making dozens of sorties to drop a platoon from the 187th Glider Infantry Regiment. Meanwhile, the rest of the 187th would hike in from Burauen, clearing the division's right flank and maintaining contact with adjacent American units to the north.

QUANDT REPORTED BACK to Swing about the unsatisfactory state of logistics he found at Manarawat.

"Something is wrong with resupply," he radioed. "There is no stockpile anywhere. Haugen ran out of rations after breakfast. Lahti moved out with little ammo though he was requesting it a week ago."

For his part, Haugen was already frustrated over the situation. Before Quandt arrived, he'd made multiple supply requests. He needed two complete 81mm mortars, more ammunition, six walkie-talkies, a back-pack radio, and plenty of batteries. He also wanted medical supplies, including syringes, alcohol, bandages, gauze, and catheters.

His men needed clothing as well. The rain was taking its toll and rotting the men's cotton uniforms. Leyte's rain was an adversary unto itself, drizzling constantly, dissolving, corroding, rusting, chilling, drenching, and drowning hope. Many troopers cut the tattered sleeves off their fatigue jackets, and several wore nothing but field-made shorts, caps, and what was left of their boots. As such, Haugen asked for five hundred pairs of socks, a hundred and fifty uniforms, mosquito nets, and twenty-five ponchos.

The supply situation had to be put in order if Swing wanted to get across the island. But back in the rear area, the quartermasters had their own troubles. So many requests came in from across the division that they were having a hard time keeping them all sorted. The Angels' logisticians were also taxed by the responsibility for the units attached to the division which increased headcount to over twelve thousand, magnifying the problem. It was, however, the attachment of anti-aircraft and tank units that allowed Swing to move his men into the mountains, but they were still additional mouths that needed to be fed.

Swing radioed to Haugen, "Many individual requests for supply for units in your area are confusing. Consolidate all requests for supply for all units in your area and submit by division radio to Div CP [command post]."

IT WOULD TAKE MORE than orderly paperwork and consolidated demands to overcome the challenges; they'd also need plenty of creativity and grit. An average division consumed three hundred tons of supplies a day, and keeping a rolling stock of ammunition, rations, radio batteries, and medical supplies would be critical to sustain Swing's campaign.

The steep, densely vegetated hills limited travel to foot traffic on narrow trails. Trucks and jeeps were out of the question, and the men could only physically carry so much weight. Locally rented pack animals were problematic as well. The lumbering carabao could carry a sizeable load but were slow, noisy, stubborn, tired easily, and unable to climb the steep, muddy hills.

Aerial delivery by C-47s was the ideal solution. But as Swing and his logisticians had already discovered, the aircraft were almost impossible to obtain. When they were available, they required forty-eight-hour advance notice and fighter plane escorts; their other responsibilities often made a synchronized sortie impossible.

Additionally, coordinating use of the big transports had to be conducted through higher headquarters—where they restricted approvals to what they deemed as "absolute essentials." That meant rations and ammunition; requests to drop much-needed uniforms and boots were denied.

Exacerbating the situation, a C-47 had crashed while dropping rations to Haugen. The plateau's small drop zone required that pilots fly in low to prevent the chutes from drifting into the jungle; the pilot failed to pull up quickly enough after his first run, auguring into a mountain five hundred yards outside Haugen's perimeter. A rescue party, following the smell of aviation fuel, hacked their way to the wreck to find both pilots dead and three aircrew badly injured. They carried the survivors out just before the Japanese found the crash site. By the time a second carrying party arrived to recover the supplies still onboard, the Japanese had taken what was left and booby-trapped the aircraft with explosives.

In the first week of December, after all C-47 air drops on Leyte were cancelled for at least ten days, Swing realized he needed an aerial supply solution that he controlled. He formed his own squadron of L-birds—his nine L-4 Piper Cubs and two L-5 Sentinels—pressing the single-engine spotter aircraft to serve as full-time cargo planes. It became one of the most improvised logistical efforts of the war.

The L-birds bumped down the Bayug airstrip in a continuous pattern of taking off almost as soon as they taxied to a stop. Personnel climbed into the back seat to either parachute into Manarawat or to push out supplies. Lightweight volunteers, under 135 pounds, rode in back to hurl out the supplies over the drop zone. It was cramped in the back seat where the passenger often had to contort his body around all kinds of supplies. Crates of machinegun ammunition weighed seventy pounds each, and the passenger had to sit with two of them in his lap until he was able to toss them out the open door.

When the weather cooperated, pilots flew from sunup until last light to get the supplies delivered. Some flew up to fifteen sorties a day. But the island's unpredictable weather plagued supply efforts for the entire campaign, and pilots were often grounded by thick, low-lying fog or clouds blanketing the plateau. The L-birds were equipped with rudimentary aviation instruments—altimeter, airspeed, turn needle, and compass—restricting pilots to visual flying conditions. The missions were not without loss; one pilot vanished in the cloud covered mountains. His crash site was never found.

BEFORE AMMUNITION CRATES OR RATIONS could be loaded into the L-birds, they first had to be moved to Bayug from the division's main supply depot back at Bito Beach. The quartermaster troops established two forward depots: one at San Pablo, and another smaller supply point at Burauen where the 187th's paragliders were preparing to follow Haugen's lead. While the engineers had completed the wood bridge traversing the swamp to the Highway, poor road conditions meant that supplies had to be taken up the coast by amphibious vehicles and landing craft to Dulag, and then inland via trucks to the two depots.

The road conditions at Dulag caused further delays. Routes west were deteriorating in the torrential rain, requiring lengthy detours. Road closures meant that instead of the eight miles to Burauen, the trucks had to travel a circuitous twenty-three, which could take eighteen hours. For the quartermasters to maintain a ready stock of staged supplies, the drivers were only allowed a few hours' sleep before making the return journey to repeat the process. If a truck got bogged in the mud or suffered a mechanical breakdown, the men had to stay with it until help arrived. Their fleet of eleven cargo trucks and five jeeps constantly shuttled between Dulag, Burauen, and Bayug.

Naturally, there were tensions. The harried logisticians radioed the forward bases, "Try and understand transportation problem when you make demands." Irritated and exhausted, the forward echelons growled to themselves, *Try to understand that we are trying to win a war up here!* The inconveniences existed at every level, including Swing's, whose latrine truck was stuck somewhere along the supply route waiting for the roads to be repaired.

But running supplies wasn't as safe or as cushy an assignment as the front-line troops presumed. On Leyte, the enemy could pop up anywhere. A small unit of Japanese ambushed a three-truck convoy on the road to Burauen one night. A trooper was shot in the leg, and the drivers executed quick U-turns to make their escape.

In spite of the continuous hustle and the incessant improvisation necessary to move supplies forward, the quartermasters' morale soared. The eighteen-hour working days confirmed their contribution to the division's offensive, and they took pride in their vital role.

The nerve center of the supply chain was the Bayug airstrip. Trucks rumbled in to unload their cargo after the long, circuitous drive, and a small contingent of men organized and readied the stacks of rations, ammunition, uniforms, batteries, and medical supplies for aerial delivery.

● ● ●

To the men on the ground, the putter of single-engine L-birds overhead meant food and provisions. Ammunition and medical supplies were dropped via parachute, while crated and canned rations were simply pushed out. Losses were approximately 10 percent, an acceptable ratio given the reduced packing time and saved parachutes.

Unfortunately, the free-falling supplies created an unexpected hazard. One man was mortally wounded by a mortar base plate, and Lee P. Turkington was killed by a plummeting rations crate while he lay in the field hospital recovering from shrapnel wounds.

Lieutenant Aubrey Lanier hands over quinine and other vital medical supplies to Sergeant Philip Schweitzer

Manarawat's field hospital grew as the number of patients and attending medics increased. Thirty-odd medics from the 221st Airborne Medical Company, carrying bulging rucksacks of supplies, marched in from San Pablo. The trip took them more than twenty-four hours via the southern trail.

While the medics stabilized the wounded, the critically injured patients needed to be evacuated to more robust facilities. Carrying them out was possible, but many were too seriously wounded to survive the journey. Litter parties required a minimum of four able-bodied men for each stretcher but ideally six. Also necessary were extra hands to relieve those of the draining work and to provide security. It was a big manpower commitment.

The L-birds, with their rugged undercarriage, could land at the small airstrip now carved out of the jungle. L-5s, with the back seat collapsed and a folding plywood shelf unfolded, had just enough room to slide a litter patient into the fuselage. The patient had to be secured as far forward as possible to maintain the plane's center of gravity, but after a bumpy takeoff while staring up through the plexiglass observation roof, he'd be on his way to surgery.

On the morning of December 5, all three of Hard Rock's battalions marched for Mahonag without any rations.

It was the beginning of what they'd call their long nightmare.

Chapter 5

"All Is Useless!"

San Pablo Command Post, Leyte Island.
18:35, Wednesday, December 6, 1944

General Swing sat down for dinner in the officers' mess tent. After a long day, he was looking forward to a plate of fried chicken and an after-dinner cocktail. The day had started off promising enough, with clear skies and no rain, providing the first break in the weather since he and the Angels had landed. But the good fortune was short-lived: just after sunrise, the Japanese launched a surprise attack on Buri Airfield, two miles northwest of Swing's command post.

The assault caught the aviation engineers, cooks, and anti-aircraft crews completely unprepared. Tan-clad Japanese, shrieking and wielding their bayonet-tipped rifles, sprung into the camp. They skewered men still sleeping in their cots and shot at others, who, panic-stricken, raced for their rifles in nothing but their boxer shorts. The shock was as complete as the pandemonium. One witness later admitted, "There was a lot of wild shooting and a lot of aimless running around."

A barefooted GI escaped the melee and raised the alarm. A hundred and fifty Japanese had emerged from the jungle like wraiths along the northern edge of the airfield, swarming in without mercy.

Because Swing's paragliders were the only infantry in the Burauen area—the other units were service and construction troops—he was ordered to retake the airstrip immediately. The thirty-odd-ton Sherman tanks of the quick reaction force were nowhere to be found (and likely stuck in the mud), but he did have two companies of paraglider troops bivouacked at the Bayug strip. The three hundred paragliders were waiting to parachute into Manarawat, and Swing immediately dispatched them to counterattack Buri.

The paragliders approached the airstrip cautiously, reporting that the besieged service troops were "firing at everything that moves and ... probably inflicting casualties among our troops."

Frank Farloni recalled a nerve-wracking moment of the attack when "out of nowhere, a Jap came toward us with his hands raised in the air, trying to surrender. We all had our rifles pointed at him. Lt. Parker commanded him to stop advancing toward us. When he didn't stop, the lieutenant fired his revolver and killed him."

A body search revealed the man was rigged with explosives.

In conjunction with the paragliders' attack on Buri, a newly landed infantry battalion from Dulag Beach was temporarily placed under Swing's command to help blunt the Japanese incursion. Swing ordered them to attack Buri from the east. At 10:30 in the morning, one of their patrols swept the airstrip's heavily vegetated northern perimeter, routing and killing a platoon of Japanese. The Imperial soldiers, caught in the pincer-attack, fell back into the surrounding swamp and rice paddies to regroup.

In the middle of coordinating the counterattack, Swing's headquarters received increasingly heated messages from his units in the mountains. At 12:45, Doug 'Tangle Foot' Quandt, at Manarawat's forward command post, radioed his request for ammunition. After Haugen's troops had stocked up for their trek to Mahonag, the stockpile was nearly depleted. Quandt needed twenty thousand rounds of rifle ammunition, thirty thousand rounds of carbine ammo, fifty thousand rounds for the belt-fed machineguns, one thousand fragmentation grenades, and another three hundred rifle grenades. He also wanted a hundred pairs of boots and three hundred pairs of socks.

A lone C-47 made one much-needed supply drop, delivering "a small quantity" of ammunition and rations. Tragically, falling crates killed one of the Angels and injured another.

Meanwhile, Haugen had arrived at Mahonag. It was little more than a farmer's clearing on the sloped side of a mountain. Previously used for growing potatoes, it was studded with tree stumps and made for a hazardous drop zone at best. Two minutes after declaring his command post established, he radioed Swing: "Have six companies at objective. Have not eaten in two days. If six thousand rations, signal supply, oil and plasma are not forthcoming, we will not be able to attack."

A few hours later, an L-bird puttered overhead, tossing out some boots and a single case of K-rations containing thirty-six meals. Clearly, Swing's supply chain was stretched thin. With more of his troops heading into the mountains, his reliance on aerial resupply grew at an alarming rate. The L-birds, limited by weather and cargo capacity, would be hard-pressed to keep up with the demand.

Fortunately, by early evening, Swing's paragliders had buttoned up the Japanese marauders at Buri. The enemy still held out in isolated pockets that would have to

An L-bird flies low over Manarawat to drop supplies

be dealt with in the morning; but they were contained for now after suffering an estimated forty dead.

But just as the sun was sinking into the deep silhouette of the jungle, an air raid alarm interrupted Swing's meal. He stepped from his mess tent to investigate the source of the alarm. Several of his staff officers joined him, abandoning their fried chicken to squint at a flight of four aircraft droning over the Bayug airstrip, a mile due west. In the dimming light, it was impossible to identify them as friend or foe, but their intention became clear when several dozen incendiary bombs whistled in. One must have made a direct hit on a stockpile of gasoline as the conflagration sent a billowing plume of oily smoke into the darkening sky.

American anti-aircraft guns cut loose with a furious barrage. The cacophony of ack-ack bursts chasing the bombers made for an impressive display, but their accuracy was less notable. The guns soon fell silent after the trigger-happy gunners expended all their ammunition, failing to hit anything. The eerie quiet was shaken by the buzz of more approaching aircraft, these much lower than the first wave.

To the men craning their necks skyward, it appeared that the waves of twin-engine aircraft lumbering in at seven hundred feet were American C-47s. Private W. C. Kitchens looked up from digging a drainage ditch and cheered.

They are finally able to supply the troops with more than a Piper Cub, he thought.

But the aircraft weren't C-47s. They were Mitsubishi Ki-57 Type 100 transport planes. Those on the ground stared in astonishment as the circular red insignia on the underside of the wings became visible. Swing's officers gawked at a man standing in the cargo door of the lead aircraft as it passed. When the armada flew over the Bayug airstrip, the sky filled with the blossoming chutes of Imperial Army paratroopers.

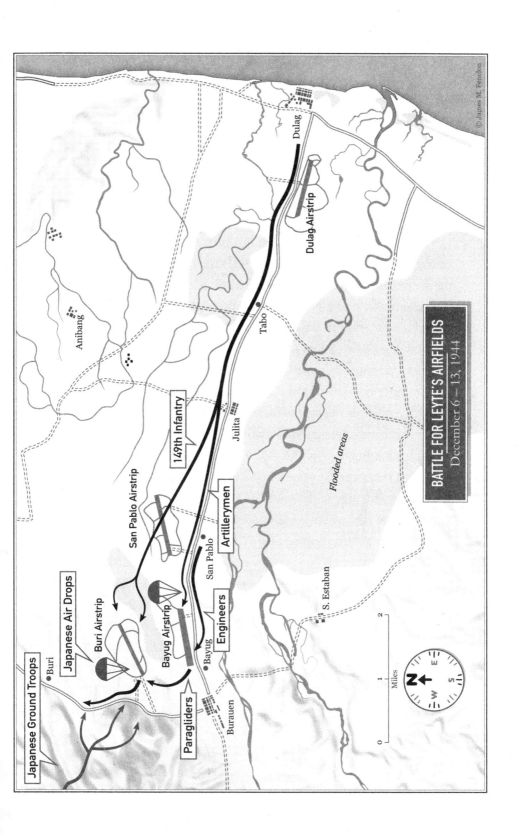

BATTLE FOR LEYTE'S AIRFIELDS
December 6 – 13, 1944

Dulag

Dulag Airstrip

Tabo

149th Infantry

Anibang

Julita

Artillerymen

San Pablo Airstrip

Flooded areas

Engineers

San Pablo

S. Estaban

Japanese Air Drops

Buri Airstrip

Buri

Bayug Airstrip

Paragliders

Bayug

Japanese Ground Troops

Burauen

N

W   E

S

Miles

0   1   2

© James M. Fenelon

Kitchens snatched up his carbine and shot at a Japanese equipment bundle that landed nearby.

"I knew even then that it wasn't a smart thing to do, but I felt quite an urge to do something, so I wasted some ammunition," he later recalled. Kitchens was soon out of the fight, shot in the shoulder by a trigger-happy comrade.

At Swing's San Pablo command post, a lieutenant colonel corralled clerks, typists, engineers, and MPs into a hurried protective perimeter around the collection of tents. Someone wisely shut down the generators, plunging the camp into darkness for fear the raiders would be attracted to the lights.

First Lieutenant John G. Mabbatt, the commander of Swing's signal company, positioned his men for defense, then turned his attention to his unit's cryptographic equipment. Concerned that the airdrop was just the first wave, Mabbatt wanted to prevent the sensitive materials from falling into enemy hands. He made plans to destroy the machines and codebooks with gasoline and thermite grenades if the raiders got too close.

More than three dozen transports zoomed over the airstrips, and within a few minutes of their descent, more than three hundred Japanese paratroopers rushed Bayug. Simultaneously, another sixty descended farther north onto the Buri airstrip. Alert troops at Dulag shot down two enemy transports attempting to belly land, and the ensuing explosions killed all aboard, ending the drama there before it started.

At Bayug airstrip, Captain David Carnahan ignored the air raid alert. They had become routine, and the target was always the cargo ships on the coast. When the bombers came overhead, he was perched—with his pants around his ankles—on one of the latrines.

Japanese paratroopers, rifles in hand, prepare to jump

When the bombs crumped in, a fuel dump erupted, along with several of the L-birds. Carnahan, with one hand holding up his pants, ran for a nearby ditch.

"The airstrip looked like Dante's *Inferno*," he said. "We were out on the strip trying to save the remnants of the airplanes when we heard them coming again. I made my ditch and looked up to watch the bombs come down, when to my horror, out of the sky poured about two hundred Jap paratroopers, coming straight down on our strip."

Carnahan organized the men closest to him and, grabbing what weapons they could, they dashed for the high ground of a small hill.

They dug in, and as others hurried to join them, Carnahan soon had a perimeter bolstered by an assorted collection of fifty quartermasters, engineers, and L-bird pilots. That was the good news. The bad news, he later recalled, was that "the only weapons we had of any power were four light machineguns belonging to the engineers, and a bunch of small arms and grenades."

Two men braved the chaos to serpentine across the field, making their way to the small operations tent on the edge of the strip. There they set alight maps and other documents detailing the Angels' mountain campaign.

The clipped bursts from Japanese 8mm submachineguns were punctuated by shrill whistles and blaring horns: the enemy was organizing into their assault units. Green and white flares—designating assembly points—arced into the sky.

Carnahan, watching the mayhem unfold, calculated the odds of his group fending off the Japanese at less than ten to one. Afraid of revealing their location, his group held their fire as the Japanese wreaked havoc.

The well-armed raiders fanned out to destroy as many American aircraft as possible. They were after bombers and fighters, but they found Swing's fleet of L-birds instead. They threw satchel charges into cockpits, hacked open fuel drums with axes, and flipped grenades into anti-aircraft positions, killing the crews hunkered in their gun pits. A pilot fleeing to safety was gunned down, but another crawled unnoticed into a drainage ditch to wait it out. With darkness enveloping the airstrip, the scene was lit by the pyres of aircraft and vehicles.

The Japanese shrieked taunts as they went about their work: "Kill a Yankee!" "Go to Hell, beast!" "Hello—where are your machine-guns?" Adding to the pandemonium, they threw ammunition crates into a burning fuel dump. The rounds popped off and sent tracers spiraling into the dark like fiery hummingbirds.

When twenty of the raiders silhouetted themselves in front of a burning cargo truck, they proved too tempting a target for Carnahan to resist.

"I gave the order to open fire," he said. "We really knocked them for a loop, and they fell back."

Across the airstrip, First Lieutenant Paul J. Pergamo rallied a platoon of combat engineers and led them into a hasty counterattack. Blasting their way forward with three belt-fed machineguns in the vanguard—one manned by Pergamo himself—they scattered several enemy squads before occupying a small hill on the strip's southwest corner.

The Japanese tried overrunning the engineers' perimeter multiple times. One attack made it within fifteen feet of Pergamo's position before the attackers were repulsed, leaving multiple dead comrades behind.

During the lulls, the Japanese threw more taunts at the surrounded Americans. "Everything is resistless! Surrender! Surrender!" they yelled. "The great Japanese Army is descending. All is useless!"

Pergamo's engineers were running low on ammunition. Technician Fifth Grade Doyle R. Lawrence volunteered to go find some. Lawrence had already proven his mettle that evening when he and a medic rushed through a hail of bullets to rescue two wounded comrades. Now Lawrence slipped out of the perimeter, belly-crawling through the dark until he reached a strip of coconut trees. He then crouched his way to the ammunition tent to find Japanese paratroopers ransacking it. He fired several bursts into the tent before retracing his route to Pergamo.

They would have to conserve their ammo until help arrived.

Fortunately, the shooting waned and the combatants settled into their isolated perimeters for a temporary stalemate. In the dark, it was impossible to know who was where or who held what, and no one wanted to move for fear of stumbling into the raiders or getting shot by a jumpy comrade. At least three Americans had already been hit by friendly fire.

"There was uncontrolled and disorganized firing, and much difficulty arose in establishing a coordinated command," admitted one observer. Sporadic and frantic shootouts erupted as the Japanese probed the American positions.

Despite the standoff, Carnahan anticipated the Japanese would attack again.

"About midnight, I took a ten man patrol out and located a fox hole about a hundred yards from our position," he wrote. "We slipped into it and began a vigil of waiting, as I figured they would make their main attack right by us. Sure enough, about 03:00 here came a Jap machinegun section of twelve men leading the main attack."

They waited until the Japanese were within thirty feet, then threw grenades and opened fire with every weapon they had.

"It was some massacre," recalled Carnahan.

He led the group back to their original perimeter, feeling that with just a few hours until sunrise, their odds had improved.

Over at San Pablo, Swing had little idea what was happening until one of his men dodged both enemy and friendly fire to make his way to the command post and deliver a report. The Japanese held the north and west sides of Bayug, with multiple groups of Americans scattered around the southern edge. As Swing's paragliders were already committed at Buri, he ordered the cannoneers of his 674th Glider Field Artillery Battalion to leave their howitzers on Dulag beach and proceed to Bayug at first light. While Bayug was the center of Swing's supply operation, it was too dangerous for the cannoneers to move at night; the surrounded troops would have to hold on.

SWING HAD UNDERESTIMATED both Tokyo's desperation and Yamashita's audacity. The Japanese were determined to seize the Burauen airstrips and destroy the fighters and bombers they thought were there. Doing so was their only hope of coping with the threat of growing American air power. If the Americans' land-based Air Force successfully relocated from New Guinea to Leyte, their air superiority in the Philippines would be complete.

Yamashita's first effort, landing sabotage teams on the airstrips, had met with disaster. For the next, he launched a coordinated strike between six hundred Imperial paratroopers and ground troops moving east from Ormoc Bay over the central mountain range.

General Sosaku Suzuki took personal command of the ground expedition and marched with seventeen hundred troops toward Burauen, while another five hundred men hiked in from the north. But their plan unraveled almost immediately: what their maps indicated was an east-west road turned out to be a foot trail. Forced to abandon their howitzers and the bulk of their supplies, the tan-clad Imperial soldiers filed into the mountains, relying only on what they carried on their backs to sustain them.

Suzuki understood the attack was a desperate gambit, but he also had faith in his men's fighting spirit—their *Yamato Damashi*—an attitude which combined honor and love of country with the certainty that their righteous cause made material strength immaterial; victory was theirs if they were brave enough to give their lives for it. A Japanese general summarized it as the belief "that a soldier imbued with *Yamato Damashi* and armed only with one small hand grenade could defeat an enemy equipped with large cannon and tanks." It fueled their brazen tactics.

Suzuki's men, strung out by the steep terrain and whittled down by Haugen's troopers, had nonetheless snaked their way over the mountains undetected to attack Buri with seven hundred soldiers. That is when they realized that in addition to their maps failing them, so had their intelligence reports: the only planes on the Burauen Airfields were abandoned wrecks and Swing's fleet of spotter aircraft.

THE NEXT MORNING, two companies of Swing's combat engineers left the command post at San Pablo to rendezvous with the artillerymen coming up from the beach. As they got closer, they passed abandoned Japanese parachutes draped over the trees, billowing silently in the breeze. The two groups formed up for their attack south of the Dulag-Burauen road. Their plan to retake the Bayug strip was simple enough: the engineers moved forward on the left flank, the cannoneers on the right. Doyle Lawrence, who had once again volunteered his services, aided them by sneaking out of the besieged perimeter to advise the reinforcements of the enemy's disposition.

As the engineers advanced across the field, the carnage bore witness to the night's violence. Smoldering aircraft and dead bodies were strewn everywhere. They didn't get far before Japanese paratroopers on the west side of the airstrip opened fire with several Nambu machineguns. The lead engineers dove for cover as bullets zipped into the group. Private Bill Bowen maneuvered forward, returning fire with his belt-fed machinegun. At the height of his advance, it jammed. He tossed it aside and drew his pistol to continue his one-man charge. He snapped off several rounds before he was riddled with enemy fire. He fell, fatally wounded, but his attack enabled the rest of his platoon to surge forward.

Michael Kalamas and several others sheltered behind a dirt pile for the night. They were well positioned to witness the engineers' counterattack as they pushed up the west side before hooking north to press the Japanese back.

The Japanese lobbed rounds from their 50mm light mortars, and the air was thick with whirling shrapnel. Kalamas, rather than running for the cover of a nearby drainage ditch, opted to stay put, afraid sprinting to safer ground might expose him to enemy riflemen. He was soon joined by a squad of engineers who slithered into position behind the dirt mound for cover.

"Someone finally brought up a .30-caliber machinegun and they tried to set it up on the strip just in front of me." he said. "Every time someone hunkered down behind it, the snipers opened up until there was a dust cloud around it. The air fairly whistled with slugs above our heads."

"The first guy got hit in the right shoulder. As I looked at his back, it turned red, and he slumped forward on top of the gun. I reached up and grabbed the back of his shirt and pulled him off the revetment. He was unconscious by then."

With bullets striking all around the gun, a sergeant slid into position behind it, squeezing off several bursts before he himself was killed.

At the same time, two troopers snaked their way forward under enemy fire. They wanted to let the Japanese know their time on the airfield was about up. Sitting on their knees, the two took turns chopping at the trunk of a tree from which the Japanese had hoisted their white and red battle flag. The tree soon fell under their blows, and they claimed their prize before scrambling back to rejoin their comrades.

As the attack progressed, Kalamas was surprised to see General Swing. "There was no mistaking his white hair under the helmet, and I thought he was nuts to walk down the strip in the open that way," Kalamas recalled.

He watched Swing stride up and down the line, waving his pistol and "barking orders as if he was on a parade ground at West Point."

On the east side, the cannoneers faced less resistance, but radio trouble meant they had to rely on runners to keep their efforts in sync with the engineers. The engineers pushed the Japanese three hundred yards north of the strip before stopping. In the process, they drained all their canteens and expended almost all their ammunition. Simultaneously, the cannoneers pushed north past the airfield, stopping in a grove of coconut trees. Shortly after 10:15, the radios were fixed, and the two groups returned to the airstrip to form a cohesive security perimeter.

David Carnahan and his men were relieved to be rescued by the reinforcements. They had made it.

Upon returning to his tent, however, Carnahan found reason to take the attack personally. His wash basin was shot full of holes, and the Japanese had skewered his cot and air mattress with a bayonet.

"They touched nothing else in my tent, the dirty dogs," he said. "If I had known that, at the time, I would have gotten more enjoyment out of killing them than I did."

He later admitted to being scared during the siege, but he took pride in his contribution to the battle. "I know that I got two Japs for sure," he wrote his wife, "one with a grenade and one with a rifle, and I figure I got a few more I can't be sure of."

While Bayug was secure, it now appeared the Buri airstrip had fallen back into enemy hands. During the night's standoff, more than half of the Japanese paratroopers escaped north to join Suzuki's ground troops at Buri.

To clarify the situation on the ground, an observation plane made a low-level pass. Heavy ground fire erupted from the north side, forcing the pilot to veer away, but from what he saw, the 40mm anti-aircraft guns had been abandoned, and a group of Americans still held the airstrip's south side. The holdouts radioed an urgent request for medical assistance, food, and ammunition; the good news was they had stripped the anti-aircraft guns, rendering them useless. They ended with a declaration that despite multiple requests for help, "No, repeat, no infantry has arrived."

A battalion of regular infantry was rushed up from Bito Beach and placed under Swing's command to wrestle back control of Buri. They had landed the previous day and had not yet seen combat. Expecting a short battle, they grabbed what ammo they could and headed to San Pablo.

Swing greeted them personally.

"Glad to see you. I'm General Swing of the 11th Airborne Division. We've been having a hell of a time here," he said.

Swing pointed the battalion commander toward Buri, where he estimated "there are about twenty-five Jap troopers. It is now 14:00. I want that strip secure by nightfall."

Swing had already attempted to get his paragliders back into action but had rescinded their movement orders after they were intercepted by yet another group of Japanese moving toward Buri. After that firefight, Swing got an update from them: they declared themselves out of the fight. "Men fatigued. Casualties heavy. Request help, need rations, ammo, water, and also medical supplies."

The regular infantry would have to make the attack on their own, their first of the war. The battalion commander organized his men in textbook fashion: two companies abreast on a four-hundred-yard front, with supporting heavy machineguns and 81mm mortars bringing up the rear.

They made good progress until they ran into a swamp. There was no time to go around, so they waded into the black, shoulder-deep water. During the slog, the two companies lost contact with each other. It took the first exhausted group over two hours to assemble on the southwest edge of the strip, and the second company finally arrived at 18:00. By then, the sun was setting, and seeing "many more Japanese" moving in the far tree line than Swing had led them to expect, they dug in. They would attack at 08:00 the next morning.

THE AFTERMATH AT BAYUG was immediately apparent. Of the eleven L-birds, Carnahan thought only one was flyable; the rest were destroyed or damaged. Making matters worse, all the cargo and personnel parachutes stored at the airstrip had gone up in flames. There were also the bodies of over a hundred and twenty dead Japanese paratroopers to deal with.

The hub of Swing's supply chain was in shambles. Without aircraft, he had no way to sustain his mountain campaign. He dispatched pilots to air bases farther north to scrounge repair parts as well as more L-birds. He then sent a message to his forward command post, "Haugen not to move beyond Mahonag. Will re-establish supply system tomorrow."

But the order arrived too late.

Chapter 6

The Long Nightmare

Central Mountain Range, Leyte Island.
Thursday, December 7, 1944

By the time Swing's message to stay in place reached Mahonag, the five-hundred-odd men of Haugen's 3rd Battalion, along with their commander, Lieutenant Colonel Edward 'Slugger' Lahti, had already marched west to seize the next ridge line. Haugen was pressing his troops forward. His job was to secure the Mahonag Pass, destroying any Japanese along the way; it was up to Swing's staff to keep the supplies flowing.

Two hours into the 3rd Battalion's advance, they were cresting a hill when the Japanese spotted them. The chatter of automatic weapons initiated the gun fight, and everyone scrambled for cover.

"I heard gun shots and dove over a log," recalled Jim Humphreys. "There was a dead Jap lying there. I have no idea who shot him."

Lieutenant John H. 'Skipper' Maloney told one of his sergeants, "Hold the platoon here, I'll be right back," then crouched his way up the hill to get a better idea of what they were up against. As he stood to follow Humphreys over the fallen tree, a bullet ripped through his left eye.

"He landed on top of me, and we were face to face," continued Humphreys. "His glasses were still on, minus one lens, and the blood was running out of his eye. I felt his body quiver, and then he was still."

Within moments, it was over; another hit and run. The Japanese fled, leaving six dead.

The peak became known as Maloney Hill for the duration of the Angels' campaign and started a habit of naming otherwise nameless hills that were often not on their maps.

Humphreys and the others collected themselves and continued single file down the narrow path. The following company, trudging up behind them, occupied the hill and dug a perimeter.

Continuing down the southside of the hill, the foot path intersected with what they suspected was the main Japanese supply trail. Its importance was self-evident. As opposed to the trail they were on, which was barely wider than an animal track, this one was five feet wide and corduroyed with thick branches and logs laid across it perpendicular to the direction of travel. It ran along the base of the hill and presumably originated somewhere on the west coast.

At the same time, the men of Haugen's 2nd Battalion, still making their way to Mahonag, ran into two hundred Japanese. The shootout pinned them down for nearly two hours, and they suffered fifteen casualties, including seven killed. It was their first taste of anything more than a short skirmish and an ominous sign they were getting deeper into enemy territory.

They opted to stay put for the night. Pairs of troopers dug their foxholes with one man watching the jungle while another shoveled. Inside the perimeter, medics tended to the wounded.

But the enemy was still out there. The slightest movement or noise triggered Japanese rifle fire, keeping everyone awake.

Leroy 'Pops' Butler was one of those who'd been alert throughout the restless night. "In the morning, we got out of our foxholes and all hell broke loose," he said. "The Jap infantry had infiltrated the area, hiding in trees and behind all types of cover."

Bullets zipped in from three sides. This was no longer the phony war troopers had grumbled about back at Burauen.

"Calvin Lincoln fired right over the top of my head, which almost deafened me, and killed a Jap in that direction," Butler continued. "I took over his field of fire and was successful in stopping several other snipers coming from the same location, about fifty yards out."

Japanese mortar rounds thumped in, and troopers ducked into the bottom of their foxholes to avoid the humming shrapnel. As the hornets' nest of Japanese swarmed around the perimeter, Colonel Norman 'Shippo' Shipley, the battalion commander, ordered a fighting retreat with one company forming a rear-guard to cover the withdrawal. The only way out was uphill.

Men fired as their buddies bounded backwards up the hill, then fell into a hasty firing position or rolled behind trees so they could return fire.

Forty-odd Japanese, their tan uniforms a blur as they surged forward, attempted to flank the rear guard. Elmer Fryar, a thirty-one-year-old private considered the 'old man' of the company, discerned the maneuver for what it was: an attempt to cut them off them from the main group.

A man behind Fryar buckled, hit in the chest. One of the belt-fed machineguns barked a few bursts in retaliation before the gunner leapfrogged back. Fryar held his ground. Bullets smacked into the tree he was using for cover. He squeezed off steady shots from his rifle, reloading after each eight-round clip *pinged* out of his empty weapon. Fryar, now hit in his left arm and shoulder, kept shooting.

Technician Fifth Grade Neal A. Retherford, lacerated by multiple grenades and blood streaming into his eyes, lurched out of the perimeter in the wrong direction. Fryar dragged him back and dressed his wounds, stemming the bleeding with two tourniquets.

Fryar, yelling commands back to the machinegunners, snapped off shot after shot as the Japanese formed for another assault. It seemed that every time he pulled the trigger, a man dropped.

Successfully stalling the attack, Fryar grabbed Retherford to join their retreating comrades. He caught up to his platoon leader, Lieutenant Norvin L. Davis, who was assisting a wounded private. The four men limped up the trail.

In front of them, a tan uniform crashed out of the undergrowth, leveling a submachine gun at the lieutenant.

"I had no chance to move," Davis later admitted.

Fryar sprung between the two men, taking the full burst in his chest and stomach. Slumping to the ground, Fryar's final effort was pulling the pin on a grenade and killing his assassin.

Davis and the others tried in vain to save him, but nothing could be done. Davis later said Fryar's last words were, "Tell my family that I got a mess of Japs before I went out."

Perhaps an embellishment, but if Fryar did say it, he was right. He was credited with saving multiple lives and personally killing twenty-seven of the enemy. Blood-trails suggested others were dragged away.

Davis and the two others hobbled on; in their condition, they were unable to carry Fryar's corpse. They soon caught up to the rear of the column where wounded troopers struggled to keep up with the main body.

Leroy Butler and another trooper aided Danny Brock, who was shot in both feet. The three of them, with Brock in the middle, heard the *fooomph* as Japanese mortar rounds sailed out of the tube. Each time, the three men hit the dirt and then picked themselves back up to stagger up the trail.

"We were very fortunate, because either the shells failed to explode, or their accuracy was lousy," recalled Butler. "We could see unexploded mortar shells protruding out of the mud."

These were likely grenades fired from a Japanese Model 89 mortar. The weapon, essentially a trench mortar, weighed just ten pounds and was crewed by one man. Its ten-inch rifled barrel could launch a grenade well over six hundred yards.

Medic John 'Muggs' McGinnis made his way up the trail, stopping to help a wounded trooper sprawled over a log. "He almost didn't have a pulse," recalled McGinnis. The man was barely conscious, and McGinnis couldn't lift him. "But I wasn't going to let him get caught by the Japanese. No way." McGinnis lingered, hoping someone would help him, but as the Japanese moved in, he made a gut-wrenching decision to overdose his patient with morphine. "It was one dose for pain and three or four to put somebody under. [He was the] only one I did that to. I did it on that one occasion," he admitted. "These are judgement calls."

Dodging the same barrage was another group struggling to carry Lieutenant Robert Norris on a cobbled-together stretcher of branches and ponchos. Norris was shot in the lower back, and the medics were unable to stop the bleeding.

Norris continually told his porters to abandon him if the Japanese got too close, but no one considered it. His men remained loyal to the end, carrying him until his life bled away. They buried him in a shallow grave beside the trail, then hurried off to catch up to the rest of the battalion. Like Fryar, the body of the twenty-four-year-old lieutenant would never be found.

Several troopers, including Butler, exhausted by over twenty-fours without sleep, swallowed a few Benzedrine tablets for a jolt of amphetamine-induced energy. The battalion kept moving, and the Japanese finally gave up the chase.

It had been another rough battle for the 2nd Battalion. Their retreat put them farther from Mahonag, and in the last twenty-four hours they suffered twenty-seven casualties, almost a full platoon.

That same day, back at Maloney Hill, a drama of a different sort unfolded. Lieutenant Miles Gale and the other hundred and twenty-odd troopers of Hotel Company were dug in, blocking the Japanese supply trail. They were milling around their foxholes when a lone Japanese began yelling from approximately twenty-five yards outside their perimeter.

The man's guttural exhortations went on for several minutes while the troopers glanced at each other in bewilderment.

What the hell is this?

When the man went silent, dozens of voices screamed in unison, "BANZAIIIIIIIIII!"

Every trooper scrambled into his foxhole.

"Adjusting our pot helmets, we got our weapons ready as we knew some charges would be coming," said Gale. "Our machineguns were set up covering the trails with a nice field of fire. Our light mortars were placed in the center of our defense, and they also covered the trails." Also in the perimeter's center were the wounded who, with nowhere to hide, felt helpless.

'Big Ed' Hogan readied his .30-caliber machinegun. He briefly reflected on how his training had prepared him for this very moment: snaking the ammo belt into the chamber, slapping the feed cover tray closed, and racking the charging handle; he had done it all automatically, without conscious thought. Now he waited, his eyes scanning for movement and his finger on the trigger.

The riflemen placed hand grenades within reach and flipped off the safeties of their M1 rifles. Some, expecting the worst, stuck knives into the mud, handle up, ready to grab in the event the Japanese broke through.

Another shrill voice erupted from the opposite side of the perimeter; it, too, was followed by several dozen unanimous screams of "BANZAI!"

We're surrounded!

While they were digging in, the enemy had been maneuvering.

The ritual whipped the shouting attackers into a feverish bloodlust and sought to induce fear in the anticipating victims. But as Gale moved across his sector of the perimeter to check on his men, he could see that "everyone was hunkered down in their foxholes with just metal helmets sticking out above ground. Weapons were trained to the front. Lots of pale faces and wide-open eyes waited for the assault. We were ready."

The two groups shouted back and forth in their call-and-response ceremony, each trying to outdo the other in the vehemence of their banzai screams. The taunts continued for what seemed like hours.

Gale continued, "This was a nerve-racking time for us, as we knew eventually we would be charged, and we had no idea of the number of troops we would be facing." Tales of "crazed, maniacal, no quarter charges" ran through Gale's mind, and he was frightened.

Rustling vegetation gave way immediately to a phalanx of shrieking Imperial Army soldiers sprinting out of the jungle shadows. In the lead were the officers—faces contorted with rage and samurai swords poised high over their heads.

They never had a chance.

The Americans' belt-fed machineguns opened fire first. The .30 caliber slugs shredded leaves and flesh alike. From their foxholes, riflemen picked off runners with well-aimed shots. The wall of lead forced the remaining attackers back.

The sudden quiet was eerie, and the men eyed the tree line expectantly. Dead and moaning Japanese lay crumpled in heaps all around the perimeter. *Was that it?*

"Nobody was keeping time, but it didn't last long," said Gale. "We had the high ground and good gun positions."

A quick check revealed good news: no one had been hit. The men wanted to search the dead for souvenirs: flags, pistols, belt buckles, and the most prized of all, swords. But recalling countless stories of a wily enemy playing possum, they stayed in their foxholes and took no chances.

"We made sure that dead Japs were really dead," said Gale. Each prostrate corpse was shot multiple times from the safety of the perimeter. No need to risk a Lazarus-like resurrection.

An hour later, it started all over again.

This time, the first cry of banzai sounded uninspired. The officer on the other side rallied his men, getting a more vigorous response. The two groups kept at it, stirring each other into a state of rage.

"The worst part," said nineteen-year-old Private Richard Keith, who was just a few foxholes down the line from Gale, "[was that] waiting for the attack, your nerves were a little jumpy. The anticipation had you strung out like a violin string, The one great fear: will I be up to it or will I let my buddies down. If I panic, cut, and run, someone may be killed. It's a genuine concern that every man has his limits. What keeps him from leaving his post is pride."

Indeed, for a unit to repel a banzai attack, each man had to play his part, to be an unfailing link in the proverbial chain. Each trooper relied on the man next to him to hold and cover his sector. Keith sat in his hole, contemplating the unknown and listening to the screams.

"It was designed to scare and intimidate," he said. "I will assure you it did both ... It was terrifying."

After a final "BANZAIIIIIII!" the Japanese charged uphill past the twisted bodies of their fallen comrades and toward the American lines.

Keith, along with every other man on the line, opened fire. Action quenched the thirsty fear of anticipation; pulling the trigger put each man back in control of his own fate. Doing *something* always felt better than doing nothing.

"At this point, a phenomenon occurred," Keith later recalled. "You are now fighting for your life. Fear temporarily leaves and training and discipline take over." Keith learned that it would always be that way. The fear, or adrenaline, or whatever a trooper wanted to call it, would creep back in no matter how many firefights he survived. It had to be overcome each time.

"We beat them back again in a short, fierce fire fight," said Miles Gale. At such a close range, the troopers hardly aimed. "It was mostly picking up a target and pulling the trigger a couple of times, then shifting a bit to pick up a new target."

"Banzai attacks are not of long duration," agreed Keith. "Either you repel them, or they overrun you."

From the jungle, a new voice yelled, "Stand up, Joe! Stand up!" and another chimed in with, "Yankee devils, die!" As the taunts grew in their fluency, one of Gale's foxhole neighbors—assuming their antagonist had learned his English in California—yelled back, "Come back here, you UCLA bastard, and I will shoot your ass off!"

The American line erupted in laughter and chanted, "UCLA bastard!" "UCLA bastard!" "UCLA bastard!" Other troopers joined in, insulting the UCLA Bastard's mother and detailing her sexual exploits. When they got bored with the jeers, they hurled a few hand grenades that seemed to chase the Bastard away.

But the Japanese weren't done. They made another attack that evening with the same result, and corpses piled up with each failed wave until there were over fifty.

It was the troopers first exposure to an enemy tactic experienced by their brothers-in-arms across the Pacific theater. The banzai charge, an unfathomable tactic from the troopers' point of view, had proven victorious over poorly armed adversaries in China and Korea, as well as exhausted, strung-out Commonwealth troops defending Malaya in 1941. But trying it against an established perimeter of disciplined, well-trained infantry was literal suicide.

"We had the firepower and knew how to use it," recalled a confident trooper. "A banzai was a 'machinegunner's delight' *if* you had a good, prepared position." The *if* was the big thing. That a heavily armed perimeter could brush such out-of-date attacks aside didn't make them any less terrifying. A rushing mass of sword and bayonet-wielding Japanese always held deadly potential, and troopers knew the odds. "It doesn't make much difference whether there are only two hundred coming up the hill or 20,000. It takes only one breaking though to get you," said a paratrooper.

The tactic was symbolic of a warped amalgamation of samurai ethic and religious dogma that gripped war-time Japan, wherein victory and death were equally glorious. When victory was unobtainable, death in battle was a worthy replacement. A charitable observer might view the ploy as an intense form of group courage, but it was culturally unrelatable to the Americans, who dismissed it as fanatical self-destruction. The promotion of the group over the individual was incomprehensible to Allied soldiers, who firmly believed that every man should be given a fighting chance to survive.

Battling the die-hard tactics of the Japanese disabused most troopers of their naïve imaginings of what war would be like. While their training prepared them to shoot the enemy, staring into the face of a dead, often teenage human brought home the gruesome realities of the job.

Nineteen-year-old Calvin Lincoln, with his rifle at the ready, cautiously approached a mortally wounded Japanese soldier. "He asked me in perfect English if I could get him a priest," Lincoln later recalled. "That stunned me. I asked him, 'Where did you learn to speak such good English?' He said, 'I graduated from Catholic University in Washington.'"

A medic gave the last rites to the man, who then asked Lincoln for a final cigarette. He died a few minutes later. "It was the first incident where I came in contact with a Japanese soldier and I talked to him," continued Lincoln. "It put a human face on the enemy. You thought they were animals, and here he spoke perfect English and was more educated than I was." Lincoln regretted having to kill people but added, "If they were shooting at me, I would obviously kill them first before they killed me. But I was never into killing."

Private Joseph R. 'Little Joe' Vannier had similar feelings. His platoon had pooled together a thousand-dollar pot for the first man to kill an enemy soldier. But when Vannier was approached as a potential winner, he bowed out.

"I hadn't thought about it before," he said, "and we quickly agreed that it was a bad idea and that all bets were off." It wasn't that Vannier was opposed to killing—he was a rifleman, and that was his job—but he didn't need to celebrate it. After several bloody firefights, he recognized a change in himself and his friends. "By now, we had our baptism of combat, and we would never again be the innocent same. We had lost our dwindling purity forever," he later lamented.

Others took a detached pride in their skill at arms. A comrade of Vannier's, Private Eugene Heath, from Portland, Oregon, was one such marksman. Heath was acclaimed for killing thirty-seven of the enemy in four days. Eleven of those he shot during a single banzai attack—and eight from more than a hundred yards away. Heath carved a notch in the stock of his M1 Garand rifle for each triumph.

Another trooper, a former high school quarterback, echoed his alma mater's touchdown tradition by decorating his helmet with a red dot for each of his kills.

Private Orville Noffke never tallied his kills, but he sought novel opportunities to exercise his marksmanship. From his foxhole, Noffke spotted a lone Japanese soldier standing idly on the supply trail below. Maybe the man was a scout, or maybe he was lost. Regardless, Noffke eyeballed the distance and drop to his target, and then with a vigorous heave, arced a hand grenade. It plunged through the branches, exploding just before it hit the Japanese's shoulder. His head came off cleanly, rolling downhill. "The corpse remained stuck in the mud in an upright position with one knee down and his rifle still in his hands leaning on the ground," recalled one of Noffke's friends. "The body stayed in this grotesque position for the next two weeks we were there."

The body count contributed to Haugen's growing tally, a statistic requested by Division HQ to estimate the enemy's remaining manpower. Haugen reported that in their first seventeen days of combat, his regiment accounted for 741 enemy dead. That was 70 percent of the division's total, with the infiltrators and Imperial paratroopers killed at the airstrips making up most of the remaining 30 percent. But Haugen's men were suffering losses, too, with twenty-nine troopers killed, forty-three wounded, and sixteen missing.

AS CHILLING AS A BANZAI ATTACK WAS, it paled in comparison to the dread that descended across the American perimeter after sunset. In dense canopy jungle, the night is as complete as a hangman's black veil, and Japanese infiltrators relished the cover of darkness to slither into their adversaries' foxholes. The stories of such ghost-like encounters were pervasive enough across Pacific battlefields to shake even the most resolute sentry.

"We were now under continuous attack from the Japanese," said First Lieutenant Randolph Kirkland, the intelligence officer from South Carolina. By blocking the corduroyed trail, Haugen's men had cut the enemy's supply line, and Japanese were desperate to eject the Americans. "We would attempt to push west in the day," Kirkland continued, "and the Japanese would swarm over us in the night."

The jungle at night is not silent. For a lonely sentry, rooting animals, rain, reptiles, and insects create an irregular cadence through which it is difficult to distinguish the rhythm of a skilled enemy stalker. And rain made the enemy's job easier. It muffled noise and smoothed the way for a silent approach through mud and wet vegetation.

Trooper Charlie Sass recalled the tension of his nighttime vigils: "You can hear everything that's not there. And your breathing is too loud, and your heart is beating too loud, and the ants are eating at you, but moving would make a sound. We learned early in the game that at night, seeing is meaningless. There's no light to see by except on those nights of the thunderstorms, when the lightning conjures up crawling silhouettes of a whole army moving across your front."

With each flash, Sass questioned what he thought he saw. *Are those bushes moving? Was that real? Was that bush there ten minutes ago?*

Machinegunner Deane Marks agreed. "After dark, one's eyes got as big as saucers. You couldn't see five feet in front of you, and your imagination would run rampant. You would visualize a Nip right out in front of you, getting ready to lob a grenade at you."

So infamous were the Japanese for their nocturnal prowling that troopers had free reign to kill anything moving at night. Shooting was a last resort, though, as accuracy was unlikely, and the muzzle flash revealed the trigger puller's location, inviting retaliation. Instead, grenades were flicked liberally at suspicious noises outside the perimeter.

If careless, friends could be just as deadly as foes in the pitch-black jungle. Leaving the foxhole was a bad idea when surrounded by nervous, trigger-happy troopers who took it as a matter of survival to shoot first and ask questions later. "When in doubt, knock it out; empty your magazine" was a popular division refrain of wisdom.

'Big Ed' Hogan witnessed two such incidents in a single night. A shadow moved; a rifle barked.

What's going on? thought Hogan, adrenaline surging.

"John, you son of a bitch, you shot me!" yelled the victim.

Another shot cut through the dark from inside the perimeter.

Who's shooting now? Are there enemy inside the perimeter? Do we have to watch our back as well as our front?

Hogan's questions remained unanswered until sunrise revealed the tragedy. A Filipino guide leaving his foxhole had been killed by a rash trooper.

SITTING IN A FOXHOLE in the pitch dark, often with a poncho propped up to ward off the rain, was lonesome work.

"With no radio, no way to read, and virtually no talking, time could not pass more slowly," said 'Big Ed' Hogan.

These moments built lifelong bonds of trust. Squad and platoon leaders rarely checked on their men after nightfall, but instead relied on individual responsibility to ensure a man was awake in each foxhole; everyone's survival depended on it. Men rotated shifts, with one trying to sleep while the other stared blankly into the darkness, bored out of his skull. Sleep only came to those who trusted their foxhole partner to watch over them.

Deane Marks shared a foxhole with Dub Westbrook and Dave Baily. To keep track of their rotating duty, they passed a watch with a luminous dial between them.

"Each guy was supposed to stay awake two hours," said Marks. "Then wake the next guy, sleep four hours, then watch for another two hours, and so on till daybreak."

Baily and Westbrook could trust Marks to stay awake, but for how long was another matter. "I would watch for a period, set the watch ahead, wake Westbrook, give him the watch, and go to sleep," Marks admitted. "I later found out that he was doing the same thing. Dave never did catch on. Perhaps he couldn't tell time. Maybe that was why he was tired all the time."

To repel organized attacks, each foxhole in the circular perimeter had a sector of fire already 'staked in'—stripped branches shoved into the ground marking a gunner's left and right limits of traverse. Each sector overlapped with those of the adjacent foxholes for mutual support.

"This worked well," said Marks. "Even in the blackest of night, you could cover your field of fire with the gun next to you. This type of staking in took place around the entire perimeter, making busting through by the Nips next to impossible."

Troopers also rigged early-warning devices in front of their fox-holes. These sometimes consisted of ration tins with pebbles inside to rattle when disturbed. The savvy cut a small hole in the tin so rain-water could not flood their life-saving contraption and render it mute. The favored technique, however, was attaching a fragmentation grenade to a tripwire strung between tree trunks. While this was the most popular method, it was not the most effective. When the tripwire pulled the out pin—releasing the spring-loaded safety lever to ignite the fuse—it audibly clicked, giving a deft quarry five seconds to hustle away from the blast. Instant fuses for just such a purpose were in the

Army's inventory, but none had found their way to the Angels.

Troopers set their helmets aside while on watch. This helped them hear better, and having the steel helmet at hand allowed them to throw it over a Japanese grenade to reduce its blast or use it as a "thunder bucket" should dysentery strike their bowels. Getting out of the hole to answer the call of nature was out of the question.

A trooper, Paul Hall, armed for watch: bayonet-tipped rifle and grenades; his helmet is by his right knee

But peeled eyes, strained ears, and taunt trip-wires weren't failsafe. One trooper sleeping on the edge of his cramped foxhole was startled awake just in time to raise his knees to protect himself from a fatal sword blow. He lost a kneecap to the vicious slice before wrestling the weapon away to slay the owner.

On another night, when someone or something tripped over mortarman's Stan Young's staked poncho, he jammed his carbine into the object and pulled the trigger several times. A leg covered in the tan puttees of an Imperial Army soldier slipped into the foxhole. Young kept an eye on the foot for the rest of the night.

George Floersch had a close call as well. A noise in front of his foxhole alerted him, and he stared into the dark but then settled back after not hearing it again.

"I was just about to get up and take another look when I looked up and could just make out the image of someone on the mound of the hole," he said.

Options ricocheted through his mind as he whipped up the carbine cradled in his lap and fired a single shot. The shadow crumpled to the ground, discharging his rifle as he fell. The shot missed Floersch—who pulled his trigger again.

Click. Nothing. It jammed.

Floersch dropped the carbine and grabbed for his trench knife with one hand while feeling for the intruder with the other. Finding the man's boot, Floersch plunged his knife repeatedly into what he thought was the man's thigh; the thrashing stopped.

Thirty minutes later, a Type 97 hand grenade arched into the foxhole, landing in Floersch's lap. He tossed it out and rolled over on top of his sleeping buddies as a geyser of shrapnel and mud peppered their hole. He chucked five of his own fragmentation grenades back. The succession of blasts was followed by silence. Floersch took stock: his buddies were okay, but his right arm was bleeding. Yelling his intent, he crawled to the foxhole behind him for medical treatment.

Another explosion detonated. One of Floersch's buddies yelled, "Oh God, someone help me!"

But he died before anyone could get to him.

• • •

On Sunday morning, December 10, Haugen sent an urgent message to Swing: "No medical supplies on hand. Desperately needed. Personal attention of CG [Commanding General] requested. Grenades urgently needed."

The destroyed L-birds, as well as the weather, hampered Swing's already stressed supply efforts. While waiting for the replacement L-birds to arrive from the 25th Liaison Squadron, the logisticians arranged for a C-47 airdrop, but attempts at Mahonag and Manarawat were aborted due to low clouds and rain. Finally, the Air Force shoved the supplies out four miles northeast of Manarawat.

After receiving Haugen's request, Swing's HQ radioed back admitting they were still wrestling the Japanese for control of the airstrips. The Japanese paratroopers, now reenforced with the rest of

Suzuki's ground troops, still occupied the Buri strip. Swing was having a devil of a time dislodging them.

In addition to Japanese tenacity, inexperience hindered Swing's units. His artillerymen, who had left their howitzers back at Bito Beach to counterattack as infantry, were having a tough go of it.

They had spent their first night in combat on the edge of the Bayug strip in a tight perimeter, continually harassed by Japanese mortars and infiltrators. The trigger-happy artillerymen were keen to keep the Japanese at bay. They threw a hundred hand grenades and expended almost fifteen hundred rounds of carbine, rifle, and machinegun ammunition. The commander later confessed that his men "may have killed one Jap" for all the effort. They also inadvertently slew one of their own with wild machinegun fire.

The chaos was more than enough to unhinge. Twenty-one-year-old Private James Billingsley watched a panic-stricken trooper a few feet away shoot himself in the head. Billingsley started out of his foxhole to help.

"Where are you going?" asked the sergeant next to him, pulling him back.

"Didn't you see what just happened?" pointed Billingsley.

"I wouldn't piss on that guy's grave," said the sergeant. "Don't you realize it's going to be that much more difficult for *us* to get out of here?"

Then the sergeant looked into Billingsley's eyes and gave him words to remember: "Never die bad! If you are going to die, die like a man!"

AT BURI, Swing's attached infantry battalion was not faring much better. Their morning attack failed after a combination of Japanese automatic weapons and friendly artillery fire crashed into their advancing ranks. After retreating, they requested 75mm artillery hammer the far side of the airstrip. Just under a hundred and fifty shells whistled overhead to detonate in the Japanese lines.

Swing was frustrated with the lack of both progress and aggression. He contemplated sending in his own paragliders to complete the job that the "lousy outfit" (his words) had left unfinished. Instead, he ordered the overwhelming use of steel to resolve the stalemate. Six hundred shells would pummel the north side of the airstrip throughout the night, with another barrage at dawn in support of the infantry's next assault.

Swing's frustration was only partially justified. His initial briefing that two dozen of the enemy held the strip was wildly inaccurate; his own intelligence officer estimated there were over six hundred. Making matters worse, the Japanese had captured six radio sets, complete with codebooks. While the Americans scrambled to reclaim the airstrip, new codes had to be distributed.

The next morning following the artillery barrage, the regular infantry made another costly frontal attack across the exposed runway. Their initial progress was promising, clearing two-thirds of the airstrip. But the Japanese refused to vacate the remaining one-third, holding it from fighting positions dug into the roots of massive trees. Additionally, roving bands of enemy riflemen kept up a steady staccato of harassing fire from the flanks. Running low on ammunition, the infantry again retreated.

It took another two days of skirmishing and mortar salvoes to dislodge the Japanese. After the infantry retook the airstrip—at the cost of a hundred and forty casualties—their commanding officer radioed Swing's HQ that he had stopped counting enemy corpses when he reached three hundred. They estimated at least another two hundred had fled west.

WITH HARD ROCK'S MEN MOVING deeper into the central mountain range, Swing needed more troops to secure his lengthening logistics trail. The division's supply chain now extended from Bito Beach by boat, up the coast to Dulag, then inland via cargo trucks to the airstrips near Burauen where L-birds took over for aerial delivery to either Manarawat or Mahonag. Swing assigned the two attached regular infantry units to defend the strips, freeing the 2nd Battalion of his 187th Paraglider Regiment to move to Mahonag, which would become the next forward logistics base. But the six-hundred-plus paragliders only made it as far as Burauen before reporting that their movement was delayed by overflowing streams and a lack of rations.

Just as Swing was getting his rear echelon reorganized, the Japanese struck again. Suzuki's troops—the two hundred who had been pushed off the Buri strip—regrouped on the west side of Burauen, where they stumbled upon an Air Force headquarters and a hospital. They attacked both in the middle of the night with mortars, hand grenades, machineguns, and rifles, killing three airmen and wounding seven. Exaggerated tales of butchered hospital patients spread like wildfire, but a hasty defense manned by Air Force cooks, drivers, and supply personnel managed to drive off the attack, killing thirty of the marauders.

At two in the morning, Swing was called upon to manage the crisis. He dispatched two infantry companies to ferret out the raiders, as well as some combat engineers to construct barbwire obstacles around both the HQ and the hospital in the event of another attack.

* * *

By Tuesday, December 12, Haugen had established his command post nine hundred yards southeast of Maloney Hill on a promontory dubbed Rock Hill in his honor. At approximately 3,000 feet in elevation, it was one of the highest points in the area and overlooked the Japanese supply trail that skirted its base. Oblong in shape, the summit was a narrow thirty-five yards wide, but its thickly vegetated three-hundred-yard length was flat. With steep slopes averaging sixty degrees, it was a first-rate defensive position.

But Haugen now had more to worry about than just the Japanese. Five days ago, his troopers marched out of Manarawat, each carrying a single K-ration that contained a breakfast, dinner, and supper meal: food for a day and a half. His men were hungry.

"Food was becoming a major problem, and we ate anything that we could chew or swallow," recalled twenty-one-year-old Sergeant James 'Bull' Hendry.

Troopers scrounged through their packs for loose cans of cheese, an old candy bar, chewing gum, or anything else they might have overlooked. In between patrolling, ambushing, and improving foxholes, hunger gnawed on their minds and stomachs. Foraging the local fauna became a common distraction. Camotes, a type of sweet potato, poinsettia roots, wild peppers, and hearts of palm were the most sought after.

The enemy also provided food. 'Bull' Hendry continued, "We found raw rice, a few cans of fish, a biscuit-like cereal, and rotten bananas and camotes in some of the dead Japs' packs."

One trooper recalled a rare treat when his platoon killed two small deer and a wild boar. "Each soldier received about one once of meat, which was his alone, to cook or eat raw, nibble or wolf down in a gulp, or to share with the wounded," he said. "Nothing was wasted. Even the bones were broken and boiled into broth."

Rumors circulated that it wasn't deer but feral dogs. But Deane Marks doubted it. "I don't think anyone was hungry enough to eat a dog. No one was any hungrier than I was, and I sure as hell could not eat a dog."

Food, always a topic of conversation amongst soldiers in the field, became the sole subject. "We would sit around and fantasize on what we were going to eat when we got home," Marks continued. "Malted milks, ice cream, T-bone steaks, and thousands of those greasy White Castle hamburgers were high on the list. Our morale was not at its highest, and being [that] most of the guys, myself included, had dysentery, didn't help either. When you had to have a bowel movement, you just passed a lot of hot water."

No rations also meant no cigarettes. Troopers relied on a K-ration's twelve cigarettes to sustain their smoking habit. Particularly hard hit were the chain-smokers, like Haugen, who seemed inseparable from the ubiquitous cigarette dangling from the corner of his mouth.

Haugen and his staff made a ceremony of their last smoke, passing it amongst themselves for each man to take a drag. When it was too small to hold, they skewered it with a small twig. Haugen, enjoying the benefits of rank, took the last puff.

Occasionally, an L-bird ventured up into the swirling mist of the steep, cloud-covered mountains in mostly futile attempts to drop supplies directly to Haugen's troops on Rock Hill. The men had cleared a patch on the summit so their bright-orange signal panels were visible to pilots, but the fog persisted.

"We could hear their engines as they circled overhead trying to spot us through a hole in the clouds so they could drop bundles of supplies to us," recalled Miles Gale. "Food, medicines, and shoes were desperately needed."

But until the weather cleared, it was safer for the L-birds to deliver supplies to Mahonag or Manarawat. From there, troopers served as pack mules to shuttle the supplies west.

Swing's quartermasters orchestrated another two C-47 missions, with one dropping at Mahonag and the other at Manarawat. At the division's forward command post at Manarawat, the drop

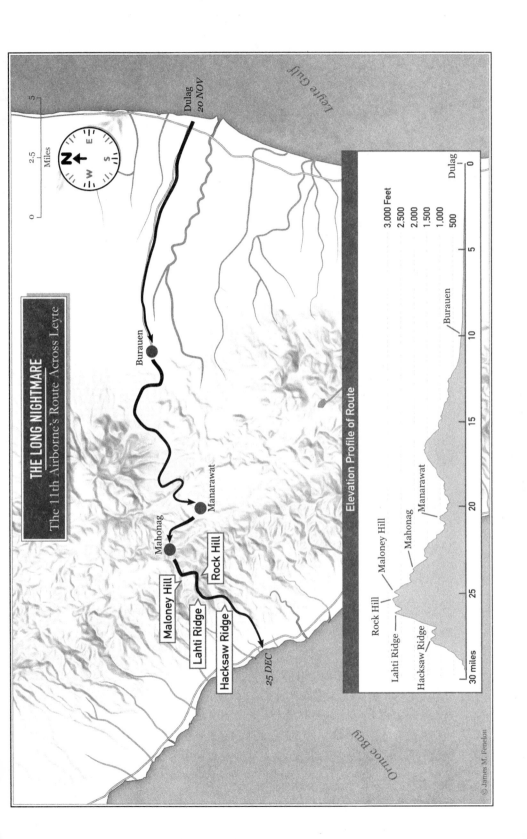

THE LONG NIGHTMARE
The 11th Airborne's Route Across Leyte

Leyte Gulf

Dulag
20 NOV

Burauen

Mahonag
Manarawat

Maloney Hill

Lahti Ridge

Rock Hill

Hacksaw Ridge

25 DEC

Ormoc Bay

Miles

N

Elevation Profile of Route

3,000 Feet
2,500
2,000
1,500
1,000
500

Dulag

Burauen

Manarawat

Mahonag

Maloney Hill

Rock Hill

Lahti Ridge

Hacksaw Ridge

0   5   10   15   20   25   30 miles

© James M. Fenelon

Troopers recover air-dropped ammuni-
tion at Manarawat

provided the first rations and medical supplies received there in two days. At Mahonag, most of the supplies drifted into the jungle, making it clear the drop zone was too small for the larger aircraft. L-birds would have to be used going forward. Haugen's troopers recovered what they could and hauled it up to their fifteen hundred comrades on Maloney and Rock Hills.

Japanese holding the next ridgeline blocked all attempts to move past Rock Hill. 'Slugger' Lahti's battalion made several unsuccessful attempts to dislodge them before dispatching George Company, led by Captain Patrick Wheeler, to bypass the ridge and cut overland to the coast, where the 7th Infantry Division was pushing north. Wheeler's company departed without food and with only a few radio batteries. Enemy scouts severed the commo wire they strung out behind them, and two days after they left, all radio contact was lost. It was a questionable decision to send out the poorly provisioned patrol. Rock Hill now had one less company to defend it, and Haugen had little idea what size of enemy units they might encounter, risking their isolation and destruction.

Perhaps it was Hard Rock's desire to compensate for the missing company, or as others have suggested, his aggressive drive to keep pushing west that led to a fatal misstep: ordering his units in the mountains to consolidate on Rock Hill. Combining the two battalions made for a stronger perimeter, but when troopers abandoned Maloney Hill to join their comrades, several hundred Japanese slipped in behind them to occupy their former positions. The enemy's speed and cunning had once again been underestimated.

A patrol from 'Shippo' Shipley's 2nd Battalion carrying up rations and ten wounded men on litters discovered the Japanese maneuver.

The lead scouts went to ground when shots rang out from Maloney Hill, forcing the lightly armed patrol to return to Mahonag.

The enemy was now lodged like a railroad spike between Haugen's command post and his supplies. The trail was blocked, and Shipley would have to find another way around. As word of the situation spread, "We have the Japs just where they want us" became a gallows' joke among the hungry on Rock Hill.

It became clear that Haugen's men were in the direct path of Suzuki's forces moving west. In addition to the several hundred Japanese atop Maloney Hill, one of Shipley's companies killed over eighty more in a single ambush along the supply trail.

But the Japanese were in disarray. The Americans' pincer attack against the west coast, as well as their two divisions in the mountains, had forced Suzuki's hand. His men needed to get back to Ormoc or risk getting cut off. Suzuki's attempts to organize his scattered units were hampered by spotty communications as some got the word, others did not.

Haugen's men now faced roving Japanese from all sides. "From our point of view, there were two groups of Japanese," said an officer. "Those survivors of the attempt to take Burauen and those survivors of the Ormoc Valley attempting to hold up in the rugged Leyte mountains. We were between these increasingly unorganized groups and an obstacle to both." Suzuki's isolated units committed themselves to either desperate acts of defense or crazed attempts to break through.

In the melee, Swing recognized opportunity. He ordered Haugen to cease his westward attack and instead hold the Mahonag Pass, locating and destroying all the Japanese moving through it.

While 'Shippo' Shipley's men continued to hold the eastern sector of the pass until the paragliders arrived, efforts to retake Maloney Hill started immediately. It wasn't going to be easy. The Japanese occupied high ground on steep terrain that forced attackers into perilously narrow uphill attacks from predictable directions. The knife-like ridges, some a mere thirty-five feet wide, limited the attacks to a single platoon. The first assault on the morning of December 13 cost Haugen ten casualties, two of whom were killed. After three hours, the withering Japanese fire forced the troopers back to Rock Hill.

THE ATTACKS RESUMED on Thursday morning, December 14. This time, Miles Gale and the rest of Hotel Company would take a crack at it. The path to Maloney Hill was now well trodden, turning it into even more of a soggy mess.

"Instead of marching, it was more like slip and slide through that mudhole," said Gale. "Mud balled up on our shoes, adding weight, and slowed down our forward progress."

Another trooper trudging uphill in the same column as Gale recalled, "With all of your equipment, you were slipping, sliding, falling. You would be covered with mud had it not been for the constant rain."

Leroy 'Pops' Butler discovered the deep mud could conceal revolting surprises. A fellow trooper stepped onto a small mound, "and it exploded like a balloon," said Butler. "I have never smelled anything quite as vile and repulsive in my life as when that aroma permeated the area. It was a Jap cadaver that had been laying there, no one knew for how long."

As the men prepared for the assault, 60mm mortar rounds warbled overhead and into the crest of the hill. 'Big Ed' Hogan recalled, "Standard practice was to aim beyond the enemy positions and gradually bring the shells closer."

This technique, called "walking in" the shells, avoided fratricide by purposely throwing the shell long, then adjusting the following based on where the first exploded. The priority was to get the rounds online with the target, and that meant a deflection: shifting the point of impact right or left. Next was adjusting the mortar's elevation to bring the shells into to the target. The mortar crews raised or lowered the tube by turning the elevation crank. In principle, it was a straightforward process, but speed and accuracy required seeing the round detonate and, in the jungle, that was often impossible. Thick vegetation and steep gorges swallowed the explosions, preventing visual confirmation and forcing observers to adjust based on sound. Smoke shells could have helped, but hand-carrying the ammunition up into the mountains meant prioritizing lethal high explosive rounds.

As the company advanced, a shell burst just in front of them. A piece of flying shrapnel struck Hogan in the shoulder. Ten hours later, they limped back to Rock Hill with one dead and six wounded in tow. They reported fifty enemy killed, but the nut remained uncracked, and the supply trail blocked.

The next day, 'Slugger' Lahti sent in most of his battalion. One of the lieutenants thought the lead company's attack got off to a poor start, observing that "when the company was trying to organize, everyone seemed to be confused. There was excessive and loud yelling by the subordinate leaders trying to assemble their men. Finally, after it was already daylight, the company started to move out."

Regardless of the confusion and delays, the attack went ahead. Miles Gale's lead scout, PFC Walter D. O'Conner, rushed a Japanese machinegun, snapping off shots as he advanced. O'Conner's marksmanship claimed nine of the enemy before his rifle malfunctioned. He dropped it and drew his pistol, killing two more. Another trooper, Paul L. McNees, charged forward to seize a second machinegun position, taking it out with a hand grenade before counterattacking Japanese cut him down. In spite of O'Conner's and McNees' destruction of two machineguns and their comrades' valiant attempts, the day ended with the Japanese still in possession of Maloney Hill. It was a heavy butcher's bill: seven Americans killed and another eighteen wounded in exchange for an estimated twenty-two Japanese.

Slumping back into their foxholes after a long, unsuccessful day, the troopers listened to one of their wounded comrades, Carl Pakes, frantically lament the loss of his helmet during the skirmish. Gale took his helmet off and slipped it onto Pakes' head, which calmed him down enough for the medics to do their work. Gale, who had already witnessed enough suffering, figured his helmet was a small price to pay for the man's peace of mind. Two of Gale's friends had died of their wounds, and while preparing them for burial, he saw their "bodies were twisted, and hands clenched tight. Mouths and eyes were open and staring." They had not gone peacefully.

Gale later grieved, "It was very hard to wrap up a good friend and buddy in a poncho and bury him in a strange place."

Late that afternoon, 'Chappie' Walker gathered troopers together for a prayer service. They collected near Rock Hill's field hospital not far from the patch of several shallow graves. Standing before them, Chappie could see his flock was exhausted, hungry, and discouraged. He shared communion from a canteen cup of water flavored with K-ration lemon powder and some crumbled crackers. 'Little Joe' Vannier's grumbling stomach tempted him to get a second serving, but his buddy nudged him back.

The thirty-three-year-old chaplain, ordained in 1938 after graduating from Pittsburgh's Xenia Theological Seminary, knew his scripture. He chose the 107th Psalm from a small Bible that he carried in his fatigue pocket. It reads in part:

> *They were hungry and thirsty, and their lives ebbed away. Then they cried out to the Lord in their trouble, and he delivered them from their distress. He led them by a straight way to a city where they could settle. Let them give thanks*

*to the Lord for his unfailing love and his wonderful deeds
for mankind, for he satisfies the thirsty and fills the hungry
with good things.*

THERE WAS FINALLY SOME GOOD NEWS. A break in the weather at Mahonag allowed the L-birds to drop food to 'Shippo' Shipley's 2nd Battalion. The L-birds flew low-level sorties for ninety minutes, and soon thereafter, carrying parties humping in crates of rations snaked around Maloney Hill and up the steep slopes of Rock Hill to deliver the food. It was better than nothing, but still not enough to go around.

Squads of twelve men were given two boxes of K-rations equating to six meals. "We decided to just throw it all into a helmet along with some water to make as much soup as we could," recalled one of the troopers. "That way everyone could get an equal portion."

It was soon obvious another Japanese unit had entered Mahonag Pass, announcing their presence with a dawn banzai attack supported by mortars. They were determined to overrun Haugen's command post.

As the first wave of tan uniforms ran uphill, several troopers watched as George Woynovich "threw the hammer down" on his belt-fed machinegun. He decimated the advancing Japanese while screaming obscenities at them. His fellow troopers were impressed by his marksmanship—and his well-crafted strings of profanity incorporating words many of them had never heard. Woynovich and his comrades, including Haugen firing his carbine, gave the attackers a bloody nose, throwing them back with a death toll of ninety-eight. It was the first of several such Japanese attempts, all using banzai tactics and all futile.

Sergeant Don Singery and Corporal John D. Moore man a .30-caliber machinegun on Manarawat's perimeter

"They came at us day and night," said a trooper later. "We'd fight them all day long, and then we'd have to hold off banzai charges at night. None of us wanted to die, you understand, but it got so bad, and we got so tired, that there were times when we just didn't care."

The fierce loyalty of a man's squad or platoon often overcame his individual fatalism. There was an unspoken code not to let each other down, and it took many forms: sometimes it was standing as an example, sometimes it was a simple word of encouragement or a bit of well-timed humor to lighten the mood. They were all on that hill together, locked in a bitter stalemate with the Japanese. It would take their collective efforts to prevail, and no one was backing down. The Japanese had run into a group of Americans with their own *Yamato Damashi*.

TWO DAYS LATER, they attacked Maloney Hill again. Haugen, suspecting the Japanese had been reinforced by at least two hundred troops, radioed 'Shippo' Shipley to dispatch a company for an attack from the north. Simultaneously, another company from Rock Hill would assault from the south. Shipley acknowledged the order and advised Haugen that the paraglider battalion, under the command of Lieutenant Colonel Harry Wilson, had arrived at Mahonag. They were in the process of taking over ambush duty and getting into position to protect the makeshift drop zone and the field hospital.

Machinegunner George Hadac advanced with Easy Company from the north. As they neared the top, the two lead scouts collapsed in a hail of bullets. Hadac and the rest of the platoon dove for cover.

"There were dead Japs all around that had been killed a few days before," remembered Hadac. "The smell, bugs, and worms got all over us, and we couldn't move—the Japs were throwing grenades at us, and we at them."

Hadac was hit in the leg by shrapnel. A medic crawled over to sprinkle sulfa powder on the wound and patch him up, saying, "I'll write you up for a Purple Heart."

Hadac replied, "Don't worry about it. We will be lucky to get out of here alive."

They did get out alive, but the joint attacks failed to dislodge the Japanese, who still held Maloney Hill. The two dead scouts lay where they fell, enemy marksmen preventing anyone from getting to them.

Haugen decided to break the ongoing stalemate with the crushing weight of steel.

At 08:30 in the morning on Monday, December 18, the first round of 75mm artillery fire whistled into Maloney Hill. It was followed by dozens more, all on target. Captain Joe D. Stokes, a forward observer for the artillery at Manarawat, had come forward to radio directions back to the gun crews. With friendly troops on both sides of the hill, it was a delicate process of walking in the rounds. Stokes did an admirable job, and Haugen was ecstatic with the skill on display.

The 75mm howitzers were fed by a steady resupply of airdropped ammunition. The cannoneers expended the shells almost as soon as they got them. They fired in support of local patrols, harassing barrages on suspected enemy bivouacs and trail junctions, and now Haugen's efforts against Maloney Hill. One of the four howitzers went out of commission when the bolts sheared off the recoil mechanism, leaving three guns in working order. But that was enough.

So steady was the harassing artillery from Manarawat that they were targeted by a company-size Japanese unit that attempted to destroy the guns. Led by a charge of bayonet-wielding infantry, shouting, "Banzai! Banzai!" Japanese sappers made a try for the Angels' artillery. Japanese trench mortars hiccupped along the perimeter attempting to make a gap for the sprinting saboteurs who were equipped with magnetic mines. Machinegun bullets sailed in as well, and medics rolled their patients into slit trenches dug for just that eventuality. The skirmish raged for two hours before the paragliders repulsed the dawn attack, killing more than twenty enemy for two wounded.

BAKER COMPANY FILED DOWN from the perimeter on Rock Hill to make their second attack against Maloney Hill. On the far side of the enemy position, Shippo set up a company-sized ambush to bag any retreating Japanese.

With artillery and mortar shells pounding the peak, four flame-thrower teams went into action. They torched the Japanese front lines with roiling balls of fire. The jets of burning fuel set everything ablaze, and thick black smoke billowed up from the inferno. The combined firestorm did the trick, breaking the backbone of the defense and cracking open a sector in the Japanese line. With his men on the edge of the perimeter, the assault commander, Captain Philip Ulrich, radioed for the artillery and mortars to cease fire. By 10:15, they were within twenty feet of the enemy foxholes, from which the defenders rolled grenades down the slope at the advancing troopers.

"We all got on line and started up the side of that hill," said Bert Marshall, a member of Baker Company. "Finally, the rifle squads got into the first row of foxholes up there."

The Japanese fled the onslaught. They scurried across and down the far side of the hill, where they ran into the waiting ambush. Troopers opened fire, raking the Japanese with everything they had. The clatter of rifles and machineguns was deafening and the slaughter complete. Within a few minutes, nearly a hundred bodies littered the kill zone.

The hill was theirs.

Troopers jumped into the foxholes, pushing out dead bodies and setting up for the expected counterattack. Artillery had torn the hill apart, and body parts were strewn everywhere. A survey found four-hundred-odd enemy dead sprawled all over the hill. Amongst the carnage, they captured two wounded prisoners.

They also discovered just how starved the Japanese were. Bert Marshall glanced at a heap of a blood stained, olive-drab American uniform on the ground. With a second look, he realized it contained human remains; he was staring at one of their missing scouts.

"He had been skinned by the Japs, and they had rolled his skin down off his arms and legs and had cut every bit of meat off his body. We found parts of his body in their mess gear."

Further searching revealed another two missing Americans were also the victims of cannibalism. Ulrich called for volunteers to bury the bodies.

Marshall, feeling sick to his stomach, recalled, "This is one thing the guys hated to do, fool with the dead. If a man was wounded, they would do anything for him, but when they were dead there was nothing anyone could do to help them."

Ulrich finally appointed three men to dig the graves. Word of the mutilations spread, injecting more bile into the already sour taste for their unrelenting enemy, and ratcheting up the sadistic terms under which the war was fought.

Leroy Butler lost two friends in the battle for Maloney Hill: his best friend, Corporal John Thistle, who had been a steady companion on every weekend pass, and Lee Turkington, who had been with Butler since their induction into the Army. Thistle was one of the victims of cannibalism, and Turkington, who barely survived the assault with serious grenade wounds to his stomach, was killed by a falling crate of mortar shells while awaiting medical treatment.

That is how friendships ended in the war: no goodbyes, no thank yous, and no time to grieve.

Deane Marks lost friends, too. "We found it hard to accept but had to. You didn't get any 'madder' at the Nips, just hated them a bit more." Sadly, the hate would only grow. 'Rusty' Cavanaugh did what he could to curb it: "Our troops were not all that humane either, and I stopped a number of our men from using the butts of their rifles to smash out the gold teeth of enemy dead."

"War is not pleasant," he added.

Nisei paratroopers Kazuo Yoshida (left) and Clarence Ohta photographed in the States prior to shipping overseas

One of the prisoners died from his wounds, while the other was taken to Rock Hill for interrogation. At Haugen's disposal were Sergeants Kazuo 'Freddie' Yoshida and Lawrence 'Larry' Kiyabu. Both hailed from Hawaii, and both were Nisei—second generation Americans of Japanese ancestry. They had volunteered to serve in the Army and for parachute training. As members of the 176th Language Detachment, they were assigned to the Angels while in New Guinea. The eleven-man unit had since been sub-divided with teams of two attached to each regiment. Yoshida and Kiyabu were in Haugen's headquarters to aid intelligence efforts in the field, as well as to conduct the rare interrogation of prisoners. As graduates of the Military Intelligence Service Language School, a six-month course where native Japanese speakers refined their fluency and learned about operational intelligence, they had a master's level understanding of the enemy.

Despite the stubborn nature of the enemy, the prisoner talked. His dog tags revealed he was in the 26th Division, which he readily confirmed. He also discussed his unit's low morale and non-existent rations. When asked if Suzuki's hidden cache of supplies was in the area, the prisoner denied it, stating that if it had been, he would not have gone nine days without food. He claimed officers were mistreating the enlisted men and hoarding food for themselves.

WITH MALONEY HILL RETAKEN, Haugen wanted the Japanese trail from Mahonag up to his command post secured for the reliable movement of supplies. Patrols between Rock Hill and Mahonag routinely bumped into Japanese units ranging in size from a few soldiers to fifty men. The arrival of the paragliders had improved the flow of rations, but it still was not enough. With each delivery, Haugen's staff strived to distribute the supplies equally. To combat his men's infamously sticky fingers, Haugen issued a decree to his battalion commanders: "Any unit found with any rations not belonging to them does not get the next issued meal. Any man found with another's equipment or in a food line illegally will be court-martialed."

To reduce the ongoing skirmishes along the trail, 'Shippo' Shipley's 2nd Battalion would start from the north of Mahonag and root out any pockets of resistance on their way to Rock Hill. But three hours into their patrol, they radioed Haugen with devastating news: they had been mauled by artillery fire. A three-round salvo exploded amongst Shipley's headquarters group, followed by three more shells erupting in geysers of mud and shrapnel along the trail. Confused accounts stated between fifteen and twenty men were wounded with at least two dead. 'Shippo' Shipley, with his leg almost severed, was out of the fight. Many of the wounded were in critical condition and not expected to live.

With the need for immediate medical help, and still unsure how far they were from Rock Hill—the map placed them anywhere from five hundred to nine hundred yards away—the battalion split up. Dog Company continued the clearing mission, while the rest of men headed back to Mahonag carrying the casualties. Major Frank S. 'Hacksaw' Holcombe assumed command of the battalion.

Where the six artillery rounds had come from was a mystery. No one believed the Japanese had that kind of firepower in the mountains, and allegations of friendly fire started almost immediately. Several troopers claimed they'd seen an American observation aircraft flying overhead just before the barrage—leading them to believe they were shelled by their own side. But American artillery units within range were adamant they had not fired.

As Dog Company followed the corduroyed trail toward Rock Hill, they passed through a deep gorge split by a stream, where they found a Japanese unit abandoning their bivouac site. The troopers assaulted, catching the enemy off-guard and killing any who opted to stay and fight.

Searching the camp, they found maps, diaries, codebooks, field equipment, and cooking utensils scattered amongst the dead. They also found an aid station with several dozen wounded, apparently on the brink of being deserted by their departing comrades. These must have been battle casualties from Maloney and Rock Hills. It was a gruesome discovery. Many of the patients were gagged and bound; some had already committed suicide. The Angels' historian wrote that "these pitiable creatures would have inspired the revolted pity of the fiercest soldier."

The troopers faced an unenviable choice. After days without food, they could barely carry their own wounded, and their medical supplies were running low. Carting out the enemy wounded was impossible. They could leave them to suffer, or they could commit a twisted act of mercy. A quiet Texan solved the dilemma, killing the wounded with a single shot, one by one.

All told, the enemy body count amounted to sixty-one dead, including, as their after-action report later admitted, the dying patients.

WITH THE ATTACKS AGAINST ROCK HILL, Haugen's wounded were in harm's way of bullets, mortar shells, grenades, and supply drops, which killed at least three. Evacuating them to safety and better medical treatment was a taxing procedure for patients and caretakers alike. Frontline medics stopped bleeding, dressed wounds, administered blood plasma, and prevented or treated shock. If necessary, a patched-up trooper was stabilized for the trek down to the regiment's rudimentary clearing station at Mahonag, where medical supplies could be dropped more reliably than atop Rock Hill.

A litter patient required eight bearers for transport, with four to six men lugging the litter and the others rotating in to ease the burden. It was a drain on Haugen's manpower, reducing vital rifles from his perimeter. The arrival of Wilson's paragliders had helped, and they regularly ranged the trails between Manarawat, Mahonag, and Rock Hills. They shouldered cases of ammunition, mortar shells, grenades, radio batteries, and rations to haul them up the steep slopes of Rock Hill. There, like army ants, they scooped up the wounded for the return journey. Carrying a case of rations, while awkward and uncomfortable, took an hour to trudge up the one-and-a-half-mile path from Mahonag. Carrying litter patients down the same route took ten hours. Once there, doctors debrided wounds and performed emergency surgeries, often working crouched under a poncho while an assistant held a flashlight.

Haugen's worst medical cases were hauled back to Manarawat, an arduous journey that required navigating a steep trail thick with sucking mud and tangled roots that tripped men struggling to keep their patients horizontal. The impractical route made Mahonag a better choice for casualty treatment, and Haugen wanted surgeons there. Swing had anticipated such needs, and two surgical teams parachuted into Manarawat. The teams each consisted of three surgeons and ten medical technicians, all of whom had qualified at Swing's New Guinea jump school. After tumbling one man at a time from L-birds, one group hiked out to Mahonag with an escort of paragliders, while the other set up at Manarawat.

An 11th Airborne medical team led by Captains Milton E. Johnston and John W. Guepe operates on a trooper to remove a bullet from his chest

Manarawat had earned several nicknames by now, including "Carnival City" and the "Million Dollar Village," both reflecting the rudimentary tents and shelters rigged together from bright red, blue, green, yellow, and white cargo parachutes. More than seventy flanked the airstrip, and with the cost of nylon in mind, the monetary moniker was understandable.

Thatched huts and two olive-drab tents were set up with cots for the patients. Those capable of walking either hiked back to Burauen with escort patrols or, if healed, headed in the opposite direction to rejoin their units in the field. When possible, L-5 Sentinels landed to fly critical casualties back to the rear-area hospitals now established at Dulag. The L-birds saved time and lives since carrying a litter to Burauen took two days.

The tireless work of the medical teams earned them lifelong respect. They stitched up countless lacerations, saved limbs, removed limbs, and even conducted a brain surgery to relieve the pain of a serious head wound. Corporal Harold Spring became one of their more legendary cases. Spring's abdomen was torn open by three bullets from a machinegun burst. With his intestines spilling out, troopers carried him to Captain Thomas Nestor. The surgeon gently placed Spring's intestines on a poncho where he washed them, stitched what holes he could find, sprinkled sulfa powder over the pile and scooped them back in. Nestor thought Spring would die during the night and had a grave dug. Miraculously, the next morning, Spring was still alive. They stabilized him for the next phase of evacuation where, once again, expectations of his death led to another grave. But a few months later, Captain Nestor received a thank you package from Spring, who was recovering in a San Francisco hospital. Inside the envelope was a *Captain Marvel* comic book.

Not all patients suffered from wounds. There were also debilitating cases of yellow jaundice and "fevers of unknown origin." Almost everyone in Haugen's regiment suffered from dysentery and the severe swelling, broken skin, and oozing of "jungle rot" sores.

Trench foot was an issue as well. Steve 'Heggy' Hegedus, whose shredded feet had plagued him since transporting Charlie Company's wounded to Manarawat, later recalled, "The first sunny day without going out on patrol or being shot at, we took off our boots and socks. I saw one guy whose skin came right off with his socks. Underneath was raw, red meat, oozing blood and fluids. How that guy ever survived the next two weeks, walking and climbing those muddy hills, I can't imagine. The pain must have been unbearable, but he never whimpered."

One of Heggy's buddies urinated on his own feet every chance he could, claiming it prevented infection.

Subjected to constant moisture, the men's jump boots were rotting off their feet. Only a lucky few received replacements, and many troopers wrapped their boots with rags or tape to keep the soles attached.

"We used the dead as our source of replenishment for footwear," recalled Captain Stephen 'Rusty' Cavanaugh. "I had to replace my boots with those of a deceased soldier that were two sizes too small, and I was forced to cut the toes out in order to wear them."

WHILE HAUGEN WAGED HIS WAR against the Japanese, Swing conducted a war of words with General Archibald V. Arnold's 7th Infantry Division, which was pushing up the west coast. Arnold's men were waiting for Swing's troops to emerge from the mountains, and the friction began when they described their imminent link-up with Swing's 11th Airborne as a "rescue." The Angels' HQ sent a curt reply: "Swing does not need or want rescue."

A source of the misperception was a 7th Infantry forward artillery observer with Haugen at Rock Hill. He sent reports to his command recounting "one hell of a fight" up in the mountains and described the 511th's situation in less than confident terms: "Their perimeter is very thin. They have no artillery support. Their ammo supply is very low." The wording annoyed Swing, who demanded all future reports from the forward observer be "censored" before transmission.

But probably the biggest culprits were a six-man patrol from Haugen's missing George Company. The troopers—grimy, gaunt, unshaved, and malnourished—filed into a 7th Infantry outpost, reporting they had been without food for four days after their company was cut off from the regiment. The other one hundred and twenty-odd men of the company were still holed up on a promontory they dubbed "Starvation Hill." A platoon from the 7th Infantry found the hill and escorted them down to the coast. They were in bad shape, with all but Captain Wheeler and eleven of his men requiring hospitalization. "The rest of the company was sick with dysentery and fever," said Wheeler, who'd lost more than thirty pounds.

General Arnold needed to push up the coast toward Ormoc Bay and was frustrated with Swing's slow progress through the mountains. Arnold left a battalion behind to contact Haugen. But just six hundred yards inland, they ran into the same type of steep ridgelines, deep gorges, and pockets of Japanese that Haugen had. When they radioed Haugen to coordinate a link-up, Hard Rock replied that his orders were to "clean up my backyard before I clean up my front yard." He would meet up with them after he accomplished his own mission.

To make it clear his division didn't need rescuing, Swing would be up front with his men when they linked up with the 7th Infantry. To get there, he first flew into Manarawat, where he found the forward operation base thriving atop the plateau. The airstrip was in good condition; parachute shelters and grass huts dotted the perimeter, and a fenced area contained a hundred carabao. Swing's combat engineers had widened the trail from Burauen for these beasts of burden, opening an alternative mode of transport for supplies.

Swing visited the wounded at the makeshift field hospital. Seeing the conditions for the first time, he boosted morale by having ice cream and cigarettes flown in. He also had several members of the band march in from Burauen while L-birds flew in their drums, clarinets, saxophones, and trombones for a jungle concert.

The next morning, Swing's entourage trekked its way to Mahonag escorted by a company of two hundred paragliders. A reporter accompanying the group noted Swing wore "freshly laundered khakis … with his two-star insignia glistening on his collar and paratrooper cap." The conspicuous stars were a sniper's dream, and a junior officer recommended the general pocket them for the journey.

"Wrathfully," the reporter wrote, "Swing turned on a staff member and, in characteristic fashion, declared that he'd be 'damned if he'd remove his damned stars for any damned Jap.'"

As Swing hiked, he was flanked by a personal five-man security detail whose mission was to ensure the Japanese did not get lucky. Swing was impressed by their discreet but obviously constant efforts to keep him safe. Even with their diligence,

The division band performs for their wounded comrades at Manarawat

though, a few miles down the trail, a bullet whizzed between Swing and one of his escorts.

The private was blunt in his admonition: "General, I don't care if you get hit or not, but you're drawing fire in my direction."

"That," said Swing, "is good enough for me." He removed his stars.

At Mahonag, Swing found another collection of wounded troopers sheltering under ponchos at the forward outpost. The location of the aid station had been shifted away from the drop zone, because despite having laid out colored signal panels to improve the pilot's aim, crates still tumbled down lethally and haphazardly. Two more men were killed the day before Swing arrived, one of them decapitated in front of his friends just after yelling in excitement, "It's raining chow, boys, it's raining chow!"

During his two-day stay, Swing invariably visited the wounded, including 'Shippo' Shipley, whose leg was barely attached. Lieutenant Foster Arnett, Haugen's boxing coach, was there, too, worrying he might lose his right arm. Arnett had charged directly into a firefight to rally fifteen troopers who had fled their foxholes under the wave of a banzai attack. Arnett careened into the fray, shouting, "Get back in the foxholes and hold those positions!" His bravery inspired the troopers to hold the line, but in the process, shrapnel mangled his right shoulder. Doc Nestor debrided the wound and removed bone fragments. But Nestor became a patient himself when both he and Arnett were struck with malaria and dengue fever.

Arnett, who lost almost thirty pounds, later recalled, "Each of us was sobbing uncontrollably and cursing through our teeth because we had lost control of ourselves and were ashamed. So they inserted each of us in this single cargo bag, and we slept the night away (for the first time in a month) like twins in a mother's womb. I shall never forget that night."

FROM ATOP ROCK HILL, Haugen eyed the next obstacle in his march west: a series of hills nicknamed Lahti Ridge. Previous reconnaissance patrols found it well defended by an undetermined number of Japanese riflemen supported by machineguns and mortars. On the morning of December 19, Haugen had the ridge pounded by three hundred and fifty artillery shells from Manarawat. He initially called in four volleys from the big 155mm guns on the west coast, but cancelled them when the explosions crept too close to his own men. The "danger-close" radius for 155s was eight hundred yards, and he was unwilling to risk that margin of error. The smaller 75mms back at Manarawat were more accurate and less dangerous. Captain Joe Stokes, the forward observer, radioed back fire directions, and he quickly had his target zeroed in. Haugen continued to rave about Stokes' willingness to be up front with his infantry, as well as his uncanny accuracy.

Two hours after the artillery ceased their salvos, the company-sized attack moved in. Up front, three men toted flamethrowers on their backs. When they were twenty-five yards from the Japanese positions, the enemy opened fire.

"As soon as we started up the saddle, our lead scout was hit by a machinegun blast full in the chest," said one of the attacking troopers. "The impact knocked him down the side of the hill. We called for mortar fire and tried to move out again but were unsuccessful."

The attackers arced in a few phosphorous grenades that, based on the screaming and smell of burning flesh, landed on target. In retaliation, the Japanese hurled hand grenades themselves. The troopers got close, but not close enough to use the flamethrowers, and the attack failed.

Haugen criticized the company commander for giving the Japanese too much time to recover from the shock of the artillery; waiting two hours after the barrage was too long. They would try again tomorrow. Haugen requested Manarawat's artillery expend a hundred rounds intermittently throughout the night, and then bludgeon the ridge again in the morning with another three hundred. Haugen wanted the defenders' nerves frayed. The Japanese, like infantry the world over, despised artillery. Nothing made a soldier feel more helpless than sheltering against the random, soul-shattering flash and thunder of an artillery barrage.

At first light the next morning, with artillery warbling overhead, 'Slugger' Lahti sent in a two-company attack. Shells crashed into the first hill at a rate of one every fifteen seconds. Forward observer Stokes was again up front with the lead platoon.

One company attacked on the left while the other flanked right. 'Little Joe' Vannier was in the vanguard of the flanking attack, where the troopers toiled up the side of a steep gully that he described as "almost vertical."

"We used bushes, vines, and limbs to pull our way up that steep incline," he said. "I still can't believe we made it up that hill."

'Bull' Hendry, shoulder to shoulder with Vannier, continued the story: "As we neared the top, the artillery and mortar fire was lifted, and the Jap machinegun and rifle fire intensified."

Crawling up with them was Staff Sergeant Harlan L. Mille from the mortar platoon. A stubborn Japanese machinegun nest was blocking the trail and had wounded several men, included Mille himself. Picking up his field telephone, he yelled hasty calculations to the crew of a lone 81mm mortar. A shell crashed in, splintering a nearby tree and killing Mille. Passing his body, Mille's commander tried to hide his tears. The men turned away. Recognizing his pain for what it was, they pretended not to notice.

As the men reached the top, a group of Japanese managed to get between them and the other company. Bullets snapped in from their front, their flank, and from behind. It was a dangerous moment with the potential for a friendly crossfire. Vannier, Hendry, and the rest of their company attached bayonets and charged the hilltop, leaving the Japanese infiltrators behind for the other company to root out.

Hendry later recalled that to avoid their bayonets, several Japanese "ducked down into their holes and we moved along the ridge, killing them with rifles and grenades. I saw at least one who killed himself by setting off a grenade in his spider hole."

Vannier was close to the botched suicide. "The Japanese soldier had put a grenade to his belly," he recalled, "and as happened so many times, it just didn't completely do the job."

The injured soldier was curled up in the bottom of his foxhole moaning in pain. Several troopers gathered around the hole. "Together, we must have fired six shots down into the agonizing hell-hole, and still the moans continued," said Vannier.

Deciding his men were wasting ammo, Captain James J. Toth ordered they bury the man. Vannier agreed with the order given the Japanese's eagerness to take as many GIs as possible with them. Why expose anyone to danger? But as a lead scout, he chose to move on, preferring the risk of another gunfight over entombing a man alive.

By 12:15, the first hill was theirs, but there were holdouts. "Most of the positions on the reverse slope were bunkers," Hendry recalled, "reinforced with logs and covered with dirt. A number of them had live Japs still in them, and we used grenades to wipe them out."

Staff Sergeant Lewis Maylock's squad rushed the next hill. Several bursts of rifle and submachine gun fire erupted as they stormed in. An officer on the first hill yelled the mortar crews into action.

Troopers, not knowing where the shells might land, scrambled for cover. One of the witnesses recalled, "Just before the expected blast, we could hear Maylock's voice splitting the jungle silence as he screamed out, 'Hold those fucking mortars. The fucking hill is ours!'

Everything was quiet for a moment, and then the whole jungle exploded in a roar of laughter."

The assault accounted for thirty-six enemy dead, with four wounded Americans and Mille the lone fatality. But many of the defenders had fled from the assault to positions on the next hill. Haugen, wanting to maintain the momentum and keep the enemy off balance, ordered 'Hacksaw' Holcombe get his 2nd Battalion up and moving. They would pass through Lahti's positions and continue the attack the next morning.

WITH HIS BOSS on the way up Rock Hill, Haugen did what he could to make a favorable impression. He assigned two officers to inspect the perimeter and had work details ensure the latrines were ship-shape. He could tidy up all he wanted, but he couldn't do much about the smell. Troopers dragged the bloated enemy corpses into the jungle, but as the heat went to work, they realized it wasn't far enough.

"The foul odor was indescribable," recalled Miles Gale. "Since those dead surrounded our hilltop, we couldn't get away from the stench."

Haugen also ordered his men to shave their twenty-some days of facial stubble. The directive was unpopular. A trooper recalled, "Talk about griping and bitching, you never heard it any better." With more fighting expected to reach the coast, another complained, "Yeah, [Swing] wants us to die clean shaven."

Few men had kept up with their razors, and Leroy Butler's platoon had just one. The men passed it around, taking turns scraping at their tangled beards without any soap or shaving cream. After hacking away, their faces were clean shaven, albeit cut to hell.

When Swing marched in with a company of Wilson's paragliders, he failed to inspire. Most of the men, keen observers of military hypocrisy, felt his arrival was grand-standing.

"When the general and his group passed through," recalled Butler, "I didn't see anyone who looked as hungry or as emaciated as we did."

Another trooper, who witnessed what he called Swing's "triumphant march to the sea," popularized Swing's new nickname, "Ipana Joe." Ipana was a wintergreen-flavored toothpaste, and Swing's big smile gave rise to his new sobriquet.

A trooper seeing Swing in his "nice khakis" summarized the growing divide between the paratroopers and their division commander: "Our general wasn't too happy with our regiment, and our regiment wasn't too happy with our general."

Haugen greeted Swing at 11:15 as he arrived at the command post. Haugen talked him through the prior day's attacks, pointing out the seized ridgeline and briefing him on Hacksaw Holcombe's ongoing push toward the west coast. Using a captured Japanese map, the two discussed Swing's evacuation plan for the wounded once they linked up with the 7th Infantry. He wanted to evacuate toward the coast rather than back the way they had come. Engineers were already using saws to cut down trees and build steps into the steepest trail sections from Mahonag. Haugen was confident the corduroyed Japanese supply trail could be used to get down to the coast—once it was cleared.

Swing, keen to get to the coast as soon as possible, asked Haugen what he thought the Japanese resistance would be.

"Negligible," replied Haugen. The growing body count, combined with intelligence reports, suggested the remaining units had been reduced to small, isolated groups.

Swing nodded, then dropped a bombshell: tomorrow, Wilson would bring up the rest of his paraglider battalion to pass through Haugen's paratroopers to connect with the 7th Infantry. Haugen didn't say much, but his actions over the next twenty-four hours provided insight into his thoughts.

Haugen paused the discussion to take a radio message from Hacksaw: the lead company was on the next knoll but had gone to ground under the hail of three enemy machineguns. The troopers were using 60mm mortars to dislodge them and would continue to attack, but the Japanese had the high ground. Hacksaw estimated they were less than a mile from the 7th Infantry.

"Get off your ass," Haugen responded evenly, "and get going."

Fifty-five minutes later, an eruption of gunfire from the next ridge confirmed Hacksaw's men were still heavily engaged. They radioed requesting a hundred 60mm mortar shells be brought forward. Hacksaw declined Haugen's offer for artillery support: the enemy was too close, so they'd use their mortars and then assault.

Hacksaw radioed again ninety minutes later with positive developments. The transmission was weak, but the message clear: "We have assaulted hill and taken it. We are pushing on." The bad news was that there was yet another hill in front them. It wasn't on their map and meant more high ground to tackle. Hacksaw also revised his estimate to the 7th Infantry: four miles.

Haugen ordered him to "push on as far as possible tonight before setting up perimeter."

It took an hour to get another two hundred yards down the trail where Hacksaw decided to stop. He reported his casualties for the day: two men killed; six wounded. They counted over thirty enemy dead.

Haugen acknowledged the report, commanding Hacksaw to resume the attack early the next morning, no later than 06:30. Meanwhile, Swing had agreed to keep Hacksaw's battalion up front until the paragliders caught up to them, at which point the fresh troops would pass through for the final push.

AT 04:00, Hacksaw's lead platoons moved forward single file through a dim pre-dawn drizzle. Each gaunt trooper, a shadowy version of his former self, slipped like a gray ghost through the jungle gloom, his bayonet fixed.

Thirty minutes later, scout Gilberto C. 'Slick' Sepulveda passed undetected into the enemy line. Behind him, two squads picked their way forward, splitting abreast into columns. Sepulveda, crouching onward, spotted a sentry and raised his bayoneted rifle. He wanted to kill the man quietly, but as he approached, his quarry turned, raising his own rifle. Sepulveda shot first, and the sentry fell. Another rifle barked, and Sepulveda crumpled. His squad fanned out forming an assault line; all six men hurled grenades. One bounced off a tree and back toward them, but it rolled away to explode harmlessly. Someone threw a phosphorus grenade, its exploding tendrils of burning magnesium blooming like a hellish flower.

The element of surprise was lost, but it was too late for the Japanese, who now felt the terror of their own infiltration tactic. The Americans' blood was up, and the advantage was finally theirs. Several troopers watched as John H. Bittorie seized it.

Bittorie, a lanky, six-foot-two New Yorker—missing his two front teeth from a State-side brawl—took the vanguard and charged uphill, firing his belt-fed machinegun from the hip. He had slung the thirty-one-pound beast over his shoulder with a piece of cargo webbing and leveled the barrel with an asbestos glove. His face was a bloody mess after running into a tree, he'd lost his helmet, and his fatigue pants had rotted into shorts. He fired burst after burst into the surprised Japanese, the muzzle flashes producing a strobe light of chaos.

"Rat's ass! Rat's ass!" screamed Bittorie between each burst.

"Rat's ass!" shrieked the troopers surging forward on each side of him as they formed into staggered skirmish lines, firing as they moved. "Banzai!" yelled a few, contributing to the bedlam.

Reaching the crest of the hill, Bittorie's assistant gunner was on his heels to help reload. They'd broken several 150-round belts in half so Bittorie could fire them while on the move and not worry about jamming. Thirty-odd troopers poured into the Japanese positions, still shouting, "Rat's ass! Rat's ass!"

The Japanese line broke.

"It was like shooting rabbits in heavy brush," recalled a trooper.

"You'd see a Japanese, and if you weren't sure if he was dead, you'd shoot his head," said another. "There were Japanese there that were alive, and you shot them. There was no place to take them, and you're too busy.... We killed anybody that moved."

Their initial volley accounted for twenty-six enemy dead. Bodies lay sprawled around cooking fires or half out of their foxholes. Some were shot while sleeping. The rolling wave of furious, smelly, and tattered paratroopers raged forward with more behind them. The Japanese fled in disarray, falling back faster than they could organize a defense. Soon the enemy body count was over a hundred.

An hour later, and with his everpresent cigarette dangling from the corner of his mouth, Haugen came upon the scene, thrilled with what he found. Hacksaw's aggression, from his perspective, "stressed the value of assault and pursuit and late-morning breakfasts."

AT 08:30, Swing and two hundred paragliders departed Rock Hill. Fifteen minutes later, the radio crackled with a snide report from the paratroopers on Lahti Ridge: the paragliders were "passing through our perimeter.... Things must be safe up the trail."

Word of Swing's plan had spread, and the troopers were incensed. *Why now? Why should they get the final glory? Where the hell have they been for the past month?*

Rumors circulated that Swing feared the appearance of his bedraggled paratroopers emerging from the jungle would confirm the Angels needed rescuing. For most troopers, it proved he had a grudge against the regiment. If Swing had other reasons, he kept them to himself.

The troopers watched from their foxholes as the paragliders trudged past. Several Japanese bodies lay sprawled on the trail itself, including one face-down corpse used as a stepping stone to avoid the quagmire. With each footfall, the unfortunate soul had been pushed deeper into the muddy slop until just the hump of his shoulders was visible. Much to the glee of Deane Marks, the machinegunner from St. Paul, unwitting paragliders, thinking the mud-covered lump was a rock, recoiled in revulsion when their weight induced a grotesque gurgling noise.

One trooper's sense of the ridiculous bubbled over at the sight of the procession. He poured the granulated TNT out of a hand grenade, replaced the fuse, pulled the pin, and rolled it onto the paragliders' trail. "They scattered and started yelling," recalled a witness. Fortunately, no one was hurt when the fuse popped.

Meanwhile, the early morning assault had turned into a pursuit. Haugen pushed his men forward, wanting to keep the Japanese off balance as they bowled downhill. If the paragliders wanted to catch up, they would have to run. Behind Haugen, the paragliders tracked their progress through the jungle by following the trail of corpses. One of them noted, "The trails everywhere were littered with enemy dead, as were the slopes of the ridge."

It was 10:00 by the time Swing and Wilson caught up to Hacksaw and Haugen, who had advanced 1,300 yards from their start point that morning. One of the paragliders' platoon leaders described the pace as "breakneck."

"It was difficult to understand how a unit engaged in bitter fighting could keep up the terrific rate of march forward," he later admitted.

It was a complete rout, but Swing thought it was time to halt and let the paragliders pass through. A runner went forward to rein in the attack, telling Captain Stephen 'Rusty' Cavanaugh that he was to hold up.

"Needless to say," the redhead later admitted, "I disregarded the order, feeling that if we paused, the enemy would have a chance to regroup and establish defensive positions."

Two hours later, a second out-of-breath runner reached Cavanaugh, reemphasizing the order. They had the Japanese on the run, and no one wanted to give them a chance to catch their breath.

"Reluctantly, we halted," said Cavanaugh, "and, exhausted, hit the prone position along the trail."

When the paragliders caught up, Haugen implored them to maintain the relentless pressure. "You must keep going as fast as possible—run if you have to—but don't give the Nips a chance to set up their weapons."

"We've got them with their pants down; you can't even stop to kill them all," he continued. "Just push through. We are behind you and will take care of them as we come to them. Just keep going, fast. Any questions?"

As Swing passed Stephen Cavanaugh resting on the side of the Japanese supply trail, he nodded in greeting, saying, "Nice job, Cavanaugh."

The captain later recollected, "It was not an extremely hearty greeting. My thoughts regarding that gentleman were at that [time] anything but complimentary."

Cavanaugh's troops used their grim silence to express their contempt.

The paragliders kept up the pressure, sweeping aside a Japanese machinegun position with a lightning-fast flanking maneuver and a white phosphorus grenade. From the top of a gorge, platoon leader Lieutenant Joseph B. Giordano watched two Japanese soldiers kneel on the edge of a stream to detonate hand grenades on their heads. Two others followed by jumping to their death from the 150-foot cliff. The enemy's self-sacrifice always struck a surreal chord with troopers, who found it incomprehensible. They could understand risking their lives, but not throwing them away. Most soldiers developed a callous response to the needless waste of life, but each suicide was subconsciously cataloged in the slideshow of horrors that would haunt them for decades, if not the rest of their lives.

An hour later, with the coast in view, Giordano signaled their location to the 7th Infantry with a purple smoke grenade. Swing was surprised to see that the wafting haze of the 7th Infantry's return signal was a still good distance away. The paragliders continued toward the coast, finding abandoned Japanese foxholes and two dead Americans left behind by the 7th Infantry. A few stay-behind snipers had to be dealt with, and Swing came forward at every pause to investigate and urge progress.

Swing was the first trooper to walk into the 7th Infantry's perimeter.

By the end of the day, Wilson's paragliders had passed through the entirety of Haugen's paratroopers, completing the Angels' cut over the mountains to slice Leyte in half. Proud of his men's accomplishment, Swing later bragged, "Have told the corps commander if he wants to walk from Burauen Airfields to Ormoc Beach, all he has to do is put a clothespin on his nose and let a man with a strong stomach guide him."

Swing later claimed to have counted 750 enemy bodies between Rock Hill and the coast, but Haugen's final tally for the day amounted to 213.

SWING WANTED ALL THE WOUNDED to be out of the mountains by Christmas, giving Haugen three days to complete his evacuation. Some, like Miles Gale shot in the right arm, descended the mountains under their own steam. The more seriously wounded were carried down by litter teams, including two hundred Filipino laborers—and all were accompanied by security details. They took frequent breaks, with the litter patients just lying there enduring the bumps and slips, sometimes cursing, but mostly just staring skyward waiting for the journey to end.

Haugen's medics set up a series of staging areas along the exit route. A litter team would deliver a patient, then lumber back up the trail to repeat the process. They shuttled over two hundred of their comrades forward, folding the regiment in on itself until, finally, it was time to leave.

Their last morning in the mountains was just like all the others: cheerless, gray, wet, and muddy. Steam rose from the ground as the heat of the rising sun evaporated the night's moisture.

"All right, on your feet. Let's move out," said a sallow-eyed, nineteen-year-old second lieutenant. It was time to leave.

Technician Fourth Grade Rod Serling recalled their descent: "We rose, the packs, the ammo belts, weaponry, all fused to us like extensions of our bodies, the weights so constant that it was all part of us, and we began to plod slowly through the ankle-deep mud—a long line of dirty, bearded sameness." Serling limped down the mountain, his shrapnel-peppered knee wrapped in bandages.

Another trooper, seeing the blue-gray waters of Ormac Bay down below, thought the muddy troopers "looked like a brown river flowing towards the sea."

Serling watched a ripple move up the line of troops as each man turned to pass back a message. "It's Christmas," whispered the man in front of him.

"I continued to lift my feet up, one after the other," said Serling, "weighted down by the fifty pounds of equipment attached to a sparse one-hundred-pound frame, and suddenly, I wasn't aware of the cold rain. I wasn't conscious of the mud that clung. I gave no thought to the sick little ache, deep inside the gut, that had been with us for so many days. Someone had just transformed the world. Two words had just reminded us that this was the earth, and this was mankind, and that people still lived, and that we did also. 'It's Christmas.'"

'Little Joe' Vannier flashed back to the prior Christmas he spent at Camp Mackall drinking a bottle of Southern Comfort with his buddy George Pelley, who was back on Rock Hill in a shallow grave.

In front of Serling, "a scratchy, discordant monotone voice" sang, 'O Come, All Ye Faithful.'

"Somebody else picked it up," he recalled, "and then we all sang. We sang as we walked through the mud. We sang as we led the wounded by the hand and carried the litters and looked back on the row of homemade crosses we left behind.... It was Christmas."

It was also Serling's twentieth birthday.

Chapter 7

Mopping Up

Leyte Island.
Tuesday, December 26, 1944

Whence the line of rag-tag troopers emerged from the hills, they handed off their wounded to waiting medical personnel, then shuffled down the beach to a cluster of waiting tents. Haugen, suffering a fever, walked out with the last platoon.

"As we passed through friendly units," said 'Bull' Hendry, "we struggled to hold our shoulders back, although it was hard to feel very military with our muddy, tattered uniforms and emaciated bodies." Leroy Butler had tightened his web belt multiple times, guessing he had dropped over thirty pounds since Thanksgiving.

Some troopers headed straight for the surf. "I recall that I was so dirty and slimy after not having my shoes off and not having a bath in thirty-three days that I went down and sat where a creek entered the ocean," recalled a corporal. "It was a place where I just sat up to my chin in the water for … I don't know how long. So soothing, it really was. I know that we all stunk pretty bad."

'Bull' Hendry found a rocking chair in a bombed house and dragged it to the shore, enjoying a rare moment of solitude. "As the sun set, I sat on that warm, dry beach smoking and drinking hot coffee," he recalled. "For the first time in weeks, we were warm, dry, safe, and clean, and our stomachs were full.... My last thought that night was that this would probably be the best Christmas I would ever know."

The next morning, trucks and landing craft transported the troopers back to Bito Beach where they had landed thirty-three days ago.

"It took us a month to fight across the island," said Kenneth Fuller, "but only about three hours to get back."

Cooks waited on the troopers, serving a belated Christmas dinner. "A day late, but so what," continued Fuller. "We had turkey and dressing, cranberry sauce, and all the traditional Christmas fixings."

As welcome as the feast was, most troopers retched it all back up. The rich food overpowered their shrunken stomachs. Their digestive weakness would dissipate over time, but their multitude of other issues needed immediate attention. They stripped off their rotting uniforms and threw them into burn piles. Medics inspected naked lines of troopers, peering between toes and fingers, under armpits and, more awkwardly, at groins and buttocks. They dabbed any tinge of festering jungle rot with silver nitrate, an ointment that dried out the fungus but turned skin a grayish-blue.

Lieutenant Miles Gale, who had not taken his boots nor socks off in over a month, sat in the surf, staring at his coal-black toenails while debriding his calluses with handfuls of sand.

Pale troopers bobbed in the ocean, letting the saltwater sterilize their cuts and wounds. It burned, but in a pleasant way, reminding them they were still alive.

"I spent a lot of time in the surf," recalled Leroy Butler, "which seemed to do a lot of good for my jungle rot. I had scars, actually for years, but the open sores healed up quite rapidly."

WHILE HAUGEN'S PARATROOPERS licked their wounds, Swing dispatched more paragliders to secure the supply trail and mop up isolated pockets of Japanese still in the Angels' sector.

"Mopping up" is an innocuous military term implying little except to those doing the mopping. MacArthur had previously announced the collapse of organized resistance on Leyte, stating that "General Yamashita has sustained perhaps the greatest defeat in the military annals of the Japanese army." But the infantry still had to clear out the unorganized resistance. And to an infantryman charged with attacking a Japanese position, the work was just as violent, deadly, and personal as any other battle. To him, it was still a full-fledged war.

As one officer put it, "Whoever coined that phrase about mopping up shouldn't be given a Christian burial. It is the most misleading statement I know, because it can be the most deadly and stressful of all the fighting." Trooper Dick Penwell agreed, saying, "When you fight someone who thinks it's an honor to die, that's the toughest job in the world."

For the paragliders, this meant chasing down infiltrators along the corduroyed supply trail and buttoning up a large group holding out on the trail's northern end near Anonang. The track there led to a peak occupied by anywhere from three hundred to eight hundred Japanese. Intelligence reports acknowledged the uncertainty; with stragglers flowing in from all directions, estimates were difficult.

Two parallel ridges peppered with caves led to the summit. The occupiers fortified the natural defenses by digging dozens of individual "spider holes." Dug six to ten feet deep, the holes sheltered occupants from artillery and allowed them to emerge unscathed just as the Americans began their advance. Additionally, well-camouflaged, log-reinforced machinegun emplacements could sweep the opposing ridge's trails at will from across the gorge.

Swing had contained the strong point—discovered earlier in the campaign by Haugen's 2nd Battalion—to deal with after completing his advance to the coast. Multiple half-hearted attempts failed to dislodge the defenders. But with the island now cut in half, it was time to eliminate the bypassed thorn.

The paragliders probed the position for three days searching for a weak spot. Each patrol returned unsuccessful, having been chased away by grenades rolled from the caves above. The frustrating efforts earned the redoubt the nickname "Purple Heart Hill."

On the night of December 28, the paragliders pummeled it with 75mm artillery from Manarawat and the heavies in Leyte Valley: 105mm and 155mm howitzers. A shell from a 155mm weighed ninety-four pounds and sounded like a freight train warbling into the target. Explosions ripped across the two ridges, sending concussion waves and shrapnel in every direction. The paragliders added to the fury by lobbing mortar shells and squeezing off long bursts from their belt-fed machineguns, the red tracers stabbing like lasers into the open caves.

As devastating as the all-night maelstrom was, the position had to be conquered to be crossed off the map. It was here that the Angels added a new weapon to their arsenal: guile. A full company, using the jungle for concealment, circled the hill in a wide arc to set up quietly on its northern side, while other units established additional blocking positions to the northwest and east. With the escape routes covered, Colonel Robert 'Shorty' Soule, the 188th Glider Infantry Regiment's commander, set his gambit in motion at 11:00 the next morning.

His assault battalion made an elaborate display of withdrawing, just as the previous failed attempts had. But rather than pull back, they button-hooked into a narrow, steep-sided gorge that masked their movement from above. They then doubled back along a wooded ridge to ascend the hill's southern slope. The troopers, hand over hand, used the vegetation to haul themselves up the steep climb. All went according to plan—until it didn't.

Private First Class John Chiesa was on point and later recalled, "We just got to the top of this hill when all hell broke loose."

Multiple machineguns opened fire, hitting a nearby trooper, who tumbled down the hill. Chiesa's platoon sergeant, attempting to direct firepower against the concealed positions, was killed by the next burst.

Downslope from Chiesa, a Japanese soldier emerged from his spider hole. "I ... turned and pulled the trigger," said Chiesa. "He was doing the same thing, but I was luckier. I hit him smack in his Adam's apple. I can still see the surprised look on his face."

The unexpected attack routed the defenders, who were already punch-drunk from the artillery barrage. Those that fled were cut down by the blocking forces guarding the escape routes. A search of the hill found 238 dead Japanese and too many severed arms and legs to count. The Angels guessed hundreds more were permanently entombed in the collapsed caves.

● ● ●

Across Leyte, the Japanese were withdrawing, or at least trying to. Yamashita, with Ormoc Bay in American hands and his supply lines severed, sent a final communique to Suzuki on Christmas day. "We shall seek and destroy our enemy on Luzon Island, thereby doing our part in the heroic struggle of the army and avenging many a valiant warrior who fell. I cannot keep back tears of remorse for tens and thousands of our officers and men fighting on Leyte Island. Nevertheless,

I must impose a still harder task on you. Please try to understand my intentions. They say it is harder to live than to die. You, officers and men, be patient enough to endure the hardships of life, and help guard and maintain the prosperity of the Imperial Throne through eternal resistance to the enemy and be prepared to meet your death calmly for our beloved country."

Suzuki and his men were on their own. They could either escape to other islands or fight on, but Yamashita was abandoning them to prepare for MacArthur's invasion of Luzon. Suzuki could not have been surprised. Updates from Manila had grown progressively worse as the battle had shifted in the Americans' favor. On December 13, Yamashita had canceled an amphibious assault on northern Leyte. Then, six days later, he informed Suzuki that no additional reinforcements or supplies should be expected, and that the three divisions sailing for Leyte had been redirected to Luzon.

Suzuki's command was in disarray, his units scattered, and he was on the run. He slipped through the Americans' pincer attack, arriving at a mountain north of Ormoc. Trying to regain control, he directed his twenty thousand men to muster there. The thousand-foot mountain, with rocky slopes on multiple sides, provided Suzuki a formidable piece of high ground. The summit was a plateau of thick forest with commanding views of the surrounding plains. Suzuki's chief of staff agreed that the "area was admirable for an extended period of defensive action." From there, Suzuki planned to wage a "Self-Supported War of Independent Actions" or, as his staff referred to it, "The Establishment of a Suzuki Kingdom." They were to hold out as long as possible, prolonging the battle and conducting raids against the Americans, driving them to exhaustion.

One of Suzuki's commanders believed that "maybe in two or three years, the Japanese would be able to stage a comeback in other areas." He mentally prepared his men to hold out for ten years, if necessary, to give their country time. It took the Americans another five months to run the holdouts to ground and officially declare Leyte liberated.

An unsent letter found in the pocket of a dead Japanese soldier documented their misery and determination: "I am exhausted. We have no food. The enemy are now within five hundred meters from us. Mother, my dear wife, and son, I am writing this letter to you by dim candlelight. Our end is near. Hundreds of pale soldiers of Japan are awaiting our glorious end and nothing else."

The extent of the Japanese suffering and losses on Leyte was incalculable. Their disorganization and piecemeal commitment of troops allowed for wide-ranging assessments at best. General Suzuki was presumed dead after American aircraft strafed his raft as he attempted to flee Leyte to a nearby island, but his chief of staff who survived the campaign estimated that almost forty-nine thousand of their soldiers were killed. However, American numbers for the same period calculated they'd killed over eighty thousand and captured just over eight hundred. By comparison, the American losses in the ground campaign were over 3,500 men dead and 12,000 wounded.

Leyte was one island in a long war, and getting to Tokyo would require seizing dozens more.

● ● ●

By Monday, January 15, 1945, Swing's Angels were bivouacked in tents on Bito Beach, back where they had started fifty-nine days ago. Having been relieved by another division, they were refitting for their next mission, but there were only rumors of when or where that might be.

To Swing's chagrin, MacArthur benched the 11th Airborne for his January 9 invasion of Luzon. Swing was frustrated at being left out of what he called the "orthodox" landing that crashed ashore a hundred and twenty miles north of the capital city, Manila. His attempts to have his division airdropped in front of the amphibious landings were rejected as too grand given that the Air Force was unable to muster enough aircraft in time. Swing complained, "[MacArthur's] staff is a pain in the neck to me so far as having little imagination [on how to utilize airborne units]." Between planners believing they had enough troops for the operation and concerns about supplying Swing's undersized division, there was little appetite for the 11th Airborne to participate.

Ten days into the Luzon campaign, however, the attack bogged down. MacArthur complained that his Sixth Army field commander, Lieutenant General Walter Krueger, was plodding despite light Japanese resistance. To spur the campaign forward, MacArthur authorized another landing—a diversion of sorts—to occupy Japanese reinforcements and reduce pressure on Krueger's two divisions still working their way toward the capital city.

The task fell to MacArthur's Eighth Army, commanded by three-star general Robert L. Eichelberger. The fifty-eight-year-old Eichelberger, whose receding gray hair revealed a tall forehead atop a long nose, had been in uniform since he was nineteen. The youngest of five children, he entered West Point in 1905, where he was classmates with George S. Patton.

Eichelberger arrived in the Pacific in August 1942, and he was soon dropped into the cauldron of New Guinea as a corps commander. With the campaign stalled, MacArthur dramatically charged Eichelberger with either securing the island or not coming back alive. Arriving on the island, Eichelberger personally took charge of the floundering 32nd Infantry Division. His decisive conduct won him both admirers and detractors, unsurprising for a commander who had fired a division commander and demanded aggressive frontline

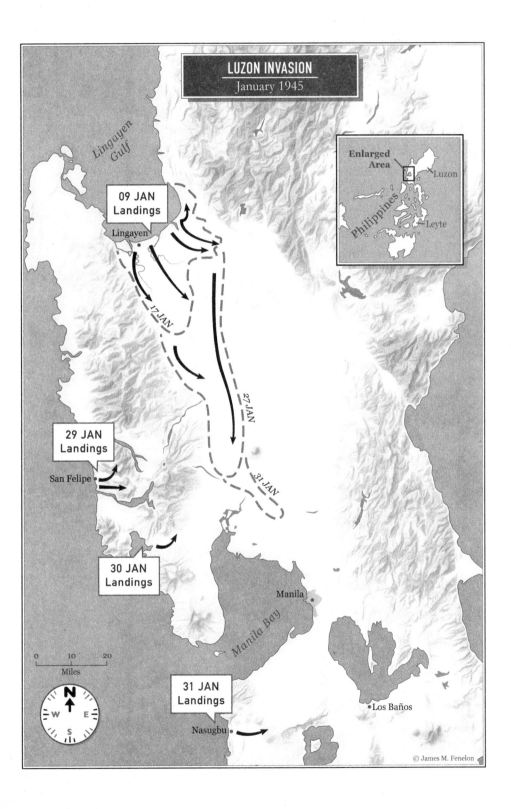

LUZON INVASION
January 1945

Lingayen Gulf

09 JAN
Landings

Lingayen

17 JAN

27 JAN

29 JAN
Landings

San Felipe

31 JAN

30 JAN
Landings

Manila

Manila Bay

0   10   20
Miles

N
W   E
S

31 JAN
Landings

Nasugbu

Los Baños

Enlarged
Area

Luzon

Philippines

Leyte

© James M. Fenelon

action from the men. But Eichelberger asked for no more than he was willing to give, putting his life on the line multiple times to ascertain ground truth and provide leadership as close to the fighting as possible. He routinely dodged enemy shellfire, and on one occasion shot and killed a Japanese rifleman.

Tellingly, Eichelberger's victory at New Guinea put him in the crosshairs of his narcissist boss. MacArthur preferred his subordinates stay out of his limelight and thwarted an attempt to award Eichelberger the Congressional Medal of Honor for his hands-on direction of the battle. Writing to the War Department, MacArthur hinted that he almost relieved Eichelberger of duty, dashing any chance for the award. After that, Eichelberger served as MacArthur's fire fighter, thrown into campaigns to stir up under-performing units or oversee mopping up operations. In the process, he earned an enviable battlefield record, but strived to avoid publicity while doing so for fear of being sidelined. Now, MacArthur, whom Eichelberger referred to as "the Big Chief" or "BC" for short, needed him to shake things up in Luzon.

Eichelberger proposed an ambitious plan: to amphibiously land the 11th's two paraglider regiments south of Manila. A few days later, Hard Rock Haugen's paratroopers would be airdropped twenty-four miles inland to link up with the advancing paragliders. Swing supported the mission, writing that "a secondary landing might turn out to be the quickest way to Manila—Eichelberger sees the possibilities."

MacArthur agreed and gave his approval, but with caveats. The operation, codenamed MIKE VI, was officially designated a "reconnaissance in force," and the initial wave was limited to a single 1,600-man regiment. Once ashore, they were to determine the "Japanese strength, deployment, and intentions." Any of Eichelberger's hopes to get himself and the rest of Swing's division into the fight were subject to the degree of enemy resistance.

Despite the caveats—what Eichelberger labeled "indefinite plans"—he and Swing readied for a full deployment, wagering the element of surprise would allow them to exploit the initial landing. After all, one man's "reconnaissance in force" was another's opportunity. Eichelberger and Swing both added vague guidance in the fine print of their field orders, advising commanders to be "prepared to advance north" after seizing their initial objectives. "North" was a veiled reference to Manila.

Eichelberger referred to his command as "Task Force Shoestring." His Eighth Army was now a skeleton organization, slimmed down from its normal compliment of several divisions to just Swing's under-sized 11th, with a hodgepodge of attached units to round up its numbers. Additionally, the Navy barely provided enough ships and escorts to land Swing's two regiments, and the Air Force had scraped together just fifty-odd transport planes, a third of what Haugen needed to drop the entirety of his regimental combat team in a single lift. But that only mattered *if* approval was given for the airdrop. MacArthur made it clear the drop could only occur if the paragliders fought their way inland far enough to make a timely link-up with the paratroopers.

If the airdrop got the green light, the Air Force agreed to fly three sorties to make up for their shortages: the first two, dropping the bulk of the troopers and two howitzers, would take place four hours apart on the same day; the third, bringing in the remaining ten howitzers and cannoneers, would drop the following morning.

Intelligence officers estimated there were seven thousand Japanese soldiers in Swing's sector south of Manila. A garrison of five hundred Japanese were estimated to be guarding the beach itself, with another five thousand farther inland close to where Haugen's troopers would drop. The assumption was that the beach garrison would fight delaying actions and the inland troops would not be committed to reinforce them.

Swing made what he could of the limited plan, writing, "Well, half a loaf is better than none, I suppose.... We're going in half airborne and half amphibious. The plan is one I've advocated for four months, only I was to go whole hog by air with another division seaborne. As you can imagine, it's an end run with a forward pass." What Swing didn't imagine was that the Japanese anticipated his end run. Intercepted radio communications kept from Swing revealed multiple broadcasts from Yamashita's headquarters informing his units to expect American airborne operations to "throw rear areas into disorder at the time of the attack upon Manila."

With the airdrop's risk mitigated by a rapid link-up with the advancing paragliders, MacArthur approved the diversionary landing. The paragliders were to hit the beach on the last day of January, giving Eichelberger and Swing eleven days to prepare.

WHILE SWING'S OFFICERS SCRAMBLED, most of the troops were oblivious to the feverish planning going on above them and enjoyed their respite from combat. Mail from home was delivered for the first time since arriving on Leyte. Private Bill Lindau sorted through a stack of sixteen letters, finding one that informed him his wife had given birth to their seven-pound, three-ounce daughter, Sara. Reflecting on the delivery date, December 11, Lindau realized he'd been crouching in the bottom of his foxhole under the weight of a Japanese mortar attack about the same time his wife was in labor.

Their footlockers, last seen stacked on New Guinea, caught up to them as well. Unfortunately, rear-echelon personnel had looted them, including a cherished bottle of whiskey that Miles Gale was looking forward to. Also coming ashore were fresh troops to fill the Angels' depleted ranks. Most went to Haugen's 511th, which suffered more than 70 percent of the division's casualties with four hundred men wounded, killed, or missing. Excluded from the numbers were the men hospitalized with fevers and disease.

"We got some replacements but did not get up to full strength," said 'Slugger' Lahti, newly promoted to Haugen's executive officer. There were other promotions as well as demotions throughout the division: Lahti reassigned most of his former headquarters' staff, feeling their poor performance in the field made them unfit for infantry service. Haugen sent Ernie LaFlamme to the paragliders, and Major Henry Burgess, the Harvard graduate who ran Swing's jump schools, took his place as commander of the 1st Battalion. Several paraglider battalion commanders were also replaced.

The new men dumping their gear onto an empty cot were surprised by their chilly reception. One recalled, "When I was assigned to the company, I felt as welcome as jungle rot. I soon learned that these silent, dirty, disgruntled guys had left a lot of their friends behind."

"They were a damaged, sorry bunch," he continued. "They needed us and didn't want us."

Deane Marks agreed. "We were so tired and burned out that all we wanted to do was to be left alone."

To get the veterans back in shape, platoon and company commanders led morning runs and calisthenics on the beach. In the afternoons, they conducted tactical exercises to instill recently learned combat lessons.

When not training, troopers returned to their habit of pilfering for entertainment. A curious squad waded through the knee-deep swamp behind Bito Beach to discover an ordnance camp. The men sloshed back with several crates of Browning Automatic Rifles (BARs) balanced on their shoulders. The automatic rifles weighed less than a belt-fed machinegun but fired the same caliber of ammunition from a twenty-round detachable magazine. Under the division's official

Table of Equipment, only Swing's paragliders were authorized the much-prized weapons.

Haugen, walking through the 1st Battalion area, spotted the men cleaning their new BARs. Henry Burgess eyed Haugen eyeing the BARs.

"He stood around and looked at them for some time," recalled Burgess, "made a comment to the effect that they were a good weapon and perhaps we should have a few more of them, and walked away."

Over the next week, many of Haugen's twelve-man squads were armed with both a belt-fed machinegun as well as a factory-fresh BAR. Burgess and his men, with help from the Angels' combat engineers, also allegedly stole two D8 Caterpillar tractors and several road graders from the same depot.

Bivouacking in tents on a secure beach ensured a return to the tedium of barracks life and labor details. Private Jerry Davis, a paratrooper in the 511th, volunteered for an unspecified work party. He was told to grab his rifle, his pack, and a full allotment of ammo and rations. Joining thirty other troopers from the division, he lined up in front of a lieutenant for further instructions.

"The lieutenant told us," Davis remembered, "that we were the grave registration detail whose mission was to return to the division's recent battle area, exhume the bodies of our fallen comrades, and bury them in two or three more or less central locations."

Quartermasters issued the group shovels, rubber gloves, ponchos, gallons of formaldehyde, and dozens of wood crosses. They flew via L-birds into Manarawat where, single file, they patrolled back up into the despised mountains. The first man they buried was one of their own party, killed during a shootout with a Japanese squad scavenging for food.

The troopers split into teams, using overhead reconnaissance photographs marked with the locations of the dead. At each shallow grave, a couple of troopers would carefully dig up the body. They had an agreement, with no questions asked, that a man could opt out of re-interring a friend. With a nod, someone else would step in to help with the solemn task.

Having dug up a comrade, Davis recalled, "One of the men from graves registration wanted to just bring in the head. He said that was all that was needed for identification." The troopers were having none of that. "We used several ponchos to make the wrap and then laced the wrapped body to a long pole," Davis continued. "We took turns, with two people carrying the body and the third person trading off at one end of the pole or the other." The three of them lugged the body almost four miles up and down hills and across a narrow river.

First Lieutenant Randolph Kirkland recalled, "We found the bodies of our own men in every conceivable posture and condition. We found that those men who had been buried in shallow graves were virtually intact and heavy.... The men who had not been buried were but bones, and they were often mixed up with Japanese bones."

"There was a site that troubled me," Kirkland continued. "Most of the American dead had been buried in shallow slit trenches." One of them, however, looked as if he had risen from the dead. His horribly mutilated body lay half out of his grave. Kirkland later learned that a besieged group of troopers, too weak to carry their wounded, gave those expected to die morphine overdoses before burying them. Kirkland suspected the dose given to this man wasn't fatal, and he later clawed his way out of his own grave only to be hacked to death by a Japanese saber.

All told, it took the men a week to complete their grisly work. They found all but twelve of their comrades, whose bodies were claimed by the jungle. With over a hundred and sixty of their comrades dead, Deane Marks later gave voice to the tormenting mixture of relief and shame that haunted many troopers. "There always was that feeling of, 'I'm glad it wasn't me.' We all felt bad for a short time when a buddy was killed, but deep inside, you were thankful to God that the shrapnel or bullet didn't take you. I never saw anyone who was willing to trade places with a corpse."

Sadly, more death loomed just over the horizon. Their tranquil beach stay was interrupted by officers passing out handbooks describing Luzon's geography, fauna, and cultural history. Map studies were followed by issuing ammunition. The Angels were headed back to war.

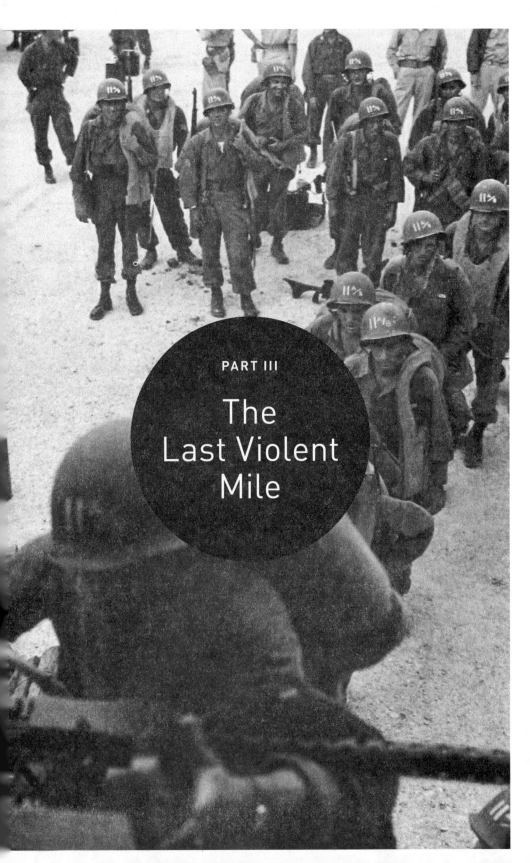

PART III

The Last Violent Mile

Chapter 8

Task Force Shoestring

Red Beach, Nasugbu, Luzon Island.
07:00, Wednesday, January 31, 1945

The naval flotilla of over a hundred assorted vessels, officially designated Task Group 78.2, held station in the dark waters off Nasugbu Beach. The convoy was poised forty miles south of Manila, ready to land 6,462 of Swing's men. But first came the air strikes: eighteen twin-engined A-20 Havoc bombers zoomed over the beach, chewing up suspected enemy positions with their forward-mounted .50-calibre machineguns. Nine P-38 Lightnings made a low pass, repeating the performance.

At 07:15, two of the escorting destroyers rotated their guns into position. With ear-splitting growls that rolled over the surf, they hurled fifty-five-pound shells into the shore, tearing apart the tree line in a series of shattering explosions.

Simultaneously, rocket-equipped landing craft angled to align their rudimentary launchers with the landing beach. Sailors hoisted the rockets into the racks, tossed the safety caps overboard, and screwed on the warheads before retreating below decks to avoid the searing back blast. The rockets lifted off with deafening *whooshes* as paired salvos arched across the pink dawn.

One of Swing's combat engineers was awed by the display, later recalling, "They all hit the beach, leaving us with the impression that nothing could live through such a rain." Sailors and Angels alike were buoyed by the absence of return fire.

Boatswains gunned their landing craft toward the beach to land the first wave of paragliders at 08:15. Seven minutes later, the radio crackled to life: they were ashore without opposition. The next wave

General Swing's glider troopers wade ashore at Nasugbu, Luzon

of eight boats muscled through the swells, and paragliders rushed over the lowered bow ramps and onto the beach. Several larger infantry landing craft pushed in as well, and troopers filed down the two lowered companionways to wade ashore through the waist-deep surf.

By the time the third wave ploughed ashore, the Japanese were shooting. As the division staff hustled out of their landing craft, several machinegun bursts sailed in from the left. Swing's assistant division commander, General Al Pierson was hit in the stomach by what felt like a baseball bat. Miraculously, the bullet struck the Army-issue compass on his belt. It would never point north again, but it saved his life.

Major 'Butch' Henry Muller, the division's intelligence officer, lay in the dunes, pinned down next to Swing. Bullets stitched the beach, and random artillery shells exploded in geysers of sand and shrapnel.

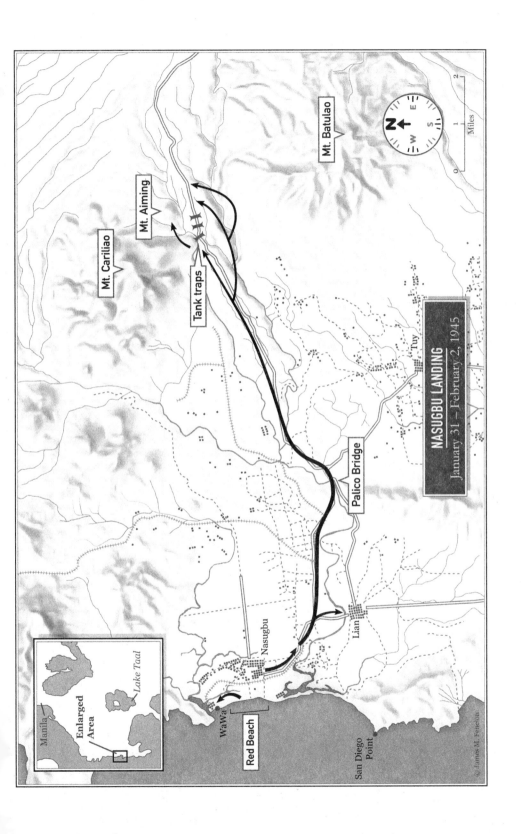

NASUGBU LANDING
January 31 – February 2, 1945

Mt. Batulao

Mt. Cariliao

Mt. Aiming

Tank traps

Palico Bridge

Tuy

Lian

Nasugbu

WaWa

Red Beach

San Diego Point

Manila

Enlarged Area

Lake Taal

Miles

0   1   2

© James M. Fenelon

Muller recalled that Lt. Colonel Bill Crawford "became exasperated because the naval gunners would not man their guns and return the enemy fire."

Crawford, Swing's operations officer—the "G-4"—announced he was going to crew the belt-fed machinegun on their landing craft himself. Waiting for a lull, he readied for a sprint.

"When he leaped to his feet," Muller remembered, "General Swing grabbed his boot and tumbled him to the sand again, telling him, 'You keep down. I need a G-4!'"

The heaviest fire came from several machineguns nested in a red-roofed building on the left flank. Not far from Swing, a naval gunfire team radioed the target to sailors offshore and within minutes rockets tore into the building, setting it and several surrounding structures ablaze. The machineguns fell silent.

The light opposition made for easy decision making. By 09:45, paragliders were fanning out to secure the beachhead. One company marched up the left flank to Wawa. Another group headed south to seize San Diego Point, while a third company rushed to set up a road-block further south at Lian.

In Nasugbu, Swing and his staff occupied a one-story school building on the town plaza for their command post. Commo teams filed in, setting up their radios and antennas. Eichelberger, still onboard his command ship and confident the plan was unfolding as hoped, authorized Swing to land the second paraglider regiment along with the rest of the division at 10:00 that morning.

Members of the beach party scrambled around the disembarking soldiers to set up their landing flags. The bright-colored markers served as guides to the forty-four vessels waiting offshore to deliver engineers, radiomen, anti-aircraft gunners, artillerymen, medics, service troops, quartermasters, ordnance specialists, cooks, the band, tons of supplies, and over eight hundred vehicles. But there was a problem. Despite prior reconnaissance and assurances, an offshore sandbar prevented the heavier-laden ships from grounding close enough to the beach for unloading.

While the paragliders marched on Wawa, Japanese machineguns resumed their chatter from the left flank, punctuated by sporadic artillery shells. An airstrike failed to silence the harassing guns, so the naval gunfire team radioed for another salvo of rockets. The paragliders halted three hundred yards away to watch the plastering. When they arrived at Wawa, they sorted through the rubble and smoke to find more than thirty twisted enemy bodies, two destroyed howitzers, and five mangled machineguns.

Waiting in Nasugbu to meet with Swing and his staff was Major Jay D. Vanderpool, a twenty-seven-year-old American intelligence officer with a unique resume. In 1935, after his divorced mother died, he dropped out of his senior year of high school to join the Civilian Conservation Corps. At nineteen, he enlisted in the Army and was assigned to Hawaii where he rose through the ranks, earning his sergeant stripes before graduating from officer training as a lieutenant in the spring of 1941. He was still in Hawaii nine months later when the Japanese attacked Pearl Harbor. In 1942, he fought on Guadalcanal with the 25th Infantry Division and in recognition of his drive and acumen, he was promoted to major. He later volunteered for a hazardous duty assignment that led him to Luzon, arriving under the cover of darkness by submarine. He had been on the island several months before the American invasion, synchronizing guerrilla activity on the west coast.

Vanderpool, titling himself "guerrilla coordinator," carried a dispatch to smooth his introduction to the locals: "Vanderpool from MacArthur: Do what will best further the allied cause." The personal missive from the revered Supreme Commander and the wide latitude it afforded, combined with Vanderpool's power to distribute US weapons and medical supplies, opened doors.

For Vanderpool to successfully navigate the local politics, he needed to be a deft combination of diplomat, tactical advisor, and consiglieri. He later recounted the state of the Luzon-based guerrillas, "There were numerous quasi-military organizations with military, economic, and political goals. Their primary loyalty was to their country ... there was no central guerrilla control or allegiance. They were, in effect, independent war lords." Their military acumen varied widely as well. While some groups were little more than street gangs led by a local tough, Vanderpool found the most professional unit to be the Hunters' ROTC, commanded by twenty-three-year-old Colonel Eleuterio L. Adevoso, a former military cadet who fought under the *nom de guerre* "Terry Magtangol." His unit, led by one-time cadets from the Philippine Military Academy and university ROTC students, knew the terrain and had been fighting the Japanese on their own terms since 1942.

Vanderpool found a good partner in the Hunters' ROTC guerrillas, who wore a mishmash of US fatigues and Japanese uniforms mixed with civilian clothes. They could not fight toe-to-toe in a pitched battle against the Japanese, but they were more than willing to raid, harass, and assist the Angels in the liberation of their island.

At noon, Eichelberger and twenty-five members of his Eighth Army staff came ashore looking for Swing. The two generals conferred, agreeing that the limited resistance, combined with Vanderpool's reports that the Japanese had withdrawn inland, meant the paragliders should push out of town to the east. Eichelberger emphasized speed, directing Swing to keep his men moving throughout the night. Their objective was Tagaytay Ridge, twenty-four miles inland, where Haugen's regiment would drop.

Eichelberger later wrote to his wife that he wasn't there to micro-manage Swing, but to spur a sense of urgency. He was growing confident in Swing's leadership, admitting, "I am very keen about this 11th Airborne. They are small in number, but they are willing to fight." Eichelberger found a kindred spirit in Swing. Both shared an aggressive willingness to take the fight to the enemy. If the troops kept pushing through such light resistance, Eichelberger saw an opportunity in his "indefinite" instructions to seize Manila and embarrass Krueger, whose Sixth Army was still well north of the capital city. The two Army commanders had little regard for each other. Krueger tended to be dismissive of Eichelberger. In turn, Eichelberger criticized Krueger for rarely visiting the front-lines and doubted his tactical acumen, writing, "If he is a great general or has any of the elements of greatness, then I am no judge of my fellow man. Beyond a certain meanness, which scares those under him, and a willingness to work, he has little to offer. He doesn't even radiate courage, which is one thing we like to think a soldier has."

By the time Eichelberger and Swing agreed to push inland, Colonel Robert 'Shorty' Soule, the commander of the 188th Para-glider Regiment, was ready. To increase his regiment's manpower, Swing attached a battalion of the 187th to the 188th, giving the bespeckled Soule a traditionally organized regiment of three battal-ions: two to attack and one in reserve to bolster the assault at any opportunity. Swing's re-organization overcame the inherit weakness of the glider regiments' two battalion structure and gave Soule an Army textbook triangular formation of three maneuver elements.

On their way out of Nasugbu, Soule's men wove their way through crowds of jubilant Filipinos celebrating the end to three years of Japa-nese occupation. Once past the gleeful mobs, they moved briskly up Route 17 in single file columns skirting each side of the one-lane gravel road. The primary artery to Tagaytay led them past open farmland punctuated with pockets of thick, lush vegetation growing up to the edge of the road.

This was Infantry 101. The sun beat down on the men's steel helmets. With their full packs and rifles slung or at the ready, they put one dusty boot in front of the other. Sweat dripped into their burning eyes while they breathed in cadence with the crunch of gravel underfoot. It all combined into a monotony that made the weight of their equipment impossible to ignore. Glancing up from their march, they would have seen the distant ridgeline that was their destination, and where the enemy lay waiting.

By midafternoon, they were five miles inland. The lead platoon picked up its pace, shuffling down a small hill toward the Palico River, intent on securing the two-hundred-foot steel-trussed bridge that spanned the river's eighty-foot-deep gorge. On the far side, the men caught a Japanese squad preparing the bridge for demolition. The paragliders' first volley of rifle fire felled six saboteurs and scattered the rest.

Seizing the bridge was a coup. For Eichelberger and Swing, its loss would have meant reversing course and a longer, southern diversion through Lian where both the road and the bridge were in pitiful condition. Combat engineers went to work immediately, disarming the explosives and replacing weakened wood crossbeams. By the next morning, they'd have the bridge fit for twelve-ton vehicular traffic.

The paragliders marched on, huffing out of the coastal plains and ascending into the mountains toward Tagaytay. They kept hiking after dark, taking advantage of the unfamiliar opportunity. Unlike a jungle trail, the road allowed for swift movement under the monochromatic glow of a full moon. At midnight, after slogging inland since that morning, the lead battalion paused to allow fresh troops to take point. They pushed through sporadic rifle fire until 04:00 when they finally stopped to rest. But two hours later, they were back on their feet.

At daybreak, the rattle of machineguns sent the point squad diving for cover. Now eleven miles inland, Route 17 threaded uphill through a draw formed by three mountains. The left was dominated by 2,100-foot Mount Cariliao, with the sharp rise of Mount Aiming at its base. One of the Angels described Aiming as "a thimble at the base of an overturned teacup." On the right, Mount Batulao rose to 2,700 feet. The heights were covered in thick scrub and riddled with caves, providing a commanding view of the road. Bullets cracked in from positions on all three mountains.

Japanese observers, eyeing the Americans through binoculars, called down artillery and mortars. As the paragliders crawled for protection, shells whistled into pre-registered points up and down the gravel road. The more immediate threat, however, were the machineguns.

While Soule's mortar teams thumped out high-explosive rounds to suppress the incoming fire, cannoneers wheeled up heavier guns: four 75mm pack howitzers of the 457th Parachute Field Artillery Battalion's Dog Battery. With their Dodge cargo trucks stalled in the surf back at Nasugbu, the crews served as primary movers, pushing, pulling, and cursing the 1,400-pound guns up hill.

The six-man crews, ignoring ricocheting bullets, muscled their gun tubes into position. Aiming over the barrel like a shotgun, each successive *WHOOOOM!* of a howitzer shattered a machinegun nest. But rifle fire still snapped overhead, and the cornucopia of 155mm, 105mm, 75mm, and 37mm shells raining down forced Soule's paragliders to withdrawal.

With the sun well up, the attached air support party, in their DUKW amphibious tractor rigged with an unwieldy SCR-399 radio, rolled forward to direct aircraft circling overhead. Twin-engined Havocs streaked out of the sky, seeking enemy howitzers and pummeling the hilltops with bombs and strafing runs. While the Japanese hunkered down, all three of Soule's battalions attacked: one moved to the left against Mount Cariliao and Mount Aiming; another went up the middle to hold the road; and the third tackled Mount Batulao on the right.

By noon, a company of paragliders led by Captain Raymond F. Lee crossed through a steep gorge on the northside of the road to ascend Aiming. Their close-quarters assault with rifles, grenades, and bayonets cleared the summit and captured a 105mm howitzer in the process. They rolled Japanese corpses out of foxholes to use the dugouts for their own defense. Lee's men spent the afternoon fending off several banzai attacks, in between which the Japanese pounded Aiming's summit with artillery. The shell fire prevented reinforcements from reaching Lee's men, who held for several tenuous hours, until the rest of their battalion fought their way up to join them.

Seizing Mount Aiming drove the first wedge into the Japanese roadblock. Simultaneously, on the right flank, Soule's 2nd Battalion cleared enemy positions up to the base of Mount Batulao, wiping out a mortar position and a 155mm howitzer. The battalion cutting up the middle knocked out a Japanese 75mm as well. The day's work resulted in ninety-one enemy dead and several captured howitzers. The Angels had made the first substantial tug at a seam that would ultimately unravel the Japanese defensive line. But it came at a heavy cost: sixteen dead paragliders and another forty-four wounded.

Friday, February 2, dawned with clear skies and good visibility, perfect weather for airstrikes and artillery barrages. For an infantryman, the morning's exhibition was a feast for the eye. Pack howitzers threw salvos against Cariliao and Batulao while the now-familiar A-20 Havocs, their canopies catching the sun as they roared overhead, bombed Japanese artillery positions. The Havocs and howitzers cleared a path, and by mid-day the paragliders humped through it to find the road ahead bisected by three Japanese anti-tank ditches. Each was nearly thirty feet wide and ranged from twenty-five to fifty feet deep. Again, the American's speed caught the enemy napping.

Two of the ditches were still rigged with explosives to collapse narrow passages left for Japanese vehicles; the third had been detonated, completely blocking the road to wheeled traffic. The paragliders continued forward on foot, sacking a command post littered with bloody medical supplies and nearly one hundred tons of abandoned ammunition.

Combat engineers bridged the ditches, and four M8 self-propelled 75mm howitzers clanked up from the beach to join the advancing columns. The tank-like armored assault guns gave Soule more firepower in his column's vanguard. That evening, L-birds buzzed in low, dropping food and ammunition. The advance had been a modest two miles, but it was close enough to Tagaytay for Eichelberger and Swing to agree: Haugen's airdrop was on.

Even so, the Japanese weren't done. Throughout the night, artillery, mortars, and machineguns harassed Soule's forward lines. Infiltrators crept through the inky jungle to assault artillery positions and forced the cannoneers to desert their guns before mustering to retake them.

THE NEXT MORNING was the big push. As the sun rose, Swing and his entourage were up front with the paragliders who, after scarfing down a few bites of cold rations, pulled themselves out of their foxholes. It was time to go to work. They trudged past the carnage of the previous day's airstrikes to close on the last hill between them and Tagaytay.

At 08:20, an hour into their trek, a low, steady droning noise caught their attention. It grew louder as the source got closer: an armada of fifty-one lumbering C-47s escorted by darting P-38 fighters. Flying in at six hundred feet, the second wave had arrived.

Haugen stood in the open cargo door of the lead aircraft, squinting against the wall of wind whipping at his uniform. Spotting the drop zone should have been easy enough, as it was atop the Tagaytay ridge-line and about as ideal as could be asked for: mostly open, plowed farmland on flat terrain, four thousand yards long and two thousand wide. While dotted with a few trees and nipa huts, the only real danger was drifting over the steep-sided slope of the ridge. The primary check-point was Lake Taal, an unmistakable body of water surrounding a flooded volcano, which formed a lake within a lake.

As the first serial of nine aircraft approached, Haugen and the pilots found the ridgeline obscured by a low cloud bank. Fortu-

C-47s fly over Lake Taal on their way to drop Colonel 'Hard Rock' Haugen's paratroopers at Tagaytay

nately, just as they passed over Route 17, a break in the clouds revealed the final checkpoint. The pilot of Haugen's aircraft, now assured of his position, led the following aircraft to the drop zone. He flipped the jump light from red to green—right on target.

Haugen glanced back into the aircraft, yelling over his shoulder, "Are you ready?" Without waiting for an answer, he bellowed, "Let's go!" then threw himself out the door. Behind him, seventeen troopers surged forward. Weighed down with equipment, they tumbled more than jumped.

Charlie Sass, jumping from another C-47, recalled, "I carried double my weight out the door—two bandoliers, rockets, grenades, BAR clips, assorted firing devices, three days of K-rations, first aid packet, shovel, two canteens, plus chute, reserve, and me. The whole rig may have toted up to four hundred pounds."

When the jump light glowed red in First Lieutenant Randolph Kirkland's aircraft, the stick of jumpers stood to attach their parachutes' static lines to the anchor line cable running the length of the cabin.

"I had thought that I would see Lake Taal," said Kirkland, "but when I peeked around the stick leader, I saw that we were above the clouds and could not see the ground. I concluded that we were still miles out. Suddenly, with no preamble, we saw a string of parachutes descending."

Kirkland was correct. They were still three miles short of the drop zone when either an equipment bundle was jarred loose, or someone jumped early. In either event, troopers seeing the floating parachute canopy believed they were over the drop zone and mistook it as the signal to jump. The resulting chain reaction was inevitable.

Kirkland continued, "Our lead officer in the door had to make a quick decision. The planes were going much too fast, and we were certainly some miles from the true drop zone. He did what I would have done—he jumped."

Kirkland followed him out the door, slapping his feet together and holding a tight body position until he felt the reassuring jerk of his chute opening. Standard procedure called for the pilots to slow their aircraft to between ninety-five and one hundred miles per hour. Exiting at a higher speed meant a rough opening shock, and Kirkland's experience was typical of many. "My musette bag with my poncho, C Rations, and bourbon disappeared into the clouds," he said. "The grenades in my pockets joined them. The opening shock well-nigh knocked me out. For some seconds, I saw confetti. Not stars."

In his aircraft, Ed Sorensen was sitting on an equipment bundle staring out the open cargo door waiting for the two-minute warning when a buddy, looking out an opposite window, yelled, "Ed, they are all jumping!"

Before the pilot could slow down, Sorensen shoved the bundle out then followed it; the remaining troopers followed him.

The sky filled with parachutes as troopers descended into the cloud bank. They were surrounded by equipment bundles floating under chutes of bright blue, red, and white. The colors allowed troopers to identify the bundles' contents of machineguns, mortars, ammunition, or medical supplies. Kirkland recalled, "I sank into the clouds and was rudely brought to reality when a palm tree whistled by me. It was a ground fog and not a cloud."

Within minutes, the first serial's 886 troopers were on the ground, including two 75mm pack howitzers and their crews. The men shrugged off their chutes, loaded their rifles, and scurried off in search of their equipment bundles or assembly areas. Trooper Jerry Davis, however, had other priorities. Not wanting to miss the jump, he and several others went AWOL from the hospital while still suffering from yellow jaundice and diarrhea. He later admitted, "I quickly got out of the harness and immediately dropped my pants. I was lucky. I made it in the nick of time. I don't know how I would have explained 'crapping my pants' on my first combat jump."

Fortunately for Davis, the enemy was nowhere to be found. Between Soule's paragliders and patrolling guerrillas, the Japanese were too occupied to muster any opposition to the airdrop. As Davis squatted on the drop zone, overhead the rumbling C-47s banked into their return route to pick up the second lift.

THE PARAGLIDERS made steady uphill progress toward Haugen's troopers until 10:15, when three hundred Japanese troops opened fire with rifles and machineguns. It was another dug-in blocking position on the road's south side. The howl of incoming artillery cut through the cacophony. The Japanese observer calling back adjustments knew his business, walking the explosions up the length of Soule's column.

Alongside the paragliders, Eichelberger and Swing and their contingent of high-ranking staff officers scrambled for cover. They were there to prod momentum, intent upon a smooth link-up with the paratroopers. So many officers were up front that the men referred to the vanguard as "the spearhead tipped with brass." Not far from Swing, the barrage killed a colonel along with seven other men. Twenty-one more were wounded, among them 'Shorty' Soule, just seven days away from his forty-fifth birthday.

Undaunted, Soule crawled half a football field back to his jeep while more shells whistled in. Soule's driver, Pius Corbett, was under the jeep, shielding himself from flying shrapnel.

"Corbett, do you want to hand me that radio?" asked Soule.

"No, sir," replied Corbett, "I don't even want to move."

Despite Corbett's reluctance, Soule got the radio and ordered his reserve battalion into the brawl. Soule, refusing medical treatment, instead crawled to a better spot to direct his artillery against the ridge. At the same time, the air support party radioed the Havocs to wing in for strafing and bombing attacks. Soule's fresh battalion rushed forward under a thunderous umbrella of howitzers, mortars, and aircraft, while on the right flank a company of paragliders swept around the hill to press a second attack. The Japanese who survived the devastating barrage were routed with hand grenades and flamethrowers.

Meanwhile, the returning C-47s flew overhead to deliver the second sortie of 906 paratroopers. By now, the ground fog had burned off, and the leading five aircraft dropped their troopers on target. However, despite instructions prior to departure, troopers in the trailing forty-odd aircraft failed to wait for the green light, jumping instead when they spotted the chutes from the first drop littering the ground.

While Swing and the Air Corps later exchanged accusations, given that the lead aircraft dropped on target and troopers had jumped against a red light, it was clear where the fault lay. It was a case of the men being out of practice, having made their last unit jump in the States.

Haugen established his command post on the edge of the drop zone, where the regiment's sergeant major found him "barking out orders and pleased with the whole thing." Despite the misdrops, the jump had gone largely to plan: many troopers landed near their objectives and headed straight to them; those who landed short of the drop zone hustled to catch up with their comrades. Only two or three equipment bundles of light machineguns couldn't be found, and injuries were relatively light: fifty-five troopers needed medical attention for scratches or sprains while three were seriously injured.

As the men scurried across the drop zone, one noted, "There was the loud sound of artillery firing a few ridges away, and because the land is rolling (with the hills terraced for farming) it was impossible to determine just where the shells were bursting." The paragliders were still flushing Japanese holdouts from their caves on the ridge's west side.

When Eichelberger and Swing arrived at Haugen's command post, Swing was irate. It might have been a performance for his boss, or a simple misunderstanding; nonetheless, Haugen's stenographer described Swing as "raising hell about lack of combat discipline and why isn't the 511th assembled and moving out." It was a puzzling tirade, as in truth, Haugen's men had already accomplished their objectives: the ridgeline was secure, the link-up with the paragliders was complete, and patrols were either at, or on their way to, roadblock positions on Route 17.

Haugen deescalated the situation with a quick summary of events, which begrudgingly satisfied Swing. With the state of affairs in order, Eichelberger, Swing, Haugen, and their combined staffs moved farther up the ridge to the Taal Vista Lodge. Once a luxurious getaway destination, the rear of the hotel had a magnificent view of the lake and its volcano. The Japanese occupied it until late 1944, when upon departure they ransacked it, taking the furniture and wrecking the plumbing. But its open, marble-floored lobby, large guest rooms, and terraced gardens made it an attractive location for a command post.

Eichelberger walked out the hotel's front entrance to get a view of Manila shimmering on the horizon, some thirty miles due north. He and Swing were both chomping at the bit to get there: Swing to keep his division in the fight, and Eichelberger to further prove his mettle. He later wrote, "Our real written orders ... were to establish ourselves on Tagaytay Ridge and stabilize conditions in that part of Luzon." But there was Manila, tantalizingly within reach, its southern door apparently wide open.

That MacArthur wanted the city secured ASAP was clear to everyone. Eichelberger believed the Big Chief was "disgusted" by Krueger's slow progress, and he concurred, referring to his rival as "old Molasses in January." Eichelberger confided to his diary, "It is evident that W. K. [Kruger] had not been able to fight the troops given to him with any kind of credible speed."

As a biographer wrote of Eichelberger's desire, "While he was unwilling to squander lives in pursuit of his military ambitions, there was nonetheless a single-minded ruthlessness about him." Swing got a glimpse of it, and before departing Leyte wrote, "If he [Eichelberger] isn't standing at the bar in the Army and Navy Club [in Manila] when Krueger walks in the door, then it won't be for lack of trying." Eichelberger later admitted his "only directives about going to Manila were oral ones, and more of a nature of permission to go rather than a directive." Eichelberger, taking MacArthur's intent as an implicit nod, ordered Swing into the city.

But the Japanese disposition in Manila was uncertain at best. Early guerrilla intelligence suggested they were evacuating, but more recent accounts indicated the construction of urban strongpoints. Eichelberger himself confessed just before launching his campaign, "We still do not know whether the Japanese are going to put up any resistance to the capture of Manila." But he dismissed the updates. "The guerrilla reports make me laugh," he wrote. "The report tonight is that Manila is being burned by the Japanese, and yet I can look right down into the town and see lights and one little fire."

Sadly, he would soon discover there was nothing to laugh about.

● ● ●

MacArthur assumed the Japanese would declare Manila an open city. His optimism that Yamashita would do as the Americans had in 1941 was contagious, and few, if any, of MacArthur's staff expected the enemy to make a stand in a capital city of almost a million civilians.

Since Yamashita abandoned Leyte, Imperial General Headquarters in Tokyo had adopted a strategy of *hondo kessen*—attrition warfare. Yamashita no longer had to defeat MacArthur, but rather, bleed him dry and delay his advance on Japan. By tying down the American divisions on Luzon, Yamashita didn't have to win; he just couldn't lose.

The shift in strategy reflected the Japanese leaders' desperate need for more time to prepare for the Allies' inevitable invasion of the home islands. Having lost the opportunity on Leyte, Japanese' soil was where the "decisive victory" would now take place.

They were mobilizing a home army of sixty divisions and thirty-four brigades—almost three million men. But arming these divisions and converting thousands of rudimentary training aircraft into kamikazes required time. Imperial soldiers and marines on Luzon, and other islands in the "national defense sphere" such as Okinawa and Iwo Jima, were ordered to buy that time with their lives.

Contemplating his options, Yamashita reasoned that Manila was too populated, its structures too flammable, and its terrain too flat for a prolonged last stand. Instead, he intended to vacate the city, withdrawing his men to fight delaying actions from mountain strongholds.

In fact, Yamashita had already departed in December, moving his headquarters and the bulk of his forces a hundred and thirty miles north. The garrison left in Manila was expected to follow him after they secured vital supplies and rendered Manila's port useless by destroying its piers, setting fuel depots alight, scuttling ships in the harbor, and demolishing several key bridges to hamper the American advance through the city. Yamashita organized his forces on Luzon into three groups: the first, a force of 152,000 in the north, under his direct command and engaged against MacArthur's landings at Lingayen Gulf; the second, on the Bataan peninsula with thirty thousand troops; and finally, eighty thousand men in the island's southern regions. Each group held their own sector centered on mountainous fortifications, from which they planned to resist as long as possible. Critical to sustaining the three groups were the sixty-five thousand metric tons of food and ammunition stockpiled in Manila supply depots. But by the time MacArthur landed in early January, only four thousand tons had been moved out of the city.

Yamashita's plans were hindered by a lack of transportation and interservice squabbling with the Imperial Navy, who posited the Americans could best be delayed by fortifying Manila's urban labyrinth and forcing them to fight for it, house by house, brick by brick. So, during December and January, as the Army withdrew from the capital city, Rear Admiral Sanji Iwabuchi moved in with nearly fourteen thousand marines, soldiers, and sailors. Iwabuchi, as directed by the commander of the Southwestern Area Fleet, was to fortify the naval air station at Nichols Field, hold the naval base at Cavite, mine Manila Bay, and ultimately destroy any naval asset he could not defend. While Yamashita was in overall command of the Philippines, Iwabuchi believed himself subject to the Army only *after* completing his naval mission. The conflicting objectives were another example of the dysfunctional decentralized approach to war that emanated from Tokyo, but the stubborn forty-nine-year-old Iwabuchi also had a personal mission in mind: redemption. The career naval officer had risen through the ranks, commanding several ships before taking the helm of the battleship *Kirishima*. Iwabuchi suffered the humiliation of not going down with the *Kirishima* when she was sunk near Guadalcanal in 1942. In a navy that held to its strong traditions, Iwabuchi's career teetered on the verge of disgrace. With perhaps his last opportunity to save face, Iwabuchi made it clear to his men they would all go down fighting, "If we run out of bullets, we will use grenades; if we run out of grenades, we will cut down the enemy with swords; if we break our swords, we will kill them by sinking our teeth deep in their throats."

Iwabuchi's troops—ad-hoc units of varying combat ability—focused on constructing defenses south of the city, where the Japanese Navy expected MacArthur to land. They were wrong; MacArthur landed north of Manila, but their fortifed buildings, emplaced landmines, and barricaded road intersections would not go to waste. With Swing's Angels poised to the south, and two of MacArthur's divisions closing from the north, the vice on Manila was tightening, setting the stage for a tragedy of unimaginable horror.

● ● ●

Back at Tagaytay Ridge, Swing tapped Haugen for the charge into the capital city. The paragliders, still wrinkling out pockets of resistance on the western slopes, had been fighting for four days without rest. Haugen's fresh troops would take point.

A convoy of the 511th's nineteen jeeps, towing nine trailers stuffed with medical supplies and radios, arrived from Nasugbu. Haugen requested his regiment's remaining thirty-nine vehicles be brought up from the beach. He was told the best he could expect was seventeen cargo trucks. The service units were still untangling the logistical mess after three days of herculean effort to finish unloading the division's supplies.

The sandbar, a hundred frustrating yards from shore, had grounded most of the larger cargo ships. Two of the escorting destroyers cruised parallel to shore, hoping to generate swells big enough to nudge the craft over the sandbar. It helped, but the heaviest laden landing ships withdrew to try again at high tide. Optimistic attempts to off load from the sandbar resulted in several vehicles stranded in the surf with swamped engines.

Crews winched the stalled trucks onto the beach, along with two disassembled L-birds. Once ashore, the wings were bolted on and the aircraft readied for flight.

An effort to float fifty-five-gallon fuel barrels ashore failed miserably. Troopers splashed through the surf, trying in vain to recover the bobbing drums as the tide washed them all out to sea. Unable to land, the same ship that had dumped them overboard sailed away with the remainder of the division's fuel, along with two self-propelled howitzers, several trucks, jeeps, and radios.

Swing prevented a fiasco by pressing every available man into service. The band's musicians hauled cargo ashore and operated bulldozers to assist engineers in grading beach access roads. The headquarters' finance staff, along with members of the adjutant general's office, humped artillery and mortar shells up Route 17. Swing's chemical officer cobbled together the division's clerks, cooks, and parachute riggers to serve as stevedores responsible for unloading rations for over eight thousand men: tons of crated artillery, mortar, and rifle ammunition, as well as grenades, medical supplies, radio batteries, and more than eight hundred vehicles.

The local populace provided them with invaluable support. Five hundred laborers recruited and paid by a civil affairs team helped organize the growing stockpiles, while guerrilla leaders, such as Colonel Jose Razon, also assisted by organizing his unit into work details. Without the extra hands, Swing's combat strength would have been sapped, forcing his infantry and artillerymen to pitch in rather than move inland.

To speed the supplies off the beach, Swing's combat engineers extended a narrow-gauge railroad track by a thousand yards. The new spur, constructed over two days and built from locally procured rails and ties, paralleled the beach before connecting to the original line, which originated in Wawa. Engineers used bulldozers to pull loaded rail cars along the new section of track before a locomotive, conducted by its Filipino crew, took over to haul men and material inland.

Adding to the urgency were swarms of Japanese speedboats, captained by suicide pilots, targeting the ships waiting to unload. They raced toward the fleet, intending to ram their explosive-laden boats into the closest Navy ship.

An observer witnessing one of the attacks later recalled, "The destroyer was trying to sink the Japanese craft with five-inch guns and pursued it. Whenever the enemy wheeled and made a direct run at the destroyer, the ship zigzagged and took to its heels.... It seemed like a crazy version of you-chase-me and I'll-chase-you.... After about fifty rounds of firing, a shell from the destroyer found its target. The boat did not sink—it disintegrated." At least six others were blasted to pieces before the others turned tail; one, however, succeeded in damaging an American ship.

In the next twenty-four hours, jittery naval gunners sunk two of their own patrol boats after mistaking the unidentified craft for more enemy suicide strikes.

AT ELEVEN THIRTY THAT NIGHT, Haugen gathered his officers at the lodge. A few dim bulbs, powered by a humming generator, provided the only light. Occasionally, the crump of an echoing artillery barrage rattled in the distance as the paragliders shelled the western slopes. Haugen stood at the front of the room, with his ever-present cigarette. Speaking loudly enough to be heard over the generator, he briefed the next day's plan.

Twenty-two men of the division's recon platoon had already departed in jeeps. They drove north up Route 17, a two-lane motorway that sloped downhill the thirty-odd miles to Manila, radioing updates as they proceeded. They'd made it fifteen miles with no enemy contact, but civilians warned them that Japanese troops were in the village of Imus just up the road.

Tomorrow morning, the regiment would follow the same route. They were to move with all possible haste, speed essential. Haugen wanted not only to capitalize on the element of surprise, but also to seize bridges that were critical for their advance as their route crossed several rivers.

Their initial objective was twenty-five miles north at Bacoor, a Manila suburb. There they'd set up blocking positions on two road junctions between Manila and the Japanese naval base at Cavite. By occupying the intersections, the paratroopers could sever any Japanese attempts to reinforce or withdraw from Manila.

'Hacksaw' Holcombe's five hundred troopers of the 2nd Battalion would be on point, departing first in seventeen olive-drab cargo trucks and a few jeeps. For support, 'Hacksaw' would have six 75mm pack howitzers with their own jeeps, a platoon of combat engineers to dismantle explosives found on the bridges, and two tracked, M8 self-propelled 75mm guns. However, quartermasters were still scrounging enough fuel to get them all rolling.

The vehicle shortage required an improvised shuttle plan. Hacksaw's battalion would drive until they either reached Bacoor or made enemy contact, at which point they'd dismount and send the trucks back for the next battalion. The rest of the regiment was on foot, marching as fast as they could until the trucks came back for them. They would leave as soon as the fuel arrived from Nasugbu.

The officers shuffled out to get their men ready. Upon receiving the word that night, Private James M. Massey, one of Haugen's machinegunners, scribbled in his journal: "Next stop, Manila."

Chapter 9

"What Bridge?"

Taal Vista Lodge, Luzon Island.
Sunday, February 4, 1945

Haugen's men were ready to roll at first light. But instead of heading toward Manila, they milled around the trucks, smoked, or curled up in ponchos to catch a few more minutes of shuteye—they were waiting for the fuel. Though some in the Army viewed waiting was a legitimate form of doing something, both Haugen and Swing despised it.

At Nasugbu, engineers and the band's musicians had toiled all night to extend the local airfield by 1,850 feet to accommodate cargo planes. They worked through a flash rainstorm and used vehicle headlights for illumination. At dawn, ten C-47s loaded with barrels of fuel circled overhead while their flight leader winged in to land. The rain-drenched field made for an uneasy touch down, so he waved off the remaining aircraft, who flew away with their precious cargo. His plane's ten fuel barrels, however, were unloaded and rushed up to an impatient Haugen.

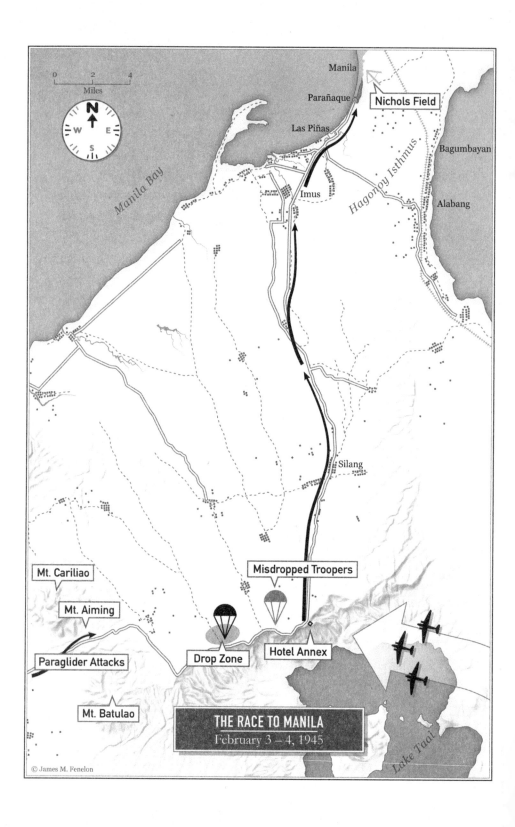

THE RACE TO MANILA
February 3 – 4, 1945

© James M. Fenelon

The paratroopers' first destination was Imus, a village twenty-two miles north, where the recon patrol found the main bridge demolished. Their further scouting located an intact bridge to the west, but it was rigged with explosives and under observation by a Japanese garrison. The recon team holed up to remain undetected and await Haugen's troops.

The advance party's two jeeps pulled away from the lodge at 05:30. An hour later, they were followed by Hacksaw Holcombe riding with Captain Stephen 'Rusty' Cavanaugh's Dog Company, crowded into the back of open-top, 2.5-ton cargo trucks. Behind them, keeping a ten-minute interval, was the remainder of Hacksaw's 2nd Battalion in more cargo trucks. Haugen accompanied this group in a jeep, followed by two more towing pack howitzers. Two tank-like M8 self-propelled howitzers with stubby 75mm barrels mounted on their turrets brought up the rear of the rolling column. The convoy passed the jeering troopers of Major Henry Burgess' 1st Battalion and the regimental headquarters staff who departed earlier on foot. They would be marching until the trucks returned for them.

A hint of what lay ahead was visible on the horizon: thick black smoke twisting up from Manila.

Leaving Tagaytay, the gravel of Route 17 became a concrete, two lane highway cutting downhill through rolling, heavily vegetated countryside. After five miles, the jungle gave way to cultivated plains dotted with farms and rice fields. The convoy made rapid progress. Swing wanted updates radioed back every thirty minutes; Haugen reported in hourly.

When they passed through the villages of Segundo, Lalann Primero, and Silang, gathered crowds greeted them with cheers, bugles, waving flags, and fingers raised in Vs for Victory. One village even assembled a four-piece band, and the quartet belted out the 'Star Spangled

Banner' to celebrate their liberation. Drivers nudged their jeeps and trucks through the crowds.

"They gave us water and bananas, papayas, and mangoes," recalled Deane Marks. "The sheer joy on their faces is hard to forget."

Upon reaching the southern outskirt of Imus, the scouts waved the column to a halt short of the demolished bridge. They briefed Hacksaw on the lay of the land, pointing out the route to the second bridge. It was two blocks west, where a Japanese-occupied compound, consisting of a long, squat building with several smaller outlying structures, overlooked the crossing. They guessed the enemy garrison was between fifty to a hundred strong.

Hacksaw's troopers dismounted, and the truck drivers wheeled around to pick up the marching 1st Battalion. Hacksaw went with 'Rusty' Cavanaugh's company to eliminate the garrison, while the executive officer, Major J. M. Cook, and Haugen led the rest of the battalion up stream to a narrow dam where they crossed the river to await developments.

Cavanaugh's troopers dropped their packs on the roadside and crouched into the town.

"One of our advanced scouts picked out a spot behind a hedge" recalled Cavanaugh, "and I could observe the enemy a few hundred yards away, quickly barricading the building and preparing for its defense."

The compound, enclosed by a four-foot-tall concrete wall, was an old Spanish barracks dating back to the 1800s.

Dog Company, famous for their 'Rat's Ass' banzai assault on Leyte, opted for stealth this time. With open ground between them and the occupied buildings, Cavanaugh organized a flanking attack. He led the assault platoon himself, swinging around to the left via a covered approach. The troopers gathered behind the compound's far wall a hundred feet from the main building. Simultaneously, Deane

Marks' machinegun crew crept forward to a position with a good view to cover them.

The clatter of machineguns initiated the attack; then rifles barked into action, sending bullets winging through windows and ricocheting off the stone exterior. That was the signal.

"We launched our attack by going over the top as a unit," said Cavanaugh, "and ran toward the building, firing at the windows and any open aperture we could see."

As they charged across the open courtyard, the Japanese in the barracks opened fire from floor-level rectangular windows and one-man foxholes dotted around the buildings. Lead scout, Arthur Chelbove, tumbled to the ground, dead, and several others staggered to the building, wounded by the hail of return gunfire.

"There was no cover," remembered a trooper.

An M8 now clanked forward, hurling 75mm shells into the compound, disintegrating the four smaller stone buildings. But the shells did little damage to the thick-walled barracks.

Sergeant Ed Sorensen's squad, sheltering on the far side of the building near a doorway, waited for the M8 to complete its bombardment. "When we reached the door," Sorensen later wrote, "I stood right next to it and waited for the ten rounds to be fired."

The 75mm shells failed to penetrate the walls, but their impact rattled the structure and kicked up plenty of dust. The troopers storming inside had a hard time seeing through the clouds of dust but found low windows, about two feet above the floor, on both sides of the barracks. John Bittorie threw himself into one, firing bursts from his Browning Automatic Rifle at tan-clad Japanese soldiers fleeing out the back of the compound. Sorensen continued, "I looked at the window to John's left and saw eight or ten Japanese falling like hay before a mowing machine. Our guns were shooting from every window. I'm certain that every one of the enemy on that side was killed."

They exited the barracks through a vehicle bay which contained sacks of rice, piles of equipment, and a 1939 US Army Dodge truck. With the building cleared and the courtyard foxholes eliminated, the shooting ceased.

What happened next has been lost in the confusion of combat. Whether due to the blinding dust inside the barracks—perhaps concealing a basement—or the fleeing Japanese circling back to reenter the barracks from the rear, the fight was not over. Regardless of how it unfolded, "a moment later, we again received heavy fire from the building," recalled Cavanaugh.

The troopers scrambled back over the compound wall. The M8 fired a few more shells at the barracks but soon gave up. The five-foot-thick walls withstood each blast. The Japanese, barricaded inside and manning the windows with rifles and automatic weapons, threw back multiple attempts to reenter the compound. Cavanaugh and Dog Company surrounded the compound for a siege as pot shots zipped back and forth.

Trooper Wilber Wilcox was angry, recalling, "If we had access to a flame-thrower ... we might have been able to save some of our soldiers' lives." The division had brought ashore more than fifty flame-throwers, but they were still sitting in Nasugbu.

"While I was trying to figure about what to do next," recalled Cavanaugh, "I was approached by a very angry representative of the regiment S-2 [intelligence section] who demanded to know why I hadn't secured 'the bridge.' I asked him, 'What bridge?' and that made him even madder."

Hacksaw had tasked him with securing the compound and he was unaware of the bridge just around the bend. He left a platoon in place to contain the Japanese and led the rest of his company to seize the crossing.

They arrived to find it already in the possession of Fox Company. While engaged in their firefight, Hacksaw had crossed over the dam and led Fox Company upstream to a position opposite the compound. While Fox's troopers took pot shots at any Japanese escaping the barracks (which probably sent them scurrying back to reoccupy it), combat engineers climbed under the bridge to gingerly deactivate two 550-pound aerial bombs rigged to blow the span.

Hacksaw, with Dog and Fox companies in tow, moved back to the dam to rejoin the rest of his battalion and resume their march on Bacoor. But they were gone.

A lingering messenger informed Hacksaw that his battalion departed twenty minutes ago under direct orders from Eichelberger and Swing. Eichelberger relished being close to the action. A non-smoker, he carried cigarettes to share with frontline troops, breaking the ice and opening the door for his considerable charm. Willing to share the risk, he frequently stated his orders as rhetorical questions. "Boys, I'm going forward. Are you with me?" They always were.

General Robert L. Eichelberger talks to a group of paratroopers on the road to Manila

Eichelberger recounted to his wife about getting Hacksaw's battalion on the move, writing, "Things were bogged down a bit, so we jazzed it up." Swing added some dash to the impromptu tactical conference when he landed in an L-bird on the highway. He joined Eichelberger in pressing the men forward. No doubt, any attempts by Hacksaw's executive officer, Major J. M. Cook, to question the change of orders in the absence of his commander were crushed under the combined weight of the generals' stars.

Swing's and Eichelberger's urgency remained palpable; they wanted to be the first into Manila. Critics might attribute their drive to seeking glory or wanting to impress MacArthur. More generous pundits would acknowledge they were aggressive combat leaders who understood that keeping the enemy off balance ultimately saved American lives. But was the race already over? Despite multiple requests from Eichelberger's staff, Krueger's Sixth Army was not reporting how close they were to the city's northern limits.

Eichelberger wrote to his wife, "The steady refusal of the Sixth Army to send me any information of our friendly troops indicates to me that they are not really in town .... If your palsy-walsy [Kruger] were in town I am sure he would be glad to tell me, so maybe he is still further away than I am."

Without confirmation to the contrary, the race was still on, and if Hacksaw wanted to regain control of his battalion, he would have to hustle to catch up.

Meanwhile, back at the barracks in Imus, twenty-three-year-old Sergeant Robert C. Steele decided to break the two-hour stalemate. If the enemy wouldn't willingly come out, he'd burn them out. Eyeing his four dead comrades sprawled in front of the walls, he slung his weapon over his shoulder and grabbed an axe and a jerrycan of fuel from one of the jeeps.

Steele's platoon opened fire as he sprinted into the compound with a leopard's grace. After he made it across the open courtyard, his men watched wide-eyed as he shimmied onto the barrack's roof. He hacked at the gable with the axe until he chopped through it. Then, twisting the cap off the jerrycan, he upended it, pouring five gallons of fuel into the building. Steele pulled the pin from a white phosphorus hand grenade and dropped it. The combination of white-hot phosphorus embers and ignited fuel set supplies and soldiers aflame. From his roost, Steele shot two Japanese trying to brave the inferno. The rest ran outside to escape the conflagration.

"As twenty to thirty Japs came scampering out the doors, we cut them to pieces," said Deane Marks, who manned one of the machineguns. Eight or nine attempted to flee via the old Dodge truck in the vehicle bay. They screeched out of the compound and onto the town's main road.

"They got halfway and ran into a Dog Company machinegun set up for just exactly that contingency," continued Marks. "All were killed."

THE ENTIRETY OF HAUGEN'S COMBAT TEAM was now on the march. The convoy, which included several captured Japanese trucks, picked up platoons of hiking 1st Battalion troopers to shuttle them forward a few miles before turning around to relay another group. Behind them, the 3rd Battalion made its way on foot. L-birds puttered overhead to report enemy sightings. Swing's intelligence officer, Major Henry Muller, sped up Route 17 in a jeep, handing out maps to officers in the strung-out columns of huffing troopers. The Shoestring Task Force brought charts only as far as Tagaytay, and Haugen was marching his men off the map. Muller's maps of Manila arrived just in time, having been delivered that morning by a P-51 pilot making a low-level pass to throw the bundle out as he buzzed the lodge.

Three miles north of Imus, Haugen's men streamed into the narrow, five-mile-wide spit of land forming the Hagonoy Isthmus, channeled between Manila Bay on the west and Laguna de Bay on the east. They'd seized the road junctions at Bacoor, and Haugen now rushed them up Route 1, paralleling the bay's shoreline as there were still bridges to seize. Haugen left his jeep to march with the squad on point. The division's assistant commander and Swing's chief of staff joined him. The high-ranking trio set the pace and spurred the men onward. Deane Marks, huffing up the same road, recalled seeing five Filipinos hung in a church yard. The locals said they were *makapilis*—traitors.

Hacksaw's Easy Company made it to Las Piñas by three thirty that afternoon; their arrival chased several Japanese over to the far side of the village's bridge. The troopers fired a volley and rushed the bridge. But heavy machinegun fire from a pillbox and a fortified schoolhouse on the opposite bank stopped them cold.

Hacksaw deployed another company to Easy's left, adding more firepower against the enemy-held school. A mortar crew managed only a single shell before they were decimated by a Japanese mortar round themselves. Hacksaw pulled Easy Company off the line, sending them upstream to circle around the flank. As the pincer attack moved in, cannoneers rolled up their two 75mm pack howitzers to join the fray. One trooper, bounding over a low wall to dodge a machinegun burst, found evidence the guerrillas were prowling the Japanese flanks. "On the other side were five dead Japs with no clothes, and they had been gutted," he recalled. "Their intestines were spread out all over the place."

Haugen, confident that Hacksaw had the Japanese at the bridge in hand, ordered Major Henry Burgess to push his 1st Battalion around to the east and keep moving up the coast. As Burgess passed Hacksaw's men, the school was engulfed in flames. Most of the defenders chose to burn to death. "The few who ran to fight another day were being cut down by the machinegunners," Burgess later recalled, "so the 1st Battalion did not stop and continued as fast as it could march."

Farther up the road, the point squad tramped into the suburb of Parañaque, six miles south of Manila's center. Burgess noted how quiet it was: no celebrating crowds, and not a single civilian on the street.

Brrrrpppppppt! Brrrrpppppppt! Brrrrpppppppt!

Bullets ricocheted off the pavement and chipped stone walls. The men went to ground under a hail of lead, a thousand feet short of the last bridge between them and Manila. A Japanese machinegun crew nestled in the bell tower of Saint Andrew's Cathedral had total command of the narrow street. From their four-story perch of brick and concrete, they swept anything that moved with their Nambu machinegun—known by US troops as a "wood-pecker" for its distinct clacking rate of fire.

In the descending darkness, the troopers maneuvered toward the cathedral in the textbook technique of fire and maneuver: those on the left side of the road, sheltering behind whatever cover they found, squeezed off shots at the arched openings of the belfry, while their comrades on the opposite side sprinted forward before the Nambu gunner traversed his gun. The process was then repeated with the left side bounding forward. In this manner, they leap-frogged closer with no one exposed for more than a few seconds. It was deliberate and effective, but it took time—there was no need to rush to one's death.

As Henry Burgess watched his troops' methodical advance, Swing's chief of staff, Colonel Irvin 'Schimmy' Schimmelpfennig, joined him. After observing the action for a few seconds, Schimmelpfennig grew impatient with the caution on display and urged Burgess to get his men moving. Burgess explained the time-consuming tactic to the artillery officer, but Schimmelpfennig remained adamant. They needed to seize the bridge.

Schimmelpfennig strode into the street toward the closest bunch of troopers—he would get them moving himself. He made it halfway to them when he fell, riddled by a burst from the belfry.

Burgess and a trooper dragged the chief of staff back into their protected doorway, but he was already dead. Burgess later remembered the thirty-three-year-old's tragic death as "sad and unnecessary."

Shortly thereafter, a squad made it close enough to the cathedral for a well-aimed rifle-launched grenade to explode in the tower. They then forced entry and, after a shootout, swarmed up the bell tower, killing three Japanese and taking two prisoners. The sullen POWs, with downcast shaved heads and torn tan shorts, were bound and handed off for interrogation.

At the river, Burgess and his entourage neared the bridge's mid-point when a torrent of bullets ripped overhead, sending them into a pile as they dove for cover. Laying there in the darkness, they watched the flickering glow of fires in Manila reflect off the river. They also spotted a series of Japanese pillboxes guarding the bridge on the far side. Burgess and Haugen agreed to wait for a daylight reconnaissance before trying to get the men across.

Stan Young, one of Burgess' mortarmen, recalled his arrival at Parañaque, "We were positioned in an alley several hundred feet south or west of the river. Our platoon leader advised us that we might receive Jap artillery fire and we could use our own judgment as to whether we wanted to dig in or not. Most of us attempted to dig in, but our foxhole in the rock and hard packed clay ended up at about two feet deep."

Haugen established his regimental command post in the cathedral, which was full of crated Japanese ammunition. Outside, paratroopers huddled in the courtyard to catch a few hours' sleep while sentries patrolled to protect their exhausted comrades.

"It was about 22:00," a trooper in the alley with Young recalled, "and a jeep came crawling along with blackout lights on. We had no instructions about vehicular traffic, and I figured it was some brass going up to our CP [command post] at the church."

He was correct. In fact, it was *the* brass: General Swing and his operations officer, Lieutenant Colonel Douglas 'Tangle Foot' Quandt, who were allegedly in search of details regarding how Schimmelpfennig had died. Instead of stopping, they kept going past the church and disappeared around the bend toward the bridge.

Young and the rest of the mortar platoon turned as a loud burst of machinegun fire reverberated from the bridge. A few minutes later, Swing and his driver emerged out of the darkness on foot, yelling at the gawkers for directions to Haugen's command post.

Trooper Howard G. Dunlop was there when Swing entered. "The next thing I heard was a loud, angry voice. I went over to where the commotion was. There was Colonel Haugen standing at ramrod attention. General Swing straight in front of him, face to face, chewing his ass. Oh, he chewed him up and down and back and forth. In essence, he was saying: 'Why did you allow my jeep to go through your position and right up to the front lines, and why wasn't my jeep stopped, didn't you know this was a US Army jeep?' He just chewed him up and down." Swing ended his tirade with the story of his jeep being shot out from under him, and Quandt remaining unaccounted for.

Haugen took the ass-chewing, then bellowed for Lieutenant Andrew B. Galligan. "Galligan, get a detail and go out there and rescue that man if he's alive, and bring back his body if he's dead."

Galligan grabbed Dunlop and a corporal for a stretcher party and led them up the narrow street toward the bridge. At the foot of the span, Galligan drew his pistol, ordered the men to stay put, and crawled to the jeep. Quandt was badly shaken, but alive. The pair snaked their way back with Galligan in the lead.

Stan Young, reflecting on Swing's "blunder," later commented, "I have always puzzled as to why *he* did not know where he was. We damn sure did not."

OMINOUSLY, SOME SIX MILES up the coast, Manila's port was ablaze. Iwabuchi's demolition of the docks and fuel storage had set bordering houses aflame. The glowing conflagration on the horizon was visible to Haugen's men. But the immediate issue was the firepower coming in at them from the far side of the river, confirming that the Japanese had mortars and howitzers supporting their pillboxes. Getting across the river appeared to be a deadly proposition.

Just before midnight, Lieutenant Colonel Lukas Hoska, commanding one of the division's glider artillery battalions, arrived at the cathedral with a proposed solution. With Swing's blessing, he grabbed a radio and crawled down to the riverbank with a spotting team. There, in Swing's favored method of expending steel instead of men, they patiently adjusted the fire of 75mm pack howitzers, blasting shell after shell into the far bank. Several of the rounds exploded across the river just thirty yards opposite Hoska's team. Shrapnel whizzed and clattered all around them.

Five hours and seven hundred rounds later, they claimed five of the pillboxes. It was a promising start, and Haugen ordered Hacksaw to cross the bridge at 05:00. That's when they discovered Hoska's efforts hadn't made a dent.

Chapter 10

The Genko Line

Parañaque Bridge, Manila.
05:00, Monday, February 5, 1945

The weak light of a hazy brown dawn revealed Haugen's paratroopers crouching past the wreck of Swing's bullet-riddled jeep. Japanese shells burst overhead as troopers hurried across the twenty-five-yard bridge in short sprints. In retaliation, the Angels' machineguns and mortars peppered the far bank. Meanwhile, the men hustling across stayed to their left to avoid a section of the span that had collapsed after Japanese sappers unsuccessfully tried to demolish the bridge. Once across, the troopers found the road blocked by dozens of ten-foot-long, thick wooden beams stacked and crisscrossed into an improvised barricade. Getting around the five-foot-tall obstacle required either scaling it or wiggling through the small gaps.

The attack was further channeled by terrain on the far side: Route 1 continued north up a quarter-mile-wide sliver of land sandwiched between Manila Bay on the left and a branch of the Parañaque River on the right. Haugen, with his front divided, sent Hacksaw's 2nd

A pre-war photograph of the bridge at Para-
ñaque; just above the dark cluster of trees is
the bell tower of Saint Andrew's Cathedral;
Manila is to the right

Battalion up the narrow strip while Major John Strong's 3rd Battalion hooked right, paralleling Hacksaw's attack from across the river.

While Hoska's howitzer sharp shooting had eliminated the closest enemy guns, Japanese artillery farther up the road subjected the crossing to heavy harassing fire. Many troopers, unwilling to risk an exposed dash over the bridge, waded through the chin-deep water instead.

A Japanese concrete pillbox to the right of the bridge fired long machinegun bursts at the shadows of scampering troopers. A squad flanked the position by crawling down the riverbank under the gun's field of fire. As they approached from behind, muffled explosions detonated inside. Facing encirclement, all nine Japanese occupants killed themselves with grenades.

The two battalions, rushing forward on such a narrow front, got mixed up in the graying dawn. Major Strong extricated his troopers, herding them across the Parañaque River's tidal flats and into flooded rice fields to occupy the right flank. At the same time, Hacksaw's men progressed into an eclectic suburb of wood, brick, stucco, and cinderblock houses along the main road, with large, luxurious houses facing the beach.

When the sun rose, it appeared as a pale orb behind the ashen pall of smoke blanketing the city. An American pilot flying overhead noted, "The spectacle was an appalling sight. The entire downtown section of the city was a mass of flames." He estimated the inferno's pyre rose two hundred feet.

By 08:30, Hacksaw's men were four hundred yards up the road when Japanese rifle and machinegun fire from pillboxes stopped them cold. A chain of pillboxes formed the spine of a series of elaborate roadblocks that included railroad ties and twelve-foot steel beams planted vertically into the road and laced with barbed-wire. Centerpieces included tractors, overturned trucks, and trolley cars in the middle of road inter-

A trooper watches Manila burn from Parañaque

sections. Oil drums filled with dirt or cement, ditches, and what seemed like miles of barbed wire obstructed the periphery. The entire area was littered with mines that were easy to spot due to the fresh dirt or broken concrete giving them away.

Machineguns barked back and forth while several rounds of air-bursting artillery sent troopers diving for cover. They suspected the Japanese were shooting at them with anti-aircraft guns leveled horizontally, but they could not spot the enemy.

Dead and wounded troopers lay where they fell. Lester Long threw himself down near a bleeding trooper. "There was a medic there, too—he was petrified. I said, 'You dumb sonuvabitch, can't you see this man is hurt?' The medic looked at me and then crawled over to the kid and lifted his helmet. The poor kid's head was gone."

The defenders in the pillboxes covered the streets and threw torrents of lead at anyone who moved. Many were constructed under huts raised on six-to-eight-foot stilts. Some of the positions had clearly been in place awhile. Covered with enough dirt that weeds had overgrown the exterior, they blended into the roadside vegetation. Bullets and bazookas merely ricocheted off their concrete hide.

Ed Sorensen watched a trooper armed with a bazooka slither forward through a ditch as bullets zinged around him. The trooper thrust the muzzle into a pillbox's firing port and pulled the trigger. *Click.* Nothing. "He had carried the bazooka all through Leyte and now to Manila," said Sorensen. "When it came time to use it, the fool thing failed him. He crawled all the way back, threw the bazooka on the ground, and actually crying, shot it full of holes."

A group of troopers attempting a left flank through an open field were sent to ground by a double-barreled 20mm anti-aircraft gun punching out rounds. They lay sweating in the muggy heat, contemplating how to crack the twelve pillboxes blocking their route.

A cry for "Medic!" propelled Jack McGrath forward from where he was hunkered down near a machinegun crew. He sprinted fifty yards to the casualty, Sergeant John D. Futch Jr., who lay in a pool of blood. McGrath tore open Futch's fatigues, revealing gaping wounds below his throat, solar plexus, and hip. "I knew Futch was dead." His pooling blood was already congealing on the broiling pavement, the sun's heat turning it brown. A nearby captain, mistaking Futch's death rattle for a sign of life, pleaded with McGrath to get him back across the bridge to the aid station.

McGrath, hoisting the corpse over his shoulders, later recalled, "I hadn't gone far, perhaps in front of the cathedral, when I could feel Futch's blood running down my back. Before I got to the corner, I felt it running down my legs, and as I continued on, I felt blood in my boots. Each step caused the blood to squeak and bubble."

The battalion surgeon confirmed McGrath's initial suspicion. On his way back to the front, McGrath clambered under the bridge. "I stripped down and tried to wash my clothes and myself," he said. "I was partially successful. War is a bloody business."

While 81mm mortars hurled rounds to harass the pillboxes, Hard Rock radioed for the armored M8 self-propelled howitzers to come forward. But they couldn't: engineers were still shoring up the damaged bridge to support their tonnage and figuring out how to deactivate the landmines. Haugen then requested an L-bird scout farther up the road to locate the concealed anti-aircraft guns. "Impracticable," Swing responded. There was too much enemy fire to risk it. They were on their own for now.

Further delays occurred when the engineers discovered that many of the landmines were really five-hundred-pound aerial bombs twenty-four inches in diameter and six feet long—placed vertically into the ground, their nose fuses replaced with low-pressure detonators. Deactivating such monsters took too much time, and blowing them in place was out of the question. Further exploration uncovered an array of standard antipersonnel and antitank mines, along with antisubmarine depth charges, artillery shells, mortar shells, and hundred-pound aerial bombs, all rigged with pressure caps. Engineers found one stretch of road peppered with buried mines every nine feet. Word spread fast, and troopers kept one eye on the ground to avoid stepping on boards, rocks, or anything that might hide a detonator.

Haugen ordered the engineers to either find a bypass or escort the M8s around the mines. He needed firepower up front, now.

Deane Marks and Bill Porteous, keen observers of the battle, were lying behind their machinegun as the first M8 clanked up the road. It paused to hurl a few 75mm shells at a pillbox, which undoubtedly rung the occupants' bells and kicked up a lot of dust but made no visible dent. The M8 then rolled through an intersection and into the sites of a Japanese 20mm. Rounds ripped down the street, and the M8 driver threw his machine intro reverse, wildly careening thirty feet backwards.

VAROOOOOOOOOOOOM!

"The sky turned black, and a concussion drove into my eyes, ears, and nose," recalled Marks. "In the blackness, for a split second,

I saw the tank upside down as high as the telephone wires. Then, a split second of dead silence. Debris started landing, mostly dirt, asphalt, and equipment from the tank. When the dust cleared, there it was, all sixteen tons, laying on its back.... One of the tank crew, possibly its commander, was inside the turret as the tank came down. As he hit the road, the tank followed. The tank severed him in half at the belt line."

None of the crew survived.

The smoldering crater was twelve feet deep and thirty feet wide. Marks' squad took a headcount, confirming two wounded. A trooper staggered back, stunned by the concussion and lacerated by shrapnel. His chest was bleeding; Marks noticed that he had *SWEET* tattooed under one nipple and *SOUR* under the other.

It became a standoff: bazookas and 75mm bounced off the pillboxes and the constant airbursts made maneuvering against them suicide. Intuition and map study led Haugen to believe the troublesome enemy guns were two miles up the coast, firing from the once-manicured grounds of Manila's Polo Club. Since he couldn't hit them with his pack howitzers, Haugen requested air support. But MacArthur's headquarters cancelled all airstrikes in Manila due to collateral damage and climbing civilian casualties.

Eichelberger and Swing personally appealed to get the restriction lifted in the Angels' sector, which, while still an urban suburb, was less populated. Haugen, awaiting the outcome, halted the attack and organized a defense in the assumption Swing would pull the right strings.

Troopers dug into yards, gardens, and fields, or set up in the rubble of houses. The wounded hobbled or were carried to the cathedral's aid station. The dead were wrapped in their ponchos. In at least one case, a shrouded body was slung onto a bamboo pole by his boot laces, equipment belt, and a rifle sling, hefted over two men's shoulders, and portaged to the rear. The litter parties returned with mortar shells and medical supplies for the frontline.

On the right flank, Strong's 3rd Battalion faced comparable trouble, with forward units pinned down along a dike. The paratroopers sought shelter at the base of the berm, wallowing in waist deep water and mud while multiple Japanese machineguns hammered away at any fleeting target.

Late that afternoon, Eichelberger and Swing received approval for their airstrikes. Red smoke grenades and signal panels were rushed up to designate friendly positions while mortars dropped white smoke rounds onto desired targets.

Deane Marks and his machinegun crew, now sheltering under an orange tractor, watched the first pass of Douglas A-20 Havocs scream into their low-level runs from over the bay. The twin-engined bombers jettisoned a string of para-frags: one-hundred-pound bombs with small parachutes that ensured they fell nose-first and slowed their descent so the aircraft could escape the blast radius. The detonations knocked out two pillboxes.

The second flight came in from the same direction but much closer, and Marks gawked wide-eyed as the bombs were released on their side of the red smoke. The detonations rattled the troopers, but no one was hurt. Not wanting to press their luck, the men pulled back.

Strong's advance on the right flank escaped a similar peril when several of the A-20s winged over into a strafing run against the paratroopers. It was another close call, with no injuries. Wondering how it happened, First Lieutenant Randolph Kirkland stood up to dust himself off. "It was only then I noticed that some shithead way back down our line had popped a red smoke grenade signaling the front line of our troops."

By sunset, Haugen's troopers had dug in to avoid the flying shrapnel from the nonstop artillery. Meanwhile, rivalries were stirred up when

Krueger's 1st Cavalry Division dismissed Eichelberger and Swing's report of their toehold in the capital. The Cav claimed they beat them by six hours. Swing later argued in his own favor, but US-issued maps showed that the Angels, while certainly in the suburbs, were still four miles south of the pre-war city limits. It was a slight Swing would remember.

Visiting Swing's headquarters in the cathedral, Eichelberger could see the capital's devastation unfolding in real time. He wrote to his wife, "The view of Manila last night was a terrible thing as the whole part of the one side of the city seemed to be on fire. Smoke and flames were going way up in the air.... What a shame it is.... It was something which I shall never forget."

On the other hand, Eichelberger's commander, The Big Chief, was oblivious to the carnage. MacArthur, from his headquarters sixty miles north of the city, was preparing for his triumphant return. As the belligerents tore the city apart—while trying to tear each other to pieces—MacArthur was planning a parade. Literally. Senior field commanders were expected to radio the names of attending officers so jeep assignments for the procession could be finalized.

It was one of the war's most striking examples of aloof leadership. MacArthur, renowned for charging bearers of inconvenient truths with disloyalty, had cowed his staff to the point none of them were willing to inform him that the capital was burning to the ground, the streets were littered with rubble and bodies, and the Japanese still held most of it. Indeed, Eichelberger's and Krueger's legions were still more than seven miles apart, with the hardest urban fighting still ahead of them.

At 06:30 on the same morning that Eichelberger wrote to his wife lamenting the flames crackling in Manila, MacArthur released a press statement announcing the capital's liberation. He said in part, "The fall of Manila was the end of one great phase of the Pacific struggle and set the stage for another ... [with] the Philippines liberated, and the ultimate redemption of the East Indies and Malaya thereby made a certainty, our motto becomes 'On to Tokyo!'"

It wasn't MacArthur's first manipulation of the press, but stateside news services rushed to echo the fantasy. "Manila Falls" read the *New York Times* headline. "Manila fell to MacArthur like a ripened plum," gushed *Newsweek*. *TIME* magazine declared, "Victory!" stating that "with MacArthur's recapture of Manila, the US passed a great milestone in World War II," and hailed the successful campaign as "a high-water mark in the inexorable rising tide of the American war effort."

Sadly, none of it was true.

Perhaps if MacArthur spent the previous night in a foxhole with Deane Marks and his machinegun crew, he would have thought twice before announcing his "victorious" conquest. Marks' night had been interrupted by "hand grenades and rifle shots and lots of hollering." Marks chucked all his hand grenades toward the commotion while next to him, Bill Porteous squeezed off several machinegun bursts.

"There was all kinds of shooting," Marks recalled. "People, barely visible, were running in every direction. Then, just as quickly as it started, all was quiet." They spent the rest of the night peering into the dark with no outlet for the adrenaline coursing through them. To a man, their fingers hovered over their triggers.

"When dawn finally came, the nightmare unfolded."

Three Japanese corpses were slumped on the road. Private Jack L. Hauser was dead, and Roy Byers in shock, his right arm nearly cleaved off by a samurai sword. His attacker lay in a heap—five close-range shots from Byer's M1 Garand rifle almost blew him in half. Bill Fairly was alive but shaken. He woke with a Japanese officer poised to strike with his sword. Just as Fairly slammed his helmet into the man's face, someone else shot the officer in the head, splattering Fairly with brain matter.

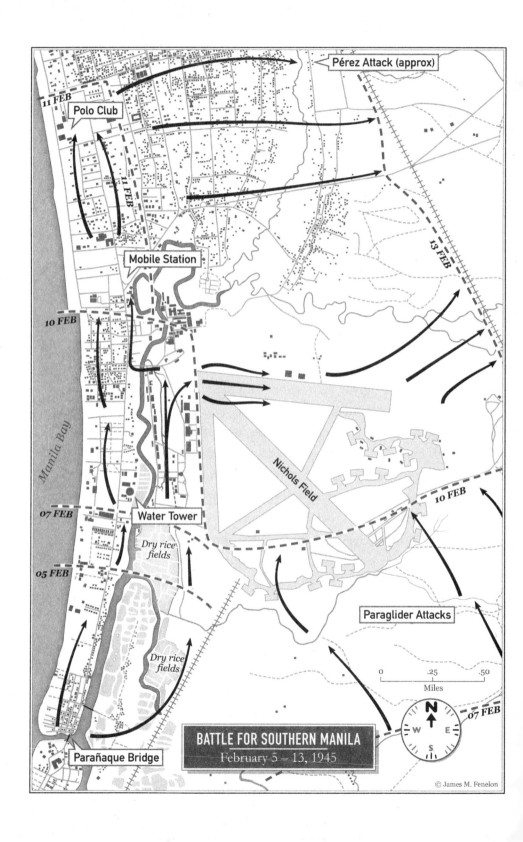

Pérez Attack (approx)

11 FEB

Polo Club

11 FEB

Mobile Station

13 FEB

10 FEB

Manila Bay

Nichols Field

10 FEB

07 FEB

05 FEB

Dry rice
fields

Water Tower

Paraglider Attacks

Dry rice
fields

0   .25   .50
Miles

N
W   E
S

07 FEB

Parañaque Bridge

BATTLE FOR SOUTHERN MANILA
February 5 – 13, 1945

© James M. Fenelon

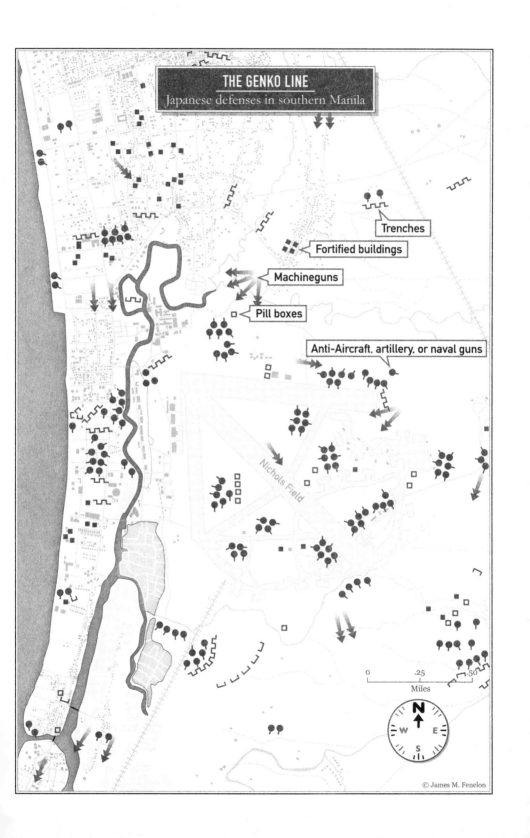

THE GENKO LINE
Japanese defenses in southern Manila

Trenches

Fortified buildings

Machineguns

Pill boxes

Anti-Aircraft, artillery, or naval guns

Nichols Field

0   .25   .50
Miles

N
W   E
S

© James M. Fenelon

Dawn also revealed a better picture of what the Angels were up against, and in light of it, Swing paused Haugen's advance. Combining reports on the ground with POW interrogations and observations from L-birds, it was clear the Japanese had constructed a formidable defense.

Most importantly, a captured Japanese map, translated by Haugen's Nisei intelligence team, disclosed the extent of what the enemy called their Genko Line. Named in honor of a thirteenth-century defensive system protecting Japan from the Mongols, the Genko Line was a fortified belt approximately two and a half miles deep, starting at the bay's shoreline and running east five-odd miles to the high ground at Laguna de Bay. Iwabuchi's troops manned over a hundred and fifty light, medium, and heavy-caliber anti-aircraft guns, bolstered by dozens of dug-in howitzers encircled by trenches. Open fields and road intersections were covered by hundreds of pillboxes positioned for mutual support—occupants of one having visibility to shoot anyone approaching the adjacent strongholds. The map also confirmed the obvious: the positions had been placed with little thought of withdrawal. Intelligence indicated that upwards of four thousand troops held the line.

The heaviest concentration of guns was at Nichols Field, a pre-war US Army airbase built in 1919, now under Imperial occupation. While air raids had cratered the runways and littered the fields with charred Japanese aircraft, it bristled with clusters of anti-aircraft batteries, bunkers, and pillboxes. The thought of traversing the wide expanse of the airfield's open, flat terrain was sobering for any infantryman contemplating an assault.

Swing and Eichelberger were on the threshold of Iwabuchi's southern defenses, and as one trooper lamented, "From now on, our advance was not measured in miles, it was measured in yards."

Swing ordered 'Shorty' Soule's paraglider regiment, still reinforced with a third battalion, to tackle the airfield from the south. While waiting for them to arrive from Tagaytay, Haugen's men held their positions and cleared their sectors. Pillboxes were the primary thorn. Troopers threaded their way around barbed wire entanglements to burn out the occupants, ideally with one of the few flamethrowers that were brought up from the beach, but more often with white phosphorus hand grenades tossed in through air vents or rear entries. Deane Marks recalled, "After the phosphorus and regular anti-personnel grenades were tossed, we would pop in for survivors and swords. I never did see any survivors. All bodies were in grotesque positions, still smoldering."

'Rusty' Cavanaugh's Dog Company was in the thick of it, earning praise from Haugen after destroying seven pillboxes and a machinegun nest. Using rifles, machineguns, grenades, and all the courage they could muster, they did it without losing a man. Their courage held, but their luck didn't. The next line of pillboxes came at the loss of fourteen wounded and three dead.

Tackling a pillbox took patience and great nerve. Leroy Butler used fear to find his courage. Of fear, he said, "To say it is a 'gut feeling' is almost a cliché. It starts there, and like adrenaline, it permeates your body and activates all nerve endings. It cleanses your mind. You become more capable of making snap and accurate decisions. The training may have dulled from fatigue, but fear—the magnificent 'upper'—clears the cobwebs and gets you back to the basics of soldiering."

A Japanese guard, standing in front of a steel pillbox, photographed in Manila a week before the American invasion

Hacksaw and Haugen organized what they called termite patrols, responsible for searching hard-won houses and bypassed buildings for pockets of hiding Japanese soldiers. The patrols, often conducted by guerrillas, required gritty dedication to ferret out zealots barricaded inside houses or hiding in the rafters of huts.

ON THE MORNING OF WEDNESDAY, February 7, Soule's paragliders launched a two-pronged attack against Nichols Field from the south. The left flank gained five hundred yards before withering anti-aircraft fire forced them back to the creek bed from where they started. The right flank fared little better. Moving up along the base of a raised railroad track, they knocked out several positions with flame-throwers but fell back under a hail of shells fired from five- and eight-inch naval guns.

Iwabuchi's troops had salvaged guns from ships sunk in Manila Bay, hauled them ashore, and positioned them to defend Nichols. The volume of incoming fire from the naval guns was so heavy and so maddening that 'Shorty' Soule sent a runner back to the division command post, advising Swing "to radio [Admiral] Nimitz and tell him the 11th Airborne has found the navy everyone is wondering about—it's on Nichols Field!"

To the west, Strong and his 3rd Battalion pushed past the rice paddies and made it to dry land near Nichols' southwest corner, where they dug into a road embankment. After a few rifle shots kicked up dirt along the top of the berm, Staff Sergeant 'Big Ed' Hogan called out to no one in particular, "See if you can spot him!"

One of the Filipino guerrillas volunteered, "I will get him!" and stood to peek over the berm. A bullet cracked and was followed by the distinct sound of a helmet liner hitting the ground.

"I turned around and saw that it belonged to one of the two Filipino guerrillas that were attached to our platoon," Hogan said. "He had been shot in the head and died instantly." Hogan didn't know the guerrilla's name, just that he was sixteen years old.

That afternoon, Swing and Eichelberger visited Haugen's command post to coordinate the next morning's push. Studying the open terrain, the two generals realized that while tanks and heavy artillery would make quick work of the fortified positions, they would have to make do with their "pop-guns," Eichelberger's term for Swing's pack howitzers. As the generals discussed the plan with Haugen, shells scudded overhead. Two of Haugen's staff officers were killed the day before, and he suspected the accuracy was due to a Japanese observation party spying from atop a distant concrete water tower. Machine-gunners sprayed it, riflemen sniped at it, and a howitzer took a couple of pot shots at it. All failed to dislodge the stubborn spotters, who continued calling in accurate fire—this time killing three engineers who were deactivating mines in the perimeter.

Fortunately, the enemy failed to capitalize on their accuracy. For reasons that flummoxed the Americans, the Japanese fired single shots rather than concentrated barrages, which would have been devastating.

Trying to find the enemy guns, Haugen put spotters up in the Saint Andrew's belfry to pinpoint muzzle flashes for retaliatory airstrikes and artillery. Thick smoke drifting in from fires in the city obscured the battlefield and hampered their efforts. The smoke was so thick in some areas that air strikes were cancelled due to poor visibility.

The next morning at 08:10, Swing again visited the front. What he found upset him. Instead of the full attack rolling forward, Haugen had sent out patrols at 06:45 and was awaiting their reports. Most troopers were still eating their breakfast rations and shaving.

First Lieutenant Kirkland was heating up his coffee over a small cook stove. "It was about ready when who should come along but General Swing. He kicked my coffee over, demanding that everyone be up and at them.... We were out and over the access road within minutes."

A trooper out in front of Kirkland recalled the attack up Nichols Field's west flank. "My squad was halfway in the field near the edge of the paved strip when all hell broke loose, with bullets flying all around me," he said. "I thought at first it was a prepared ambush of machinegun and mortar fire from the sound of the firing, but I was wrong in my guess. It turned out to be 20mm anti-aircraft guns, made in the USA, but captured by the Japs."

'Big Ed' Hogan, scurrying across the same bomb-pocked field, had his rifle shot out of his hands while surveying the scene from behind a burned-out Japanese fighter plane. His platoon leader lay dead, and the attack stalled under overwhelming firepower. Japanese gunners fired yellow smoke rounds as markers, which gave troopers a warning before the next two or three rounds crashed in. Troopers lay still, baking under the hot sun for hours, afraid to move for fear of drawing fire. The lucky tumbled into shell craters as digging into the hardpacked ground was impossible. "This was a tough day for us.... For the most part, it was running from one bomb crater to another for cover," Hogan said.

Deane Marks, now suffering from the bone-aching symptoms of dengue fever, dove into the closest shell hole to find it occupied by his commanding officer and several other troopers. The lieutenant told Marks to move on—there were already too many men in the crater.

"I just looked at him and laid my carbine over my knees with the muzzle pointed right at his belly," Marks recounted. "I didn't say a word, just put my hand on the carbine and said, 'There's artillery out there, sir.' That was the end of it."

One of Marks' machinegun crew, a replacement who joined them after Leyte, was out of ammo. "He thought he was a one-man army," recalled Marks. He shot blindly into trees, doorways, or bunkers—anywhere he thought the enemy might be hiding. Marks added, "He would unload a couple of clips from his M1 into obviously dead Japs."

The trigger-happy newbie asked for more ammo. "We told the asshole, 'Club 'em to death.'" The crew let him sweat, but then, realizing an unarmed man was a liability to their own safety, they threw him a few eight-round clips, beseeching him, "No shooting until you see the whites of their eyes." "He never learned," sighed Marks.

Twelve Marine Douglas SBD dive bombers circled overhead before peeling out of formation for a timely attack. The aircraft—designated SBDs for "Scout Bomber, Douglas," and nicknamed "Slow But Deadly"—used the dive brakes mounted on the trailing edge of their wings to reduce speed in a dive and increase accuracy. They buzzed over the airfield in their graceful parabolas, the sun glinting off their canopies as anti-aircraft shells exploded amongst them. Troopers watched the SBDs' high explosive payloads rip into the Japanese positions.

"What is difficult to describe, and almost impossible to understand, was the complete silence coming from the Jap artillery and ack-ack positions," recalled a trooper. "There was not even the ever-present small arms fire. The SBD bombers must have devastated the area, as well as crushing the morale of the Jap soldiers."

It gave the men the break they needed to withdraw.

Despite the setbacks, Strong's 3rd Battalion occupied the west edge of the airfield, driving the first wedge into the Genko Line, but like every other gain, it came with a price.

By the end of the day, Hacksaw's 2nd Battalion, which had led the brunt of the fighting thus far, was down to less than two hundred men—they'd jumped into Tagaytay with five hundred and two troopers. The headcount of Strong's 3rd Battalion was barely three hundred. Hotel Company alone had one officer left and barely enough riflemen to fill the ranks of two understrength platoons. Across the board, Haugen's regiment was down by six hundred troopers.

Haugen needed more men. He radioed Swing's headquarters, calling for troopers injured in the parachute drop to be sent forward. Sprained ankle or not, if a man could pull a trigger, he was needed. But still, the wounded flowed back to the Parañaque aid station in Saint Andrew's Cathedral. From Parañaque, patients were driven the fifty-four miles back to Nasugbu where the division field hospital was established in the town's school. All along the evacuation chain, troopers were aided by both the Filipino volunteers ranging the battlefield to carry the wounded as well as local nurses toiling beside surgeons in dimly lit field hospitals.

One of the more critical patients was Jerry Davis, who wrestled with diarrhea until being shot in the head not long after crossing the Parañaque bridge. His helmet offered little protection from the bullet that cracked his skull and left him paralyzed. Fortunately, the surgeons at Nasugbu operated quickly, relieving the pressure and giving him back some movement. Davis would have a complete recovery, but for him, the war was over.

Not far behind him was Lieutenant Miles Gale, who had been with the regiment since day one. A Japanese anti-aircraft round shredded his left shoulder, and he was fortunate not to lose his arm. After surgery, Gale learned that his former Fort Polk roommate, Lieutenant Edward Stoeckly, was killed in the same battle at Nichols Field.

"We had a good friendship, and Ed had one ambition," lamented Gale, "which was to get this war over soon so he could get home to his hardware business in Indiana."

To speed access to life-saving surgeons, Swing's 221st Airborne Medical Company and members of the 7th Portable Surgical Hospital opened a facility at Las Piñas, where critical patients were stabilized before the trip to Nasugbu. Soon after that, engineers completed construction of an airfield near Imus. Patients requiring urgent care were flown to facilities on New Guinea or Leyte, and by mid-February, more than 640 patients were evacuated by air.

Cargo trucks stuffed with supplies headed against the flow of casualties. The division's lifeline wound upward from the coast like a centipede. "We had a supply line fifty-four miles long and fifty to two hundred yards wide," said Major John Conable, Swing's quartermaster. Conable kept twenty-five olive-drab cargo trucks constantly on the move. The demanding schedule made routine maintenance difficult, and the gravel road between Nasugbu and Tagaytay regularly chewed up tires.

Unsurprisingly, Swing's quartermasters were again shorthanded, making nineteen-hour days routine. "At each end of the run, we would check each driver to be sure he was alert enough to make another trip," recalled Conable. "There was a place at each end for the sleepy drivers to catch a little sleep." To give the drivers well-earned breaks, members of the division band got behind the wheel. Because no one could be spared to ride shotgun, drivers often steered with their left hand on the wheel while their right rested on a carbine pointed out the window. They braved snipers and floored it through several ambushes, losing just one truck.

Swing seemed to be omnipresent, orchestrating his division's momentum and pushing the limits of effective control. Often, while puttering overhead in an L-bird, he directed the pilot to land on the highway so he could see for himself what was happening on the ground.

Eichelberger's staff arranged for C-47 cargo drops atop Tagaytay ridge, where the Taal Lodge served as a supply depot. The airdrops shortened Swing's supply line; on one day alone, C-47s dropped fifty-four tons of vital supplies.

The most pressing need at the front was artillery ammunition. A week into the campaign, Eichelberger and Swing requested six thousand more shells. A paltry 470 arrived by air but would have to suffice until the rest were delivered by ship at Nasugbu. Nineteen thousand additional rounds were being prepared for a follow-on shipment.

The "just in time" supply situation meant any delays rippled into the forward units' ability to wage war. Colonel Harry D. Hildebrand had the unglamorous but vital responsibility of protecting the division lifeline from bypassed Japanese units. He had a battalion of paraglider infantry and artillery support from the 457th Parachute Field Artillery to guard the supply line. The 331 cannoneers of the 457th dropped onto Tagaytay with ten howitzers the day after Haugen's regiment and provided artillery support from their positions around the lodge. The true saviors of the supply line, however, were the guerrillas, some two thousand in number, coordinated by Major Vanderpool. They guarded bridges, manned outposts, and patrolled Route 17 to keep Japanese ambushes and saboteurs at bay. Henry 'Butch' Muller, Swing's intelligence officer, later recounted, "The major and his coalition of guerrilla units became a major asset to our division throughout the Luzon campaign, with the provision of intelligence, harassment of small enemy units, and defense of our extended supply lines."

The supplies, having snaked up from Nasugbu, were stockpiled at Parañaque, from where they were either shuttled forward by jeeps or hand-carried by troopers. Flat tires were a problem; one jeep alone lost six tires in a single day from running over shrapnel. Getting supplies to Strong's 3rd Battalion required crossing the Parañaque River in rubber rafts, then slogging through ankle-deep rice paddies for a thousand yards while dodging enemy mortar fire. Wounded supply personnel were replaced by the battalion's kitchen staff.

ON FEBRUARY 9, Haugen's paratroopers resumed punching their way up the coast block by block, moving into more densely populated neighborhoods. One- and two-story tin-roofed apartments lined both sides of the streets, shops were flush with the road, and along the bay were mansions surrounded by stone walls, protecting garages and swimming pools.

Haugen pushed his battalion commanders to use the fire from their pack howitzers like battering rams. Even if the 75mm shells couldn't penetrate the pillboxes, the jarring concussions rattled defenders' nerves and shattered their resolve. In one case, Haugen ordered four hundred rounds into a single target; in another, he directed a ten-minute barrage of 360 rounds with a shell exploding on target every two seconds.

"We must have plenty of fire, as much as possible," he demanded over the radio. Haugen sacked an artillery spotter who fussed over pinpoint accuracy at the expense of magnitude. Haugen wanted to smash forward, block by block, shell by shell. He radioed Hacksaw, "You can have up to 1,500 rounds of fire between now and dark. Use this fire and give the position hell."

Corporal Richard A. 'The Rat' Laws, a mortarman, and his assistant gunner, Willard J. 'Wink' Lamb, did their best to meet the spirit of Haugen's mandate. Laws, nicknamed 'The Rat' for his fondness of replying, "Rat's ass" to almost every request made of him, was a former bakery salesman from Detroit, Michigan. Now, he and Wink—who had pierced his left ear back in the States—were responsible for the 3rd Battalion's last 81mm mortar. Four had parachuted into Tagaytay. "We were now down to one—mine! The other three had been abandoned as their crews were lost," wrote Laws. Both of his officers were gone as well, one wounded and one dead, leaving Laws in charge. "When we jumped, I was eighth in command in the mortar platoon, and now I'm the leader."

As two rifle companies bounded into the attack, Laws' mortar was on standby. When Japanese machineguns stymied their advance,

Laws and Lamb went into action. After each round crashed to earth, Laws received adjustments over a field telephone.

The concussion of each round soaring out of the tube dug the baseplate deeper into the mud. After several shots, Laws paused firing while he and Lamb shoveled the mortar's bipod level with the base. If they didn't adjust it, the lower base elevated the tube, which made rounds fall short of the target.

'Wink' and 'The Rat' maintained a steady rate of fire for hours. While Laws sighted and kept the mortar level, Lamb dropped rounds down the tube. Filipino ammo bearers kept them supplied with shells. The pair used high-explosive rounds with delayed action fuses, allowing the shells to penetrate the roof of a building or pillbox before exploding inside. The results were devastating.

Finally, with the call, "No more targets," the two slumped to the ground, exhausted. All told, they fired nearly two hundred and fifty rounds.

"We knocked out twenty-three pillboxes and a hundred and eighteen Japs, Wink and I," said Laws.

They were later hailed by a rifleman shouting, "You saved our ass today!" Their deft skills helped the battalion worm deeper into the Genko Line and occupy the northwest corner of Nichols Field.

To Haugen's east, Soule's paragliders, with the aid of multiple artillery barrages of their own, chipped their way forward like an icepick. They took out a cluster of six anti-aircraft guns with an airstrike and captured two of the five-inch naval guns; their own cannoneers then turned the weapons against the enemy. The Japanese counterattacked. Three hundred men charged across open ground into a downpour of artillery shells that eviscerated them.

THE FOLLOWING MORNING, on Saturday, February 10, Soule launched his next attempt to take Nichols Field. Against withering flat trajectory anti-aircraft fire, Soule's men improved their toehold only slightly. The gains came with heavy casualties, including one of Soule's battalion commanders, who was cut down by a Japanese machinegun on just his second day in command. One notorious enemy gunner killed several troopers from eight hundred yards away. Despite multiple airstrikes, the chain of Japanese defenses repelled all the attacks.

The same was true to the west, where Haugen's paratroopers were held up in the urban labyrinth. The primary thorn was a Japanese heavy machinegun barricaded in a fortified Mobile Oil gas station. Occupying the center of a Y-intersection, the station provided the gunners with a perfect field of fire covering the road up which Haugen's men were advancing. The gas station's familiar red Pegasus logo was an incongruous sight to troopers ducking through Manila's rubble.

With the no-man's-land of the fire-swept street as a boundary, troopers worked their way forward house by house. George Company was on the right side of the road with a company from the 2nd Battalion on the left. They alternated attacks with the lead company, shooting across the street and hitting an enemy-held house with flanking fire while the other attacked it. That worked until they ran out of houses.

George Company's last house on the right side provided cover but was too far away from the Mobile station to take it out. Across the street, a narrow alley bordered by an eight-foot cement block wall could provide protection from the enemy machinegunners. Between the wall and the Y-intersection was an overgrown field where the weeds appeared tall enough to conceal one or two men crawling into hand grenade range.

Each time a man poked his head around the corner for a glance, bullets kicked up the pavement and sent him sprawling backwards. Captain Pat Wheeler, the George Company commander, was hit and killed while rushing across the road. Two more men, trying to drag his body back to cover, were also gunned down.

Next up, First Lieutenant Randolph Kirkland backed up twenty feet to get a running start. As Kirkland recounted, "When I reached the street, I was at Mach 0.3 and accelerating." Bullets pinged and whined, chipping the asphalt as he sprinted across the road, leapt over the three corpses, and made it to the protection of the far wall. "They couldn't traverse that gun fast enough to track me," he continued.

The wall ran the width of the block, stretching from George Company's street to the next road farther west. Predictably, the Japanese had another machinegun on that side, too.

Kirkland conferred with an officer and several troopers who'd come up from the left side and were sheltering behind the wall. To determine their chances of getting around either side, they extended a helmet on the end of a rifle. Each time they tried it, the helmet drew an immediate burst of fire. With the exits too well covered and without demolitions to breech the wall, they decided to sit out the stalemate until sunset. Recovering the three bodies lying in the street would have to wait. It wouldn't be until the next day that word reached 'Big Tom' Mesereau that Wheeler, his fellow officer, friend, and classmate, was dead.

Meanwhile, Krueger's divisions pressed in from the north. Their increasing proximity gave the Angels the benefit of heavy artillery support, which pummeled Nichols Field with sixteen salvos of 155mm and eight inch howitzer concentrations. The Japanese defenders felt the earth shake under the weight of the bigger shells and understood they were now up against more than Swing's pop-guns, which never seemed to run out of ammo. Living under almost constant artillery fire is a soul-draining experience of helplessness. There is nothing to do but take it and pray.

With the northern phalanx inching closer, MacArthur transferred control of the 11th Airborne from Eichelberger to Krueger. The reassignment facilitated tightening the noose around Manila. While the logistics of determining who was where got ironed out, and Krueger finalized his assault plan, he ordered Swing to pause his attacks. The Angels spent the time consolidating their perimeter: the paratroopers cleared their sector of holdouts and tied their lines together with the paragliders on Nichols Field's southwest corner, forming a net around the contested airfield.

Iwabuchi's troops, even with multiple flanks on the brink of collapse, held their pledge, remaining steadfast in their defense. Of their adversary's resolution, a trooper wrote, "The Japs defended Nichols Field as if the Emperor's palace itself were sitting on the center runway." Some of their resolution was fueled by devotion to the Emperor, and some of it by lies ranging from the unlikely to the absurd.

Radio Tokyo assured those defending Manila that their brothers were mopping-up what remained of the decimated 11th Airborne Division. At the same time, Yamashita's headquarters bolstered morale by issuing a communiqué proclaiming that "US and British troops in Western Europe surrendered unconditionally." To give his Luzon garrison a further boost, Yamashita declared, "Our air units sank 150 ships in Lingayen Bay." That his men in the field had gone weeks without seeing a single Japanese aircraft in the sky went unremarked.

The Americans took advantage of the wild propaganda to sow confusion and doubt in Yamashita's ranks. They dropped a million surrender leaflets across Luzon, exposing the lies with contrasting facts and pointing out the horrible Japanese supply situation. Some of the leaflets called into question Japanese leaders' samurai honor for failing to take responsibility for their obvious failures.

Those on the ground hardly noticed such efforts, however. The 11th Airborne had taken fourteen POWs, but prisoners were still hard to come by, even when the troopers were in the mood to take them. One patrol tried, but the man stabbed himself through the neck with his bayonet rather than face capture. Henry Burgess' men accounted for three of the prisoners, but admitted they were only taken alive "because of confusion of identity with Filipinos."

THREE GUERRILLAS ranging beyond Haugen's lines at dawn on Sunday, February 11, reported the Japanese had seemingly abandoned their positions during the night. Feeler patrols from the 3rd Battalion picked their way forward three hundred yards past the abandoned Mobile Oil station without firing a shot. With the Americans converging from both the south and the north, the defenders fled east to bolster defensive positions there.

First Lieutenant Randolph Kirkland was with the patrols. "We passed a Japanese warehouse that was being merrily looted by locals." They focused on stockpiles of rice and other foodstuff, while Kirkland got his hands on a case of *shōchū*, a distilled alcohol. A quick swig reminded him of rum, so the patrol stuffed as many bottles as they could into their backpacks. Kirkland later poured his liberated liquor into several Japanese canteens for safer transport. He enjoyed spiking his morning coffee for the rest of the campaign.

The patrols also found a deserted hospital. All the occupants—wounded Japanese soldiers—had been executed by their withdrawing comrades. The troopers found one of the dead men in a closet, where he'd apparently tried to hide.

Haugen worried briefly about the looters, radioing Swing "to send some MPs [military police] or someone to stop it. We can't." They were too busy moving north, and by noon, they had covered the 1,500 yards to Manila's Polo Club on Libertad Avenue, which served as the

Angels' limit of advance. With Krueger's forces descending into the center of town, the avenue became a sector boundary to reduce fratricide.

The Polo Club was in a shambles. The grounds were upturned by multiple barrages and airstrikes seeking out the dug-in Japanese guns. Two detonated caches of Japanese ammunition and stores of burning fuel sent black smoke roiling over an already hellish landscape. The site must have been sobering for Swing and Haugen, both avid polo players. The club, even in its sad state, was a reminder of the capital's reputation as the "Pearl of the Orient."

Bordering the club was Dewey Boulevard, where couples once strolled to bask in the postcard-perfect sunsets on Manila Bay. The wide promenade was now pitted by countless artillery shells and marred by an improvised Japanese airfield. Manila's majestic neoclassic government buildings, such as the Central Post Office, the Legislature, and the Treasury, formerly rivaling anything in Washington, DC, were charred sanctuaries for Japanese zealots.

Termite patrols fanned out from the polo grounds, searching through houses for the inevitable holdouts. Hacksaw Holcombe, wanting to get a better view down the street, climbed atop a bunker he thought was empty. When the Japanese soldiers hiding inside blew themselves up, the detonation catapulted Hacksaw head over heels. He was dazed but unscratched. Another trooper ducked into a bunker to escape incoming Japanese mortar rounds. Sitting on a bench while waiting out the barrage, the trooper lifted the edge of a poncho hung from the ceiling to discover two Japanese peering out the front gun slit. He backed out quietly, leaving a smoking hand grenade in his old seat.

When the Angels reached their northern boundary, Krueger divided the city into three sectors, assigning each to a division. The 37th Infantry would continue their southward attack while the 1st Cavalry swung around to the east to link up with Swing's troops, who were now authorized to resume their assault on Nichols Field.

In preparation for the next attack, Haugen visited a front-line command post located in a large, Spanish-style stucco house near the Polo Club. Outside, troopers dug foxholes in the courtyard as anti-aircraft shells exploded in the street. Inside, Haugen and the officers huddled over a map laid out on a twelve-foot-long oak table.

A 40mm anti-aircraft round screamed in through a window, gouging into the table before exploding. The blast shook the room, knocking everyone to the floor.

After a few seconds, they all stood, ears ringing, to dust themselves off, stunned and amazed at their close call. Everyone except Haugen; he remained on the floor, turning gray, with a piece of shrapnel buried in his chest.

A pair of medics loaded Hard Rock onto a stretcher and rushed him to a jeep for evacuation. Private Richard Loughrin recalled that Haugen "was smiling, wanly, then he asked for a cigarette. Someone lit it and put it in his mouth. He held it with his lips and let it droop from one corner of his mouth as he always did."

Haugen waved weakly as the jeep pulled away. And just like that, the man who forged the regiment into a reflection of his own warrior ethos was gone. Before the news began to spread, command transitioned to Haugen's executive officer, thirty-one-year-old Lieutenant Colonel Edward 'Slugger' Lahti.

Lahti, like Haugen, conducted himself in a no-nonsense manner and was known for his "poorly suppressed state of simmering anger." It was on Leyte that his men had learned, as one of them put it, "He was a good man to go to war with, but a bad man to cross. His patience was limited, as was his charm and gentility." What Lahti might have lacked in popularity, he made up for in respect. His rise through the ranks and his West Point commission had only burnished his humble origins; he still prized hard work and diligence over entitlement and politics. Lahti's standards were high, but his subordinates always knew where they stood. Now, with responsibilities only tragedy could bestow, Lahti found himself in command of the regiment.

WHILE THE AMERICANS AND JAPANESE CLASHED for control of the capital, civilians found themselves caught between the back-and-forth artillery duels and the raging infernos gutting their city. During the battle, the Americans alone fired more than 42,000 shells, ranging in caliber from 60mm mortars to earth-shaking 155mm artillery. The number of Japanese shells that fell in the city is impossible to determine.

The flow of refugees escaping the city grew steadily. They emerged like an army of forlorn ghosts from the rubble-strewn streets. 'Slugger' Lahti's paratroopers, with the help of guerrillas, ushered the refugees away from the frontlines whenever possible. The guerrillas set up checkpoints, searching refugees for weapons and looking for Japanese soldiers in civilian clothes.

Charlie Sass, who witnessed the exodus, recalled, "I remember the people coming out of Manila, small groups of them, all ages, carrying what they could. Some of them were resting and crying in ditches."

First Lieutenant Kirkland was there, too. "They all carried pitifully meager possessions. Many pushed little carts. One small boy pushed his grandmother in a baby carriage. None had any food or water."

The refugees, with eyes red from smoke and tears, told the troopers about the orgy of violence occurring behind them, but the full horror failed to sink in until witnessed firsthand.

Kirkland, figuring his battalion would continue their fight deeper into the city, conducted a solo reconnaissance patrol past the divisions' boundary. Winged by Japanese shrapnel, he ducked into the Red Cross' two-story headquarters. In the entry way, a man was in shock; Kirkland guessed every bone in his legs had been smashed in multiple places.

Kirkland continued into the building. "The entire first floor was crammed with women of all ages who had been raped repeatedly and then had their breasts sawed off by dirty bayonets. The place was airless and hot. There was one hysterical nurse slumped in a corner. She was in shock and helpless. So was I."

Kirkland was staring at the aftermath of a soul-crushing atrocity.

Red Cross workers had been providing refugees shelter and emergency aid to those wounded in the crossfire. The hundred-odd patients, refugees, and staff were limping through, though quarters were tight: cots lined the hallways, and nine German Jewish refugees occupied the women's bathroom. They were all making the best of the cramped conditions—until four Japanese naval troops entered the back door.

Gunshots and screams were followed by slaughter. The Japanese soldiers bayonetted women protecting their children, then bayonetted the children, including a ten-day-old infant. They shot nurses and doctors and ran through helpless patients lying on cots; an officer then shot each victim in the head. They killed several of the Jewish refugees hiding in bathroom stalls. In less than thirty minutes, the floors were slick with blood and more than fifty people were murdered.

The site left Kirkland speechless. "I could only think to go for help. I pressed my aid kit into the lone nurse's hand and fled." He sprinted back to his battalion aid station where Captain Charles E. Van Epps reluctantly agreed to return with Kirkland. Upon seeing the victims, Van Epps ordered his medics to truck the survivors back for aid.

Major Henry Burgess, vividly recalling the horrid spectacle, said, "Many nursing women had been bayoneted in their breasts, some had the tendons in the back of their necks severed by sabers and could no

longer hold their necks up. Small children and babies had been bayoneted.... We had been admonished to keep our medical supplies for
ourselves and not to help others. Of course, we couldn't, and didn't
refuse them assistance."

Patrols crossing deeper into the city sadly discovered the Red
Cross rampage was not an isolated incident. Mutilated and charred
bodies lay everywhere. "They were piled in the ditch and laying every
which way on the hillside. One look was all I could handle," lamented
a trooper. Corpses, strung up by the Japanese, hung from balconies
and telephone poles. Thirty-six civilians were machinegunned in front
of the general hospital and there were countless decapitations.

Sergeant Edmund Harris was checking on his platoon's positions.
"The area had been shelled and burned, and there were almost no
buildings undamaged," he later recounted.

"A hundred yards away, a figure emerged from the rubble and
moved slowly toward us. As the figure came closer, we recognized a
woman pulling a little wagon with a tiny passenger. She was looking
for a doctor, but what she needed was a miracle. The expression of
her face was a mixture of pain and hopelessness. One look in the little
wagon and part of me died. I believe it was a little girl, about three
years old. She was sitting upright, but I don't know how. Her little
face had been blown away from the eyes down. No teeth, no jaw, no
tongue, no trachea, no esophagus. A burst from a Japanese machinegun, according to the mother."

The woman had also lost her two other children and her sister.
As the mother pulled the wagon past the trooper's foxholes, the
brown-eyed little girl stared at Harris.

"I lived with that look the rest of the war, and to this day I can
picture that pitiful little body and those beautiful eyes that exposed
the soul of a three-year-old who was an innocent victim of war. I
heard from a medic that the little girl died later that day."

Medic Bernard Coon waded into the flow of refugees with his aid bag. "One lady, her foot was missing, but she was walking. I don't know how she could do it; the pain must have been terrible." He patched up another woman with forty-two Japanese bayonet wounds, and there was a nine-year-old boy, whose arm had been torn out of its socket. As Coon tried to re-set it, the boy pleaded, "Give me a gun, and I'll go back and kill them all."

The destroyed environs of Manila

What started as grotesque Japanese reprisals against suspected guerrillas descended into wider, methodical rape and murder. Captured diaries and documents confirmed the systemic nature of the barbarity: "45–150 guerrillas were disposed of tonight. I personally stabbed and killed 10," a Japanese soldier confided to his diary. Two days later, the same author scribbled, "Burned 1,000 guerrillas to death tonight." A document issued from Iwabuchi's headquarters made the policy clear, "All people on the battlefield with the exception of Japanese military personnel, Japanese civilians, and Special Construction Units will be put to death." Executioners were instructed to be mindful of conserving ammunition and advised that when disposing of dead bodies, "they should be gathered into houses which are scheduled to be burned or demolished. They should also be thrown in the river."

At Nasugbu, Eichelberger's Eighth Army established a refugee camp and an emergency hospital dedicated to aiding the civilian casualties flowing out of Manila. At its peak, the camp fed and sheltered ten thousand refugees, including a hundred ninety German, Austrian, Italian and Norwegian Jews who had been hiding in the surrounding area. Vanderpool and the guerrillas were hard at work procuring and distributing food. Vanderpool later recalled, "The project entailed buying up all available chickens, pigs, rice, corn, and vegetables, establishing kitchens, and feeding a lot of hungry people."

The Angels only witnessed a portion of the atrocities in Manila, and American units continued to make grisly discoveries throughout the city. Post-war investigations estimated one hundred thousand men, women, and children died in Manila. For the Angels, the barbarity steeled already hardened hearts. Kirkland later wrote that "the Japanese had simply gone berserk in the center city, raping and killing with a childish, mindless ferocity that forever blotted their absurd claim to be a superior race. We certainly treated them as vermin to be destroyed from then on."

● ● ●

On Monday morning, February 12, a flight of SBDs buzzed over Nichols Field to soften up the defenses for Swing's next attempt to seize the field.

After the airstrike cut down at least sixty-seven defenders, the paragliders dashed forward in concert with protective artillery barrages advancing in front of them. They attacked under the watchful eyes of gunners whose skills were well-honed in the art of marching fire.

The open runways were littered with wrecked aircraft, pitted with shell craters, and studded with land mines. The profusion of weapons arrayed against Soule's paragliders represented almost every caliber available to the Imperial forces. There were anti-aircraft guns varying in size from 20mm to 90mm, a few 25mm machine cannons, and hundreds of mortars ranging from the small trench variety to 150mm. The big guns included dozens of naval 120mms complemented by

75mm howitzers and several anti-tanks guns; machinegun positions were ubiquitous.

A paraglider battalion attacked out of Lahti's perimeter, sweeping across the top of the field with two self-propelled 75mm M8s in support. The armor crews exhausted their ammunition against 20mm gun positions before withdrawing to resupply. Simultaneously from the south, Soule's two other battalions resumed their familiar yard-by-yard advance against the indurate Japanese defenses, but this time they had a new trick.

The enemy's dug-in guns exposed little more than the barrel, but most lacked overhead protection. The paragliders' 81mm mortar crews were now armed with a game-changing device, "Time and Super-Quick" fuses. The fuses gave gunners the flexibility to set the charge to explode either on impact or just before, as an airburst. Airbursts eliminated the need for a direct hit—a close enough detonation eviscerated Japanese crews with shrapnel whirling down from above. White phosphorous rounds, with their searing embers, also claimed several gun positions.

Firepower and determination carried the day, and except for a few isolated positions, the paragliders secured the field by sunset. Their tally included sixty-seven enemy dead, twenty-five machineguns captured or destroyed, and twenty-four 25mm guns knocked out, along with a lone 75mm field gun. With no time to savor the win, Swing readied the division to pivot east against the most daunting bastion of the Genko Line, Fort William McKinley. The fort, originally a US Army base built in 1901, was the last bastion for Iwabuchi's naval troops in the Angels' sector. Sacking the fort, however, required taking out another cluster of Japanese anti-aircraft guns and crossing over three miles of dried rice fields. From the fort's west side, two 5-inch naval guns fired rounds that traveled that distance in eight seconds.

Swing's units would leapfrog east by bounds to a north-south-running railroad track designated as the first phase line. The raised tracks made for a natural barrier, and the paratroopers and para-gliders pushing simultaneously to occupy it gave Swing a point for getting his infantry abreast for the second phase.

The attack kicked off the next morning. From Henry Burgess' view on the northern flank, he recalled, "At one time in the open, rolling country, one could see seven infantry battalions attacking on a line supported by tanks and self-propelled guns ... just like they do it in the movies!"

Burgess was right: there were many actions that day worthy of Hollywood. Suppressing fire and quick bounds was the key to getting across the flat, billiard table-like terrain. One of Burgess' troopers sprinted like mad for his next spot of cover when a shell exploded against his backpack. His comrades watched in amazement as cans of Spam, tins of cheese, crackers, and cigarettes flew in every direction. The packrat trooper, described by a buddy as "'a walking grocery store,' was up and running, with his shattered pack flapping against his ass, minus all that stuff which saved his life."

Twenty-one-year-old Private First Class Manuel Pérez was crossing the same field. Manny, as his friends called him, was tired. He and the rest of his squad had spent their violently repetitive morning overpowering a succession of stubborn enemy emplacements. As lead scout, Manny was up front for each assault using his rifle and a shower of hand grenades to clear the way.

During his advance, he gunned down five Japanese caught in the open—not bad for a trooper who struggled on the rifle range during basic training, proving that Army instructors not only

Trooper Manuel Pérez, Jr.

produced marksmen but killers as well. Pérez developed his reputation as deadly gunslinger on Leyte, where his commander noted, "His detection of the enemy was very sharp and his reaction with weapons was very quick and effective."

By mid-day, Manny and his squad had destroyed eleven pillboxes, but one more blocked their way forward. The twelfth position, the largest of the group, held twin-mounted heavy machineguns with a commanding view. The guns steadily belted out rounds with a deep *CHUG, CHUG, CHUG!*

With .50-caliber bullets snapping past them, Manny and the troopers surveyed the terrain. Getting to the bunker required crossing two hundred yards of dried rice fields. As Lieutenant Ted Baughn contemplated their next move, someone yelled, "There goes Pérez!" Baughn turned to see Manny in a flat-out run. "I yelled for him to get down—which had no effect on his concentration."

The platoon poured in suppressing fire as Manny dashed to the guns' flank. He flopped down twenty yards from the gun pit, shooting four of the defenders, then overhanded a fragmentation grenade. Within a heartbeat of the explosion, he was up and racing toward the guns. He found the dazed and wounded crew crawling toward a tunnel and emptied eight shots into them. Taking a knee, he reloaded before pursuing four of the fleeing Japanese, one of whom decided to turn and fight.

"I can remember the Jap with his fixed bayonet charge Pérez," said Sergeant Richard Sibio. The Japanese threw his rifle like a spear, knocking Pérez's rifle out of his hands. Pérez scooped up the Arisaka rifle and attacked. Sibio continued, "We saw him beat the Jap and bayonet him with his [own] fixed bayonet."

Charging ahead with the Japanese rifle at the ready, Manny bayonetted two more defenders before beating the last three to death with the butt of the rifle. All told, Pérez's one-man charge officially accounted for twenty-three enemy dead. Troopers in his platoon, however, disputed the Army's tally. Sergeant Max Polick, Manny's squad leader, who witnessed his role in taking out the previous eleven pillboxes, later commented, "Among his grenades, rifle, and bayonet, the count of dead Japs was more like seventy-five." Others in the platoon agreed with Polick's number. Several witnesses stated emphatically that Pérez had taken out the majority, if not all, of the eleven previous pillboxes.

To the south, fresh from their victory at Nichols Field, the paragliders ran into trouble of a different kind. Their morning started off with a tempting target: a large concentration of Japanese troops in the open, perfect for an airstrike.

Anthony K. Genematas eyed the dive bombers circling overhead, "but before our front lines could be marked, the planes began their attack." The SBD pilots dropped their payload on Colonel Norman Tipton's front line. The bombs whistled in, exploding into steel shards that sliced through the troopers. A medic wading into the bloodshed recalled, "I have never—and hope to never again—witness such a scene of human carnage. In addition to many ugly wounds, body parts were scattered all around. We stuffed those parts into mattress covers for the quartermaster's graves registration to sort and identify later."

Casualty reports trickled in: eight killed and twenty-six wounded. In a fraction of a second, an entire platoon was gone. But still, the battalion surged forward.

"There was no choice except to 'push straight to the front and keep going,'" wrote one of Tipton's company commanders of the open terrain. Before the attack, Tipton implored his officers, "Don't give the little bastards a chance to get set.... It is damned good defensive terrain, and so I repeat—hit hard and keep moving. Don't stop for anything."

It was damned good defensive terrain, and Tipton's men chewed on every yard of it, crawling forward on their bellies to stay under the guns. Volleys of suppressing fire flew in both directions. Japanese 120mm anti-aircraft guns threw softball sized rounds with a furious staccato. In retaliation, the paragliders traversed a captured five-inch naval gun to support their attack.

Tipton's howitzers and mortars fired ammunition as fast as it was brought forward. To keep as much manpower on the assault line, Tipton pressed the battalion's cooks into service to cart up ammunition or water and carry back the wounded. When possible, they used jeeps to speed across the open expanse and drove several on their rims after shrapnel shredded the tires. Their support helped the paragliders roll headlong toward the rail line, capturing or destroying ten 25mm guns and eight heavy machineguns along the way. The regimental historian documented the stats with an almost palatable weariness: "Total pillboxes to date: 300."

Characteristically, the defenders fought to the last man. And heedless of the Americans' onslaught across all fronts, Iwabuchi urged those still alive to counter-attack. His instructions were clear: "Prior

to the all-out suicide attack, wounded will be made to commit suicide and documents and material will be burnt.... In the all-out suicide attack, every man will attack until he achieves a glorious death. Not even one man must become a prisoner. During the attack, friends of the wounded will make them commit suicide." His directive ensured his men's annihilation.

The Angels, having made the railroad tracks, dug in along the raised embankment. Late that afternoon, in the paragliders' sector, hundreds of screaming Japanese with swords, bayonet-tipped rifles, and even spears sprinted toward the waiting riflemen. By the time the free-for-all was over, four

A trooper poses with a spear used by Japanese attackers during a failed banzai attack

paragliders were dead, and medics scrambled to treat twenty
wounded. Out front, it was a massacre. Close to two hundred and
fifty Japanese soldiers lay dead, sixty of them roasted by a single
trooper with a flamethrower.

That same night, farther up the rail line, Henry Burgess' troopers
recovered their casualties. In the dark, litter parties moved into the
perimeter carrying the wounded. Behind them were the shadows of
marching men, three abreast, their boots silent on the dirt road.

Troopers manning belt-fed machineguns on both sides of the road
caught on first; the marching troops were Japanese! In the gloom,
there appeared to be hundreds of them.

The gunners opened fire simultaneously, raking the column at
point-blank. The Japanese, caught by surprise, fled in every direction,
some straight into the lines. Medic Jack McGrath recalled, "One
inspired Jap came through our perimeter at top speed. He fell into a
hole occupied by Ed Davis."

Davis, face down in the bottom of his foxhole and terrified he
would be stabbed in the back, grabbed the only weapon he had, a
hand grenade. He pulled the pin and reached back with his left hand,
jamming the grenade against his adversary's spine.

The detonation evaporated Davis' hand and killed his attacker,
who probably never knew what hit him. Ignoring his appalling injury,
Davis tried to re-man his machinegun. A buddy rushed to his aid,
taking over the gun while McGrath put a tourniquet on the stump.

The confused Japanese withdrew, leaving forty-two dead. The
next morning, Swing, seeing the corpses piled up across the entirety
of the rail line, ordered his engineers forward with bulldozers. With
the aid of civilian labor, the bodies were tossed into communal graves
by the dozen.

To help Swing crack Fort McKinley, the 1st Cavalry sent him
several M18 Hellcat tank destroyers. To the uninitiated, the M18s

were tanks, but they had thinner armor, an open top, and a long-range, high-velocity 76mm main gun.

Medic Jack McGrath was with a squad trying to talk a hesitant M18 commander into aiding their assault against a Japanese-held trench. "He informed us that his armor would not stop a rifle bullet."

Sergeant Russell W. Appleyard tugged at his own olive-drab fatigue shirt, asking, "Do you think this will?"

The commander, finding no logical counter argument, rumbled forward to fire three rounds into the trench. McGrath and Appleyard's squad sheltered behind the Hellcat to avoid the muzzle blast. Spinning out of the second explosion was something McGrath thought looked like a soccer ball. After the third shot, the squad went forward to investigate.

"When we reached the trench, it was an unholy mess," recalled McGrath. "One Jap was on his knees, his spine was blown away, and he was bent over backwards. Hanging down his back like a dirty shirt was his face. There was no skull. I knew then what the soccer ball was—it was his skull. There he was, two small holes for eyes, a little bubble for a nose and mouth like the artist used to draw for Orphan Annie.... The trench was ours."

The Hellcats' firepower enthralled the paratroopers. One enthusiast reported the crews were so good that they needed just two shells to zero in and destroy a target at four thousand yards. With their support, the pillboxes fell one by one, and the troopers advanced another thousand yards.

As the Angels closed on McKinley, flames erupted from within the fort. The occupiers were burning their supplies. Detonations of ammunition stockpiles shook the ground and hurled flaming debris skyward. 'Slugger' Lahti observed the inferno from a few hundred yards away. A six-inch piece of shrapnel zipped out of the explosion and tore through his right bicep. He muttered, "I think I've been hit" and sat down as his map fluttered to the ground. After nearby troopers bandaged his arm, Lahti collected himself, then headed to the aid station. It took twenty stitches to close what he described as "a beautiful cut about seven inches long." When he returned to the front a few hours later with his arm in a sling, the Japanese still held the fort.

In the face of growing casualties and a literal uphill battle, Swing ordered his men to stand down and stand back. He called for the Air Force to unleash napalm. Essentially jell-thickened gasoline, napalm's liquid fire stuck to anything it touched. When dropped from low altitudes, the ensuing conflagration engulfed an area seventy feet wide and almost two hundred long. The searing heat was enough to suck the air out of an engulfed pillbox or cave. It was a horrible way to die.

First in were sixteen P-38s, rolling in to drop their napalm payloads from less than a hundred feet. Through the billowing black smoke, a flight of ten A-20 Havocs made another low-level strike, followed by twenty-seven SBDs hitting surrounding targets. After that, artillery barrages thundered into the fort all night.

To bag any of the soldiers trying to escape McKinley, Swing pulled Strong's 3rd Battalion off the line and trucked them south to replace guerrillas holding a roadblock. Their orders: "Simply hold the line and block the escape of the Jap survivors from Manila and Fort McKinley." Strong established his command post in an abandoned schoolhouse at Bagumbayan on the shore of Laguna de Bay. While two attached M18 Hellcats and the machinegun platoon blocked the road running along the lakeshore, the three rifle companies dug a defensive line across a series of small hills to the west. To Strong's south, Easy Company set up another roadblock at Alabang. With the Japanese on a hill five hundred yards to their front, little action was expected. And as First Lieutenant Kirkland recalled, "The battalion was seriously depleted and worn by this time, and we welcomed a comparatively quiet assignment."

But there were a few clashes. A Japanese howitzer hit one of the Hellcats, killing most of the crew. An L-bird trying to spot the enemy position was shot down, but the pilot managed to crash land in no-man's-land, where a squad of paratroopers rescued the crew.

From the roadblock, they could hear airstrikes and artillery mopping up around Fort McKinley four miles away. The fort had fallen on February 17 when Tipton's paragliders entered with rifles at the ready and tallied 961 dead Japanese.

A FEW NIGHTS LATER at the Bagumbayan roadblock, Kirkland listened to puttering engines out on the lake. A hysterical eruption of gunfire ended the noise. A guerrilla unit stationed farther south sank a forty-foot barge and scattered three others. As predicted, scores of Japanese were fleeing south, and with one of their evacuation routes identified—moving barges down the lake after dark—Kirkland plotted a scheme to interdict their next attempt. He and his six-man intelligence section procured a 60mm mortar and fifty illumination shells, then set up on the sandy beach opposite the schoolhouse. Kirkland sweet-talked the remaining tank destroyer crew into joining them. The Hellcat's main gun and turret-mounted, belt-fed heavy machinegun would take out the barges, while Kirkland's crew would provide illumination. In turn, the intelligence men dug their foxholes around the Hellcat to defend the crew.

The Japanese had developed a healthy respect for the Hellcat's lethal firepower and often made efforts to take them out after sunset. Infiltration patrols of four to six men specially equipped with explosives slithered through perimeters in search of the armored targets. Sometimes the demolitions were strapped to their bodies, and sometimes they were mounted on eight-foot ramming poles. In either case, their objective was to destroy the Hellcats. Shooting an explosive-laden saboteur often blew him up, so the Hellcat's crews appreciated the protection of Kirkland's men.

With the trap set, Kirkland and his commander, Captain John A. Coulter, sacked out on the sandy beach, fifty feet away from the mortar and the Hellcat. Kirkland later wrote, "The weather was muggy but clear, and we both felt snug and smug."

That lasted until about 02:00 when Kirkland woke to the sound of movement on the road just a yard from his head. He squinted into the gloom to confirm his fear: it was a column of Japanese marching south, four abreast with rifles slung. "They were clearly bluffing their way out, and it was working," he recalled. Somehow, they had paraded past the machinegun roadblock. After they passed, Kirkland and Coulter dashed for the schoolhouse to radio the troopers at Alabang to expect company in about forty-five minutes.

Just as they completed their call, all hell broke loose at the roadblock. The four belt-fed machineguns were blazing away at what must have been another column of enemy troops trying the same gambit. The machinegunners had been surprised, alerted to the enemy only when they were just four feet from the guns.

Under the command of twenty-five-year-old Sergeant Mills T. Lowe, the machinegun crews were strung along a fence line between the lake and a ravine, with one on the far side of the road. Lowe, manning a gun himself, was widely considered one of the best soldiers in the division. Kirkland, who counted himself among Lowe's admirers, described him as "a relatively small and spare man ... quiet and somewhat religious. He never raised his voice and never lost his temper or criticized. I discovered that the men in his platoon simply revered him. A small hint of disappointment from him was intolerable to each and every man under him." Despite his quiet demeanor, or perhaps because of it, one of Lowe's comrades called him a "tough SOB," and a "typical regular army type that wouldn't let you get too close to him; he preferred to be a loner, except for a couple of close buddies."

Lowe's twenty-four-man platoon, reduced from forty, was in for the fight of their lives. Their initial bursts cut down the front ranks of the advancing column, sending those in the rear running helter-skelter. Sergeant Howard Ferguson grabbed the 60mm mortar and fired illumination rounds to explode over the roadblock. The yellowish light cast by the flares as they swung below their descending parachutes made for an eerie, shadowy scene with dark figures darting in and out of view.

Across from Kirkland and Coulter, a group of ten or twelve Japanese vaulted the small fence surrounding the schoolhouse and huddled in its shadow. Both men opened fire, Kirkland with his M1911 pistol and Coulter with a carbine. "I couldn't miss at that range, even with a shaky hand," admitted Kirkland. One of the enemy slipped behind the building, where a cleaver-wielding mess sergeant killed him.

The Japanese at the roadblock regrouped, then threw themselves forward in a frontal charge against Lowe's machinegun positions. The guns barked again and again, their almost continuous *rat-tat-a-tat* cutting through the night. The dull *crump* of exploding hand grenades added to the bedlam.

The firefight alerted the infantry on the other side of the ravine, but they could only watch the distant flares arcing overhead and wonder what was happening.

During the waves of banzai attacks, the growing mounds of corpses became a problem. One of the troopers recalled, "We had to move the gun three times because the pile of Nips kept blocking the field of fire after each attack." There had been several hand-to-hand battles, and Lowe felled at least eight with his bayonet. Two of the guns were overheating, causing ammunition in the chamber to cook off due to the heat of the glowing barrels. All four crews' ammunition was running low.

Back at the schoolhouse, Japanese soldiers emerged out of the dark from multiple directions. Kirkland figured the first group must have been engaged at the second roadblock and were fleeing straight back. He watched a group of them drag a canoe into the water, then pile in to make their escape. The lieutenant in the Hellcat swiveled his heavy machinegun into action, shredding both the crew and their canoe. As the lieutenant leaned out of the turret, a Japanese soldier hiding by the treads shot him in the face. The bullet tore up through his chin and knocked out several front teeth before exiting out his nose. Sergeant Ferguson shot the Japanese and rushed the lieutenant across the road to the aid station at the schoolhouse.

At the roadblock, Lowe had to do something about his men's dwindling ammunition. He rallied several others to sprint forward with him into the piles of enemy corpses. They grabbed seven Japanese machineguns, two trench mortars, and all the ammunition they could find. Lugging their loot, they scurried back to their foxholes.

Resupplied, the machinegunners staved off two more frantic attacks before the rising sun ushered in a macabre calm.

Kirkland hoofed it up the road to find Lowe standing at his machinegun position staring at the cluster of huts on the far side of the clearing. One was engulfed in flames after three direct hits from a captured trench mortar. As the two men stood together, they could hear chanting drifting toward them.

"Presently, there were explosions," Kirkland said. "While we stood watching, a hand came sailing through the air to drop at our feet. The surviving Japanese were committing suicide."

It had been a night of pandemonium and terror. Miraculously, the paratroopers suffered only two wounded, the Hellcat lieutenant and a trooper shot through the thigh while running with two boxes of ammo for Lowe. Kirkland, as the battalion's intelligence officer, began the grisly task of searching the enemy dead. "I counted 342 Japanese dead in front of Sgt. Lowe," he said. "I counted seventy-one in front of the S-2 [intelligence] section, I can't remember how many we killed in the schoolhouse yard, but it would have been a dozen or so." As Kirkland counted, a Filipino man, whose house had been ransacked by the Japanese, kicked one of the corpses, asking the dead man, "Did you get your rice, Tojo?"

Lowe, who had been serving as the platoon leader since they dropped at Tagaytay, was awarded a battlefield promotion to second lieutenant for his leadership. The Army's standard policy was to transfer newly commissioned officers to another unit, which worried Lowe's platoon. He'd been their rock, steadily leading by example. The son of a North Carolina peanut farm sharecropper, Lowe grew up in an austere home without indoor plumbing. He had a workmanlike childhood that required diligence and a strong work ethic, traits the Army rewarded with rapid promotions. While hunting had made him a

Sergeant Mills T. Lowe photographed prior to his battlefield commission

skilled outdoorsman, Lowe thrived in all aspects of his military vocation. In garrison, his "rifle [was] speck-free, his fatigues consistently immaculate, his boots consistently mirror polished." While on Leyte, he kept himself as professionally presentable as the conditions allowed. "The rest of us were wet and muddy," remembered one of his comrades, "Lowe was just wet." He also exhibited a humble nonchalance to personal courage, shrugging off recognition after he dodged enemy fire to save one of his men's lives with the deft application of a tourniquet. Later, he singlehandedly recaptured a machinegun that the Japanese had seized during the battle for Nichols Field.

When Lowe's men, as a body, petitioned he stay with the platoon after his promotion, both 'Slugger' Lahti and Lowe's commander agreed.

"I ran into Lowe later," said Kirkland, "and noted that he was his same quiet, modest self, but that he was no longer so attached to his Bible studies. I think that he found joy in desperate battle and [was] unable to make peace with his dirty hands. He was no longer innocent."

Lowe wasn't alone in the struggle of lost innocence. To the immediate west, Lieutenant Grant Neuteboom was staring down at a Japanese prisoner wounded in the previous night's melee. He'd been shot in the shoulder and was suffering from uncontrollable diarrhea. The man tugged at Neuteboom's leg, sobbing, "Japs no good, Japs no good."

Neuteboom radioed battalion headquarters at the schoolhouse informing them he had a prisoner. "They said they didn't need any more," recalled Neuteboom. "At that moment, at that precise moment, I could have stopped to clean and wash and comfort that pitiful wretch, so in need of compassion. The men would have helped me if I had only led the way. I know that now, in retrospect, but at the time, it never occurred to me. That is the terrible part. I simply nodded to the Filipinos, and they dragged him off and shot him. My only defense is that I had lived like an animal so long, I had seen so much killing, that I was incapable of feeling any more moral outrage. Neither side was taking prisoners at that time. We were shooting the wounded because they were shooting our wounded."

THAT HIS ANGELS WERE STRETCHED THIN and undermanned did not dissuade Swing from wading into the enemy. Indeed, the tougher things got, it seemed the more he thrived. He made up for his shortages by shuffling battalions between regiments, and attaching and detaching artillery batteries, engineer platoons, and medical squads as needed to maintain the momentum of his attacks. He embraced improvisation and flaunted convention to keep the Angels punching above their weight.

In one example, he pinched together a task force of anti-aircraft gunners to conduct an amphibious landing north of Nasugbu. Lacking naval gunfire support, the men fired bazookas over the ramps of their landing craft for five minutes to serve as their pre-invasion barrage.

While Swing's infantry laid siege to Fort McKinley, he formed another ad hoc unit to deal with a large group of Japanese occupying positions on the shores of Laguna de Bay. The Pierson Task Force, commanded by Swing's assistant division commander, Brigadier General Albert Pierson, was composed of a paraglider battalion, a battalion of regular infantry brought ashore by Eichelberger, guerrillas, a company of Sherman tanks, a platoon of combat engineers, and medics. One of Swing's artillery battalions provided fire support. The Japanese garrison holding Mabato Point was mostly remnants of the naval troops, anti-aircraft gunners, and ground crews that had fled the Genko Line. With their backs to the lake, they occupied a series of fortified caves and tunnels that served as a catacomb-like complex of living quarters, supply depots, communication centers, and gun positions. Swing was content to let them wither.

He wrote, "Right now [we] have got a bunch of Japs, about two hundred left, neatly surrounded about two miles south of McKinley on the shore of Laguna de Bay. There were about six hundred to start with; we're killing them off with artillery and TD [tank destroyer] fire night and day. There's no particular hurry, and I'm just going to 'waste' ammunition until they are exterminated." The task force found napalm was particularly effective against the caves as it burned off camouflage covers and evaporated oxygen, suffocating the occupants.

An attempt was made to spare the defenders' lives. As the Angels' historian wrote of the surrounded position, "The situation was hopeless for the Nips. We knew it, and we thought they did." A captured Japanese sergeant major told his interrogators that his men "were disgusted with their officers and would like to surrender." A Japanese-speaking guerrilla volunteered to deliver the terms: at noon, the Americans would stop firing for thirty minutes to allow anyone who desired to come out with their hands up.

At 12:30, after no one emerged from the redoubt, the attack resumed. Some tried to escape rather than surrender, but they were trounced upon by well-placed guerrilla ambushes. The Angels' final estimate calculated nine hundred of the enemy perished in the senseless siege.

Swing again cobbled together a solution when Krueger charged him with securing the naval base on the Cavite Peninsula. The Air Force had already dropped more than two hundred and fifty tons of bombs onto the base, but because the peninsula jutted out into Manila Bay and threatened Allied shipping, it needed to be cleared. Lieutenant Colonels Doug Quandt and Henry Muller formed a task force from the only units not engaged at the front: the reconnaissance platoon, the headquarters' defense platoon, a handful of guerrillas, a three-man civil affairs team, and two radio operators. Led by Swing's personnel officer, Lieutenant Colonel Glenn McGowan, the fifty men landed under the cover of darkness via patrol boat. At first light, the recon men took out a lone twelve-man Japanese gun crew and dismantled their anti-aircraft gun. Mission accomplished.

By the Angels' count, their sacking of the Genko Line accounted for twelve hundred pillboxes, more than three hundred machineguns, forty-four heavy guns of all sorts, and 5,210 of the enemy. The architect, Rear Admiral Iwabuchi, went down with his men. While under siege in the Agriculture and Commerce Building, Iwabuchi called his men together one last time, telling them, "If anyone has the courage to escape, please do so. If not, please take your lives here." He then committed *seppuku* by slicing open his own stomach.

IT WOULD TAKE SEVERAL MORE WEEKS to fully secure Manila, but Swing was already eyeing his next mission, perhaps the Angels' most important of the war. Swing wanted a rifle company for an operation behind the lines, and 'Slugger' Lahti, after consulting the unit roster, selected Baker Company, with a strength of eighty men—the highest in the regiment.

Lieutenant John Ringler, Baker Company's commander, without context or explanation, hopped into the back seat of Lahti's jeep to meet with General Swing. He was nervous. "A thousand things can race through your mind as to what I or the company did since our jump on Tagaytay Ridge that the division commanding general is directing my presence," he admitted.

Chapter 11

"You're not Marines"

Parañaque, Luzon.
Wednesday, February 21, 1945

Ringler climbed out of the jeep and strode up the shaded walkway leading to the two-story stucco house that served as the division command post. His conversation with Swing was short: Baker Company would parachute near a prison camp, and after overcoming the Japanese garrison, the men would liberate two thousand civilian internees. The briefing left Ringler with lots of questions, but when Swing asked him if he had any, he simply said no. The general was there to convey the mission's importance, not impart details. Ringler knew he would get the specifics soon enough.

The Americans had already liberated three other such camps since January, and in each, the internees were suffering from starvation and disease. The Japanese invasion of the Philippines caught not only the world by surprise, but also the thousands of foreign civilians living there. Expatriate business owners, clergy, contractors, missionaries, professors, and medical staff—along with their spouses and children—had no means to escape. In time, the Japanese herded them into several fenced internment camps, where they remained under guard for three years.

The Japanese commandants issued limited rice rations but encouraged gardens and sometimes allowed internees to purchase food from the local population. But as the war progressed, they forbid outside contact and reduced the distribution of food and medical supplies to a trickle. The deprivation worsened after the Americans attacked Leyte.

MacArthur, after witnessing the deplorable condition of the freed internees, urged Swing to liberate a fourth internment camp shortly after the Angels had landed on Luzon. But at the time, Swing had his hands full breaking the Genko Line, and the camp near Los Baños was several dozen miles to his south. But while the Angels bashed into Manila, Major Jay Vanderpool, the guerrilla coordinator, dispatched Lieutenant Colonel Gustavo Ingles to collect information about the camp. Ingles operated with the local guerrillas and clandestinely met with some of the internees, learning that one or two of them were dying every day from malnourishment or disease. He also heard growing fears that the Japanese garrison might either evacuate the internees—or worse, execute them as the Americans drew closer. Massacre rumors were rampant amongst the internees, and freshly dug ditches outside the camp's barbed-wire fence underscored their concern.

The revelations increased the mission's urgency, and while Vanderpool did not relish the idea of a guerrilla-only raid, he gave Ingles wide latitude to initiate his own rescue if necessary. In the event of a crisis, Vanderpool's contingency planning was critical. "I thought, should the executions start, we would just have to go with what we had available at the time," he said. "Hence, the dual planning and preparations for the raid."

Vanderpool's guerrilla headquarters was across the street from Swing's command post. The two headquarters shared an officers' mess, and it was there that Vanderpool and his intelligence officer, Colonel Marcelo Castillo, kept Swing and his intelligence officer, 'Butch' Muller, apprised of their reconnaissance efforts. Castillo, a guerrilla and US Naval Academy graduate, provided Muller enough information for him to draft a detailed map of the camp, including the locations of the internee barracks, guard posts, and concealed routes of approach.

Ringler received a full briefing from Muller and Swing's operations officer, Doug 'Tangle Foot' Quandt. Huddled over maps and hand-sketched diagrams, the group reviewed the plan and finalized the details of Baker Company's role.

The camp at Los Baños was located on a sixty-acre campus of the University of the Philippines' College of Agriculture. The internees lived in a complex of eighteen long, rectangular bamboo and grass shacks. Two barbed-wire fences, each six feet tall, surrounded the compound, with machinegun pillboxes and guard posts fortifying the perimeter. Working in the raiders' favor, the camp's defenses were arranged primarily to prevent escape rather than fend off attackers. The guerrillas estimated there might be as many as a hundred and twenty-five Japanese guards.

Bigger threats loomed nearby. A mile and a half west of the camp, the guerrillas identified a Japanese infantry company manning two howitzers and four heavy machineguns. And eight miles up the main road was an eighty-man outpost with two more howitzers. Scattered throughout the province were another six thousand troops of General Masatoshi Fujishige's 8th Tiger Division. If Fujishige reacted swiftly, it was thought he could reach Los Baños with a sizable force within three hours.

The main consideration was getting the internees safely out of enemy territory. Many of them were elderly, and some forty-odd were bed ridden. All suffered from malnutrition and weakened physical states. Walking out was infeasible, as was driving a roundtrip column of cargo trucks to the camp through the Japanese positions. Quandt, seeing the camp was just two miles inland from Laguna de Bay, came up with the solution. The lake offered a direct route behind the lines. Amphibious vehicles—amtracs—could launch from the American-held shore and emerge close to the camp. The lake route minimized exposure and protected internees from hostile fire during evacuation.

The final plan, largely developed with intelligence provided by the guerrillas, called for a simultaneous land, air, and water operation.

While Colonel 'Shorty' Soule was designated the raid's overall task force commander, Muller had already set the plan's first phase in motion by having Lieutenant George Skau's reconnaissance platoon join the guerrillas already keeping the camp under surveillance. The twenty-two-man recon platoon and fifty select guerrillas had three tasks: taking out the guards and marking both Ringler's drop zone as well as the amtrac's beach landing site with smoke grenades. The smoke would aid navigation, as both elements would be approaching in the dim light of dawn.

The assault's kick-off signal would be Ringler's opening parachute. Once on the ground, Ringer's paratroopers would rush to join the assault, setting up a perimeter around the camp and organizing the internees for evacuation. At the same time, Henry Burgess, newly promoted to lieutenant colonel, would be churning across Laguna de Bay in fifty-seven amtracs carrying 350 troopers from his 1st Battalion. The operation's lynch pin was a diversionary attack by a battalion of 'Shorty' Soule's paragliders. Their assault south toward Los Baños would occupy the two Japanese units while guerrillas throughout the area launched raids on Japanese outposts.

The biggest intelligence coup was provided by escaped internee Prentice 'Pete' Miles, who'd been an engineering contractor before the war. Three prisoners had slipped under the wire to contact the guerrillas, who then guided Miles to Swing's command post on the evening of Tuesday, February 20, 1945, just three days before the raid. Getting out of the camp wasn't difficult, and intrepid internees did so regularly to forage for food. Getting back in, however, was the tricky part, and guards had shot two internees trying to do just that.

Miles revealed two key details: there were eighty guards, and every morning at 06:45, those not on duty conducted their daily calisthenics. For thirty minutes, most of the camp's garrison would be conveniently assembled and unarmed. The assault's H-Hour was set for 07:00.

Plan in hand, Ringler returned to brief his troopers. The dark-haired, twenty-six-year-old lieutenant had assumed command of Baker Company just before the jump into Tagaytay. One of his men, Charles Thollander, later recalled his first impression of Ringler, saying, "He didn't seem like the kind who'd let you get close to him, not friendly at all, but you knew this man was the right man for this company." Ringler demonstrated an even-tempered demeanor. He never raised his voice, nor did he smile. A trooper later quipped, "I've got a pet fish with a friendlier smile." While Ringler was reserved, he understood the burden of leadership and was always up front, close to the action. When asked why he took the same risks as those he led, Ringler reflected briefly before answering, "It's the toughest thing an officer has to do—send people into harm's way. The least you can do is be there."

Ringler would again be in the vanguard, jumping first from the lead aircraft. "My plan was to drop at a low altitude and as close as possible outside the camp to surprise the Jap garrison and to avoid a concentration of enemy ground fire," he said. "The three rifle platoons would assemble on their own leaders and move directly to their objective areas to engage the enemy."

He told his platoon leaders they would be dropping twenty-odd miles behind the lines into a dry rice paddy eight hundred yards west of the camp. To fill out their depleted ranks, they'd be integrating troopers from the machinegun platoon, rounding up their headcount to a hundred and twenty-five men.

After receiving platoon-specific missions, the troopers readied their gear and commenced with the usual pre-mission banter. The naysayers started first with, "This is a suicide jump." "Few of us will return." The optimists shrugged them off, countering with, "This is what we have trained so long and hard for." "This will be the ultimate battle." "This is the highlight of our combat career."

For all the uncertainty, Trooper John Holzem recalled, "For no amount of money could anyone have bought a seat on the plane from a [Baker Company] trooper."

The sense of purpose was contagious. Keen to make the jump were three Filipinos who had been with the company for several weeks. Serving as guides, interpreters, and ammo bearers, the teenagers were viewed by most troopers as members of the unit. Ringler left it up to the platoon sergeants: if the guerrillas wanted to jump, they would get parachutes and fifteen minutes of instruction.

ON THE MORNING OF FEBRUARY 23, all the pieces were in motion. All of them, that is, except Swing. He originally planned to jump with Ringler's men but changed his mind, instead opting to ride in on an amtrac. Rather than spending the night at the amtracs' staging area, however, he'd spent it at the division command post in Parañaque. The officer assigned to fetch him, Lieutenant Robert S. Beightler, along with his jeep driver, took a wrong turn in the dark. Swing was howling mad. When Beightler later recounted getting lost, he admitted, "Discretion prevents me from telling you some of the words the general used." They finally arrived at the lake just as the

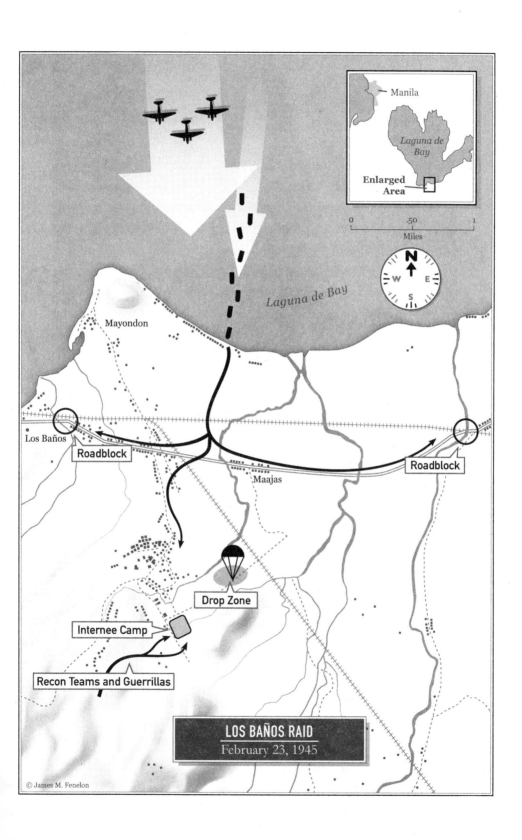

Manila

Laguna de Bay

Enlarged Area

0   .50   1
Miles

N
W   E
S

Laguna de Bay

Mayondon

Los Baños

Roadblock

Roadblock

Maajas

Drop Zone

Internee Camp

Recon Teams and Guerrillas

LOS BAÑOS RAID
February 23, 1945

© James M. Fenelon

last amtrac lumbered into the dark water and churned away—Swing would be sitting this one out.

Meanwhile, at the Los Baños camp, the recon teams and guerrillas crept into position. They'd spent the night slowly slinking their way around the perimeter, some groups taking ten hours to circuitously get to the drop on their assigned guard post. However, half the teams were still on the move when the drone of approaching aircraft heralded 07:00. The nine C-47s cruised in at seven hundred feet, and in the cargo door of each aircraft, a jumper stood poised, craning to spot the drop zone. They flew over the amtrac column, churning across the lake and toward the two columns of red smoke curling up from a rice field just further inland.

The green jump light flashed on. Ringler shoved out the bundle containing a belt-fed machinegun and jumped after it.

INSIDE THE BARBED-WIRE COMPOUND, the internees were mustering for their morning roll call. One of them pointed toward the horizon and yelled, "Look over there! Airplanes!"

"American or Japanese?"

"Oh, pray God they're Americans!"

"They're flying right toward us!"

"Something's falling from them!"

Their first thought was of food. *The planes are dropping food?*

Carol Terry, a missionary, watched the small armada fly in before she joined the chorus. "Stars!" she shouted. "I see stars! They're American!"

The crowd soon realized that the descending objects were men.

Terry recalled, "Everyone started screaming with joy.... It became a vibrant song of heart and soul." For her, it meant the end, one way or another, of three and a half years of imprisonment.

Gunfire erupted from every direction, immediately changing the internees' euphoria to panic. Eighteen-year-old Margaret Squires recalled, "Gunfire ricocheted around us as we ran back into the barracks and threw ourselves on the dirt center aisle that ran its length."

The Japanese guards in the exercise yard stopped their workout, staring wide eyed at the airdrop. The steady *Pop! Pop! Pop!* of rifle fire sent bullets whizzing into the confused mass, and within seconds, several crumpled bodies lay where they fell. The survivors sprinted away in every direction, some for the hills, some for their rifles.

Skirmishes broke out all along the perimeter. The recon teams and guerrillas not in position sprinted forward, engaging their targets on the move. Soon they were swarming in from three sides of the camp.

Sergeant Terry R. Santos, a slim Filipino American from California, led his team toward the two pillboxes they were responsible for eliminating. Santos and three other Americans had started with a squad of twelve guerrillas, but by the time they arrived on target, just one remained, Private Pastor Gatdula. The rest had drifted off on other routes or stopped short due to wearing partial Japanese uniforms that made them likely targets. As Santos' group rushed forward, the alerted Japanese gunner opened fire, wounding three of the men with a wild burst before an unscathed Santos took him out.

Another recon team, led by Sergeant Cliff Town, spotted a group of six Japanese guards and cut them down from a hundred yards with well-aimed automatic fire.

The internees huddled in their barracks, ducking as bullets punched through the thatched walls. Several pulled their thin mattresses over themselves. Jesse Tribble, who'd given his mattress to a woman and her children, tried to hide behind his cardboard suitcase. Guards fired several shots at them, missing Tribble but hitting the woman and her daughter. Neither was seriously wounded.

British internee Lewis Thomas Watty watched a recon man and some guerrillas cut their way through the fence near his barracks.

"We were all taking what cover was available from flying bullets, but when we saw him, we forgot bullets, danger, and everything else, and dashed out cheering." Watty pointed the raiders toward the guards' barracks and then watched their attack, later describing it as "a pretty piece of work."

Ringler's paratroopers charged into the camp seventeen minutes after their drop. By then, most of the guards were already dead or fleeing. The prisoners poured out of their barracks to greet their rescuers.

"There was much jubilation," recalled Ringler, "with everybody wanting to hug the men and congratulate them. My effort was to eliminate all of that and immediately get the people organized."

With over two thousand internees in the camp, Ringler found it easier said than done. Many were still hiding, others wandered around gawking, and several took advantage of the pandemonium to rush past the corpses of their former jailers and raid the Japanese food supplies.

The approaching sound of armored vehicles caused another wave of panic.

"Jap tanks! Jap tanks!" someone yelled. Again, the internees scattered.

Ringler's bazooka team sprinted forward, but it was a false alarm. The grinding racket was the arriving amtracs. Their clanking was so loud that several guards fled, fearing a full-scale tank attack. The driver of the lead vehicle steered past a silent pillbox and crashed through the front gate.

The amtracs had navigated their seven-mile course through the lake's inky gloom using a hand-held compass; they'd hit the beach just as Ringler's aircraft flew over. At the shoreline, several of the amtracs split off, with one group rambling west to occupy key high ground while a second peeled east to set up a roadblock.

Two pack howitzers went into action upon unloading at the landing site. Sergeant Harry Van Divner, a radioman, later recalled, "A Jap heavy machinegun commenced firing from high ground to the right of the beach, three or four hundred yards away.... I heard some slamming and banging; the artillerymen were preparing to fire on the Jap machinegun. They fired white phosphorus and few other rounds, and the Japs shut up—we heard nothing more from them."

The rest of the amtracs continued toward the camp, preceded by combat engineers waving their mine detectors over the road. Colonel Henry Burgess rode in the first vehicle through the gate. He surveyed the scene. "I was appalled at the condition of the internees," he said. "None of us was prepared for what we found, most of the men weighing no more than 110 pounds, and the women resembling sticks. A few children had survived and were very weak."

Burgess was anxious. The clock was ticking, and he wanted everybody out of there. Behind him, the long line of amtracs were already turning around to lower their ramps for loading.

Many internees wandered through the camp, unaware this was a raid and that the rescuers had no intention of sticking around. Ringler's paratroopers swarmed through the sixty-acre camp, yelling and cajoling them toward the rows of idling amphibious vehicles.

"Lady, you've got five minutes to get to an amtrac," a trooper told Carol Terry.

"What's an amtrac?" she asked.

"Now you've got two minutes to get in that amtrac." The trooper moved on as Terry scrambled to throw a few pieces of clothing into a suitcase.

The internees were still moving too slowly. Most were packing what few scraps of clothes or utensils they had left in the world. The camp's carpenter pleaded to take all his tools. One trooper encountered a woman refusing to leave without her Persian cat. "She's been gone since Tuesday," she cried. She suspected foul play of her fellow starving internees. "I'm afraid they've eaten her."

A trooper noticed a gaunt woman scowling at her rescuers. When questioned, she replied, "Night after night, I've dreamed of this day, and in all my dreams of rescue, I was rescued by Marines. You're not Marines."

At 07:45, Ringler found Burgess. Both were anxious to get the evacuation underway. Yelling only motivated those within earshot, but Ringler observed that several buildings had caught fire during the shootout, and the flames were chasing the internees toward the amtracs.

"Fire the barracks," Burgess ordered.

Ringler sent a lieutenant and a group of troopers to the rear of the camp to torch the place as they worked their way back.

Soon the camp was ablaze, and the evacuation gained momentum. One trooper, lighter in hand, took a few seconds to cut down the camp's Japanese flag, tossing it to medic Jack McGrath as a souvenir.

Several internees too weak to walk were carried on stretchers by troopers who set them down gingerly in an amtrac before sprinting off to find more people in need of help. For trooper Richard Penwell, the sight of the emaciated women and children was too much. "The only flashbacks I get are of them ... the starved people," he later confided.

Private Don Langford watched, too. "You couldn't believe those skinny little people, lugging those big suitcases with everything they had in the world."

A priest paused his exodus to kneel in thanksgiving of his deliverance. A trooper gently nudged him back to his feet, pleading, "Come on, Father. Let's get the hell out of here."

Each amtrac could carry almost thirty internees, and troopers shuttled babies, the feeble, and suitcases up the ramps. First aboard were the sick and those too weak to walk. Passengers were allowed one suitcase; anything more was left behind.

A flock of habit-cloaked nuns was loaded onto an amtrac whose driver had painted the sobriquet *The Impatient Virgin* on its bow. The scene evoked more than one snicker.

Amtrac driver Arthur J. Coleman watched several internees shuffle into his idling vehicle. "[They] looked very thin and were dressed in well-worn and tattered clothing. They were very hungry and ate our rations without asking for them," he said. "They ate everything but the boxes."

They also eyed his smokes. "I wanted to smoke but had very few to share. I lit one and tried to hide it, but to no avail." When an internee asked if he could have the butt of Coleman's cigarette when he was done, Coleman passed out the pack.

In the middle of the loading, someone pointed to a culvert and yelled, "There's a Jap in there!" A guerrilla flipped a grenade into the ditch, then delivered the coup de grace with a few point-blank shots from his carbine.

When the amtracs were filled with the first fifteen hundred evacuees, the drivers threw the monsters into gear and headed to the lake. Trailing behind, the paratroopers, recon men, and guerrillas formed a cordon around the remaining eight-hundred-odd internees, escorting them to the beach. There they would wait for the amtracs to return for the second lift. It was a hot, dusty two-mile march, but the mood was jubilant.

In the distance, the thump of artillery explosions rolled across the hills. 'Shorty' Soule's diversionary attack drew out and killed well over two hundred of the enemy. While Shorty's feint was obviously working, at least one Japanese outpost was aware of the rescue. As the raiders and the internees waited on the beach, a few mortar shells whistled in. No one was hit, but for the exhausted internees unaccustomed to the sights and sounds of battle, it must have been terrifying.

After an anxious hour, the first amtracs returned at 11:45. Several split off to pick up the roadblock teams while everybody loaded up. As they churned back across the lake, a few Japanese artillery shells exploded within feet of the amtracs, showering the occupants with geysers of water. Behind them, the camp burned, its grounds littered with forty-eight Japanese corpses.

The rescuers pulled off one of the war's most audacious raids with surprisingly few casualties: two guerrillas were wounded, and two, Captain Anselmo Soler and Sergeant Anastacio Castillo, were killed; several recon men were wounded, and an amtrac driver was shot in the hand. Shorty's diversionary force suffered two killed and three wounded.

WHEN THE INTERNEES ARRIVED at the far shore, medics greeted them and transferred the litter patients into waiting ambulances while military policemen helped the rest into olive-drab cargo trucks. Once loaded, they were driven twenty miles north to dorms prepared for them in an old prison. American Red Cross volunteers

handed out cigarettes and candy while ladling steaming cups of bean soup. A nun dropped her Hershey Bar, "but even though it had mud on it, I ate it," she remembered. "I was starving." The internees were also given writing paper so they could inform loved ones of their rescue.

The O'Hara family is interviewed after their liberation from the Los Baños prison camp; two amtracs idle behind them

Medics examined and registered them as they settled in, including the youngest: three-day-old Kathleen

McCoy. Among the 2,147 rescued were a preponderance of Americans, but also British, Australians, Canadians, Norwegians, Poles, Dutch, Italians, French, and a Nicaraguan. Over a hundred were hospitalized for various ailments, including fever, dysentery, beriberi, malnutrition, and exhaustion. Six were treated for battle wounds.

Later that afternoon, cooks served a meal of vegetables and meat with tomato soup. So many internees came back for third or fourth helpings, the kitchen was busy until midnight.

When the last of the troopers arrived—a group from one of Burgess' roadblocks—the internees waiting in the food line noticed them. One of the combat engineers was heartened by what happened next. "There wasn't a sound, like a graveyard," he said. "Then they began to clap. The feeling I had was one of humility, and as if I had been touched by something. I was almost moved to tears. It was awesome, pleasant, and warm. It's hard to explain."

Radioman John Fulton felt the same, later saying, "I can't really describe the joy I felt while helping those prisoners out of their barracks and heading them toward the amtracs. The looks on their faces I can never forget."

Many troopers later voiced the same elusive sentiment. Time and distance eventually helped them understand their emotions and they later looked back upon the unique mission with pride for the simplest of reasons: that day, they were saving lives instead of taking them.

Chapter 12

"We're Going to Step in It Today"

Southern Luzon.
February 24 – May 1, 1945

The day after the rescue was notable for its absence of laurels. While at least three reporters witnessed the raid, including two who rode in amtracs and Frank Smith of the *Chicago Daily Times,* who parachuted in, there was even bigger news unfolding fifteen hundred miles away. The photograph of six Marines raising the US flag on Iwo Jima snagged front page headlines.

Not that the rescuers had time to relish the limelight. Swing was readying the division for another attack, and Henry Burgess' battalion of paratroopers was already returning to the front.

'Butch' Muller, seeing Swing get back to business after such an accomplishment, thought, *This is the way it must be with a first-class unit. You do one job, and you get right on to the next. There is no time for glory in the infantry.*

With the collapse of the Genko Line, and Manila liberated, Krueger's Sixth Army divided Luzon into sectors to facilitate securing the rest of the island. The 11th Airborne drew several sectors in central Luzon, an area of approximately fifty-five thousand square miles. Swing joked that Krueger's planners tracked his division on a different scale map than the other divisions: "Right now, I've got more territory to cover than the 37th [and] 1st Cavalry [Divisions]. In a way, it's a compliment, but the men can't keep it up endlessly."

Swing's units were stretched thin—all on the frontlines, all operating without reserves, and all under strength. First Lieutenant Kirkland commented on the manpower shortages, "Our masters tasked regiments and battalions that were—present for duty—only battalions and companies."

Thinning the ranks at the same rate as the bullets and shrapnel was disease. Many troopers, with insufficient time to recover after Leyte, were worn down and unable to fend off jaundice and other jungle maladies. Machinegunner Deane Marks was a prime example: his swollen joints screamed with each step. "My eyeballs were yellow, as was my skin," he said. "My urine was colored like Coca-Cola, and stool like white putty." The battalion surgeon took one look at him, tied a tag labeled "hepatitis/dengue" to his uniform, and ordered him to the aid station.

In February, Swing's medics tallied 985 battle casualties and hospitalized another 945 with hepatitis, diarrhea, yellow jaundice, and various undetermined fevers. Non-combat injuries took an additional seventy-three men off the line, and the division psychiatrist diagnosed ninety others with battle fatigue.

Taking a smaller but no less deadly toll was friendly fire. After one night-time shooting, a trooper—refusing to name the victim—recalled, "The next few hours were spent in disbelief regarding GI John Doe, who came all the way from Toccoa, Mackall, Benning, Polk, Stoneman, New Guinea, Leyte … to almost the end of Luzon, only to die because some jackass, fresh off the boat, panicked and shot before he looked or challenged." The shooters were transferred to other units for their own safety but had to manage their guilt themselves.

Fratricide numbers were not tracked, but an Army study suggested that between 16 and 24 percent of American deaths in the Pacific could potentially be attributed to friendly fire. A trooper later ruefully admitted, "I hate to say this, but I know for sure that a lot of our people were killed by friendly fire. I know that." One of his peers agreed, confessing, "When everybody's wound up tight and their bowels are churning, it takes only one yell or one shot to get the whole show going, and too many people get hurt that way. We shoot anything—rocks, trees, the moon, each other."

Wounded men trickled back to their units when healed, and fifty-seven of the battle fatigue cases returned after a short hospital stay, but it wasn't enough. Replacements were the lifeblood of combat units, and Swing needed fresh troops. Without them, units wilted away.

"No replacements of my own," Swing complained. "The stuffy Army staff doesn't like airborne and won't do anything about getting me any." They did attach the 158th Regimental Combat Team—the Bushmasters—to Swing's command, but that was an expedient, short-term solution. Swing also worked with Major Vanderpool to assign guerrillas to each infantry battalion. The guerrillas became an integral part of the division. The Angels, short of machineguns, mortars, and bazookas, armed the guerrillas with captured Japanese weapons. Troopers held mixed opinions on working with the irregular units, with some questioning their effectiveness. But as First Lieutenant Kirkland said, "The bare truth is that we desperately needed these guerrilla forces."

Despite his division being down by almost two thousand men, Swing remained undaunted. It took him several days to ready the division for the push into the island's center. While his staff moved the command post back into the lodge atop Tagaytay Ridge, the perennially toiling quartermasters packed up the supplies at Parañaque to follow them. Maintenance and supply issues still hounded Swing: a third of his cargo trucks were redlined for lack of tires, and twelve of the sixteen tanks attached to the 11th Airborne were out of commission waiting for spare parts. Operationally supporting the new campaign meant more tentacle-like supply lines. The engineers went to work cutting new roads, widening dirt trails for vehicles, and spanning rivers, but "the most astounding" feat, according to the division historian, was gouging a narrow switch-back road out of an almost vertical cliff.

ARRAYED AND WAITING at strategic points throughout central Luzon were the thirteen thousand soldiers of the *Fuji Heidan*. Their commander, Colonel Masatoshi Fujishige, a thirty-year veteran of infantry service and a self-described expert in land warfare, intended to drag the Americans to a standstill. Fujishige deployed his units on high ground overwatching the region's limited road network. By denying the Americans the use of roads, he'd block their advance and prevent them from cutting across the island. He was ready for a fight, and he had wide latitude to conduct his defense as he saw fit. Some of that freedom was due to Yamashita organizing his forces for independent action, but most of it was due to a complete breakdown in communications after the fall of Manila. Since then, Fujishige had received no instructions or updates from Yamashita's headquarters.

Fujishige was operating under many of the same constraints as Swing: his men were split into multiple groups; he lacked sufficient transportation; he wanted tank support; and his units were undermanned and a composite of specialties (infantry, naval troops, and Air Force personnel). His dearth of transportation meant limited mobility, arguably one of the greatest assets to a ground commander.

After the Los Baños raid, Fujishige ordered more troops to reinforce the line between Lake Taal and Laguna de Bay. Arriving in the middle of the night, they brought a reign of terror with them. Japanese soldiers, fanning out ostensibly in search of guerrillas, instead waged a one-sided war against civilians. Those escaping the massacre warned their neighbors, who also fled. Each time they paused to catch their breath, the victims' shrill screams compelled them to keep running. By the time local guerrillas mustered, they found eight dead, but shrieks echoing out of the dark confirmed the carnage had just started.

Families sought shelter at a nearby chapel, barricading themselves inside. The soldiers tried bashing through the doors with rifle-butts but gave up and instead blocked the exits. Then they torched the building. When the Japanese faded back into the night, the smoldering chapel contained three hundred charred corpses of men, women, and children. Several more victims, cut down by swords and bayonets, surrounded the pyre.

A mile north of Los Baños, in the small village of Malinta, a Japanese squad herded villagers at gunpoint into a bamboo grove, prodding the hesitant forward with bayonets. Edmundo Manzanilla escaped the bloodbath that took the lives of sixty neighbors.

"My two elder sisters played dead," he recalled, "but the child in each of their arms was repeatedly bayoneted every time it cried."

Manzanilla and the few other escapees saw that the Japanese were not alone. They were reinforced by rampaging YOIN, a paramilitary group of pro-Japanese Filipinos. The YOIN were volunteer units equipped and commanded by the Imperial Army. They participated in the massacres, cutting down their neighbors with a fury fueled by a hatred for American imperialism that outweighed compassion for their own countrymen.

PATROLLING PARATROOPERS stumbled across other atrocities. Lieutenant Robert Fuller later recalled, "My platoon came across a Filipino man tied to a small tree with his hands behind him. He looked dead, as he was just hanging there with his guts falling out of his belly."

Sprawled on the ground in front of the man were a woman and three children—all four murdered.

"When we cut the man loose from the tree," Fuller continued, "we were surprised to discover he was still alive."

The man, Timoteo Buado, worked at a nearby sugar factory, and the dead woman was his wife. Japanese soldiers stabbed her and two of the children as Buado, lashed to the tree, was forced to watch. Another soldier tossed the couple's infant into the air to be skewered on a bayonet. An officer then disemboweled Buado, leaving him there to die with his intestines hanging out. Fuller's medics bandaged Buado as best they could, then rushed him to the field hospital where surgeons saved his life.

Guerrilla Jose Honrado, searching for his family at Los Baños, found them in a relative's living room, piled together and decaying into an amorphous "waxen solid mass."

The total deaths amounted to more than fifteen hundred victims, many of them unidentifiable due to fire and decomposition. It is unclear if the "inhuman butchery of the Japanese," as Fuller described it, was in retribution for freeing the internees at Los Baños or part of the Japanese's wider, systemic slaughter of civilians. What is clear is that the local guerrilla leader, Colonel Romeo Espino, had anticipated such atrocities and raised his concerns to Colonel Gustavo Ingles before the Angels' raid. Ingles, representing Vanderpool's guerrilla headquarters, assured Espino he'd arrange protection with the Americans.

Ingles later lamented, "To this day, the relatives of the massacred persons have not forgiven us. I still maintain that because of the failure of the US Army to occupy and give adequate protection to the town of Los Baños, many Filipinos had to die as a result of the liberation of the internment camp. While this was never the intention prior to the raid, it came out that way, as many feared it would."

Ingles claimed Espino's concerns were radioed to Vanderpool, who confirmed he'd coordinate protection with 'Butch' Muller, Swing's intelligence officer. For his part, though, Muller insisted the request never reached him or any of the other planners. Nor did any of them expect such vengeful barbarity. "We didn't foresee it," he admitted. "That was a mistake, a fault. We probably should have seen it. Now, if we had foreseen it, what could we have done?"

Muller ticked off the options: prevent the guerrillas from participating—so fleeing guards couldn't report local participation? Delay the raid until American forces were closer and in strength to defeat the *Fuji Heidan*? Equip the guerrillas to better defend the area? Encourage a civilian evacuation? All options would have required more time, and the raid's urgency was driven by suspicions of a pending internee massacre. Tragically, one bloodbath was avoided only to set the stage for another.

The atrocities appalled Colonel Henry Burgess, who wrote to his fiancée, "No one at home knows what the Jap is like. In this small town of Los Baños, all the houses were burned after first tying the occupants inside. A ten-day-old baby was brought in with a bayonet wound. A small girl about three years old was in with two large stabs in the back. There is a great deal of difference in the impression created between hearing such doings and seeing them."

The division historian agreed, writing, "No wonder we developed an un-Christian-like hate for the Japs as we discovered their vicious, criminal methods of fighting."

The guerrillas sought retribution against both the Japanese and those aiding them. When John Ringler's Baker Company passed through a village whose residents had hanged several collaborators, the troopers bristled at the frontier-style justice. Ringler passed through the column of marching troopers, urging them forward to avoid trouble. "This is their affair. We have our own business, so move on."

When the same troopers saw the charred chapel and the Los Baños chief of police counting the victims' blackened skulls, Ringler gave them a different message, impressing on them, "I want you to walk by and look at this hell. Don't turn away. Don't ever doubt why we are here."

The grisly spectacle struck a chord in Charles Sass. "That was a hard emotional experience, and its with me to this day. We could have hiked around those places and never known. At times, I wish we had."

Medic Jack McGrath witnessed a guerrilla tribunal that he described as "a scene from Dante's *Inferno*." The room was crowded with the curious, the accusers, and the accused, bound by chains, ropes, or handcuffs.

"These people were being knocked about and cut like you couldn't believe. The floor was carpeted with blood, so much of it you could hardly walk," recalled McGrath. "You walked by sliding your feet along the floor. One Filipino asked me if I wanted to box, and with that, he hit one of the prisoners in the face. I declined the offer."

McGrath watched an interrogator force one of the accused to eat a piece of his own severed ear. "When asked how it tasted, he said very good. These prisoners were being subjected to pain—lots of it. No one cried out, no one pleaded for mercy. I had formed the opinion the Filipinos were a brave lot; even their traitors were brave. I mean this in a complimentary way. They impressed me then, and were to impress me more before the day ended."

The tribunal moved outside, where an American officer tried to end the exhibition, but McGrath and several other troopers "hooted" him down.

McGrath continued, "The prisoners were brought out in groups of three and four. They were tortured, then killed; not one asked for mercy. They were all brave men. There must have been twenty, all told. Then for the *pièce de résistance*, a woman was brought out. Her arms were bound behind her. Another woman, good looking and well dressed, started punching the bound one. She did this to the cheers of the Filipinos in the audience."

The prisoner—with a sign around her neck listing her crimes—was then marched through the crowd. Her guilt was by association: marriage to a Japanese officer who was the alleged mastermind of several local atrocities. Her punishment was death.

"She was tied to a stake," said McGrath. "Straw was placed around her legs up to her knees. Five gallons of alcohol were poured over her, and she was set alight. Not once did she cry, not during her beating or when the flames got her." Recalling the scene, McGrath said, "Sherman was right." War is hell.

HELL IT WAS, and the month of March ushered in more of it, wrapped in a flurry of activity and preceded by bad news: thirty-seven-year-old Colonel Orin 'Hard Rock' Haugen was dead. He'd died two weeks earlier after succumbing to his wounds during his evacuation flight, but the news was just now reaching the front. Undoubtedly, Haugen's wife and their adopted seven-year-old son had already received a telegram from the War Department. It would likely be several more days before his two brothers fighting on Iwo Jima heard the news. Among his troopers, word of his death spread quickly, but no one had time to mourn. The war continued, and the division was on the march.

Swing's advance into the center of the island put his knack for dizzying improvisation to the test. He split up the division, attacking on multiple fronts to sweep east around both sides of Lake Taal. With his forces divided, Swing watched the battle unfold while crossing his fingers and "hoping that I can effect a junction south of the lake before the Japs realize what I am trying to do." He urged speed to keep the enemy off balance and give his small units the tactical advantage.

He left one of the 188th's Paraglider battalions near the Genko Line, while the other sliced down the west coast to seize Ternate, the division's first objective. *Fuji Heidan* units occupied the area, launching their depth-charge-laden suicide boats against Allied shipping in Manila Bay.

The paragliders preceded their assault with a heavy artillery barrage, followed by tanks threading their way forward around buried depth charges rigged with pressure plates. Three guerrilla companies threw themselves into the enemy as well. An American observer complimented their combat prowess, describing them as "wily and reliable mountain soldiers." After twenty-four hours of running gun battles, the Japanese garrison effectively withdrew via a series of delaying skirmishes, losing two hundred and seventy-six men in the process.

The paragliders captured numerous machineguns, mortars, and howitzers, then swiftly flanked down the coast, trapping 1,350 Japanese, who'd be dealt with piecemeal by the now well-armed guerrillas.

At the same time, the Bushmasters of the 158th Combat Team raced south to seize Batangas Bay, liberating one of the islands' best deep-water harbors for Allied shipping. The 187th Paragliders attacked east across the top of Lake Taal, clearing Mount Sungay and Hill 660 along the way. Hill 660 fell to the guerrillas' zeal and the Americans' willingness to use them as bait. The paragliders made a frontal attack while sending the guerrillas around the two flanks for an envelopment. A trooper later confessed, "As expected, the swarms of Filipinos in their white shirts and shorts drew heavy fire as they advanced over the open ground and rice paddies."

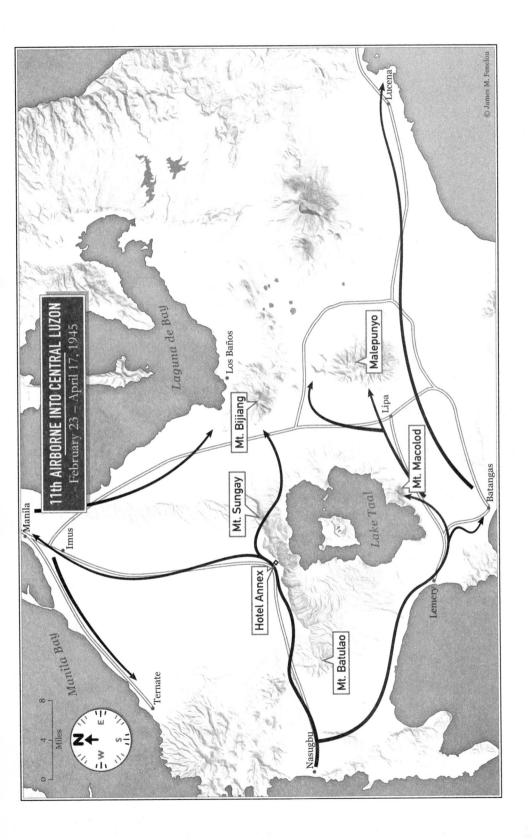

11th AIRBORNE INTO CENTRAL LUZON
February 23 – April 17, 1945

Manila

Imus

Ternate

Manila Bay

Laguna de Bay

Los Baños

Mt. Bijiang

Mt. Sungay

Hotel Annex

Lake Taal

Mt. Batulao

Nasugbu

Lemery

Batangas

Mt. Macolod

Lipa

Malepunyo

Lucena

© James M. Fenelon

Miles
0   4   8

N

The distraction allowed the paragliders to advance under a creeping artillery barrage until they were close enough to open fire. They took the position and, as noted in their after-action report, "chalked up thirty-eight dead Nips." No mention was made if any guerrillas died in the assault.

The guerrillas were vital to Swing's campaign, and he knew it. "The only thing that keeps my lines open and allows me to spread so thin is the fact that we have five thousand guerrillas and have them attached to all the infantry, artillery, and engineer units."

"Am so darn proud of my guerrillas," he gushed. "Finally persuaded Army to give me uniforms for them. With their big straw hats and white shirts, they were easy meat for a Jap machinegun—since receiving the uniform and watching our men work, they can now take a cave full as neatly as anybody." Swing authorized the guerrillas to wear the division patch over their left breast pocket and credited them with killing nearly two thousand Japanese.

The 187th now moved south between Laguna de Bay and Lake Taal, shoulder-to-shoulder with Lahti's paratroopers on the left flank. But here, Fujishige's line held, and his mortars and artillery arrested the Angels' march south. The Japanese strongpoint atop Mount Bijiang—the highest promontory in the area—overlooked the highway and gave them command of the surrounding countryside. They repelled several of 'Slugger' Lahti's patrols attempting to reconnoiter the thousand-foot-tall mountain.

First Lieutenant Randolph Kirkland accompanied the next attempt. As 3rd Battalion's intelligence officer, he wanted to know firsthand what they were up against. He described the terrain as a "bare open field stretched from the top down to the road. A tongue of mixed banana plants, bamboo, and hardwood trees split the open field but stopped about 150 yards from the top. The bare open pastureland was broken up by ridges and rolling terraces. Over on the right of the field, facing the hill from the road, there was a wooded approach that became a part of the wooded crest."

The platoon leader led his men up the open field toward the crest. When Kirkland drew the lieutenant's attention to the concealed route offered by the thicket, the officer replied "that he wanted to keep it simple, to go straight up and back." Kirkland, accompanied by two guerrillas, opted to shadow the platoon from the thicket. Reaching the end of the brush line, Kirkland watched the platoon spread out for their approach.

"About then," Kirkland recalled, "I was taken with an urgent return of my chronic dysentery and dropped my pants and squatted. The two greenhorn guerrillas thought this immensely amusing and giggled at my discomfiture."

As Kirkland hunkered down, bullets ripped over his head and into the laughing guerrillas, both dead before they hit the ground.

"I rolled over into a nearby erosion ditch, struggling to get my pants up."

To his right, at least two Japanese machineguns raked the platoon. Then a salvo of 81mm mortar shells crashed in. The concussion slammed Kirkland to the ground. Bleeding from his ears and nose, he shrank as a line of Japanese infantry emerged from the hill's wooded crest, their bayonet-tipped rifles catching the sun. He was calculating his odds of escape when several more shells screamed in, this time bursting amid the Japanese. The barrage, called in by the platoon leader, chased the Japanese back into the woods. Kirkland scrambled downhill, confirmed the four Americans collapsed in the open field were dead, and joined the platoon in their retreat. Together they staggered to their foxholes, toting four wounded comrades.

"It had not been a day to be proud of," Kirkland later wrote.

Kirkland estimated two hundred Japanese held the hill. They were well dug in and were supported by numerous machineguns and, based on the pattern and frequency of the shelling, at least four 81mm mortars.

The next attack, a double effort, would include Captain Stephen 'Rusty' Cavanaugh's Dog Company. Cavanaugh conducted his own reconnaissance and concluded, "The western approach was the least desirable, and I decided to attempt a movement up the southern slope of the mountain." Item Company's commander, however, opted to use the same exposed route as before.

It was to be a textbook envelopment, but unorthodox, as the two companies were from different battalions and had no radio contact between them. Item Company was making the primary effort up the west side, while Dog Company came up from the south as a diversionary attack. Cavanaugh's troopers would help Item Company consolidate on the crest, then return to the regiment's perimeter.

At precisely 08:30 on Tuesday morning, March 13, 1945, twelve P-38 Lightnings swooped in, dropping one-hundred-pound bombs on the crest of Mount Bijiang. While their timing was impeccable, their accuracy wasn't. Only a third of their ordnance exploded on target. They winged back around, making several strafing runs that Cavanaugh judged to be right where he wanted them.

Cavanaugh recalled, "The company moved off the road and into a column of platoons, with an increased interval between men and platoons. As the company began moving up the gradual slope of the mountain, the terrain was, as I recall, rather open with a few small, shallow ravines running up the slope, and with little vegetation."

Artillery crashed in after the P-38s flew away, and a Dog Company trooper recalled that "shells were still coming in when we got to the foot of the mountain. I remember the shelling was so close that shrapnel was raining down on our steel helmets." When the shelling stopped, the staccato of Item Company's rifles and machineguns echoed from the other side of the mountain.

Halfway up, Japanese bullets zipped in from the left. Scout Raymond Cegiacnik went down with his jawbone torn away. Medics were on him in an instant, but he died after they couldn't stem the bleeding. Cavanaugh shifted his platoons to the right and continued uphill. By mid-afternoon, Dog Company had seized the mountain with two men killed, but as far as Cavanaugh could tell, they hadn't inflicted any enemy losses. He deployed his men for the expected Japanese counterattack, positioning 1st Platoon on the left and 2nd Platoon on the right, while 3rd Platoon held the rear. In the middle of them, Cavanaugh placed his command element, along with their lone 60mm mortar in a small depression.

Surveying the broad, open terrain, which was cultivated for farming, Cavanaugh realized "the defensive position was less than desirable in that the area was too large to be fully defended with the troops available." But the "big problem," he said, "[was] we'd come up the hill with scaled down packs and with no entrenching tools, nothing to dig in with. I was a very upset company commander, kicking myself for not anticipating the need for digging in."

Some troopers scraped shallow ditches with their helmets. They all broiled in the seething heat, and most drained their canteens to slake their thirst.

The Japanese announced their counterattack with a salvo of mortar shells against the two forward platoons.

"I remember vividly seeing the bobbing back of a Japanese soldier about fifty yards from me as he apparently was loading and firing a mortar," said Cavanaugh. "I must have fired three clips at that bobbing back, and I don't think I ever hit him."

Elmer Hudson was nearby. "I could see several shells in the air coming right down my throat! I protected my face with my right arm in front and caught five pieces of shrapnel in the arm, saving a hit to my head." The concussion threw Hudson back about twenty feet, and shrapnel peppered both his legs. A medic injected him with morphine and dragged him behind a dike before rushing off to aid others.

The artillery forward observer with Cavanaugh yelled adjustments into his radio, but the enemy's proximity required finesse. "I recall the artillery shells coming in from our supporting battery passing so close over our heads that we could almost have touched them." But they only enjoyed the benefit of a few shells before calling off the dangerous barrage. The 60mm mortar thumped out three or four rounds, chasing off an enemy machinegun crew.

The Japanese charged forward into a wall of lead unleashed by two of Cavanaugh's machineguns and the entirety of the 3rd Platoon. "Its effect was murderous," said one of the troopers. "When no more movement could be seen, the fire lifted." Smoke drifting in from a spreading fire reduced visibility.

The situation was grim. Troopers had one grenade apiece, were low on rifle ammo, and had no machinegun ammo. A sergeant and several men stripped the dead and wounded of their ammo to refill the machinegun belts—both used the same caliber ammunition. Two troopers worked together per belt and soon had four belts ready. Those lasted just a few minutes, but they kept the enemy at bay and out of hand grenade range. Cavanaugh radioed for an urgent resupply but had no idea how long that would take.

"About this time, my radio operator turned to say something to me and took a bullet through the mouth," he said.

The casualty reports came in: 1st Platoon's commander was shot in the head, losing an eye; the executive officer was hit in the shoulder; and twenty-odd others were wounded. Cavanaugh took a round through his shoulder and another through the front of his helmet, which miraculously skirted the steel rim before punching out the side. Dog Company was down by almost 30 percent, and then the radio went dead. It was time to go.

"I passed the word to the 3rd Platoon which guarded the rear of the perimeter to be prepared to cover our withdrawal through its position," recalled Cavanaugh.

The forward platoons peeled back through the perimeter. They moved so fast they almost forgot one of the wounded. But Billy Pettit and LeRoy 'Richie' Richardson slithered back to get him.

"The enemy did not pursue," continued Cavanaugh, "perhaps because the 3rd Platoon laid down such a heavy volume of covering fire." After accounting for his troopers, Cavanaugh was one of the last men off the hill.

On the west side of the mountain, Item Company was faring little better. They, too, were under heavy machinegun fire. Elmer Blake fired a rifle grenade at a machinegun he estimated to be about a football field away. One of his buddies watched the grenade's trajectory with a critical eye. "When we saw it go straight up, we knew we were in trouble, and we all hit the dirt. But not so! The grenade landed right on the Japanese position!"

But it was a dud, and so was the second.

The Japanese crew, deciding the third grenade might do the trick, grabbed their gun and fled. Several fell to American rifle fire as they scurried uphill.

Item Company escaped downhill with their wounded, leaving three dead comrades behind. But one of them was still alive. Twenty-seven-year-old Medic Bernard 'Bernie' B. Coon was running to aid a wounded scout when he was knocked off his feet by a shot to the arm. Another trooper helped him up when a second burst ripped into his other arm, flipping him back down.

Coon lay helpless, the two debilitating wounds preventing him from getting up or reaching the medical supplies in his backpack.

"If you have never lain wounded in enemy territory and watched your fellow men pull back and leave you," said Coon, "then you cannot appreciate my feelings at this time."

"Because of the continued bleeding, I decided my end was rather near, so I spent several minutes in thought with my mother and family and prayed they would not take it too hard, as I was tired anyhow and needed a rest after many long hours of combat, death, and torn and wrecked bodies."

Coon slept to slow his heart rate, but nearby movement startled him awake shortly after sunset. It wasn't the comrades he'd hoped had come back for him, but two Japanese soldiers searching the dead.

The scavengers wanted Coon's medical pack and rolled him onto his back to fumble with the clasp. Coon played dead but feared his pounding heart would give him away. They cut off the pack, took Coon's wristwatch, and moved off. Coon kept his eyes closed until he fell back asleep.

He woke to the heat of dawn and Japanese voices drifting over from the woods. He lay still, staring at the sky. A flight of American aircraft circled lazily overhead.

"One ship just peeled off and seemed to be diving right at me," recalled Coon. "I saw the flash from its four machineguns, and that thump, thump I heard hitting the ground wasn't rain drops." Four planes passed overhead, bombing and strafing the hilltop. Coon passed the time watching flies lay eggs on his raw, torn flesh. He attempted to escape that night but was too weak to get to his feet. His next attempt the night after was more successful. When he managed to pull himself into a sitting position with his heels, Coon—sunburned, thirsty, and weak—lurched down the hill. After several hours, he made the four miles back to Item Company's perimeter. He recovered, but spent the next two years in the hospital, enduring seven operations, including a bone graft.

For the next two days, the Angels pummeled Mount Bijiang around the clock. Pack howitzers lobbed shell after shell into it, pausing their barrages only for airstrikes. A guerrilla patrol ranged the mountain, confirming the mauling had forced the Japanese to abandon their strongpoint. They found three hundred foxholes, as well as dugouts for fifteen machineguns and six mortars.

A company of paratroopers occupied Bijiang until units from the 1st Cavalry relieved Swing's troopers holding the line between Lake Taal and Laguna de Bay. But there would be no rest. Swing trucked them eighty-five miles around Lake Taal for the next phase of his campaign: pushing east across the entire island.

SWING DESCRIBED HIS NEXT SERIES of moves as biting off a chunk at a time—the Sixth Army staff called it a "daring stroke." With Fujishige's loss of mobility, Swing recognized an opportunity to cut off Japanese escape routes into southern Luzon—if he could get to the east coast fast enough.

For his foot race across the island, Swing formed ad-hoc combat teams—attaching and detaching battalions between regiments, treating them as interchangeable parts. The 187th Paragliders, after linking up with the 158th's Bushmasters in the Batangas sector, peeled off to lay siege to a Japanese strongpoint at Mount Macolod on the southeast edge of Lake Taal. Meanwhile, the 188th's 2nd Battalion paired with Lahti's 3rd Battalion, leapfrogged east, and established a roadblock south of Lipa. Two days later, more paragliders pushed past them to meet the 1st Cavalry coming down from Los Baños. The two divisions—on parallel routes—now sped for the east coast. The cavalry was to the north, and the Angels to the south.

Swing, reconnoitering thirty miles ahead of his division in an L-bird, ordered his pilot to land at Lucena on the west shoulder of the Bicol Peninsula. A guerrilla greeted Swing, telling him the Japanese had abandoned the city and there were enough guerrillas to defend it—if they could be properly armed. Seeing an opportunity, Swing handed over his pistol and promised reinforcements soon.

Arriving back at his command post, Swing ordered the division's observer pilots to shuttle the reconnaissance platoon to Lucena in their L-birds. He then cobbled a paraglider company, a few pack howitzers, and ninety guerrillas into a makeshift task force. They boarded landing craft and puttered around the coast—twenty-two miles behind the lines—to join the recon platoon. Once united, they slashed east, organizing guerrillas and occupying towns, including Sariaya, Tayabas, Pagbilao, and finally Antimonan on the east coast.

Fujishige, under the weight of the growing encirclement, ordered his scattered units to regroup at his mountain garrison at Malepunyo. They tried, but the Angels harried them every step of the way. To delay the hounds, the Japanese torched villages and towns as they passed through, and in one ten-mile stretch of road, they demolished five bridges.

By April 8, the Angels had successfully cut off the Bicol Peninsula. In his forty-five-mile end run to the coast, Swing bypassed several of Fujishige's strongpoints—leaving them to be systematically destroyed one chunk at a time.

WITH THE JAPANESE IN DISARRAY and their escape routes cut off, Swing now focused on eliminating—or "reducing," in Army terms—the isolated pockets. The first Japanese strongpoint rested atop Mount Macolod and backed up against Lake Taal. Its summit rose more than three thousand feet, and several small hills skirted the base. Its north and west slopes were nearly vertical, and on its south and east sides, steep ridges split by densely wooded ravines channeled any approach into predictable routes. 'Butch' Muller estimated the Japanese held the mountain with a battalion, maybe more.

Fujishige had personally planned Macolod's defenses, stating with confidence, "My positions were so well placed and camouflaged that they could not be seen by ground or air observations. This was the best position in Southern Luzon." His troops took a month to prepare the fortifications, building a network of interconnected caves, trenches, and camouflaged machinegun emplacements to cover the approach routes. They also had numerous howitzers, including two massive Japanese Type-7 30cm's—known to the Americans as twelve-inch guns. The two beasts, with ranges of over seven miles, were destroyed early in the siege.

Time was on Swing's side, and the 187th Paragliders waged a protracted campaign to chip away at the defenders one hill or cave at a time. Their firepower included four artillery battalions as well as three M2 4.2-inch—"four-deuce"—mortars. The cannoneers used delayed fuses to penetrate the bunkers before exploding. Airdropped napalm and flaming oil drums rolled into ravines burned away camouflage to expose pillboxes and caves, which were demolished by tank salvos, sealing the helpless occupants inside. The Army flung so much ordnance at the mountain that troops nicknamed it "Million Dollar Hill." It took a month of methodical work, and progress was slow, but the deliberate tactics produced steady results and reduced friendly casualties. Fujishige's losses were estimated to be between six hundred and fourteen hundred soldiers.

THE SECOND AND FAR MORE IMPOSING strongpoint was a thirty-square mile area of mountain fortifications near Malepunyo. But before wading into the main attack, Swing wanted the foothills cleared of Japanese howitzers, several of which were lobbing shells at

American supply columns on the highway. Destroying those guns would open traffic between Batangas Bay and Manila.

Pushing up into the foothills with the rest of his company was nineteen-year-old glider-rider Earl L. Urish, a recently arrived replacement. The division was receiving trickles of new men; none were qualified paratroopers or glidermen, however. Some were allegedly untrained Air Force ground crew converted to riflemen out of desperation. Urish had arrived with a group from Camp Hood, Texas. They were split up, with Urish and three of his buddies assigned to the same company. The new arrivals spent their first twenty-four hours in combat unarmed before someone scrounged up some bolt-action 1903 Springfield rifles for them. A few days later, wounded men surrendered their semi-automatic rifles to arm the replacements with modern weapons.

Urish, now part of a belt-fed machinegun crew, trudged across an open, dry agricultural field crisscrossed with irrigation ditches. The machinegun balanced over his shoulder was heavy, and sweat made the metal ammo box dangling in his left hand slippery. He padded forward next to Feling, his teenage Filipino sidekick who carried Urish's rifle, the machinegun's spare barrel, and his own carbine. The foothills were still a mile away with the mountains looming in the distance.

A short, high-pitched whine, followed by a thunderous explosion, interrupted Urish's daydream about Illinois cornfields. "Just up the skirmish line, three men disappeared in a cloud of smoke and dust," he said. "Everyone hit the dirt." A buddy of Urish's from Camp Hood never got up, decapitated by shrapnel.

Troopers dove into the closest irrigation ditches. "They were wide enough for one man, but were filled with men three deep as the shells kept roaring in."

Urish and his crew were caught in the open, "so we could only hug the ground and pray." They dashed back the way they came, seeking the protection of a stream bed half a mile behind them. The whistle of incoming shells sent them sprawling. "Each time we hit the ground, I held the machinegun in front of me for whatever little protection it might afford. After each shell exploded, everyone jumped up and ran until the next whining roar."

They grabbed the wounded and scooped up weapons. When Urish and Feling slid into the stream bed, they had the machinegun, six rifles, a carbine, and a Tommy gun. The stock of a rifle slung over Feling's back was split by a jagged three-inch piece of shrapnel. As they caught their breath, friendly artillery scudded overhead and into the foothills. A few feet away from Urish, his battalion commander spoke calmly into a radio, directing the artillery with colorful interjections of profanity.

The company was regrouping when General Swing arrived. "We're going to go back up there and get those little yellow bastards," he roared.

A paraglider sitting next to Urish muttered, "You go ahead, Joe. We've already been there." They would go back up, but not that day. They were dog-tired, and it was clear the enemy held the hills in strength. Paraglider Eli Bernheim was at his unit's command post when word reached Colonel George Pearson that two of his junior officers were killed in the open fields.

"Colonel Pearson sat down on a stump, took off his helmet, and began to weep softly," wrote Bernheim. "I suppose no one but a former combat infantryman can understand that kind of compassion in such a huge man."

"The battle for Malepunyo had begun on a low note," admitted a witness.

A few days later, an L-bird spotted muzzle flashes from Japanese artillery positions on Malaraya Hill and radioed for counter-battery fire. First Lieutenant Kirkland watched the unique barrage, later recalling, "I became aware that our artillery was firing at a great rate but in a peculiarly random sequence. The guns further away had fired first, then those closer in, and last of all our nearby mortars. The air was alive with the swish of traveling shells. Suddenly, Malaraya Hill simply exploded."

The cannoneers were using Time on Target fire—a controlled technique that allowed multiple batteries to fire on the same target so that all the ordnance hit simultaneously. Kirkland continued, "This is cruelly effective because the chosen moment of devastation arrives without a hint of preparation. There would be no ranging shots to alert the enemy."

Major John Strong's 3rd Battalion of paratroopers and a platoon of guerrillas followed the shells in, storming Malaraya Hill. They found three knocked-out 150mm howitzers alongside the mangled wrecks of several other smaller-caliber artillery pieces.

The paratroopers and guerrillas dug in, their entrenching tools chipping the rocky ground. It was arduous work, but they hacked shallow foxholes as best they could. Their first night on the hill was quiet until a few hours before sunrise—when the taunting started. "Hey Joe, I'm coming! Hey Charlie, wait for me!" The troopers stayed silent, knowing any response would reveal their position. The gibes grew more menacing: "I'm going to slit your throat!" "Hey Bill, light a match, it will be the last light you will ever see!"

An artillery observer whispered fire directions into his radio, and within seconds, a white phosphorus shell exploded outside the perimeter, followed by a second, right on target. The searing detonations triggered a frenzied banzai attack against the perimeter's north side. The men opposite could do nothing but scan their sectors and wait, while behind them, machinegun bursts and rifle volleys punctuated the screams.

The artillery observer kept the cannoneers busy. A trooper later recalled, "The artillery kept firing and walking their guns closer by five yards after each round, until it seemed they were laying their rounds right on top of us." For the next two hours, the ground shook with each impact.

At the height of the attack, newly commissioned Lieutenant Mills Lowe scrambled into one of his men's foxholes. Lowe wanted the machinegun moved to a more advantageous position, and without debating the request, he hoisted it back to his own foxhole. Lowe and his assistant gunner, twenty-three-year-old Solon M. Hayes, got the gun up and firing with well-practiced speed. Lowe was on the trigger, and Hayes fed him ammo. Their workmanlike hammering kept the attackers back, but their high rate of fire overheated the gun. Troopers in foxholes on either side of Lowe's saw the barrel glowing red.

The strobe light of each machinegun burst gave away their position, and bullets snapped out of the dark at the two troopers hunkered behind their gun. A hail of hand grenades and wild rifle fire erupted, and the machinegun fell silent; both Lowe and Hayes were down. Their stand cost Hayes his life and Lowe his right eye, but they'd turned the tide, and when the sun rose, the perimeter remained unbroken.

A trooper seeing Lowe's jagged injury in the graying light recalled the horrifying sight. "At the time, I thought his whole face was shot away," he said. "All you could see was the blood and dangling flesh." Trooper Ed Baumgarten stood over the lifeless body of his friend Solon Hayes. "I vividly remember lifting his poncho to see if it was really him. I was devastated. I didn't think God was fair to allow such a thing to happen." Baumgarten was tormented by thoughts of seesawing guilt. *Had I been with him, he might not have been killed—or I might have been killed with him.* But those thoughts had to be compartmentalized to be dealt with later, if ever.

Baumgarten and several troopers disposed of the enemy corpses. "I didn't count them, but it took us most of the morning to drag the bodies to the cliff edge of the mountain and toss them over."

Malaraya Hill overlooked a narrow valley cutting into the Malepunyo mountains, and its capture put Swing on the doorstep of what intelligence reports suggested was Colonel Masatoshi Fujishige's headquarters.

'Slugger' Lahti and his battalion commanders took turns flying over the twisted knot of ridgelines in an L-bird. Their reconnaissance revealed several hills and valleys not plotted on their maps and confirmed Fujishige had selected formidable terrain for his defense. The flights also provided a good idea of what they were up against: the Japanese held the high ground, and getting to them required threading up what one observer described as "a welter of conical hills covered with tangled rain forest and bamboo thickets, surrounded by precipitous slopes and interlaced with sharp ridges."

Hidden under all the foliage were Fujishige's camouflaged emplacements, caves, tunnels, supply dumps, howitzers, an underground hospital, and four thousand men waiting to make their final stand. They'd hauled in six months of food and enough ammunition to last two years. They were ready for a fight.

The route to the range's highest peak appeared clear of Japanese positions, and seizing it could upend Fujishige's line. The Angels' first foray into the mountains was a questionable "straight up the middle" maneuver that underestimated the Japanese' advantages. 'Hacksaw' Holcombe's Easy Company would make the attack. Reviewing the plan, Hacksaw turned to his executive officer and voiced his qualms bluntly, stating, "We're going to step in it today."

Despite the misgivings, initial progress was promising. Easy Company gingerly navigated trails mined with buried artillery shells and picked their way through the slope's thick vegetation. They made it as far as the hill's western approach, expending six thousand rounds of machinegun ammo in the process. But as they ascended, Hacksaw's prediction came true. Japanese holding the heights as well as the surrounding hills eviscerated the lead platoon. In an instant, ten men went down—four killed and six wounded. The company commander radioed they could only take the hill with more artillery support. Troopers grabbed the wounded and limped down the hill, leaving their dead behind. They suffered another dozen casualties during their two-hour withdrawal.

The failed attack forced introspection and more aerial observation. For ease of reference, the nameless mountains were labeled by their elevations, such as Hill 2380—at 2,380 feet. The spine of Fujishige's defense seemed to run along a ridge of four mountains separated by thousand-foot-deep chasms. The ridge ran in a north-south line and was dominated by two center peaks, Hill 2380 and Hill 2375, both suspected of harboring key enemy positions. The ridge's backdoor was guarded from the east by Mount Mataasna Bundoc and it, too, was thought to contain numerous enemy positions.

The additional terrain study also revealed a better route into the ridgeline. From the south, each mountain more or less masked the next from enemy fire. By working their way across the ridge, the attackers could use the rugged terrain to shield themselves from the next mountain.

Swing knew preventing his enemies' escape was just as important as destroying their strongholds. Ringing the base of the mountain mass would require the entirety of his division and then some. To help Swing tighten his noose, Sixth Army attached two cavalry units that established positions on the north and northeast sides. On the southeast boundary, Swing placed a battalion of paragliders, along with his anti-aircraft battalion. Lahti's paratroopers, wading in from the southwest, would make the main attack and tighten the knot, mountain by mountain.

But there was a hiccup that required Swing to modify his plan and address what he later referred to as some "unsavory" and "sad business." On Sunday evening, April 22, 1945, Swing received word from his higher headquarters that the 1st Cavalry units on the north side of the Malepunyo perimeter "could not get the men to advance." General Oscar Griswold was blunt: if Swing wanted his northern sector secure, he'd have to bolster the cavalry with his own units to prevent a withdrawal. Swing ordered the 188th Paragliders to prepare for movement, then shuffled some gunners from his anti-aircraft battalion to fill in the resulting void.

The next morning, when Swing and the paragliders arrived by truck, they saw most of the cavalrymen stripped to their undershirts relaxing in the shade of a coconut grove. Swing found the regimental commander in his tent five thousand yards from where the frontline should have been.

"He stated unequivocally that his regiment was licked," recalled Swing, "[and] that they were shocked because one squadron commander had been killed in the fight on the 21st, and try as he could, he could not get his outfit to advance." When Swing asked the colonel to escort him to his forward most troops, he demurred, citing pressing administrative duties, and instead assigned a captain to the task.

They traveled by jeep, then on foot, to a platoon nestled into the foothills overlooking the Onipa River. Below them, at the water's edge, Swing saw what he described as "scores of Japanese sitting around campfires and bathing in the river." Noting the enemy was in range of the outpost's machineguns as well as supporting artillery, Swing asked the platoon leader what he was waiting for. The lieutenant replied, "We have been ordered not to fire for fear the Japs will retaliate and drive us from this position."

Disgusted, Swing ordered his paragliders to take over the lines. Getting everything and everyone else into position took several more days. Engineers needed seventy-two hours of around-the-clock work to ford a river and widen a supply trail to the northern-blocking units. Swing judged the time and effort to be worth it, telling his men, "The Japs are not any different than you or any other soldiers. When somebody gets behind you, you're very nervous. You're looking both ways."

With his enemy caged, Swing saw no reason to needlessly risk lives. Death and destruction, combat's unforgiving handmaidens, made casualties inevitable, but Swing raged against senseless slaughter. "It makes me sick when I read about the casualties on Iwo Jima," he wrote. "It can be done more scientifically. There is no doubt in any of our minds but what this 'Howlin' Smith' [USMC General Holland Smith] is actually howling mad. We laugh at the fruitless method of the Jap in his banzai attack, and yet allow that fanatic to barge in using up men as though they were a dime a dozen, and apparently boasting about it."

Swing was no less critical of his own unit's tactics, beseeching his men to "not act like 'fat heads'" on the battlefield and to avoid suffering casualties "by reason of our own stupidity." He demanded "that every member of this division employ the individual measures for his own protection which we have spent two years in acquiring." Swing held himself to the same standard, wanting to obliterate Malepunyo's garrison with as few of his own casualties as possible. To do that, he planned to unleash a tempest of steel rather than spill his men's blood rooting out a stubborn enemy cave by cave, foxhole by foxhole.

On Leyte, the jungle had largely negated Swing's firepower, but here on Luzon, he could dispense with subtlety and hurl every advantage of modern warfare at Malepunyo: napalm, fragmentation bombs, timed fuses, air bursts, and heavy mortars.

While Japanese soldiers despised the Americans' reliance on technology over an honorable warrior spirit, Swing's response to their feudal-like cult of death was his own cult of oblivion, wherein personal risk was replaced with shock and awe.

As one veteran described the realities of killing, "You shoot him in the back, you blow him apart with mines, you kill or maim him the quickest and most effective way you can with the least danger to yourself. He does the same to you. He tricks you and cheats you, and if you don't beat him at his own game, you don't live to appreciate your own nobleness." Like all American soldiers, the Angels couldn't care less about meeting the Japanese on equal terms; they wanted to win and go home. Save the stories of fair play for children's books about knights or musketeers.

Like history's most famous artilleryman, Napoléon Bonaparte—who referred to his largest cannons as *belles filles* or beautiful daughters—Swing loved his howitzers, and during his Luzon campaign the Angels' artillery fired an average of over fifteen hundred shells a day. But still he observed, "It is amazing how despite all training maneuvers, movies, lectures, and what not, the doughboy will never realize until he has seen it what artillery can do for them."

Everyone, the Japanese especially, were about to witness what artillery could do.

Swing's cannoneers towed their howitzers into place. He had seven artillery battalions and stockpiles of shells surrounding the mountains, ready to unleash more shells in forty-eight hours than other units did in five weeks.

The days leading up to the assault also included largely fruitless attempts to encourage surrender. The Angels broadcast calls for surrender via loudspeakers and airdropped leaflets over the ridgeline. The leaflets encouraged at least one Japanese officer to give up. He emerged from the hills waving the paper over his head. After yielding his sword, he readily answered his interrogators' questions. When asked if the leaflets were effective, he said the leaflets were much sought after by Japanese soldiers as they had run out of toilet paper.

SWING SCHEDULED THE ATTACK for April 27, 1945, but pilots flying preparatory airstrikes were having trouble distinguishing their targets in the rolling sea of green mountains. Their first target was the suspected command post atop Hill 2380, but they needed eyes on the ground to confirm they were hitting it.

Thus, on Thursday morning, April 26, Captain Stephen 'Rusty' Cavanaugh led a group to the top of Hill 2362; from there he observed the airstrikes. Rusty passed corrections via radio to the air support party located at the base of the hill, who in turn radioed the pilots. The support party's vehicle-mounted radios prevented them from having direct observation of the target, creating a less-than-ideal game of telephone.

The first nine A-20s rolled in at 09:35. Cavanaugh radioed, "Ginger 3, this is Rusty. The last plane is way, way off. He dropped the bombs a good six hundred yards south of the target."

Most of the other bombs fell short as well, impacting on the near slope, but secondary explosions suggested Fujishige lost at least one ammunition dump.

The next pilot was closer. "Ginger 3, this is Rusty. Two napalms dropped, one napalm in the target area, one was low in the target area. And they still insist on flying west to east." Cavanaugh adjusted the pilots' flight path and got them on target. Smoke roiled up from the mountain.

The second airstrike went in against another mountain but was interrupted by the arrival of a third flight, which caused several of the bombs to fall past the target. The final strike was the most successful, with 90 percent of the bombs detonating on target, followed by well-aimed strafing runs.

That night, the thunder and flash of howitzers ripped across the foothills as Swing heralded his campaign with a massive artillery barrage that sent round after round hammering into the ridgeline. Dawn's pink sunlight glinted off five thousand empty shell casings littered around the gun pits.

AT 08:45 THE NEXT MORNING, Captain John Ringler's Baker Company—the heroes of Los Baños—advanced west through the valley floor toward their objective, suitably designated Ringler Ridge.

For all the steel falling out of the sky and the thousands of men surrounding the mountains, the attack's first wave was just three infantry companies. Another 1,700 artillery shells whistled over the troopers and crashed into the surrounding higher elevations. The cannoneers mixed in smoke rounds to obscure Ringler's movement from any Japanese observer brave enough to stick his head up.

Early in their march, lead scouts found the bodies of two hundred mutilated Filipinos. Based on the decomposition, Ringler estimated they'd been dead for a month. He radioed it in and kept the men moving; they were on a timeline. They picked their way through a coconut grove, and after a brief skirmish that flushed out a single Japanese rifleman, they made it to the base of the ridge.

To their right, Able Company headed to Hill 2218 after waiting out a napalm strike. The battalion mortar teams walked a barrage of 81mm high explosive rounds up the trail ahead of the advancing troopers. They, too, ascended their objective unopposed, but the chatter of a gunfight echoed from the east.

The Ciceri task force—an ad-hoc unit made up of Lahti's Charlie Company and F Troop from the 8th Cavalry Regiment—was attacking Mount Mataasna Bundoc. Sergeant Edward Reed Jr.'s squad was on point when the lead scouts crumpled under the ripping fire of two

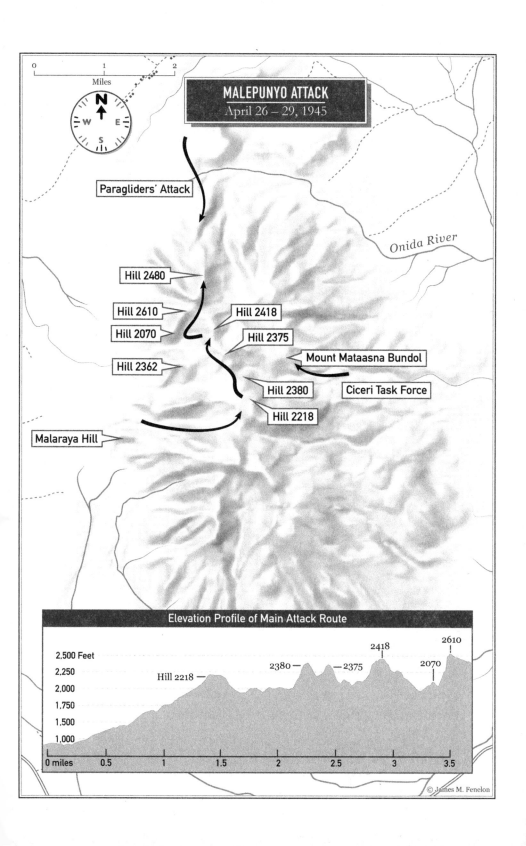

MALEPUNYO ATTACK
April 26 – 29, 1945

Paragliders' Attack

Onida River

Hill 2480

Hill 2610   Hill 2418

Hill 2070   Hill 2375

Hill 2362   Mount Mataasna Bundol

                 Ciceri Task Force

                 Hill 2380

                 Hill 2218

Malaraya Hill

Elevation Profile of Main Attack Route

2,500 Feet   2418   2610
2,250   2380 — — 2375   2070
2,000   Hill 2218 —
1,750
1,500
1,000

0 miles   0.5   1   1.5   2   2.5   3   3.5

© James M. Fenelon

machineguns. Reed flopped down, snaking fifty yards toward the first enemy position. He inched close enough to flip a grenade into the four-man nest. The blast killed three of them, and Reed shot the fourth. Now wounded, he serpentined another forty yards to the second gun, where a single grenade took out the crew. With bullets zipping overhead, Reed dragged one of the wounded scouts to safety, then returned to do the same for the other.

Meanwhile, Able Company took Hill 2380 without firing a shot. Empty foxholes and corpses indicated the Japanese had at least one company atop the hill, but they must have fled from the incoming artillery. Troopers ducked as rifle fire cracked in from the next hill.

They radioed for help and got it from a 75mm pack howitzer a half mile away atop the rugged promontory of Hill 2362. A trooper, spotting the sun glinting off the howitzer, said, "It had been dragged, wrestled, hoisted over miles of swamp, up a ravine and then by pure muscle and guts, straight up that crag along with a gun crew and a hundred rounds of ammunition." The crew nudged the howitzer into position and bore sighted over the barrel. It took several shots, but the fifth explosion silenced the incoming fire. From their vantage point, the crew systematically blasted caves in front of the advancing infantry.

The Angels' 75mm howitzer overlooking Malepunyo from atop Hill 2362

Charlie Sass, a trooper in Ringler's company, appreciated their work. "Our artillery boys never got the credit they deserved," he said. "They were taking the caves out, one or two at a time. No fast fire, just slow and steady. Not much noise either. Just a whistle and a big whump and a lot of smoke, rocks, and dirt falling down the hillside."

In the distance, a flight of eighteen A-20s worked over the far mountaintops with napalm and parachute bombs. After one strike, the troopers cheered while dozens of enflamed Japanese thrashed in pain as their ammunition belts exploded. "There was no respect for a worthy foe to be found on either side," Kirkland explained.

By 15:00, the first phase of the operation was almost complete. Able Company was expecting a patrol from the Ciceri task force on Mount Mataasna Bundoc to clear the saddle between them. The task force commander, Major John Ciceri, radioed that they were blocked by a stubborn enemy emplacement. Could Able attack the position from behind?

The thirteen-man patrol moved cautiously into the bamboo thicket. One of the troopers recalled, "Our lead scout, PFC Trevor E. Jarrard, went down the trail about a hundred and fifty yards, and he was hit and killed."

From Abel's perimeter, Sergeant Pat Berardi heard the eruption of gunfire. He grabbed two troopers, and together they all sprinted down into the saddle to assist. The thicket's dense vegetation was ideal concealment, and the Japanese had dug one-man foxholes along the trail. Enemy riflemen seemingly popped out of the ground from nowhere, letting rip with several bursts that cut through the three would-be rescuers. Berardi was badly wounded, and the other two men were dead.

Berardi attacked. Overhanding grenades, he followed the explosions with several shots from his rifle, killing the closest Japanese. He then took command of the patrol to get the wounded out of the kill zone. Among them was Berardi's close friend, Staff Sergeant Richard Sibio, who'd been shot through the stomach and hit in the spine. The two men had served side-by-side since January 1943 when they were drafted in Ohio. Berardi was carrying his friend out when he was hit again, shot in the back. Sibio later lamented, "Pat Berardi tried to help me, and he was fatally wounded." Berardi died at the field hospital.

That evening, a momentary lull settled across the battlefield. Baker Company dug in along the spine of Ringler Ridge. "Looking down in late afternoon from the high ground, we could see fog drifting into the flatlands and creeping into the gullies, swallowing the trees," recalled Charlie Sass. "The tops of the foothills still poked through the haze."

Ringler positioned Sass' platoon on a narrow, fifteen-foot-wide spur, spread out over fifty yards. "As the dark came on, we felt reasonably secure. We'd done this drill hundreds of times. There was no perimeter, just a long string of people with two or three to each position and three machineguns on the high end.... Trip lines were out. Grenades with pins loosened sat side by side. An extra clip tucked into the rifle sling. We had our last, long drink of warm water; agreed on who would take what hours of watch—a few whispers, and then quiet."

As the troopers settled in for the night, long columns of Filipinos slogged up the muddy supply line to deliver rations, water, and ammo. Harassing fire employing Time on Target salvos continued through the night. The day's total of twenty casualties included eight dead.

SASS BLINKED AT THE RISING SUN from the cramped confines of his foxhole. The day's plan of attack called for him and the rest of Baker Company to carry the ball. Also up early that morning were the Air Force pilots, initiating the day's complex choreography of fire support. Sass and his fellow troopers must have felt confident as the spectacle unfolded on the dot of 08:00. A flight of eighteen A-20s roared overhead united by a single purpose: to decimate Hill 2418, Baker Company's destination. Napalm splattered across the crest, engulfing it in flames, followed by parachute bombs drifting in to explode on target. Before the buzz of the Havocs' engines faded away, the thunder of artillery roared from the valley below. A thousand rounds crashed into Hill 2418, while other batteries, including the monstrous four-deuce mortars, smothered the surrounding hills with smoke.

With the smokescreen wafting over the mountains, Ringler dispatched his scouts, and the company plodded forward at six minutes after ten. Trooper Sass considered their vanguard mission a "very questionable honor." They passed through Able Company, then pushed up the narrow trail to Hill 2418. They bumped into a few shell-shocked Japanese but brushed them aside without any casualties of their own.

Ascending the top of the mountain, Sass took in the view. "From our place, we could see for miles, far up and down the valley. The colors looked like a valley in upstate New York, green and brown and yellow. Our place was nothing but gray grit, rock, and a terrible smell." Napalm and artillery had burned off all the vegetation and ground everything else to dust; the air reeked of gasoline.

After catching their breath and filling their canteens from water dropped by an L-bird, Lahti ordered Ringler to move against Hill 2610.

Cresting the next rise, Ringler determined that the only feasible route keeping them on the high ground was over Hill 2070—another battalion's objective. While the radio crackled with Lahti orchestrating the change in plan, howitzers sent a few shells into Hill 2070 to confirm their registration before unleashing 675 rounds into the crest. Ringler's men followed the barrage and took 2070 without incident. The recent plastering made digging in easier.

To the east, the Ciceri task force took over Able Company's old positions on Hill 2380. Troopers threw phosphorus grenades to burn the grass and reveal Japanese foxholes. When the occupants fled the conflagration, they were mowed down by rifle fire and 60mm mortars.

Lahti's 2nd Battalion and several guerrilla units filed in behind the advance units to secure the hilltops, ensuring the Japanese did not slip back around to reoccupy them.

Meanwhile, the 188th Paragliders were busy on the northern perimeter, attacking that morning at 10:00. Both battalions swept forward behind tank destroyers, and on the right flank, flame-thrower teams incinerated eight caves. A few enemy mortar rounds sailed in, wounding eighteen paragliders, but they seized their objective for the day.

ON THE THIRD, and what Swing hoped would be the final, day of the battle, 'Slugger' Lahti's paratroopers were poised to take Hill 2610 with a dangerous gambit.

The morning of April 29 dawned bright and clear, offering perfect visibility for artillery and airstrikes. At 08:00 a flight of P-38s circled overhead, the pilots craning in their cockpits to spot the target. Columns of red smoke wafted up from the hills occupied by Swing's units, and on the crest of Hill 2610, a single white phosphorus shell splashed into its distinct blossom of white-hot embers. The pilots had their mark.

Just seven hundred yards from the target, Ringler and Baker Company got as low as they could. For a one-thousand-pound bomb, the distance was considered "danger close" and the flight line had been verified multiple times to minimize fratricide. As soon as the final airstrike was completed, Ringler's men were to assault Hill 2610 in the hope that the ordnance had numbed the Japanese into inaction.

The P-38s, armed with one-thousand-pound bombs, circled once more, then barreled out of the sky. The first nine aircraft roared over in single file, their bombs bracketing the crest, some falling short and some falling long. The second flight, with the target now well defined, dropped twelve bombs on the button. Each explosion's detonation caused landsides.

The reverberating shockwaves thumped the nearby troopers like the concussion of a passing freight train. As the third flight circled, Ringler grabbed the radio, demanding, "Call off the planes, one man wounded, several with bloody noses."

Lahti confirmed, "Last flight cancelled," then he ordered Ringler to "coordinate artillery concentrations using at least five hundred rounds, including smoke; shift fires to north slope of Hill 2610. Let me know when you move out."

During the salvos, the troopers topped off canteens and loaded up with ammo. When the howitzers ceased fire, they went forward. Charlie Sass recalled the plan: "The understanding was—get to the top, as fast as you can, as many as you can, don't slow down, don't look back, and when you get there, spread out, cover the guys coming behind you. Simple stuff, actually."

To keep the Japanese occupied during their climb, Lahti—overhead in an L-bird with a radio and binoculars—directed the fire of tank destroyers blasting the opposite side of the hill. But Ringler ordered him to stop when shrapnel and spall rained into his men.

They formed loose skirmish lines and rushed up the near vertical slope. "We grabbed at rocks, roots, bushes, and pulled and pushed and dragged each other up when we had to. The closer we got to the crest, the faster we moved," said Sass. "Then there were one, two, three, a dozen men up there and soon, our platoon, our whole damned company."

By 10:45, they were on top without firing a shot, thinking the enemy had fled. But troopers tossing phosphorus grenades into caves found out differently. The explosions flushed out eight or ten Japanese at a time—some on fire from the scorching phosphorus. When the enemy scrambled out, the troopers opened fire in what Sass called a "turkey shoot."

With the enemy in disarray and undoubtedly unnerved by the morning's bombardment, the troopers methodically took out the caves. "We could clean house on our terms, one cave at a time," continued Sass. "Phosphorous. Flamers. A can of gasoline with a charge taped to it worked sometimes, or you could dig a charge above a cave and blow it in." They tied blocks of TNT to grenades to increase the blast, but found the grenade just blew the blocks apart instead of detonating them. One cave disgorged a pack of thirty-odd feral dogs; one darted out with a human arm in its mouth.

The Japanese who stayed in their caves were entombed in them; those that fled were cut down almost immediately. But the defeated still had a few surprises left.

A crowd of troopers searching the dead for souvenirs were surprised by a satchel charge sailing out of a cave. Private Albin P. Scott caught it and whipped it back just as it exploded. The airburst showered eighteen troopers with fragments, killing a guerrilla as well as an artillery observer. Scott's hand was shredded, and his upper body peppered, but he'd live.

On another section of the hill, bullets ripped out of the ground where the Japanese had rigged camouflaged covers for their underground bunkers. Lahti urged his L-bird pilot to fly low and he tossed out a flamethrower to deal with the stubborn holdouts.

Baker Company counted 123 enemy dead, the combined victims of airstrikes, artillery, bullets, and grenades. Countless more were buried in caves or flung into gorges by artillery concussions.

Troopers searching the caves and bunkers found several radios and generators. Others found a Japanese map confirming they'd destroyed Fujishige's headquarters. Of Fujishige himself, there was no sign. He'd slipped away with his staff, making it to a hill outside the Angels' sector.

Two companies from Lahti's 3rd Battalion filed up to reinforce the position. George Company, passing over Hill 2610, radioed Lahti they could take the last mountain, 2480. It was a paraglider objective, but Swing gave permission, and the paratroopers occupied it unopposed, completing the link-up with the northern blocking force.

Malepunyo was reduced. Total Japanese casualties were impossible to calculate with various after-action reports claiming anywhere between 632 to 1,600. Swing's tactics were sound, and he limited Lahti's casualties to twelve killed and seventy wounded.

The next morning, groans for help caught the attention of First Lieutenant Kirkland. "During the night, a wounded Jap tried to come up the hill to our lines to surrender. The riflemen on outpost simply shot him. He lay outside our perimeter groaning and calling out until dawn."

Kirkland and Jose Honrado, a Japanese-speaking guerrilla, climbed down the hillside to investigate. They loaded the wounded prisoner onto Kirkland's back, and with Jose pushing, they clambered uphill. During the ascent it became obvious, in a foul manner, that in addition to being shot in the chest, the Japanese soldier was suffering from dysentery. They laid him on a stretcher, confiscated his diary, and then went to get cleaned up.

When they returned, the prisoner was gone; Kirkland's intelligence team had tossed him over the cliff.

"I could detect no remorse," recalled Kirkland. Most troopers were unapologetic about such acts. "When you saw what they did to the Filipinos, you didn't bring back prisoners," said one. Another later conceded, "We did not take the crown for taking the most captives."

Staring at the empty stretcher, Kirkland thought, *So ends another pointless day in the high hills of Luzon.*

Chapter 13

Home Alive in Forty-Five

Lipa, Luzon.
Wednesday, May 2, 1945

Escaping the death throes of the *Fuji Heidan*, Japanese stragglers slipped east, sometimes in groups and sometimes alone. The unlucky bumped into the blocking units surrounding the mountain range or blundered into vengeful locals. A diary recovered from one of Fujishige's dead men documented their plight: "The crisis is great now. Artillery shells drop like drops of rain. The end has come. I'm going to die bravely. I pray for the country's everlasting good fortune. I'm completely surrounded."

The men were hungry, disorganized, and often lost, but their faith and courage remained undaunted, as did their willingness to fight. The cannoneers of Swing's 457th artillery battalion clashed with a group of ninety-five Japanese who all went down swinging.

When Swing was satisfied that the largest groups had been delt with—after clearing ravines and collapsing more caves—Lahti's paratroopers marched out of the mountains, turning Malepunyo over to the guerrillas on May 2.

355

The exhausted troopers filtered out of the line and back to the outskirts of Lipa, where they looked forward to setting up a camp and getting some rest. Lahti observed all the other units built their camps in the open, under the "direct rays of the heat." Lahti found a coconut grove for his regiment. It was ten miles from the rest of the division, providing both shade and distance from the flagpole.

Swing, predictably, wanted the camp closer. He told Lahti to move, saying, "You can't keep the road open during the rainy season."

Lahti, predictably, wanted to stay put. "If I can't, then you can throw me out," he countered.

"All right, Lahti, God damn it, keep the area!" Swing replied in exasperation.

Lahti later wrote, "I was never intimidated by Swing, but many of his subordinates were. My purpose was to always do the best for the benefit of the men in my command. I never backed away from this position as long as I could honestly and logically defend it."

Lahti assigned First Lieutenant Kirkland as the regiment's Road Officer. His job was to oversee the construction of an all-weather road to Lipa before June's rainy season hit. Kirkland marshalled a platoon of the division's engineers and put them to work. They surveyed the route, used a crusher to make gravel out of coral, and supervised the local laborers hired to "do the pick, shovel and spreading work." Rollers completed the packing, and Kirkland made sure "that the material was spread evenly, the surface crowned, i.e., higher in the center, and both sides ditched."

Back at camp, the troopers erected rows of six-man pyramidal tents under the palm trees. Each tent had surrounding drainage ditches and raised floors made from bamboo to keep their cots and gear dry when the rains came.

The men's footlockers caught up with them. Again, the rear echelons charged with watching over them had looted them instead.

Kirkland complained, "My footlocker had been smashed in, and everything non-issue had been stolen." One of Kirkland's fellow officers, anticipating such pillaging, had boobytrapped his footlocker. It had exploded, and the contents were splattered with the thief's blood. "There was never a complaint or investigation," added Kirkland with approval.

On May 8, the end of the war in Europe was announced. The news was met with little fanfare by those settling into their camps and looking forward to sleeping on a cot for the first time in more than three months. One Angel recalled hopefully, "Perhaps our days of fighting on a shoe-string were almost over, but we knew that the Japs were still plenty strong, we hadn't made much of a dent in China, and we hadn't set foot on the home islands of Japan."

A more celebrated date for the Angels was Friday, May 11: the first day since landing on Luzon that they'd not killed an enemy soldier. Or as Swing wrote, "After 101 days of killing Japs, we failed to bag any game on the 102nd." His staff dutifully tallied the daily numbers and calculated the average at 98.3 per day.

SWING EXPECTED THE CAMPS to be ship-shape. Hundreds of the pyramid tents were erected in strict military fashion: spaced evenly in long, straight rows, providing the comforting appearance of military order. There were hardstand parking lots for vehicles, mess facilities, showers, latrines, and a flagpole outside the headquarters' tent.

The showers, due to a shortage of pipes, were fed by water hauled in by trucks. Swing wanted the water pumped to the showers and appealed to the Sixth Army's commander, Walter Krueger, for six thousand feet of three-inch pipe to keep his men clean. The request ran Swing afoul of the Sixth Army quartermasters, who viewed it as "excessive." Their report on the administrative kerfuffle noted, "The

[11th Airborne's] camp bears little resemblance to that contemplated in our construction directives and is scattered over a large area. Materials issued for mess halls and authorized structures have been diverted to other structures, some with authority and some without." They also noted the "difficulty in controlling the commanding general [Swing]." But with Krueger's approval of Swing's request, no one dared buck it. Swing got his pipes.

"Life in the camp among the coconuts became downright agreeable," recalled First Lieutenant Kirkland. "We built a little amphitheater out of coconut logs; it had a small stage, and we rigged up lights and a sound system." There were boxing matches, USO shows, and nightly movies, including Humphrey Bogart's and Lauren Bacall's *The Big Sleep* and *This is the Army* with Alan Hale.

But the most popular entertainment, according to Kirkland, was a local orchestra. "It had the most gorgeous singer you can imagine. [She] had a bell-like voice that was twice her size," he said. "Her rendition of 'Rum and Coca-Cola' was guaranteed to raise wild cheers, especially when she slapped her thigh on 'Working for the Yankee Dollar.'"

There was also plenty of food. Good food.

Henry Burgess wrote to his fiancée, contrasting the camp to his six months on New Guinea, where "we had fresh meat about once a month and fresh potatoes but once. Here we have them five and six times a week. The old soldiers are getting suspicious, believing no one eats this well unless there is a tough mission in the air. But we believe it is due to the end of the war in Europe."

The old soldiers were right. Underlying the attempts at normalcy was the tension of uncertain futures. Kirkland recalled, "There was a fatalistic sense that we were certainly winning [the war], but the catch phrase, 'Home alive in forty-five' had changed to 'The Golden Gate in forty-eight.'" Ground-pounding GIs and Marines could not see how the war would end without an invasion of Japan. Contemplating an airdrop into the home islands, a trooper summed up what everyone thought, declaring, "I felt our mission was suicide. I could not see many of us coming out of this operation alive."

The rumor pendulum swung wide, ranging from shipping home to airborne operations into China or Formosa [Taiwan]. The most pervasive had the division heading back to the States. Unfounded gossip with such universal appeal took on a life of its own, gaining enough momentum to induce complacency or ruin morale when the bubble burst.

Swing set the record straight as soon as he heard it, issuing a division-wide memo to quash the scuttlebutt: "It has come to my attention that persistent rumors to the effect that the division will be home in July exists among personnel of the division.... I caution you to pay no heed to unfounded rumors and be ever on the alert."

Many troopers felt they had earned more than a few days' rest under the hot sun. "Most of us thought that we would get a rest with some time in Australia. After all, we had not been in what might be called a 'developed' country since coming overseas," complained a trooper. "When we realized that we were not going to Australia, we were somewhat downhearted."

Swing's solution to idle hands and wandering minds was work. He gave the men four days to rest before mandating a return to a six-day training week. Monday through Saturday started with morning calisthenics, followed by classes and field exercises to codify basics of soldering with lessons learned during the Luzon campaign: squad tactics, marksmanship, first aid, and field sanitation. Then there were the dreaded foot marches with full packs, conducted both day and night.

The Angels established formal schools for teaching Japanese weapons and tactics, bomb disposal, scouting, and patrolling.

Machinegun and mortar ranges were set up for crew qualification. Flamethrower training got a lot of attention, too. When they invaded Japan, Swing wanted each squad in the division to have two trained operators.

Swing also took the opportunity to open another jump school. The engineers hammered together a jump tower, mock aircraft doors, and other training aids for the instructors' use. The nearby airfield was improved to facilitate the training, and the engineers laid eleven hundred feet of pierced steel planking to extend it. They also built an all-weather taxiway in addition to aircraft hardstands.

The return to the routines of garrison life included the unavoidable tedium of daily bugle calls, kitchen duty, shining boots, a dress code for the officers' mess (tie required), and manning guard posts.

Guard duty, a requirement since roving bands of Japanese still slinked about, was typically boring. Men walked their post until relieved, mostly shooing away unauthorized civilians. Sentries Teddy Burke and 'Little Joe' Vannier noticed a popular hut just outside their camp. They finally asked a passing trooper what the attraction was. A prostitute was peddling her negotiable affections in exchange for food, blankets, cigarettes, or American cash.

There was plenty of other recreation for the less adventurous. A division R&R camp on the coast offered boating, volleyball, fishing, and uninterrupted sleep. Unit commanders issued frequent passes for the men to visit surrounding villages. A lucky few visited Manila, which was in the process of rebuilding. In late May, the first of Swing's battalions rotated to the capital city for garrison duty, patrolling the neighborhoods with the regularity of beat cops. Swing cringed at the thought of what trouble his men might get into. "Will get more grey hairs from that than during the entire campaign."

The division held a parade for visiting dignitaries and organized several award ceremonies. First Lieutenant Kirkland received a Silver

Star but was jaded about the accolade. "Strangers to the system tend to believe that medals are given to award the recipient. That is seldom the case. Medals are passed out to encourage others to be foolish and zealous. The citation says that I did valiant things with utter disregard for my personal safety. Not so. There was no safe place. If there had been one within reach, I would have been in it."

Notably absent from the awards ceremonies was Manny Pérez, who stormed the Genko Line—only to be killed three weeks later. He was awarded the Medal of Honor posthumously. Also missing was Robert Steele, who broke the stalemate at Los Piños with gasoline and a phosphorus grenade—killed in Manila. His Distinguished Service Cross was sent home to his family. Mills Lowe's Distinguished Service Cross was awarded *in absentia,* as he was in hospital. All told, the Angels suffered 1,679 casualties on Luzon, 353 of which were fatalities.

ON WEDNESDAY, June 6, MacArthur announced the end of organized resistance on Luzon. There was still plenty of unorganized resistance, however. The rotating combat patrols, conducted concurrently with training and recreation, made for an odd juxtaposition of activities. A trooper quipped, "We went about work and play, shooting straggling Japs in the mornings and playing softball in the afternoon."

There were still thousands of Japanese soldiers wandering the countryside, some actively looking for a fight, but more likely just trying to find something to eat. Troopers happening upon them rarely took the time to discern into which category their quarry fell. The guerrillas were often dispatched to investigate civilian sightings and proved very good at patrol work.

To encourage troopers to take prisoners, three-day passes to Manila were offered to any patrol that brought in a live Japanese soldier. A trooper admitted, "As attractive as that pass was, it was difficult to get."

In one case, two Japanese approached a patrol with their hands raised. The first men fell to his hands and knees—with a machinegun strapped to his back; the second opened fire. "Luckily, no one was killed," said a paraglider, "but there were a few nasty wounds. Suffice it to say, every weapon on that patrol was turned on the two Japanese until there was no doubt they were both dead."

In another case, a lone Japanese soldier wielding a knife tied to a bamboo pole charged pell-mell downhill into a patrol. They tried capturing him—by shooting him in the legs—but he kept jabbing his spear at anyone trying to disarm him. "Had to kill him," shrugged a witness.

They did get the occasional prisoner. A squad from Lahti's Charlie Company found four Japanese bathing in a river. When they rushed to their rifles to confront the Americans, three were gunned down. The fourth soldier was captured when a dud grenade foiled his attempted suicide. In all, the Angels managed to successfully capture 128 prisoners.

Replacements benefited from the patrols' on-the-job training opportunities. Incorporated into the veteran-led squads, the new men glimpsed the stress of combat and refined their fieldcraft.

The patrols were inconsistently violent. Most were boring, with no enemy contact, while others, such as the twelve-man squad led by Private Joe Siedenberg—a veteran of Leyte and Luzon—got into a sharp firefight that ended with twenty-seven enemy dead. On the next day's patrol, Siedenberg died from gunshot wounds suffered while dragging a replacement back to safety.

Sometimes the troopers were their own enemy, as when a company of paratroopers was dispatched in response to a sighting of Japanese stragglers. In a poorly coordinated pincer attack, two platoons unknowingly converged on each other through tall kunai grass. Blurry movement in the undergrowth was followed by a burst of rifle fire, sending everyone to ground. When the two groups heard each other yelling commands in English, the firing petered out—but not before one man had been shot in the leg. "I couldn't see him," lamented the trigger-puller. "He was in front of us." After months of combat, the Angels were still learning.

Locals guided another patrol to a pile of several dozen decomposing bodies. The Japanese had bayonetted the civilians and shoved them off a cliff. The enemy's atrocities and code of non-surrender broiled the Americans' psyche into charred toast. Of his men's evolving character, Henry Burgess wrote to his aunt, "It is tough, deadly tough, and hard. No soldier in the world is as cold, relentless, and cruel as an aroused American."

Exposure to the non-stop violence either desensitized a man or drove him insane. That many of the Angels grew almost nonchalant to savagery was not in doubt. A patrol of paratroopers and guerrillas set up an overnight ambush near Lake Taal. At dawn, a long column of Japanese troops marching down the trail was silhouetted against the eastern sun, their mushroom-shaped helmets and long rifles distinct telltales.

The patrols' belt-fed machineguns opened with long, sharp bursts when the bulk of the Japanese were in the kill zone. The slaughter cut down more than eighty men.

The guerrillas dragged the corpses into a pile at the troopers' behest. According to one witness, the mound of tangled arms and legs was ten or twelve feet high. Impressed by their own grisly handiwork, some of the troopers took turns ascending the corpses to pose for photographs atop their grotesque monument of triumph.

IN NORTHERN LUZON, the fighting was still ongoing. Krueger's divisions had pushed General Yamashita—the Tiger of Malaya—and his force of over fifty thousand men through the Cagayan Valley and up into the northern mountains. To prevent their escaping the island, Krueger wanted to cut off their access to the port at Aparri. He gave Swing thirty-six hours' notice to airdrop a combat team to seize the port and link up with an American division advancing toward the mountains.

Swing was unsurprised. "I pleaded with the Sixth Army staff to drop the whole division up here two months ago when they were having such a helluva time," he wrote. "Had they done so, we would have been on the Japs' tail and cleared out the valley six weeks ago and saved a lot of casualties the other divisions had in making their frontal attack. As it was, they let the Japs withdraw the greater part of their garrison at the northern end of the valley.... Do you wonder that sometimes I think I'll lose my mind?"

Swing was mystified by his peers' adherence to what appeared to him as First World War era tactics. Seeing their "frontal attacks all along the line," Swing wrote, "I thank my lucky stars that all our fighting has been more or less on our own [with] no higher echelon ordering me to butt my head against a stone wall."

Swing formed the Gypsy Task Force, presumably a tongue-in-cheek reference to its cobbled-together roster of a thousand-odd troopers: five companies of paratroopers, a company of engineers, radio operators, four howitzers and their cannoneers, a platoon of medics, parachute riggers, an ordnance team, and a handful of press officers. In addition to dropping paratroopers from sixty-eight aircraft, the mission would also use seven gliders—the first use of the engineless craft in the Pacific theater.

When American-led guerrillas rolled into Aparri without firing a shot, it was presumed the airdrop would be scrubbed, but for reasons unclear, Krueger ordered the mission to proceed.

The paratroopers boarded their aircraft just as the gliders were towed aloft. The gliders—carrying the howitzers and several jeeps festooned with communications equipment—needed a one-hour head start. One of the troopers watching the awkward craft lumber into the sky behind the tug said, "It was magnificent, those big silent boxes floating against the blackness."

Several hours later, the armada droned over the drop zone, and at 09:06 the first trooper leapt out the door. The ground winds gusted up to twenty-five miles an hour, and combined with the rutted landing field caused seventy-two injuries. The hurt troopers suffered from broken or sprained ankles, dislocated shoulders, and a few broken legs.

"The rice paddy was so hard it was like concrete. It had baked hard from the sun," recalled Trooper Bert Marshall. "I had come in backwards and hit so hard I saw stars.... When I got up, I was dizzy."

Parachute failures killed two men.

Since their objectives had already been taken, the task force spent the next three days marching seventy-five miles to meet with the 37th Infantry Division. The troopers, loaded down with bazookas, 81mm mortars, and machineguns, sweltered in the heat. Soaring temperatures required thirty-minute breaks every hour. The uneventful slog flushed a lone Japanese soldier, the only action of the entire operation.

Charles Sass later referred to the jump—that put two platoons in the hospital and bagged one enemy combatant—as a "modest disaster." Jack McGrath agreed, calling it a "joke," and cautioned, "If you should ever meet a man who made the jump at Aparri, you don't owe him a drink."

Yamashita and thousands of his bedraggled legion, running out of food and ammunition, were now trapped in the mountains—where Krueger and MacArthur were content to keep them bottled up.

Four days after the airdrop at Aparri, on Saturday, June 30, MacArthur declared the Luzon campaign closed. Securing it had cost the Americans just under thirty-eight thousand casualties.

All eyes were now on Japan.

The American campaign clawed closer to Japan one island at a time, with the butcher's bill growing at a staggering rate: sixty-six thousand casualties for the islands of Iwo Jima and Okinawa. The nearly complete decimation of the defending Japanese garrisons, combined with the well-publicized civilian mass suicides during the battle for Saipan, left little hope for a Japanese surrender. From several island-based airfields, flights of American B-29 Superfortresses continued to strike Japan's home islands. The persistent air raids wreaked havoc on Japanese industry, ports, and urban areas. Tokyo was devastated by incendiary bombing, which enflamed more than half the city, killing and wounding hundreds of thousands of civilians and leaving several million more homeless.

Swing's troopers followed the war's progress on the radio and by reading the *Stars and Stripes* newspaper. And they wondered, *What's next?* Swing was in the dark himself and could only speculate. "Still have no intimation as to what our role is in the next operation," he wrote. "It will probably be about a four-corps show on the island of Kyushu and in late fall or at least before Christmas. Don't know whether we will go in Airborne or not—but am sure General Doug will use us. I have a sneaking idea that he believes as we do, that we can handle just about twice as many Japs as any of the others."

The prospect of invading Japan ensured the troopers took their training seriously, but Swing knew they could only "think, eat, and dream of war" for so long before burning out. His sports programs once again provided a welcome distraction from the weariness of an uncertain future.

After the 511th PIR football team won the division championship, 'Slugger' Lahti was looking for bigger game to keep his squad on the field. When Swing learned Lahti had arranged a face-off against the Navy's team on the Fourth of July, he was nonplussed.

"How stupid can you two be?" Swing asked rhetorically.

'Slugger' Lahti and his Special Service Officer didn't answer.

"The Navy will fly in players from all over the Pacific for this Army-Navy Game," said Swing. The gridiron rivalry between the two services was legendary, and Swing guessed that the Navy would stack the deck with "ringers." He canvassed the division for his own all-star players and reinforced Lahti's roster with the best he could find. Captain 'Big Tom' Mesereau would again be coaching the team.

At least thirty thousand troops and sailors attended the head-to-head match in Manila's Rizal Stadium. If the Navy stacked the deck, the Angels held their own, ending the game with a scoreless tie. In the words of one admiral who was present, "The game was well worth the thought and effort expended."

Four of the Angels' US Navy opponents for the July 4, 1945, football game in Manila

CHANGES WERE IN THE WIND, and replacements continued to arrive by the truckload, enough to both fill the casualty-depleted ranks and increase the division's manpower. The War Department, recognizing the Army's airborne units were undermanned for the missions expected of them, authorized a new table of equipment and organization that boosted the headcount from eight thousand to more than twelve thousand. Swing was excited by the prospects, writing, "It will certainly be a grand striking force by November."

The division's structure was reorganized as well. Instead of a lone parachute regiment—'Slugger' Lahti's 511th—there would now be two, and the Army assigned a new parachute regiment freshly arrived from the States to the 11th Airborne. But rather than keep it intact,

Swing deactivated that regiment, doling out the men to beef up his own units. He then chartered the 188th Paraglider to convert fully to a parachute outfit. This meant adding a third battalion and getting all the men jump qualified. Troopers uninterested in volunteering for the parachute school were transferred to the 187th, which retained a mixture of parachute and glider infantry troops.

Swing's approach kept his original units' linage intact and ensured combat veterans were sprinkled across the division, but the transition ruffled a few feathers. The reshuffling of personnel meant new leadership in well-established units, sometimes at the expense of combat-experienced Angels.

'Big Ed' Hogan later recalled, "Dick Ostrom, who had been promoted to buck sergeant … was now told he wasn't a sergeant after all. Another guy, a sergeant from the States with no combat experience, was now the assistant squad leader in the first squad. It was a devastating blow to Ostrom as well as to the rest of us, but with the Army, nothing could be done."

New leaders found earning the veterans' respect took more than the rank insignia on their uniforms. Some went about it the wrong way. A fresh-faced second lieutenant took charge of Stan Young's mortar platoon. When the lieutenant gave a nonsensical order, "March at attention!" the platoon ignored him. The enraged officer ordered the platoon to drop for push-ups. They did, all except Young, whose shoulder injury prevented him from doing push-ups.

"[The] others turned and saw me standing and stood up. Soon our entire mortar platoon was standing."

The lieutenant, sensing his withering authority, pleaded, "I know you guys had it rough in combat, but I went through OCS [officer candidate school] and that was tough, too."

All of the men laughed except Joe Otaviano, who yelled, "Lieutenant, get the [hell] out of here!" He did, and the platoon never saw him again, nor was their insubordination questioned. "We never heard any more about it," said Young.

ON MONDAY, August 6th, at fifteen minutes after eight in the morning, an American B-29 dropped an atomic bomb on the Japanese city of Hiroshima. After a blinding flash and rolling shockwave of destruction, more than seventy thousand Japanese were vaporized in a matter of seconds. It was followed by a second bomb on a few days later, devastating Nagasaki and killing another thirty thousand men, women, and children.

The Angels, hearing the newscast, did not know what to make of the bombs or if they would even change the course of the war. First Lieutenant Kirkland recalled, "Our training routine was not altered by the news that atomic bombs had been dropped .... Most of us expected the Japanese to go down fighting. There was a great sense, however, that we had indeed won and that the end was within reach."

The potential end of the war left him with mixed emotions. "I myself had the most peculiar sense of regret. I was becoming competent in my military trade and found that I really did not want it to end just yet. I was not alone. Major [John] Ciceri ... confided to me that he had been a truck driver in civilian life and did not want to go back to that." Kirkland later admitted, "We should have all been elated."

Twenty-four hours after the second bomb was dropped, on the night of Friday, August 10, the Japanese announced their willingness to discuss capitulation.

"Word spread from tent row to tent row that the Japanese had indeed surrendered," gushed Stan Young. "Jubilation! Laughing, crying, back slapping, hand shaking, quiet reflection, what a mix of emotions. I have had many happy moments in my life, but without a doubt, this was the happiest."

Speaking for the division, the unit historian wrote, "We had been watching for so long the Jap tactics of dying rather than surrendering that we expected to have to kill every one [of them] before the war was declared over. Least of all did we look for a formal peace."

Jack McGrath thought the news unbelievable. "I couldn't visualize the war ever ending. I thought this is what I would be doing all my life. Common sense would tell you that can't be, but that's the way I felt."

At 05:30 the next morning, MacArthur's staff ordered Swing to get his division ready to fly, first to Okinawa, then mainland Japan. Aircraft would be landing at three airfields for the Angels' airlift—they'd be leaving that day.

For Kirkland, the day started just like any other. He was out on the 81mm mortar range preparing to instruct students on crew drills. He had set up the range in an open pasture four hundred yards long. At the far end was an abandoned village that Kirkland confirmed was empty.

After the first shell exploded near the target, Kirkland was "aghast to see a civilian down at the impact point trying to do something with a carabao."

"To my horror," he recalled, "I discovered that all the villagers had returned home during the night."

The first round killed one of the village's water buffalo.

Kirkland demanded the village elder evacuate everyone, but the man refused. They were through running from Japanese and American soldiers. They were staying.

"Being a kind and understanding twenty-four-year-old, I gave him one hour to leave and returned to our mortar position."

The hour ticked by. When it ended, Kirkland ordered the mortar crew to fire a smoke round upwind of the village. "I hoped that the acrid white phosphorous smoke would change their minds," he said.

The sergeant adjusted the mortar's elevation. But firing into a strong headwind and using an under-sized propellent charge, the round fell short, exploding in the village. The thatched houses burst into flames, and through his binoculars, Kirkland saw the villagers scattering in terror.

"I stood in shock. This I had not intended," he admitted. "My shame for this act of undefendable stupidity remains."

As everyone stared downrange at the growing fire, a messenger arrived: everyone back to camp immediately. The regiment was leaving in two hours.

THE AIRLIFT BECAME A CLASSIC ARMY SNAFU—the ol' hurry-up-and-wait routine as everyone reacted to a series of improvised, countermanded, and confused loading plans. The type and number of aircraft were only known when they landed, and the cobbled-together armada consisted of more than five hundred C-47s, C-46s, and bombers. The first of Lahti's men lifted off at 17:12 that afternoon. The rest of the division followed over the next four days while the rear echelons moved by ship.

Houston Jolley and four other paratroopers made themselves as comfortable as possible in the back of a B-25 Mitchell bomber for their flight. "The pilot came to the door of the bomb bay and told us that the five chutes that were behind us were for the crew in case of trouble." The men responded with blank stares, unwilling to acknowledge the pilot's directive. "We agreed among ourselves that if trouble developed, the pilot was in for a great surprise."

Of his divisions' nine-hundred-mile flight to Okinawa—which moved 11,100 troops and 1,161,000 pounds of equipment—Swing wrote, "That's a record for an air movement to date, and we'll establish a new one when we lift for Tokyo." But getting to Tokyo would take longer than he expected, and the Angels sat on Okinawa for the next two weeks.

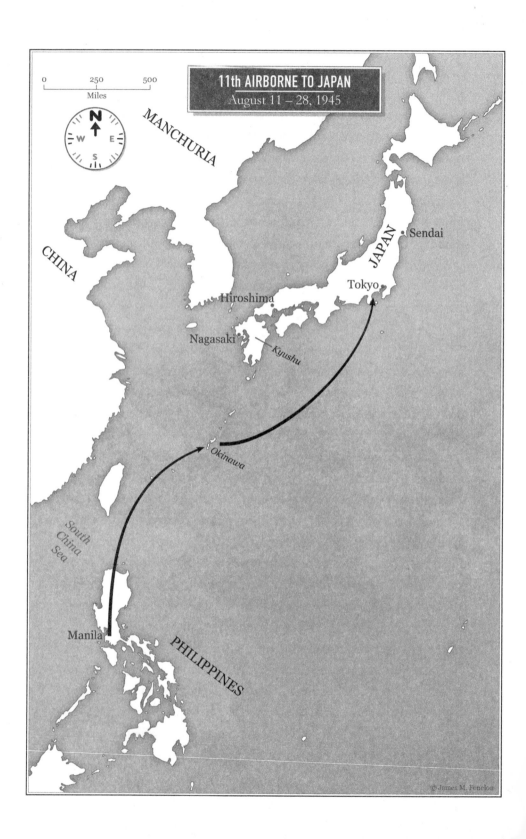

Mostly they waited, lounging in their two-man pup tents while weathering monsoons or baking in the heat. Swing shared their frustration. "So many of the brass hats are nervous about the reaction of the [Japanese] civil population—to me they're just a bunch of monkeys, and the sooner we get in there and start putting the heat on, the quicker they'll realize that they are really beaten and that we're coming in as conquerors, not paying guests." Swing, keen to get moving, radioed an urgent message back to Manila requesting permission to airdrop two battalions as a vanguard to secure an airfield near Tokyo. The Angels had already conducted test jumps from the B-24 bombers on hand. The request was denied without much consideration, however, as plans were underway to ensure the Army and Navy landed in Japan simultaneously. Politics and egos had to be considered.

The delays were due to bad flying weather and ongoing negotiations related to the terms of the surrender—a wrinkle unknown to the Angels. Even after the detonation of two atomic bombs and the Soviets attacking into Manchuria, the Japanese Supreme Council and the Cabinet were divided on how to end the war.

Those wanting to end the war immediately knew the country was devastated and couldn't take much more; they advocated accepting the American's unconditional terms, with the additional guarantee the Emperor would retain his position. The militants' perspective was summarized by Admiral Soemu Toyoda, who said, "We cannot say that final victory is certain, but at the same time we do not believe we will be positively defeated." His faction advocated additional terms: self-disarmament, control of any war crime trials, and no Allied occupation. Opponents proffered that such autonomous terms would be categorically rejected by the Americans and viewed as a refusal to surrender.

After listening to the arguments, Emperor Hirohito broke the stalemate: Japan would accept the terms of the surrender and "bear the unbearable to restore peace." Only after suffering through another B-29 airstrike, foiling a coup attempt, and quelling a kamikaze pilot revolt did a Japanese delegation fly to Manila to discuss the details of the surrender.

Not everyone was complaining about the delays. "The [time] we spent on Okinawa was one of the happiest of my whole time in the service," admitted Steve 'Heggy' Hegedus. "We had no responsibilities or duties. Best of all, nobody was shooting at us."

Houston Jolley and some of his friends got their hands on a five-gallon can of medicinal alcohol. Mixing it with grapefruit juice, they opened "Tavern Number One" for cocktails.

Despite the surrender announcement, most troopers speculated it was an elaborate trap. After all, they argued, Tokyo's propaganda had led the world to expect the Japanese would fight to the last man, woman, and child. Hegedus observed, "Nobody knew what would happen when the Americans would land. Would there be some kind of last-ditch defense by the citizenry? ... Would some fanatic band of veterans stage one last banzai attack?"

'Bloody' Swan harbored the same fears, recalling "I wondered whether I would be returned home in a body bag, or, if this occupation failed, would I then be taken prisoner? Of course, that could never happen. I knew that the Japanese were never known to take prisoners since the early days of the war. So why would they take prisoners now?"

Their worries were stoked by caveat-wielding intelligence officers describing the situation in Japan as "unpredictable." While opposition was "not anticipated," they emphasized that "some resistance in the form of espionage, sabotage, assassinations, and organization of underground movements may be expected from fanatical civilians and secret societies."

THE AIR FORCE used the delays to assemble an armada of silver C-54 Skymaster transport planes for the airlift. The four-engine beasts could make the roundtrip flight from Okinawa to Tokyo without refueling. On the morning of August 28, the Americans' advance party flew into Atsugi Airfield, located twenty-three miles southwest of Tokyo. They arrived in forty-eight aircraft and were greeted by a nervous delegation of Japanese officers and officials who were there to coordinate the formal surrender. US Air Force personnel got to work verifying the runway's suitability for heavy traffic while communications technicians erected antennas and radios for transmitting updates back to Manila. Engineers fanned out, sweeping the area for landmines.

Glider troopers board their C-54 on Okinawa for their flight to Japan

Richard 'The Rat' Laws and fifteen other combat-loaded troopers guarding an air traffic control team and their portable radar unit were some of the first Angels into Japan. They never strayed far, sleeping on the ground, with two men always on guard. It was obvious that the Japanese wanted to avoid trouble as well. Civilian policemen had established a security cordon outside the airfield's perimeter to keep the curious at bay. Any troublemakers who made it past them would have to deal with patrolling Imperial Naval troops armed with bayonets and wooded clubs. As a precaution, all authorized Japanese personnel inside the perimeter wore arm bands for identification. Signs of recent trouble were close: a line of aircraft, stripped of propellers and guns, sat just off the runway. It was a safeguard after a group of rebellious Kamikaze pilots attempted to hijack the aircraft for a final blaze of glory.

The remainder of the 11th Airborne would arrive two days later, simultaneously with American and British Marines landing amphibiously at Yokosuka's naval base.

General Swing arrives at Atsugi Airfield outside of Tokyo

FORTY-EIGHT HOURS LATER, on August 30, the first wave of transports roared over Atsugi Airfield at 06:00. The C-54s flew in groups of nine, each holding a "V of V" formation: three leading aircraft, with just a few feet between wingtips, arranged in a V, with three more aircraft on each flank holding their own tight Vs. The aerial armada passed overhead at 1,500 feet before making a lazy wide turn to land. Swing's aircraft touched down first with more than a hundred and twenty Skymasters following. They landed at the rate of one every three minutes, each depositing forty well-armed troopers before taxiing for the return flight to Okinawa. Swing's men fanned out to set up a three-mile-deep perimeter around the airfield.

"We were on full alert," recalled Steven Hegedus, sitting behind a belt-fed machinegun, "and by evening we had the entire airfield surrounded, but had still not seen even one Japanese." All troopers had live ammunition at the ready, but to avoid accidents, their weapons remained unchambered.

The rest of the division would fly in over the next several days, but Swing's immediate task was to pave the way for MacArthur's arrival later that afternoon. The advance party had already established the Angels' temporary command post in a large olive-drab tent. Nearby, a group of Japanese officers waited to formally surrender the airfield. Swing, however, had little interest in playing diplomat; he was a soldier on a mission. He wore his helmet, fatigues, a holstered pistol, a leather ammunition bandoleer, and shined jump boots. He ignored the cultural advisor's request to have tea with his former adversaries and allow them to retain their swords. Instead, Swing set an authoritarian tone.

"You get the goddamn bunch over here without their sabers," said Swing, "and we'll have the arrangements made right here on the airfield."

'Butch' Muller recalled, "A Japanese general told Swing he was the commanding general of Atsugi Air Base. Swing's curt reply was, 'All right, you can be the commanding general of Atsugi Air Base if you wish, but just keep the hell out of my way.'"

Eichelberger flew in a few hours later, and the two generals set about ensuring everything was in order for MacArthur's arrival. Swing's next task was securing the Yokohama dockyards. As the Angels' commandeered cargo trucks rumbled toward the harbor, Japanese troops manning roadblocks saluted and, in some cases, stood at attention with their backs turned as the Americans passed. Cultural misunderstanding and strained nerves almost resulted in a few hotheads gunning down their humbled adversaries, but interpreters restored calm after explaining the respectful gesture.

The troopers were stunned. Hundreds of armed Japanese soldiers guarded the procession route without raising even a fist in anger. It was surreal—none of them could imagine this happening back home if the situation were reversed. 'Butch' Muller observed, "The Japanese had surrendered as hard as they had fought."

At 14:00, MacArthur's gleaming C-54, with 'Bataan' painted on the nose, landed at Atsugi. The aircraft door swung open, and MacArthur emerged wearing his khaki uniform, famous crushed cap, and aviator sunglasses. He stood at the top of the stairs, corncob pipe clenched between his teeth, soaking in the moment. It had taken a long, brutal war to get there, and he was taking his time.

A trooper witnessing the Supreme Commander's arrival was impressed. "He's on the steps, and the press is going crazy, and he's posing—literally posing—for a good five minutes. Turning one way then another. Never smiling. Appearing godly. Totally in charge."

There was later criticism of MacArthur's "crass showmanship," but to 'Butch' Muller, present at the event, "he looked extremely dignified—every inch the conqueror."

Major Thomas 'Big Tom' Mesereau in Atsugi, Japan

Swing had ensured the proper amount of pomp for the occasion. An American flag waved in the breeze from atop one of the hangers, the Angels' band played the national anthem, and a seventy-man honor guard stood at attention at the base of the stairs. Two rows of six-foot-tall paratroopers, commanded by Major 'Big Tom' Mesereau, formed a cordon to MacArthur's waiting car. Eichelberger and Swing enforced the minimum six-foot height requirement for the honor guard to impress both the reporters as well as intimidate the Japanese. At least one member of the guard detail, John Bandoni, had put cardboard shims into his jump boots to make sure he participated in the historic event. Each trooper sported a helmet emblazed with "11 A/B" on the front, stenciled in white. MacArthur wasn't the only press-savvy general in the Army.

MacArthur descended to greet the reporters, but first shook hands with Eichelberger, then Swing. In a sea of smiling, khaki-clad officers, Swing—in his olive-drab combat fatigues and steel helmet—stood out like a cactus in a rose garden. After a brief statement, MacArthur inspected the honor guard, then approached Swing's band conductor. "Thank you very much. I want you to tell the band that that's about the sweetest music I've ever heard."

A waiting motorcade, sandwiched between cargo trucks full of Swing's armed troopers, escorted MacArthur into Yokohama. In the lead was a Japanese fire truck, its wailing siren heralding the advance of Japan's new emperor. As the vehicles passed, Japanese soldiers along the route again stood at attention, their backs turned. Eichelberger wasn't taking any chances: on the seat beside him, within arm's reach, was a hand grenade. The formal surrender ceremony would take place in a few days, and until then, MacArthur would be staying at the well-appointed New Grand Hotel.

ON THE MORNING OF SEPTEMBER 2, General Swing stood on the crowded deck of the US battleship, *Missouri*. The ship was packed with dignitaries, admirals, generals, and more than a thousand sailors all craning for a peek at the Japanese surrender delegation. Tokyo Bay teemed with more than two hundred Allied vessels: battleships, destroyers, mine sweepers, cargo transports, and submarines.

Swing was one of forty American generals standing at attention in a formation flanking the ceremony. From the second row, he had a clear view of the proceedings. A group of admirals and Allied representatives stood behind MacArthur, who stepped up to several microphones and addressed the world:

> We are gathered here, representatives of the major warring powers, to conclude a solemn agreement whereby peace may be restored.
>
> The issues involving divergent ideals and ideologies have been determined on the battlefields of the world, and hence are not for our discussion or debate.
>
> Nor is it for us here to meet, representing as we do a majority of the peoples of the earth, in a spirit of distrust, malice, or hatred.

But rather it is for us, both victors and vanquished, to rise to that higher dignity which alone befits the sacred purposes we are about to serve, committing all of our peoples unreservedly to faithful compliance with the undertakings they are here formally to assume.

It is my earnest hope, and indeed the hope of all mankind, that from this solemn occasion a better world shall emerge out of the blood and carnage of the past—a world founded upon faith and understanding, a world dedicated to the dignity of man and the fulfillment of his most cherished wish for freedom, tolerance, and justice.

The terms and conditions upon which the surrender of the Japanese Imperial Forces is here to be given and accepted are contained in the Instrument of Surrender now before you.

As Supreme Commander for the Allied Powers, I announce it my firm purpose, in the tradition of the countries I represent, to proceed in the discharge of my responsibilities with justice and tolerance, while taking all necessary dispositions to ensure that the terms of surrender are fully, promptly, and faithfully complied with.

He concluded by inviting the Japanese representatives to sign the surrender documents. When they finished, MacArthur added his signature. A retinue of Allies followed, including a Russian who Swing described as "a big tough-looking bruiser," who had "a hard time handling [his pen] with his big fist."

Punctuating the event was an armada of several hundred B-29s and carrier-based fighter planes droning low overhead.

With the formalities completed, an officer climbed up from the lower deck where he'd been watching the ceremony. He was a towering figure: six-foot-four, weighing 210 pounds, and brimming with confidence. His cap was adorned with the oak leaf rank of a major; over his left breast pocket he wore shined parachute wings, and tucked under his arm was a .45-automatic pistol in a shoulder holster. It was 'Big Tom' Mesereau—personally selected by Swing to hand-carry copies of the surrender documents, including sound recordings and movies, to Washington, DC.

The Japanese surrender aboard the USS Missouri; *Swing is standing out of frame to the left while Major 'Big Tom' Mesereau looks on from the lower deck, his hands clasped in front of him*

Mesereau had seen his fair share of the war: from Charlie Company's first deadly day of combat on Leyte to the dust and heat of the Genko Line, and finally to the deck of the USS *Missouri*. It was a dreamlike moment of reflection for someone not expecting to live long enough to see it. At last, the nightmare was over, and Mesereau was heading home.

The Ol' Gray Mare

Yokohama Harbor, Japan.
11:00, Sunday, September 2, 1945

S wing made it back to the Yokohama docks just in time to thumb his nose at the 1st Cavalry Division, his Manila city-limit rivals. When the cavalrymen debarked from their ships, setting foot on Japanese soil for the first time, Swing signaled his band to belt out, "The Old Gray Mare, She Ain't What She Used to Be."

Paratroopers heckled them as they marched past, shouting, "Welcome to Japan!" "What took ya so long?"

When the cavalrymen arrived in Tokyo for occupation duty, they erected a billboard proclaiming in over-sized letters, "1st Cavalry Division – 1st in Manila – 1st in Tokyo." They wisely stationed armed guards around it.

The plumb assignment of garrison duty in the capital allegedly belonged to the Angels. As the story goes—and most troopers believe it to be true—a bank robbery scuttled those plans, causing MacArthur to banish "Ali Baba Swing and his 8,000 thieves" to northern

Japan. But in reality, Swing knew before he landed at Atsugi that his division was destined for the rural Sendai province.

Navigating Japan's destroyed transportation network by truck and train was another adventure of fits and starts. Once in Sendai, the Angels commandeered the largest buildings they could find for billets and settled in for occupation duty. Their first assignment was working with local police to confiscate caches of weapons ranging from machineguns to homemade spears—an eerie glimpse into an invasion that would have been a senseless bloodbath.

Prior to Japan's surrender, the 11th Airborne was destined to invade the Japanese home island of Kyushu. Their role in Operation OLYMPIC, along with fourteen other divisions, would have been just the first phase of the invasion. The Japanese had 900,000 troops waiting for them—almost a 1:1 ratio to the invaders.

The Americans' casualty estimates for the invasion were speculative and varied wildly, but the number put in front of President Truman during a planning meeting was a staggering 193,500. The report's authors admitted their numbers were inaccurate given that "the scale of Japanese resistance in the past has not been predictable." While civilian deaths were outside the purview of such reports, that dedicated resistance could be expected by the several million conscripted civilians of the Patriotic Citizens Fighting Corps suggested the invasion would be an unprecedented apocalypse for both sides. Fortunately, the world was spared such an Armageddon-like devastation.

With hostilities ended, the US War Department developed a point system for demobilization, and by the end of 1945, most of Swing's combat veterans were shipping back to the States. And so it was that in dribs and drabs, some of the war's most elite soldiers unceremoniously disappeared back into civilization.

The war's victors continued to press the vanquished, seeking justice in the courts where war crime tribunals determined the fate of

The Angels' Lieutenant Bernard J. 'Bud' Stapleton raises the American flag atop the
Nippon News building in Tokyo on September 5, 1945

the Angels' former adversaries. General Tomoyuki Yamashita, whose tactical flexibility and use of terrain kept a force of fifty thousand troops in the field until the end of the war, walked out of Luzon's mountains to surrender on the same morning that Swing stood on the deck of the USS *Missouri*. Yamashita never left Luzon and was hanged there for war crimes in 1946. The same fate befell General Masatoshi Fujishige—the architect of Malepunyo's mountain defenses. Allied military tribunals sentenced over nine hundred Japanese war criminals to death and imprisoned several thousand more. Many others escaped Allied judgement by taking their own lives.

In March 1974, twenty-nine years after the war was over, Second Lieutenant Hiroo Onoda emerged from the Philippine jungle to give himself up. He was the last of Yamashita's known holdouts, his sword still razor-sharp and his rifle loaded.

SWING REMAINED IN COMMAND of the 11th Airborne Division until 1948. His Angels stayed in Japan until mid-1949, then they rotated back to the States. Several duty stations followed until the division's flag was folded on July 1, 1959. There was a brief resurrection in 1963 as the 11th Air Assault Division, but that experiment ended after two years.

Many of the Angels continued to serve in uniform. Stephen 'Rusty' Cavanaugh fought in Korea and Vietnam, where he commanded the covert Special Operations Group. John Bittori—credited with leading the 'Rat's Ass' charge on Leyte—served in airborne units for most of his career and retired as a command sergeant major. Robert H. 'Shorty' Soule retired as a major general. John Ringler and Edward Lahti both retired as full colonels.

Thomas 'Big Tom' Mesereau beat everyone home, flying back to the States with an empty briefcase. At the last minute, the powers that be decided it was safer to send the surrender documents by sea rather than air. To maintain the ruse however, Mesereau flew back to Washington, DC, where he received a well-publicized home coming. After a short visit with his family, he returned to Japan and later, after ten years of service, joined his father-in-law in the restaurant business.

Mills Lowe wanted to make the Army his career, but his glass eye took that option off the table. He returned to Virginia, where he earned a living as a pipe-fitter, learned to hunt with his good eye, and raised a family. Lowe didn't talk much about his war experience, but his daughter remembers that his body was so riddled with shrapnel that he always set off metal detectors at the airport.

Like Lowe, most of the Angels returned to civilian life. Randolph Kirkland resumed his pre-war mechanical engineering career with General Electric. Henry Burgess finished law school and served in the Wyoming House of Representatives and Senate. Machinegunner Deane Marks went to college on the GI Bill and raised a family of four after marrying Clare, whom he'd met at Camp Polk.

Rod Serling, attempting to purge his post-traumatic demons through writing, studied literature in college and later struck fame as the creator and host of *The Twilight Zone*. "I was bitter about every-thing," he admitted, "and at loose ends when I got out of the service, I think I turned to writing to get it off my chest." Serling's wounded knee plagued him for the rest of his life, and his children remember him collapsing when it gave out on him without warning. His knee injury was a physical symptom of deeper trauma, and he later wrote, "Shrapnel wounds and mangled, bullet-ridden bodies are not the only casualties of war. There are casualties of the mind. Every war pro-duces a backwash, a residue of pain and grief."

Time and distance gradually numbed the memories for some fortunate veterans, while others struggled to find their own form of therapy and excise what is now known as post-traumatic stress. But after World War II, it was hard to find help. Most put their heads down and marched forward into their new lives, but some tragically chose suicide. The trope of the disenfranchised combat veteran became all too real for those seeking purpose or comradeship in a post-war society increasingly infatuated with the distractions of commerce. As the country moved on, many veterans still had one foot in the past, processing the horrors of war.

"I try to forget the war, but I can't," said Miles Gale decades later. "Hunting down and killing people called 'the enemy' is not a great achievement. Weekly nightmares full of fighting, kicking, and screaming follow after all these years." Another veteran was haunted by the memory of a decaying Japanese corpse whenever it rained. He had seen the body on Leyte—the dead man lay beside the trail, a puddle forming in his empty chest cavity as rain drops rolled down his waxy skin.

Some, like Charles Sass, floundered. He bummed around New York City for several months, sleeping on the streets before collecting himself and going back to college. Some veterans coped with alcohol; others repressed their experiences, refusing to talk about them. For many, it was always there, just below the surface—a simmering anger or impatience its only tell.

The veterans who came to terms with the war often valued their experiences for the perspective it gave them. Trooper Richard Penwell summarized it simply by saying, "The war helped me appreciate life more."

As William Walter put it, "I was so hungry! That's one of the emotions you experience in war: pain, hunger, heartbreak, love, hate, and fear. All the emotions—you're kind of living on the edge. Everything is on a serrated, raw edge. You're more alive than any point in your life since you experience every emotion."

Those emotions, forged on the anvil of combat and shared with members of their unique fraternity, bonded them together in profound ways. In later reflections, many veterans admitted—even if only to themselves—that they missed it. Not the blood and violence, but the communal experience of youth and being alive in the face of so much death. Certainly, there was nothing romantic about the war's filth, privation, fear, agony, and tragedy, but paradoxically it revealed a nobility of sacrifice that's rarely exposed in civilized society.

"I wouldn't trade anything for those days," commented a trooper. "We had some very good times and also some bad and sad times during the war, but we always stayed together, no matter what."

In a letter home to his parents in December 1944, Private Richard Mueller shared his ruminations after the long nightmare of Leyte, writing, "These men I'm with are really close, and our company officers are good leaders and have to go through everything we do and much more at times. You can see the pain on their faces when someone dies or is hurt because of the orders they had to issue. We're all scared and sometimes just can't do everything we should, but everyone understands the other man's feeling and helps out whenever necessary. If I have to be here at all, these are the men I want around me, that's for damn sure."

The Angels' war was personal, but not unique. Tens of thousands of Americans fought and hacked their way through the jungles of the Pacific, and unsurprising patterns emerged as to how they coped with the stress of combat. A war-time survey of infantry divisions fighting the Japanese found that the majority of officers and enlisted men cited their need to not let the other men down as a reason they kept fighting. This sentiment outweighed patriotism, prayer, and hatred of the enemy as sources of strength in the face of terror.

Patriotism, often ascribed as one of the Greatest Generation's outstanding traits, might have factored into volunteering or refusing a draft deferment, but those motives shifted as men transitioned from civilians to front-line soldiers.

Paratrooper Robert Marich, remembering how his initial desire to serve contrasted with the realities of combat, said, "We were gung-ho, and people the next day [after the attack on Pearl Harbor] were lined up all over the place to enlist and get back at the Japanese. And the whole thing was for mother, God, country, and apple pie, you know."

"That is pure bullshit," he continued. "When you're engaged in a fight for your life, you don't think about mother, God, country, and the flag and all of that. That's the least of it; that's one thing that never enters your mind. The only thing you're worried about is getting killed, and your buddy next to you getting killed. You have a friend there that's like your brother. And he guards you and you guard him. The company commander doesn't say, 'All right fellas, this is for the country and mother and apple pie! Let's go get 'em!' That's bullshit."

Marich's observations would resonate with most combat veterans. In the thick of battle, survival—"fighting for your skin"—meant subordinating personal interests. In other words, the choreography of combat, as writer Sabastian Junger put it, "requires that each man make decisions based not on what's best for him, but on what's best for the group. If everyone does that, most of the group survives. If no one does, most of the group dies. That, in essence, is combat."

"Your relationship with the men around you is closer than anything you can imagine," said Charles Sass. "These men are all part of you—even the guys you don't like, and there are plenty of those. You depend on each other."

That dependence bred a fierce loyalty. Decades after the war, Robert Marich recalled a haunting memory from Leyte. Private Bill Hesselbacher lay bleeding to death on a muddy trail, shot three times in the head and neck. Lawrence 'Lorney' E. DuBay grabbed his rifle and sprinted down the hill to Hesselbacher.

"Don't go down there!" screamed Marich.

But DuBay, as recalled by another trooper, "was really fast; he could run like the devil. He was the first down there. As soon as he got down there, the Japs shot him through the chest."

Holding back his emotion, Marich continued, "They were both killed. His friend had been butchered; he went down there to save him, and he was butchered. Nobody else would have done that. This kid didn't care. He was my friend.... It's all you had; your buddy was all you had."

DuBay was wrapped in a red cargo parachute and buried next to Hesselbacher. The two men were a pair of tragic stories among tens of thousands killed in circumstances not of their choosing. War provided them all occasions to see and experience both the best and the worst that mankind could offer. All they could hope for in response was that they'd find the courage to give the best of themselves when called upon. Sadly, finding that courage sometimes came at their own expense.

"A good soldier will die before he'll let down his fellow soldiers," said trooper James H. Billingsley, staring into the distance as if it was a portal to the past. "He will die first."

Acknowledgments

Writing the Story of the 11th Airborne Division

It is a well-known dictum of human observation that witnesses invariably view unfolding action from their own, often narrow, perspective. That is especially true of soldiers in combat, particularly those enduring weeks of sleepless nights in a muddy jungle where days bled into a blurry green morass of sameness. Add to that the threat of violence as well as the distraction of hunger, and the immediacy of the present becomes inevitable. As trooper Dick Ostrom recalled of his wartime experiences, "Back then we had only three days—today, yesterday, and the next day. No Mondays, Wednesdays, or Sundays."

Verifying personal accounts and connecting the dots to specific skirmishes required a lot of cross-referencing while sifting through unit journals, orders, and after-action reports. The points of connection were often, tragically, dates of death. Veterans might chronicle an event out of sequence or incorrectly recall a date, but their stories often framed events in relation to a killed or wounded comrade. In the post-war decades, the division's veterans collated and curated unit casualty rosters which were critical artifacts in tying together events.

Additionally, the Angels' various association newsletters also served as peer-review journals with veterans batting their combat stories back and forth to reconstruct events and hammer personal recollections into a collective record. While I put forth my best effort to build on their foundation, any errors are my responsibility alone.

Sussing out some of the geographic locations on Leyte was particularly challenging. Given the inaccurate period maps and the severe mountainous terrain that almost defies description, it is surprising anyone knew where they were, let alone notated the correct grid references. With the help of trooper Joseph Vannier's detailed descriptions of Rock Hill and the 511th PIR's intelligence reports, I mapped the Angels' route through the central mountains. The battles on Luzon were better charted, and I am in debt to Chris Salvano at California State University and Katherine Strickland at the University of Texas at Austin (my *alma mater*), both of whom unearthed period maps allowing me to plot the division's progress as they bashed into Manila's Genko Line and across the island.

Many fine institutions and individuals helped me connect the dots to tell this story. For period records, I relied heavily on the US National Archives and the US Army Heritage and Education Center, where Justine Melone was both kind and diligent in her efforts to track down documents. I'm thankful for the hospitality of my friends Cathy and Fernando Grajales, as well as Jim and Lisa Dymski who opened their homes to me while I conducted my research. Laura Jowdy at the Congressional Medal of Honor Society dug through her archives to find several witness accounts of Elmer Fryar's and Manuel Pérez's courageous actions. Toni Kiser at the National World War II Museum in New Orleans provided invaluable oral histories and greatly facilitated my onsite research. Fiona Garnes at the MacArthur Museum in Brisbane, Australia tracked down some very esoteric but vital details for me, and Jim Zobel of the MacArthur Memorial was always willing to help; I appreciate his patient assistance. Walter Borneman, accomplished author and MacArthur biographer, leaned in several times to assist. I spent hours on the phone with historian and author Jon Parshall, who was also kind enough to read several passages of an early draft. His insight into the dramatic nuances of the Pacific war were invaluable. Don Patton, the relentless cofounder of the World War II History Round Table, was free with his rolodex and gladly connected me with several experts, including Kimmy Tanaka at Historic Fort Snelling. Her help filled in many details of the Angels' Nisei in the Language Detachment. The research skills of my longtime friend Jennifer Manning uncovered numerous period documents, allowing me to burnish many of the book's incidents and personalities.

I would not have been able to accurately include the contributions of the Filipino guerrillas without the time and effort of Cecilia Gaerlan, the executive director of the Bataan Legacy Historical Society. Additionally, Dr. Ricardo T. Jose of the University of the Philippines provided transcripts of war crime trials that revealed the horror of the atrocities on Luzon. He was also kind enough to give feedback on several excerpts regarding those valiant men and women who stood against the Imperial Army and suffered the heinous consequences. While this book is primarily an account of the 11th Airborne Division, it was the guerrillas' contribution on Luzon, which General Henry 'Butch' Muller described as "at least equal to the addition of two more regiments" that allowed the Angels to punch above their weight.

Breathing life into this narrative are the words of the veterans themselves, and several of their children entrusted me with their fathers' legacies, including Brian Loughrin, Craig Davis, Matt Hall, Freddy Arthur, Anne Serling, Mick Robson, Susan Lowe Bevins, Sara Miley, and Thomas Mesereau, Jr. I remain thankful for their faith and support.

The outstanding team at Regnery carried the book across the finish line with grace and enthusiasm: Tom Spence, president and publisher, always made himself available. Tony Daniel, editor, was a staunch supporter, and his feedback was valuable and deeply appreciated. John Caruso designed a fantastic jacket, and Josh Taggert's interior layout and design pulled it all together. Special thanks to Michael Baker for his dedication and invaluably rigorous copyediting. A big salute goes to my agent, David Hale Smith, who was consistent in his support and encouragement. I'd also like to thank David Mamet (whom I've never met) for pointing me toward the "No Admittance" door.

On a personal level, I'm greatly thankful for the time and efforts of Mark Bristol, Steve Jensen, Chris Shore, Julie Paasche, Robert Lindsey, and several members of my family, all of whom read early drafts of the manuscript and provided invaluable feedback. They all helped me hone a manuscript that I'm proud of. And last, but far from least, is my wife, Melanie. She not only provided notes and feedback throughout this process, but also provided an endless stream of encouragement, wisdom, and whiskey sours. I couldn't have done it without her.

In memory of James D. Hornfischer, agent, mentor, and friend. He is missed.

Bibliography

Selected Sources

The following abbreviations appear in the endnotes and bibliography:

11ABN 11th Airborne Division
127ENG 127th Airborne Engineer Battalion
152AAB 152nd Airborne Anti-Aircraft Battalion
408AQM 408th Airborne Quartermaster Company
511SIG 511th Airborne Signal Company
511PIR 511th Parachute Infantry Regiment
711ORD 711th Airborne Ordnance Maintenance Company
AHEC Army Heritage and Education Center
DRL Donovan Research Library
GO General Order
FO Field Order
NARA National Archives and Records Administration, College Park, Maryland.
NOLA National WWII Museum in New Orleans, LA.
Voice *Voice of the Angels*, the official newsletter of the 11th Airborne Division
WA *Winds Aloft*, Official News Bulletin of the 511th Parachute Infantry Association

Books

11th Airborne Division. Atlanta, Georgia: Albert Love Enterprises, 1944.

511th PIR Association. *511th Parachute Infantry Regiment*. Paducah, Kentucky: Turner Publishing Company, 1997.

Bergerud, Eric. *Touched with Fire: The Land War in the South Pacific*. New York: Penguin Books, 1996.

Blair, Clay. *Ridgway's Paratroopers: The American Airborne in World War II*. Garden City, New York: Dial Press, 1985.

Burgess, Henry A. *Looking Back: A Wyoming Rancher Remembers the 11th Airborne and the Raid on Los Baños*. Missoula, Montana: Pictorial Histories Publishing Company, Inc., 1993.

Cannon, Hardy D. *Box Seat Over Hell: The True Story of America's Liaison Pilots and Their Light Planes in World War Two*. San Antonio, Texas: Alamo Liaison Squadron, 2007.

Cannon, M. Hamlin. *Leyte: The Return to the Philippines*. *U.S. Army in World War II*. Washington, DC: Office of the Chief of Military History, Department of the Army, 1954.

Chaze, Elliott. *The Stainless Steel Kimono*. New York: Simon and Schuster, Inc., 1947.

Eichelberger, Robert L. *Dear Miss Em: General Eichelberger's War in the Pacific, 1942–1945*. Westport, Connecticut: Greenwood Press, 1972.

Flanagan, Edward M., Jr. *The Angels: A History of the 11th Airborne*. Novato, California: Presidio Press, 1989.

———. *The Angels: A History of the 11th Airborne Division 1943–1946*. Washington, DC: Infantry Journal Press, 1948.

Frank, Richard B. *Downfall: The End of the Imperial Japanese Empire*. New York: Random House, 1999.

Henderson, Bruce. *Rescue at Los Baños: The Most Daring Prison Camp Raid of World War II*. New York: William Morrow, 2015.

Hogan, Edward W. *A Dogface's War: A Paratrooper's Story of WWII in the Philippines*. Lincoln, Nebraska: iUniverse, 2007.

Kitchen, William C. *Angels at War*. Self-published, 2014.

Lahti, Edward H. *Memoirs of an Angel*. Self-published, 1994.

LeRoy, Bob. *From My Foxhole to Tokyo*. Boring, Oregon: CPA Book Publisher, 1992.

McManus, John C. *Fire and Fortitude: The US Army in the Pacific War, 1941–1943*. New York: Dutton Caliber, 2019.

———. *Island Infernos: The US Army's Pacific War Odyssey, 1944*. New York: Dutton Caliber, 2021.

11th Airborne Division Association. *11th Airborne.* Edited by Robert J. Martin. Paducah, Kentucky: Turner Publishing Company, 1993.

Mitchell, Harris, T. *The Story of the First Airborne Battalion.* Rockville, Maryland: Twinbrook Communications, 1992.

O'Donnell, Patrick K. *Into the Rising Sun.* New York: Free Press, 2002.

Rottman, G. & A. Takizawa. *Japanese Paratroop Forces of World War II.* New York: Osprey Publishing, 2005.

Serling, Anne. *As I Knew Him: My Dad, Rod Serling.* New York: Citadel Press, 2013.

Scott, James M. *Rampage: MacArthur, Yamashita, and the Battle of Manila.* New York: W. W. Norton & Company, Inc., 2018.

Smith, Robert Ross. *Triumph in the Philippines: U.S. Army in World War II.* Washington, DC: Center of Military History, United States Army, 1991.

Stouffer, Samuel A., et al. *The American Soldier: Combat and Its Aftermath, Vol. II.* Princeton, New Jersey: Princeton University Press, 1949.

Talbot, Carol T. and Virginia J. Muir. *Escape at Dawn.* Wheaton, Illinois: Tyndale House Publishers, Inc., 1988.

Wiegand, Brandon T. *Index to the General Orders of the 11th Airborne Division in World War II.* Creighton, Pennsylvania: D-Day Militaria, 2004.

Periodicals and Newspapers

The *I Co. Beacon,* newsletter of the 511th PIR's Item Company, published and edited by Joseph R. Vannier. As this publication rarely used article titles, content is cited in the endnotes as *I Co. Beacon* with author, issue date, and page number.

Abernathy, William C. "Prelude The Los Baños Decision." *WA,* no. 10 and no. 11 (July/October 1989): 33.

Alverson, Frank. "2610." *Voice,* no. 49 (August 15, 1982): 25.

Bandoni, John. "A Memorable Experience." *WA,* no. 27 (Spring 1994): 27.

Baughn, Ted. "Congressional Medal of Honor, PFC Manuel Pérez, Jr." *WA,* no. 3 (October 1987).

Baumgarten, Ed. "Mail Call." *WA,* no. 88 (Summer 2009): 35.

Bengtson, Roy H. "Unit History." *WA,* no. 18 (Winter 1991): 20.

Beightler, Robert S. "A Swing and a Miss." *WA,* no. 10/11 (July/October 1989): 30.

———. "Lieutenant Foster Arnett." *WA,* no. 12 (January 1990): 7.

Bigart, Homer. "Los Baños Rescue." *Voice* 125 (December 1999): 49.

Bostick, Deane E. "The 11th." *Voice,* no. 97 (July 15, 1992): 24.

Broestl, Robert S. "History of the 11th ABN DIV 408 Quartermaster Co. 1942–45." *Voice,* no. 102 (January 15, 1994): 42.

Burger, Donald. "How I Became a Trooper." *WA*, no. 48 (Summer 1999).

Burgess, Henry. "The Japanese Attack across Leyte into the Burauen Airfield." *Voice*, no. 83 (June 15, 1989): 23.

———. "Joe Swing & His 10,000 Thieves." *Voice* no. 85 (November 15, 1989): 25.

Butler, Leroy D. "Geronimo #13 or the South Pacific as I Saw It, Part I." *WA* no. 53 (Fall 2000): 21.

———. "Geronimo #13 or the South Pacific as I Saw It, Part II." *WA*, no. 54 (Winter 2001): 26.

———. "Geronimo #13 or the South Pacific as I Saw It, Part III." *WA*, no. 55 (Spring 2001): 13.

———. "Thanksgiving–Christmas 1944." *WA*, no. 57 (Fall 2001): 11.

Carnahan, David H. "1944 Letter." *Voice*, no. 80 (November 15, 1988): 43.

Carrico, Jane. "CSM John Bittorie." *WA*, no. 96 (Summer 2011): 14.

Carroll, Robert A. "The 11th Airborne Division Provisional Reconnaissance Platoon and the Los Baños Raid." *WA*, no. 66 (Winter 2004): 12.

Cavanaugh, Stephen E. "A Call to Arms, Part I." *WA*, no. 93 (Fall 2010): 6.

———. "Imus—Gateway to Manila." *WA*, no. 50 (Winter 2000): 12.

———. "Mt. Bijiang—What Really Happened (I Think)." *WA*, no. 49 (Fall 1999): 114.

———. "Rats Ass Charge." *WA*, no. 7 (October 1988): 17.

———. "Survival of the Fittest." *WA*, no. 62 (Winter 2003): 17.

———. "Vigueur de Dessus, Strength from Above (and I Needed it)." *WA*, no. 70 (Winter 2005): 10.

Coon, Bernie. "A Walk with God." *WA*, no. 32 (Summer 1995): 36.

Culbertson, Charles. "Jumping into History." *Voice* 125 (December 1999): 48.

Davis, Jerry T. "511th PIR New Guinea: May–November, 1944." *WA*, no. 49 (Fall 1999): 25.

———. "Combat Jump." *WA*, no. 9 (April 1989): 7.

———. "The Longest Night." *WA*, no. 22 (Winter 1993): 14.

———. "A Slow Boat Home." *WA*, no. 23 (Spring 1993): 36.

———. "The Strangest Detail." *WA*, no. 49 (Fall 1999): 84.

Doherty, George. "John Santucci, I Co. Makes Ripley's 'Believe It or Not.'" *WA*, no. 47 (Spring 1999).

———. "Letter to Richard Hoyt, undated." *Voice*, no. 68 (August 15, 1986): 20.

———. "Lt. General Joseph M. Swing and the 11th Airborne Division." *Voice*, (Newsletter #84, September 15, 1989): 44.

———. "New Guinea." *Voice*, no. 99 (January 15, 1993): 11.

———. "Tech. Sgt. Miles [sic] T. Lowe Awarded a Field Commission." *Voice*, no. 90 (January 15, 1991): 27.

———. "Tomorrow I Will Be a Paratrooper." *Voice*, no. 81 (January 15, 1989): 3.

———. "Welcome to the Jungle." *Voice*, no. 102 (October 15, 1993): 6.

Dubes, William L. "Company D Stories." *WA*, no. 77 (Fall 2006): 23.

Dunlop, Howard G. "Strange Happenings in Combat." *WA*, no. 57 (Fall 2001): 9.

Eichelberger, Robert L., "The Dash for Manila." *Saturday Evening Post* (September 10, 1949): 26.

Ermatinger, Ralph E. "Hunger, Leyte, 1944." *WA*, no. 4 (January 1988): 9.

Farrell, F. W. "Letter to Richard Hoyt, undated." *Voice*, no. 16 (March 15, 1975): 2.

Flanagan, Edward M., Jr. "Joseph May Swing." *Voice*, no. 68 (August 15, 1986): 29.

Fletcher, Bob. "Hill 2610." *Voice*, no. 50 (November 15, 1982): 7.

Floersch, George C. "And the 'Fox' Showed Up for Snacks." *WA*, no. 33 (Fall 1995): 21.

———. "Another Remembrance of C Company's First Battle." *WA* 25 (Fall 1993): 29.

———. "Do You Remember When the 511th Landed on the Beach of Leyte?" *WA*, no. 66 (Winter 2004): 10.

———. "What Happened to PFC George Floersch?" *WA* 29 (Fall 1994): 9.

Ford, Charlie. "I Stole the Liquor." *WA*, no. 43 (Spring 1998).

Farloni, Frank. "Farloni's Tour of the Philippines." *Voice* 127 (June 2000): 39.

Foster, Arnett D. "Boxing Team." *WA*, no. 49 (Fall 1999): 32.

———. "In Memorium—Thomas A. Nestory, MD." *WA*, no. 49 (Fall 1999): 128.

Fuller, Kenneth D. "Los Baños Address, 23 February 2005." *WA*, no. 71 (Spring 2005): 30.

———. "Los Baños – Another Point of View." *WA*, no. 34 (Winter 1996): 46.

———. "Some Recollections of an Old Airborne Soldier." *WA*, no. 67 (Spring 2004): 4.

Gale, Miles. "The 11th Airborne Reviews for General Henri Giraud." *WA*, no. 33 (Fall 1995): 11.

———. "Accidental Death in the 11th Airborne." *WA*, no. 25 (Fall 1993): 36.

———. "Banzai." *WA*, no. 22 (Winter 1993): 18.

———. "A Chance Meeting." *Voice*, no. 52 (April 15, 1983): 10.

———. "Farewell to New Guinea." *WA*, no. 37 (Fall 1996): 24.

———. "The Guinea Moonshiners." *WA*, no. 44 (Summer 1998).

———. "Getting Ready for a Training Jump." *Voice*, no. 77 (May 15, 1988): 6.

———. "Home Sweet Home." *WA*, no. 31 (Spring 1995): 21.

———. "Jungle School." *WA*, no. 49 (Fall 1999): 27.

———. "Letter to editor, undated." *Voice*, no. 67 (June 15, 1986): 9.

———. "Letter to Richard Hoyt, dated September 23, 1978." *Voice*, no. 96 (April 15, 1992): 11.

———. "Leyte to Luzon, A Vivid Remembrance." *WA*, no. 49 (Fall 1999): 87.

———. "More About Leyte." *WA*, no. 26 (Winter 1994): 17.

———. "New Guinea 1944." *Voice*, no. 81 (January 15, 1989): 31.

———. "The New Guinea Water Works." *Voice*, no. 104 (July 15, 1994): 13.

———. "On the Trail in Leyte." *WA*, no. 27 (Spring 1994): 19.

———. "A Paratrooper Sea Voyage — Crossing the Pacific Ocean, Spring of 1944." *WA*, no. 4 (January 1988): 6.

———. "Remembrances of Miles Gale." *WA*, no. 20 (Summer 1992): 19.

———. "Scouts Out." *WA*, no. 36 (Summer 1996): 31.

———. "The Valiant Plan." *WA*, no. 34 (Winter 1996): 37.

Gay, Glibert H. "Camp Stoneman." *WA*, no. 49 (Fall 1999): 21.

———. "Tokyo Rose." *WA*, no. 3 (October 1987).

Genematas, Anthony K. "Company E, 187th Regiment: HQ Second Battalion, Nasugbu to Manila." *Voice*, no. 58 (August 15, 1984): 12.

Gleich, Pete. "Partners in Victory: 672nd Amphibian Tractor Bn. Finally Receives due Honors for Los Baños Rescue, Part I." *Voice* 173 (December 2011): 25.

Greer, Harold. Undated letter. *Voice*, no. 96 (April 15, 1992): 28.

Haan, Fred. "The Prisoner." *WA*, no. 32 (Summer 1995): 42.

Hadac, George. "A Trooper's Story." *WA*, no. 46 (Winter 1999).

Hale, Murray M. "Company D Stories." *WA*, no. 92 (Summer 2010): 9.

Hammrich, Edward A. "A Short, Personal History of My Time in the 11th Airborne Division." *Voice* 115 (July 15, 1997): 26.

Harrison, Joe. "Nichols Field." *WA* no. 38 (Winter 1997).

Heath, Eugene P. "Expert Marksmanship." *WA*, no. 5 (April 1988): 10.

Hegedus, Steve M. "Big Red Rising Sun and Little Red Dots." *WA*, no. 39 (Spring 1997).

———. "A Bowel Movement Can Be Hazardous to Your Health." *WA* 29 (Fall 1994): 30.

———. "Burial Detail and the C Company Ambush." *WA* 25 (Fall 1993): 25.

———. "Company Medics, A-511, a Tribute." *WA* no. 4 (January 1988): 2.

———. "Lowly Paratroop Sgt. Stares Down Big Navy Brass." *WA*, no. 53 (Fall 2000): 32.

Hendry, James B. "Fighting." *WA*, no. 18 (Winter 1991): 23.

———. "Letter to the Editor." *Voice*, no. 34 (April 15, 1979): 7.

———. "A Night of Peace." *WA*, no. 2 (October 1988): 1.

———. "Mahonag to the Sea." *WA*, no. 49 (Fall 1999): 54.

Hogan, Ed. "The Longest Night II." *WA*, no. 53 (Fall 2000): 27.

Holzem, Jim. "Jim Holzem's Story." *Voice*, no. 48 (June 15, 1982): 10.

———. "Newspaper Reporter Jumped at Los Baños." *Voice*, no. 66 (March 15, 1986): 40.

Hoyt, Richard L. "The Dash to Manila." *Voice* 109 (January 1996): 24.

———. "Editor's Note." *Voice*, no. 87 (April 15, 1990): 7.

———. "How I Became a Paratrooper." *Voice*, no. 23 (December 1, 1976): 2.

———. "Leyte Operations (6 December 1944)." *Voice*, no. 73 (July 15, 1987): 11.

———. "Los Baños, the Aftermath." *Voice*, no 147 (June 2005): 16.

———. "Recollections of General Joe Swing." *Voice*, no. 60 (January 15, 1985): 31.

Humphreys, Jim. "Mail Call, a letter to Joseph Vannier." *WA*, no. 37 (Fall 1996): 46.

Hudson, Elmer. "The Last Mountain – or – Die Another Day." *WA*, no. 87 (Winter 2009): 25.

Ingles, Gustavo C. "The Los Baños Reprisals." *Voice* 117 (January 1998): 32.

Ito, George. "Linguist Paratroopers." *Voice* 111 (July 15, 1996): 27.

Jenkins, Edward L. "Combined Air-Ground Operations on Luzon." *Military Review* 25, no. 11 (February 1946): 30.

Johansen, Herbert O. "'Banzai' at Burauen." *Air Force Magazine* 28, no. 3 (March 1945): 4.

Jolley, Houston. "Personal Recollections 1943–1946, Part I." *Voice*, no. 90 (January 15, 1991): 8.

———. "Personal Recollections 1943–1946, Part II." *Voice*, no. 91 (April 15, 1991): 6.

Jones, Charlie. "Company D Stories." *WA*, no. 97 (Fall 2011): 17.

Jones, Harold. "The Saga of E Company." *WA*, no. 6 (July 1988): 4.

Jose, Ricardo T., PhD. "Japanese Accounts of the Battle of Manila." PX Publications (2014).

Kalamas, Michael. "Letter to the Editor." *Voice*, no. 101 (July 15, 1993): 5.

Karberg, Paul F. "511th Infantry." *Voice*, no. 23 (December 1, 1976): 8.

Karst, O.R. "Through the Eyes of the Pilot." *Voice* 117 (January 1998): 34.

Keith, Richard E. "The 96-Hour Day, Tagaytay Ridge to Nichols Field." *Voice* 167 (June 2010): 22.

———. "The Fog of War." *Voice* 183 (June 2014): 22.

———. "Letter to the Editor." *Voice* 187 (June 2015): 16.

———. "The Saga of Purple Heart Hill." *WA*, no. 67 (Spring 2004): 16.

Kenny, Pat. "Co. E, 187th P/G Infantry Disaster." *Voice*, no. 75 (January 15, 1988): 21.

Kinghorn, Anderson M. "Addendum to 127th History from Company B Commander." *Voice* 111 (July 15, 1996): 32.

Kitchens, William C. "Div HQ & Spec Troops." *Voice*, no. 33 (February 15, 1979): 6.

Kocher, Leo. "Another 'Point of View' of the Los Baños Raid. A Collection of Articles from Various Newspapers." *WA*, no. 75 (Spring 2006): 12.

Krivdo, Michael E. "Major Jay D. Vanderpool, Advisor to the Philippine Guerrillas." *Veritas* 9, no. 1: 22.

Lahti, Edward. "Combat Jump." *WA*, no. 9 (April 1989): 11.

———. "A Hero is Dead–Dr. Lee E. Walker." *WA*, no. 39 (Spring 1997).

———. "Letter to George Doherty, dated January 28, 1992." *Voice*, no. 96 (April 15, 1992): 22.

———. "The Southern Luzon Campaign." *WA*, no. 12 (January 1990): 23.

Laws, Richard. "Colonel Lahti's Mortars." *WA*, no. 43 (Spring 1998).

———. "The Day the Riflemen Clapped Their Hands." *WA*, no. 44 (Summer 1998).

———. "First Man in Japan." *WA*, no. 52 (Summer 2000): 4.

———. "Pilot Trouble." *WA*, no. 65 (Fall 2003): 8.

Leroy, Bob P. "My Christmas in Combat." *Voice* 113 (January 15, 1997): 32.

Light, William H. "Notes about Orin Haugen's Early Life." *Voice*, no. 100 (April 15, 1993): 9.

Long, Lester. "Los Baños Anniversary." *WA*, no. 56 (Summer 2001): 12.

Lorio, James W. "The Fighting Angels." *WA*, no. 6 (July 1988): 9.

———. "Orin Doughty Haugen." *WA*, no. 4 (January 1988): 10.

Loughrin, Richard N. "Mortally Wounded in Action." *WA* no. 10 and no. 11 (July/October 1989): 11.

MacMillan, Bob. "Yamashita Gives Up." *Yank Magazine* 4, no. 17 (October 12, 1945): 3.

Manzanilla, Edmundo. "Los Baños–Another Point of View." *WA*, no. 34 (Winter 1996): 47. [Reprinted from the May 16, 1995, issue of the *Philippine Star* newspaper.]

Marks, Deane. "The Day the Tank Blew Up, Part I." *WA*, no. 9 (April 1989): 12.

———. "The Day the Tank Blew Up, Part II." *WA*, no. 10 and no. 11 (July/October 1989): 8.

———. "The Day the Tank Blew Up, Part III." *WA*, no. 12 (January 1990): 12.

———. "No One Smiled on Leyte." *WA*, no. 7 (October 1988): 25.

———. "A Terrible Day on Leyte." *WA* 21 (Fall 1992): 32.

Marshall, Bert W. "The Jump on Los Baños." *Voice* no. 68 (August 15, 1986): 35.

———. "The Marshall Brothers, Part I." *WA*, no. 25 (Fall 1993): 6.

———. "The Marshall Brothers, Part II." *WA*, no. 26 (Winter 1994): 6.

———. "The Marshall Brothers, Part III." *WA*, no. 27 (Spring 1994): 7.

Massey, Jim. "The Paratrooper Machine Gunner in Jungle Warfare." *WA*, no. 7 (October 1988): 16.

McGovern, Barney. "1318th Para Surgical Team." *Voice*, no. 105 (October 15, 1994): 8.

———. "Glorious Medical Paratroopers." *Voice* 110 (April 15, 1996): 28.

McGowan, Glenn J. "Clarification." *Voice*, no. 91 (April 15, 1991): 15.

———. "Yanks Down Under." *Voice* 113 (January 15, 1997): 38.

McGrath, Jack. "The Day Geronimo Cried." *WA*, no. 87 (Winter 2009): 18.

———. "Decision At Fort McKinley." *WA*, no. 53 (Fall 2000): 19.

———. "The Hell We Call War." *WA*, no. 41 (Fall 1997).

———. "Second Opinion." *WA*, no. 42 (Summer 1997).

———. "A Tale of Two Flags." *WA*, no. 34 (Winter 1996): 36.

———. "Unrequited Love." *WA*, no. 52 (Summer 2000): 3.

McSweeny, D. J. "C-127th Engineers." *Voice*, no. 48 (June 15, 1982): 16.

Merritt, Herbert. "More about Leyte." *WA*, no. 48 (Summer 1999).

Miley, Buzz. "The Hand Grenade." *WA*, no. 4 (January 1988): 8.

———. "Moonlight Requisition." *WA*, no. 3 (October 1987).

Miller, Earl L. "Carlos Palvarosa." *Voice*, 130 (March 2001): 42.

———. "The Continuing Saga of the Los Baños Raid." *WA*, no. 44 (Summer 1998).

———. "Letter to the editor, dated September 10, 1979." *Voice*, no. 39 (April 15, 1980): 7.

———. "A Vignette of the Los Baños Jump." *Airborne Quarterly* (Spring 2001): 64.

Misculin, George. "Remembers His Tomorrow." *Voice* 126 (March 2000): 42.

Mueller, Richard. "A Trooper Writes Home." *WA*, no. 26 (Winter 1994): 25.

Muller, Henry J. "The Day the War Ended." *WA*, no. 73 (Fall 2005): 4.

———. "The Japanese Airborne Attack on Elements of the 11th Airborne." *Voice* 185 (December 2014): 28.

———. "Planning for Los Baños." *Voice* 121 (December 1998): 32.

———. "The Reluctant Boatman." *WA*, no. 65 (Fall 2003): 16.

Neuteboom, Grant H. "A Few Memories of Leyte and Friends." *Voice*, no. 102 (January 15, 1994): 15.

Ostrom, Dick. "A Lasting Friendship." *WA*, no. 48 (Summer 1999).

Piasecki, Eugene G. "The Knollwood Maneuver, the Ultimate Airborne Test." *Airborne Quarterly* (Winter 2012): 33.

Porteous, Bill. "That Crappy Crapper." *WA*, no. 27 (Spring 1994): 35.

Quandt, Douglas P. "Fifth Wheel." *Voice*, no. 54 (September 15, 1983): 5.

———. "Salute to General Swing." *Voice*, no. 49 (August 15, 1982): 9.

Quesada, Francisco B. "Guerrillas & 11th A/B Division, Nasugbu to Manila." *Voice*, no. 44 (March 15, 1981): 8.

Repplier, Banning. "This Barringer Grad Is 'Making Good.'" Unknown Newark, New Jersey newspaper, circa early 1945.

Renfroe, Colbert G. "The 511th Regiment's First Battle on Leyte." *WA*, no. 5 (April 1988): 8.

———. "Was C Company Ambushed?" *WA* 23 (Spring 1993): 18.

Ridgway, Matthew B. "Letter to Daniel S. Campbell, dated February 13, 1985." *Voice*, no. 61 (June 15, 1985): 37.

Ringler, John M. "The Los Baños Raid." *WA*, no. 49 (Fall 1999): 103.

Roberts, Donald J. "Angels to the Rescue." *WA*, no. 58 (Winter 2002): 26.

Sass, Charles J. "Anonymous Pictures." *WA*, no. 52 (Summer 2000): 17.

———. "Attack on Mount Malipunyo." *WA*, no. 100 (Summer 2012): 9.

———. "Colonel John Ringler, The Compassionate Captain." *WA*, no. 65 (Fall 2003): 3.

———. "Fifteen Minutes of Fame." *WA*, no. 61 (Fall 2002): 23.

———. "First Sergeant X." *WA*, no. 40 (Summer 1997).

———. "Just Part of the Family." *WA*, no. 45 (Fall 1998).

———. "K.I.S.S." *WA*, no. 44 (Summer 1998).

———. "Mail Call, Letter to George Doherty." *WA*, no. 73 (Fall 2005): 38.

———. "On a Couple of Hot Summer's Nights." *WA*, no. 41 (Fall 1997).

———. "Perimeter Thoughts at Night." *WA*, no. 39 (Spring 1997).

———. "Somebody Worth Remembering." *WA*, no. 59 (Spring 2002): 15.

Santos, Terry R. "Recon Platoon at Los Baños." *WA*, no. 49 (Fall 1999): 101.

Schlobohm, George J. "Letter to the Editor." *Voice*, no. 66 (March 15, 1986): 40.

Sibio, Richard and Max Polick. "Posthumous Award of Distinguished Service Cross to Pat Berardi." *WA*, no. 20 (Summer 1992): 23.

Smith, Frank. "How Sky Army Took Ridge on Manila Bay." *Voice*, no. 41 (September 15, 1980): 4. [Reprinted from an undated 1945 issue of the *Chicago Times* newspaper.]

Smith, Jacques. "Untitled Article." *WA*, no. 35 (Spring 1996): 48. [Reprinted from the September 2, 1995, issue of the *Times-Picayune* newspaper.]

———. "The Leyte Tapioca Pudding Tree." *WA*, no. 53 (Fall 2000): 26.

Solow, Abe. "Letter to Editor." *Voice*, no. 80 (November 15, 1988): 44.

Sorensen, Edward L. "Company D Stories." *WA*, no. 95 (Spring 2011): 7.

Spring, Harold J. "An Account of One Soldier's Will to Live." *WA*, no. 16 (June/July 1991): 13.

———. "Wounded in Action." *WA*, no. 4 (January 1988): 14.

Squires, Margaret. "Los Baños Diary." *WA*, no. 82 (Winter 2008): 12.

Squires, Martin. "Aw Mom!" *WA*, no. 10/11 (July/October 1989): 36.

Stout, Roy E. "Supply—Nasugbu to Tagaytay." *Voice* 129 (December 2000): 44.

Swan, Harry A. "Gotta Be One Helluva Shot." *WA*, no. 39 (Spring 1997)

———. "A Mortarfying Experience in Tactics." *Voice*, no. 90 (January 15, 1991): 25.

———. "The Occupation of the Japanese Mainland." *WA*, no. 32 (Summer 1995): 43.

Swindler, Henry R. "C/127th Engineers in the Los Baños Mission." *Voice* 176 (September 2012): 16.

Tassone, Sam. "Unit History." *WA*, no. 18 (Winter 1991): 20.

Tench, C. T. "Advance Party: Mission Surrender." *Infantry Journal* (August 1946): 30.

Teulle, Chuck. "News Briefs." *Voice*, no. 15 (January 15, 1975).

Thollander, Charles. "Letters Home." *WA*, no. 39 (Spring 1997).

Thomas, Frederick. "Colonel Orin D. Haugen 'The Rock' as I Knew Him." *WA*, no. 10 and no. 11 (July/October 1989): 1.

———. "Letter from Frederick Thomas, Sergeant Major, to Judge Loughrin September 13, 1984." *WA*, no. 57 (Fall 2001): 22.

———. "Regimental Combat Jump." *WA*, no. 9 (April 1989): 4.

Underwood, Matt. "Partners in Victory: 672nd Amphibian Tractor Bn. Finally Receives Due Honors for Los Baños Rescue, Part III." *Voice* 176 (September 2012): 23.

Unknown Author. "The 187th in the Leyte Campaign." *Voice* 122 (March 1999): 33.

Unknown Author. "Air Troops Razz Cavalry Men." *Voice*, no. 41 (September 15, 1980): 4. [Reprinted newspaper article datelined, Yokohama, September 2, 1945.]

Unknown Author. "Col. Orin Haugen, Capt. T. J. James Reported Dead." *Asheville Citizen-Times* (Asheville, North Carolina; March 6, 1945): 1.

Unknown Author. "Communicating in the Pacific Proves Challenging." *Voice* 199 (June 2018): 20.

Unknown Author. "Los Baños." *Voice* 125 (December 1999): 46.

Unknown Author. "Lt. Maylock." *Voice*, no. 108 (July 15, 1995): 14.

Unknown Author. "Reunion '95." *WA*, no. 33 (Fall 1995): 40.

Unknown Author. "Seven Dwarfs." *Voice*, no. 25 (June 1, 1977): 10.

Unknown Author. "Silver Star Posthumously to PFC. Bill Bowen." *Voice*, no. 92 (June 15, 1991): 14.

Unknown Author. "Sniper Fire from Church Near Parañaque." *Voice* 122 (March 1999): 27.

Unknown Author. "Somebody Had to Do It, WWII Airborne Surgeon Recalls Action at Front." *Voice*, no. 70 (January 15, 1987): 19.

Urish, Earl. "11th Airborne Honor Guard Protected MacArthur." *Voice* 124 (September 1999): 39.

———. "Easter Weekend in Southern Luzon." *Voice* 118 (March 1998): 36.

Van Divner, Harry H. "Los Baños, A Report from the Beach." *WA*, no. 37 (Fall 1996): 31.

Vannier, Joseph R. "From Out of the Past on Christmas Eve." *WA*, no. 44 (Summer 1998).

———. "Giving Thanks on Bito Beach." *WA* no. 38 (Winter 1997).

———. "The I Company Beacon, May 25, 1997." *Voice* 115 (July 1997): 32.

———. "Pearl Harbor Day on Maloney Ridge." *WA*, no. 36 (Summer 1996): 7.

Varrone, Lou. "Congressional Medal of Honor." *WA*, no. 3 (October 1987).

———. "The Congressional Medal of Honor." *Voice* 123 (June 1999): 44.

Wagers, Harry. "Trooper Has Wet Dream." *WA*, no. 26 (Winter 1994): 26.

Walker, Lee E. "A Handful of Memories from New Guinea." *WA*, no. 31 (Spring 1995): 2.

———. "What's for Dinner Sarge?" *WA*, no. 27 (Spring 1994): 2.

Walker, 'Ripcord.' "LTG Joseph M. Swing and the 11th Airborne Division." *Voice*, no. 61 (March 15, 1985): 24.

Walter, William R. "Company D Stories." *WA*, no. 77 (Fall 2006): 14.

Watty, Lewis T. "Personal Journal." *Voice* 159 (June 2008): 15.

———. "A POW's Memory of the Raid." *Voice* 125 (December 1999): 50.

Webb, David. "The Poncho." *WA*, no. 4 (January 1988): 15.

Young, Stan. "Luzon Liberation: My Memories." *WA*, no. 52 (Summer 2000): 8.

———. "One and One-Half Months on Leyte." *WA*, no. 49 (Fall 1999): 42.

———. "The War Is Over." *WA*, no. 75 (Spring 2006): 10.

Wilcox, Wilber. "The Assault on Manila." *WA*, no. 78 (Winter 2007): 19.

Orders, Reports, and Monographs

XIV Corps. *After Action Report M1 Operation.* (July 29, 1945). AHEC.

11ABN. *Historical Summary: 25 February 1943 to 10 February 1945.* n.d. NARA.

———. *11th Airborne Division History: February 1943 to May 1945.* NARA.

———. *Airborne Operations: Letter to the Commandant, the Cavalry School, Ft. Riley, Kansas.* (September 18, 1946). NARA.

———. *Division Artillery Unit Journal.* NARA.

———. *FO* (1944). NARA.

———. *FO* (1945). NARA.

———. *G1 (Personnel) Journal.* NARA.

———. *G2 (Intelligence) Journal*. NARA.

———. *G2 (Intelligence) Periodic Reports*. NARA.

———. *G2 (Intelligence) Summary of Enemy Airborne Activities*. NARA.

———. *G3 (Operations) Journal*. NARA.

———. *G3 (Operations) Periodic Reports*. NARA.

———. *G4 (Supply) Journal*. NARA.

———. *GO* (1943). NARA.

———. *GO* (1944). NARA.

———. *GO* (1945). NARA.

———. "History." (May 13, 1945). NARA.

———. *History of Operation, Luzon*. (August 3, 1945). NARA.

———. *Historical Narrative, 30 June 1945 to 30 Sept. 1945*. n.d. NARA.

———. *History of 11th Airborne Division Band for Year of 1945*. (February 14, 1946). NARA.

———. *Location of 11th Airborne Division Command Posts from April 1944 to Present*. NARA.

———. *Memorandums* (1943). NARA.

———. *Memorandums* (1943). NARA.

———. *Memorandums* (1945). NARA.

———. *Medical History, Second Quarter of 1944*. (July 1, 1944). NARA.

———. *Medical History for Period January–March 1945*. (April 8, 1945). NARA.

———. *Operation KING II, Leyte Campaign*. (May 28, 1945). NARA.

———. *Operations Report, Operation MIKE VI*. n.d. NARA.

———. Press Relations Office. "List of General and Staff Officers and Unit Commanders, 11th Airborne Div." (April 9, 1945). NARA.

———. *Report After Action with the Enemy, Operation MIKE VI, Luzon Campaign*. (January 24, 1946). AHEC.

———. *Report on the Los Baños Operation*. (March 17, 1945). NARA.

———. *Standing Operating Procedure Troop Carrier-Airborne Operations*. (September 25, 1944). NARA.

———. *Training Memorandums*. (1945). NARA.

———. *Unit History, 20–30 June 1945*. n.d. NARA.

———. *Warning Order No. 2*. (January 22, 1945). NARA.

127ENG. *K-2 Operation (October 20, 1944 to December 25, 1944)*. (January 12, 1945). NARA.

———. *Organization History*. n.d. NARA.

152AAB. *Historical Report of 152 AB AA Bn, in Leyte Campaign*. (January 10, 1945) NARA.

———. *Historical Report of 152 AB AA Bn, in Luzon, P.I. Campaign.* (July 12, 1945). NARA.

187GIR. *Chronological Narrative Mike 6 Operation, 25 January 1945 to 24 February 1945.* [Reprinted in *Voice*, no. 48 (June 15, 1982): 3.]

———. *The Leyte Campaign (Oct. 20, 1944 to Dec. 25, 1944).* (October 2, 1946). NARA.

———. GO (1945) NARA.

188GIR. GO (1943) NARA.

———. *Historical Report of the 188th Paraglider Infantry in K-2 Operation, Leyte, P.I.* (January 17, 1945) NARA.

———. *Historical Report of the 188th Paraglider Infantry in [MIKE VI] Operation, Luzon, Philippine Islands.* (no date) NARA.

———. *Part I: 1 January 45 to 30 Jan 45.* (no date) NARA.

———. *Part II: Luzon, Philippine Islands Campaign, 31 Jan. 1945 to 30 Jun. 1945.* (no date) NARA.

———. *Part III: Luzon, Philippine Islands Campaign, 1 Jul. 1945 to 31 Dec. 1945.* (no date) NARA.

———. *Maps and Sketches Illustrating the Operations of the 11th Airborne Division.* (September 1947) NARA.

408AQM. *Historical Operational Report K-2 Operation (Leyte).* (January 1, 1945) NARA.

511SIG. *Historical Record and History 511th Airborne Signal Company.* NARA.

———. *Operational Historical Report on KING TWO Operation.* (no date) NARA.

511PIR. GO (1944) NARA.

———. *FO # 10, Operation MIKE 6.* (January 27, 1945) NARA.

———. *FO # 19.* (February 25, 1945) NARA.

———. *FO# 34.* (August 26, 1945) NARA.

———. *Occupation of Japan, Unit History 30 June–30 September.* NARA.

———. *Regimental History.* (no date) NARA.

———. *Regimental History: Leyte Campaign.* (no date) NARA.

———. *Regimental Journal.* NARA.

———. *S1 (Personnel) Journal.* NARA.

———. *S2 (Intelligence) Journal.* NARA.

———. *S3 (Operations) Journal.* NARA.

———. *S4 (Supply) Journal Summary, 3 Feb. to 1 Jul.* NARA.

———. *Unit History (Period: 26 January 45 to 31 March 45 Incl.).* (March 26, 1946) NARA.

———. *Luzon Report.* (no date, missing first several pages). NARA.

711ORD. *Historical Report.* (January 15, 1945) NARA.

Cook, John M. *The Operations of Company D, 511th Parachute Infantry 11th Airborne Division, Near Lipa, Luzon Philippine Islands, 13 March 1945. (Personal Experience of a Battalion Executive Officer).* DRL.

Barnum, Richard V. *The Operations of the 3rd Battalion, 511th Parachute Infantry (11th Airborne Division) in the Advance Through the Mahonag-Anas Pass to the West Coast of Leyte, 27 November–25 December 1944. (Personal Experience of a Mortar Platoon Leader).* DRL.

Coulter, John A. *The Operations of the Headquarters Company, Third Battalion, 511th Parachute Infantry, (11th ABN VID) in the Attack on Manila, 3-13 FEB, 1945. (Personal Experience of a Company Commander).* DRL.

Eighth Army. *Report of the Commanding General Eighth Army on the Nasugbu and Bataan Operations, MIKE VI and MIKE VIII.*

Faulkner, Lyman S. *The Operations of the 511th Parachute Infantry Regiment (11th Airborne Division) in the Mount Malepunyo Mountain Mass, East of Lipa, Luzon, Philippine Islands, 12 April–2 May 1945. (Personal Experience of a Regimental Intelligence Officer).* DRL.

Giordano, Joseph B. *The Operations of Company G 187th Glider Infantry Regiment (11th Airborne Division) in the Breakthrough to the Ormoc Corridor, 22–23 December 1944 (The Leyte Campaign, Personal Experience of a Platoon Leader).* DRL.

Grigg, Martin C. *The Operations of the 1st Battalion, 149th Infantry (38th Infantry Division) in the Battle for the Buri Airstrip, Leyte, P.I. 7–11 December 1944 (Personal Experience of a Company Commander).* DRL.

Holcombe, Frank S. *The Operations of the 2nd Battalion, 511th Parachute Infantry (11th Airborne Division) in the Jump on Tagaytay Ridge and the Advance to Manila 3–4 February 1945 (Luzon Campaign).* DRL.

Hoppenstein, Isaac. *The Operations of the 187th Glider Infantry Regiment (11th Airborne Division) in the Landing at Nasugbu, Luzon, Philippine Islands 31 January–3 February 1945. (Personal Experiences of a Regimental Supply Officer).* DRL.

Jeffress, Edwin B. *Operations of the 2nd Battalion, 511th Parachute Infantry (11th Airborne Division) in the Battle for Southern Manila, 3–10 February. (Personal Experience of a Battalion Intelligence Officer).* DRL.

Kennington, Robert E. *The Operations of the Los Baños Force (1st Battalion, 511th Parachute Infantry and 1st Battalion, 188th Glider Infantry) 11th Airborne Division, in the Liberation of the Internees from the Los Baños Internment Camp, Luzon, Philippine Islands, 23 February 1945. (Personal Experience of a Battalion Operations Officer).* DRL.

Leister, Albert P. *Operations of the 11th Airborne Division from Nasugbu to Manila, 31 January–4 February 1945.* DRL.

Merritt, John. *The Operations of Company 'G' 187th Glider Infantry Regiment (11th Airborne Division) in the Attack on Nichols Field, Luzon, Philippine Islands, 13–15 February 1945. (Personal Experience of a Company Commander).* DRL.

Military Commission, *People of the Philippines vs. Shizuo Yokoyama,* Vol. XX. (January 18, 1949)

Parachute Maintenance Company. *Historical Record of Leyte Campaign, from 18NOV44 to 25DEC44.* (no date) NARA.

Sixth Army. *Memorandum to Colonel Leaf [Office of the G4].* (February 16, 1945) NARA.

———. *Memorandum to: Engineer. [Office of the Chief of Staff]* (June 24, 1945) NARA.

———. "G2 Weekly Report No. 75." (February 14, 1945) AHEC.

———. [Aparri Report] *Memorandum to: AC of S, G-3 (June 29, 1945).* NARA.

Stahl, David C. *Ōoka Shōhei's Writings on the Pacific War: The Failure of the Campaign for Leyte Island.* Yale University Dissertation (UMI No: 9523234): 1994.

Tomochika, Yoshiharu, Major General. "The True Facts of the Leyte Operation." November 5, 1946. AHEC.

Transport Squadron Fourteen, US Pacific Fleet. *War Diary: November 1994.*

US Pacific Fleet. *Report of Surrender and Occupation of Japan.* (February 11, 1946)

US Pacific Warfare Board. *Report No. 11, Parachute Field Artillery.* (June 19, 1945) DRL.

Vanderpool, Jay D. "Letter of Instruction, Los Baños Patrol." (February 10, 1945) AHEC.

Walsh, Louis A., Jr. *Report on Airborne Operations in the Pacific.* (March 30, 1945) AHEC.

Papers, Letters, Collections, Personal Narratives, and Diaries

Augustin, James H. "Once an Angel." n.d. AHEC.

Bandoni, John R. *Army Stories.* Author's collection.

Baugh, Ted. "Undated Letter to Jerard Vlaminck." Printed in *Voice* no. 47 (January 15, 1982): 10.

Burgess, Henry A. *Letter to Edward M. Flanagan, September 25, 1984.* AHEC.

———. "Reminiscences of the 11th Airborne Division Raid on Los Baños." (April 10, 1981). AHEC.

Cole, Edward J. "Military History of Edward J. Cole." AHEC.

Coleman, Arthur J. *Letter to Edward M. Flanagan, August 14, 1984.* AHEC.
———. *Letter to Edward M. Flanagan, August 31, 1984.* AHEC.
Davis, Jerry T. "80 Years of Dogs: The Memoirs of Jerry T. Davis from 1924 through 2006."
Doherty, George. "Tomorrow I Will Be a Paratrooper." AHEC.
Eichelberger, Robert L. *Diary.* AHEC.
Grimmer, Robert H. "WWII Memoirs." AHEC.
Ingles, Gustavo C. *Letter to Edward M. Flanagan, October 25, 1984.* AHEC.
Ito, George. *Letters to the author,* December 2003.
Kirkland, Randolph W. Jr. *Long Ago and Far Away.* V8.1, October 3, 2013.
Massey, James. "Diary."
O'Hara, James G. "Letter to Bob Fletcher, August 16, 1982." Reprinted in *Voice,* no. 50 (November 15, 1982): 22.
Swing, Joseph M. "Dear General, WWII Letters, 1944–1945. Letters from General Joseph M. Swing to General Peyton C. March." 11th Airborne Division Association, 1987.
———. "Diary." Extracts printed in *Voice,* no. 20 (March 1, 1976): 6.
Vanderpool, Jay D. *Letter to Edward M. Flanagan, May 29, 1984.* AHEC.
———. *Letter to Edward M. Flanagan, August 20, 1984.* AHEC.
———. *Letter to Edward M. Flanagan, September 17, 1984.* AHEC.
Vignola, James B. "In the 11th Airborne Division." AHEC.
Walsh, Louis A., Jr. "Los Baños–A Raid in Force." (March 30, 1945) AHEC.
Wentink, James J. *Letter to Edward M. Flanagan, June 2, 1988.* AHEC.

Interviews, Questionnaires, and Oral History Transcripts
Augustin, James H. *WWII Veteran Survey.* AHEC.
Bernheim, Eli D. *WWII Veteran Survey.* AHEC.
Billingsley, James H. *Oral History.* NOLA.
Davis, Jerry T. *WWII Veteran Survey.* AHEC.
Jones, Harold. *Oral History.* NOLA.
Langford, Don. Interview by Craig Davis on February 3, 2001.
Laws, Richard A. *WWII Veteran Survey.* AHEC.
Marich, Robert. *Oral History.* NOLA.
Muller, Henry. Author interview on August 20, 2020.
Muller, Henry. Interview by Craig Davis on February 10, 2001.
Penwell, Richard F. *Oral History.* NOLA.
Santos, Terry. Interview by Craig Davis on January 27, 2001.
Schweitzer, Philip. *WWII Veteran Survey.* AHEC.
Smith, Jacques B. *Oral History.* NOLA.

Strobel, Clarence. *Oral History*. NOLA.

Swing, Joseph M. *Oral Reminiscences*. Interviewed by D. Clayton James on August 26, 1971. AHEC.

Tyre, Bailey O. *WWII Veteran Survey*. AHEC.

Whitehead, Herbert S. *WWII Veteran Survey*. AHEC.

Weber, William E. Interview with author. July 27, 2019. [Weber was an officer in the 187th GIR.]

Weber, William E. *WWII Veteran Survey*. AHEC.

Miscellany

Eichelberger, Robert L. *MacArthur and the Eighth Army*. Dictations by Eichelberger found in the Jay Luvaas Collection. AHEC.

Enemy Publications no. 415. *Combat Regulations for Island Garrison Forces (Shubi) (Provisional) and Study of Island Defense*. Originally issued December 25, 1943, translated version dated October 12, 1945.

GHQ, SWPA Military Intelligence Section G-2, "Ultra Intelligence Bulletins." AHEC.

Jacobs, Edward W. (Secretary to General Swing). "History Notes." NARA.

"Journey into the Past: 11th Airborne Division Battlegrounds." Set of four VHS tapes filmed, edited, and narrated by George Doherty.

Loughrin Journal. In mid-December of 1944, PFC Richard Loughrin was assigned as Col. Haugen's scribe "to write down all of the Colonel's oral orders and radio messages he told me to record. Col. Haugen had complained that officers were not obeying his oral orders as he had given them and were saying he never gave them in that exact manner. From that time on, I was always six or seven feet from him throughout every day." The Loughrin notes often mirror events documented in the regiment's official journals (*S1, S2*, etc.): but usually with more detail and additional observations. Loughrin noted not only the date but the time, down to the minute, of each entry. His notes were invaluable to reconstructing the dreary days on Leyte as well as Luzon, and I'm grateful to Loughrin's son, Brian, and Craig Davis for helping me track them down.

War Department, Press Branch. "Medal of Honor to Infantryman Who Gave Life to Save Platoon Leader." April 27, 1945.

Photo Credits

Page 21: Courtesy of Anne Serling; page 28: Author's collection; page 44: Courtesy of the Robson family; page 57: Courtesy of the Kirkland family; page 124: Author's collection; page 150: Courtesy of the Hall family; page 168: Bancroft Library, University of California at Berkeley; page 292: Courtesy of

Susan L. Blevins; page 378: Carl Mydans/The *LIFE* Picture Collection/Shutterstock. All other photos from US Army archives.

Notes

Prologue

1. *The single-file column of American* ... The opening moments of Charlie Company's first combat engagement are based on several sources: Colbert Renfroe, "The 511th Regiment's First Battle on Leyte," *WA*, April 5, 1988, 5; ———, "Was C Company Ambushed?" *WA*, Spring 1993, 18; George Floersch, "Another Remembrance of C Company's First Battle," *WA*, Fall 1993, 29. **2.** *A trooper staggered back up* ... This was Private Arthur Deszez. **3.** *A trooper next to Floersch* ... This was Private Randall Dobbs.

Chapter 1: You're in the Army Now

1. *201 Edward Street* ... Date and time of meeting confirmed via MacArthur's personal diary, courtesy of Jim Zobel at the MacArthur Memorial; meeting description based on notes from Swing, Joseph M. *Oral Reminiscences*, interview by D. Clayton James, Army Heritage and Education Center, August 26, 1971. Glenn McGowan, "Yanks Down Under," *Voice*, January 15, 1997, 38. **2.** *Swing's rigid posture carried* ... George Doherty, "Lt. General Joseph M. Swing and the 11th Airborne Division," *Voice*, September 15, 1989, 44. **3.** *"He personified a general officer* ... " William Weber, interviewed by author, July 27, 2019. **4.** *He had little tolerance for verbosity* ... 'Ripcord' Walker, "LTG Joseph M. Swing and the 11th Airborne Division, *Voice*, March 15, 1985, 24. **5.** *"If he said, 'Frog,'* ... Clay Blair, *Ridgway's Paratroopers: The American Airborne in World War II* (Garden City, New York: Dial Press, 1985), 18. **6.**

"You could almost see flames... ibid. **7**. *"tactful and charming ...* Douglas Quandt, "Salute to General Swing," *Voice*, August 15, 1982, 9. **8**. *Born in Jersey City, New Jersey ...* Swing, Joseph, *Oral Reminiscences*, 1. **9**. *"rough-housing ...* Blair, Clay, *Ridgway's Paratroopers*, 17. Classmates of Bradley and Eisenhower via *Howitzer*, West Point 1915 Yearbook. **10**. *Swing spent the next two decades ...* Highlights of Swing's early career taken from *Army Register of Officers: 1916, 1918, 1919, 1920, 1921, 1924, 1933*; and from Swing, Joseph, *Oral Reminiscences*, 16. **11**. *Swing had earned the one star ...* Edward Flanagan, "Joseph May Swing," *Voice*, August 15, 1986, 29. **12**. *In February 1943 ...* ibid. **13**. *Swing's 11th Airborne Division was built ...* The division's initial officer cadre came from the 76th Inf Div and Airborne Command, while the enlisted cadre came from the 88th Inf Div and Airborne Command, per 11ABN, *Historical Summary*, 1. **14**. *The 11th was the first ...* 11ABN, *11th Airborne Division History*, 1. **15**. *The initial thirteen weeks ...* The thirteen weeks of basic were March 15 to June 21, 1943; the twelve weeks of unit training were June 27 to September 12, 1943; glider orientation flights took place in July and August; 11ABN, *History*, 3. **16**. *On Thursday, February 25 ...* 11ABN, *GO*, 1943. **17**. *Once the full complement of ...* 11th Airborne Division Association, *11th Airborne*, ed. Robert J, Martin (Paducah, Kentucky: Turner Publishing Company, 1993), 11; Edward M. Flanagan Jr., *The Angels: A History of the 11th Airborne* (Novato, California: Presidio Press, 1989), 58. Additionally, extensive notes on the division's TO&E can be found in Rottman, Gordon, *US Airborne Units in the Pacific Theater 1942–45* (Osprey, 2007), 25. **18**. *"My first impression ...* This was Edward A. Hammrich via, Martin, Robert, *11th Airborne*, 13. **19**. *Simultaneously arriving at Mackall ...* 11ABN, *11th Airborne Division History*, 2. **20**. *Among the listed qualification ...* Jump into the Fight! Parachute Troops – US Army recruiting pamphlet, July 11, 1942. **21**. *"I thought I would ...* Davis, Jerry, *WWII Veteran Survey*, 2. **22**. *"I wanted to see if ...* 11ABN, *11th Airborne Division History*, 3. **23**. *Richard Laws, a teenage bakery ...* Laws, Richard, *WWII Veteran Survey*, 2. **24**. *"not an exceptionally bright ...* William Light, "Notes about Orin Haugen's Early Life," *Voice*, April 15, 1993, 9. **25**. *To overcome his lack ...* 511th PIR Association, *511th Parachute Infantry Regiment*, 7; Frederick Thomas, "Colonel Orin D. Haugen 'The Rock' as I Knew Him," *WA*, July/October 1989, 1. **25a**. *"bull-dog tenacity"* and *"distaste for disciplinary ...* Howitzer, West Point 1930 Yearbook, 132. **25b**. *sea-roaming Viking ...* ibid. **26**. *Promoted to captain, he ...* This was the 501st Parachute Infantry Battalion via Harris Mitchell, *The Story of the First Airborne Battalion* (Rockville, Maryland: Twinbrook Communications, 1992), 87. **27**. *By late 1942 ...* 511th PIR Association, *511th Parachute Infantry Regiment*, 6. He was promoted to colonel a few months later. James Lorio, "Orin Doughty Haugen," *WA*, January 1988, 10. **28**. *"Bulldozers and graders were ...* Miles Gale, "Remembrances of Miles Gale," *WA*, Summer 1992, 19. Gale was drafted in February 1941, went to OCS in October 1942, went to Jump School in November 1942, and was ordered to the 511th in December 1942. **29**. *"I was constantly in mud ...* Polidoro, Mike, *The I Co. Beacon*, Oct. 1996, 3. **30**. *During roll call ...* George Floersch, "And the 'Fox' Showed Up for Snacks," *WA*, Fall 1995, 21. **31**. *George Doherty thought his ...* George Doherty, "Tomorrow I Will Be a Paratrooper," *Voice*, January 15, 1989, 3. **32**. *"demanding,*

extensive, and tough … 11th Airborne Division Association, *11th Airborne*, 10. **33.** *"Everything was double time* … Leroy Butler, "Geronimo #13 or the South Pacific as I Saw It, Part I," *WA*, Fall 2000, 21. **34.** *"They made us run from* … William Walter, "Company D Stories," *WA*, Fall 2006, 14. This was Bill Dubes; Staff Sergeant Al Barreiro was later killed in action on Leyte. **35.** *"the paratroops would be hard to* … quoting General William 'Bud' Miley from James Fenelon, *Four Hours of Fury* (New York: Scribner, 2019), 41. **36.** *"I am lying on my bunk* … Charles Thollander, "Letters Home," *WA*, Spring 1997. **37.** *Red, Pinky, Blacky, Whitey* … Nicknames collected from various *WA*, *I Co. Beacon*, and *Voice* articles. **38.** *"crude, undignified, derogatory* … Vannier, Joseph, *The I Co. Beacon*, November 1996, 10. **39.** *"I never heard so much* … Thollander, Charles, "Letters Home." **40.** *"I have to laugh at* … ibid. **41.** *"I can't say that* … Cole, Edward, *Military History of Edward J. Cole*, 4. **42.** *It wasn't long before* … 511th PIR Association, *511th Parachute Infantry Regiment*, 7. **43.** *The gasping pace* … Ten minutes is cited in Frederick Thomas, "Letter From Frederick Thomas, Sergeant Major, to Judge Loughrin September 13, 1984," *WA*, 22. **44.** *"Ten pounds of red mud stuck to* … Meeker, Lewis, *The I Co. Beacon*, September 1996, 5. **45.** *One of Haugen's platoon leaders* … Charles Muse, Charles, *The I Co. Beacon*, Oct. 1996, 5. **46.** *"You are the best!...* Lorio, James, "Orin Doughty Haugen," 10. **47.** *"Paratrooper's fancy boots* … from Angolia, John, *Heroes in our Midst*, vol. 2, 430. *"AMERICAN PARATROOPERS HAVE* … from Angolia, John, *Heroes in our Midst*, vol. 4, 173. **48.** *For further inspiration, they* … Cole, Edward, *Military History of Edward J. Cole*, 3. **49.** *"Whatever it was that* … ibid. **50.** *"We have swell officers* … Thollander, Charles, "Letters Home." **51.** *It was an intimidating* … Lahti, Edward, *Memoirs of an Angel*, 37. Some troopers remember standing at attention naked, but most say they were wearing boxers. **52.** *In 1931, seeking further* … Lahti biography details collected from *Howitzer*, West Point 1938 Yearbook; 11ABN, *List of General and Staff Officers and Unit Commanders*; Lahti, Edward, *Memoirs of an Angel*. **53.** *"blunt and rough* … Kirkland, Randolph, *Long Ago and Far Away*, 74. **54.** *In late February* … Thollander, Charles, "Letters Home." **55.** *"People used to wonder why* … Carter, Ross, *Those Devils in Baggy Pants*, ii. **56.** *"Fights were a rather commonplace* … James Hendry, "Fighting," *WA*, Winter 1991, 23. **57.** *"I was billeted temporarily in* … quoting Maxwell D. Taylor in Blair, Clay, *Ridgway's Paratroopers*, 18. **58.** *"Goddamn rowdy paratroopers* … Edward Lahti, "Letter to George Doherty, dated January 28, 1992," *Voice*, April 15, 1992, 22. **59.** *"We were in a state of* … Flanagan, Edward, *The Angels* [1989], 42. **60.** *"It made you feel limp* … Elliott Chaze, *The Stainless Steel Kimono* (New York: Simon and Schuster, Inc., 1947), 5, 104. **61.** *The fifty-year-old general* … 11th Airborne Division Association, *11th Airborne*, 13; 11ABN, *11th Airborne Division History*, 2. The average for the officers was higher: twenty-four. **62.** *Swing had designed the division* … 11ABN, *11th Airborne Division History*, 1-A; F. W. Farrell, "Letter to Richard Hoyt, undated," *Voice*, March 15, 1975, 2. **63.** *"The 101st got the head* … Terry Santos interviewed by Craig Davis, January 27, 2001. **64.** *It cannot be truthfully* … Walker, 'Ripcord,' "LTG Joseph M. Swing and the 11th Airborne Division," 24. **65.** *John Bandoni benefited* … Bandoni, John, *Army Stories*, 2. **66.** *"That's about the* … Vannier,

Joseph, *The I Co. Beacon*, n.d., 5. **67.** *"Has anybody here been ...* Joseph Vannier, "Pearl Harbor Day on Maloney Ridge," *WA*, Summer 1996, 7. **68.** *each morning at 05:45 ...* 11ABN, GO #04, 1943; 11th Airborne Division Association, *11th Airborne*, 14. **69.** *"yellow" for practice ...* 188GIR, GO #7, 1943. **70.** *Guards wore a pressed uniform ...* 188GIR, GO #2, 1943. **71.** *They completed basic training in late June ...* 11ABN, History, 3. **72.** *Tactical field exercises were conducted ...* 511SIG, *Historical Record and History 511th Airborne Signal Company*, 3; 11ABN, *Training Memorandum No. 4*, 1943; 11ABN, *Training Memorandum No. 6*, 1943. **73.** *Toward the end of basic training ...* 11ABN, *Historical Summary*, 1. In May and June 1943, the parachute units attended jump school, and at some date thereafter Swing restored the wearing of jump boots, potentially to increase the allure of volunteering for the division's own parachute school. **74.** *The glider units meanwhile ...* 11th Airborne Division Association, *11th Airborne*, 15; 11ABN, History, 3. The July to August glider training was at Laurinburg-Maxton AFB. **75.** *"The Air Force had some formula ...* William Kitchen, *Angels at War* (Self-Published, 2014), 89. **76.** *In late July, General Swing ...* Swing, Joseph, *Diary*, Swing and Quandt in Algiers, June 11 to July 24, 1943; 11ABN, History, 4. **77.** *The lives of 157 ...* Connor, Joseph, "Know the Enemy" *WWII Magazine*, February 2021, 28. **78.** *He extended the division's work week ...* 11ABN, *Training Memorandum No. 6*, 1943; 11ABN, *Training Memorandum No. 7*, 1943; 11ABN, *11th Airborne Division History*, 5. During the fall training period, the men went through expert infantry tests, and approximately 86 percent of the division's infantrymen passed. **79.** *He visited units in the field ...* 11th Airborne Division Association, *11th Airborne*, 14. **80.** *"cruel to be kind ...* Walker, 'Ripcord,' "LTG Joseph M. Swing and the 11th Airborne Division," 24. **81.** *"until only the steel and ...* 11th Airborne Division (Atlanta, Georgia: Albert Love Enterprises, 1944), 2. **82.** *"I want your people free to be ...* 11ABN, *Training Memorandum No. 6*, 1943; Walker, 'Ripcord,' "LTG Joseph M. Swing and the 11th Airborne Division," 24. **83.** *"The General's Walk ...* 11ABN, *11th Airborne Division History*, 4. The first one occurred on Friday, March 19, 1943, at 16:00. See Martin, Robert, *11th Airborne*, 14; 11ABN, *11th Airborne Division History*, 4. **84.** *"If you fell out ...* Richard Hoyt, "Recollections of General Joe Swing," *Voice*, January 15, 1985, 31. **85.** *"Our regiment was not beloved ...* Stephen Cavanaugh, "Vigueur de Dessus, Strength from Above (and I needed it)," *WA*, Winter 2005, 10. Also see interview with Steven Cavanaugh by Rebecca Webb: http://cda.morris.umn.edu/~webbrl/Haugen/ **86.** *At the end of basic training ...* 11ABN, *Training Memorandum No. 3*, 1943. **87.** *"glorified infantrymen ...* Polidoro, Mike, *The I Co. Beacon*, October 1996, 2. **88.** *The distances of the marches ...* 11ABN, *Training Memorandum No. 4*, 1943. Five miles in one hour (5 mph); nine miles in two hours (4.5 mph); twelve miles in three hours (4 mph); eighteen miles in six hours (3 mph); twenty-five miles in eight hours (3.1 mph); Haugen's record was twenty-five miles in six and a half hours (3.8 mph). The US Army's expert infantry standard as of April 22, 2021, is twelve miles in three hours (4 mph) with a thirty-five pound ruck-sack, in addition to personal equipment and water. **89.** *The foot marches were ...* Cole, Edward, *Military History of Edward J. Cole*, 4. **90.** *"Hey, Whitehead, I'm going ...* Richard Laws, "Colonel Lahti's Mortars," *WA*, Spring

1998. **91.** *Unsurprisingly, the marches* ... 511th PIR Association, *511th Parachute Infantry Regiment,* 13; 11th Airborne Division Association, *11th Airborne,* 14. **92.** *"a couple of guys had blood* ... Carpino, Frank, *The I Co. Beacon,* February 1997, 3. **93.** *"Men just outdid themselves* ... Cole, Edward, *Military History of Edward J. Cole,* 4. **94.** *After the long, record-setting march* ... Meeker, Lewis, *The I Co. Beacon,* June 1997, 3. **95.** *"The men griped about the long* ... 11ABN, *11th Airborne Division History,* 4. **96.** *The first occurred in mid-August* ... 11ABN, GO #*14,* 1943; 11ABN, GO #*15,* 1943. The division's first fatalities (Private Allen B. MacDonald and Tech. 4 Ralph E. Johnson) occurred on August 17, 1943. **97.** *The fatalities included the* ... Miles Gale, "The 11th Airborne Reviews for General Henri Giraud," *WA,* Fall 1995, 11. This demonstration was for French General Henri Giraud on September 16, 1943; see 11ABN, GO #*17,* 1943. These men were from 674th GFAB. **98.** *"Now the men are* ... Henry Burgess, *Looking Back: A Wyoming Rancher Remembers the 11th Airborne and the Raid on Los Baños* (Missoula, Montana: Pictorial Histories Publishing Company, Inc., 1993), 28. **99.** *Ten more troopers died* ... 11th Airborne Division Association, *11th Airborne,* 16; 11ABN, GO #*18,* 1943, This took place on October 29, 1943. Sadly, the troopers had wanted to jump for their own safety and to lighten the plane, but the co-pilot refused and ordered them to ride the plane in. **100.** *The death of nineteen-year-old* ... 11ABN, GO #*20,* 1943. DiPangrazio is often cited as regiment's first fatality, but he was actually the third after MacDonald and Johnson. **101.** *"It was an awakening moment* ... 511th PIR Association, *511th Parachute Infantry Regiment,* 10. **102.** *First Lieutenant Robert H. Kliewer* ... 11th Airborne Division Association, *11th Airborne,* 125. **103.** *"Gory, gory* ... 11ABN, GO #*21,* 1943. Private David E. Heltzel and PFC Conner Karrick, 511th Sig. CO, on November 20, 1943, during a night glider-landing. **104.** *"Guadalmackall* ... 11ABN, *11th Airborne Division History,* 8. **105.** *"Dehydrated* ... ibid., 9. **106.** *Swing's next attempt* ... ibid. **107.** *"Any of your angels* ... Flanagan, Edward, *The Angels* [1989], 396. There are many stories claiming the origins of the "Angels" nickname, from New Guinea to Los Baños, but Flanagan confidently states it came into heavy usage at Camp Polk. **108.** *But some high-spirited troopers* ... 11ABN, *11th Airborne Division History,* 7. **109.** *There was also the story* ... William Walter, "Company D Stories," *WA,* Fall 2006, 14. **110.** *The 11th Airborne's initial training* ... 11ABN, *11th Airborne Division History,* 5; Eugene Piasecki, "The Knollwood Maneuver, the Ultimate Airborne Test," *Airborne Quarterly,* Winter 2012, 33. **111.** *Over a series of days starting* ... Edward M. Flanagan, Jr., *The Angels: A History of the 11th Airborne Division 1943-1946* (Washington, DC: Infantry Journal Press, 1948), 16. **112.** *"We were housed in 'real'* ... Harold Jones, "The Saga of E Company," *WA,* July 1988, 4. **113.** *The food was better too* ... Flanagan, Edward, *The Angels* [1948], 16. **114.** *A squad of troopers purchased* ... Carpino, Frank, *I Co. Beacon,* February 1997, 3. **115.** *"He lost very few fights* ... Miles Gale, "Letter to editor, undated," *Voice,* June 15, 1986, 9. Unfortunately, I was unable to confirm Curcio's first name and have used 'John' as a place holder. My apologies. **116.** *'Big' Tom Granillio* ... George Doherty, "Letter to Richard Hoyt, undated," *Voice,* August 15, 1986, 20. Granillio was also known for being the leader of the Black Widow gang. **117.** *Swing's men were run through* ... Flanagan, Edward, *The Angels* [1948], 16. **118.** *In the first* *week of February* ... ibid. **119.** *"The salient feature of the maneuvers* ... ibid., 17. **120.** *"We had everything as far as* ... Flanagan, Edward, *The Angels* [1989], 64; Miller, Earl, "Letter to the Editor," 7. **121.** *"We learned that our bayonets* ... Burgess, Henry, *Looking Back*, 29. **122.** *Swing assigned 'Hard Rock' Haugen* ... this was at DeRidder Army Air Base, Flanagan, Edward, *The Angels* [1989], 65. **123.** *"Swing was in a hurry* ... ibid. **124.** *"We're going to have our* ... Donald Burger, "How I Became a Trooper," *WA*, Summer 1999, 2. **125.** *"We had two days of orientation* ... Richard Hoyt, "Editor's Note," *Voice*, April 15, 1990, 7. **126.** *While he wore US Army* ... Contrary to Flanagan, Edward, *The Angels* [1989], 41, Swing's record of only one jump is based on multiple sources, including Blair, *Ridgway's Paratroopers*, 34; Matthew Ridgway, "Letter to Daniel S. Campbell, dated February 13, 1985," *Voice*, June 15, 1985, 37; and Ridgway, *SOLDIER: The Memoirs of Matthew B. Ridgway* (Harper & Brothers, 1956), 153. Additionally, not a single 11th Airborne veteran recollection includes Swing jumping with the troops—contrary, by way of example, to those who served in the 82nd Airborne Division with Jim Gavin. **127.** *In mid-1942* ... LoFaro, Guy. *The Sword of St. Michael: The 82nd Airborne Division in World War II* (Boston, Massachusetts: Da Capo Press, 2011), 41; Blair, Clay, *Ridgway's Paratroopers*, 34. **128.** *"about a half hour of basic* ... this was Major Warren R. Williams CO of 1/504 PIR via Blair, Clay, *Ridgway's Paratroopers*, 34. **129.** *"I'd rather fall off an airplane* ... ibid., 35. Ridgway then took the group to Ohio for a glider flight at Wright Field. The flight went well, but the landing did not. As the glider approached to land, the wheel-release mechanism jammed, preventing the pilot from dropping the wheels, which were intended for take-off only and had no brakes. As the glider careened down the runway heading for an idling bomber, the pilot yelled, "Jump!" Swing and Ridgway dove out the troop door at almost thirty miles an hour while the glider continued rolling forward. They narrowly avoided the collision. **130.** *Burgess managed the jump school* ... Flanagan, Edward, *The Angels* [1989], 66. **131.** *"Monday, we jogged and tumbled* ... ibid., 67. **132.** *"We presumed that Polk* ... ibid., 69. **133.** *Rumors ceased in mid-April* ... Flanagan, Edward, *The Angels* [1948], 19; Davis, Jerry, *WWII Veteran Survey*, 6. This was on April 15, 1944. **134.** *"We began to load up on* ... Butler, Leroy, "Geronimo #13 or The South Pacific as I Saw It, Part I," 21. **135.** *"Strangely, we did not discuss* ... Murray Hale, "Company D Stories," *WA*, Summer 2010, 9. **136.** *By April 28, 1944* ... 11ABN, *History*, 5. **137.** *They learned where the onboard* ... Flanagan, Edward, *The Angels* [1948], 19. **138.** *The camp served hearty food* ... Flanagan, Edward, *The Angels* [1989], 70. **139.** *They returned to camp* ... Gilbert Gay, "Tokyo Rose," *WA*, October 1987. **140.** *Harry Wagers, from Haugen's 3rd Battalion* ... Harry Wagers, "Trooper Has Wet Dream," *WA*, Winter 1994, 26. **141.** *"The division accumulated a record number* ... Flanagan, Edward, *The Angels* [1989], 71. Crawford was reassigned to the 188th GIR; the other officer was named Buckhalt, and allegedly the armored officers were brought in to testify from their stretchers, this from *Long Ago and Far Away* by Randolph W. Kirkland, Jr., who served with Crawford. **142.** *"They were wearing 'our' jump boots* ... Deane Bostick, "The 11th," *Voice*, July 15, 1992, 24. **143.** *When Haugen learned that a Marine* ... The timing of this march varies, but the most commonly recorded is a USMC record of 4 hours and the 511th at 3 hours, per

Thomas, Frederick, "Colonel Orin D. Haugen 'The Rock' As I Knew Him," 1; Bert Marshall, "The Marshall Brothers, Part I," *WA,* Fall 1993, 6; and Gilbert Gay, "Camp Stoneman," *WA,* Fall 1999, 21. **144.** *With their time at Stoneman complete* ... Flanagan, Edward, *The Angels* [1948], 19. **145.** *The first would debark on May 5, 1944* ... 11ABN, *History,* 6. **146.** *Straining under the weight of a rifle and two duffel bags* ... Miles Gale, "A Paratrooper Sea Voyage — Crossing the Pacific Ocean, Spring of 1944," *WA,* January 1988, 6. **147.** *Senior officers were assigned staterooms* ... Edward Lahti, *Memoirs of an Angel,* 40; Schweitzer, Philip, *WWII Veteran Survey,* 18. **148.** *With so many troopers shuffling* ... Flanagan, Edward, *The Angels* [1948], 20. **149.** *"Perhaps the most memorable part* ... Paul Karberg, "511th Infantry," *Voice,* December 1, 1976, 8. **150.** *After a series of stunning victories* ... Scott, James, *Rampage,* 32. **151.** *The Allies were regaining territory on multiple fronts* ... This Pacific summary is based on M Hamlin Cannon, *Leyte: The Return to the Philippines. U.S. Army in World War II* (Office of the Chief of Military History, Department of the Army, 1954), 2–46.

Chapter 2: Bugs, Breasts, and Beer!

1. *Twenty-one days after departing San Francisco* ... 11ABN, *History,* 6. This was on May 26, 1944. **2.** *Temperatures soared in the crowded* ... Karberg, Paul, "511th Infantry," 8. **3.** *"unbearable* ... One of many examples; see Schweitzer, Philip, *WWII Veteran Survey,* 18. **4.** *"At 04:00am, the decks were* ... Miles Gale, "A Chance Meeting," *Voice,* April 15, 1983, 10. **5.** *"For washing and shaving* ... Karberg, Paul, "511th Infantry," 8. **6.** *They were fed two meals a day* ... Flanagan, Edward, *The Angels* [1989], 73. **7.** *The monotonous daily routine at sea* ... 11ABN, *Training Memo, No. 3, Shipment No. 1855,* no date. **8.** *The troopers organized skits* ... Flanagan, Edward, *The Angels* [1948], 21. **9.** *Officiated by a sailor dressed as King Neptune* ... Flanagan, Edward, *The Angels* [1989], 76; Lahti, Edward, *Memoirs of an Angel,* 40. **10.** *"Now hear this* ... Miles Gale, "The Valiant Plan," *WA,* Winter 1996, 37; Butler, Leroy, "Geronimo #13 or the South Pacific as I Saw It, Part I," 21. **11.** *"We got our first glimpse* ... George Doherty, "New Guinea," *Voice,* January 15, 1993, 11. **12.** *"The land rose rather steeply* ... Edward Hogan, *A Dogface's War: A Paratrooper's Summary of WWII in the Philippines* (Lincoln, Nebraska: iUniverse, 2007), 15; Dick Ostrom, "A Lasting Friendship," *WA,* Summer 1999. Ed Hogan was known as "Big Ed," because Ed Bolte was already "Little Ed." **13.** *Swing, having already arrived* ... 11ABN, *History,* 6. He arrived May 19, 1944. **14.** *Their camp was in a broad jungle* ... 11ABN, *Medical History, Second Quarter of 1944,* 1. This was a former Fifth Air Force base. **15.** *"gave way to the oppressive* ... Doherty, George, "New Guinea," 11. **16.** *"DOBODURA-TOKYO ROAD* ... ibid. **17.** *Each unit found piles of cots* ... 11ABN, *Medical History, Second Quarter of 1944,* 1. **18.** *Swing's engineers developed a framing system* ... Flanagan, Edward, *The Angels* [1989], 80. **19.** *"Even with the side rolled up* ... Miles Gale, "The Guinea Moonshiners," *WA,* Summer 1998; Flanagan, Edward, *The Angels* [1989], 81. **20.** *Showers were* *rudimentary contraptions* ... Doherty, George, "New Guinea," 11; 11ABN, *Medical History, Second Quarter of 1944*, 2. **21.** *"All bathers will wet up* ... 11ABN, *Memorandum*, June 2, 1944. **22.** *"This setup didn't encourage* ... Lahti, Edward, *Memoirs of an Angel*, 42. **23.** *Miles Gale shuddered at* ... Miles Gale, "Getting Ready for a Training Jump," *Voice*, May 15, 1988, 6. **24.** *"In five or ten minutes the fire* ... Bill Porteous, "That Crappy Crapper," *WA*, Spring 1994, 35. **25.** *"seemed to change his mind almost* ... Lahti, Edward, *Memoirs of an Angel*, 42. **26.** *The men constructed huts* ... Doherty, George, "New Guinea," 11; Unknown Author, "Seven Dwarfs," *Voice*, June 1, 1977, 10; Houston Jolley, "Personal Recollections 1943-1946, Part I," *Voice*, April 15, 1991, 8. **27.** *Guard duty was conducted* ... 511PIR, GO #23, 1944. **28.** *Church worship services* ... 11ABN, *Memorandum*, September 16, 1944. **29.** *At the same time, Swing established* ... 11ABN, *11th Airborne Division History*, 12; 11ABN, *Historical Summary*, 1, By the time the Angels left New Guinea, 75 percent of the enlisted men and 82 percent of officers were qualified parachutists. As in the States, Burgess ran the school and went through it as well. See Flanagan, Edward, *The Angels* [1989], 83. **30.** *Enough had gone through the division's schools* ... This change was made clear in the division's period documents and field orders, but it was an internal reference and not recognized officially by the Army. **31.** *The Air Force also made twelve* ... 11ABN, *11th Airborne Division History*, 12. This was all in concert with the 54th Troop Carrier Wing. 11ABN, *Training Memorandum No. 8*, September 3, 1944, says twelve gliders for this. Additionally, some troopers attended advanced training as jumpmasters and pathfinders, via 11ABN, *Memorandum*, August 11, 1944; and via 11ABN, *Memorandum*, September 28, 1944. **32.** *A few members of the Angels' reconnaissance* ... 11ABN, *11th Airborne Division History*, 12. **33.** *The Angels took their lessons to heart* ... Miles Gale, "Jungle School," *WA*, Fall 1999, 27. Lessons were run by ANGAU at Higatura. **34.** *The trick of waving a white surrender flag* ... Stahl, David, *Ōoka Shōhei's Writings on the Pacific War*, 302. The use of fake surrenders is well documented and is explained in this excerpt: "Japanese soldiers on New Guinea battlefronts also tried frequently to deceive the enemy with white surrender flags. The idea of using any and every means to kill the enemy, even when outnumbered twenty to one or fifty to one, had permeated the minds of the officers and soldiers on front lines throughout the Pacific. ... The Japanese soldiers who fought on the front lines throughout the Pacific felt that the Americans' material (superiority) was 'cowardly.' The thought that 'anything goes' originated from this feeling." **35.** *Training exercises emphasized* ... 11ABN, *Training Memorandum No. 4*, August 10, 1944. **36.** *"the ugliest mountains in the world* ... Hogan, Edward, *A Dogface's War*, 15. **37.** *"I remember that when* ... Harold Greer, Undated Letter, *Voice*, April 15, 1992, 28. **38.** *"was a very scary situation* ... George Doherty, "Welcome to the Jungle," *Voice*, October 15, 1993, 6. **39.** *"I swear, as big as cats* ... Marich, Robert, *Oral History*. **40.** *"Being tough paratroopers* ... Butler, Leroy, "Geronimo #13 or the South Pacific as I Saw It, Part I," 21. **41.** *Acting as a single unit* ... This was an infantry battalion supported by an artillery battery of four 75mm howitzers, a platoon of engineers, a platoon of heavy machineguns, and a medical section, as per 11ABN, *Training Memorandum No. 5*, July 23, 1944. **42.** *Failures were those of troops ...* 11ABN, *Memorandum*, August 19, 1944; 11ABN, *11th Airborne Division History*, 12. **43.** *One of Haugen's men ...* Miles Gale, "New Guinea 1944," *Voice*, January 15, 1989, 31. **44.** *A demonstration of Japanese ...* Flanagan, Edward, *The Angels* [1989], 88; Burgess, Henry, *Looking Back*, 37. **45.** *"bomber-size mosquitoes ...* 11ABN, *11th Airborne Division History*, 11; Doherty, George, "New Guinea," 11; Jerry Davis, "511th PIR New Guinea: May–November 1944," *WA*, Fall 1999, 25. **46.** *Everyone smelled like a ...* Lahti, Edward, *Memoirs of an Angel*, 41. **47.** *for the men in the field ...* Walker, 'Ripcord,' "LTG Joseph M. Swing and the 11th Airborne Division," 24. **48.** *The threat was real ...* Flanagan, Edward, *The Angels* [1989], 88. **49.** *"something like a liquefied ...* Lee Walker, "What's for Dinner Sarge?" *WA*, Spring 1994, 2. **50.** *One man in paratrooper ...* Davis, Jerry, "511th PIR New Guinea: May–November 1944," 25. **51.** *"just plain ugly ...* Gale, Miles, "Jungle School," 27. **52.** *Photos by the dozens ...* Miles Gale, "Accidental Death in the 11th Airborne," *WA*, Fall 1993, 36. Gale's description of Papuans from, Gale, Miles, "Jungle School," 27. **53.** *The initial interest faded ...* Lee Wallace, "A Handful of Memories from New Guinea," *WA*, Spring 1995, 2. **54.** *Those WACs interested in ...* Marich, Robert, *Oral History*. **55.** *The cooks in Hard Rock's ...* 511th PIR Association, *511th Parachute Infantry Regiment*, 18. **56.** *Doodlebug racing required participants ...* Vannier, Joseph, *The I Co. Beacon*, May 1996, 5. **57.** *the twelve-ounce ...* 11ABN, *Memorandum: Sale of Non-Gratuitous QM Items*, July 20, 1944. **58.** *Two men in Mile Gale's platoon ...* Gale, Miles, "The Guinea Moonshiners." **59.** *Moonshine production became a ...* Swift, Volney, *I Co. Beacon*, February 1997, 5. **60.** *One plucky trooper fermented ...* Carmesin, Johnny, *I Co. Beacon*, February 1999, 2. **61.** *an open-air amphitheater ...* 11ABN, *11th Airborne Division History*, 11, with seating for 12,000. **62.** *"Movies were shown several nights ...* Hogan, Edward, *A Dogface's War*, 16. **63.** *Conducted by Warrant Officer John Bergland ...* Band notes: 11ABN, *GO #40*, 1944; 511th PIR Association, *511th Parachute Infantry Regiment*, 9; ninety men from 11ABN, *11th Airborne Division History*, 11; 11ABN, *History of 11th Airborne Division Band for Year of 1945*, 1, says eight-four men in January 1945; Chuck Tuelle, "News Briefs," *Voice*, January 15, 1975. **64.** *Sports were a big morale ...* 11ABN, *11th Airborne Division History*, 11. **64a.** *Mesereau had been playing ...* "T.A. Mesereau Is West Point Cadet," *The Kingston Daily Freeman*, Kingston, New York, July 3, 1939, 8; "It's A Shade Hot but Mesereau's Eleven Tries It," *The Record*, Hackensack, NJ, December 14, 1944, 27. **65.** *"raising hell ...* Arnett Foster, "Boxing Team," *WA*, Fall 1999, 32. Ransdell's full name is from a George Company manifest; Preston Carter was later KIA. **66.** *"think, eat, and dream of war ...* Banning Repplier, "This Barringer Grad Is 'Making Good,'" Unknown Newark, New Jersey, newspaper, early 1945. **67.** *"wild horses, over trained ...* Stephen Cavanaugh, "A Call to Arms Part I," *WA*, Winter 2000, 6. **68.** *"noncombatants ... labor battalions ...* 11ABN, *11th Airborne Division History*, 14. **69.** *"I ought to shoot that thing ...* Bat story based on, Light, William, "Notes about Orin Haugen's Early Life," 9; Marshall,

Bert, "The Marshall Brothers, Part I," 6; and Vannier, Joseph, *The I Co. Beacon*, January 2, 1997, 7. **70.** *"ruthless martinet* ... Bernheim, Eli, *WWII Veteran Survey*, 4. **71.** *"constant state of sweat* ... Gale, Miles, "Accidental Death in the 11th Airborne," 31. **72.** *Four of the cases were* ... This according to Bernheim, Eli, *WWII Veteran Survey*, 4. **73.** *They were paid to fight* ... Doherty, George, "New Guinea," 11. **74.** *"Personally," said First Lieutenant Randolph* ... Kirkland, Randolph. *Long Ago and Far Away*, 50. **75.** *Serving as transport drivers* ... Burgess, Henry, *Looking Back*, 43. **76.** *"I don't want you officers* ... Harry 'Bloody' Swan quoted in Light, William, "Notes About Orin Haugen's Early Life," 9. **77.** *"Stanley, you have over* ... Glenn McGowan, "Clarification," *Voice*, April 15, 1991, 15. Col. 'Shimmy' Schimmelpfennig's recollection. **78.** *"Sparks flew, but no court* ... Davis, Jerry, "511th PIR New Guinea: May–November 1944," 25. **79.** *Ali Baba Swing and* ... Bernheim, Eli, *WWII Veteran Survey*, 6. **80.** *"I decided I wanted that* ... Burgess, Henry, *Looking Back*, 41. **81.** *"moonlight requisition* ... Miley, Buzz, "Moonlight Requisition." Buzz was the son of General 'Bud' Miley, CG of the 17th Abn Div. The pistol numbers are from comparing the TO&Es as found in Rottman, Gordon, *US Airborne Units in the Pacific Theater 1942–45*, 20 (1,753 pistols) with Rottman, Gordon, *US Airborne Units in the ETO 1944–45*, 27 (ten pistols). **82.** *"I wasn't really sure what* ... Charlie Ford, "I Stole the Liquor," *WA*, Spring 1998; Ford, Charlie, *The I Co. Beacon*, January 1997, 8. That this was Magadieu is based on the division's officer roster. Ford's two bottles met an unfortunate fate: he broke one digging it up and never found the other. **83.** *On Monday, October 12, 1944* ... Flanagan, Edward, *The Angels* [1989], 94. **84.** *"It was very hard to get him* ... Based on a combo of Flanagan, Edward, *The Angels* [1989], 95, and Swing, *Oral Reminiscences*, 22. **85.** *Once secured, Leyte's central location* ... Cannon, M, *Leyte: The Return to the Philippines*, 3. **86.** *Only a small group of* ... 11ABN, *11th Airborne Division History*, 14. **87.** *The engineers dismantled* ... Miles Gale, "Farewell to New Guinea," *WA*, Fall 1996, 24. **88.** *They loaded over seventeen hundred* ... Loaded transports on November 7, 1944, and sailed on November 11, per 408AQM, *Historical Operational Report K-2 Operation (Leyte)*, 1. The historical record of how many ships the Angels boarded varies by source. I have used nine as per the recollections of General Swing's assistant div. commander and the USS *Gilliam's War Diary*, which indicates nine APAs and AKAs left New Guinea. **89.** *"Accumulation* ... 408AQM, *Historical Operational Report K-2 Operation (Leyte)*, 2. **90.** *On Saturday, November 11* ... Details of Task Unit 79.15.1 from the USS *Gilliam* (APA 57) *War Diary*. The TF was composed of the following ships: *Cambria* (APA 36), *Monrovia* (APA 31), *Rixey* (PH 3), *Gilliam* (APA 57), *Cavalier* (APA 37), *Feland* (APA 11), *Golden City* (AP 169), *Thuban* (AKA 19), *Chara* (AKA 58), *Brain* (DD 630), *Gansevoort* (DD 608), *Luce* (DD 522), and *Chauncey* (DD 667). The following ships joined enroute to Leyte: *Calvert* (APA 32), *Twiggs* (DD59), *Halligan* (DD584), and *Haraden* (DD 585). **91.** *After two* *days at sea ...* 511SIG, *Operational Historical Report on KING TWO Operation*, 2. The announcement was made on November 13, 1944.

Chapter 3: "We Can Still Win"

1. *While escorting destroyers lingered offshore ...* Transport Squadron Fourteen, *War Diary*, 7; 11ABN, *Operation KING II, Leyte Campaign*, 2. USS *Monrovia*, *War Diary (Month of November)*, 4, described the frontage "from Abuyog to Tarragona." USS *Cambria* (APA 36), *War Diary for the Month of November 1944*, 2. **2.** *Just twenty minutes after dropping anchor ...* USS *Feland, War Diary, November 1944*, 5; Leroy Butler, "Thanksgiving–Christmas 1944," *WA*, Fall 2001, 11. **3.** *"Flash Red, Control Yellow ...* USS *Cavalier* (APA 37), *War Diary – November 1944*, 3. **4.** *Gunners on the USS* Thuban *...* USS *Thuban* (AKA 19), *War Diary for the Month of November 1944*, 6. **5.** *"There was shooting all over ...* Deane Marks, "No One Smiled on Leyte," *WA*, October 1988, 25. **6.** *Once ashore, sergeants herded ...* Vignola, James, "In the 11th Airborne Division," 1, writes, "There was a company formation on the beach, and I kept thinking a Japanese plane or planes could fly over us and strafe our whole outfit." **7.** *"The Navy made no bones ...* Flanagan, Edward, *The Angels* [1989], 105. **8.** *The USS* Monrovia *emptied its ...* USS *Monrovia, War Diary (Month of November)*, 2–7. **9.** *The 11th, in addition to ...* Cannon, M, *Leyte: The Return to the Philippines*, 191. Convoy from New Guinea: nine APAs, two AKAs from Flanagan, Edward, *The Angels* [1989], 106. 11ABN, *Operation KING II, Leyte Campaign*, 7, states: seven APAs, two AKAs, one APH, and one Liberty Ship; the division's G-4 journal for November 21, 1944, confirms supplies were also delivered via LSTs. **10.** *"turmoil ...* George Floersch, "Do You Remember When the 511th Landed on the Beach of Leyte?" *WA*, Winter 2004, 10. **11.** *Swing's quartermaster troops ranged ...* 408AQM, *Historical Operational Report K-2 Operation (Leyte)*, 2. **12.** *"[They] were fun to watch ...* Marks, Deane, "No One Smiled on Leyte," 25. **13.** *Reasons for the delays were numerous ...* Cannon, M, *Leyte: The Return to the Philippines*, 307. **14.** *MacArthur's staff dismissed engineering ...* John McManus, *Island Infernos: The US Army's Pacific War Odyssey, 1944* (New York: Dutton Caliber, 2019), 504. **15.** *Most importantly, the three airstrips ...* 11ABN, FO #1, November 19, 1944. **16.** *To ready the fields ...* Airstrip all from: Cannon, M, *Leyte: The Return to the Philippines*, 124, 187–188. **17.** *It was partly a self-induced ...* ibid., 222. **18.** *However, the effective strength ...* ibid., 222 cites 12,804 men. **19.** *MacArthur's ground commander ...* ibid., 221, cites replacements as 5,289; ibid., 306, for committing his reserve divisions, which were 32nd and 77th Infantry Divisions (ibid., 222). **20.** *Swing's division, initially placed ...* Flanagan, Edward, *The Angels* [1989], 106. **21.** *Having been commissioned after ...* Yamashita bio based on Scott, James, *Rampage*, 31–35. **22.** *"Old Potato Face ...* Bob MacMillan, "Yamashita Gives Up," *Yank Magazine*, October 12, 1945, 3. **23.** *"He may be a great orator ...* Scott, James, *Rampage*, 35. **24.** *"Never suggest in your report ...* ibid., 35. **25.** *"The tiger attacks its prey ...* ibid., 43. **26.** *"More than seven thousand ...* ibid., 45. **27.** *"If you can crush ...* ibid., 46. **28.** *There was spirited debate ...* This debate is well documented in Tomochika, Yoshiharu, "The True Facts of the Leyte Operation," 6. **29.** *Imperial General Headquarters settled* ... Cannon, M, *Leyte: The Return to the Philippines*, 51. **30.** *There were almost 432,000* ... ibid., 51, 93. **31.** *His predecessor, Lieutenant General Shigenori Kuroda* ... ibid., 50; Yamashita replaced Kuroda on October 9; see also Tomochika, Yoshiharu, *The True Facts of the Leyte Operation*, 8, for insight into the strategic squabbles between Kuroda and his staff. **32.** *"Good, they have picked* ... Cannon, M, *Leyte: The Return to the Philippines*, 93. **33.** *"We were determined to* ... ibid., 94; Tomochika was chief of staff of the 35th Army quoted from Tomochika, Yoshiharu, "The True Facts of the Leyte Operation," 15. **34.** *"Where is Leyte?* This was Lt. Gen. Akira Muto, Cannon, M., *Leyte: The Return to the Philippines*, 51. **35.** *Yamashita issued the* Shō Ichi Go ... This was on October 21, 1944, as per Cannon, M., *Leyte: The Return to the Philippines*, 103. **36.** *Three days later, however* ... American losses: one light carrier, two escort carriers, two destroyers, and one destroyer escort. Ibid., 92. **37.** *But Tokyo-based propaganda* ... Tomochika, Yoshiharu, "The True Facts of the Leyte Operation," 19. See page 13 for the effects of Tokyo's misinformation; McManus, John, *Island Infernos*, 470. **37a**. *The Japanese fared little* ... McManus, John, *Island Infernos*, 469. **38.** *"The main battle is fought* ... ibid., 7. Suzuki had been Yamashita's chief of staff in Singapore per Scott, James, *Rampage*, 50. **39.** *His troops had spent* ... Since April 1944. Cannon, M, *Leyte: The Return to the Philippines*, 50; "The 35th Army forced the men of the 16th Division to fight according to a strategy of engaging the landing American forces at the shoreline, and then gradually falling back to interior positions." Quoted in Stahl, David, *Ōoka Shōhei's Writings on the Pacific War*, 291. **40.** *The convoys landing on the* ... Cannon, M, *Leyte: The Return to the Philippines*, 103; McManus, John, *Island Infernos*, 499. **41.** *Yamashita advocated to his* ... ibid., 221. **42.** *He was overruled* ... This had taken place on November 9–10, as per Cannon, M., *Leyte: The Return to the Philippines*, 221. **43.** *"If our Emperor has consented* ... Scott, James, *Rampage*, 49. **43a**. *The Emperor and the* ... Richard Frank, *Downfall: The End of the Imperial Japanese Empire* (New York: Random House, 1999), 89. **44.** *The Japanese convoys, hampered by* ... Over ten thousand tons of supplies; see Cannon, M., *Leyte: The Return to the Philippines*, 102. **45.** *Ten thousand of those troops* ... This on November 9, 1944; see Cannon, M, *Leyte: The Return to the Philippines*, 101, 254. **46.** *"All personnel must be able* ... Enemy Publications No. 415, *Combat Regulations for Island Garrison Forces*, 5. **47.** *"The Army operates on the* ... ibid., 3, 42. **48.** *After their first night on the beach* ... 11ABN, *Location of 11th Airborne Division Command Posts from April 1944 to Present*, 1. The 11th ABN CP was at Sungi from November 19 to 24. **49.** *It was time for the 11th* ... 11ABN, FO #1, November 19, 1944; see Cannon, M, *Leyte: The Return to the Philippines*, 222. **50.** *two divisions would push across the* ... These were 1st Cav and 24th Inf Div; see Flanagan, Edward, *The Angels* [1948], 31. **51.** *Swing's 11th, with another* ... The US 96th Div on the right; see Cannon, M, *Leyte: The Return to the Philippines*, 223. **52.** *"Monday morning, we replace* ... Hogan, Edward, *A Dogface's War*, 17. **53.** *"I had some feeling of trepidation* ... Butler, Leroy, "Thanksgiving—Christmas 1944," 11. **54.** *"No one thought they would* ... Keith, "The Saga of Purple Heart Hill," *WA*, Spring 2004, 16. **55.** *There was a reason* ... Beach description based on

Flanagan, Edward, *The Angels* [1948], 31. **56.** *Their priority was to build ...* Cannon, M, *Leyte: The Return to the Philippines*, 11. **57.** *The engineers drove wooden ...* Flanagan, Edward, *The Angels* [1948], 31. **58.** *Setting up water points ...* 127ENG, *K-2 Operation (October 20, 1944, to December 25, 1944)*, January 12, 1945, 1. **59.** *They also carved out a ...* 11ABN, *Operation KING II, Leyte Campaign*, 11, confirms the initial use of eleven liaison/spotter aircraft, which are also mentioned in Unknown Author, "Communicating in the Pacific Proves Challenging," *Voice*, June 2018, 20; 680-lbs for an L-4 is per Cannon, Hardy, *Box Seat Over Hell: The True Story of America's Liaison Pilots and Their Light Planes in World War Two* (San Antonio, Texas: Alamo Liaison Squadron, 2007), 124; Stinson at 1,495 lbs. from ibid., 128. **60.** *On Monday, the 20th of November ...* The 511th PIR was relieving the 17th Infantry Regiment. **61.** *Since Haugen couldn't wait for ...* The division had access to four LCTs and ten DUKWs; see 11ABN, *Operation KING II, Leyte Campaign*, 7. **62.** *Their destination was the ...* Flanagan, Edward, *The Angels* [1948], 31. **63.** *They arrived just before sunset ...* 511PIR, *Regimental History*, 1; 511PIR, *Regimental History: Leyte Campaign*, 1. **64.** *As part of taking over ...* 11ABN, *G3 (Operations) Journal*, November 22, 1944. Haugen had sent squads from 1/511 PIR to guard seven bridges between Dulag and Palo. **65.** *Private George Floersch and his ...* Floersch, George, "Do You Remember When the 511th Landed on the Beach of Leyte?" 10. **66.** *A two-mile section ...* Road conditions per 11ABN, *G3 (Operations) Journal*, 21, November 22, 1944. **67.** *Most of the palm trees ...* Description of the beach based on period photos and Cannon, M., *Leyte: The Return to the Philippines*, 75. **68.** *Seven hours later ...* 511PIR, *Regimental History*, 1; 11ABN, *FO #1*, November 19, 1944. The relief was to be effected in order: 1st BN [November 20], 3rd BN and Regt HQ [November 23], 2nd BN [November 26]; 1/511 relieved the 17th Infantry Regiment's 1st BN. **69.** *At the same time ...* 11ABN, *G3 (Operations) Journal*, November 22, 1944. **70.** *He'd been able to commit ...* This was a regiment of the 32nd Inf; see Cannon, M., *Leyte: The Return to the Philippines*, 254. **71.** *After complaints of the ...* 11ABN, *G3 (Operations) Journal*, November 22, 1944. **72.** *That same day ...* 11ABN, *G1 (Personnel) Journal*, November 24, 1944. **73.** *The 23rd of November ...* 511PIR, *Regimental History*, 2. The 511th's Regt HQ left for Burauen and established the CP in the 1BN perimeter at 14:00. **74.** *Joseph Vannier woke for breakfast ...* Joseph Vannier, "Giving Thanks on Bito Beach," *WA*, Winter 1997, 75. *"The pilot was determined ...* Lahti, Edward, *Memoirs of an Angel*, 49. **75.** *The same evening ...* Cannon, M, *Leyte: The Return to the Philippines*, 257. **76.** *"At this point, it was ...* Marks, Deane, "No One Smiled on Leyte," 25. **77.** *Locals reported a large ...* 511PIR, *Regimental History: Leyte Campaign*, 3. **78.** *On Friday morning ...* 711ORD, *Historical Report*, 2. **79.** *The airstrip's 4,920-foot runway ...* Cannon, M, *Leyte: The Return to the Philippines*, 124. **80.** *Swing's signal company went to work ...* 511SIG, *Operational Historical Report on KING TWO Operation*, 3; G3 Journal, November 24. **81.** *Quartermaster crews worked day ...* 11ABN, *G4 (Supply) Journal*, November 21, 1944; Parachute Maint. Co, *Historical Record of Leyte Campaign*, 1. **82.** *Well away from the main ...* 408AQM, *Historical Operational Report K-2 Operation (Leyte)*, 3. **83.** *The parachute maintenance section ...* Parachute Maint. Co,

Historical Record of Leyte Campaign, 1. **84.** *Captain Thomas Jordan* ... 408AQM, *Historical Operational Report K-2 Operation (Leyte)*, 3. **85.** *"Destroy by offensive action* ... 11ABN, FO #2, November 25, 1944. **86.** *The one hundred and thirty men* ... 511PIR, *Regimental History*, 2. **87.** *Other companies would follow* ... 11ABN, *G3 (Operations) Journal*, November 24, 1944; 511PIR, *Regimental History*, 2, left at 08:00 on November 24 while Recon Plt. left November 23 at 06:30; 11ABN, *G3 (Operations) Journal*, November 22, 1944. **88.** *But Able Company made better* ... 11ABN, *G3 (Operations) Journal*, November 24, 1944; 511PIR, *Regimental History*, 2. **89.** *"Scaled distances may be* ... Period maps, *Leyte Special*, 1944. **90.** *The maps barely hinted* ... Cannon, M, *Leyte: The Return to the Philippines*, 21. **91.** *As the troopers headed* ... Vannier, Joseph, "Giving Thanks on Bito Beach." **92.** *Additional reserves, estimated to be* ... 11ABN, FO #2, November 25, 1944. **93.** *Neither of those patrols* ... 511PIR, *Regimental History*, 3. **94.** *"The easiest way to* ... Miles Gale, "The New Guinea Water Works," *Voice*, July 15, 1994, 13. **95.** *Their small backpacks contained* ... Vannier, Joseph, "Giving Thanks on Bito Beach." **96.** *the heaviest loads during* ... Bob LeRoy, *From My Foxhole to Tokyo* (Boring, Oregon: CPA Book Publisher, 1992), 133. **97.** *In the rain* ... ibid., 134; 511PIR, *Regimental History: Leyte Campaign*, 6. **98.** *"We threw the top* ... Bert Marshall, "The Marshall Brothers, Part II," *WA*, Winter 1994, 6. **99.** *That afternoon, one of the* ... 11ABN, *G4 (Supply) Journal*, November 25, 1944. **100.** *The pilot marked the location* ... 511PIR, *S2 (Intelligence) Journal*. 511 was yellow, 187 purple, 188 green, and artillery units red. **101.** *It was a hit-and-run* ... 511PIR, *Regimental History*, 3. **102.** *At 07:30 the next morning* ... ibid.; 511PIR, *S1 (Personnel) Journal*, November 26, 1944. **103.** *Private George Floersch was* ... Floersch, George, "Another Remembrance of C Company's First Battle," 29.

Chapter 4: The Mud Rats

1. *LaFlamme was still trying to* ... 511PIR, *S1 (Personnel) Journal*, November 27, 1944; 511PIR, *Regimental History*, 3; 11ABN, *G3 (Operations) Journal*, November 27, 1944. This was 3rd PLT as confirmed in 511PIR, *Regimental History: Leyte Campaign*, 5. Renfroe had more information, as he was in the vanguard of the battle, but no one sought him out, and his attempts to provide details were apparently rebuffed. **2.** *The fact that only three* ... 511PIR, *S1 (Personnel) Journal*, November 27, 1944. **3.** *LaFlamme radioed Swing's HQ* ... ibid.; sunset was at 19:13. **3a.** *Major 'Slugger' Lahti disagreed* ... Kirkland, Randolph, *Long Ago and Far Away*, 79. **4.** *Haugen, with Mesereau and* ... Thirty men and six WIA via 511PIR, *S2 (Intelligence) Report*, November 29, 1944, written by Jeffress. **5.** *"Darkness was setting in* ... 511th PIR Association, *511th Parachute Infantry Regiment*, 60. **6.** *The regimental surgeon* ... Steve Hegedus, "Company Medics, A-511, A Tribute," *WA*, January 1988, 2; Unknown Author, "Somebody Had to Do It, WWII Airborne Surgeon Recalls Action at Front," *Voice*, January 15, 1987, 19; Silver Star citation via 11ABN, *GO #28*, 1945. **7.** *Just after sunrise* ... 511PIR, *S1 (Personnel) Journal*, November 28, 1944. **8.** *Lieutenant Merkel Varner* ... Silver

Star citation via 11ABN, *GO #18*, 1945. **9.** *Swing needed to keep* … Swing, *Oral Reminiscences*, 17. **10.** *One crashed at Buri* … Flanagan, Edward, *The Angels* [1989], 125; 187GIR, *The Leyte Campaign (Oct. 20, 1944 to Dec. 25, 1944)*, October 2, 1946, 5. Crashes per 11ABN, *G2 (Intelligence) Periodic Report*, November 27, 1944; 11ABN, *G2 (Intelligence) Journal*, November 26, 1944. **11.** *Unsure if these were* … 11ABN, *G3 (Operations) Journal*, November 27, 1944. **12.** *As an additional precaution* … This was A & B Co's from the 767th Tank Battalion. **12a.** *Furthermore, a map found* … 511PIR, *Regimental History*, 3. Map interpreted per 511PIR, *S1 (Personnel) Journal*, November 28, 1944; 11ABN, *G2 (Intelligence) Summary of Enemy Airborne Activities*, 1. **13.** *Swing shrugged off* … 11ABN, *FO #3*, November 28, 1944. **14.** *"Where did you train* … Swing, *Oral Reminiscences*, 17. **15.** *Manarawat plateau was occupied* … 511PIR, *S1 (Personnel) Journal*, November 28, 1944. Baker Company first occupied the plateau. Terrain description based on Flanagan, Edward, *The Angels* [1989], 117. **16.** *With Hard Rock isolated* … 511PIR, *Regimental History*, 4; 511PIR, *Regimental History: Leyte Campaign*, 5. The 1st and 3rd BNs were moving, while the 2nd BN was at Burauen. **17.** *Lieutenant Colonel Norman E. Tipton* … 1,000 feet from 11ABN, as per *11th Airborne Division History: February 1943 to May 1945*, 19. Tipton details from 11ABN, *Press Relations Office, List of General and Staff Officers*. **18.** *Wheeler and Mesereau had* … Lahti, Edward, *Memoirs of an Angel*, 53. Wheeler's unit was also reinforced with at least two 81mm mortar teams; see *Howitzer*, West Point 1943 Yearbook; and "Becomes Bride in Rites at Noon," *Evening Sun*, Hanover, Pennsylvania, January 20, 1943, 1. **19.** *Earlier that morning* … A dozen men plus Haugen via 511PIR, *S2 (Intelligence) Report*, November 29, 1944, written by Jeffress. **20.** *"We left our rations* … 511th PIR Association, *511th Parachute Infantry Regiment*, 60. **21.** *At 0:800 the next morning* … 511PIR, *Regimental History*, 5, this on November 30. The 511PIR, *Regimental History: Leyte Campaign*, 5, claims Tipton led this patrol, and 511PIR, *Regimental History*, 5, implies both the 1st BN CO and Tipton went, but the multiple 511th journals [S1, S2, etc.] refer only to Wheeler leading the patrol, which makes more tactical sense, as it would have been irresponsible for senior leadership to leave the main unit while so much else was going on. **22.** *"somewhat blind* … 511th PIR Association, *511th Parachute Infantry Regiment*, 20. This inner monologue is based on thoughts shared by Swan, which were certainly shared by others. **23.** *"I had no idea* … Stan Young, "One and One-Half Months on Leyte," *WA*, Fall 1999, 42. **24.** *They arrived at the* … 511PIR, *Regimental History*, 6; Marks, Deane, "No One Smiled on Leyte," 25. Estimated fifty-two EKIA via 511PIR, *S2 (Intelligence) Report*, November 29, 1944, written by Jeffress. **25.** *After holding out for* … 511th PIR Association, *511th Parachute Infantry Regiment*, 20. **26.** *They won't die from* … Hegedus, Steve, "Company Medics," 2. **27.** *"It pelted rain incessantly* … Young, Stan, "One and One-Half Months on Leyte," 42. **28.** *"It was a miserable* … 511th PIR Association, *511th Parachute Infantry Regiment*, 20. **29.** *In the graying dawn* … 511PIR, *Regimental History*, 5. **30.** *"The fellow we carried* … Young, Stan, "One and One-Half Months on Leyte," 42. **31.** *"With nowhere to go* … Jim Massey, "The Paratrooper Machine Gunner in Jungle Warfare," *WA*, October 1988, 16. Additional details from Massey's citation via 11ABN, *GO #57*, 1944. **32.**

'Bloody' Swan took a knee ... This was First Lieutenant Armfin Olsen's mortar section and Sergeants Spencer Halgren and Thomas Thompson per Harry Swan, "A Mortarfying Experience in Tactics," *Voice,* January 15, 1991, 25. **33.** *Captain Wheeler scooped up a* ... Wheeler details from his award citation via 11ABN, GO #57, 1944, Wheeler was later KIA. **34a.** *"All I could see* ... "Captain Wheeler Given Silver Star," *Evening Sun,* Hanover, PA, February 5, 1945, 1. **34.** *While they suffered one man* ... 11ABN, *G3 (Operations) Journal,* December 2, 1944. Massey and Wheeler were later both awarded the Silver Star for their actions; four WIA from 3rd BN PIR casualty list found in *Voice* (no. 103, April 15, 1994): 23. **35.** *Wheeler's men reorganized and* ... 511PIR, *Regimental History,* 5; Swan, "where we later joined A Company" from Swan, Harry, "A Mortarfying Experience in Tactics," 25. Captain Tom Brady was mortally WIA the next day, on December 2, 1944. **36.** *"Even though others were* ... Vannier, Joseph, "Pearl Harbor Day on Maloney Ridge," 7. **37.** *"Footsteps of men who* ... Miles Gale, "Scouts Out," *WA,* Summer 1996, 31. **38.** *"These tiny, black, thread-like* ... Kirkland, Randolph, *Long Ago and Far Away,* 77. **39.** *"You could see the sky* ... Steve Hegedus, "Burial Detail and the C Company Ambush," *WA,* Fall 1993, 25. Hegedus refused to name the men out of respect for their deplorable burials, and while further research has verified his story and identified at least one of the men, if not both, I will respect his wishes. Two days after this incident, a dead Japanese soldier was found wearing a pair of US jump boots. **40.** *After spending the night* ... 11ABN, *G3 (Operations) Journal,* November 30, 1944. This was Guerrilla Camp 755, which, given its proximity to Burauen, was most likely at Abuyagon. **41.** *But at some point* ... The version in Flanagan's *The Angels* [1989] varies from later accounts provided by survivors. **42.** *After the meeting* ... Flanagan, Edward, *The Angels* [1989], 129; thirty-eighth jump from Lorio, James, "Orin Doughty Haugen," 10; Unknown Author, "Col. Orin Haugen, Capt. T.J. James Reported Dead," *Asheville-Citizen Times,* March 6, 1945, 1. **43.** *Men slashed at the* ... Flanagan, Edward, *The Angels* [1948], 43; 127ENG, *K-2 Operation (October 20, 1944, to December 25, 1944),* 2. This was 1st PLT of C Co. **44.** *With the entire regiment* ... 11ABN, *G3 (Operations) Journal,* November 30, 1944. **45.** *"The going was* ... Young, Stan, "One and One-Half Months on Leyte," 42. **46.** *Eleven of them, having* ... 511PIR, *Regimental History,* 7. **47.** *Swing tapped Colonel Nicholas Stadtherr's* ... 511PIR, *S2 (Intelligence) Journal,* November 27, 1944. This was A Battery. **48.** *To drop a full battery* ... Flanagan, Edward, *The Angels* [1948], 45. **49.** *To pull it off* ... ibid., 42. **50.** *In case of fortune* ... ibid., This was at the Taclobán airfield, and despite stories to the contrary, 11ABN, *Operation KING II, Leyte Campaign,* 10, confirms that the Fifth Air Force blessed the unconventional airdrop; "RESCUE" on side of aircraft confirmed per 11ABN, *Airborne Operations,* 1. **51.** *The artillery crews and a* ... 511PIR, *S2 (Intelligence) Journal,* November 28, 1944. **52.** *Clouds were often too low* ... and *"Bastards would not let* ... 11ABN, *G3 (Operations) Journal,* December 2, 1944. **53.** *Finally, the weather cleared* ... Flanagan, Edward, *The Angels* [1948], 42. **54.** *It took seven sorties* ... 11ABN, *Division Artillery Unit Journal,* December 4, 1944. **55.** *On December 4* ... 11ABN, FO #4, December 4, 1944. **56.** *Filipino guerrillas reported that* ... ibid., and also 11ABN, *G3 (Operations) Journal,* November 30, 1944. This intelligence was provided by the

7th Inf. Div. **57.** *Quandt squeezed into the* ... Flanagan, Edward, *The Angels* [1948], 43. **58.** *Initially, a seven-man team* ... 511SIG, *Operational Historical Report on KING TWO Operation*, 4. **59.** *Instead, an officer* ... ibid. This group included S/Sgt Martin F. Buck, Tec 3 John Fulton, and Tec 5 Keith H. Martin, with a SCR-694 radio that weighed 19.5 pounds, but all components were close to 200 lbs. It had a fifteen-mile range via voice and almost thirty via morse. **60.** *Swing ordered platoons from* ... Godfrey is based on content from 152AAB, *Historical Report of 152 AB AA Bn, in Leyte Campaign.* **61.** *The day after Quandt arrived* ... 11ABN, *G3 (Operations) Journal*, December 4, 1944. This was the 2nd PLT, C Co, 1/187th per 187GIR, *The Leyte Campaign.* **62.** *Meanwhile, the rest of the 187th* ... 11ABN, *FO #4*, December 4, 1944. The 187th movement also included three batteries from the 152 AA BN; 187GIR, *The Leyte Campaign*, 6. **63.** *"Something is wrong with resupply* ... 11ABN, *G3 (Operations) Journal*, December 5, 1944. **64.** *As such, Haugen asked* ... 11ABN, *G4 (Supply) Journal*, December 4, 1944. **65.** *So many requests came* ... 408AQM, *Historical Operational Report K-2 Operation (Leyte)*, 9. **66.** *"Many individual requests for* ... 511PIR, *S1 (Personnel) Journal*, December 4, 1944. **66a.** *An average division consumed* ... McManus, John, *Island Infernos*, 517. **67.** *The lumbering carabao could* ... The carabao were abandoned at Manarawat per Flanagan, Edward, *The Angels* [1948], 45. **68.** *When they were available* ... 11ABN, *G3 (Operations) Journal*, November 28, 1944; 11ABN, *Operation KING II, Leyte Campaign*, 10. **69.** *"absolute essentials* ... 11ABN, *G4 (Supply) Journal*, December 2, 1944. **70.** *A rescue party, following* ... Flanagan, Edward, *The Angels* [1948], 46; Herbert Merritt, "More about Leyte," *WA*, Winter 1994, 8. **71.** *In the first week of December* ... 11ABN, *G4 (Supply) Journal*, November 30, 1944. **72.** *He formed his own squadron* ... Liaison aircraft numbers are per 11ABN, *Operation KING II, Leyte Campaign*, 11: nine L-4s and two L-5s. I have used the number in this report for consistency. However, 408AQM, *Historical Operational Report K-2 Operation (Leyte)*, 8, claims eight L5s, which is consistent with the Div's TO&E, but other sources claim as many as seventeen. Swing was also assisted by the C-47s of the 11th Cargo Supply Squadron at Tacloban and a division re-supply team at the same strip. [408AQM, *Historical Operational Report K-2 Operation (Leyte)*, 8]; see also 11th Cargo Resupply Sq. in Cannon, M, *Leyte: The Return to the Philippines*, 310. **73.** *Lightweight volunteers, under 135* ... Captain Davy Carnahan was chief of the aerial delivery; the pilots were under the direction of Major Edwin Horloff, Division Artillery Air Officer, as per Flanagan, Edward, *The Angels* [1948], 46; 135 lbs from Flanagan, Edward, *The Angels* [1989], 138. **74.** *Some flew up to fifteen* ... 408AQM, *Historical Operational Report K-2 Operation (Leyte)*, 8. **75.** *The missions were not* ... 11ABN, *G3 (Operations) Journal*, December 5, 1944. This was Lt. John A. Ricks per Flanagan, Edward, *The Angels* [1948], 47. **76.** *The quartermaster troops established* ... 408AQM, *Historical Operational Report K-2 Operation (Leyte)*, 7. **77.** *While the engineers had completed* ... ibid., 9. Causeway completion details from 11ABN, *Operation KING II, Leyte Campaign*, 9. **78.** *If a truck got bogged* ... 408AQM, *Historical Operational Report K-2 Operation (Leyte)*, 6–9. **79.** *"Try and understand transportation* ... 11ABN, *G4 (Supply) Journal*, November 30, 1944. **80.** *The inconveniences existed at* ... ibid. **81.** *A small unit of Japanese ambushed* ...

408AQM, *Historical Operational Report K-2 Operation (Leyte)*, 10. **82.** *Trucks rumbled in to unload* … ibid., 8. **83.** *Losses were approximately 10 percent* … ibid. **84.** *Lee P. Turkington was killed* … Report of first supply casualty is in 11ABN, *G3 (Operations) Journal*, December 5, 1944; Jack V. Jones was wounded on December 4 and died the next morning; Trooper Lee P. Turkington was WIA by a grenade and then hit by re-supply drop of mortar shells; Roy Bengston, "Unit History," *WA*, Winter 1991, 20, says it was rations; but Jacques Smith, "The Leyte Tapioca Pudding Tree," *WA*, Fall 2000, 26, says it was a crate of boots. **85.** *Thirty-odd medics from the* … 11ABN, *G3 (Operations) Journal*, December 5, 1944. These medics were from the 221st Airborne Medical Company. **86.** *L-5s, with the back seat collapsed* … 11ABN, *11th Airborne Division History: February 1943 to May 1945*, 18, says forty-four men were flown out by these aircraft; the first casualty was flown out on December 4, 1944, the same day the engineers completed their work. **87.** *On the morning of December 5* … 11ABN, *G3 (Operations) Journal*, December 5, 1944; 511PIR, *Regimental History: Leyte Campaign*, 5.

Chapter 5: "All Is Useless!"

1. *But the good fortune was* … The attack was launched at 06:30, Cannon, M., *Leyte: The Return to the Philippines*, 299. **2.** *"There was a lot of wild* … Herbert Johansen, "'Banzai' at Burauen," *Air Force Magazine*, March 1945, 4. **3.** *The three hundred paragliders* … This was 1/187 GIR. Cannon, M., *Leyte: The Return to the Philippines*, 298; two companies per 187GIR, *The Leyte Campaign*, 7; Henry Burgess, "The Japanese Attack across Leyte into the Burauen Airfield," *Voice*, June 15, 1989, 23. **4.** *"firing at everything that* … Cannon, M., *Leyte: The Return to the Philippines*, 300. **5.** *Frank Farloni recalled a* … Frank Farloni, "Farloni's Tour of the Philippines," *Voice*, June 2000, 39. **6.** *At 10:30 in the morning, one of their* … This was 1/382nd Inf Regt of the 96th Inf Div ('The Deadeyes'); Cannon, M, *Leyte: The Return to the Philippines*, 300. Private Ova A. Kelly of the 382nd was posthumously awarded the Medal of Honor for his critical role in this attack. **7.** *At 12:45, Doug 'Tangle Foot' Quandt* … 11ABN, *G4 (Supply) Journal*, December 6, 1944; these numbers are based on: ten cases [3,000 rds each] of carbine ammo, fifty cases [1,000 per crate, containing four metal boxes of 250 rds each] of ammo for the belt-fed machineguns, forty cases [25 each] of hand grenades, along with another thirty cases of [10 each] rifle grenades. **8.** *A lone C-47 made one* … 511PIR, *S3 (Operations) Journal*, December 6, 1944. **9.** *Tragically, falling crates killed* … 511PIR, *Regimental History*, 8. **10.** *Previously used for growing potatoes* … Flanagan, Edward, *The Angels* [1948], 44. **11.** *Two minutes after declaring* … 511PIR, *S3 (Operations) Journal*, December 6, 1944. **12.** *Fortunately, by early evening* … Cannon, M, *Leyte: The Return to the Philippines*, 300. **13.** *But just as the sun was* … 408AQM, *Historical Operational Report K-2 Operation (Leyte)*, 10. Time of airdrop at 18:40 is based on 11ABN, *Division Artillery Unit Journal*; 127ENG, *K-2 Operation (October 20, 1944 to December 25, 1944)*, 2; Burgess, Henry, "The Japanese Attack across Leyte into the Burauen Airfield," 23; and Flanagan, Edward, *The Angels* [1948], 47. **14.** *American anti-aircraft guns* …

Flanagan, Edward, *The Angels* [1948], 49. **15.** *They are finally able to* ... William Kitchens, "Div HQ & Spec Troops," *Voice,* February 15, 1979, 6. **16.** *They were Mitsubishi Ki-57* ... Rottman, G. & Takizawa, A., *Japanese Paratroop Forces of World War II* (New York: Osprey Publishing, 2005), 47, the Allies referred to these transports as "Topsy." **17.** *"I knew even then that it* ... Kitchen, William, *Angels at War,* 103. Kitchen does not directly state that he was shot by friendly fire but does state that his comrades were shooting from behind him and that he was hit in the back; the conclusion is obvious. **18.** *At Swing's San Pablo* ... 11ABN, *G3 (Operations) Journal,* December 7, 1944. This was Lieutenant-Colonel Douglas C. Davis. **19.** *Someone wisely shut down* ... Henry Muller, "The Japanese Airborne Attack on Elements of the 11th Airborne," *Voice,* December 2014, 28. **20.** *First Lieutenant John G. Mabbatt* ... 511SIG, *Operational Historical Report on KING TWO Operation,* 6. **21.** *More than three dozen transports* ... 187GIR, *The Leyte Campaign,* 7. **22.** *Alert troops at Dulag* ... Rottman, G. and A. Takizawa, *Japanese Paratroop Forces of World War II,* 47; Cannon, M., *Leyte: The Return to the Philippines,* 300. In all, there were apparently fifty-one Japanese aircraft, including transports, bombers, and fighter escorts. **23.** *At Bayug airstrip, Captain David Carnahan* ... David Carnahan, "1944 Letter," *Voice,* November 15, 1988, 43. Carnahan was later awarded the Silver Star for his leadership. **24.** *Two men braved the chaos* ... 11ABN, GO #51, 1944, citation for PFC David S. Taylor. **25.** *The clipped bursts from* ... Richard Hoyt, "Leyte Operations (6 December 1944)," *Voice,* July 15, 1987, 11. **26.** *Green and white flares* ... 11ABN, *G2 (Intelligence) Journal,* December 8, 1944. **27.** *A pilot fleeing to safety* ... This was probably Captain Felix Coone. Flanagan, Edward, *The Angels* [1948], 50. **28.** *With darkness enveloping the airstrip* ... Hoyt, Richard, "Leyte Operations," 11. **29.** *The Japanese shrieked taunts* ... ibid.; Cannon, M, *Leyte: The Return to the Philippines,* 300. **30.** *"I gave the order* ... Carnahan, David, "1944 Letter," 43. **31.** *Across the airstrip, First Lieutenant Paul J. Pergamo* ... Flanagan, Edward, *The Angels* [1948], 50. Pergamo was in the 127AEB; see 11ABN, GO #30, 1945. **32.** *Technician Fifth Grade Doyle R. Lawrence* ... 127ENG, *Organization History,* 26. **33.** *At least three Americans* ... 11ABN, *G3 (Operations) Journal,* December 7, 1944. **34.** *"There was uncontrolled and* ... Cannon, M, *Leyte: The Return to the Philippines,* 302. **35.** *"About midnight, I took* ... Carnahan, David, "1944 Letter," 43. **36.** *Over at San Pablo, Swing* ... This was Tech4 Herman C. Hellman per Parachute Maint. Co, *Historical Record of Leyte Campaign,* 1, and 11ABN, GO #44, 1944. **37.** *As Swing's paragliders were already* ... Cannon, M, *Leyte: The Return to the Philippines,* 302. **38.** *The Japanese were determined* ... ibid., 294. **39.** *General Sosaku Suzuki took personal* ... ibid., 313. The chief of staff, Wachi, and six staff officers accompanied Suzuki. He departed Lubi on December 1 with the 26th Inf Div, per Tomochika, "The True Facts of the Leyte Operation," 28. Given that sources and captured intelligence vary on the size of Suzuki's expedition and that Japanese units on Leyte were all understrength, 1,700 is based on an estimation using the size of a battalion (~1,100) and a regiment (~3,800) as well as the following: as per 11ABN, *Operation KING II, Leyte Campaign,* 5, those units moving east were elements of the 26th Div cobbled together and known as Shigamatsu Force of 1,500 to 2,000; it is difficult to know how many of those troops took part in the

Burauen attack before returning west. According to Cannon, M., *Leyte: The Return to the Philippines*, 305, "Only a little more than a battalion of the 26th Div, which was to assist the 16th Div, managed to reach the airstrips.." The 16th Div apparently dispatched ~350 men according to Stahl, David, *Ōoka Shōhei's Writings on the Pacific War*, 294. 11ABN, *Operation KING II, Leyte Campaign*, 5, provides these numbers: "Remnants of the 16th Div estimated to be another 1,500 men, only 500 of whom could be considered combat effectives … ~200 reached a heavily wooded area north of Buri airstrip." According to GHQ, *SWPA Ultra Bulletin No. 563* (November 21–22, 1944), the Japanese expected there to be 300 to 500 hundred Allied aircraft on Leyte. **40.** *But their plan unraveled* … Paragraph based on: Tomochika, "The True Facts of the Leyte Operation," 19–28; Stahl, David, *Ōoka Shōhei's Writings on the Pacific War*, 274. **41.** *A Japanese general summarized* … Tomochika, "The True Facts of the Leyte Operation," 5. Also based on Stahl, David, *Ōoka Shōhei's Writings on the Pacific War*, 302. **42.** *Suzuki's men, strung out* … This was the 16th Div's attack per Stahl, *Ōoka Shōhei's Writings on the Pacific War*, 294. **43.** *Their plan to retake* … 127ENG, *K-2 Operation (October 20, 1944 to December 25, 1944)*, 2. The artillerymen were commanded by Lieutenant-Colonel Lukas E. 'Luke' Hoska Jr. The two units formed a provisional regiment under the command of Lieutenant-Colonel Douglas C. Davis, the combat engineer's commander. **44.** *Doyle Lawrence, who had once* … 127ENG, *Organization History*, 26. Lawrence was killed the next day. **45.** *Smoldering aircraft and dead bodies* … 127ENG, *K-2 Operation (October 20, 1944, to December 25, 1944)*, 3. **46.** *Private Bill Bowen maneuvered* … Unknown Author, "Silver Star Posthumously to PFC Bill Bowen," *Voice*, June 15, 1991, 14. **47.** *Michael Kalamas and several* … Michael Kalamas, "Letter to the Editor," *Voice*, July 15, 1993, 5. **48.** *With bullets striking all around* … This was Lloyd L. Peters per 127ENG, *Organization History*, 27. **49.** *At the same time* … This flag is now at West Point, and the two engineers were Houston Jolley and Allen Osborne per *Voice of the Angels* newsletter, No. 60. January 1985. Main account is from Jolley, Houston, "Personal Recollections, Part I," 8. **50.** *"There was no mistaking* … Kalamas, Michael, "Letter to the Editor," 2. **51.** *On the east side* … 127ENG, *K-2 Operation (October 20, 1944, to December 25, 1944)*, 3. **52.** *"They touched nothing else* … Carnahan, David, "1944 Letter," 43. **53.** *While Bayug was secure* … Cannon, M, *Leyte: The Return to the Philippines*, 302–303. **54.** *To clarify the situation* … 11ABN, *G3 (Operations) Journal*, December 7, 1944. **55.** *The holdouts radioed an* … 11ABN, Division Artillery Unit Journal, December 7, 1944; 32nd AA Brigade, *Report of Antiaircraft Action in the Leyte Campaign*, 4. **56.** *"Glad to see you* … These were elements of 1/149th Inf Reg, 38th Inf Div; see Cannon, M., *Leyte: The Return to the Philippines*, 303; Grigg, Martin, *The Operations of the 1st Battalion, 149th Infantry (38th Infantry Division) in the Battle for the Buri Airstrip*, 6. **57.** *Swing had already attempted* … 11ABN, *G3 (Operations) Journal*, December 7, 1944. **58.** *"Men fatigued. Casualties heavy* … ibid. **59.** *The battalion commander organized* … Cannon, M, *Leyte: The Return to the Philippines*, 303. **60.** *It took the first exhausted group* … ibid., 303; Grigg, Martin, *The Operations of the 1st Battalion, 149th Infantry (38th Infantry Division) in the Battle for the Buri Airstrip*, 8. **61.** *Of the eleven L-birds* … Japanese KIA from, Hoyt, Richard, "Leyte Operations," 11.

Regarding additional Japanese casualties: the 187GIR captured a document [found in 11ABN, *G2 (Intelligence) Periodic Report*, December 23, 1944] wherein the chief of staff, of the Japanese 16th Div states his unit's casualties were 630 and that the 300 paratroopers were "almost entirely wiped out." The number of destroyed aircraft vary; again, I have used eleven from 11ABN, *Operation KING II, Leyte Campaign*, 11, which states, "All but one of these planes were destroyed when Japanese parachutists attacked ... " (which reflects what Carnahan found). The Fifth Air Force provided fifteen planes and pilots from the 25th Liaison Squadron to continue aerial resupply work. Robert Broestl, "History of the 11th ABN DIV 408 Quartermaster Co. 1942–45," January 15, 1994, 42, states eleven out of seventeen L-birds were destroyed; parachutes per Parachute Maint. Co, *Historical Record of Leyte Campaign*, 1. **62.** *He then sent a message ...* 511PIR, *S1 (Personnel) Journal*, December 7, 1944.

Chapter 6: The Long Nightmare

1. *By the time Swing's message ...* Chapter title from: Bakken, Vincent H, "Leyte, which turned out to be one long nightmare ... " 511th PIR Association, *511th Parachute Infantry Regiment*, 70; 511PIR, *Regimental History*, 8. **2.** *"Hold the platoon here ...* 511th PIR Association, *511th Parachute Infantry Regiment*, 26. **3.** *"He landed on top of me ...* Jim Humphreys, "Mail Call, a letter to Joseph Vannier," *WA*, Fall 1996, 46. The dead Japanese is most likely the man killed by Lieutenant Randolph Kirkland, who led a recon patrol up the hill earlier that same day; Kirkland, Randolph, *Long Ago and Far Away*, 83. **4.** *The Japanese fled, leaving ...* 511PIR, *S1 (Personnel) Journal*, December 7, 1944. **5.** *The peak became known as ...* Vannier, Joseph, *I Co. Beacon*, November 1997, 2, claims they named it that same night. I Co. took the hill, then H Co. occupied it; I Co. came back up occupy half of the perimeter; Jerry Davis, "The Longest Night," *WA*, Winter 1993, 14. **6.** *As opposed to the trail ...* 511PIR, *S2 (Intelligence) Journal*, December 7, 1944; Ed Hogan, "The Longest Night II," *WA*, Fall 2000, 27. Another segment of the supply trail had been found by the Recon PLT on November 30. **7.** *At the same time ...* two hundred per 11ABN, *11th Airborne Division History*, 20. **8.** *The shootout pinned them ...* 511PIR, *S1 (Personnel) Journal*, December 7, 1944; 511PIR, *Regimental History*, 8. **9.** *"In the morning, we ...* , Leroy Butler, "Geronimo #13 or the South Pacific as I Saw It, Part II," *WA*, Winter 2001, 26. This was on the morning of December 8, 1944. **10.** *"Calvin Lincoln fired right ...* Butler, Leroy, "Thanksgiving–Christmas 1944," 11. **11.** *Forty-odd Japanese, their ...* forty-odd numbers from War Department, Press Branch. *Medal of Honor to Infantryman Who Gave Life to Save Platoon Leader*, 1. This was E Co, fighting the rear-guard action. **12.** *One of the belt-fed machineguns ...* George Hadac, "A Trooper's Story," *WA*, Winter 1999. **13.** *Fryar held his ground ...* 11ABN, *11th Airborne Division History*, 20. **14.** *Fryar, yelling commands back ...* ibid.; Smith, Jacques, *Oral History*. **15.** *He caught up to his platoon leader ...* the wounded private was Marvin D. Douglas per War Department, Press Branch. *Medal of Honor to Infantryman Who Gave Life to Save Platoon Leader*, 1. **16.** *Fryar sprung* *between the* … Fryar was posthumously awarded the division's first Medal of Honor. Details of Fryar's action: Medal of Honor Citation; 511th PIR Association, *511th Parachute Infantry Regiment*, 31; War Department, Press Branch. *Medal of Honor to Infantryman Who Gave Life to Save Platoon Leader*, 1. **17.** *"Tell my family that I* … War Department, Press Branch. *Medal of Honor to Infantryman Who Gave Life to Save Platoon Leader*, 1. **18.** *Leroy Butler and another* … The other man was J.D. Perry; Butler, Leroy, "Thanksgiving—Christmas 1944," 11; Butler, Leroy, "Geronimo #13 or the South Pacific as I Saw It, Part II," 26. **19.** *Its ten-inch, rifled barrel* … Eric Bergerud, *Touched with Fire: The Land War in the South Pacific* (New York: Penguin Books, 1996), 319. **20.** *"He almost didn't have* … Patrick O'Donnell, *Into the Rising Sun* (New York: Free Press, 2002), 21. *Dodging the same barrage* … Butler, Leroy, "Geronimo #13 or the South Pacific as I Saw It, Part II," 26. **21.** *They buried him in* … Butler, Leroy, "Thanksgiving–Christmas 1944," 11. **22.** *Several troopers, including Butler* … ibid. **23.** *Their retreat put them* … 511PIR, *Regimental History*, 8, says fifteen casualties the day before and twelve today, with six KIA. **24.** *"Adjusting our pot helmets* … All Gale this section from Miles Gale, "Banzai," *WA*, Winter 1993, 18. **25.** *'Big Ed' Hogan readied his* … Hogan, Edward, *A Dogface's War*, 19. *"The worst part* … Keith, Richard, "The Saga of Purple Heart Hill," 16; Whitehead, Herbert, *WWII Veteran Survey*, 7. Whitehead agreed with Keith about fear; when answering the question, "What factors improved moral?" he answered, "The discharge of your weapon." He also stated that "after initial contact, the fear was gone and morale high." **26.** *"We beat them back* … Gale, Miles, "Banzai," 18. **27.** *"Banzai attacks are not* … Keith, Richard, "The Saga of Purple Heart Hill," 16. **28.** *"Stand up, Joe* … Kliewer, Bob. *I Co. Beacon*, November 1996, 6. **29.** *"Come back here, you* … Gale, Miles, "Banzai," 18. **30.** *Corpses piled up with* … fifty-two killed per 511PIR, *S2 (Intelligence) Journal*, December 8, 1944. **31.** *"We had the firepower* … Miles Gale, "On the Trail in Leyte," *WA*, Spring 1994, 19. **32.** *"It doesn't make much* … Lindau, Bill, *With Tar Heels on Leyte*. The News and Observer, Raleigh, NC, February 11, 1945, 14. **33.** *"He asked me in perfect* … O'Donnell, Patrick, *Into the Rising Sun*, 161. **34.** *"I hadn't thought about* … All Vannier content from Vannier, Joseph, "Pearl Harbor Day on Maloney Ridge," 7. **35.** Heath was acclaimed for … 11ABN, *11th Airborne Division History: February 1943 to May 1945*, 21; Eugene Heath, "Expert Marksmanship," *WA*, April 1988, 10. **36.** *Another trooper, a former* … Steve Hegedus, "Big Red Rising Sun and Little Red Dots," *WA*, Spring 1997. This was Robert Williams; he added nine after one ambush. He had more than two dozen total. **37.** *"The corpse remained stuck* … LeRoy, Bob, *From My Foxhole to Tokyo*, 212. **38.** *Haugen reported that in* … 741 from 511PIR, *S2 (Intelligence) Journal*, December 9, 1944. I have noted Japanese casualty numbers as found in the official reports, but readers are advised that for a myriad of reasons, the counts can be over estimated. 1,054 EKIA is from 11ABN, *G2 (Intelligence) Periodic Report*, December 9, 1944. **39.** *But Haugen's men were* … 511 numbers are from 511PIR, *S1 (Personnel) Journal*, December 9, 1944, I included 'injured' in the wounded count. **40.** *"We were now under* … Kirkland, Randolph, *Long Ago and Far Away*, 86. **41.** *"you can hear everything* … Charles Sass, "Perimeter Thoughts at Night," *WA*, Spring 1997. **42.** *"After dark, one's eyes* … Marks,

Deane, "No One Smiled on Leyte," 25. **43.** *"When in doubt ...* Charles Sass, "First Sergeant X," *WA,* Summer 1997. **44.** *What's going on?* Hogan, Ed, "The Longest Night II," 27. **45.** *"I would watch for a ...* Marks, Deane, "No One Smiled on Leyte," 25. **46.** *"This worked well even ...* ibid. **47.** *The favored technique however ...* Miley, Buzz, *The Hand Grenade,* 8. **48.** *One trooper, sleeping on ...* George Floersch, "What Happened to PFC George Floersch?" *WA,* Fall 1994, 9. **49.** *On another night, when ...* Young, Stan, "One and One-Half Months on Leyte," 42. **50.** *"I was just about to ...* Floersch, George, "What Happened to PFC George Floersch?" 10. **51.** *"No medical supplies on hand ...* 511PIR, S3 *(Operations) Journal,* December 10, 1944. **52.** *While waiting for the replacement ...* 11ABN, G3 *(Operations) Journal,* December 9, 1944. This drop took place at Ananog; 11ABN, G3 *(Operations) Journal,* December 10, 1944. **53.** *After receiving Haugen's request ...* 11ABN, G3 *(Operations) Journal,* December 10, 1944. **54.** *"May have killed one ...* 11ABN, *Division Artillery Unit Journal,* December 10, 1944. This was on December 8. **55.** *They also inadvertently slew ...* 11ABN, G3 *(Operations) Journal,* December 9, 1944. **56.** *"Where are you going ...* Billingsley, James, *Oral History,* also confirmed in 11ABN, G3 *(Operations) Journal,* December 9, 1944. **57.** *Their morning attack failed ...* 11ABN, *Division Artillery Unit Journal,* December 9, 1944; Grigg, Martin, *The Operations of the 1st Battalion, 149th Infantry (38th Infantry Division) in the Battle for the Buri Airstrip,* 9. **58.** *After retreating, they requested ...* 11ABN, *Division Artillery Unit Journal,* December 9, 1944. **59.** *"lousy outfit ...* 11ABN, G3 *(Operations) Journal,* December 9, 1944. **60.** *Instead, he ordered the ...* ibid. **61.** *His initial briefing that ...* Grigg, Martin, *The Operations of the 1st Battalion, 149th Infantry (38th Infantry Division) in the Battle for the Buri Airstrip,* 10. **62.** *Making matters worse was ...* 11ABN, G3 *(Operations) Journal,* December 9, 1944. **63.** *But the Japanese refused ...* 11ABN, *Division Artillery Unit Journal,* December 10, 1944. **64.** *Running low on ammunition ...* Grigg, Martin, *The Operations of the 1st Battalion, 149th Infantry (38th Infantry Division) in the Battle for the Buri Airstrip,* 11. **65.** *After the infantry retook ...* 11ABN, *Division Artillery Unit Journal,* December 12, 1944; vs. more than three hundred via Grigg, Martin, *The Operations of the 1st Battalion, 149th Infantry (38th Infantry Division) in the Battle for the Buri Airstrip,* 15. **66.** *With Hard Rock's men ...* 11ABN, FO #5, December 8, 1944; 11ABN, G3 *(Operations) Journal,* December 9, 1944. **67.** *Swing assigned the two ...* 11ABN, FO #6, December 12, 1944. **68.** *But the six-hundred-plus ...* 11ABN, G3 *(Operations) Journal,* December 10, 1944. **69.** *They attacked both in ...* 11ABN, G3 *(Operations) Journal,* December 11, 1944, indicates sixteen, but Cannon, M., *Leyte: The Return to the Philippines,* 305, says thirty. I have used thirty given the number of Suzuki's troops that made it down from the mountains and that the G3 report was early in the fighting, which may account for the difference in EKIA. **70.** *At two in the morning ...* 11ABN, G3 *(Operations) Journal,* December 11, 1944; 2/188 led by Major [Thomas L. 'Tommy'] Mann and a company from the attached infantry; 11ABN, G3 *(Operations) Journal,* December 11, 1944. **71.** *Oblong in shape, the ...* Rock Hill description based on terrain and Vannier, Joseph, "Pearl Harbor Day on Maloney Ridge," 7; Flanagan, Edward, *The Angels* [1948], 59; Barnum, Richard, *The Operations of the 3rd Battalion, 511th Parachute Infantry,* 18. **72.** *"Food was* *becoming a ...* 511th PIR Association, *511th Parachute Infantry Regiment*, 26. **73.** *"Each soldier received about ...* Ralph Ermatinger, "Hunger, Leyte, 1944," *WA,* January 1988, 9. **74.** *"I don't think anyone ...* Marks, Deane, "No One Smiled on Leyte," 25. **75.** *Haugen and his staff ...* Young, Stan, "One and One-Half Months on Leyte," 42. **76.** *The men had cleared ...* Barnum, Richard, *The Operations of the 3rd Battalion, 511th Parachute Infantry,* 19. **77.** *"We could hear their ...* Miles Gale, "More About Leyte," *WA,* Winter 1994, 17. **78.** *Swing's quartermasters orchestrated another ...* 11ABN, *G3 (Operations) Journal,* December 12, 1944. **79.** *At the division's forward ...* 11ABN, *G3 (Operations) Journal,* December 12, 1944. **80.** *Wheeler's company departed without ...* G Co. left on December 11, 1944, per 511th PIR Association, *511th Parachute Infantry Regiment,* 26; 511PIR, *Regimental History: Leyte Campaign,* 6; see also Harry Swan, "Gotta Be One Helluva Shot," *WA,* Spring 1997; story of G Co, from 11ABN, *G3 (Operations) Journal,* December 13, 1944; 511PIR, *S3 (Operations) Journal,* December 15, 1944; David Webb, "The Poncho," *WA,* January 1988, 15. **81.** *The lead scouts went ...* 511PIR, *Regimental History,* 10; this on December 12. **82.** *The trail was blocked ...* ibid., 11. **83.** *"We have the Japs just ...* Bob Leroy, "My Christmas in Combat," *Voice,* January 15, 1997, 32. **84.** *In addition to the ...* 511PIR, *Regimental History,* 10, "During night (9-10) F Co, [in ambush pos] killed 85 Japs." **85.** *The Americans' pincer attacks against ...* US 77th Division landed at Deposito, three miles south of Ormoc on December 7, 1944. **86.** *Suzuki's attempts to organize ...* Tomochika, Yoshiharu, *The True Facts of the Leyte Operation,* 29; Cannon, M, *Leyte: The Return to the Philippines,* 305. **87.** *"From our point of ...* Kirkland, Randolph, *Long Ago and Far Away,* 87. **88.** *He ordered Haugen to ...* 11ABN, FO #6, December 12, 1944. **89.** *While 'Shippo' Shipley's men ...* 11ABN, *G3 (Operations) Journal,* December 12, 1944. **90.** *The knife-like ridges ...* Flanagan, Edward, *The Angels* [1948], 59. **91.** *The first assault on ...* 511PIR, *Regimental History,* 11, 08:00 attack by I Co. **92.** *"Instead of marching, it ...* Gale, Miles, "More About Leyte," 17. **93.** *"With all of your equipment ...* Keith, Richard, "The Saga of Purple Heart Hill," 16. **94.** *"and it exploded like ...* Butler, Leroy, "Geronimo #13 or the South Pacific as I Saw It, Part II," 26. **95.** *"Standard practice was to ...* Hogan, Edward, *A Dogface's War,* 24. **96.** *Ten hours later, they ...* 511PIR, *Regimental History,* 11; Approx. seventy EKIA via 511PIR, *S3 (Operations) Journal.* **97.** *"when the company was ...* Barnum, Richard, *The Operations of the 3rd Battalion, 511th Parachute Infantry,* 25. This December 15 attack was by I Co., reinforced with a PLT from HQ Co. and supported by H Co. **98.** *O'Conner's marksmanship claimed ...* 11ABN, GO #06, 1945; Gale, Miles, "More About Leyte," 17. **99.** *Another trooper, Paul L. McNees ...* 11ABN, GO #57, 1944. **100.** *In spite of O'Conner's ...* 511PIR, *Regimental History,* 12; 511PIR, *S3 (Operations) Journal,* December 15, 1944. **101.** *It was a heavy ...* 511PIR, *Regimental History,* 12, I Co.; five KIA, eight WIA; H Co; five WIA, HQ Co.; two KIA, five WIA, twenty-two EKIA. **102.** *Gale took his helmet ...* Gale, Miles, "More About Leyte," 17. **103.** *"bodies were twisted, and ...* Gale, Miles, "On the Trail in Leyte," 19; Joseph Vannier, "The I Company Beacon," *Voice,* July 1997, 32; Miles Gale, "Leyte to Richard Hoyt, dated Sep. 23, 1978," *Voice,* April 15, 1992, 11. Pete Diffenbaugh, a platoon leader in H Co., and Sgt. Enio DiLuigi were both shot and died of their wounds. **104.** *Late that afternoon, 'Chappie' Walker* ... LeRoy, Bob, *From My Foxhole to Tokyo,* 79. **105.** *He shared communion from* ... Vannier, Joseph, *I Co. Beacon,* May 1997, 3; Vannier, Joseph, *I Co. Beacon,* September 1996, 6. **106.** *The thirty-three-year-old chaplain* ... Edward Lahti, "A Hero is Dead—Dr. Lee E. Walker," *WA,* Spring 1997. **107.** *The L-birds flew low-level* ... Sixty degrees per Flanagan, Edward, *The Angels* [1948], 59; 511PIR, *Regimental History,* 11; 511PIR, *S3 (Operations) Journal,* December 15, 1944. **108.** *"We decided to just* ... Kenneth Fuller, "Some Recollections of an Old Airborne Solder," *WA,* Spring 2004, 4. **109.** *It was soon obvious* ... 11ABN, *G3 (Operations) Journal,* December 16, 1944. **110.** *"threw the hammer down* ... Ford, Charles, *The I Co. Beacon,* June 1997, 5. **111.** *Woynovich and his comrades* ... 11ABN, *G3 (Operations) Journal,* December 16, 1944; "In fact, Colonel Haugen had been personally involved in numerous fights and was gaining a reputation as a true fighter." From Cavanaugh, Stephen, "A Call to Arms, Part I," 6. **112.** *It was the first* ... Barnum, Richard, *The Operations of the 3rd Battalion, 511th Parachute Infantry,* 29. **113.** *"They came at us day* ... John A. Hash quoted in Charles Culbertson, "Jumping into History," *Voice,* December 1999, 48. **114.** *Haugen, suspecting the Japanese* ... 11ABN, *G3 (Operations) Journal,* December 16, 1944. Shipley to dispatched E Co. for an attack from the north, simultaneously another attack by B Co. from Rock Hill would go in from the south; *Loughrin Journal,* December 16, 1944. **115.** *Shipley acknowledged the order* ... ibid. Wilson commanded 2/187 GIR; this battalion, plus C Co. that had jumped into Manarawat, were temporarily under direct divisional control. **116.** *"There were dead Japs* ... Hadac, George, "A Trooper's Story." **117.** *The cannoneers expended the* ... 11ABN, *Division Artillery Unit Journal,* December 15, 1944. **118.** *So steady was the* ... 11ABN, *G3 (Operations) Journal,* December 16, 1944. **119.** *The skirmish raged for* ... Flanagan, Edward, *The Angels* [1989], 192. **120.** *On the far side of the* ... This was E Co. set up in Shippo's ambush position. **121.** *By 10:15, they were* ... *Loughrin Journal,* December 18, 1944. **122.** *"We all got on line* ... Marshall, Bert, "The Marshall Brothers, Part II," 6. **123.** *Within a few minutes* ... 511PIR, *S3 (Operations) Journal,* December 18, 1944; this was E Co.; 511PIR, *Regimental History,* 12. **124.** *Troopers jumped into the* ... ibid. **125.** *A survey found four-hundred-odd...* 511PIR, *Regimental Journal,* December 18, 1944. **126.** *Amongst the carnage, they* ... *Loughrin Journal,* December 18, 1944. **127.** *"He had been skinned* ... Marshall, Bert, "The Marshall Brothers, Part II," 6. Accounts of cannibalism are confirmed by multiple sources, including 511PIR, *Regimental Journal,* December 18, 1944; *Loughrin Journal,* December 18, 1944; Butler, Leroy, "Geronimo #13 or the South Pacific as I Saw It, Part II," 26; and 11ABN, *G3 (Operations) Journal,* December 19, 1944. **128.** *Leroy Butler lost two friends* ... See Bengtson, Roy, *Unit History,* 20; Butler, Leroy, "Geronimo #13 or the South Pacific as I Saw It, Part II," 26; Butler, Leroy, "Thanksgiving–Christmas 1944," 11; and Butler, Leroy, "Geronimo #13 or the South Pacific as I Saw It, Part I," 21. **129.** *"We found it hard* ... Marks, Deane, "No One Smiled on Leyte," 25. **130.** *Our troops were not* ... Cavanaugh, Stephen, "A Call to Arms, Part I," 6. **131.** *One of* the prisoners ... Fred Haan, "The Prisoner," *WA,* Summer 1995, 42. **132.** *At Haugen's disposal were* ... George Ito, "Linguist Paratroopers," *Voice,* July 15, 1996, 27; Ito, George, *Letters to the author.* Yoshida earned a Bronze Star for tapping a Japanese communication wire that ran along the supply trail on December 10. The language/intelligence course was at Camp Savage, Minnesota. **133.** *When asked if Suzuki's ...* 11ABN, G2 *(Intelligence) Periodic Report*, December 19–20, 1944; cannibalism from 11ABN, G2 *(Intelligence) Periodic Report*, December 17–18, 1944. **134.** *With Maloney Hill retaken ...* 511PIR, S1 *(Personnel) Journal*, December 19, 1944; 511PIR, *Regimental History*, 12. **135.** *Patrols between Rock Hill and ...* 11ABN, G2 *(Intelligence) Periodic Report*, December 18–19, 1944, outlines these skirmishes. **136.** *"Any unit found with ... Loughrin Journal*, December 19, 1944. **137.** *A three-round salvo exploded ...* 511PIR, *Regimental History*, 12, "Killed 2, wounded 20 (3 of these died); 511PIR, *Regimental Journal*, December 18, 1944. **138.** *Dog Company continued the ...* Deane Marks, "A Terrible Day on Leyte," WA, Fall 1992, 32. It was HQ Co. 2/511 and F Co. that headed back to Mahonag with the casualties, E Co. was already on Maloney Hill from the previous day's successful attack; see *Loughrin Journal*, December 17, 1944. **139.** *Major Frank S. 'Hacksaw' Holcombe ...* Jack Chambers, the executive officer, initially assumed command before Haugen put Major Frank S. 'Hacksaw' Holcombe in command. **140.** *Several troopers claimed they'd ...* Wentink, James, *Letter to Edward M. Flanagan*. **141.** *As Dog Company followed the ...* 511PIR, *Regimental History*, 12. **142.** *"these pitiable creatures would ...* Flanagan, Edward, *The Angels* [1948], 57; Tomochika, "The True Facts of the Leyte Operation," 35, provides chilling confirmation of this policy: "Commanders, employing persuasive language, frequently requested seriously wounded soldiers at the front to commit suicide. This was particularly common among personnel of the 1st Div, and it was pitiful. However, the majority died willingly. Only Japanese could have done a thing like this, and yet I could not bear to see the sight." **143.** *A quiet Texan solved the ...* Kirkland, Randolph, *Long Ago and Far Away*, 91. I have chosen not to disclose the name of this trooper, who was later killed in action. **144.** *All told the enemy body ... Loughrin Journal*, December 18, 1944. **145.** *With the attacks against ...* ibid., and 511PIR, *Regimental Journal*, December 18, 1944. **146.** *The arrival of Wilson's paragliders ...* 511PIR, *S3 (Operations) Journal*, December 18, 1944. **147.** *They shouldered cases of ...* 511PIR, *Regimental Journal*, December 16, 1944; *Loughrin Journal*, December 16, 1944; 511PIR, *S3 (Operations) Journal*, December 18, 1944. Contents of request from 511PIR, *S1 (Personnel) Journal*, December 16, 1944; 11ABN, *Division Artillery Unit Journal*, December 19, 1944. The scope of the supply effort is hard to convey without sounding hyperbolic; the paragliders did the yeoman's work bringing up supplies. **148.** *Carrying a case of rations ...* 511PIR, *Regimental History*, 13; *Loughrin Journal*, December 19, 1944. **149.** *The impractical route made ...* 511PIR, *Regimental Journal*, December 16, 1944; *Loughrin Journal*, December 16, 1944. **150.** *Swing had anticipated such ...* 11ABN, G3 *(Operations) Journal*, December 14, 1944. Each surgical team consisted of three officers and ten enlisted men each; they were attached to the div on October 10, 1944. Various details from: 11ABN, G1 *(Personnel) Journal*, November 29, 1944; 11ABN, G3 *(Operations) Journal*, December 14, 1944; Barney McGovern, "The 1318th Para Surgical Team," *Voice*, October 15, 1994, 8; "Glorious Medical Paratroopers," *Voice*, April 15, 1996, 28; and 11ABN, *History*, 11. **151.** *"Carnival City ... Undated* newspaper clipping, "Isolated Leyte Paratroopers Live in Silk-Lined Foxholes." **152.** *When possible, L-5 Sentinels ...* Flanagan, Edward, *The Angels* [1948], 44. **153.** *The L-birds saved time ...* 11ABN, *History*, 11. **154.** *Corporal Harold Spring became ...* Harold Spring, "Wounded in Action," *WA*, January 1988, 14; ———, "An Account of One Soldier's Will to Live," *WA*, June/July 1991, 13; Sam Tassone, "Unit History," *WA*, Winter 1991, 20. **155.** *"fevers of unknown origin ...* 408AQM, *Historical Operational Report K-2 Operation (Leyte)*, 12; fevers per *Loughrin Journal*, December 20, 1944. **156.** *"The first sunny day ...* Steve Hegedus, "A Bowel Movement Can Be Hazardous to Your Health," *WA*, Fall 1994, 30. **157.** *Only a lucky few ...* Marks, Deane, "No One Smiled on Leyte," 25. **158.** *"We used the dead ...* Cavanaugh, Stephen, "A Call to Arms, Part I," 6. **159.** *"Swing does not need ...* 11ABN, *G3 (Operations) Journal*, December 13, 1944; *Loughrin Journal*, December 19, 1944. **160.** *"Their perimeter is very ...* 11ABN, *G3 (Operations) Journal*, December 16, 1944. **161.** *A platoon from the ...* Cannon, M, *Leyte: The Return to the Philippines*, 322. **162.** *They were in bad ...* 511PIR, *S1 (Personnel) Journal*, December 21, 1944, G Co, had one officer and eleven men capable of making the trip. **163.** *"The rest of the ...* "Captain Wheeler Given Silver Star," *The Evening Sun*, Hanover, PA, February 5, 1945, 1. **164.** *But just six hundred ...* Cannon, M., *Leyte: The Return to the Philippines*, 323. **165.** *"clean up my backyard ...* 11ABN, *G3 (Operations) Journal*, December 16, 1944. **166.** *To get there, he ...* 11ABN, *G3 (Operations) Journal*, 18 and December 22, 1944, confirms Quandt was there, too. Swing wrote hyperbolically in a letter to his father-in-law, "As a matter of fact, I've walked clean across the 'd—' island, and it wasn't the most pleasant jaunt I ever took," but multiple sources have him flying into Manarawat, most notably 188GIR, *Historical Report of the 188th Paraglider Infantry in K-2 Operation*, 5, which confirms F Co. accompanied him from there. **167.** *Swing's combat engineers had ...* 127ENG, *K-2 Operation* (October 20 to December 25, 1944), 4. Carabao details from 188GIR, *Historical Report of the 188th Paraglider Infantry in K-2 Operation*, 5. **168.** *Seeing the conditions for ...* 11ABN, *G3 (Operations) Journal*, December 18, 1944; 11ABN, *G3 (Operations) Journal*, December 20, 1944. Smokes and ice cream per *G-1 Journal (November 29 to December 6, Periodic Report No. 3)*. Band and ice cream confirmed via 11ABN, *Operation KING II, Leyte Campaign*, 14. **169.** *"freshly laundered khakis ...* Repplier, Banning, "This Barringer Grad is 'Making Good.'" **170.** *Swing was impressed by ...* 11ABN, *Security Escort Memo*, dated December 28, 1944. **171.** *"General, I don't care ...* Repplier, Banning, "This Barringer Grad is 'Making Good.'" **172.** *At Mahonag, Swing found ...* *Loughrin Journal*, December 19, 1944. **173.** *Two more men were ...* 11ABN, *G3 (Operations) Journal*, December 18, 1944. The tragic story of Melvin B. Levy's death, as recounted by his best friend Rod Serling, can be found in Anne Serling, *As I Knew Him: My Dad, Rod Serling* (New York: Citadel Press, 2013), 55. **174.** *Lieutenant Foster Arnett ...* Robert Beightler, "Lieutenant Foster Arnett," *WA*, January 1990, 7. **175.** *"Get back in the ...* Young, Stan, "One and One-Half Months on Leyte," 42. **176.** *"Each of us was sobbing ...* Arnett Foster, "In Memoriam—Thomas D. Nestory, MD," *WA*, Fall 1999, 128. **177.** *From atop Rock Hill ...* 511th PIR Association, *511th Parachute Infantry Regiment*, 26, Sometimes called South Hill, Lathi Hill was heavily defended, and repeated attempts to seize it had failed. **178.** *Previous reconnaissance patrols found* ... H Co. made recon of west ridge (aka Hacksaw); Flanagan, Edward, *The Angels* [1948], 49. **179.** *On the morning of December 19* ... 11ABN, *Division Artillery Unit Journal*, December 18, 1944. **180.** *He even called in* ... ibid. These were batteries from 52nd FA, 24th Inf Div. **181.** *The "danger-close" radius* ... 511PIR, *S1 (Personnel) Journal*, December 19, 1944. **182.** *Captain Joe Stokes* ... *Loughrin Journal*, December 19, 1944. **183.** *Two hours after the* ... 511PIR, *S1 (Personnel) Journal*, December 19, 1944, this was H Co.; *Loughrin Journal*, December 19, 1944. **184.** *When they were twenty-five* ... *Loughrin Journal*, December 19, 1944. **185.** *"As soon as we started* ... Grant Neuteboom, "A Few Memories of Leyte and Friends," *Voice*, January 15, 1994, 15. **186.** *Haugen criticized the company* ... *Loughrin Journal*, December 19, 1944; 511PIR, *Regimental Journal*, December 19, 1944; 11ABN, *Division Artillery Unit Journal*, December 19, 1944. **187.** *Shells crashed into the* ... *Loughrin Journal*, December 20, 1944; 11ABN, *Division Artillery Unit Journal*, December 20, 1944. **188.** *Forward observer Stokes was* ... *Loughrin Journal*, December 20, 1944. **189.** *One company attacked on* ... 511PIR, *S1 (Personnel) Journal*, December 20, 1944. The two-company attack was H and I Cos. H Co. attacked on the left while I Co. flanked right and got to the top of the hill first. **190.** *"almost vertical* ... Vannier, Joseph, *I Co. Beacon*, November 1997, 3. **191.** *"As we neared the top* ... 511th PIR Association, *511th Parachute Infantry Regiment*, 26; James Hendry, "Letter to the Editor," *Voice*, April 15, 1979, 7. **192.** *Crawling up with them* ... Barnum, Richard, *The Operations of the 3rd Battalion, 511th Parachute Infantry*, 27. 193. *It was a dangerous moment* ... 511PIR, *Regimental History*, 13. **194.** *"ducked down into their* ... 511th PIR Association, *511th Parachute Infantry Regiment*, 26. **195.** *"The Japanese soldier had* ... Vannier, Joseph, *I Co. Beacon*, November 1997, 3. **196.** *By 12:15, the first hill* ... *Loughrin Journal*, December 20, 1944. **197.** *"Most of the positions* ... 511th PIR Association, *511th Parachute Infantry Regiment*, 26. **198.** *"Just before the expected* ... Unknown Author, "Lt. Maylock," *Voice*, July 15, 1995, 14. **199.** *The assault accounted for* ... *Loughrin Journal*, December 20, 1944; 511PIR, *Regimental History*, 13. **200.** *They would pass through* ... Flanagan, Edward, *The Angels* [1948], 59; *Loughrin Journal*, December 20, 1944. **201.** *He assigned two officers* ... *Loughrin Journal*, December 21, 1944. Cook and Goodlet were the two officers. **202.** *"The foul odor was* ... Gale, Miles, "On the Trail in Leyte," 19. **203.** *"Talk about griping and* ... Fuller, Kenneth, "Some Recollections of an Old Airborne Soldier," 4. **204.** *Few men had kept* ... Butler, Leroy, "Geronimo #13 or The South Pacific as I Saw It, Part II," 26; Butler, Leroy, "Thanksgiving–Christmas 1944," 11. **205.** *When Swing marched in* ... *Loughrin Journal*, December 21, 1944; 511PIR, *S3 (Operations) Journal*, December 21, 1944. **206.** *"When the general and* ... Butler, Leroy, "Thanksgiving–Christmas 1944," 11. **207.** *"triumphant march to the* ... Ford, Charles, *I Co. Beacon*, January 1997, 4. **208.** *"Our general wasn't too* ... Jones, Harold, *Oral History*. **209.** *Haugen greeted Swing at* ... Swing/Haugen conversation is based on details from *Loughrin Journal*, December 21, 1944. **210.** *The growing body count* ... 11ABN, *G2 (Intelligence) Journal*, December 21, 1944. **211.** *Haugen paused the discussion* ... 511PIR, *S1 (Personnel) Journal*, December 21, 1944. **212.** *"We have assaulted hill...* 511PIR,

Regimental Journal, December 21, 1944. **213.** *The bad news was...* 511PIR, S2 *(Intelligence) Journal*, December 21, 1944. **214.** *At 04:00, Hacksaw's lead ...* 11ABN, G2 *(Intelligence) Journal*, December 21, 1944. This was D Co. **215.** *Thirty minutes later, scout...* ibid. **216.** *a lanky, six-foot-two New Yorker ...* Bittorie description based on Marks, Deane, "No One Smiled on Leyte," 25. "Rat's ass!" claim has also been attributed to Dave Vaughn in Edward Sorensen, "Company D Stories," *WA*, Spring 2011, 7, but most agree it was Bittorie who initiated it. In all the chaos, it's easy to understand the confusion. **217.** *They'd broken several ...* Cavanaugh, Stephen, *Rats Ass Charge*, 7; George Schlobohm, "Letter to the Editor," *Voice*, March 15, 1986, 40. **218.** *"Rat's Ass ... Loughrin Journal*, December 22, 1944; 511PIR, *Regimental Journal*, December 22, 1944. While accounts of what was yelled vary, all agree on 'Rat's ass!' and others include "Banzaiiiiiiiiii!" "Hubba, Hubba!" and the regiment's favorite chant, "48 ... 49 ... 50 ... SOME SHIT!" **219.** *"It was like shooting ...* Charlie Jones, "Company D Stories," *WA*, Fall 2011, 17. **220.** *"You'd see a Japanese ...* This was Edwin Sorenson of D Co., 511th PIR, per O'Donnell, Patrick, *Into the Rising Sun*, 165. **221.** *Their initial volley accounted ... Loughrin Journal*, December 22, 1944. **222.** *Soon the enemy body ...* 511PIR, *Regimental History*, 14. This was D Co. with F Co. **223.** *"stressed the value of ... Loughrin Journal*, December 22, 1944. **224.** *At 08:30, Swing and ...* 511PIR, S3 *(Operations) Journal*, December 22, 1944. **225.** *"passing through our perimeter ...* 511PIR, *Regimental History*, 14. **226.** *For most troopers, it ...* James Hendry, "Mahonag to the Sea," *WA*, Fall 1999, 54. **227.** *Much to the glee of Deane Marks ...* Marks, Deane, "No One Smiled on Leyte," 25. **228.** *"They scattered and started ...* Davis, Jerry, *80 Years of Dogs*, 34. **229.** *Meanwhile, the early morning ... Loughrin Journal*, December 22, 1944. **230.** *"The trails everywhere were ...* Giordano, Joseph, *The Operations of Company G 187th Glider Infantry Regiment*, 13. **231.** *It was 10:00 by ...* 511PIR, S1 *(Personnel) Journal*, December 22, 1944; *Loughrin Journal*, December 22, 1944. **232.** *"breakneck ...* and *It was difficult ...* Giordano, Joseph, *The Operations of Company G 187th Glider Infantry Regiment*, 13. **233.** *"Needless to say ...* Cavanaugh quoted in Jane Carrico, "CSM John Bittorie," *WA*, Summer 2011, 14. Lt. Barnum claimed, "At this point, D Co. had advanced to the foothills and had to withdraw about two miles to allow the 187th to take over." Barnum, Richard, *The Operations of the 3rd Battalion, 511th Parachute Infantry*, 29. **234.** *Two hours later, a ...* Giordano, Joseph, *The Operations of Company G 187th Glider Infantry Regiment*, 13. **235.** *"We've got them with ...* ibid. **236.** *"Nice job, Cavanaugh ...* Cavanaugh, Stephen, "A Call to Arms, Part I," 6. **237.** *From the top of a gorge ...* Giordano, Joseph, *The Operations of Company G 187th Glider Infantry Regiment*, 14. **238.** *An hour later, with ... Loughrin Journal*, December 22, 1944. **239.** *Swing was surprised to ...* ibid. Apparently, the 7th Inf. Div. had only moved six hundred yards inland from the coast and claimed it took them six days to bring up their supplies. **240.** *A few stay-behind snipers ...* Giordano, Joseph, *The Operations of Company G 187th Glider Infantry Regiment*, 16. **241.** *Swing was the first trooper ...* ibid., 3. **242.** *By the end of the ...* 11ABN, G2 *(Intelligence) Journal*, December 21, 1944. **243.** *"Have told the corps ...* Swing, Joseph, *Dear General*, letter dated December 24, 1944. **244.** *Swing later claimed to ...* 511PIR, S2

(Intelligence) Journal, December 22, 1944, for a total of 1,943 to date. **245.** *Swing wanted all the* ... *Loughrin Journal*, December 22, 1944. **246.** *The more seriously wounded* ... Marshall, Bert, "The Marshall Brothers, Part I," 6; two hundred locals from 511PIR, *S1 (Personnel) Journal*, December 24, 1944. **247.** *Haugen's medics set up* ... 511PIR, *S1 (Personnel) Journal*, December 22, 1944; *Loughrin Journal*, December 22, 1944. 1/511 stayed at Mahonag, 3/511 moved eight hundred yards up to where the Rat's Ass attack took place, and 2/511 set up a perimeter in the foothills. These points served as shuttle stops for the wounded carrying parties. **248.** *They shuttled over two hundred* ... via 511PIR, *S1 (Personnel) Journal*, December 22, 1944. The two hundred count is based on the 511th's final Leyte casualty numbers of 86 KIA, 249 WIA, 11 IIA, 16 DOW; presuming several troopers were evacuated back to Burauen via Manarawat, I used "over two hundred" in this sentence. **249.** *"All right, on your feet* ... Serling essay via Walker, Gerald, ed., *My Most Memorable Christmas* (Pocket Books, 1963). **250.** *Serling limped down the* ... Serling, Anne, *As I Knew Him*, 56. One of Serling's wrists was also hit by shrapnel. **251.** *"looked like a brown* ... 511th PIR Association, *511th Parachute Infantry Regiment*, 74. **252.** *'Little Joe' Vannier flashed* ... Joseph Vannier, "From Out of the Past on Christmas Eve," *WA*, Summer 1998.

Chapter 7: Mopping Up

1. *When the line of rag-tag* ... A total of 168 patients were evacuated per 11ABN, *Operation KING II, Leyte Campaign*, 12. **2.** *Haugen, suffering a fever* ... *Loughrin Journal*, December 25, 1944. **3.** *"As we passed through* ... James Hendry, "A Night of Peace," *WA*, October 1988, 1. **4.** *Leroy Butler had tightened* ... Butler, Leroy, "Geronimo #13 or The South Pacific as I Saw It, Part II," 26. **5.** *"I recall that I* ... Walter, William, "Company D Stories," 14. **6.** *As the sun set* ... Hendry, James. "A Night of Peace," 1. **7.** *The next morning, trucks* ... 511PIR, *Regimental History*, 15. **8.** *"It took us a month* ... Fuller, Kenneth, "Some Recollections of an Old Airborne Soldier," 4. **9.** *As welcome as the* ... Walter, William, "Company D Stories," 14. **10.** *Lieutenant Miles Gale, who* ... Miles Gale, "Leyte to Luzon, a Vivid Remembrance," *WA*, Fall 1999, 87. **11.** *"I spent a lot* ... Butler, Leroy, "Geronimo #13 or The South Pacific as I Saw It, Part II," 26. **12.** *"General Yamashita has sustained* ... Scott, James, *Rampage*, 51. **13.** *"Whoever coined that phrase* ... Fuller, Kenneth, "Some Recollections of an Old Airborne Soldier," 4. **14.** *"When you fight someone* ... Richard Penwell, *Oral History*, NOLA. **15.** *For the paragliders* ... 11ABN, *FO #8*, December 25, 1944. **16.** *The track there led* ... 11ABN, *G2 (Intelligence) Periodic Report*, December 24, 1944, not the "1,000 Japanese" as mentioned in Flanagan, Edward, *The Angels* [1989], 192. **17.** *Additionally, well-camouflaged, log-reinforced* ... 187GIR, *The Leyte Campaign*, 10; 11ABN, *G2 (Intelligence) Periodic Report*, December 28, 1944. **18.** *Swing had contained the* ... Lahti, Edward, *Memoirs of an Angel*, 58. **19.** *"Purple Heart Hill* ... multiple attempts by 2/188 per Flanagan, Edward, *The Angels* [1989], 192. **20.** *The paragliders added to* ... ibid., 193; Flanagan, Edward, *The Angels* [1948], 160. **21.** *A full company, using* ... This was F Co. **22.** *With the escape routes* ...

There were multiple attacks, but the main effort was on December 29, 1944. **23.** *His assault battalion made* ... This was 2/188. **24.** *"We just got to* ... Chiesa was in E Co. per 188. Flanagan, Edward, *The Angels* [1989], 193. Roscoe Kelly was Chiesa's platoon sergeant. **25.** *A search of the* ... 238 EKIA via 11ABN, G2 *(Intelligence) Periodic Report*, December 28, 1944. **26.** *The Angels guessed hundreds* ... Flanagan, Edward, *The Angels* [1989], 193; Flanagan, Edward, *The Angels* [1948], 160. **27.** *"We shall seek and* ... Scott, James, *Rampage*, 50. **28.** *On December 13, Yamashita* ... Cannon, M, *Leyte: The Return to the Philippines*, 362. **29.** *He slipped through the* ... ibid., 314. **30.** *Trying to regain control* ... Stahl, David, *Ōoka Shōhei's Writings on the Pacific War*, 303; Stahl quotes 20,000 holdouts (the number I used); McManus, John, *Island Infernos*, 539, states "about fifteen thousand." **31.** *"area was admirable for* ... Tomochika, Yoshiharu, "The True Facts of the Leyte Operation," 41–50. **32.** *They were to hold* ... Cannon, M, *Leyte: The Return to the Philippines*, 362; prolonged, self-sustaining holding actions (*jikatsu jikyū*) from Stahl, *Ōoka Shōhei's Writings on the Pacific War*, 279. **33.** *"maybe in two or* ... This was General Gyosaku Morozumi via interrogation in Tomochika, "The True Facts of the Leyte Operation," 7. **34.** *"I am exhausted* ... Scott, James, *Rampage*, 50. **35.** *The extent of the Japanese suffering* ... Numbers are from Cannon, M, *Leyte: The Return to the Philippines*, 365. Japanese estimated there were 61,800 on the island; American numbers combine Sixth and Eighth Army numbers for a total of 80,557 EKIA, and 828 POWs. Of those, the 11th ABN claimed 5,760 EKIA and 12 POWs, a 23:1 kill ratio as per 11ABN, *11th Airborne Division History: February 1943 to May 1945*, 22. The 511th claimed a 45:1 kill ratio in 511th PIR Association, *511th Parachute Infantry Regiment*, 30. The US also lost 2,500 sailors and aviators in the battle. **36.** *Having been relieved by* ... This was the 96th Div; see Cannon, M, *Leyte: The Return to the Philippines*, 365. **37.** *Despite Swing's hopes, MacArthur* ... Jacobs, Edward W, *History Notes*, December 29, 1944. **38.** *the "orthodox" landing* ... Swing, Joseph, *Dear General*, letter dated December 24, 1944. **39.** *His attempts to have* ... Robert Ross Smith, *Triumph in the Philippines. US Army in World War II* (Washington, DC: Center of Military History, United States Army, 1991), 221. **40.** *"[MacArthur's] staff is a pain in the neck* ... Swing, Joseph, *Dear General*, letter dated December 24, 1944. The Angels were transferred to the Eighth Army on December 26, 1944. **41.** *Eichelberger arrived in the* ... John McManus, *Fire and Fortitude: The US Army in the Pacific War, 1941–1943* (New York: Dutton Caliber, 2019), 308. **42.** *"a secondary landing might* ... Swing, Joseph, *Dear General*, letter dated December 30, 1944. **43.** *MacArthur agreed and gave* ... Smith, Robert, *Triumph in the Philippines*, 222. **44.** *Eichelberger labeled "indefinite plans* ... Eichelberger, Robert, *Diary*, January 27, 1945. **45.** *"prepared to advance north* ... 188GIR, *Historical Report of the 188th Paraglider Infantry in [MIKE VI] Operation, Luzon, Philippine Islands*, 24. **46.** *"Task Force Shoestring* ... Robert Eichelberger, *Dear Miss Em: General Eichelberger's War in the Pacific, 1942–1945* (Westport, Connecticut: Greenwood Press, 1972), 206. **47.** *If the airdrop got* ... first pass was Regt HQ, 2nd BN, 3rd BN (-two cos.), and commo PLT per Edward Lahti, "Combat Jump," *WA*, April 1989, 11. Initially two howitzers, then the other ten per US Pacific Warfare Board, *Report No. 11, Parachute Field Artillery*, June 19, 1945, 1. **48.** *A garrison of five hundred* ...

Smith, Robert, *Triumph in the Philippines*, 223; 11ABN, *FO #10*, February 24, 1945. **49.** *The assumption was that ...* Eighth Army, *Report of the CG Eighth Army on the Nasugbu and Bataan Operations*, 38. **50.** *"Well, half a loaf ...* Swing, Joseph, *Dear General*, letter dated January 25, 1945. **51.** *"throw rear areas into ...* GHQ, SWPA, *Ultra Bulletins*, No. 582 (December 10–11, 1944) and No. 587 (December 15–16, 1944). **52.** *While Swing's officers scrambled ...* 188GIR, *Part I*, 2. **53.** *Private Bill Lindau sorted ...* Lindau, Bill, *With Tar Heels on Leyte*. The News and Observer, Raleigh, NC, February 11, 1945, 14. **54.** *Unfortunately, rear-echelon personnel ...* Gale, Miles, "Leyte to Luzon," 87. **55.** *Also coming ashore were ...* Eighth Army, *Report of the CG Eighth Army on the Nasugbu and Bataan Operations*, 35, says 956 replacements, getting them to ~8,200; see also Flanagan, Edward, *The Angels* [1989], 215. **56.** *Most went to Haugen's ...* Casualty numbers from Jacobs, Edward W, *History Notes*, December 30, 1944. 11th ABN totals were cited as KIA: 126, DOW: 30, SWA: 47, LWA: 315, MIA: 14, for a total of 532. 511PIR casualty numbers via 511PIR, *S1 (Personnel) Journal*, December 24, 1944, reported as, KIA: 85, DOW: 16, SWIA: 2, MIA: 13, IIA: 11, WIA: 251, for a total of 378, which is 71.05% of the div's total. **57.** *"We got some replacements ...* Lahti, Edward, *Memoirs of an Angel*, 67; replacement numbers per 11ABN, *G1 (Personnel) Journal*, December 20 to December 27, 1944, *Periodic Report No. 6*, indicates that just over three hundred and thirty men arrived, but due to the division's records ending in December, it is difficult to determine how many replacements arrived in total. **58.** *There were other promotions ...* Summarized from Kirkland, Randolph, *Long Ago and Far Away*, 92; Flanagan, Edward, *The Angels* [1989], 209; Hoppenstein, Isaac, *The Operations of the 187th GIR in the Landing at Nasugbu*, 12. **59.** *"When I was assigned ...* Charles Sass, "Just Part of the Family," *WA*, Fall 1998. **60.** *"We were so tired ...* Marks, Deane, "No One Smiled on Leyte," 25. **61.** *A curious squad waded ...* Henry Burgess, "Joe Swing & His 10,000 Thieves," *Voice*, November 15, 1989, 25. **62.** *"He stood around and ...* ibid. **63.** *"The lieutenant told us ...* Jerry Davis, "The Strangest Detail," *WA*, Fall 1999, 84. The initial collection points were Manarawat and Rock Hill, and later Dulag; the officer in charge of this detail was Lt. Melvin A. Levins along with a dental officer. See 408AQM, *Historical Operational Report K-2 Operation (Leyte)*, 11. **64.** *The first man they buried ...* Kirkland, Randolph, *Long Ago and Far Away*, 93. **65.** *"One of the men ...* Davis, Jerry, *80 Years of Dogs*, 34. **66.** *"There was a site ...* Kirkland, Randolph, *Long Ago and Far Away*, 94. **67.** *"There always was that feeling ...* Marks, Deane, "No One Smiled on Leyte," 25. **68.** *Map studies were followed ...* Augustin, James, *Once an Angel*, 26; Hoppenstein, Isaac, *The Operations of the 187th GIR in the Landing at Nasugbu*, 11.

Chapter 8: Task Force Shoestring

1. *The naval flotilla of ...* 11ABN, *Warning Order No. 2, Annex No 1*: Troop List, Total Personnel: 8,942 total, 6,462 by sea and 2,480 by air; fifteen days from Sixth Army, *Memorandum to Colonel Leaf*, 1; 11ABN, *Report After Action with the Enemy, Operation MIKE VI*, 38, these included thirty-two LCIs (Landing Craft,

Infantry), eight LSMs (Landing Ship, Medium), and six LSTs (Landing Ship, Tank) and four APDs. **2.** *At 07:15, two of the* ... 11ABN, *History,* 13. **3.** *"they all hit the* ... D.J. McSweeny, "C-127th Engineers," *Voice,* June 15, 1982, 16. **4.** *Boatswains gunned their landing* ... Time via Hoppenstein, Isaac, *The Operations of the 187th GIR in the Landing at Nasugbu,* 18; 11ABN, *History,* 13. **5.** *The next wave of* ... This was 1/188 GIR, Hoppenstein, Isaac per *The Operations of the 187th GIR in the Landing at Nasugbu,* 18. Higgens boats confirmed via Smith, Robert, *Triumph in the Philippines,* 224. **6.** *By the time the* ... Incoming fire started at 09:12 per Hoppenstein, Isaac, *The Operations of the 187th GIR in the Landing at Nasugbu,* 19. The third wave landed between 08:30 and 09:00. **7.** *"became exasperated because the* ... Flanagan, Edward, *The Angels* [1989], 225. **8.** *Not far from Swing* ... Hoppenstein, Isaac, *The Operations of the 187th GIR in the Landing at Nasugbu,* 20. **9.** *paragliders were fanning out* ... Anthony Genematas, "Company E, 187th Regiment: HQ Second Battalion, Nasugbu to Manila," *Voice,* August 15, 1984, 12. There were lots of unit movements at this time: C Co. [CO Captain Malcolm Stanford] headed south for Lian; E Co. [CO George Ori] proceeded to Wawa and relieved G Co. of 188th; C Co. was relieved by A Co. 188 so they could move to vic. San Diego Point. G Co. 187 [CO Lt. Harrison Merritt] attacked and cleared San Diego Point; see 11ABN, *G3 (Operations) Periodic Reports No. 1,* January 31, 1945. **10.** *In Nasugbu, Swing and* ... Leister, Albert, *Operations of the 11th Airborne Division from Nasugbu to Manila,* 12; CP loc. per Leister, Albert, *Operations of the 11th Airborne Division from Nasugbu to Manila,* 8. **11.** *Despite prior reconnaissance and assurances* ... Eighth Army, *Report of the CG Eighth Army on the Nasugbu and Bataan Operations,* 5. **12.** *While the paragliders marched* ... Hoppenstein, Isaac, *The Operations of the 187th GIR in the Landing at Nasugbu,* 20. While this was going, 1/187 landed, moving off the beach to assemble at the Don Pedro Sugar Central as division reserve. In the early afternoon, they were attached to the 188th, which had pushed toward Tagaytay Ridge. **13.** *The paragliders halted three hundred* ... ibid., 23. **14.** *When they arrived at* ... 11ABN, *Report After Action with the Enemy, Operation MIKE VI,* 27. **15.** *Waiting in Nasugbu to* ... Vanderpool, Jay, *Letter to Edward M. Flanagan, May 29, 1984.* Vanderpool was born in 1917 and commissioned on April 5, 1941; other Vanderpool details from Bruce Henerson, *Rescue at Los Baños: The Most Daring Prison Camp Raid of World War II* (New York: William Morrow, 2015); and Krivdo, Michael, *Major Jay D. Vanderpool,* 22. **16.** *titling himself "guerrilla coordinator* ... and following details from Vanderpool, Jay, *Letter to Edward M. Flanagan, May 29, 1984.* **17.** *His unit, led by* ... Francisco Quesada, "Guerrillas & 11th A/B Division, Nasugbu to Manila," *Voice,* March 15, 1981, 8. **18.** *Vanderpool found a good* ... Jim Holzem, "Jim Holzem's Story," *Voice,* June 15, 1982, 10. **19.** *The objective was Tagaytay Ridge* ... Eighth Army, *Report of the CG Eighth Army on the Nasugbu and Bataan Operations,* 16; guerrilla reports from Hoppenstein, Isaac, *The Operations of the 187th GIR in the Landing at Nasugbu,* 23. **20.** *"I am very keen about* ... Eichelberger, Robert, *Dear Miss Em,* 206. **21.** *He saw an opportunity* ... Eichelberger, Robert, *Dear Miss Em,* 215. **22.** *"If he is a great* ... Eichelberger, Robert, *Dear Miss Em,* 214. **23.** *Once past the gleeful* ... 11ABN, *11th Airborne Division History,* 24. 188 GIR was racing up Hwy 17, while 187

GIR was clearing Nasugbu and Wawa. **24.** *By midafternoon, they were* ... Eighth Army, *Report of the CG Eighth Army on the Nasugbu and Bataan Operations*, 14. **25.** *On the far side* ... 11ABN, *G3 (Operations) Periodic Reports No. 1*, January 31, 1945; Smith, Robert, *Triumph in the Philippines*, 225. **26.** *For Eichelberger and Swing* ... Eighth Army, *Report of the CG Eighth Army on the Nasugbu and Bataan Operations*, 16. **27.** *Combat engineers, commanded by* ... 127ENG, *Organization History, Section IV*, 2. This was A Co, 127 AEB. **28.** *At midnight, after slogging* ... 1/187 took point here until 00:30 as per 11ABN, *G3 (Operations) Periodic Reports No. 2*, February 1, 1945. **29.** *They pushed through sporadic* ... 11ABN, *G3 (Operations) Periodic Reports No. 2*, February 1, 1945. At 02:20, first resistance encountered. **30.** *"a thimble at the* ... Leister, Albert, *Operations of the 11th Airborne Division from Nasugbu to Manila*, 16. **31.** *As the paragliders crawled* ... 11ABN, *G3 (Operations) Periodic Reports No. 2*, February 1, 1945. **32.** *four 75mm pack howitzers* ... Douglas Quandt, "Fifth Wheel," *Voice*, September 15, 1983, 5; 11ABN, *Operations Report, Operation MIKE VI*, 2. The CO of D Batt./457 PFAB was Capt. Lou Burris; see Hoppenstein, Isaac, *The Operations of the 187th GIR in the Landing at Nasugbu*, 22. **33.** *But rifle fire still* ... Leister, Albert, *Operations of the 11th Airborne Division from Nasugbu to Manila*, 17. One 155, seven 105s, six 75s, and 37s with ~250 men; ~400 infantry in the caves and trenches of Mt. Aiming per 11ABN, *Report After Action with the Enemy, Operation MIKE VI*, 28; Smith, Robert, *Triumph in the Philippines*, 226. **34.** *With the sun well up* ... From Eighth Army, *Report of the CG Eighth Army on the Nasugbu and Bataan Operations*, 46; Flanagan, Edward, *The Angels* [1989], 235; Leister, Albert, *Operations of the 11th Airborne Division from Nasugbu to Manila*, 17. **35.** *While the Japanese hunkered* ... Flanagan, Edward, *The Angels* [1989], 235. The 1/188 attacked left while 1/187 went up the road/held the middle and 2/188 went south toward Batulao. The Recon/pathfinders appear to have hiked around Cariliao to the north; OPFOR numbers in this area per Smith, Robert, *Triumph in the Philippines*, 224. **36.** *By noon, a company* ... 11ABN, *G3 (Operations) Periodic Reports No. 2*, February 1, 1945. This was A Co.; Lee was KIA on March 19, 1945; see Smith, Robert, *Triumph in the Philippines*, 226. **37.** *Their close-quarters assault* ... Flanagan, Edward, *The Angels* [1989], 235. **38.** *Lee's men spent the* ... 11ABN, *Report After Action with the Enemy, Operation MIKE VI*, 2; 11ABN, *G3 (Operations) Periodic Reports No. 2*, February 1, 1945. It was the rest of 1/188 that joined A Co. atop Mt. Aiming. **39.** *The battalion cutting up* ... According to map from Flanagan, Edward, *The Angels* [1989], 233; 11ABN, *Report After Action with the Enemy, Operation MIKE VI*, 2; 1/197 cut up the middle. **40.** *But it came at* ... 11ABN, *G3 (Operations) Periodic Reports No. 2*, February 1, 1945, states casualties for period ending 18:00 were twelve KIA, forty-one WIA; but 11ABN, *Operations Report, Operation MIKE VI*, 2, states that in the first twenty-eight hours, there were sixteen KIA, forty-nine WIA. **41.** *Friday, February 2, dawned* ... This attack was at 08:30 per 11ABN, *G3 (Operations) Periodic Reports No. 3*, February 2, 1945. **42.** *Pack howitzers threw salvos* ... Some of these positions were as far away as three miles to the east, at Kaytitingal; see Flanagan, Edward, *The Angels* [1948], 73. **43.** *Two miles east of* ... 11ABN, *Report After Action with the Enemy, Operation MIKE VI*, 28; enemy at Aga, etc. via Eighth Army, *Report of the CG Eighth Army* *on the Nasugbu and Bataan Operations,* 12. **44.** *The paragliders continued forward* ... Flanagan, Edward, *The Angels* [1948], 73; 11ABN, *G3 (Operations) Periodic Reports No. 3,* February 2, 1945. **45.** *Combat engineers bridged the* ... 11ABN, *Operations Report, Operation MIKE VI,* 2. This was the 127 AEB. **46.** *The day's advance had* ... 11ABN, *G3 (Operations) Periodic Reports No. 3,* February 2, 1945, says casualties for period to 18:00 were four KIA, eight WIA. **47.** *Infiltrators crept through the* ... This was the 675 GFAB per Flanagan, Edward, *The Angels* [1989], 236. **48.** *At 08:20, an hour* ... 11ABN, *G3 (Operations) Periodic Reports No. 4,* February 3, 1945. **49.** *It grew louder as* ... Walsh, Louis, *Report on Airborne Operations in the Pacific,* 2, says fifty-eight aircraft; Coulter, John, *The Operations of the Headquarters Company, 3rd BN, 511 PIR in the Attack on Manila,* says fifty-one. **50.** *Fortunately, just as they* ... Walsh, Louis, *Report on Airborne Operations in the Pacific,* 2. Several men from the recon platoon and a four-man pathfinder team were already there; they had snaked around the Japanese positions to mark the DZ with smoke grenades, but the low clouds obscured their signals. **51.** *"Are you ready* ... Frederick Thomas, "Regimental Combat Jump," *WA,* April 1989, 4. Haugen as first man to jump and jump master confirmed by *Loughrin Journal,* February 3, 1945. **52.** *"I carried double my* ... Charles Sass, "K.I.S.S.," *WA,* Summer 1998. **53.** *"I had thought that* ... Kirkland, Randolph, *Long Ago and Far Away,* 97. **54.** *Kirkland was correct, they* ... Eighth Army, *Report of the CG Eighth Army on the Nasugbu and Bataan Operations,* 17. The distance varies by source, but this report says six miles; an observer who jumped with the 511 says between three to five miles; Leister, Albert, *Operations of the 11th Airborne Division from Nasugbu to Manila,* 22, says five. I have used four to split the difference; see also Holcombe, Frank, *The Operations of the 2nd BN, 511 PIR in the Jump on Tagaytay Ridge,* 9. **55.** *Standard procedure called for* ... per 11ABN, *Standing Operating Procedure Troop Carrier-Airborne Operations.* Speed was not to be less than 95 MPH nor more than 100 MPH; Red Light: ten minutes from DZ, flashed on and off. At two min from DZ, red light turned on and left on, then green light to jump. **56.** *"My musette bag, with* ... Kirkland, Randolph, *Long Ago and Far Away,* 98. **57.** *"Ed, they are all* ... Sorensen, Edward, "Company D Stories," 7. **58.** *Within minutes, the first* ... US Pacific Warfare Board, *Report No. 11, Parachute Field Artillery,* 3. **59.** *"I quickly got out* ... Jerry Davis, "Combat Jump," *WA,* April 1989, 7. **60.** *Between Soule's attack and patrolling* ... Vanderpool, Jay, *Letter to Edward M. Flanagan, May 29, 1984.* **61.** *The paragliders made steady* ... 11ABN, *G3 (Operations) Periodic Reports No. 4,* February 3, 1945. **62.** *"the spearhead tipped with* ... Flanagan, Edward, *The Angels* [1989], 242. **63.** *"Corbett, do you want* ... Flanagan, Edward, *The Angels* [1989], 242; The XO was Lieutenant Colonel 'Mortime' O'Kane, and the reserve BN was the 1/187; Flanagan, Edward, *The Angels* [1989], 243, says Soule went into the attack, but 11th Airborne Division Association, *11th Airborne,* 40, says he called in more artillery, which seems more likely to me; the ridge was thereafter referred to as 'Shorty Ridge.' **64.** *Soule's fresh battalion rushed* ... Multiple artillery units contributed to this barrage, including 675 FA, D Batt, 457 PFAB, elements of Cannon Company from the 21st, and probably the attached tank destroyers as well; 11ABN, *G3 (Operations) Periodic Reports No. 4,* February 3, 1945; 11ABN, *Operations Report, Operation MIKE*

VI, 3; flank attack and flamethrowers per 11th Airborne Division Association, *11th Airborne*, 40. **65.** *Meanwhile, the returning C-47s* ... 11ABN, *G3 (Operations) Periodic Reports No. 4*, February 3, 1945. Second pass was 1st BN, and two cos. from 3rd BN, Regt HQ Co., Srvc Co., and part of 221 Med Det, per Lahti, Ed, "Combat Jump," 11. Lahti also says reporter Frank Smith jumped with him. **66.** *By now, the ground* ... Five aircraft from Smith, Robert, *Triumph in the Philippines*, 227. **67.** *However, despite cautions prior* ... Eighth Army, *Report of the CG Eighth Army on the Nasugbu and Bataan Operations*, 17. Again there are discrepancies in the numbers of aircraft, Leister, Albert, *Operations of the 11th Airborne Division from Nasugbu to Manila*, 22, says forty-eight, while Coulter, John, *The Operations of the Headquarters Company, 3rd BN, 511 PIR in the Attack on Manila*, says forty-seven. **68.** *While Swing and the* ... Leister, Albert, *Operations of the 11th Airborne Division from Nasugbu to Manila*, 8, 22, 28. **69.** *"barking out orders and* ... Thomas, Frederick, "Regimental Combat Jump," 4; *Loughrin Journal*, February 4, 1945; 511PIR, *Unit History*, 1; 511PIR, *S1 (Personnel) Journal*, February 4, 1945. **70.** *Only two or three* ... 11ABN, *G3 (Operations) Periodic Reports No. 4*, February 3, 1945; Holcombe, Frank, *The Operations of the 2nd BN, 511 PIR in the Jump on Tagaytay Ridge*, 10; and Lahti, Ed, "Combat Jump," 11, say three severely injured, fifty-five lightly injured; 511PIR, *S4 (Supply) Journal Summary, 3 Feb. to 1 Jul.*, 1; Smith, Robert, *Triumph in the Philippines*, 229. **71.** *"There was the loud* ... Frank Smith, "How Sky Army Took Ridge on Manila Bay," *Voice*, September 15, 1980, 4. [Reprinted from an undated 1945 issue of the *Chicago Times* newspaper] **72.** *The paragliders were still...* 11ABN, *G3 (Operations) Periodic Reports No. 3*, February 2, 1945. **73.** *"raising hell about lack* ... *Loughrin Journal*, February 3, 1945. **74.** *It was a puzzling* ... Holcombe, Frank, *The Operations of the 2nd BN, 511 PIR in the Jump on Tagaytay Ridge*, 10; 511PIR, *Field Order # 10*. According to Smith, Robert, *Triumph in the Philippines*, 229, "Haugen had all troops under his control by 14:00." From Eighth Army, *Report of the CG Eighth Army on the Nasugbu and Bataan Operations*, 17, "By 1400, the two regiments had occupied all high ground along Tagaytay Ridge, and patrols moved as far as Silang w/out incident." **75.** *Haugen deescalated the situation* ... *Loughrin Journal*, February 3, 1945. **76.** *Once a luxurious getaway* ... Hotel description based on multiple sources, but mostly Smith, Frank, "How Sky Army Took Ridge on Manila Bay," 4. **77.** 11ABN, *G3 (Operations) Periodic Reports No. 4*, February 3, 1945. **78.** *"Our real written orders* ... Eichelberger, Robert, *Dear Miss Em*, 218. **79.** *"disgusted ... old Molasses in January* ... Both from Eichelberger, Robert, *Dear Miss Em*, 214. **80.** *"While he was unwilling* ... McManus, John, *Fire and Fortitude*, 337. McManus provides an excellent biographical sketch of Eichelberger. **81.** *"If he [Eichelberger] isn't standing* ... Swing, Joseph, *Dear General*, letter dated January 25, 1945. **82.** *"only directives about going* ... Eichelberger, Robert, *Dear Miss Em*, 218; Smith, Robert, *Triumph in the Philippines*, 229. Eichelberger later claimed MacArthur's chief of staff, General Sutherland, had given him verbal orders to attack Manila. **83.** *"We still do not* ... Eichelberger, Robert, *Dear Miss Em*, 204. **84.** *"The guerrilla reports make* ... Eichelberger, Robert, *Dear Miss Em*, 209. **85.** *His optimism that Yamashita* ... For more insight into MacArthur's thought process, see Scott, James,

Rampage, 128. **86.** *Since Yamashita abandoned Leyte* ... Smith, Robert, *Triumph in the Philippines*, 90; Stahl, *Ōoka Shōhei's Writings on the Pacific War*, 278. **87.** *Having lost the opportunity* ... Frank, Richard, *Downfall*, 84. **88.** *They were mobilizing a* ... ibid., 85; Stahl, *Ōoka Shōhei's Writings on the Pacific War*, 280. **89.** *Contemplating his options, Yamashita* ... Smith, Robert, *Triumph in the Philippines*, 240. **90.** *Instead, he intended to* ... Scott, James, *Rampage*, 51. **91.** *In fact, Yamashita had* ... ibid., 53, 287. **92.** *The garrison left in* ... Scott, James, *Rampage*, 51; Smith, Robert, *Triumph in the Philippines*, 240. **93.** *Yamashita organized his forces* ... Smith, Robert, *Triumph in the Philippines*, 94. These numbers are just for those elements directly under Yamashita. Ultra intercepts revealed there were a total of 287,000 Japanese troops on Luzon; see Drea, Edward, *MacArthur's Ultra: Codebreaking and the War Against Japan, 1942–1945*, University of Kansas, 1992, 184. **94.** *Critical to sustaining the* ... Smith, Robert, *Triumph in the Philippines*, 92. **95.** *Yamashita's plans were hindered* ... ibid., 243. **96.** *Iwabuchi, as directed by the* ... This was Vice Admiral Denshichi Okochi, 14,000 troops in Manila per Smith, Robert, *Triumph in the Philippines*, 241–244. **97.** *While Yamashita was in* ... ibid. **98.** *The career naval officer* ... Jose, Ricardo, "Japanese Accounts of the Battle of Manila," 6. **99.** *"If we run out of* ... From the *Diary of Lt. Hoichiro Miyazawa* quoted in Jose, Ricardo, "Japanese Accounts of the Battle of Manila," 22. **100.** *Iwabuchi's troops—ad-hoc units* ... Smith, Robert, *Triumph in the Philippines*, 245. **101.** *Back at Tagaytay Ridge* ... 11ABN, G3 *(Operations) Periodic Reports No. 4*, February 3, 1945. **102.** *The sandbar, a hundred* ... Hoppenstein, Isaac, *The Operations of the 187th GIR in the Landing at Nasugbu*, 19. **103.** *It helped, but the* ... Eighth Army, *Report of the CG Eighth Army on the Nasugbu and Bataan Operations*, 51. **104.** *Crews winched the stalled* ... Hoppenstein, Isaac, *The Operations of the 187th GIR in the Landing at Nasugbu*, 22. This was the Air Section, 457th PFAB. **105.** *An effort to float* ... Eighth Army, *Report of the CG Eighth Army on the Nasugbu and Bataan Operations*, 51. **106.** *Unable to land, the* ... Stout, Roy, "Supply—Nasugbu to Tagaytay," 44; Flanagan, Edward, *The Angels* [1989], 236. **107.** *The band's musicians hauled* ... McSweeny, D.J, "C-127th Engineers," 16; Eighth Army, *Report of the CG Eighth Army on the Nasugbu and Bataan Operations*, 51. **108.** *The headquarters' finance staff* ... 11ABN, *Operations Report, Operation MIKE VI*, i; 11ABN, *Report After Action with the Enemy, Operation MIKE VI*, 49. Six days of Class I rations per Eighth Army, *Report of the CG Eighth Army on the Nasugbu and Bataan Operations*, 51; see also Hoppenstein, Isaac, *The Operations of the 187th GIR in the Landing at Nasugbu*, 15. **109.** *Five hundred laborers, recruited* ... Hoppenstein, Isaac, *The Operations of the 187th GIR in the Landing at Nasugbu*, 31; 11ABN, *Report After Action with the Enemy, Operation MIKE VI*, 40. This was managed by a Civil Affairs team that landed with the division. **110.** *To speed the supplies* ... 11ABN, *Report After Action with the Enemy, Operation MIKE VI*, 40; Sixth Army, *Memorandum to Colonel Leaf*, 2; Leister, Albert, *Operations of the 11th Airborne Division from Nasugbu to Manila*, 13; Eighth Army, *Report of the CG Eighth Army on the Nasugbu and Bataan Operations*, 53. **111.** *"The destroyer was trying* ... Robert Eichelberger, "The Dash for Manila," *The Saturday Evening Post*, September 10, 1949, 26. **112.** *At least six others* ...

11ABN, *Report After Action with the Enemy, Operation MIKE VI*, 27. **113.** *In the next twenty-four* ... USS Lough (DE 586), *War Diary for the Month of February 1945*, 16. **114.** *At eleven thirty that night* ... Field order details via *Loughrin Journal*, February 3, 1945. **115.** *A few dim bulbs* ... 11ABN, *G3 (Operations) Periodic Reports No. 4*, February 3, 1945. **116.** *They'd made it fifteen* ... Holcombe, Frank, *The Operations of the 2nd BN, 511 PIR in the Jump on Tagaytay Ridge*, 12. **117.** *Their initial objective was* ... *Loughrin Journal*, February 3, 1945. **118.** *By occupying the intersections* ... Holcombe, Frank, *The Operations of the 2nd BN, 511 PIR in the Jump on Tagaytay Ridge*, 11; Smith, Robert, *Triumph in the Philippines*, 222. **119.** *'Hacksaw' Holcomb's five hundred* ... Holcombe, Frank, *The Operations of the 2nd BN, 511 PIR in the Jump on Tagaytay Ridge*, 7, says he had 502 troopers, but minus his two jump injuries gave him a total of 500 on February 3. **120.** *For support, 'Hacksaw' would* ... M-8s confirmed in Holcombe, Frank, *The Operations of the 2nd BN, 511 PIR in the Jump on Tagaytay Ridge*. **121.** *However, quartermasters were still* ... Leister, Albert, *Operations of the 11th Airborne Division from Nasugbu to Manila*, 23; Eighth Army, *Report of the CG Eighth Army on the Nasugbu and Bataan Operations*, 52. **122.** *"Next stop, Manila* ... Massey, James, *Diary*, February 3, 1945.

Chapter 9: "What Bridge?"

1. *At Nasugbu, engineers and* ... 11ABN, *G3 (Operations) Periodic Reports No. 4*, February 3, 1945; 11ABN, *Report After Action with the Enemy, Operation MIKE VI*, 40. **2.** *At dawn, ten C-47s* ... Leister, Albert, *Operations of the 11th Airborne Division from Nasugbu to Manila*, 23; Eighth Army, *Report of the CG Eighth Army on the Nasugbu and Bataan Operations*, 52. **3.** *Their further scouting located* ... Flanagan, Edward, *The Angels* [1989], 251. **4.** *The nine jeeps of* ... Wentink, James, *Letter to Edward M. Flanagan*, February 9, 1988. Advance party was eight men, and the lead jeep was commanded by Corporal James Wentink; departure time per Jeffress, Edwin, *Operations of the 2/511th in the Battle for Southern Manila*, 19. **5.** *Haugen accompanied this group* ... Holcombe, Frank, *The Operations of the 2nd BN, 511 PIR in the Jump on Tagaytay Ridge*, 12; *Loughrin Journal*, February 4, 1945; 511PIR, *S4 (Supply) Journal Summary*, 2; 11ABN, *G3 (Operations) Periodic Reports No. 5*, February 4, 1945; 11ABN, *Operations Report, Operation MIKE VI*, 3. I have used Loughrin's timeline throughout. **6.** *Two tank-like M8* ... *Loughrin Journal*, February 4, 1945; 511PIR, *S3 (Operations) Journal*, February 4, 1945. The towed arty were howitzers of the 674th GFAB; see Flanagan, Edward, *The Angels* [1989], 250. **7.** *The convoy passed the* ... 511PIR, *S3 (Operations) Journal*, February 4, 1945. **8.** *Leaving Tagaytay, the gravel* ... Eighth Army, *Report of the CG Eighth Army on the Nasugbu and Bataan Operations*, 6–28. **9.** *Swing wanted updates radioed* ... *Loughrin Journal*, February 3, 1945. **10.** *One village even assembled* ... Deane Marks, "The Day the Tank Blew Up, Part II," WA, July/October 1989, 8. **11.** *"They gave us water* ... Deane Marks, "The Day the Tank Blew Up, Part I," WA, April 1989, 12. **12.** *Upon reaching the southern* ... this at 11:00 via Holcombe, Frank, *The Operations of the 2nd BN, 511 PIR in the*

Jump on Tagaytay Ridge, 12. **13.** *Hacksaw went with 'Rusty' Cavanaugh's* ... ibid.
14. *Cavanaugh's troopers dropped their* ... Stephen Cavanaugh, "Imus—Gateway
to Manila," *WA*, Fall 2010, 12. **15.** *"One of our advanced* ... ibid.; Jeffress, Edwin,
Operations of the 2/511th in the Battle for Southern Manila, 24. This near Mabolo,
at the first objective, the road intersection near Cavite. **16.** *The compound, enclosed
by* ... Holcombe, Frank, *The Operations of the 2nd BN, 511 PIR in the Jump on
Tagaytay Ridge*, 12. **17.** *The clatter of machineguns* ... Jeffress, Edwin, Operations
of the 2/511th in the Battle for Southern Manila, 22; 11ABN, History, 14; 11ABN,
G3 (Operations) Periodic Reports No. 5, February 4, 1945. **18.** *"We launched our
attack* ... Cavanaugh, Stephen, "Imus—Gateway to Manila," 12. **19.** *Lead scout,
Arthur Chelbove* ... Wilber Wilcox, "The Assault on Manila," *WA*, Winter 2007,
19. **20.** *"There was no cover* ... ibid. **21.** *An M8 now clanked* ... Richard Hoyt,
"The Dash to Manila," *Voice*, January 1996, 24; Wilcox, Wilber, "The Assault on
Manila," 19. **22.** *"When we reached the* ... Sorensen, Edward, "Company D
Stories," 7. **23.** *"A moment later, we* ... Cavanaugh, Stephen, "Imus—Gateway to
Manila," 12. **24.** *The M8 fired a few* ... Holcombe, Frank, *The Operations of the
2nd BN, 511 PIR in the Jump on Tagaytay Ridge*, 12. **25.** *"If we had access* ...
Wilcox, Wilber, *The Assault on Manila*, 19. **26.** *"While I was trying* ... Cavanaugh,
Stephen, "Imus—Gateway to Manila," 12. **27.** *While Fox's troopers took* ...
127ENG, *Organization History, Section IV*, 3; McSweeny, D.J, "C-127th
Engineers," 16. The source says they were 250kg bombs. I have converted to the
nearest poundage for my fellow non-metric readers. **28.** *A lingering messenger
informed* ... Eichelberger visiting the front is verified in multiple accounts including
Loughrin Journal, February 4, 1945; 11ABN, *Operations Report, Operation
MIKE VI*, 4. **29.** *A non-smoker, he* ... *"Boys, I'm going forward* ... McManus,
John, *Fire and Fortitude*, 320–323. **30.** *"Things were bogged down* ... Eichelberger,
Robert, *Dear Miss Em*, 210. **31.** *Swing added some dash* ... Holcombe, Frank, *The
Operations of the 2nd BN, 511 PIR in the Jump on Tagaytay Ridge*, 12. **32.** *"The
steady refusal of* ... Eichelberger, Robert, *Dear Miss Em*, 212. **33.** *Eyeing his four
dead* ... Cavanaugh, Stephen, "Imus—Gateway to Manila," 12. **34.** *Steele's platoon
opened fire* ... Flanagan, Edward, *The Angels* [1989], 252. Steele was later awarded
the Distinguished Service Cross; he was killed two days later. **35.** *"As twenty to
thirty* ... Marks, Deane, "The Day the Tank Blew Up, Part II," 8. All told, "84
enemy dead were counted," per Walsh, Louis, *Report on Airborne Operations in
the Pacific*, 3. **36.** *The convoy, which now* ... Howard Dunlop, "Strange
Happenings in Combat," *WA*, Fall 2001, 9; captured Japanese trucks also via
Walsh, Louis, *Report on Airborne Operations in the Pacific*, 4. **37.** *Muller's maps
of Manila* ... Henry Muller interviewed by author, August 20, 2020. **38.** *Haugen
left his jeep* ... Flanagan, Edward, *The Angels* [1989], 255. They were General
Albert Pierson and Colonel Irvin 'Schimmy' Schimmelpfennig. **39.** *Deane Marks,
huffing up* ... This at Zapote; see Marks, Deane, "The Day the Tank Blew Up, Part
II," 8. **40.** *But heavy machinegun fire* ... Flanagan, Edward, *The Angels* [1989], 253.
41. *As the pincer attack* ... This was F Co. and E Co., ibid., 254. **42.** *"On the other
side* ... O'Donnell, Patrick, *Into the Rising Sun*, 185. **43.** *Haugen, confident that
Hacksaw* ... *Loughrin Journal*, February 4, 1945. **44.** *"The few who ran* ...
Flanagan, Edward, *The Angels* [1989], 254; Eighth Army, *Report of the CG Eighth*

Army on the Nasugbu and Bataan Operations, 28; Jeffress, Edwin, *Operations of the 2/511th in the Battle for Southern Manila*, 24. **45.** *"sad and unnecessary …* Flanagan, Edward, *The Angels* [1989], 263. **46.** *Shortly thereafter, a squad …* Virgil L. Adamson fired the grenade per Unknown Author, "Sniper Fire From Church Near Parañaque," *Voice*, March 1999, 27. **47.** *They forced entry and …* 511PIR, *S2 (Intelligence) Journal*, February 4, 1945; Walsh, Louis, *Report on Airborne Operations in the Pacific*, 22. **48.** *Laying there in the …* Flanagan, Edward, *The Angels* [1989], 264. **49.** *"we were positioned in …* Stan Young, "Luzon Liberation— My Memories," *WA*, Summer 2000, 8. **50.** *Haugen established his regimental …* Walsh, Louis, *Report on Airborne Operations in the Pacific*, 22. **51.** *"It was about 22:00 …* Fuller, Kenneth, "Some Recollections of an Old Airborne Soldier," 4. There are several contradictory accounts of Swing's jeep trying to cross the bridge. I have pieced this account together using the most common elements from multiple eyewitness accounts. The jeep was driven by Manuel C. DeBaca. **52.** *"The next thing I …* Dunlop, Howard, "Strange Happenings in Combat," 9. **53.** *Galligan grabbed Dunlop and …* this was Corp. Rex S. Curtiss per 511PIR, *S1 (Personnel) Journal*, February 7, 1945. **54.** *At the foot of …* 11ABN, GO #30, 1945. Galligan, Howard Grant Dunlop, and Sgt. Aldo Benedetti from comms PLT were on the detail. Galligan, from Highland Park, Pennsylvania, would be killed two days later on February 6, 1945. **55.** *"blunder …* "I have always puzzled … Young, Stan, "Luzon Liberation—My Memories," 8. It is interesting to note this lesson documented in 511PIR, *Luzon Report, Section II: Summary of Lessons Learned*, 39: "[In] units where higher commanders habitually visit the front line, guards should be posted to prevent vehicles from passing beyond the front lines." **56.** *The glowing conflagration on …* Flanagan, Edward, *The Angels* [1989], 260. **57.** *But the immediate issue …* Eighth Army, *Report of the CG Eighth Army on the Nasugbu and Bataan Operations*, 28. **58.** *Just before midnight …* Hoska was CO of the 675th GFAB; despite previous accounts, Hoska was not alone per 11ABN, GO #26, 1945: "at extreme risk to himself personally conducted an observer party to a forward position and directed fire which reduced the enemy positions." **59.** *Five hours and seven hundred ̇…* 11ABN, *Operations Report, Operation MIKE VI*, 4; it might have been as many as a thousand rounds per 11ABN, *Report After Action with the Enemy, Operation MIKE VI*, 4.

Chapter 10: The Genko Line

1. *Shells burst overhead and …* At 04:00 per Eighth Army, *Report of the CG Eighth Army on the Nasugbu and Bataan Operations*, 29; 11ABN, *Operations Report, Operation MIKE VI*, 4; 11ABN, *G3 (Operations) Periodic Reports No. 6*, February 5, 1945; Marks, Deane, "The Day the Tank Blew Up, Part III," 12. **2.** *Haugen, with his front …* 11ABN, *G3 (Operations) Periodic Reports No. 6*, February 5, 1945. **3.** *Many troopers, unwilling to …* Kirkland, Randolph, *Long Ago and Far Away*, 101. **4.** *Facing encirclement, all nine …* Lester Long, "Los Baños Anniversary," *WA*, Summer 2001, 12. **5.** *Hacksaw's men progressed into …* Smith, Robert, *Triumph in the Philippines*, 239. **6.** *"The spectacle was an …* Scott,

James, *Rampage*, 198. **7.** *A chain of pillboxes* ... Long, Lester, "Los Baños Anniversary," 12. **8.** *Centerpieces included tractors, overturned* ... Smith, Robert, *Triumph in the Philippines*, 246. **9.** *They suspected the Japanese* ... Eighth Army, *Report of the CG Eighth Army on the Nasugbu and Bataan Operations*, 29. **10.** *"There was a medic* ... Long, Lester, "Los Baños Anniversary," 12. **11.** *Many were constructed under* ... Walsh, Louis, *Report on Airborne Operations in the Pacific*, 24. **12.** *"He had carried the* ... Sorensen, Edward, "Company D Stories," 7. **13.** *A group of troopers* ... Deane Marks, "The Day the Tank Blew Up, Part III," *WA*, January 1990, 12. **14.** *They lay sweating in* ... *Loughrin Journal*, February 5, 1945. **14a.** *"I knew Futch was* ... Jack McGrath, "Second Opinion," *WA*, Summer 1997. **15.** *But they couldn't: engineers* ... Walsh, Louis, *Report on Airborne Operations in the Pacific*, 4; 127ENG, *Organization History, Section IV*, 3; *Loughrin Journal*, February 5, 1945. **16.** *"Impracticable," Swing responded* ... 511PIR, *S3 (Operations) Journal*, February 5, 1945. **17.** *Further delays occurred when* ... 11ABN, *G3 (Operations) Periodic Reports No. 6*, February 5, 1945; Anderson Kinghorn, "Addendum to 127th History from Company B Commander," *Voice*, July 15, 1996, 32. **18.** *Further exploration uncovered an* ... 11ABN, *Report After Action with the Enemy, Operation MIKE VI*, 29; Smith, Robert, *Triumph in the Philippines*, 246; Flanagan, Edward, *The Angels* [1948], 81. **19.** *Word spread fast and* ... Long, Lester, "Los Baños Anniversary," 12. **20.** *The M8 then rolled* ... Veteran accounts often confuse the M8 for M18 tanks, but the unit journals make it clear they were initially supported by M8s, and the M18 arrived later. **21.** *"The sky turned black* ... Marks, Deane, "The Day the Tank Blew Up, Part III," 12. **22.** The tattooed trooper was Art Ousterhoudt. **23.** *The smoldering crater was* ... Kinghorn, Anderson, "Addendum to 127th History," 32. **24.** *The targets were beyond* ... 511PIR, *S1 (Personnel) Journal*, February 5, 1945. **25.** *But MacArthur's headquarters cancelled* ... *Loughrin Journal*, February 5, 1945. **26.** *In at least one case* ... Joe Harrison, "Nichols Field," *WA*, Winter 1997. **27.** *On the right flank* ... Coulter, John, *The Operations of the Headquarters Company, 3rd BN, 511 PIR in the Attack on Manila*, 9. **28.** *Late that afternoon, Eichelberger* ... *Loughrin Journal*, February 5, 1945. **29.** *The detonations knocked out* ... Airstrike details from *Loughrin Journal*, February 5, 1945; Marks, Deane, "The Day the Tank Blew Up, Part III," 12. **30.** *"It was only then* ... Kirkland, Randolph, *Long Ago and Far Away*, 101. **31.** *Meanwhile, rivalries were stirred* ... 11ABN, *Operations Report, Operation MIKE VI*, 4. For discussion on wartime city limits, see Smith, Robert, *Triumph in the Philippines*, 231. **32.** *"The view of Manila* ... Eichelberger, Robert, *Dear Miss Em*, 211. **33.** *MacArthur, from his headquarters* ... Scott, James, *Rampage*, 287. **34.** *Senior field commanders were* ... ibid., 207. **35.** *He said in part* ... Scott, James, *Rampage*, 203; see also *New York Times*, February 6, 1945. **36.** *"Manila Falls" read the* ... These headlines from, Scott, James, *Rampage*, 203; *TIME Magazine* (vol. 45, issue 7), February 12, 1945, 19. **37.** *"hand grenades and rifle* ... Marks, Deane, "The Day the Tank Blew Up, Part III," 12; 511PIR, *S1 (Personnel) Journal*, February 7, 1945; E Co. broke up attack in hand-to-hand with one KIA, three WIA, and eleven EKIA. **38.** *Most importantly, a captured* ... *Loughrin Journal*, February 6, 1945; Jeffress, Edwin, *Operations of the 2/511th in the Battle for Southern Manila*, 29. **39.** *Named in honor of* ... Smith, Frank, "How

Sky Army Took Ridge on Manila Bay," 4; *History of Operation, Luzon,* 2; Flanagan, Edward, *The Angels* [1948], 81. Smith says fourteenth century, but my research indicates the line was named after the Genkō Bōrui line, a twelve-mile stone wall built in anticipation of a Mongol invasion in 1274 AD. **40.** *The map also confirmed* ... Smith, Robert, *Triumph in the Philippines,* 246. **41.** *Intelligence suggested the line* ... 11ABN, *Report After Action with the Enemy, Operation MIKE VI,* 29. **42.** *While air raids had* ... Smith, Robert, *Triumph in the Philippines,* 265. **43.** *"From now on, our* ... Flanagan, Edward, *The Angels* [1948], 81. **44.** *Swing ordered 'Shorty' Soule's* ... Smith, Robert, *Triumph in the Philippines,* 266; Eighth Army, *Report of the CG Eighth Army on the Nasugbu and Bataan Operations,* 29. **45.** *While waiting for them* ... *Loughrin Journal,* February 6, 1945. **46.** *"After the phosphorus and* ... Marks, Deane, "The Day the Tank Blew Up, Part III," 12. **47.** *'Rusty' Cavanaugh's Dog Company* ... *Loughrin Journal,* February 7, 1945. **48.** *The next line of pillboxes* ... *Loughrin Journal,* February 10, 1945. **49.** *"To say it is* ... Leroy Butler, "Geronimo #13 or The South Pacific as I Saw It, Part III," *WA,* Spring 2001, 13. **50.** *Hacksaw and Haugen organized* ... 511PIR, *Luzon Report, Section II: Summary of Lessons Learned,* 36; *Loughrin Journal,* February 10, 1945. **51.** *On the morning of* ... Left flank was 1/187; they made it as far as Canales Creek as per 187GIR, *Chronological Narrative Mike 6 Operation, 25 January 1945 to 24 February 1945.* [Reprinted in *Voice,* June 15, 1982, 3.] **52.** *Moving up along the* ... 188GIR, *Historical Report of the 188th Paraglider Infantry in [MIKE VI] Operation,* 6. **53.** *Iwabuchi's troops had salvaged* ... Smith, Robert, *Triumph in the Philippines,* 246. **53a.** *"to radio [Admiral] Nimitz* ... Eichelberger, Robert, *Dear Miss Em,* 216; Soule's quote has several versions, including swapping Admiral Halsey for Nimitz, but Eichelberger's letter was written at the time, and I've used it. **54.** *To the west, Strong's* ... Smith, Robert, *Triumph in the Philippines,* 266. **55.** *"I will get him* ... Hogan, Edward, *A Dogface's War,* 32; Richard Keith, "The 96-Hour Day, Tagaytay Ridge to Nichols Field," *Voice,* June 2010, 22. **56.** *That afternoon, Swing and* ... *Loughrin Journal,* February 7, 1945. **57.** *Studying the open terrain* ... Sixth Army, *G2 Weekly Report No. 75,* 17; "pop-guns ... Eichelberger, Robert, *Dear Miss Em,* 211. **58.** *Two of Haugen's staff* ... *Loughrin Journal,* February 6, 1945. **59.** *Machinegunners sprayed it, riflemen* ... ibid., February 7, 1945. **60.** *For reasons that flummoxed* ... Walsh, Louis, *Report on Airborne Operations in the Pacific,* Tab C, 3. **61.** *The smoke was so* ... 511PIR, *S1 (Personnel) Journal,* February 10, 1945. **62.** *Instead of the full* ... *Loughrin Journal,* February 8, 1945. **63.** *"It was about ready* ... Kirkland, Randolph, *Long Ago and Far Away,* 103. **64.** *"my squad was halfway* ... Harrison, Joe, "Nichols Field." **65.** *Japanese gunners fired yellow* ... Marks, Deane, "The Day the Tank Blew Up, Part III," 12. **66.** *"This was a tough* ... Hogan's platoon leader was Lt. Edward Stoeckly; see Hogan, Edward, *A Dogface's War,* 32. **67.** *"I just looked at* ... Marks, Deane, "The Day the Tank Blew Up, Part III," 12. **68.** *"He thought he was* ... ibid. **69.** *"What is difficult to* ... Keith, Richard, "The 96-Hour Day, Tagaytay Ridge to Nichols Field," 22; Smith, Robert, *Triumph in the Philippines,* 268. **70.** *Despite the setbacks, Strong's* ... 188GIR, *Historical Report of the 188th Paraglider Infantry in [MIKE VI] Operation,* 6. **71.** *By the end of the day* ... Flanagan, Edward, *The Angels* [1989], 271. 2/511 had 187 men left from the 502 that jumped at Tagaytay. **72.** *The headcount of Strong's ... Loughrin Journal*, February 10, 1945. **73.** *Hotel Company alone had ...* Keith, Richard, "The 96-Hour Day," 22, states the three rifle platoons were down to fifty-nine troopers. **74.** *Across the board, Haugen's ... Loughrin Journal*, February 10, 1945 states, "51 dead, 400 WIA, we are short 601 men now." **75.** *He radioed Swing's headquarters ... Loughrin Journal*, February 8, 1945. **76.** *All along the evacuation ...* George Doherty, "John Santucci, I Co. Makes Ripley's 'Believe it or Not,'" *WA*, Spring 1999; George Misculin, "Remembers His Tomorrow," *Voice*, March 2000, 42; Hoppenstein, Isaac, *The Operations of the 187th GIR in the Landing at Nasugbu*, 29. **77.** *One of the more ...* Jerry Davis, "A Slow Boat Home," *WA*, Spring 1993, 36. **78.** *"We had a good ...* Miles Gale, "Home Sweet Home," *WA*, Spring 1995, 21. **79.** *To speed access to ...* 11ABN, *Medical History for Period January–March 1945*, 2; 127ENG, *Organization History, Section IV*, 3; Sixth Army, *Memorandum to Colonel Leaf*, 3. **80.** *Patients requiring urgent care ...* Flanagan, Edward, *The Angels* [1948], 89. **81.** *"We had a supply ...* Flanagan, Edward, *The Angels* [1989], 253. This supply line quip has various sources with variable distances. I chose the Conable's, Div's supply officer and edited the distance to reflect the actual map mileage. **82.** *Conable kept twenty-five olive ...* Sixth Army, *Memorandum to Colonel Leaf*, 2. **83.** *The demanding schedule made ...* Smith, Robert, *Triumph in the Philippines*, 234. **84.** *At each end of ...* Flanagan, Edward, *The Angels* [1989], 253. **85.** *To give the drivers ...* Sixth Army, *Memorandum to Colonel Leaf*, 2. **86.** *Often, while puttering overhead ...* Leister, Albert, *Operations of the 11th Airborne Division from Nasugbu to Manila*, 25. **87.** *Eichelberger's staff arranged for ...* Smith, Robert, *Triumph in the Philippines*, 234; 11ABN, *Report After Action with the Enemy, Operation MIKE VI*, 39/49. **88.** *A paltry 470 arrived ...* Eighth Army, *Report of the CG Eighth Army on the Nasugbu and Bataan Operations*, 54/62. **89.** *Nineteen thousand additional rounds ...* Sixth Army, *Memorandum to Colonel Leaf*, 3. **90.** *They braved snipers and ...* Flanagan, Edward, *The Angels* [1948], 89. **91.** *Colonel Harry D. Hildebrand had ...* Hoppenstein, Isaac, *The Operations of the 187th GIR in the Landing at Nasugbu*, 31. **92.** *The 331 cannoneers of ...* 11ABN, *Operations Report, Operation MIKE VI*, 3; 11ABN, *G3 (Operations) Periodic Reports No. 5*, February 4, 1945; 331 personnel per US Pacific Warfare Board, *Report No. 11, Parachute Field Artillery*, 3. **93.** *The true saviors of ...* two thousand via 11ABN, *History of Operation, Luzon*, 2; 11ABN, *Report After Action with the Enemy, Operation MIKE VI*, 4. **94.** *"The major and his ...* Henry Muller, "The Reluctant Boatman," *WA*, Fall 2003, 16. **95.** *The supplies, having snaked ...* Smith, Robert, *Triumph in the Philippines*, 234. **96.** *Flat tires were a ...* 511PIR, *S4 (Supply) Journal Summary*, 2. **97.** *Wounded supply personnel were ...* ibid. **98.** *One- and two-story ...* Walsh, Louis, *Report on Airborne Operations in the Pacific*, Tab C, 3. **99.** *"We must have plenty ...* based on multiple comments from *Loughrin Journal*, February 8 and 9, 1945. **100.** *Corporal Richard A. 'The Rat' Laws ...* Richard Laws, "The Day the Riflemen Clapped Their Hands," *WA*, Summer 1998. **101.** *"We were now down ...* Richard Laws, "Pilot Trouble," *WA*, Fall 2003, 8. Law's account says they were down to just one mortar, but John Coulter's account indicates there were two. The wounded officer was Richard Barnum. Law's casualty numbers confirmed per

511PIR, *S3 (Operations) Journal*, February 10, 1945. **102.** *To Haugen's east, Soule's ...* this was 1/187, 187GIR, *Chronological Narrative Mike 6 Operation.* **103.** *Three hundred men charged ...* 188GIR, *Historical Report of the 188th Paraglider Infantry in [MIKE VI] Operation*, 7. **104.** *The following morning ...* Abe Solow, "Letter to Editor," *Voice*, November 15, 1980, 44. **105.** *including one of Soule's battalion commanders ...* The killed battalion commander was Major Charles Loeper. **106.** *One notorious enemy gunner ...* 511PIR, *S2 (Intelligence) Journal*, February 9, 1945. **107.** *The primary thorn was ...* Kirkland, Randolph, *Long Ago and Far Away*, 106. The account of Wheeler's death and the Mobile gas station are heavily based on Kirkland's account, coupled with map study and plotted unit locations. **108.** *Their increasing proximity gave ...* Smith, Robert, *Triumph in the Philippines*, 267. **109.** *With the northern phalanx ...* This was at 13:00. Initially, Eichelberger's Eighth Army was still responsible for suppling Swing's troops while Kruger's Sixth Army managed their tactical advances. **110.** *While the logistics of ...* Smith, Robert, *Triumph in the Philippines*, 268. **111.** *"The Japs defended Nichols ...* Flanagan, Edward, *The Angels* [1948], 85. **112.** *Radio Tokyo assured ...* Walsh, Louis, *Report on Airborne Operations in the Pacific*, Tab C, 3; "US and British troops ..." Sixth Army, *G2 Weekly Report No. 75*, 21; extract from diary captured in Manila. **113.** *They dropped a million ...* Sixth Army, *G2 Weekly Report No. 75*, 13; Eighth Army, *Report of the CG Eighth Army on the Nasugbu and Bataan Operations*, 39. **114.** *The 11th Airborne had ...* Fourteen POWs from 511PIR, *S2 (Intelligence) Journal*, February 19, 1945; the prisoner stabbing himself with own bayonet per the same, February 17, 1945. **115.** *"because of confusion ...* Burgess, Henry, *Looking Back*, 100. **116.** *Three guerrillas, ranging beyond ...* this in Pasay, *Loughrin Journal*, February 11, 1945. **117.** *"We passed a Japanese ...* Kirkland, Randolph, *Long Ago and Far Away*, 107. **118.** *The patrols also found ...* ibid. **119.** *"to send some MP's ...* Loughrin Journal, February 9, 1945. **120.** *Two detonated caches of ...* Smith, Frank, "How Sky Army Took Ridge on Manila Bay," 4. **121.** *Another trooper ducked into ...* Kirkland, Randolph, *Long Ago and Far Away*, 106. **122.** *The 37th Infantry would ...* Smith, Robert, *Triumph in the Philippines*, 263, 268. **123.** *In preparation for the ...* Haugen's death is largely based on Loughrin's eye-witness account in Richard Loughrin, "Mortally Wounded in Action," *WA*, July/October 1989, 11, and *Loughrin Journal*, February 11, 1945. Swing had apparently left just prior to the fatal explosion. **124.** *"poorly suppressed state of ...* Kirkland, Randolph, *Long Ago and Far Away*, 74. **125.** *"[Lahti] was a good man ...* ibid., 54. **126.** *During the battle, the ...* Scott, James. *Rampage*, 316. **127.** *The flow of refugees ...* 11ABN, *Report After Action with the Enemy, Operation MIKE VI*, 59. **128.** *'Slugger' Lahti's paratroopers ...* Loughrin Journal, February 11, 1945. **129.** *The guerrillas set up ...* ibid., February 7, 1945. **130.** *"I remember the people ...* Charles Sass, "Anonymous Pictures," *WA*, Summer 2000, 17. **131.** *"They all carried pitifully ...* Kirkland, Randolph, *Long Ago and Far Away*, 107. **132.** *"rape and slaughter ...* Richard Keith, "Letter to the Editor," *Voice*, June 2015, 16. **133.** *"The entire first floor ...* Kirkland, Randolph, *Long Ago and Far Away*, 109. For a full account of the grisly atrocity, see Scott, James, *Rampage*, 302–310. **134.** *"Many nursing women had ...* Flanagan, Edward, *The Angels* [1989], 266. **135.** *"They were piled in ...* Sass, Charles, "Anonymous

Pictures," 17. **136.** *Corpses, strung up by* ... Charles Sass, "Mail Call, Letter to George Doherty," *WA,* Fall 2005, 38; Genematas, Anthony, "Company E, 187th Regiment," 12; Scott, James, *Rampage,* 311. **137.** *"The area had been* ... 511th PIR Association, *511th Parachute Infantry Regiment,* 66. **138.** *"One lady, her foot* ... O'Donnell, Patrick, *Into the Rising Sun,* 186. **139.** *What started as grotesque* ... Scott, James, *Rampage,* 252. **140.** *"45–50 guerrillas were* ... Diary extract via Jose, Ricardo, "Japanese Accounts of the Battle of Manila," 22. **141.** *"All people on the* ... Document dated February 13, 1945, via ibid., 19. **142.** *"they should be gathered* ... The full text of the order can be found in ibid., 20. **143.** *At Nasugbu, Eichelberger's Eighth* ... 11ABN, *Report After Action with the Enemy, Operation MIKE VI,* 40. **144.** *The camp, at its* ... XIV Corps, *After Action Report M1 Operation,* Part II, 36. **145.** *"The project entailed buying* ... Vanderpool, Jay, *Letter to Edward M. Flanagan, Sep. 17, 1984.* **146.** *Post-war investigations estimated* ... Scott, James, *Rampage,* 422. **147.** *"the Japanese had simply* ... Kirkland, Randolph, *Long Ago and Far Away,* 107. **148.** *After the airstrike cut* ... 188GIR, *Historical Report of the 188th Paraglider Infantry in [MIKE VI] Operation,* 8. **149.** *The open runways were* ... Smith, Robert, *Triumph in the Philippines,* 268. **150.** *There were the anti-aircraft* ... ibid., 246; 188GIR, *Historical Report of the 188th Paraglider Infantry in [MIKE VI] Operation,* 6. **151.** *The armor crews exhausted* ... Genematas, Anthony, "Company E, 187th Regiment," 12. **152.** *While the enemy's guns* ... Walsh, Louis, *Report on Airborne Operations in the Pacific,* Tab C, 3. **153.** *The paragliders' 81mm mortar* ... Genematas, Anthony, "Company E, 187th Regiment," 12. **154.** *Their tally for the* ... 188GIR, *Part II: Luzon, Philippine Islands Campaign, 31 Jan. 1945 to 30 Jun. 1945,* 7. **155.** *With no time to* ... Contact was made at 18:15 per *Loughrin Journal,* February 11, 1945. **156.** *"At one time in the* ... Burgess, Henry, *Letter to Edward M. Flanagan, Sep. 25, 1984.* **156a.** *"a walking grocery store* ... Sass, Charles, "Anonymous Pictures," 17. **157.** *Twenty-one-year-old Private* ... Unknown Author, "Reunion '95," *WA,* Fall 1995, 40; Pérez, Manuel Jr, Draft Registration Card. Born in Oklahoma on March 3, 1923, he had grown up in Chicago. Pérez was killed on March 14, 1945. **158.** *"His detection of the* ... Ted Baughn, "Congressional Medal of Honor, PFC Manuel Pérez, Jr.," *WA,* October 1987. **159.** *By mid-day, Manny* ... War Department, "Public Relations Press Release (undated)," 1. **160.** *"There goes Pérez* ... Baughn, Ted, "Congressional Medal of Honor." **161.** *Taking a knee, he* ... Flanagan, Edward, *The Angels* [1948], 90. **162.** *"I can remember the* ... Flanagan, Edward, *The Angels* [1989], 282. **163.** *All told, Pérez's one-man* ... Citation says eighteen, but the math adds up to twenty-three. **164.** *"among his grenades, rifle* ... Polick quoted in Varrone, Lou, "The Congressional Medal of Honor," *WA,* October 1999, 44. **165.** *Several witnesses were emphatic* ... ibid. **166.** *Their morning started off* ... Genematas, Anthony, "Company E, 187th Regiment," 12. **167.** *"but before our front* ... ibid. **168.** *"I have never—and* ... Augustin, James, "Once an Angel," 32. **169.** *Casualty reports trickled in* ... Numbers from Pat Kenny, "Co. El. 187th P/G Infantry Disaster," *Voice,* January 1988, 21. Eight KIA according to Bernheim, Eli, *WWII Veteran Survey,* 9. **170.** *"There was no choice* ... Merritt, John, *The Operations of Company G 187th GIR in the Attack on Nichols Field,* 12. **171.** *Tipton's howitzers and mortars* ... Genematas, Anthony, "Company E, 187th

Regiment," 12. **172.** *"Total pillboxes to date* ... 188GIR, *Historical Report of the 188th Paraglider Infantry in [MIKE VI] Operation*, 9. **173.** *"Prior to the all-out* ... Jose, Ricardo, "Japanese Accounts of the Battle of Manila," 20. **174.** *Late that afternoon, in* ... 511PIR, *S3 (Operations) Journal*, February 14, 1945; Walsh, Louis, *Report on Airborne Operations in the Pacific*, Tab C, 7; spears also reported in 511PIR, *S2 (Intelligence) Journal*, February 10, 1945. **175.** *In the dark, litter* ... This at 19:45 on February 13, via 511PIR, *S2 (Intelligence) Journal*, February 14, 1945. **176.** *"One inspired Jap came* ... Jack McGrath, "Decision at Fort McKinley," *WA*, Fall 2000, 19; Baugh, Ted, *Undated Letter to Jerard Vlaminck*, 10. Some accounts position this as a deliberate attack, but most make the mutual surprise clear, as confirmed in 511PIR, *S2 (Intelligence) Journal*, February 14, 1945;, and *Loughrin Journal*, February 13, 1945. **177.** *The next morning, Swing* ... *Loughrin Journal*, February 15, 1945; Augustin, James, "Once an Angel," 41. **178.** *"He informed us that* ... Jack McGrath, "Unrequited Love," *WA*, Summer 2000, 3. **179.** *The Hellcats' firepower enthralled* ... *Loughrin Journal*, February 15, 1945. **180.** *One enthusiast reported the* ... ibid., February 16, 1945. *The occupiers were burning* ... 188GIR, *Historical Report of the 188th Paraglider Infantry in [MIKE VI] Operation*, 13; 511PIR, *S2 (Intelligence) Journal*, February 16, 1945. **181.** *Detonations of ammunition stockpiles* ... Genematas, Anthony, "Company E, 187th Regiment," 12. **182.** *'Slugger' Lahti observed the* ... Lahti, Edward, *Memoirs of an Angel*, 75; Flanagan, Edward, *The Angels* [1989], 284. **183.** *When dropped from low* ... *Impact* (September 1944, Vol 2, no. 9), 49; *Impact* (August 1945, Vol III, no. 8), 48. **184.** *First in was a* ... *Loughrin Journal*, February 16, 1945; 188GIR, *Historical Report of the 188th Paraglider Infantry in [MIKE VI] Operation*, 13. **185.** *"Simply hold the line* ... Kirkland estimated there were forty-five men in the HQ at this time. The E Co. roadblock at Alabang was holding the crossroads leading to Cavite/Manila, as per Kirkland, Randolph, *Long Ago and Far Away*, 113. **186.** *The fort had fallen* ... 188GIR, *Historical Report of the 188th Paraglider Infantry in [MIKE VI] Operation*, 13; 961 per Flanagan, Edward, *The Angels* [1948], 89. **187.** *A few nights later, at* ... This attack and the account of Mills Lowe is based on Randolph Kirkland's eyewitness recounting of what he saw and is supplemented with other details. See Kirkland, Randolph, *Long Ago and Far Away*, 113–119, and 511PIR, *S1 (Personnel) Journal*, February 20–21, 1945. **188.** *Shooting an explosive-laden* ... saboteurs via Walsh, Louis, *Report on Airborne Operations in the Pacific*. **189.** *among Lowe's admirers* ... Lowe as "one of the best," via Kirkland, 50. **190.** *"tough SOB* ... George Doherty, "Tech. Sgt. Miles [sic] T. Lowe Award a Field Commission," *Voice*, January 15, 1991, 27. **191.** *"We had to move the* ... Lindau, Bill, "Nips Get Rough Handling from N.C. Paratroopers," *News and Observer*, Raleigh, North Carolina, June 17, 1945, 6. **192.** *At least eight* ... Doherty says eight; Kirkland says twelve. The seven enemy machineguns were being carried by a Japanese heavy weapons company decimated in the first burst. **193.** Battlefield promotion via 511PIR, *S1 (Personnel) Journal*, February 23, 1945; a bulldozer was later used to bury the dead in a mass grave; see Kirkland, 121. **194.** *"rifle [was] speck-free* ... and *"The rest of us* ... Both from Lindau, Bill, "With Tar Heels on Leyte," *News and Observer*, Raleigh, North Carolina, February 11, 1945, 14; Susan Lowe Bevins, interview with author; recaptured machinegun story recounted in Lindau, Bill, "Nips Get Rough Handling from N.C. Paratroopers," *News and Observer*, Raleigh, North Carolina, June 17, 1945, 6; tourniquet story via LeRoy, Bob, *From My Foxhole to Tokyo*, 186. **195.** *"They said they didn't …* Neuteboom, Grant, *I Co. Beacon*, January 1998, 10. **196.** *In one example, he …* 152AAB, *Historical Report of 152 AB AA Bn, in Luzon, P.I. Campaign*, 3; Flanagan, Edward, *The Angels* [1948], 132. **197.** *The Pierson Task Force …* Flanagan, Edward, *The Angels* [1948], 89. The task force was 1/187, 3/19 Inf. Regt, A Co., 44th TB, combat engr. PLT, medic PLT, and 457th PFAB. 11ABN, *11th Airborne Division History*, 33 says 2/19th inf. (from 24th DIV); 188GIR, *Part II: Luzon, Philippine Islands Campaign*, 8, says 675 arty, not 457 arty; 188GIR, *Maps and sketches illustrating the operations of the 11th Airborne Division*, 66. **198.** *The Japanese garrison holding …* Walsh, Louis, *Report on Airborne Operations in the Pacific*, 8. **199.** *With their backs to …* Flanagan, Edward, *The Angels* [1948], 91. **200.** *"Right now [we] have …* Swing, Joseph, *Dear General*, letter dated February 21, 1945. **201.** *"The situation was hopeless …* This section based on Flanagan, Edward, *The Angels* [1948], 91; Walsh, Louis, *Report on Airborne Operations in the Pacific*, Tab J, 1. **202.** *The Air Force had …* Edward Jenkins, "Combined Air-Ground Operations on Luzon," *Military Review*, February 1946, 30. **203.** *Lieutenant Colonels Doug Quandt …* Flanagan, Edward, *The Angels* [1989], 290. **204.** *By the Angels' count …* 5,210 is from 11ABN, *Report After Action with the Enemy, Operation MIKE VI*, 6; but Smith, Robert, *Triumph in the Philippines*, 268, states, "The DIV and its air and arty support had killed perhaps 3,000 Japs in the metropolitan area." **205.** *"If anyone has the …* This on February 26, 1945; Jose, Ricardo, "Japanese Accounts of the Battle of Manila," 23. **206.** *It would take several …* This on March 3, 1945. **207.** *Swing wanted a rifle …* This on February 21, 1945; the lieutenant was Bill Abernathy per Lahti, Edward, *Memoirs of an Angel*, 77; eighty from Ringler, John, *511th Parachute Infantry Regiment*, 37. **208.** *"A thousand things can …* John Ringler, "The Los Baños Raid," *WA*, Fall 1999, 103.

Chapter 11: "You're not Marines"

1. *The Americans had already …* These three other camps were at Santo Thomas, Bilibid Prison, and Cabanatuan. **2.** *MacArthur, after witnessing the …* This on February 10, 1945. There are several versions of how the 11th Airborne was assigned the Los Baños mission; the most plausible is found in XIV Corps, *After Action Report M1 Operation, Part I*, 159, wherein it states that GHQ decided on February 4, 1945, to assign the rescue to the 11ABN, but they were too engaged at the time. Per Gen. Albert Pierson, the Div XO, "I was present when Eichelberger told Swing that Los Baños would be his mission. Muller and Quandt started planning the mission immediately." The mission was officially assigned to 11ABN in a Field Order issued to XIV Corps by Sixth Army on February 10, 1945. 11ABN then issued its own Field Order (#18) on February 21, 1945. That the division had started planning for the rescue while still on Leyte seems highly implausible. **3.** *Ingles operated with the …* Lewis Watty, "Personal Journal," *Voice*, June 2008, 15.

4. *He also heard growing fears* ... XIV Corps, *After Action Report M1 Operation*, 161. **5.** *Massacre rumors were rampant* ... 511th PIR Association, *511th Parachute Infantry Regiment*, 68. Guerrilla message sent on February 18, 1945: "Have received reliable information that Japs have Los Baños scheduled for massacre." **6.** *The revelations increased the* ... Doubts expressed by Vanderpool, Jay, *Letter of Instruction, Los Baños Patrol*; Vanderpool, Jay, *Letter to Edward M. Flanagan, May 29, 1984*. **7.** *"I thought, should the excursions* ... Vanderpool, Jay, *Letter to Edward M. Flanagan, Aug. 20, 1984.* The guerrilla contingency plan was also confirmed in a speech by Henry 'Butch' Muller to the Manila Liberation Commemoration on February 5, 1999, in San Diego, California. **8.** *Vanderpool's guerrilla headquarters was* ... ibid. **9.** *The two headquarters shared* ... Vanderpool, Jay, *Letter to Edward M. Flanagan, May 29, 1984*; Vanderpool, Jay, *Letter of Instruction, Los Baños Patrol.* **10.** *Castillo, a guerrilla and* ... Ingles, Gustavo, *Letter to Edward M. Flanagan, Oct. 25, 1984*; XIV Corps, *After Action Report M1 Operation, Part I*, 161. **11.** *The camp at Los Baños* ... Sixty acres via Burgess, Henry, *Reminiscences of the 11th Airborne Division Raid on Los Baños*, 8; Homer Bigart, "Los Baños Rescue," *Voice*, December 1999, 49. **12.** *The compound was surrounded* ... Donald Roberts, "Angels to the Rescue," *WA*, Winter 2002, 26. **13.** *Working in the raiders'* ... 11ABN, *Report After Action with the Enemy, Operation MIKE VI*, 31. **14.** *The guerrillas estimated there* ... Eighty via XIV Corps, *After Action Report M1 Operation, Part I*, 164. Guerrilla estimates of 100–125 via Ingles, Gustavo, *Letter to Edward M. Flanagan, Oct. 25, 1984*. **15.** *A mile and a* ... the Japanese infantry company was at a gravel quarry with two 155mm howitzers; the outpost northwest of the camp at the San Juan River had two 75mm howitzers; see XIV Corps, *After Action Report M1 Operation*, 164. **16.** *The main consideration was* ... ~2,300 for planning purposes from Walsh, Louis, *Los Baños – A Raid in Force*, 3. **17.** *Many of them were* ... Bigart, Homer, "Los Baños Rescue," 49. **18.** *While Colonel 'Shorty' Soule* ... 11ABN, *Report on the Los Baños Operation*, 2; XIV Corps, *After Action Report M1 Operation, Part I*, 161. **19.** *The twenty-two-man recon* ... Fifty from Kennington, Robert, *The Operations of the Los Baños Force*, 6; 11ABN, *11th Airborne Division History*, 36. Recon PLT was sixteen men with 150 guerrillas; Walsh, Louis, *Report on Airborne Operations in the Pacific*, 9, states fifty guerrillas. **20.** *At the same time* ... Sources vary on the number of amtracs and the paratroopers they carried. For consistency, I used 11ABN, *Report on the Los Baños Operation*, 2; Burgess, Henry, *Reminiscences of the 11th Airborne Division Raid on Los Baños*, 6, states there were 412 men. **21.** *The operation's lynch pin* ... Vanderpool, Jay, *Letter to Edward M. Flanagan, May 29, 1984*. **22.** *Three prisoners had slipped* ... 511PIR, *S2 (Intelligence) Journal*, February 20, 1945; 511PIR, *S2 (Intelligence) Journal*, February 20, 1945. The three internees were Pete Miles, Freddy Zervoulakos, and Ben Edwards. **23.** *Miles revealed two key* ... In 511PIR, *S2 (Intelligence) Journal*, February 20, 1945, Miles said "Jap garrison of 80 men in poor condition, 2,130 prisoners." Smith, Robert, *Triumph in the Philippines*, 428, says 250 guards, but others, including XIV Corps, *After Action Report M1 Operation, Part I*, 164, say eighty guards. **24.** *The dark-haired, twenty-six-year-old* ... 511th PIR Association, *511th Parachute Infantry Regiment*, 37. **25.** *"He didn't seem like* ... Charles Thollander quoted in Charles

Sass, "Colonel John Ringler, The Compassionate Captain," *WA,* Fall 2003, 3. **26.** *"I've got a pet* ... ibid. **27.** *"My plan was to* ... 511th PIR Association, *511th Parachute Infantry Regiment,* 37; "The Continuing Saga of the Los Baños Raid," *WA,* Summer 1998; "A Vignette of the Los Baños Jump," *The Airborne Quarterly,* Spring 2001, 64. **28.** *He told his platoon* ... Eight hundred via Kennington, Robert, *The Operations of the Los Baños Force,* 7; rice from Walsh, Louis, *Los Baños – A Raid in Force,* 3. **29.** *To fill out their* ... William Abernathym, "Prelude ... The Los Baños Decision," *WA,* October 1989, 33, says eight-nine men; 11ABN, *Report on the Los Baños Operation,* 2, says 125 men. **30.** *"This is a suicide jump* ... Holzem, Jim, "Jim Holzem's Story," 10. **31.** *"for no amount of* ... ibid. **32.** *Keen to make the* ... Roger Miller, "Carlos Palvarosa," *Voice,* March 2001, 42; Bert Marshall, "The Jump on Los Baños," *Voice,* August 15, 1986, 35; three were Rosendo Castello, Robert Fletcher, and Carlos "Oscar" Palvarosa, a former corporal in the Philippine Scouts. **33.** *He originally planned to* ... 11ABN, *Report on the Los Baños Operation,* 3. **34.** *"Discretion prevents me from* ... Robert Beightler, "A Swing and a Miss," *WA,* July/October 1989, 30. The amtracs were gone by ~05:30, with the first into the water at 05:15 per 11ABN, *Report on the Los Baños Operation,* 3. **35.** *The nine C-47s cruised* ... 11ABN, *11th Airborne Division History,* 35; O.R. Karst, "Through the Eyes of the Pilot," *Voice,* January 1998, 34. **36.** *They flew over the* ... 11ABN, *Report on the Los Baños Operation,* 3. **37.** *The green jump light* ... Karst, O.R, "Through the Eyes of the Pilot," 34. **38.** *"Look over there! Airplanes* ... Carol Talbot and Virginia Muir, *Escape at Dawn* (Wheaton, Illinois: Tyndale House Publishers, Inc., 1988), 234. **39.** *"Gunfire ricocheted around us* ... Margaret Squires, "Los Baños Diary," *WA,* Winter 2008, 12. **40.** *The recon teams not* ... Robert Carroll, "The 11th Airborne Division Provisional Reconnaissance Platoon and the Los Baños Raid," *WA,* Winter 2004, 12; Martin Squires, "Aw Mom!" *WA,* July/October 1989, 36. **41.** *Sergeant Terry R. Santos* ... Terry Santos, "Recon Platoon at Los Baños," *WA,* Fall 1999, 101. **42.** *Santos and three other* ... Santos, interview; Gatdula based on Ingles, Gustavo, *Letter to Edward M. Flanagan, Oct. 25, 1984.* **43.** *The rest had drifted* ... Kenneth Fuller, "Los Baños Address, 23 February 2005," *WA,* Spring 2005, 30. **44.** *Another recon team, led* ... Carroll, Robert, "The 11th Airborne Division Provisional Reconnaissance Platoon and the Los Baños Raid," 12. **45.** *Jesse Tribble, who'd given* ... Talbot, Carol, *Escape at Dawn,* 237. **46.** *"We were all taking* ... Lewis Watty, "A POW's Memory of the Raid," *Voice,* December 1999, 50. **47.** *Ringler's paratroopers charged into* ... At 07:17 per Kennington, Robert, *The Operations of the Los Baños Force,* 14; 11ABN, *Report on the Los Baños Operation,* 4. **48.** *"There was much jubilation* ... Talbot, Carol, *Escape at Dawn,* 240. **49.** *"Jap tanks! Jap tanks* ... ibid. **50.** *The grinding racket was* ... The entire cadre of the 672nd Amphibian Tractor Battalion's officers and enlisted men volunteered; see Pete Gleich, "Partners in Victory: 672nd Amphibian Tractor Bn. Finally Receives due Honors for Los Baños Rescue, Part I," *Voice,* December 2011, 25. **51.** *Their clanking was so* ... Underwood, Matt, "Partners in Victory, Part III," 23. **52.** *The driver of the* ... Burgess, Henry, *Letter to Edward M. Flanagan, Sep. 25, 1984.* **53.** *The amtracs had navigated* ... 7.4 miles to be specific, per 11ABN, *Report on the Los Baños Operation,* 3. **54.** *At the shoreline, several* ... 11ABN, *Report on the*

Los Baños Operation, 4; Henry Swindler, "C/127th Engineers in the Los Baños Mission," *Voice*, September 2012, 16. **55.** *"A Jap heavy machinegun* ... Harry Van Divner, "Los Baños, A Report from the Beach," *WA*, Fall 1996, 31. **56.** *The rest of the amtracs* ... 11ABN, *Report on the Los Baños Operation*, 4. **57.** *"I was appalled at* ... Talbot, Carol, *Escape at Dawn*, 242. **58.** *"Lady, you've got five* ... ibid., 243. **59.** *The camp's carpenter pleaded* ... Coleman, Arthur, *Letter to Edward M. Flanagan, Aug. 31, 1984.* **60.** *"She's been gone since* ... This was Lt. Benjamin Rooth per Bigart, Homer, "Los Baños Rescue," 49. **61.** *"Night after night I've* ... Flanagan, Edward, *The Angels* [1948], 98. **62.** *Yelling was only motivating* ... Roberts, Donald, "Angels to the Rescue," 26. **63.** *Ringler sent a lieutenant* ... 511th PIR Association *511th Parachute Infantry Regiment*, 37; this was Lt. Bill Hettlinger. **64.** *One trooper, lighter in* ... Jack McGrath, "A Tale of Two Flags," *WA*, Winter 1996, 36. **65.** *"The only flashbacks I* ... Penwell, Richard, *Oral History.* **66.** *"You couldn't believe those* ... Don Langford, interviewed by Craig Davis, February 3, 2001. **67.** *"Come on, Father* ... Unknown Author, "Los Baños," *Voice*, December 1999, 46. **68.** *Passengers were allowed one* ... Marshall, Bert, "The Jump on Los Baños," 35. **69.** *A flock of habit-cloaked* ... Unknown Author, *Los Baños*, 46. **70.** *"[They] looked very thin* ... All Coleman quotes from Coleman, Arthur, *Letter to Edward M. Flanagan, Aug. 14, 1984*; and from Coleman, Arthur, *Letter to Edward M. Flanagan, Aug. 31, 1984.* **71.** *"There's a Jap in* ... ibid. **72.** *In the distance, the* ... 511th PIR Association, *511th Parachute Infantry Regiment*, 37. **73.** *The paragliders diversionary attack* ... 11ABN, *Report on the Los Baños Operation*, 4. **74.** *After an anxious hour* ... Kennington, Robert, *The Operations of the Los Baños Force*, 16. **75.** *Behind them, the camp* ... 511PIR, S2 *(Intelligence) Journal*, February 24, 1945, states forty-eight EKIA, while most accounts give the number as over 200 EKIA. The S2 report was written the day of the attack and is the least biased. The surprise attack was so complete most of the guards fled, and as the mission was to rescue the internees, they were not pursued. **76.** *The rescuers pulled off* ... 511PIR, S3 *(Operations) Journal*, February 23, 1945; Ingles, Gustavo, *Letter to Edward M. Flanagan, Oct. 25, 1984*; Coleman, Arthur, *Letter to Edward M. Flanagan, Aug. 31, 1984.* **77.** *Shorty's diversionary force suffered* ... 11ABN, *Report on the Los Baños Operation*, 5. **78.** *When the internees arrived* ... 11ABN, *Report on the Los Baños Operation*, 3. **79.** *"but even though it* ... Unknown Author, *Los Baños*, 46. **80.** *The internees were* ... Watty, Lewis, "A POW's Memory of the Raid," 50. **81.** *Medics examined and registered them* ... Kathleen was the daughter of Oscar McCoy; there was also Mrs. Louise Franciso and her nine-day-old baby, Elizabeth, Bigart; see Homer, "Los Baños Rescue," 49. **82.** *Among the 2,147 rescued* ... XIV Corps, *After Action Report M1 Operation, Part II*, 35, Among the 2,147 rescued, there were Americans, [1,583] British, [323] Australians, [32] Canadians, [144] Norwegians, [10] Poles, [22] Dutch, Italians, [16] French, [1] and a Nicaraguan. **83.** *Over a hundred were* ... XIV Corps, *After Action Report M1 Operation, Part II*, 35. **84.** *Later that afternoon, cooks* ... Unknown Author, *Los Baños*, 46; food line from XIV Corps, *After Action Report M1 Operation, Part II*, 35. **85.** *"There wasn't a sound* ... Swindler, Henry, "C/127th

Engineers in the Los Baños Mission," 16. **86.** *"I can't really describe ...* 511th PIR Association, *511th Parachute Infantry Regiment,* 68.

Chapter 12: "We're Going to Step in It Today."

1. *While at least three ...* Ellis, Steve, *Los Baños' Freedom Day* (*VFW* Magazine, February 1979), 42. The AP's Dean Schedler rode in the lead amtrac per Leo Kocher, "'Another 'Point of View' of the Los Baños Raid. A collection of articles from various newspapers," *WA,* Spring 2006, 12; Frank Smith from Jim Holzem, "Newspaper Reporter Jumped at Los Baños," *Voice,* March 15, 1986, 40; United Press writer Francis McCarthy and Dean Schedler, who both rode in amtracs. **2.** *this is the way ...* Henry Muller interviewed by Craig Davis, February 10, 2001. **3.** *The 11th Airborne drew ...* 11ABN, *11th Airborne Division History,* 37. **4.** *"Right now, I've got ...* Swing, Joseph, *Dear General,* letter dated March 8, 1945. **5.** *"Our masters tasked regiments ...* Kirkland, Randolph, *Long Ago and Far Away,* 123. **6.** *Many troopers, with insufficient ...* Holcombe, Frank, *The Operations of the 2nd BN, 511 PIR in the Jump on Tagaytay Ridge,* 5. **7.** *"My eyeballs were yellow ...* Marks, Deane, "The Day the Tank Blew Up, Part III," 12. **8.** *In February, Swing's medics ...* 11ABN, *Medical History for Period January–March 1945,* 3, In March 1945: Disease: 1,499; Injury: 209; Battle Casualties: 387; of the diseases, 96 were hepatitis, 56 diarrhea, and 325 fever of undetermined origin. **9.** *The next few hours ...* Marks, Deane, "The Day the Tank Blew Up, Part III," 12. **10.** *The shooters were transferred ...* Loughrin *Journal,* February 7, 1945. **11.** *Fratricide numbers were ...* The studies were conducted on New Georgia and Bougainville and summarized in Bergerud, Eric, *Touched with Fire,* 380. **12.** *"I hate to say ...* Billingsley, James, *Oral History.* **13.** *"When everybody's wound up ...* Charles Sass, "On a Couple of Hot Summer's Nights," *WA,* Fall 1997. **14.** *"No replacements of my ...* Swing, Joseph, *Dear General,* letter dated March 4, 1945. **15.** *Swing also worked with ...* 511PIR, FO #19, February 25, 1945. **16.** *The guerrillas became an ...* Swing, Joseph, *Dear General,* letter dated March 23, 1945; Kirkland, Randolph, *Long Ago and Far Away,* 123. **17.** *"The bare truth is ...* Kirkland, Randolph, *Long Ago and Far Away,* 123. **18.** *Despite his division being ...* Swing, Joseph, Letter to Eichelberger dated July 28, 1948, Swing wrote, "Effective strength of about 6,500." **19.** *While his staff moved ...* CP moved on March 3, 1945, per 11ABN, *Report After Action with the Enemy, Operation MIKE VI,* 39; 511PIR, *Luzon Report, Phase V,* 18. **20.** *Maintenance and supply issues ...* Swing, Joseph, *Dear General,* letter dated April 5, 1945. **21.** *The engineers went to ...* Flanagan, Edward, *The Angels* [1948], 99; 511PIR, *S1 (Personnel) Journal,* March 4, 1945. **22.** *Arrayed and waiting at ...* Smith, Robert, *Triumph in the Philippines,* 426. **23.** *Their commander, Colonel Masatoshi Fujishige ...* Lahti's memoir contains a transcript from a post-war interview with Fujishige, Lahti, Edward, *Memoirs of an Angel,* 108. **24.** *By denying the Americans ...* Smith, Robert, *Triumph in the Philippines,* 426. **25.** *He was operating under ...* Lahti, Edward, *Memoirs of an Angel,* 118. **26.** *After the Los Baños raid ...* many arrived on the night of February 25, 1945, 11ABN, *Report After Action with the Enemy, Operation MIKE VI,* 17.

27. *By the time local* ... Ingles, Gustavo, *Letter to Edward M. Flanagan, Oct. 25, 1984.* **28.** *Families sought shelter at* ... Richard Hoyt, "Los Baños—The Aftermath," *Voice,* June 2005, 16. The chapel was at Calamba, described in one guerrilla account as "about a klick away from the college gate"; Charles Sass, "Attack on Mount Malipunvo," *WA,* Summer 2012, 17; three hundred victims from the testimony of the Los Baños chief of police via Military Commission, *People of the Philippines vs. Shizuo Yokoyama,* 90. **29.** *Several more victims, cut* ... Gustavo Ingles, "The Los Baños Reprisals," *Voice,* January 1998, 32. Espino was the CO of the Red Lions Unit, PQOG guerrillas. **30.** *"My two elder sisters* ... Kenneth Fuller, "Los Baños – Another Point of View," *WA,* Winter 1996, 47. **31.** *They were reinforced by* ... Ingles, Gustavo, "The Los Baños Reprisals," 32. **32.** *"My platoon came across* ... This took place near Mt. Makiling, at the Sugar Factory; see Fuller, Kenneth, "Some Recollections of an Old Airborne Soldier," 4; Fuller, Kenneth, "Los Baños – Another Point of View," 46. **33.** *"waxen solid mass* ... Kirkland, Randolph, *Long Ago and Far Away,* 131. **34.** *The total deaths amounted* ... Military Commission, *People of the Philippines vs. Shizuo Yokoyama,* 48. **35.** *"inhuman butchery of* ... Fuller, Kenneth, "Los Baños – Another Point of View," 46. One of the witnesses testifying at the post-war trail had this to say: "My personal belief, I mean my honest belief, is that they wanted to kill every Filipino whom they could meet at that time when the American Army was coming back, so that not a single male Filipino would be in a position to welcome and help the United States Army." Military Commission, *People of the Philippines vs. Shizuo Yokoyama,* 43. **36.** *"To this day the* ... and *Ingles claimed Espino's concerns* ... Flanagan, Edward M., *Angels at Dawn* (Presidio Press, 1999), 213. **37.** *"We didn't foresee it* ... Muller, Henry interviewed by Craig Davis. **38.** *"No one at home* ... From letter dated March 13, 1945, in Burgess, Henry, *Looking Back,* 103. **39.** *"No wonder we developed* ... Flanagan, Edward, *The Angels* [1948], 77. **40.** *"This is their affair* ... Sass, Charles, "Colonel John Ringler, The Compassionate Captain," 3. **41.** *"That was a hard* ... ibid. **42.** *"a scene from Dante's* ... This tribunal was at Santa Rosa per Jack McGrath, "The Hell We Call War," *WA,* Fall 1997. **43.** *Colonel Orin 'Hard Rock' Haugen* ... 511PIR, *S1 (Personnel) Journal,* March 1, 1945. Haugen died of his wounds on February 22, 1945, but it took several weeks for word to make it back to his unit. **44.** *"hoping that I can* ... Swing, Joseph, *Dear General,* letter dated March 8, 1945. **45.** *He left one of* ... 2/188 stayed in the vicinity of the Genko Line; 1/188 moved against Ternate. **46.** *The paragliders preceded* ... 188GIR, *Historical Report of the 188th Paraglider Infantry in [MIKE VI] Operation,* 16, the tanks were from A Co, 44th Tank Bn. **47.** *"wily and reliable mountain* ... 188GIR, *Part II: Luzon, Philippine Islands Campaign,* 11. This is in specific reference to the Ocompo guerrillas. **48.** *After twenty-four hours* ... 11ABN, *Report After Action with the Enemy, Operation MIKE VI,* Annex 30. **49.** *The paragliders captured* ... 188GIR, *Part II: Luzon, Philippine Islands Campaign,* 11; Smith, Robert, *Triumph in the Philippines,* 427. **50.** *At the same time* ... 11ABN, *11th Airborne Division History,* 37. **51.** *"As expected, the swarms* ... Flanagan, Edward, *The Angels* [1989], 310; this was C Co. 1/187 on March 8, 1945. **52.** *"The only thing that* ... Swing, Joseph, *Dear General,* letter dated March 4, 1945. **53.** *"and of course saved* ... Swing, Joseph, *Dear General,* letter dated March 23, 1945.

54. *They repelled several of* ... First by H Co. on March 9; on March 10, another patrol had six WIA. **55.** *"A bare open field* ... Kirkland, Randolph, *Long Ago and Far Away*, 125. This was on March 11. **56.** *Together they staggered to* ... Richard Keith, "The Fog of War," *Voice*, June 2014, 22; 511PIR, *S1 (Personnel) Journal*, March 11, 1945. **57.** *"The western approach was* ... and following from Stephen Cavanaugh, "Mt. Bijiang—What Really Happened (I Think)," *WA*, Fall 1999, 114. **58.** *It was to be* ... Cook, John, *The Operations of Company D, 511 PIR, Near Lipa, Luzon*, 13. **59.** *"shells were still coming* ... Elmer Hudson, "The Last Mountain — or — Die Another Day," *WA*, Winter 2009, 25. **60.** *When the shelling stopped* ... Cook, John, *The Operations of Company D, 511 PIR, Near Lipa, Luzon*, 16; this was at 09:45. **61.** *Scout Raymond Cegiacnik went* ... William Dubes, "Company D Stories," *WA*, Fall 2006, 23. **62.** *He deployed his men* ... Cook, John, *The Operations of Company D, 511 PIR, Near Lipa, Luzon*, 20. **63.** *Some troopers scraped shallow* ... Burger, Donald, "How I Became a Trooper." **64.** *"I could see several* ... Hudson, Elmer, "The Last Mountain," 25. The medic was Al Harr. **65.** *"Its effect was murderous* ... Cook, John, *The Operations of Company D, 511 PIR, Near Lipa, Luzon*, 21. **66.** *Those lasted just a few* ... ibid., 23. **67.** *Dog Company was down* ... Cook states D Co. strength was originally ninety-five men; by sustaining four KIA and twenty-four WIA, they were down 29.4% strength. **68.** *They moved so fast* ... Hudson, Elmer, "The Last Mountain," 25. **69.** *After accounting for his* ... Cook, John, *The Operations of Company D, 511 PIR, Near Lipa, Luzon*, 26. **70.** *"When we saw it* ... Thompson, Phil, *The I Co. Beacon*, May 1998, 4. **71.** *Item Company escaped downhill* ... ibid.; I Co, casualties via 511PIR, *Unit History*, 14. **72.** *"If you have never* ... Bernie Coon, "A Walk with God," *WA*, Summer 1995, 36. Multiple letters found in *WA #34*, Winter 1996, 51. **73.** *For the next two* ... 511PIR, *Unit History*, 16, 75mm fire by of 674th GFAB, airstrikes by A-20s and P-38s. **74.** *A guerrilla patrol ranged* ... 511PIR, *S1 (Personnel) Journal*, March 19, 1945. **75.** *They found three* ... Keith, Richard, "The Fog of War," 22; 511PIR, *Luzon Report, Phase V*, 24. **76.** *A company of paratroopers* ... This relief occurred on March 23, 1945. **77.** *Swing trucked them around* ... 11ABN, *History of Operation, Luzon*, 4; 11ABN, *Report After Action with the Enemy, Operation MIKE VI*, 7. Eighty-five miles via Swing, Joseph, *Letter to Eichelberger dated July 28, 1948*. **78.** *"daring stroke* ... Smith, Robert, *Triumph in the Philippines*, 433; XIV Corps, *After Action Report M1 Operation, Part I*, 189. **79.** *The 187th Paragliders* ... 11ABN, *History of Operation, Luzon*, 4. The Bushmaster link-up was at Balibag on March 23, 1945. **80.** *Meanwhile, the 188th's 2nd Battalion* ... ibid.; linked up with 1st Cav. Two days later, the roadblock was on March 25 to protect the DIV's right flank. **81.** *Arriving back at his* ... Flanagan, Edward, *The Angels* [1948], 110. The paragliders were B Co. 188 GIR. **82.** *Fujishige, under the weight* ... This on March 12, 1945, 11ABN, *Report After Action with the Enemy, Operation MIKE VI*, 8; Lahti, Edward, *Memoirs of an Angel*, 113. **83.** *To delay the hounds* ... 188GIR, *Historical Report of the 188th Paraglider Infantry in [MIKE VI] Operation*, 23. **84.** *By April 8, the* ... 11ABN, *Report After Action with the Enemy, Operation MIKE VI*, 8. **85.** *In his forty-five-mile* ... 11ABN, *History of Operation, Luzon*, 4; 188GIR, *Historical Report of the 188th Paraglider Infantry in [MIKE VI] Operation*, 23. 2/188 took Lipa Hill, then moved east, bypassing the enemy strongpoint at Malepunyo, and continued sixty miles across southern Luzon to cut off any escape route into the Bicol Peninsula. **86.** *The first Japanese strongpoint* ... 11ABN, *History of Operation, Luzon,* 4. The local name for Macolod is Maculot. **87.** *'Butch' Muller estimated the* ... Muller, Henry, "The Reluctant Boatman," 16. **88.** *"My positions were so* ... Lahti, Edward, *Memoirs of an Angel,* 115. **89.** *The two beasts, with ranges* ... Muller, Henry, "The Reluctant Boatman," 16; XIV Corps, *After Action Report M1 Operation, Part I,* 173. **90.** *Their firepower included four* ... This included the 760th, 756th and 472nd, 675th w/ 105s, as well as three M2 4.2-inch rifled mortars, a company of medium tanks, and a company tank destroyers per Unknown Author, "The 187th in the Leyte Campaign," *Voice,* March 1999, 33. **91.** *"Million Dollar Hill* ... 44th Tank Battalion, *Tank Tracks, Tennessee to Tokyo,* 37. **92.** *Fujishige's losses were estimated* ... 11ABN, *History of Operation, Luzon,* 4. 1,342 EKIA per XIV Corps, *After Action Report M1 Operation, Part I,* 195;.11ABN, *Report After Action with the Enemy, Operation MIKE VI,* 22, says approx. six hundred EKIA; Macolod cleared by April 21, 1945. **93.** *The second and far* ... Edward Lahti, "The Southern Luzon Campaign," *WA,* January 1990, 23. **94.** *But before wading into* ... 11ABN, *History of Operation, Luzon,* 5. **95.** *Pushing up into the* ... Earl Urish, "Easter Weekend Southern Luzon," *Voice,* March 1998, 36. **96.** *The division was receiving* ... 511PIR, *S1 (Personnel) Journal,* April 1, 1945. Seventy-seven replacements, all non-jumpers; Air Force personnel via Kirkland, Randolph, *Long Ago and Far Away,* 133. **97.** *"Colonel Pearson sat down* ... Flanagan, Edward, *The Angels* [1989], 330. **98.** *"The battle for Malepunyo* ... Kirkland, Randolph, *Long Ago and Far Away,* 137. **99.** *"I became aware that* ... ibid., 138. **100.** *They found three knocked* ... 11ABN, *Report After Action with the Enemy, Operation MIKE VI,* 21. This was on April 7; see 11ABN, *History of Operation, Luzon,* 5. **101.** *"Hey Joe, I'm coming* ... Doherty, George, "Tech. Sgt. Miles [sic] T. Lowe Awarded a Field Commission," 27. **102.** *At the height of* ... ibid.; this attack was on April 21; Solon Hayes was born December 5, 1921, per LeRoy, Bob, *From My Foxhole to Tokyo,* 97. **103.** *"at the time I* ... Doherty, George, ibid. **104.** *"I vividly remember lifting* ... Ed Baumgarten, "Mail Call," *WA* (Summer 2009), 35. **105.** *Malaraya Hill overlooked a* ... 11ABN, *History of Operation, Luzon,* 5. **106.** *"a welter of conical* ... Faulkner, Lyman, *The Operations of the 511th PIR in the Mount Malepunyo Mountain Mass,* 6. **107.** *Hidden under all the* ... Flanagan, Edward, *The Angels* [1948], 114. Four thousand Japanese troops per Smith, Robert, *Triumph in the Philippines,* 434. **108.** *They'd hauled in six* ... Lahti, Edward, *Memoirs of an Angel,* 116. **109.** *"We're going to step* ... Faulkner, Lyman, *The Operations of the 511th PIR in the Mount Malepunyo Mountain Mass,* 9. This attack from Hill 2362 against Hill 2380. **110.** *They made it as* ... 511PIR, *S3 (Operations) Journal,* April 22, 1945. **111.** *In an instant, ten* ... Faulkner, Lyman, *The Operations of the 511th PIR in the Mount Malepunyo Mountain Mass,* 9. **112.** *The company commander radioed* ... 511PIR, *S3 (Operations) Journal,* April 22, 1945. **113.** *The ridge ran in* ... Faulkner, Lyman, *The Operations of the 511th PIR in the Mount Malepunyo Mountain Mass,* 9. **114.** *The additional terrain study* ... conducted on April 21 per 511PIR, *Luzon Report, Phase V,* 27. **115.** *To help Swing tighten* ... 11ABN, *History of Operation, Luzon,* 5; Faulkner, Lyman, *The Operations of the 511th PIR in the*

Mount Malepunyo Mountain Mass, 5. A battalion from 7th Regt & 8th Cavalry Regt had cleared to the northern edge of Malepunyo and had advanced into its eastern side. **116.** *On the southeast boundary* ... This was 1/187 and the 152nd AAA. **117.** *Lahti's paratroopers, wading in* ... Main effort quote via 11ABN, *History of Operation, Luzon*, 5. Ciceri TF was also known as TF 58 with C Co. 511 & F Troop, 7th Cav Regt. **118.** *"unsavory" and "sad business* ... In Swing, Joseph, *Letter to Eichelberger dated July 28, 1948*, Swing wrote, "I recommended the relief of Colonel Grady and General Hoffman." **119.** *Engineers needed seventy-two* ... Faulkner, Lyman, *The Operations of the 511th PIR in the Mount Malepunyo Mountain Mass*, 9; 188GIR, *Part II: Luzon, Philippine Islands Campaign*, 16. **120.** *"The Japs are not* ... Swing, *Oral Reminiscences*, 14. **121.** *"It makes me sick* ... Swing, Joseph, *Dear General*, letter dated March 8, 1945. **122.** *"not act like 'fat heads* ... 11ABN, *Memorandum*, February 21, 1945. **123.** *"You shoot him in* ... this is Bill Maudlin quoted in Stouffer, Samuel, *The American Soldier: Combat and Its Aftermath, Vol. II*, 159. **124.** *"It is amazing how* ... Swing, Joseph, *Dear General*, letter dated March 4, 1945. **125.** *He had seven artillery* ... ibid.; 511PIR, *Luzon Report, Phase V*, 27. **126.** *The leaflets encouraged at* ... Kirkland, Randolph, *Long Ago and Far Away*, 139. **127.** *"Ginger 3, this is* ... Video "Attack on Hill 2380, 1945." [https://www.youtube.com/watch?v=hwwcfn_Bzn4], accessed on April 9, 2022. **128.** *Most of the other* ... 511PIR, *S3 (Operations) Journal*, April 26, 1945. **129.** *Dawn's pink sunlight glinted* ... Faulkner, Lyman, *The Operations of the 511th PIR in the Mount Malepunyo Mountain Mass*, 11. **130.** *At 08:45 the next* ... 511PIR, *Luzon Report, Phase V*, 27. **131.** *The cannoneers mixed in* ... 511PIR, *S3 (Operations) Journal*, April 27, 1945; 511PIR, *Luzon Report, Phase V*, 27. **132.** *Early in their march* ... 511PIR, *S1 (Personnel) Journal*, April 29, 1945. Bodies found on April 27, 1945. **133.** *They picked their way* ... 511PIR, *S3 (Operations) Journal*, April 27, 1945. **134.** *The battalion mortar teams* ... 511PIR, *Luzon Report, Phase V*, 27; Faulkner, Lyman, *The Operations of the 511th PIR in the Mount Malepunyo Mountain Mass*, 12. **135.** *They too ascended their* ... 511PIR, *Luzon Report, Phase V*, 27; 511PIR, *S3 (Operations) Journal*, April 27, 1945. **136.** *Sergeant Edward Reed, Jr.'s squad* ... 11ABN, *GO #120*, 1945. **137.** *Meanwhile, Able Company took* ... 511PIR, *Luzon Report, Phase V*, 27; Faulkner, Lyman, *The Operations of the 511th PIR in the Mount Malepunyo Mountain Mass*, 12. **138.** *Empty foxholes and corpses* ... 511PIR, *Luzon Report, Phase V*, 27. **139.** *"It had been dragged* ... This howitzer was on Hill 2362 per Sass, Charles, "On a Couple of Hot Summer's Nights." **140.** *It took several shots* ... 511PIR, *Luzon Report, Phase V*, 31, This was against Hill 2375. **141.** *"Our artillery boys never* ... Sass, Charles, "On a Couple of Hot Summer's Nights." **142.** *In the distance, a* ... 511PIR, *Luzon Report, Phase V*, 27. **143.** *"There was no respect* ... Kirkland, Randolph, *Long Ago and Far Away*, 139. **144.** *Able Company was expecting* ... 511PIR, *S3 (Operations) Journal*, April 27, 1945. **145.** *The thirteen-man patrol* ... 511PIR, *Luzon Report*, 27; Richard Sibio and Max Polick, "Posthumous Award of Distinguished Service Cross to Pat Berardi," *WA*, Summer 1992, 23. **146.** *"Our lead scout, PFC Trevor E. Jarrard* ... Sibio, Richard, "Posthumous Award of Distinguished Service Cross to Pat Berardi," 23. **147.** *Among them was Berardi's* ... James Lorio, "The Fighting Angels," *WA*, July 1988,

9; Sibio, Richard, "Posthumous Award of Distinguished Service Cross to Pat Berardi," 23. **148.** *"Pat Berardi tried to* ... Flanagan, Edward, *The Angels* [1989], 283. **149.** *"Looking down in late* ... Sass, Charles, "On a Couple of Hot Summer's Nights." **150.** *As the troopers settled* ... Faulkner, Lyman, *The Operations of the 511th PIR in the Mount Malepunyo Mountain Mass,* 12; eight hundred per 511PIR, *S4 (Supply) Journal Summary,* 4. **151.** *Harassing fire employing Time* ... 511PIR, *Luzon Report, Phase V,* 29. **152.** *The day's total of* ... Faulkner, Lyman, *The Operations of the 511th PIR in the Mount Malepunyo Mountain Mass,* 13. But 511PIR, *S3 (Operations) Journal,* April 27, 1945, says: A Co. had two KIA, three WIA; C Co. had five KIA and seven WIA; F Troop had one KIA and one WIA. **153.** *The day's plan of* ... 511PIR, *Luzon Report, Phase V,* 29; Faulkner, Lyman, *The Operations of the 511th PIR in the Mount Malepunyo Mountain Mass,* 13. The hills hit with smoke were Hill 2070 and Hill 2610. **154.** *"very questionable honor* ... Sass, Charles, "On a Couple of Hot Summer's Nights." Able Company was on Hill 2375. **155.** *They bumped into a* ... 511PIR, *Luzon Report, Phase V,* 29. **156.** *"From our place we* ... Sass, Charles, "On a Couple of Hot Summer's Nights." **157.** *Meanwhile, the 188th Para-Gliders* ... 188GIR, *Part II: Luzon, Philippine Islands Campaign,* 18. **158.** *The morning of April 29* ... Faulkner, Lyman, *The Operations of the 511th PIR in the Mount Malepunyo Mountain Mass,* 16. **159.** *Just seven hundred yards* ... Baker Company was on Hill 2070. 511PIR, *Luzon Report, Phase V,* 30; Faulkner, Lyman, *The Operations of the 511th PIR in the Mount Malepunyo Mountain Mass,* 15. 511PIR, *S3 (Operations) Journal,* April 29, 1945, says 600 yards, but map measurement is 700. **160.** *To keep the Japanese* ... Fletcher, Bob, "Hill 2610," 7. **161.** *"We grabbed at rocks* ... Sass, Charles, "On a Couple of Hot Summer's Nights." **162.** *They tied blocks of* ... Frank Alverson, "2610," *Voice,* August 15, 1982, 25. **163.** *One cave disgorged a* ... Kirkland, Randolph, *Long Ago and Far Away,* 134. **164.** *Private Albin P. Scott* ... James O'Hara, "Letter to Bob Fletcher, Aug. 16, 1982," *Voice,* November 15, 1982, 22; Bert Marshall, "The Marshall Brothers, Part III, *WA,* Spring 1994, 7; Eighteen WIA per 511PIR, *Luzon Report, Phase V,* 30; Faulkner, Lyman, *The Operations of the 511th PIR in the Mount Malepunyo Mountain Mass,* 15; Alverson, Frank, "2610," 25. **165.** *Lahti, urged his L-bird* ... 511PIR, *Luzon Report, Phase V,* 30. **166.** *Baker Company counted 123* ... 511PIR, *S1 (Personnel) Journal,* April 29, 1945. **167.** *Troopers searching the caves* ... 511PIR, *Luzon Report, Phase V,* 31. **168.** *He'd slipped away with* ... Lahti, Edward, *Memoirs of an Angel,* 116–118. **169.** *George Company, passing over* ... 511PIR, *Luzon Report, Phase V,* 30; Lahti, Ed, "The Southern Luzon Campaign," 23. **170.** *Total Japanese casualties were* ... 632 EKIA per Faulkner, Lyman, *The Operations of the 511th PIR in the Mount Malepunyo Mountain Mass,* 17; 1,600 per 11ABN, *Report After Action with the Enemy, Operation MIKE VI,* 23. **171.** *Swing's tactics were sound* ... 511PIR, *Luzon Report, Phase V,* 32. These are numbers for April 12 to May 4, 1945. **172.** *"During the night a* ... Kirkland, Randolph, *Long Ago and Far Away,* 139. **173.** *"When you saw what* ... Penwell, Richard, *Oral History.* **174.**

"*We did not take* ... Smith, Jacques, *Oral History.* **175.** "*so ended another pointless* ... Kirkland, Randolph, *Long Ago and Far Away*, 139.

Chapter 13: Home Alive in Forty-Five

1. "*The crisis is great now* ... Flanagan, Edward, *The Angels* [1948], 120. **2.** *The cannoneers of Swing's* ... 11ABN, *History of Operation, Luzon*, 5; Flanagan, Edward, *The Angels* [1948], 119. **3.** *The exhausted troopers filtered* ... 11ABN, *History of Operation, Luzon*, 5. They were all out by May 10, 1945. **4.** "*You can't keep the* ... This exchange based on Lahti, Edward, *Memoirs of an Angel*, 89. **5.** "*do the pick, shovel* ... Kirkland, Randolph, *Long Ago and Far Away*, 142. **6.** *Back at camp, the* ... Fuller, Kenneth, "Some Recollections of an Old Airborne Soldier," 4. **7.** "*My footlocker had been* ... Kirkland, Randolph, *Long Ago and Far Away*, 142. **8.** "*Perhaps our days of* ... Flanagan, Edward, *The Angels* [1948], 135. **9.** *A more celebrated date* ... 11ABN, *Report After Action with the Enemy, Operation MIKE VI*, 9. **10.** "*After 101 days of* ... Swing, Joseph, *Dear General*, letter dated May 20, 1945, 1. Various unit histories range from 94 (11ABN, *11th Airborne Division History*, 39.) to 105 (11ABN, *History of Operation, Luzon*, 6). Swing is correct, as January 31 to May 11 is 101 days. **11.** *His staff dutifully tallied* ... 11ABN, *Report After Action with the Enemy, Operation MIKE VI*, 9. **12.** *Swing wanted the water* ... and "*excessive* ... , etc., Sixth Army, *Memorandum to: Engineer*, 1. **13.** "*Life in the camp* ... Kirkland, Randolph, *Long Ago and Far Away*, 147. **14.** "*We had fresh meat* ... Burgess, Henry, *Looking Back*, 104. **15.** "*There was a fatalistic* ... Kirkland, Randolph, *Long Ago and Far Away*, 149. **16.** "*I felt our mission* ... Grimmer, Robert, *WWII Memoirs*, 24. **17.** "*It has come to my* ... 11ABN, *Memorandum*, February 25, 1945. **18.** "*Most of us thought* ... Schweitzer, Philip, *WWII Veteran Survey*, 20. **19.** *Monday through Saturday started* ... 11ABN, *Training Memorandum No. 12*, June 13, 1945; 11ABN, *Training Memorandum No. 4*, May 4, 1945. **20.** *The Angels established formal* ... 11ABN, *Training Memorandum*, May 19, 1945; Kirkland, Randolph, *Long Ago and Far Away*, 144. **21.** *When they invaded Japan* ... 11ABN, *Training Memorandum No. 15*, July 13, 1945. **22.** *The nearby airfield was* ... 127ENG, *Organization History, Section IV*, 9. **23.** *The return to the* ... 187GIR, GO #18, July 18, 1945. **24.** *Sentries Teddy Burke and* ... Vannier, Joseph, *The I Co. Beacon*, May 1996, 3. **25.** *Unit commanders issued frequent* ... 11ABN, *Memorandum*, July 24, 1945. **26.** "*Will get more grey* ... Swing, Joseph, *Dear General*, letter dated May 28, 1945. **27.** "*Strangers to the system* ... Kirkland, Randolph, *Long Ago and Far Away*, 129. **28.** *All told, the Angels* ... 11ABN, *History of Operation, Luzon*, 6. **29.** *There was still plenty* ... 511PIR, *Luzon Report*, 34. **30.** "*We went about work* ... Flanagan, Edward, *The Angels* [1948], 135. **31.** *The guerrillas were often* ... 188GIR, *Part II: Luzon, Philippine Islands Campaign*, 20. **32.** "*As attractive as that* ... Augustin, James, "Once an Angel," 34. **33.** "*Luckily, no one was* ... ibid. **34.** "*Had to kill him* ... Strobel, Clarence, *Oral History.* **35.** *The fourth soldier was* ... 511PIR, *S3 (Operations) Journal*, May 21, 1945. **36.** *In all, the Angels* ... 11ABN, *History of Operation, Luzon*, 6. **37.** *On the next day's* ...

Flanagan, Edward, *The Angels* [1948], 130. **38.** *"I couldn't see him* ... Doherty, George, *Tomorrow I Will Be a Paratrooper* [AHEC], 65. **39.** *"It is tough, deadly* ... Burgess, Henry, *Looking Back*, 104. **40.** *At dawn, a long* ... Marich, Robert, *Oral History.* **41.** *To prevent their escape* ... Devlin, Gerard, *Silent Wings* (St. Martin's Press, 1985) 366. They'd drop on Camalaniugan airport, four miles south of Aparri, via 11ABN, *History of Operation, Luzon*, 6. **42.** *"I pleaded with the* ... Swing, Joseph, *Dear General*, letter dated July 3, 1945. **43.** *"frontal attacks all along* ... Swing, Joseph, *Dear General*, letter dated August 17, 1945. **44.** *Swing formed the Gypsy* ... 11ABN, *History of Operation, Luzon*, 6; Sixth Army, *[Aparri Report] Memorandum*, 1. Gypsy TF was 1,020 men from 1/511, G and I Cos., C Co., 127th Engrs, C Bat, 457th PFAB, a medic PLT, sixteen riggers, and elements of the ordnance, chemical, signal, intel, and press officers. Guerrillas seized Aparri on June 21, 1945. **45.** *The paratroopers boarded their* ... 11ABN, *Unit History, 20 – 30 June 1945*, 3. The seventy-five aircraft were fourteen C-46s, six CG-4A gliders, one CG-13 glider, fifty-four C-47s; see Sixth Army, *[Aparri Report] Memorandum*, 1. **46.** *"It was magnificent, those* ... Charles Sass, "Somebody Worth Remembering," *WA*, Spring 2002, 15. **47.** *Several hours later, the* ... Lahti, Edward, *Memoirs of an Angel*, 92; 11ABN, *11th Airborne Division History*, 40; Two KIA per Sixth Army, *[Aparri Report] Memorandum*, 2. **48.** *"The rice paddy was so* ... Marshall, Bert, "The Marshall Brothers, Part III," 7. **49.** *Since their objectives had* ... 11ABN, *History of Operation, Luzon*, 6; 127ENG, *Organization History, Section IV*, 9; Sixth Army, *[Aparri Report] Memorandum*, 2. **50.** *The uneventful slog flushed* ... 11ABN, *11th Airborne Division History*, 40; Sixth Army, *[Aparri Report] Memorandum*, 4, "To all appearances, the enemy had vacated the premises at least a week previous." **51.** *"modest disaster* ... Charles Sass, "Fifteen Minutes of Fame," *WA*, Fall 2002, 23. **52.** *"If you should ever* ... Jack McGrath, "The Day Geronimo Cried," *WA*, Winter 2009, 18. **53.** *Yamashita and thousands of* ... 11ABN, *Unit History, 20 – 30 June 1945*, 5. **54.** *Four days after the* ... 11ABN, *Report After Action with the Enemy, Operation MIKE VI*, 23. **55.** *Securing it had cost* ... Smith, Robert, *Triumph in the Philippines*, 692, 8,310 KIA, 29,560 WIA. **56.** *"Still have no intimation* ... Swing, Joseph, *Dear General*, letter dated May 28, 1945. The OLYMPIC plans outlined in Richard Frank's *Downfall* indicate that the 11th Airborne would have been in floating reserve as part of Kruger's Sixth Army. **57.** *"How stupid can you* ... Lahti, Ed, "The Southern Luzon Campaign," 23; Lahti, Edward, *Memoirs of an Angel*, 90. **58.** *At least thirty thousand* ... USS *Teton* (AGC-14), *War Diary for July 1945*, 1. **59.** *"The game was well* ... ibid. **60.** *"It will certainly be* ... Swing, Joseph, *Dear General*, letter dated July 3, 1945. **61.** *But rather than keep* ... this was the 541st PIR, 188th details via 188GIR, *Part III: Luzon, Philippine Islands Campaign, 1 Jul. 1945 to 31 Dec. 1945*, 1; July 20, 1945, per GO #144, HQ Sixth Army. **62.** *Troopers uninterested in volunteering* ... Edward Hammrich, "A Short, Personal History of My Time in the 11th Airborne Division," *Voice*, July 15, 1997, 26. **63.** *"Dick Ostrom who had* ... Hogan, Edward, *A Dogface's War*, 37. **64.** *"[The] others turned and* ... Stan Young, "The War is Over," *WA*, Spring 2006, 10. I added "hell" to Otaviano's quote as the original had just a dashed line, and readers can insert their favorite profanity. **65.** *After a blinding flash* ... Frank, Richard, *Downfall*, 286. **66.** *"Our training routine was* ...

Kirkland, Randolph, *Long Ago and Far Away*, 149. **67.** *"Word spread from tent …* Young, Stan, "The War is Over," 10. **68.** *"We had been watching …* Flanagan, Edward, *The Angels* [1948], 147. **69.** *"I couldn't visualize the …* O'Donnell, Patrick, *Into the Rising Sun*, 212. **70.** *At 05:30 the next …* 11ABN, *Historical Narrative, 30 June 1945 to 30 Sept. 1945*, 2. **71.** *"aghast to see a …* Kirkland, Randolph, *Long Ago and Far Away*, 150. **72.** *The type and number …* 11ABN, *Historical Narrative*, 2; 17:12 per 511PIR, *Occupation of Japan*, 1. Aircraft numbers were 151 C-47s, 351 C-46s, and 100+ bombers. **73.** *"The pilot came to …* Houston Jolley, "Personal Recollections 1943-1946, Part II," *Voice*, April 15, 1991, 6. **74.** *"That's a record for …* Swing, Joseph, *Dear General*, letter dated August 17, 1945; equip stats via 11ABN, *Historical Narrative*, 2. **75.** *"So many of the …* Swing, Joseph, *Dear General*, letter dated August 24, 1945. **76.** *Swing, keen to get moving …* Eichelberger, Robert, *Diary*, August 20, 1945. **77.** *Even after the detonation …* Frank, Richard, *Downfall*, 290-299. This is a simplified view of the machinations that were unfolding. I recommend *Downfall* for those wanting full insight. **78.** *"The [time] we spent …* Steve Hegedus, "Lowly Paratroop Sgt. Stares Down Big Navy Brass," *WA*, Fall 2000, 32. **79.** *"Tavern Number One …* Jolley, Houston, "Personal Recollections, Part II," 6. **80.** *"Nobody knew what would …* Hegedus, Steve, "Lowly Paratroop Sgt. Stares Down Big Navy Brass," 32. **81.** *"I wondered whether I …* Harry Swan, "The Occupation of the Japanese Mainland," *WA*, Summer 1995, 43. **82.** *"unpredictable …* and *"not anticipated …* 11ABN, FO #34, August 25, 1945, Intelligence Annex. **83.** *On the morning of August 28 …* US Pacific Fleet, *Report of Surrender and Occupation of Japan*, 10. **84.** *Richard 'The Rat' Laws and …* Laws, Richard, "First Man in Japan," 4. The advance party included 150 troopers from the 11 ABN. **85.** *Civilian policemen had established …* C.T. Tench, "Advance Party: Mission Surrender," *Infantry Journal*, August 1946, 30. **86.** *Signs of recent trouble …* Eichelberger, Robert, *MacArthur and the Eighth Army*. **87.** *The aerial armada passed …* Tench, C.T, "Advance Party: Mission Surrender," 30. **88.** *More than a hundred …* Three minutes per US Pacific Fleet, *Report of Surrender and Occupation of Japan*, 11. **89.** *They fanned out to …* 4,200 troops per 11ABN, *Historical Narrative*, 3. **90.** *"We were on full …* Hegedus, Steve, "Lowly Paratroop Sgt. Stares Down Big Navy Brass," 32. **91.** *The advance party had …* Tench, C.T, "Advance Party: Mission Surrender," 30. **92.** *Eichelberger flew in a …* Eichelberger, Robert, *Diary*, August 30, 1945. **93.** *"You get the goddamn …* Henry Muller, "The Day the War Ended," *WA*, Fall 2005, 4. At this time, Muller was with Eichelberger's Eighth Army staff. **94.** *The next task was …* 511PIR, *Field Order # 34*, August 26, 1945. **95.** *At 14:00, MacArthur's gleaming …* US Pacific Fleet, *Report of Surrender and Occupation of Japan*, 11. **96.** *"He's on the steps …* Jacques Smith, "Untitled Article," *WA*, Spring 1996, 48. [Reprinted from the September 2, 1995, issue of the *Times-Picayune* newspaper] **97.** *At least one member …* John Bandoni, "A Memorable Experience," *WA*, Spring 1994, 27. **98.** *"Thank you very much …* LIFE Magazine (September 10, 1945), 30. **99.** *Eichelberger wasn't taking any …* Eichelberger, Robert, *MacArthur and the Eighth Army*. **100.** *On the morning of …* US Pacific Fleet, *Report of Surrender and Occupation of Japan*, 104. **101.** *From the second row …* Swing, Joseph, *Dear General*, letter dated September 2, 1945. **102.** *A retinue of Allies followed …* ibid. **103.** *"We are gathered here …* MacArthur's address at the surrender ceremony available at the website of the US Navy. "From the Papers of Richmond Kelly Turner, Box 33," Archives Branch, *Naval History and Heritage Command*. **104.** *With the formalities completed* ... *Voice of the Angels* (No. 98, 15 Oct. 1992), 28; 'Big Tom' Mesereau can be seen at the surrender ceremony on the cover of *Yank* magazine. He is identified by his shoulder holster and jump wings. **105.** *He was a towering figure* ... Swing, Joseph, *Dear General*, letter dated August 17, 1945.

Epilogue: The Ol' Gray Mare

1. *When the cavalrymen debarked* ... Unknown Author, "Air Troops Razz Cavalry Men," *Voice*, September 15, 1980, 4. [Reprinted newspaper article datelined "Yokohama," September 2, 1945]; Swing, Joseph, *Dear General*, letter dated September 2, 1945. **2.** *"1st Cavalry Division – 1st* ... Earl Urish, "11th Airborne Honor Guard Protected MacArthur," *Voice*, September 1999, 39. **3.** *The plumb assignment of* ... Multiple mentions, but most specific in Bernheim, Eli, *WWII Veteran Survey*, 18; Tyre, Bailey, *WWII Veteran Survey*, 6; Weber, William, *WWII Veteran Survey*, 6. **4.** *Their role in Operation OLYMPIC* ... D-Day was planned for November 1, 1945, and would have included nine Army divisions, three Marine divisions, two regiments with another two divisions in reserve. Frank, Richard B. *Downfall*, 205. **5.** *The Japanese had 900,000* ... ibid., 900k via page 203; and 1:1 on page 340. **6.** *The Americans' casualty estimates* ... all from ibid., 139. **7.** *While civilian deaths were* ... Frank, Richard B. *Downfall*, 190. **8.** *With hostilities ended, the* ... 127ENG, *Organization History, Section IV*, 12. **9.** *General Tomoyuki Yamashita, whose* ... Scott, James, *Rampage*, 442. **10.** *Thomas 'Big Tom' Mesereau beat* ... Interview with Thomas A. Mesereau, Jr. **11.** *Mills Lowe wanted to* ... Susan Lowe Bevins, interview. **12.** *"I was bitter about* ... Serling, Anne, *As I Knew Him*, 60. **13.** *"Shrapnel wounds and mangled* ... ibid., 61. **14.** *"I try to forget* ... Gale from O'Donnell, Patrick, *Into the Rising Sun*, 174; Gale, Miles, "More About Leyte," 17. **15.** *Another veteran was haunted* ... Miller, Marvin. *The 11th Airborne Brick*, 116. **16.** *Sass bummed around New York* ... O'Donnell, Patrick, *Into the Rising Sun*, 290. **17.** *"The war helped me* ... Rausch, Kenneth, *The I Co. Beacon*, January 1999, 2. **18.** *"I was so hungry* ... O'Donnell, Patrick, *Into the Rising Sun*, 166. **19.** *"I wouldn't trade anything* ... Penwell, Richard, *Oral History*. **20.** *"These men I'm with* ... Letter dated December 8, 1944, reprinted in Richard Mueller, "A Trooper Writes Home," *WA*, Winter 1994, 25. **21.** *This sentiment outweighed patriotism* ... Stouffer, Samuel, *The American Soldier: Combat and Its Aftermath*, Vol. II, 164. **22.** *"We were gung-ho* ... Marich, Robert, *Oral History*. **23.** *"fighting for your skin* ... Stouffer, Samuel, *The American Soldier: Combat and Its Aftermath*, Vol. II, 169. **24.** *"requires that each man* ... Junger, Sabastian, *War* (Twelve, 2010), 120. **25.** *"Your relationship with the* ... O'Donnell, Patrick, *Into the Rising Sun*, 219. **26.** *"Don't go down there* ... combo of Marich, Robert, *Oral History*; O'Donnell, Patrick, *Into the Rising Sun*, 157. **27.** *"A good soldier will die* ... Billingsley, James, *Oral History*.

Index

Adevoso, Eleuterio L. (Terry Magtangol), 214

Aiming, Mount, Luzon, 217–218

Aircraft
  B-24 Liberator bombers, 373
  B-25 Mitchell bomber, 371
  B-29 Superfortresses, 366, 368, 374, 380
  C-46 Commando, 371
  C-47 cargo plane (Skytrain)/DC-3 (Douglas), 22, 26, 28, 34, 101, 110, 114–115, 121–122, 151, 156, 219–220, 222–223, 233, 265, 304, 371
  C-54 Skymaster transport planes, 375–377
  CG-4A cargo gliders, 20, 26
  Douglas A-20 Havoc bombers, 209, 217–218, 223, 253, 287, 343, 347–349
  Douglas SBD Dauntless dive bombers, 263, 279, 283, 287
  L-4 Piper Cubs, 83, 98, 115
  L-5 Stinson (Sentinel), 83, 100–101, 108, 112–113, 115, 118, 172
  L-birds, 115–118, 121, 125–126, 133, 151, 154, 156, 163, 172, 175, 204, 219, 229, 241, 258, 332
  Mitsubishi Ki-57 Type 100 transport planes, 122
  Mitsubishi A6M Zero, 87
  P-38 Lightnings, 67, 72, 87, 209, 219, 287, 326, 350
  P-51 Mustangs, 241

Alabang, Philippines, 287, 289

Alamo Scout School, 46

Angaur, 60

"The Angels," xv–xvi, 2, 4, 6, 15, 29, 32, 38–39, 42, 44, 46–49, 51–52, 56, 59–60, 65–66, 68, 71–73, 79–80, 83, 86, 88–89, 98–99, 101, 110, 112, 114, 119, 121, 125, 132, 136, 150, 154, 168, 170, 172, 174, 184, 187, 193–195, 197–198, 202, 204, 206, 214–215,, 217–218, 247, 252, 254, 258, 260, 270–273, 279–280, 284, 286, 294–296, 298, 314–316, 318, 324, 331–332, 338, 342, 346, 353, 357, 358–359, 361–363, 367, 369–371, 373, 376–378, 383–387, 389, 394–395

Anti-aircraft guns
  20mm anti-aircraft gun, 67, 250–251, 262, 279–280
  25mm machine cannons, 279–280, 284
  40mm anti-aircraft guns, 67, 132, 274
  120mm anti-aircraft guns, 279, 284

Antimonan, Philippines, 332

Aparri, Philippines, 364–365

Appleyard, Russell W., 286

Army, Imperial Japanese
  26th Division (Japanese), 168
  8th Tiger Division (Japanese), 299
  Banzai attacks, 140–146, 163–165, 176, 183, 218, 236, 284, 290, 336, 341, 374
  Fuji Heidan, 316, 318, 322, 355

Army, U.S.
  1st Cavalry Division, 254, 285, 314, 331, 340, 383
  7th Infantry Division, 80–81, 83–85, 98, 158, 173–175, 181–182, 187
  7th Portable Surgical Hospital, 264
  8th Cavalry Regiment, 344
  11th Air Assault Division, 386
  11th Airborne Division, see "the Angels"
  Ciceri Task Force, 344, 347, 347
  Gypsy Task Force, 364
  Pierson Task Force, 294
  25th Infantry Division, 213
  25th Liaison Squadron, 151
  32nd Infantry Division, 198
  33rd Infantry Division, 55
  37th Infantry Division, 273, 314, 365